Amsterdam

"All you've got to do is decide to go
and the hardest part is over.

So go!"

TONY WHEELER, COFOUNDER – LONELY PLANET

Contents

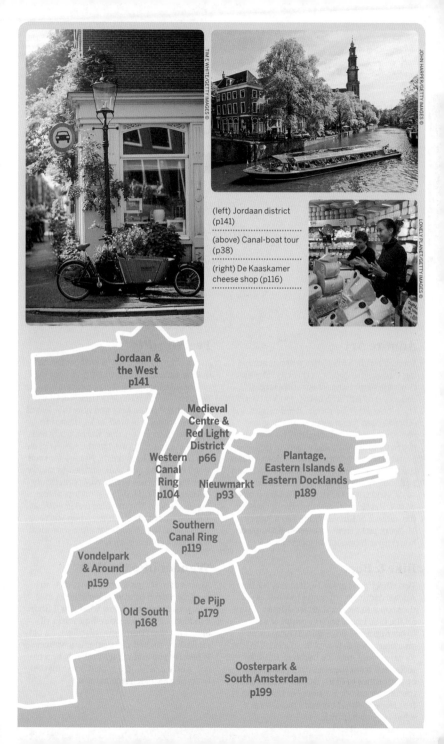

(left) Jordaan district (p141)

(above) Canal-boat tour (p38)

(right) De Kaaskamer cheese shop (p116)

Jordaan &
the West
p141

Medieval
Centre &
Red Light
District
p66

Western
Canal
Ring
p104

Nieuwmarkt
p93

Plantage,
Eastern Islands &
Eastern Docklands
p189

Southern
Canal Ring
p119

Vondelpark
& Around
p159

De Pijp
p179

Old South
p168

Oosterpark &
South Amsterdam
p199

Welcome to Amsterdam

Seventeenth-century buildings. Joint-smoking alien sculptures. Few cities meld history with modern urban flair like Amsterdam.

Admire Art

You can't walk a kilometre without bumping into a masterpiece in this city. The Van Gogh Museum hangs the world's largest collection by tortured native son Vincent. A few blocks away Vermeers, Rembrandts and other Golden Age treasures fill the gloriously restored Rijksmuseum. The Museum het Rembrandthuis offers more of Rembrandt via his etching-packed studio, while the newly doubled-in-size Stedelijk Museum pulls out Mondrian among its modern stock. And when the urge strikes for a blockbuster, the Hermitage Amsterdam delivers: the outpost of Russia's State Hermitage Museum picks from its three-million-piece home trove to mount mega exhibits.

Bike & Boat

Two wheeling is a way of life here. It's how Amsterdammers commute to work, go to the shop and meet a date for dinner. With all the bike rental shops around, it's easy to gear up and take a spin. If locals aren't on a bike, they may well be in a boat. With its canals and massive harbour, this city reclaimed from the sea offers countless opportunities to drift. Hop in a canal boat (preferably an open-air one) or one of the free ferries behind Centraal Station for a wind-in-your-hair ride.

Feel *Gezellig*

Amsterdam is famously *gezellig*, a Dutch quality that translates roughly as convivial or cosy. It's more easily experienced than defined. There's a sense of time stopping, an intimacy of the here and now that leaves all your troubles behind, at least until tomorrow. You can get that warm, fuzzy feeling in many situations, but the easiest place is a traditional brown *café*. Named for their wood panelling and walls stained by smoke over the centuries, brown *cafés* practically have *gezelligheid* (cosiness) on tap, alongside good beer. You can also feel *gezellig* at any restaurant after dinner, when you're welcome to linger and chat after your meal while the candles burn low.

Wander into the Past

Amsterdam is ripe for rambling, its compact core laced by atmospheric lanes and quarters. You never know what you'll find: a hidden garden, a shop selling velvet ribbon, a *jenever* (Dutch gin) distillery, an old monastery-turned-classical-music-venue. Wherever you end up, it's probably by a canal. And a *café*. And a gabled building that looks like a Golden Age painting.

Why I Love Amsterdam

By Karla Zimmerman, Author

I love walking around Prinsengracht in the morning. Houseboats bob, bike bells *cling cling*, flower sellers lay out their wares. The old merchants' houses tilt at impossible angles, and it's easy to imagine an era when boats unloaded spices out the front.

I love that you can drink under a windmill without affectation in the city. I love how candles burn in all bars and restaurants and that friends linger over dinner long after the last bite has been consumed. And I love chocolate sprinkles on bread for breakfast. Excellent idea!

For more about our authors, see p328.

Above: Bloemenmarkt (p128)

Amsterdam's
Top 10

VANGOGH
GAUGUIN

Van Gogh Museum (p170)

1 Housing the world's largest collection by artist Vincent van Gogh, the museum is as much a tour through the driven painter's troubled mind as it is a tour through his body of work. More than 200 canvases are on display, from his dark, potato-filled early career in the Netherlands through to his later years in sunny France, where he produced his best-known work with its characteristic giddy colour. Paintings by contemporaries Gauguin, Toulouse-Lautrec, Monet and Bernard round out the retrospective. NEW WING, VAN GOGH MUSEUM, DESIGNED BY ARCHITECT KISHO KUROKAWA

⊙ **Old South**

Brown Cafés (p48)

2 For the quintessential bite of Amsterdam, pull up a stool in one of the city's famed *bruin cafés* (brown *cafés;* traditional Dutch pubs). The true specimen has been in business a while and gets its name from centuries' worth of smoke stains on the walls. Brown *cafés* have candle-topped tables, sandy wooden floors and sometimes a house cat that sidles up for a scratch. Most importantly, brown *cafés* induce a cosy vibe that prompts friends to linger and chat for hours over drinks – the same enchantment the *cafés* have cast for 300 years. HOPPE BROWN *CAFÉ* (P81)

🍷 *Drinking & Nightlife*

LONELY PLANET/GETTY IMAGES ©

Vondelpark (p159)

3 On a sunny day it seems the whole city converges on this sprawling equivalent of New York City's Central Park. Couples kiss on the grass, friends cradle beers at the outdoor *cafés*, while others trade songs on beat-up guitars. Street performers work the crowds and kids rush the playgrounds. It's all very democratic, and sublime for people watching. The English-style layout offers an abundance of ponds, lawns, thickets and winding footpaths that encourage visitors to get out and explore the free-wheeling scene.

⊙ *Vondelpark & Around*

Rijksmuseum (p172)

4 The Netherlands' top treasure house has reopened in its entirety after a 10-year renovation and it does not disappoint. The crowds huddle around Rembrandt's humongous *Night Watch* and Vermeer's *Kitchen Maid* in the Gallery of Honour, but that just means the remaining 1.5km of rooms are free for browsing antique ship models, savage-looking swords, crystal goblets and magic lanterns. You could spend days gaping at the beautiful and curious collections tucked into the nooks and crannies. What's more, free sculpture-studded gardens surround the monumental building.

⊙ *Old South*

Jordaan (p141)

5 If Amsterdam's neighbourhoods held a 'best personality' contest, the Jordaan (once the workers' quarter) would win. Its intimacy is contagious, with modest old homes, offbeat galleries and vintage shops peppering a grid of tiny lanes. This is the place for jovial bar sing-alongs and beery brown *cafés*, the neighbourhood where you could spend a week wandering the narrow streets and still not discover all the hidden courtyards and tucked-away eateries. By now you know the Dutch propensity for *gezelligheid* (conviviality); the Jordaan is a font of it.

⊙ *Jordaan & the West*

Outdoor Markets *(p58)*

6 Amsterdam is market-mad, and its streets hold spreads from silks and coins to organic cheeses and bike locks. The Albert Cuypmarkt is king of the lot. Here Surinamese and Indonesian immigrants mix with locals at stalls hawking rice cookers, spices and Dutch snacks, such as sweet *stroopwafels* (syrup-filled waffles). Flowers fill the Bloemenmarkt, while porcelain teapots and other bric-a-brac tempt at Waterlooplein Flea Market. The Oudemanhuis Book Market has been selling tomes for a few centuries. Then there's the antiques market, farmers' market, art market... BLOEMENMARKT (P128)

Shopping

King's Day *(p23)*

7 For decades it was Queen's Day, but there's a new monarch in the house. So now it's King's Day (Koningsdag), celebrated on King Willem-Alexander's birthday of April 27 (unless it falls on a Sunday – as in 2014 – in which case it's celebrated the day before). Whatever the name, whatever the date, it's really just an excuse for a gigantic drinking fest and for everyone to wear ridiculous orange outfits, the country's national colour. There's also a free market citywide (where anyone can sell anything) and rollicking free concerts.

Month by Month

7

8

Canal Trips *(p35)*

8 Amsterdam has more canals than Venice and getting on the water is one of the best ways to feel the pulse of the city. You could catch the vibe by sitting canal-side and watching boats glide by: myriad *cafés* seem purpose-built for this sport. Or you could stroll alongside the canals and check out some of the city's 2500 houseboats. Better yet, hop on a tour boat and cruise the curved passages. From this angle, you'll understand why Unesco named the waterways a World Heritage Site.

🏃 *Canals*

Anne Frank Huis *(p106)*

9 Seeing Anne Frank's melancholy bedroom and her actual diary, sitting alone in its glass case, is a powerful experience that draws a million visitors annually. Step through the revolving bookcase of the 'Secret Annexe' and up the steep stairs into the living quarters. It was in this dark and airless space that the Franks observed complete silence during the day, outgrew their clothes, pasted photos of Hollywood stars on the walls and read Dickens, before being mysteriously betrayed. STATUE OF ANNE FRANK, BY SCUPLTOR MARI ANDRIESSEN

◉ *Western Canal Ring*

Cycling *(p30)*

10 Bicycles are more common than cars in Amsterdam. Everyone rides: young, old, club-goers in high heels, cops on duty, bankers in suits with ties flapping in the breeze. Pedal power is what moves the masses to work, to shop and to socialise at the *cafés*. Renting a bike not only puts you shoulder to shoulder with locals, it gives you easy access to the city's outer neighbourhoods and their cool architecture and museums, as well the windmill-dotted countryside and its time-warped villages.

 By Bike

What's New

Rijksmuseum

After a 10-year renovation, the nation's premier art trove, the Rijksmuseum, reopened in its entirety, splashing Rembrandts, Vermeers and 7500 other masterpieces over 1.5km of galleries. (p172)

King's Day

Willem-Alexander became king of the Netherlands in 2013, so no more Queen's Day parties. Now it's King's Day, with a new date – April 27 – to honour the new monarch's birthday. (p23)

Stedelijk Museum

The Stedelijk, Amsterdam's modern-art museum, finally popped the top on 'the Bathtub', its new wing that nearly doubles the space for Monets, Mondrians, glassworks, posters and textiles. (p175)

Verzetsmuseum Junior

Late 2013 saw the opening of this engaging addition to the Verzetsmuseum, which puts the Netherlands' Resistance efforts into context for kids through the experiences of four children. (p194)

Van Dyck Bar

Big-name DJs spin bangin' tunes at Van Dyck Bar, a super-stylish, Ibiza-meets-Miami-vibed club that opened near Leidseplein in 2013. (p132)

Amsterdam & Region Day Ticket

This new, cost-saving travel pass goes beyond the tram/metro system, adding on night buses, airport buses, Connexxion buses to south Amsterdam, and EBS buses to Haarlem and Zaanse Schans. (p273)

Droog

Dutch design superstar Droog expanded its uber-cool store with a mod cafe, a gallery to show off one-of-a-kind products, and a trippy garden with a very big mushroom. (p101)

Cafe Modern

Cafe Modern is one of many stylish eateries that have popped up around the EYE Film Institute in Amsterdam-Noord. The owners have opened the area's first boutique hotel (three rooms) above it. (p87)

Andaz Amsterdam

Conceived by designer Marcel Wanders, this hotel in the city's former library combines surreal decor such as giant cutlery and Delftware-like carpets with state-of-the-art amenities. (p227)

REM Eiland

Cutting-edge Amsterdam design firm Concrete converted a 22m-high former pirate broadcasting rig into REM Eiland, an amazing platformed restaurant and bar overlooking the IJ. (p148)

Vondelpark

More and more chic wine bars, candlelit *cafés* and in-the-know foodie restaurants keep opening west of Vondelpark, especially around Amstelveenseweg. (p162)

For more recommendations and reviews, see **lonelyplanet.com/Amsterdam**

Need to Know

For more information, see Survival Guide (p269)

Currency
Euro (€).

Language
Dutch and English.

Visas
Generally not required for stays up to three months. Some nationalities require a Schengen visa.

Money
ATMs widely available. Credit cards accepted in most hotels but not all restaurants. Non-European credit cards are sometimes rejected.

Mobile Phones
Local SIM cards can be used in European and Australian phones. Standard North American GSM 1900 phones will not work.

Time
Central European Time (GMT/ UTC plus one hour).

Tourist Information
The VVV main office (www.iam sterdam.com; Stationsplein 10; ⊘9am-6pm Mon-Sat, 10am-5pm Sun; 🚊4/9/16/24/25 Centraal Station), located outside Centraal Station, offers maps, guides, transit passes, accommodation booking services and ticket purchases for attractions.

Daily Costs
The following are average costs per day:

Budget: less than €100
➡ Dorm bed €22–35

➡ Supermarkets and lunchtime specials for food €15

➡ Boom Chicago discount ticket €11–17

Midrange: €100–200
➡ Double room €125

➡ Three-course dinner in casual restaurant €30

➡ Concertgebouw ticket €40

Top end: more than €200
➡ Four-star hotel double room €230

➡ Five-course dinner in top restaurant €50

➡ Private canal boat rental for two hours €90

Advance Planning

Six months before Book your hotel, especially if you'll be visiting in the summer.

Two months before Check calendars for the Concertgebouw, Muziekgebouw aan 't IJ, Melkweg and Paradiso, and buy tickets for anything that looks appealing.

Two weeks before Make dinner reservations at De Kas or Bordewijk, and check the city's festival program (www. amsterdamfestivals.com).

A few days before Buy tickets online to the Van Gogh Museum, Anne Frank Huis and Rijksmuseum. Reserve walking or cycling tours.

Useful Websites

Lonely Planet (www.lonely planet.com/amsterdam) Destination information, hotel bookings, traveller forum and more.

I Amsterdam (www.iamsterdam. com) City-run portal packed with sightseeing, accommodation and event info.

Dutch News (www.dutchnews.nl) News tidbits and event listings.

Overdose.am (www.overdose. am) Art, music and fashion to-dos.

Amsterdam Hotspots (www. amsterdamhotspots.nl) Hip eats, drinks, sleeps and parties.

WHEN TO GO

Summer (June to August) is peak tourist season, with warm weather and lots of daylight for cycling. March to May is tulip time.

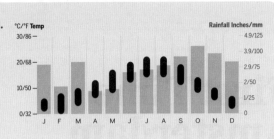

Arriving in Amsterdam

Schiphol airport Trains to Centraal Station depart every 10 minutes or so from 6am to 12.30am, €3.90; taxi €47.

Centraal Station In central Amsterdam with most tram lines connecting it to the rest of the city; taxis queue near the front entrance.

Bus station Buses arrive at Amstelstation, south of the centre, with an easy metro or train link to Centraal Station.

For much more on **arrival** see p270

Getting Around

GVB passes in chip-card form are the most convenient option for public transport. Buy them at VVV offices or from tram conductors. Always wave your card at the pink machine when entering and departing.

➡ **Walking** Central Amsterdam is compact and easy to cover by foot.

➡ **Bicycle** This is the locals' main mode of getting around. Rental companies are all over town; bikes cost about €13.50 per day.

➡ **Tram** Fast, frequent and ubiquitous, operating between 6am and 12.30am.

➡ **Bus & Metro** Primarily serve the outer districts; not much use in the city centre.

➡ **Ferry** Free ferries depart for northern Amsterdam from docks behind Centraal Station.

➡ **Taxi** Expensive and not very speedy given Amsterdam's maze of streets.

For much more on **getting around** see p272

Sleeping

Resting your head in Amsterdam can be expensive. Book as far in advance as possible (especially for summer bookings, and for weekends anytime) to get the best deals and to secure the place you want.

Hostels are plentiful, with most geared to youthful party animals. Hotels typically are small (less than 20 rooms) and ramble over several floors in charming old buildings. Canal-side addresses cost more, while places by the Red Light District or Damrak – though cheaper – tend towards the seedy side. In general, everything is pretty expensive.

Useful Websites

➡ **I Amsterdam** (www. iamsterdam.com) Wide range of options from the city's official website.

➡ **Citymundo** (www. citymundo.com) Reliable broker for apartment rentals; three-night minimum required.

➡ **Hotels.nl** (www.hotels.nl) For deals on larger properties.

For much more on **sleeping** see p222

First Time Amsterdam

For more information, see Survival Guide (p269)

Checklist

➡ Make sure your passport is valid for at least six months after your arrival date

➡ Inform your debit-/credit-card company of your travel

➡ Arrange appropriate travel insurance

➡ Call your mobile provider to enquire about roaming charges or getting an international plan

What to Pack

➡ Good walking shoes – Amsterdam is best appreciated on foot

➡ Umbrella, because it can be rainy

➡ Netherlands electrical adapter

➡ A small day-pack (the smaller the better to avoid having to check it when visiting museums)

Top Tips for Your Trip

➡ Plan your time – lengthy queues can add an hour or so to each museum visit.

➡ Make reservations for dinner at midrange and top-end eateries. Many restaurants are small and customers like to linger. Without a reservation, you might well miss out on your spot of choice.

➡ Sightsee by foot. Walking is one of the best ways to get around the compact city – it's quick, cheap and provides the opportunity to wander by hidden lanes and shops you might otherwise miss.

What to Wear

Locals dress stylishly but practically (they're riding bicycles, after all). Most people wear jeans and hip boots for an evening out.

Pack layers of clothing, bearing in mind that Dutch weather is notoriously fickle and there can be chilly spells even in summer. In spring, summer and autumn, a light trench coat or jacket and a small travel umbrella will mean you're prepared for the weather but can still blend in with the crowd. In winter, bring a proper heavy coat to ward off the near-freezing temperatures (and you'll still want that umbrella).

Be Forewarned

Amsterdam is a safe and manageable city and if you use your common sense you should have no problems.

➡ Some restaurants and businesses close for two to six weeks in summer, usually in July or August, when owners go on holiday.

➡ Be alert for pickpockets in tourist-heavy zones such as the Bloemenmarkt and Red Light District; avoid deserted streets in the Red Light District at night.

➡ Be careful around the canals. Most aren't fenced.

➡ It is forbidden to take photos of women in the Red Light District windows, and this is strictly enforced.

➡ The trams stop running at 12.30am, after which you'll have to wait for less convenient and more expensive night buses.

Money

ATMS are everywhere, and will generally accept Visa, MasterCard, Cirrus or Maestro cards. There is nearly always a transaction surcharge for cash withdrawals with foreign cards.

Most hotels accept credit cards, but a fair number of restaurants, shops and other businesses (including Dutch Railways) do not, or accept only European cards with security chips. Some businesses levy a 5% surcharge (or more) on credit-card purchases. Always check first.

To change money, try GWK Travelex (p277), which has offices at Centraal Station, Leidseplein and Schiphol airport.

For more information, see p277.

Touring the canals (p35)

Taxes & Refunds

Value-added tax (VAT, or 'BTW' in Dutch) is a sales tax levied on most goods and services. It's 6% for restaurants, hotels, books, transport and museum admissions. It's 21% for most other items. The tax should already be included in the price.

It's sometimes possible for visitors to claim a VAT refund; see p59 for details.

Tipping

➡ **Hotels** Porters expect €1–2 per bag; not typical for cleaning staff.

➡ **Bars** Not expected.

➡ **Restaurants** Round up to the next euro, or around 5%; a 10% tip is considered generous. If your bill comes to €9.50, you might leave €10.

➡ **Taxis** Tip 5–10% of the fare, or round up to the nearest euro.

Etiquette

➡ **Greetings** Do give a firm handshake and double or triple cheek kiss.

➡ **Pot smoking** Don't smoke dope or drink beer on the streets.

➡ **Cigarette smoking** Don't smoke cigarettes in bars or restaurants.

➡ **Bluntness** Don't take offense if locals give you a frank, unvarnished opinion. It's not considered impolite, rather it comes from the desire to be direct and honest.

➡ **Cycling paths** Don't walk in bike lanes (which are marked by white lines and bicycle symbols), and do look both ways before crossing one.

Visitor Pass

The I Amsterdam Card (p275) is handy for quick visits to the city. It provides admission to more than 30 museums and includes a local transit pass, a canal cruise, and restaurant and shop discounts. If you just visit a few museums per day it'll pay for itself.

Language

English is widely spoken, especially by younger locals. Most restaurants and cafes have menus in Dutch and English; most museums have information posted in both languages.

See p281 for more information.

Top Itineraries

Day One

Old South (p168)

 Begin with the biggies: tram to the Museum Quarter to ogle the masterpieces at the **Van Gogh Museum** and **Rijksmuseum**. They'll be crowded, so make sure you've pre-booked tickets. Modern art buffs might want to swap the **Stedelijk Museum** for one of the others. They're all lined up in a walkable row.

> **Lunch** Slow-food favourite Gartine (p79) grows ingredients in its garden.

Medieval Centre (p71)

Spend the afternoon in the Medieval Centre. Explore the secret courtyard and gardens at the **Begijnhof**. Walk up the street to the **Dam**, where the **Royal Palace**, **Nieuwe Kerk** and **Nationaal Monument** huddle and provide a dose of Dutch history. Bend over and take your *jenever* (Dutch gin) like a local at **Wynand Fockink**.

> **Dinner** Do elegant Dutch for dinner at Hemelse Modder (p99).

Red Light District (p74)

Venture into the Red Light District. A walk down **Warmoesstraat** or **Oudezijds Achterburgwal** provides an eye-popping line-up of fetish gear shops, live sex shows, smoky coffeeshops and, of course, women in day-glo lingerie beckoning from crimson windows. Then settle in to a brown *café* (pub), such as **In 't Aepjen**, **In de Olofspoort** or **'t Mandje**.

Day Two

De Pijp (p179)

 Browse the **Albert Cuypmarkt**, Amsterdam's largest street bazaar, an international free-for-all of cheeses, fish, *stroopwafels* (syrup-filled waffles) and bargain-priced clothing. Then submit to the **Heineken Experience** to get shaken up, heated up and 'bottled' like the beer you'll drink at the end of the brewery tour.

> **Lunch** Bite into a burger at The Butcher (p183) on Albert Cuypstraat.

Southern Canal Ring (p119)

Make your way over to the Southern Canal Belt and stroll along the grand Golden Bend. Visit **Museum Van Loon** for a peek into the opulent canal-house lifestyle, or get a dose of kitty quirk at the **Kattenkabinet**. Browse the **Bloemenmarkt** and behold the wild array of bulbs.

> **Dinner** Fork into organic dishes canalside at Buffet van Odette (p127).

Southern Canal Ring (p119)

When the sun sets, it's time to par-tee at hyperactive, neon-lit **Leidseplein**. If you get here before 7.30pm weekdays (6pm weekends), check at the **Uitburo** for concerts or show tickets. **Paradiso** and **Melkweg** host the coolest agendas. Otherwise the good-time clubs and *cafés* around the square beckon. Try beery **Café de Spuyt** or historic **Eijlders**.

Day Three

Vondelpark (p159)

Take a spin around beloved **Vondelpark**. Long and thin – about 1.5km long and 300m wide – it's easy to explore via a morning jaunt. All the better if you have a bicycle to zip by the ponds, gardens and sculptures. **Café Vertigo, 't Blauwe Theehuis** and other eateries in the park offer sustenance.

> **Lunch** Head to the Western Canals for Dutch classics at Bistro Bij Ons (p112).

Western Canal Ring (p104)

Immerse yourself in the **Negen Straatjes** (Nine Streets), a tic-tac-toe board of oddball speciality shops. The **Anne Frank Huis** is also in the neighbourhood, and it's a must. The claustrophobic rooms, their windows still covered with blackout screens, give an all-too-real feel for Anne's life in hiding. Seeing the diary itself – filled with her sunny writing tempered with quiet despair – is moving, plain and simple.

> **Dinner** Balthazar's Keuken (p147) cooks whatever deliciousness is on hand.

Jordaan (p141)

Spend the evening in the Jordaan, the chummy district touted as the Amsterdam of yore. Hoist a glass on a canalside terrace at **'t Smalle**, join the drunken sing-along at **De Twee Zwaantjes**, or quaff beers at heaps of other *gezellig* (cosy) haunts.

Day Four

Nieuwmarkt (p93)

Mosey through **Waterlooplein Flea Market**. Doc Martens? Buddha statues? Electric saw? These goods and more fill the stalls. Rembrandt sure loved markets, if his nearby studio is any indication. **Museum het Rembrandthuis** gives a peek at the master's inner sanctum, including his curio-packed cabinet and paint-spattered easel. Neighbouring **Gassan Diamonds** gives the bling lowdown via free tours.

> **Lunch** Try a hot-spiced Surinamese sandwich at Tokoman (p98).

Plantage, Eastern Islands & Eastern Docklands (p189)

Wander over to the Plantage to check out the intriguing **Verzetsmuseum** (Resistance Museum) or sea t reasures at **Het Scheepvaartmuseum**. Then it's time for an only-in-Amsterdam experience: drinking organic beer at the foot of an authentic windmill at **Brouwerij 't IJ**. Snap your photos before knocking back too many glasses of the strong suds.

> **Dinner** Dine in the glass greenhouse at De Kas (p204).

Oosterpark (p199)

You've been a sightseeing trooper, zipping through most of Amsterdam's neighbourhoods over the past four days. An evening spent plopped on **De Ysbreeker**'s terrace, looking out over the bustling, houseboat-strewn Amstel river, is a well-deserved treat.

If You Like...

Art

Van Gogh Museum It has the world's largest collection of the tortured artist's paintings, from his early work to his final pieces. (p170)

Rijksmuseum The Netherlands' mightiest museum bursts with Rembrandts, Vermeers, delftware and kilometres more, now showing in all their glory in the beautifully restored building. (p172)

Stedelijk Museum The new 'Bathtub' wing has doubled capacity for the groovy modern trove by Picasso, Chagall, Mondrian, Warhol, Lichtenstein and the CoBrA chaps. (p175)

Museum het Rembrandthuis You almost expect to find the master himself still nipping around his old paint-spattered studio and handsome home. (p95)

Hermitage Amsterdam This satellite of Russia's Hermitage Museum features one-off, blockbuster exhibits showing everything from Matisse cut-outs to Byzantine treasures. (p125)

FOAM (Fotografiemuseum Amsterdam) Changing exhibitions feature world-renowned photographers such as Sir Cecil Beaton, Annie Leibovitz and Henri Cartier-Bresson. (p121)

Markets

Albert Cuypmarkt Amsterdam's largest and busiest market has been selling flowers, clothing, household goods and food of every description for more than 100 years. (p188)

Bloemenmarkt (p128)

LONELY PLANET/GETTY IMAGES ©

Waterlooplein Flea Market The city's famous flea market piles up curios, used footwear, electronic gear, New Age gifts and cheap bicycle parts for bargain hunters. (p97)

Oudemanhuis Book Market Located in a moody, old, covered alleyway, this place is lined with second-hand booksellers and is a favourite with academics. (p89)

Noordermarkt The Noorderkerk's front plaza has been a market since the early 1600s; antiques and organic fare are the offerings these days. (p157)

Bloemenmarkt The 'floating' flower market (it actually sits on pilings) is the place to bag your beautiful bloomin' bulbs. (p128)

Beer

Café Belgique Pouring the best lambic beers, Trappist brews and golden ales, this atmospheric beer *café* (bar) is the next best thing to being in Belgium. (p81)

Brouwerij 't IJ The tasting room of Amsterdam's leading organic microbrewery has a cosy, down-and-dirty beer-hall feel. Bonus: it sits under a windmill. (p197)

De Bierkoning They don't call this shop the 'beer king' for nothing; it stocks 950 brews plus beer glasses and beer guidebooks. (p90)

Gollem The pioneer of Amsterdam's beer *cafés* still pours a bountiful selection in its tiny, brew-paraphernalia-covered space. (p82)

Brouwerij de Prael This laudable local brewery employs people overcoming mental illness. Its organic beers are named after famous Dutch singers. (p85)

Hedonistic Pursuits

Dampkring This coffeeshop stalwart has a comprehensive, well-explained menu, a Cannabis Cup–winning product and a George Clooney Hollywood pedigree. (p114)

Condomerie Het Gulden Vlies Puts the 'pro' back in prophylactic with its tasteful setting and huge array of condoms for sale. (p92)

Kokopelli Life gets a whole lot more colourful (literally) with a serving of magic truffles from this classy, smart shop. (p92)

Prostitution Information Get frank information about the women in the windows on the centre's walking tour. (p74)

Casa Rosso Jaw-dropping tricks with lit candles and more at the city's most popular sex show (a hen's-night favourite). (p88)

Webers When you need a PVC catsuit with whip holster, this little shop can do the fitting. (p103)

Windmills

De Gooyer It's hard to beat drinking freshly made organic beers at the foot of an 18th-century spinner. (p191)

Riekermolen Rembrandt used to sketch by this windmill, south of the city at Amstelpark's edge. (p203)

Zaanse Schans A whole village of blades turns in the North Sea breeze, a 20-minute train ride from the city. (p220)

National Windmill Day Here's your chance to peek inside the country's 600 twirlers; held the second Saturday in May. (p23)

For more top Amsterdam spots, see the following:
- ➡ Eating (p43)
- ➡ Drinking & Nightlife (p48)
- ➡ Entertainment (p56)
- ➡ Shopping (p58)

Parks & Gardens

Vondelpark A mash-up of ponds, lawns, thickets and winding footpaths beloved by picnickers, dope smokers, kissing couples and frolicking children. (p161)

Museumplein The festive green space between the Rijksmuseum, Van Gogh Museum and Stedelijk Museum packs a crowd for winter ice skating and summer lazing. (p176)

Oosterpark Political monuments and grey herons dot the sweeping expanse of this park, built for nouveau riche diamond traders a century ago. (p201)

Hortus Botanicus When Dutch ships sailed afar in the 1600s, the tropical seeds they brought back were grown in this wonderful garden. (p191)

Amsterdamse Bos The Amsterdam Forest sprawls with thick trees and open fields, crisscrossed with cycling and walking paths, and home to rowing ponds and a goat farm. (p202)

Westerpark Abutting a former gasworks-building-turned-edgy-cultural-centre, the west side's rambling, reedy wilderness has become a hipster hangout. (p146)

Frankendael Park This formal garden with a gushing fountain and Greek-god statues sits behind a Louis XIV–style mansion. (p201)

Active Endeavours

Cycling in Amsterdam-Noord It's surprisingly easy to ride into the countryside and spin by time-warped villages and cow-dotted pastures. (p87)

Walking Tours The city has a slew of options for lacing up your shoes and seeing the sights. (p273)

Cycling Explore the city from a different perspective with a pedal around the canals. (p30)

Ice Skating Museumplein's pond turns into Amsterdam's favourite rink come winter, looking like the top of a wind-up jewellery box. (p176)

Sustainable Options

De Ridammerhoeve Feed the kids (both kinds) at the organic goat farm and cafe in Amsterdamse Bos. (p202)

De Kas Sit in a greenhouse and fork into meals whose components were grown just a few steps away. (p204)

Recycled Bicycles Rent wheels that have been rescued from scrap parts and refurbished for economical use. (p30)

Boerenmarkt This organic farmers' market sets up on Saturdays at Noordermarkt and Nieuwmarkt at the Waag. (p103)

De Winkel Van Guus Browse the 100% ecofriendly products at this light, bright concept store. (p155)

Hemp Works All the clothing and bags are made with organic fibres, plus there's an exclusive label of Dutch-made wares. (p89)

Architecture

Rijksmuseum Pierre Cuypers' magnificent, iconic design from 1875 harks back to earlier times, with Renaissance ornaments carved in stone around the facade. (p172)

ARCAM Amsterdam's Centre for Architecture is a one-stop shop for architectural exhibits, guidebooks and maps. (p193)

NEMO Renzo Piano's green-copper, ship-shaped science museum is a modern classic. (p192)

Scheepvaarthuis This grand 1916 building encrusted with nautical detailing and stained glass is the first true Amsterdam School example. (p97)

Eastern Docklands If you're looking for one place to see the cutting edge of Dutch architecture, the Docklands is the place. (p191)

Beurs van Berlage The 1903 financial exchange building is a temple to capitalism, with tile murals and other decor that venerates labour. (p71)

Het Schip A pilgrimage site for design buffs, this 1920s housing project is the pinnacle of Amsterdam School style. (p146)

Offbeat Museums

Kattenkabinet A creaky old canal house filled with kitty-cat art from the likes of Picasso, Steinlen and Rembrandt. (p123)

Houseboat Museum Get a feel for the compact, watery lifestyle aboard a 23m-long sailing barge. (p143)

Tassenmuseum Hendrikje This entire museum is devoted to handbags, from 16th-century pouches to Madonna's modern arm candy. (p121)

Pianola Museum Bursting with musical keys from the early 1900s, this little place is an extraordinary paean to the player piano. (p143)

Electric Ladyland Prepare for a trippy time at the world's first museum of fluorescent art, glowing with psychedelic rocks, rice and rabbits. (p145)

History Lessons

Anne Frank Huis The Secret Annexe, Anne's melancholy bedroom and her actual diary are all here, serving as chilling reminders of WWII. (p106)

Oude Kerk The senior citizen of Amsterdam's structures, now more than 700 years old, with many famous Amsterdammers buried under the floor. (p70)

Amsterdam Museum Intriguing multimedia exhibits take you through the twists and turns of Amsterdam's convoluted history. (p73)

Verzetsmuseum Learn about WWII Dutch Resistance fighters during the German occupation. Learn too about the minority who went along with the Nazis. (p194)

Stadsarchief The city's rich archives offer remarkable displays, like Anne Frank's stolen-bike report from 1942. (p121)

Month by Month

January

Yes, it's cold. Yes, it's dark. But the museum queues are nonexistent and there is more time to relax in a cosy cafe in front of a crackling fireplace.

✯ Amsterdam Fashion Week

Amsterdam's fashion scene takes flight during Fashion Week (www.amsterdam fashionweek.com) with catwalk shows, parties, lectures and films. Many events – free and ticketed – are open to the public. There's a July festival, too.

March

Early spring weather can be fickle but if it complies, you can get a jump-start on tulip viewing (and the crowds) at Keukenhof (p211).

✯ 5 Days Off

Electronic music festival 5 Days Off (www.5daysoff. nl) puts on dance parties at the Melkweg (p136) and Paradiso (p136) towards the beginning of the month.

April

Days are getting longer, temperatures are rising and flowers are in full bloom in the lead-up to the show-stopping King's Day party, the highlight of Amsterdam's annual calendar.

✯ King's Day

One of the biggest – and arguably best – street parties in Europe, King's Day (Koningsdag) celebrates the birthday of King Willem-Alexander on 27 April (26 April if the 27th is a Sunday). Uproarious partying, music and *oranjekoorts* (orange fever) aside, there's a giant flea market.

◉ World Press Photo

A gripping exhibition of the year's best photojournalism (www.worldpressphoto.org) debuts in the Oude Kerk in late April, and stays on display until June.

May

Amsterdam follows Remembrance Day (4 May) observances with Liberation Day (5 May) festivities, and flourishing cafe terraces make this mild month a perfect time to linger in the city.

◉ National Windmill Day

On the second Saturday in May, 600 windmills throughout the country unfurl their sails and welcome the public into their innards. Look for windmills flying a blue pennant.

June

The start of summer sees live music, theatre and dance take to leafy outdoor spaces, as well as to the city's most celebrated performance venues.

✯ Holland Festival

Highbrow and pretentious meets lowbrow and silly when the country's biggest performing arts extravaganza, the month-long festival (www.hollandfestival.nl), takes over Amsterdam.

☆ Vondelpark Open-Air Theatre

A popular Amsterdam tradition, the Vondelpark Open-Air Theatre (p166) features classical music, dance, musical theatre, cabaret and children's shows in a wonderful park setting from early June to late August.

◉ Open Tuinen Dagen

The Open Garden Days in the third weekend in June bring a unique opportunity to view some 30 private gardens along the canals (www.opentuinendagen.nl).

July

The days are long, the sun is shining, so who cares if the crowds are clogging Amsterdam's streets and canals? It only adds to the party atmosphere.

⚗ Amsterdam Roots Festival

Early July's four-day roots festival (www.amsterdamroots.nl) programs world music in key venues around town, culminating in the vibrant Roots Open Air all-day fest at the Oosterpark.

⚗ Over het IJ Festival

Off-beat venues at the NDSM-werf shipyards in Amsterdam-Noord (p87) host unconventional performing-arts productions for 10 days in early July during the Festival across the IJ (www.overhetij.nl).

August

A welter of events take place during Amsterdam's high summer, yet the city has less sweltering temperatures than many other European cultural capitals and relatively few summer closures.

⚗ Amsterdam Gay Pride

Amsterdam flies the rainbow flag from around late July to early August during Amsterdam Gay Pride (www.weareproud.nl). Among the plethora of parties and events is the world's only waterborne Gay Pride Parade, on the Prinsengracht and Amstel.

⚗ Grachtenfestival

Classical musicians pop up in canal-side parks and hidden gardens during mid-August's 10-day Grachtenfestival (www.grachtenfestival.nl). The highlight of the 'Canal Festival' is the free concert on a floating stage in the Prinsengracht.

September

Summer may be technically over but September is one of the best months to visit Amsterdam. There are some superb festivals along with fair weather and fewer crowds.

⚗ Jordaan Festival

Practitioners of the nostalgic, tears-in-your-beer folk music called *levenslied* – a speciality of the tight-knit Jordaan – take the stage in the mid-September, weekend-long festival (www.jordaanfestival.nl).

October

A kaleidoscope of autumnal hues colour Amsterdam's parks and gardens and while the weather may remain mild, low-season prices kick in and queues thin out.

⚗ Amsterdam Dance Event

An electronic music powwow on a massive scale (www.amsterdam-dance-event.nl) sees 800 DJs and some 200,000 clubbers attending 300 events all over the city over five long, sweaty days and nights late in October.

November

Cultural events and reduced low-season rates make up for the shortening days and chilly nights, while the arrival of Sinterklaas heralds the start of the festive season.

◉ Museumnacht

On the first Saturday in November around 50 museums throughout the city stay open till 2am for 'Museum Night', scheduling live music, DJs and art-fuelled parties (www.n8.nl). It's arranged by N8, an organisation connecting under 35s with art.

⚗ Sinterklaas Intocht

St Nicholas arrives by boat from Spain for the Sinterklaas Intocht (www.sintinamsterdam.nl) in mid- to late November and parades on his white horse to the Dam and Leidseplein to the delight of the city's child population.

(Top) Amsterdam Gay Pride Parade
(Bottom) Amsterdam Light Festival

International Documentary Film Festival

Ten days in late November are dedicated to screening fascinating true stories from all over the world (www.idfa.nl).

Cannabis Cup

By day, late November's four-day Cannabis Cup (www.cannabiscup.com) is a hilarious mix of garden show and trade fair (with awards for the best grass, biggest reefer and top 'pot comedian'), while evenings are one long after-party.

December

Winter-magic blankets the city (as, some years, does snow), ice-skating rinks set up in open spaces, including the Museumplein, and the city is a vision of twinkling lights.

Amsterdam Light Festival

The twin highlights of this six-week-long festival (www.amsterdamlight-festival.com) include a Boulevard Walk of Light along the Amstel, passing magnificently lit monuments; and a magical, mid-December Christmas Canal Parade of illuminated boats floating along the canals.

New Year's Eve

Fireworks light up the skies in a spark-showering spectacle and countless parties take place around the city. Event locations vary annually; check with the tourist office to find out where to ring in the new year.

PAUL BENNSEN/GETTY IMAGES ©

HILDA ELISABETH AARDEMA/GETTY IMAGES ©

With Kids

Breathe easy: you've landed in one of Europe's most kid-friendly cities. The famous Dutch tolerance extends to children and Amsterdammers are cheerfully accommodating to them. Virtually all quarters of the city – except the Red Light District, of course – are fair game for the younger set.

Riding in a *bakfiets* (cargo bike)

CRAIG PERSHOUSE/GETTY IMAGES ©

Outdoor Activities

Green spaces, parks and canals galore provide plenty of fresh-air fun for the little (and not-so-little) ones.

Parks & Playgrounds

A hot favourite with kids of all ages is the vast play space of the Vondelpark (p161), with leafy picnic spots and duck ponds, as well as cool space-age slides at its western end and a playground in the middle of the park. Westerpark (p146) also has a terrific playground, while Sarphatipark (p181) and Oosterpark (p201) shouldn't be overlooked as great open spaces to let the kids run free. Canoeing, a tree-climbing park, horse riding, paddle boats and a goat farm are among the fun activities in the huge, forested Amsterdamse Bos (p202).

Winter Magic

Kids will love the skating rinks and outdoor merriment at the winter carnivals that spring up in public spaces such as the Museumplein (p176). Don't miss uniquely Dutch festive-season treats such as *poffertjes* (small pancakes) and gingery-cinnamon *speculaas* (cookies), traditionally eaten around Sinterklaas (Saint Nicholas' Eve; 5 December), which are served up at rustic market stalls.

Canals

Take to the canals – by bike! – on a unique pedal-powered ride on the city's beautiful canals. See p30 for more information.

Artis Royal Zoo

The extrovert monkeys, big cats, shimmying fish and dazzling planetarium will keep young eyes shining for hours at Artis Royal Zoo (p192), while teenagers and adults will love the beautifully landscaped grounds. You can combine a zoo visit with a canal cruise aboard the Artis Royal Zoo Express (p193). The cruise departs from near Centraal Station and travels via the IJ before dropping you off at the zoo; it loops back to Centraal along some of the city's prettiest canals.

Museum Fun

Amsterdam has plenty of museums that are accessible, educational and, above all, fun.

NEMO

A tailor-made, hands-on science museum, NEMO (p192) is useful for answering all those 'how' and 'why' questions.

Tropenmuseum

The children's section devoted to exotic locations at the Tropenmuseum (p201) is a winner in any language.

Joods Historisch Museum

There is a great kids' display on Jewish life in Amsterdam at the Joods Historisch Museum (p96).

Verzetsmuseum

A brand-new section at the Verzetsmuseum (p194) known as the Verzetsmuseum Junior puts the Dutch Resistance into context for kids through the experiences of four children: Eva, Jan, Nelly and Henk.

Beach Fun

BovenNEMO

Amsterdam's most futuristic beach is the rooftop BovenNEMO – translation: on top of NEMO (p192) – which opens from June to August. As well as the tremendous city views, the 'beach' has olive trees, an ice-cream stand, lawn chairs and even sand (well, sand pits), although there's no swimming. It's completely free (no NEMO entrance fee required).

City Beaches

Around 10 'urban beaches' pop up on Amsterdam's outskirts each summer around the IJ. While most cater to adults (complete with cocktails and DJs), some are more family friendly – check with the tourist office for locations. Enjoy the river views, but don't hope to swim.

Scheveningen

If you want an actual beach, with sand, salt water and waves, head for the long sandy coast at Scheveningen (p218), near Den Haag. It's an easy day trip from Amsterdam, but you'll also find plenty of hotels – and restaurants – that cater to families.

Rainy-day Ideas

It's prudent to have a rainy-day plan in your back pocket. In fact, it might be so much fun that kids will hope the sun doesn't come back out all day.

TunFun

Set 'em loose for a romp in the underground, all-round pleasure centre TunFun (p103).

Cinema

Kids can eat popcorn and watch new releases at the art-deco Pathé Tuschinskitheater (p137) or the intimate, atmospheric Movies (p154) while adults revel in the historic environs.

Indoor Pools & Saunas

The recreational Zuiderbad (p178) is a good place to take the kids swimming on a rainy day. Adults will enjoy the palatial vintage interior. The exquisite art-deco jewel Sauna Deco (p118) welcomes children until 8pm.

Centrale Bibliotheek Amsterdam

The city's stunning, contemporary Centrale Bibliotheek Amsterdam (p193) has a whole floor dedicated to children's activities, including comfy reading lounges and plenty of books in English. Check out the weekly story times (some in English) for younger visitors. Teenagers can take advantage of the free computer terminals and wi-fi.

Kid-friendly Cuisine

While Amsterdam's foodie scene continues to explode with adventurous and sophisticated offerings, you can still find plenty of fare that junior diners will enjoy.

Sandwich Shops

A *broodje* (filled bread roll) or *tosti* (toasted sandwich) always hits the spot. Scores

Above: Skating on frozen canals

Left: Het Scheepvaartmuseum (p191)

of shops throughout the city specialise in these staples; try Broodje Bert (p79).

Pancakes

The city is full of this kid-pleasing delight. Top choices include Pancakes! (p112) and Pancake Bakery (p112).

For true pancake aficionados, a trip aboard the 'pancake boat', **De Pannen-koekenboot** (Pancake Boat; ☑636 88 17; www.pannenkoekenboot.nl; Ms Van Riemsdijkweg; adult/child from €23.50/18.50; ☺by reservation), is definitely in order. Brunch and evening cruises depart from the NDSM-werf in Amsterdam-Noord, reached by a free ferry.

Burgers

Gourmet burgers made from organic ingredients are going gangbusters in Amsterdam. Best burger bets are Burger-meester (p193), at several locations including Plantage, and The Butcher (p183) in De Pijp.

Fries

Fries slathered in mayonnaise or other sauces are a favourite with all ages. Wil Graanstra Friteshuis (p112) is a local institution.

Ice Cream

Many ice-cream shops are seasonal: come April or May, look out for them in most high foot-traffic areas. Year-round, try the chocolate-dipped waffle cones at Jordino (p146).

Cafes & Restaurants

Particularly kid-friendly cafes and restaurants include Moeders (p149), Het Groot Melkhuis (p166), Café Toussaint (p164) and NeL (p134).

Markets

Kids love browsing the markets for both familiar and exotic treats. Try the Albert Cuypmarkt (p188) for *stroopwafel* (syrup waffles), fruit smoothies, chocolates, sweets and fresh fruit. Or pick up ingredients here and take a picnic to the nearby Sarphatipark.

Kid-friendly Shops

Dozens upon dozens of shops cater for children, who will adore deliberating over toys and sweet treats.

Check out De Beestenwinkel (p102) for stuffed-animal toys, Joe's Vliegerwinkel (p102) for kites, Mechanisch Speelgoed (p156) for nostalgic wind-up toys, De Winkel van Nijntje (p178) for merchandise related to Dutch illustrator Dick Bruna's most famous character – the cute rabbit Miffy (Nijntje in Dutch) – and Tinkerbell (p138), a toy-and-more store fronted by a mechanical bear blowing bubbles.

Het Oud-Hollandsch Snoepwinkeltje (p156) has jar after jar of Dutch penny sweets.

By Bike

Bicycles are more common than cars in Amsterdam. To roll like a local get a two-wheeler: rent one from the many outlets around town or your accommodation, and the city becomes your playground. It's the quintessential activity while visiting and makes it remarkably easy to get around.

LONELY PLANET/GETTY IMAGES ©

Cycling past the Royal Palace (p68)

Hiring a Bike

Many visitors rent a bike late in their stay and wish they'd done so sooner. Rental shops are everywhere; you'll have to show a passport or European national ID card and leave a credit card imprint or pay a deposit (usually €50). Prices for basic 'coaster-brake' bikes average €13.50 per 24-hour period. Bikes with gears and hand-brakes, and especially theft insurance, cost more.

Bike City (Map p320; ☎626 37 21; www.bike city.nl; Bloemgracht 68-70; bikes per 4/24hrs from €10/13.50; ⊙9am-6pm) Bikes carry no advertising so you'll look like a local.

Black Bikes (☎670 85 31; www.black-bikes. com; Nieuwezijds Voorburgwal 146; ⊙8am-8pm Mon-Fri, 9am-7pm Sat & Sun) Sign-less company, with cargo bikes for toting kids.

Damstraat Rent-a-Bike (☎625 50 29; www. rentabike.nl; Damstraat 20-22; ⊙9am-6pm) Lots of tandem bikes.

MacBike (☎620 09 85; www.macbike.nl) The most touristy (with logos) but has the most locations.

Recycled Bicycles (☎06 8505 9329; www. recycledbicycles.org; Spuistraat 84a; ⊙hrs vary Mon-Sat) Rents bikes rebuilt from scrap parts for just €5 per day.

Bike Tours

A bike tour is an ideal way to get to know Amsterdam. Bike rental is included in prices (tour companies also rent bikes). Be sure to reserve in advance. Countless great options include the following:

Orangebike (Map p308; ☎354 17 81; www. orange-bike.nl; Prins Hendrikkade 506; bike tours €19.50-29.50; ⊙office 9am-6pm) Traditional city and countryside tours (including a beach tour) plus themed options like the Snack Tour, sampling *bitterballen* (croquettes) and *jenever* (Dutch gin), and Eastern Harbour or Amsterdam School architectural tours. Also has an outlet at Oudezijds Voorburgwal 147.

Mike's Bike Tours (p135) A range of fantastic, often youth-oriented tours around town, the harbour and further afield south along the Amstel river, past dairy farms and windmills.

Yellow Bike (☎620 69 40; www.yellowbike.
nl; Nieuwezijds Kolk 29; city/countryside tours
€25/31.50) The original. Choose from city tours
or the longer countryside tour through the pretty
Waterland district to the north.

Road Rules

➡ Helmets aren't compulsory. Most Dutch
cyclists don't use them and they don't come
standard with rental.

➡ Amsterdam has 400km of bike paths. Use
the bicycle lane on the road's right-hand side,
marked by white lines and bike symbols.

➡ Cycle in the same direction as traffic and
adhere to all traffic lights and signs.

➡ Hand signal when turning.

➡ After dark, a white headlight and red tail light
are required by law.

➡ Park only in bicycle racks near train and tram
stations and in certain public squares (or risk
removal by the police).

Cycling Tips

➡ Most bikes come with two locks: one for the
front wheel (attach it to the bike frame), the
other for the back. One of these locks should
also be attached to a fixed structure (preferably
a bike rack).

➡ Cross tram rails at a sharp angle to avoid
getting stuck.

➡ Watch out for vehicles, other bikes and
oblivious pedestrians.

➡ Ring your bell as a warning as often as
necessary.

Buying a Bike

Cheap bikes are available from Recycled
Bicycles. Check out Fietsfabriek (p187) for
one-of-a-kind wheels.

Cycling Beyond the City

You don't have to pedal far from
Amsterdam to reach idyllic, windmill-
dotted landscapes. LF routes (*landelijke*

NEED TO KNOW

Bike Paths Route planner **Route-
craft** (http://routecraft.com) calculates
the best bike paths.

MacBike Maps Fun, city bike-maps
covering themes such as Rembrandt
sites, gay hot spots, Amsterdam
Noord's countryside and more. They
cost a euro or two and are available
at tourist offices, as well as MacBike
shops.

Assistance If your bike has been
stolen, call the police on ☎0900 88
44 or go to www.politie.nl/aangifte
and fill out the declaration form.

---

fietsroutes; long-distance routes somewhat
like bike highways) criss-cross the country.
Look out for the widely available Falk/
VVV *Fietskaart met Knooppuntennetwerk*
(cycling network) map series, with keys in
English.

By Numbers

➡ Total number of bikes in Amsterdam: 881,000

➡ Total number of cars: 220,000

➡ Total number of bike racks: 225,000

➡ Number of spaces at Centraal Station's bike-
parking garage: 2500

➡ Number of bikes stolen in Amsterdam each
year: 180,000

Top Cycling Spots

➡ **Vondelpark** (p161) Urban oasis.

➡ **Eastern Islands & Eastern Docklands** (p191)
Contemporary architecture.

➡ **Amsterdamse Bos** (p202) Enchanting
woodlands.

➡ **Herengracht** (p108) Historic canal houses.

➡ **Amstelsluizen** (p124) Riverside riding by the
locks.

Like a Local

Get on your bike, head to the nearest bruin café *and take a free course in Dutch culture by simply observing what goes on around you. It's one thing to witness local life and another to actually immerse yourself in it.*

The Other Side coffeeshop (p135)

LONELY PLANET/GETTY IMAGES ©

Embrace the *Gezellig* Culture

This particularly Dutch quality, which is most widely found in old *bruin cafés* (bars), is one of the best reasons to visit Amsterdam. It's variously translated as snug, friendly, cosy, informal, companionable and convivial, but *gezelligheid* – the state of being *gezellig* – is something more easily experienced than defined. There's a sense of time slowing, and of a connection with the present that allows you to forget your troubles (for now, at least). This warm and fuzzy feeling can be achieved in a variety of places and situations, often while nursing a brew with friends during *borrel* – an informal gathering over drinks (see p52 for more information). And nearly any cosy establishment lit by candles probably qualifies.

Find Your Way Around

Navigate the Country

'Holland' is a popular synonym for the Netherlands, yet it only refers to the combined provinces of Noord (North) and Zuid (South) Holland. (Amsterdam is Noord-Holland's largest city; Haarlem is the provincial capital.) The rest of the country is not Holland, even if locals themselves often make the mistake.

Navigate the City

Amsterdam's concentric canals and similarly named streets make it all too easy to get lost. Some pointers: a *gracht* (canal), such as Egelantiersgracht, is distinct from a *straat* (street), such as Egelantiersstraat. A *dwarsstraat* (cross-street) that intersects a *straat* is often preceded by *eerste, tweede, derde* and *vierde* (first, second, third and fourth; marked 1e, 2e, 3e and 4e on maps).

Eerste Egelantiersdwarsstraat, for example, is the first cross-street of Egelantiersstraat (ie the nearest cross-street to the city centre). Streets preceded by *lange* (long) and *korte* (short) simply mean the longer or shorter street. Be aware too that seemingly continuous streets regularly change name along their length.

Pedal Power

It takes spending all of five minutes in Amsterdam to realise that locals bike everywhere. Literally everywhere. They bike to the dentist, to work, to the opera and to brunch; they bike in snow, rain, sunshine and fog. So don't just rent a bike for a quick spin around the Vondelpark – get on the beaten path by biking everywhere, too. Dressing up to bike to dinner and a show, or to drinks and a club, is a typical Dutch pastime that locals shrug off but visitors marvel over. Put on a suit or a cocktail dress and pedal away. No matter what you wear or where you're going, you'll blend in (and have fun doing it).

Another great opportunity to join the locals is on National Cycling Day. It's held on the second Saturday in May, in conjunction with National Windmill Day, and includes family cycling trips along special routes.

Soak Up Dutch History

One of the best ways to experience Amsterdam's unique history – from the highs of the Golden Age to the tragic years of German occupation – is to join the crowds at one of the city's many history-oriented celebrations. On Liberation Day (5 May) Amsterdammers join together to celebrate the end of German occupation in 1945; it's jubilantly commemorated with speeches, concerts and street parties. The Dam, Vondelpark and Museumplein are generally the centre of festivities.

Another interesting, if more sombre, local experience is to trek down to the Dam on Remembrance Day (4 May), when King Willem-Alexander lays a wreath for the victims of WWII at the Nationaal Monument on the Dam. At 8pm sharp, the city solemnly observes two minutes' silence.

Orange Fever

If you've ever attended a sporting event where the Dutch are playing, you'll already be familiar with *oranjegekte* (orange craze), also known as *oranjekoorts* (orange fever). The custom of wearing the traditional colour of the Dutch royal family, the House of Orange-Nassau, was originally limited to celebration days for the monarchy, such as Queen's Day (Koninginnedag), now King's Day (Koningsdag). But particularly since the 1974 FIFA World Cup, when tens of thousands of orange-clad football supporters cheered on every game, the ritual of wearing outlandish orange get-ups – clothes, scarves, wigs, fake-fur top hats, face paint, feather boas, you name it – has become a Dutch phenomenon. To really celebrate like a local, you know what colour to wear.

Burning of the Christmas Trees

It's a strange Dutch tradition that makes even normally jaded adults positively wide-eyed: the burning of the Christmas trees. Think of it as a pagan version of Sinterklaas, a time when people of all ages take to the streets to create massive bonfires of festive trees past their prime, to usher in the New Year without 'dead wood', so to speak. The event usually takes place about a week after New Year's. Museumplein is a good spot to check out the madness.

Join in the Festivities

Explore the unique character of Amsterdam's diverse neighbourhoods by partying with the locals at a neighbourhood festival.

Revel in the city's rich Surinamese and African heritage at the food-and-football Kwaku (p203) festival, held in Bijlmerpark each weekend from mid-July to early August.

Listen to classic Jordaan ballads during the **Jordaan Festival** (www.jordaanfestival.nl).

Or grab your platinum blonde wig and platform shoes for the hysterically fun **Hartjesdagen Zeedijk** (Days of Hearts) festival, held on the third weekend of August. Dating back to medieval times, it features street theatre, a transvestite parade and all kinds of costumed extroverts on and around Zeedijk.

Locals party like it's King's Day during the **Uitmarkt** (www.uitmarkt.nl) festival, which kicks off the cultural season in late August/early September.

For Free

Although the costs of Amsterdam's accommodation and dining can mount up, there is a bright side. Not only is the entire Canal Ring a Unesco World Heritage Site (read: free, living museum), but virtually every day you'll find things to do and see that are free (or virtually free, at least).

Free Sights

➡ **The I Amsterdam Card** (p273) is a great money-saving card offering discounts and freebies at shops, attractions and restaurants. Students and seniors should bring ID and flash it at every opportunity for reduced admission fees.

➡ **Civic Guard Gallery** (p71) Stroll through the monumental collection of portraits, from Golden Age to modern.

➡ **Rijksmuseum Gardens** (p172) Even many locals don't know that the Renaissance and baroque gardens are free and open to the public (including occasional sculpture exhibitions). Let your pre-Raphaelite spirit run free as you explore the rose bushes, hedges and statues.

➡ **Begijnhof** (p69) Explore the 14th-century hidden courtyard and its clandestine churches. Wander the gardens, peek in the medieval church and drink in the silence.

➡ **Stadsarchief** (p121) You never know what treasures you'll find in the vaults of the city's archives.

➡ **Gassan Diamonds** (p96) Distinguish your princess from marquise, river from top cape.

➡ **Albert Cuypmarkt** (p188) Amsterdam's biggest market, and the city's many other bazaars, are all free to browse.

➡ **ARCAM** (p193) A fascinating look at Amsterdam's architecture – past, present and future.

Free Entertainment

➡ **Top tip**: even if you pay for entertainment at the Concertgebouw, Bimhuis or Muziekgebouw aan 't IJ, your ticket serves as a voucher for a free tram ride to and from the venue and a free drink in the concert hall lobby.

➡ For discounted last-minute tickets, visit **Uitburo** (www.amsterdamsuitburo.nl).

➡ **Concertgebouw** (p177) Sharpen your elbows to get in for Wednesday's lunchtime concert, often a public rehearsal for the performance later that evening.

➡ **Muziektheater** (p101) Free classical concerts fill the air during lunch on Tuesdays.

➡ **Bimhuis** (p197) Jazz sessions hot up the revered venue on Tuesday nights.

➡ **Openluchttheater** (p166) Vondelpark's outdoor theatre puts on concerts and kids' shows throughout summer.

➡ **EYE Film Institute** (p87) Has pods in the basement where you can watch free films.

➡ **Badcuyp** (p187) All-ages jazz shows bring the neighbourhood out to listen on Sunday afternoons.

➡ **Mulligans** (p133) Free music sessions and gigs at the city's best-known and loved Irish pub.

➡ **Festivals** (p23) Many festivals and events, including the ultimate party, King's Day, are totally free. (Well, you might want to bring some euros for beer and a cheap orange wig.)

Free Transport

Amsterdam's flat terrain makes it ideal for walking as well as cycling. If you're catching a lot of public transport, you'll save considerably by using an OV-chipkaart (p272).

Free ferries depart behind Centraal Station to NDSM-werf, northern Amsterdam's edgy art community 15 minutes up harbour, and to the EYE Film Institute, five minutes across the river.

Canal houses lining the Keizersgracht

 # Canals

Amsterdammers have always known their Canal Ring, built during the Golden Age, is extraordinary. Unesco made it official in 2010, when it listed the waterways as a World Heritage Site. Today the city's canals outnumber those in Venice, and Amsterdam also has three times as many bridges – more than any other city worldwide.

Names & Layout

In Dutch a canal is a *gracht (khrakht)* and the main canals form the central *grachtengordel* (canal ring). These beauties came to life in the early 1600s, after Amsterdam's population grew beyond its medieval walls and city planners put together an ambitious design for expansion. The concentric waterways they built are the same ones you see today.

CORE CANALS

Starting from the core, the major semicircular canals are the Singel, Herengracht, Keizersgracht and Prinsengracht. An easy way to remember them is that, apart from the singular **Singel** (which originally was a moat that defended Amsterdam's outer limits), these canals are in alphabetical order.

The **Herengracht** is where Amsterdam's wealthiest residents moved once the canals were completed. They built their mansions alongside it (particularly around the Golden Bend), hence its name, which translates to Gentlemen's Canal.

Almost as swanky was the **Keizersgracht** (Emperor's Canal), a nod to Holy Roman Emperor Maximilian I.

NEED TO KNOW

Canal Safety

Virtually none of Amsterdam's canals are fenced or otherwise blocked off by barriers. If you're travelling with young children, keep a close eye out to ensure they don't take an unexpected plunge.

Ice skating was part of the Dutch psyche long before scarfed figures appeared in Golden Age winterscapes. The first skates were made from cow shanks and ribs, had hand-drilled holes and were tied to the feet. When canals and ponds freeze over, everyone takes to the ice. Beware, though: drownings occur each year. Stay away from the ice unless you see large groups of people and be very careful at the edges and under bridges – areas with weak ice.

Boating Rules & Advice

➡ Stay on the waterways' right (starboard) side.

➡ Commercial traffic (including tour boats) has right of way.

➡ The speed limit is 7.5km per hour (the top speed for many electric rental boats).

➡ Life jackets/vests aren't compulsory (but are strongly recommended).

➡ Drinking alcohol while in control of a boat is illegal.

➡ Shouting and amplified music is also illegal on board.

➡ Many bridges have low clearance (less than 2m).

➡ Docking is permitted anywhere in the city except beneath bridges, on narrow waterways, junctions or adjacent to rescue steps, or locations signposted as prohibited.

➡ Switch on your lights at dusk.

The **Prinsengracht** – named after William the Silent, Prince of Orange and the first Dutch royal – was designed as a slightly cheaper canal with smaller residences and warehouses. It also acted as a barrier against the working-class Jordaan beyond.

RADIAL CANALS

The canals cutting across the core canals like spokes on a bicycle wheel are known as radial canals. From west to east the major radial canals are Brouwersgracht, Leidsegracht and Reguliersgracht, also in alphabetical order.

The **Brouwersgracht** (Brewers Canal) is one of Amsterdam's most beautiful waterways. It takes its name from the many breweries that lined the banks in the 16th and 17th centuries.

Leidsegracht was named after the city of Leiden, to which it was the main water route.

Peaceful **Reguliersgracht** was named after an order of monks whose monastery was located nearby. Today it's often better known as the 'canal of seven bridges' and its iconic scenery isn't lost on canal-boat operators.

Bridges

Some truly striking bridges straddle the city's waterways.

Spanning the Singel, the **Torensluis** (Singel 165a) was built in 1648, making it Amsterdam's oldest bridge (also its widest, at 39m). The Blauwbrug (p124) crosses the Amstel river, with fish sculptures and imperial-crowned street lamps dotting the way. And you've probably seen the iconic Magere Brug (p124) in photos or films, stretching over the Amstel, twinkling beneath the glow of 1200 tiny lights. In the Western Islands, look out for the charming, narrow Drieharingenbrug (p147).

Houseboats

Some 2500 houseboats line Amsterdam's canals. Living on the water became popular after WWII, when a surplus of old cargo ships helped fill the gap of a housing shortage on land. The Prinsengracht displays a particularly diverse mix of houseboats. You can climb aboard one and explore the cramped, er, cosy interior at the Houseboat Museum (p143), or book to stay overnight on the water yourself in true Amsterdam style.

Greener Canals

While Amsterdam's canals certainly aren't crystal clear (around 12,000 to 15,000 bicycles are pulled from the canals each year),

Canals by Neighbourhood

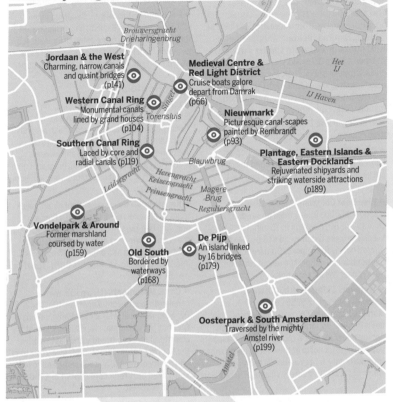

Brouwersgracht
Drieharingenbrug

Jordaan & the West
Charming, narrow canals
and quaint bridges
(p141)

**Medieval Centre &
Red Light District**
Cruise boats galore
depart from Damrak
(p66)

Het
IJ

IJ Haven

Western Canal Ring
Monumental canals
lined by grand houses
(p104)

Torensluis
Singel

Nieuwmarkt
Picturesque canal-scapes
painted by Rembrandt
(p93)

Southern Canal Ring
Laced by core and
radial canals (p119)

**Plantage, Eastern Islands &
Eastern Docklands**
Rejuvenated shipyards and
striking waterside attractions
(p189)

Herengracht
Keizersgracht
Prinsengracht
Leidsegracht

Blauwbrug

Magere
Brug
Reguliersgracht

Vondelpark & Around
Former marshland
coursed by water
(p159)

Old South
Bordered by
waterways
(p168)

De Pijp
An island linked
by 16 bridges
(p179)

Oosterpark & South Amsterdam
Traversed by the mighty
Amstel river
(p199)

Amstel

they're cleaner today than ever before in the city's history.

In part this is due to the locks, most of which close three times per week to allow fresh water to be pumped from the IJsselmeer lake. This creates a current that flushes the stagnant canal water out through open locks on the other side of the city and out to sea – check out the mighty Amstelsluizen (p124) on the Amstel in the Southern Canal Ring. What's more, the canals are regularly patrolled by specialised cleaning boats. And since 2005, houseboats have been required to connect to the city's sewerage system. All should be connected by 2016.

These efforts have made a significant difference, as evidenced by the wildlife the canals now attract. Some 20 fish and crab species now live happily below the water's surface. They, in turn, attract a wide variety of water birds such as gulls, herons, ducks, coots and cormorants. You might even see – or more likely, hear – neon-green ring-necked parakeets circling above. These, of course, aren't native; their presence in the city dates from 1976, when a pet-shop owner tormented by a pair of parakeets screeching in store, high-tailed them to the Vondelpark and let them loose. The birds soon bred and there are now more than 2000 pairs in the city.

Looking ahead, Amsterdam's city council is planning to allow only electric tour boats on its central canals. It's also considering a one-way boat-traffic system to further reduce emissions and noise pollution and to keep the waterways as pristine as possible.

Tours

Sure they're touristy, but canal cruises are also a delightful way to see the city. Several operators depart from moorings at Centraal Station, Damrak, Rokin and opposite the Rijksmuseum. Costs are similar (around €14 per adult). To avoid the steamed-up glass window effect, look for a boat with an open-seating area. On a night tour you'll see the bridges lit up (though these tours usually cost a bit more).

➡ **Artis Royal Zoo Express** (p193) A great way to combine a trip to the zoo with a canal tour.

➡ **Canal Bus** (p272) Offers a handy hop-on, hop-off service. Its 19 docks around the city are located near landmarks including the big museums.

➡ **Blue Boat Company** (Map p310; www. blueboat.nl) Blue Boat's main tour (adult/child €13/6.50) clocks in at 75 minutes. Evening cruises (adult/child €15.50/14) are offered hourly from 7pm to 9pm from April to September and at 8pm the rest of the year. The dock is near the Max Euweplein.

➡ **Wetlands Safari** (Map p300; www. wetlandssafari.nl; 📞5355 26 69; ⏱9.30am Mon-Fri, 10am Sun) OK, so it's not a canal tour, but it is an exceptional 5½-hour boat trip (per person incl transport & picnic €43). Participants get a bus to just north of the centre, then canoe through boggy, froggy wetlands and on past windmills and 17th-century villages. There's also an electric-boat tour option. Departure is from the tourist office opposite Centraal Station.

➡ Filled with historical info, *Canal* magazine (€3.50; available in English) has an illustrated walking and cycling route along the canals. It's available from Amsterdam's tourist offices as well as some museums, hotels and bookshops.

Boat Rentals

➡ **Canal Bike** (Map p322; www.canal.nl; ⏱10am-6pm Apr-Oct, to 10pm in summer) These pedal boats allow you to splash around the canals at your own speed. Landing stages are by the Rijksmuseum, Leidseplein, Anne Frank Huis and the corner of Keizersgracht and Leidsestraat. Deposit of €20 required. Affiliated with Canal Bus.

➡ **Kanoschool** (www.kanoschool.nl; 1hr kayak tours €10, kayak rental per hr €10) Rents one- and two-person canoes for paddling along the canals (waterway map and tips supplied; photo ID required as a deposit) and runs weekly one-hour canoe tours. Also has SUPs (stand-up paddle boards).

➡ **Canal Motorboats** (Map p303; www. canalmotorboats.com; Zandhoek 10a; 📞422 70 07; ⏱9am-sunset) Has small aluminium boats (per hr €50; maximum six passengers) that are electric, silent, eco-friendly and easy to drive (no boat licence required). Staff give you a map and plenty of advice, and will come and rescue you if need be. Credit card imprint or €150 cash deposit required.

Lonely Planet's Top Choices

Prinsengracht (p109) The liveliest of Amsterdam's inner canals, with cafes, shops and houseboats lining the quays.

Reguliersgracht (p124) From here you can peer through the arches of seven bridges.

Brouwersgracht (p143) Among some seriously tough competition, Amsterdammers swear this is the city's most beautiful canal.

Herengracht (p108) Amsterdam's stateliest canal takes in the city's most prestigious real estate along the Golden Bend.

Bloemgracht (p143) This gorgeous canal is home to a large number of fine, gabled houses.

Egelantiersgracht (p143) An elegant and serene canal that feels like you have it (practically) to yourself.

Best Canal-Related Museums

Houseboat Museum (p143) Discover how *gezellig* (convivial, cosy) houseboat living can be aboard this 1914 sailing barge-turned-museum.

Het Grachtenhuis (p110) 'Canal House' tours explain how the canals and houses were integral in Amsterdam city planning.

Best Canal Festivals & Events

King's Day (p23) During one of Europe's biggest street parties, plenty of action takes place around the city's famous waterways.

Grachtenfestival (p24) The 'Canal Festival' sees classical musicians play alongside and on the water aboard a barge.

Amsterdam Gay Pride (p24) Amsterdam proudly hosts the only waterborne gay pride festival in the world.

Open Tuinen Dagen (p24) 'Open Garden Days' offer the opportunity to view dozens of private gardens along the canals.

Sinterklaas Intocht (p24) Even St Nicholas sails into town; his arrival by boat heralds the start of Christmas season.

Amsterdam Light Festival (p25) Highlights include a magical, mid-December Christmas Canal Parade of illuminated boats floating along the waterways.

Best Houseboat Accommodation

Houseboat Ms Luctor (p231) A beautiful 1913-built self-contained boat with mahogany panelling, moored in a quiet location near Centraal Station.

B&B Le Maroxidien (p234) Dutch hospitality in a former freighter with three exotically themed cabins in its guest wing.

Frederic Rentabike (p227) Not only rents bikes but a range of houseboats on the Prinsengracht, Brouwersgracht and Bloemgracht.

Best Canal-Side Dining

Café Restaurant Open (p151) On top of a disused 1920 railway bridge, with pivoting windows and an open kitchen.

De Belhamel (p112) At the head of the Herengracht, this superb restaurant's canal-side tables are an aphrodisiac.

Buffet van Odette (p127) Simple, creative cooking overlooking the Prinsengracht's crooked canal houses.

Gebr Hartering (p195) Exquisitely presented contemporary Dutch dishes compete with the impossibly romantic canal-side location.

Best Canal-Side Drinking

't Smalle (p151) Dock right by the charming stone terrace of this 18th-century former *jenever* (Dutch gin) distillery.

Café P 96 (p152) The summertime terrace of this late-night watering hole is aboard a houseboat.

Het Papeneiland (p152) A 1642 gem on the corner of the Prinsengracht and Brouwersgracht canals.

De Ysbreeker (p204) Hot spot overlooking the houseboat-dotted Amstel.

Café de Jaren (p82) Sip drinks on the balcony, watch the Amstel flow by, and the afternoon vanishes.

Café Binnen Buiten (p185) The best canal-side terrace in Amsterdam's 'Latin Quarter', De Pijp.

Museums & Galleries

Amsterdam's world-class museums draw millions of visitors each year. The art collections take pride of place – you can't walk a kilometre here without bumping into a masterpiece. Canal-house museums are another local speciality. And, of course, the freewheeling city has a fine assortment of oddball museums dedicated to everything from hash to houseboats.

All the Art

The Dutch Masters helped spawn the prolific art collections around town. You've probably heard of a few of these guys: Jan Vermeer, Frans Hals and Rembrandt van Rijn. They came along during the Golden Age when a new, bourgeois society of merchants and shopkeepers were spending money to brighten up their homes and workplaces with fresh paintings. The masters were there to meet the need, and their output from the era now fills the city's top museums.

Other Treasures

The Netherlands' maritime prowess during the Golden Age also filled the coffers of local institutions. Silver, porcelain and colonial knick-knacks picked up on distant voyages form the basis of collections in the Rijksmuseum, Amsterdam Museum, Het Scheepvaartmuseum and Tropenmuseum.

Canal-House Museums

There are two kinds: the first preserves the house as a living space, with sumptuous interiors that show how the richest locals lived once upon a time, as at Museum van Loon. The other type uses the elegant structure as a backdrop for unique collections, such as the Kattenkabinet for cat art.

Contemporary Galleries

Van Gogh and the Golden Age masters grab all the glory, but Amsterdam's art scene goes well beyond them. Several contemporary galleries dot the city, providing outlets for avant-garde and emerging artists. Many galleries, such as W139 in the Red Light District, began as squats and then moved into the mainstream over the years. Gallery-dense neighbourhoods include the Jordaan and the Southern Canal Ring.

How to Beat the Crowds

Queues at the Van Gogh Museum, Rijksmuseum, Anne Frank Huis and others can easily reach an hour, particularly in summer. Want to avoid the mobs? Here are some strategies:

➡ **Take advantage of e-tickets** Most sights sell them and there's little to no surcharge. They typically allow you to enter via a separate, faster queue. Note that, in most cases, you need to be able to print the tickets.

➡ **Go late** Queues are shortest during late afternoon and evening. Visit after 3pm for the Rijksmuseum and Van Gogh Museum (also open Friday nights), and after 6pm for the Anne Frank Huis (open late nightly in summer).

➡ **Try tourist offices** You can also buy advance tickets at tourist offices, but often the queues there are as lengthy as the ones at the sights.

➡ **Buy a discount card** In addition to saving on entrance fees, discount cards commonly provide fast-track entry.

How to Save Money

Discount cards can save you lots of cash, as long as you choose wisely. There are three main options:

➡ **I Amsterdam Card** (p273) Good for quick visits to the city. Provides admission to more than 30 museums (many of the same venues as the Museum Card), plus a GVB transit pass, a canal cruise, and restaurant and shop discounts. You'll need to visit three or so museums per day to make it pay for itself.

➡ **Museumkaart** (p275) This card works well if you plan to be in the Netherlands a while. It provides free entry to some 400 museums nationwide for a year. Great for queue-jumping; no transit pass or other perks though.

➡ **Holland Pass** (p273) It's similar to the I Amsterdam Card, but without the rush for usage; you can visit sights over a prolonged period. It gets a bit tricky to figure out how much money you're saving because you pick from 'tiers' of attractions (the most popular/expensive sights are top-tier). It also includes a local transit pass.

Museums & Galleries by Neighbourhood

➡ **Medieval Centre & Red Light District** (p71) Spans the sacred (several church museums) to the profane (Sexmuseum; Hash, Marijuana & Hemp Museum).

➡ **Nieuwmarkt** (p96) Museum Het Rembrandthuis and the Joods Historisch Museum anchor the area.

➡ **Western Canal Ring** (p108) Anne Frank Huis draws the mega-crowds; smaller, canal-focused museums pop up, too.

➡ **Southern Canal Ring** (p121) Home to the Hermitage Amsterdam plus several quirky museums.

➡ **Jordaan & the West** (p143) Off-the-beaten path collections from tulips to houseboats to fluorescent art.

➡ **Old South** (p168) Holds the Museum Quarter and its big three: Van Gogh Museum, Rijksmuseum and Stedelijk Museum.

➡ **De Pijp** (p181) Crowds amass to learn about brewing at the Heineken Experience.

➡ **Plantage, Eastern Islands & Eastern Docklands** (p191) NEMO, Het

NEED TO KNOW

Opening Hours

➡ Most museums: 10am to 5pm, some close on Monday.

➡ The Van Gogh Museum stays open to 10pm Fridays.

➡ The Anne Frank Huis stays open to 9pm or 10pm daily in summer and Saturdays year-round.

Costs

➡ Tickets: typically €6–15.

➡ Kids under 13 often get in for free or half-price.

➡ Audio guides €2–5.

Top Tips

➡ Pre-book tickets for the big museums.

➡ Queues are shortest during late afternoon and evening.

➡ Friday, Saturday and Sunday are the busiest days.

➡ Many hotels sell surcharge-free tickets to the big museums as a service to guests; be sure to ask your front-desk staff.

Advance Purchase Recommendations

➡ **Van Gogh Museum & Rijksmuseum** No surcharge for e-tickets; puts you in a faster queue.

➡ **Anne Frank Huis** Small surcharge for e-tickets with set entry times; lets you bypass the queue.

➡ **Stedelijk Museum** No surcharge for e-tickets; lets you bypass the queue.

➡ **Heineken Experience & Madame Tussauds Amsterdam** E-tickets provide a small discount over regular admission; puts you in a faster queue.

➡ **Het Grachtenhuis** E-tickets provide a small discount over regular admission, but mostly they ensure access for the limited-space tours.

Scheepvaartmuseum and the Verzetsmuseum are scattered around the neighbourhood.

➡ **Oosterpark & South Amsterdam** (p201) Colonial trinkets at Tropenmuseum, avant-garde art at Cobra Museum.

Lonely Planet's Top Choices

Van Gogh Museum (p170) Hangs the world's largest collection of the tormented artist's vivid swirls.

(p172) Rembrandts, Vermeers, crystal goblets and magic lanterns pack the nation's sprawling treasure chest.

Anne Frank Huis (p106) The Secret Annexe and Anne's claustrophobic bedroom provide an unnerving insight into life during WWII.

Pianola Museum (p143) Listen to rare jazz and classical tunes unrolling on vintage player pianos.

Best Art Museums

Museum Het Rembrandthuis (p95) Immerse yourself in the old master's paint-spattered studio and handsome home.

Stedelijk Museum (p175) Renowned modern art from Picasso to Mondrian to Warhol fills the newly revamped building.

Hermitage Amsterdam (p125) The outpost of Russia's Hermitage Museum picks from its rich home trove to mount mega exhibits.

FOAM (p121) Hip photography museum with changing exhibits by famous shutterbugs.

Best History Museums

Amsterdam Museum (p73) Whiz-bang exhibits take you through seven centuries of the city's intriguing history.

Verzetsmuseum (p194) Find out how the Dutch Resistance operated when the Germans occupied the country during WWII.

Best Unusual Museums

Tassenmuseum Hendrikje (p121) A museum of handbags and purses throughout history, with lots of sparkling celebrity clutches.

Kattenkabinet (p123) Art devoted to cats (including works by Picasso and Rembrandt) fills a rambling old canal house.

Electric Ladyland (p145) The world's first museum of fluorescent art offers a trippy glow-in-the-dark experience.

Torture Museum (p73) Eerie galleries show branding tongs, skull crackers, a guillotine and the Iron Maiden of Nuremberg.

Sexmuseum Amsterdam (p71) The naughty art and artefacts make for a fun, silly browse.

Best Canal-House Museums

Museum Van Loon (p126) This opulent old manor whispers family secrets in its shadowy rooms.

Museum Willet-Holthuysen (p123) Peruse sumptuous paintings, china and a French-style garden with sundial.

Best Underappreciated Museums

Tropenmuseum (p201) Contains a whopping collection of ritual masks, spiky spears and other colonial booty.

Het Scheepvaartmuseum (p191) The Maritime Museum features ancient globes, spooky ship figureheads and a replica schooner to climb.

Museum Ons' Lieve Heer op Solder (p78) Looks like an ordinary canal house, but hides a relic-rich 17th-century church inside.

Best Galleries & Arts Centres

Walls Gallery (p138) Edgy space in a former garage that shows up-and-coming artists.

W139 (p77) Ponder political, hot-button multimedia works in the thick of the Red Light District.

Civic Guard Gallery (p71) Stroll through the monumental collection of portraits, from Golden Age to modern day.

De Appel (p97) Count on having your mind expanded at this hip, contemporary arts centre.

Best for Kids

NEMO (p192) Kid-focused, hands-on science labs inside; an artificial beach with sand and ice cream is located on the roof.

Joods Historisch Museum (p96) The children's section replicates a Jewish home, with a hands-on music room and kitchen for baking.

Madame Tussauds Amsterdam (p71) Youth get excited to see their favourite celebrities and heroes up close (albeit in wax).

Eating a herring, Albert Cuypmarkt (p188)

Eating

We'll just call Amsterdam's hot global eats and locally sourced fare our little secret. Wherever you go, meals – from Indonesian rice tables to mod Moroccan plates – are something to linger over with friends as the candles burn low on the tabletop.

NEED TO KNOW

Price Ranges

In our listings we've used these price ranges for the cost of a main dish at dinner:

€ less than €12

€€ €12–25

€€€ more than €25

Opening Hours

Most restaurants open 11am to 2.30pm for lunch, 6 to 10pm for dinner.

Reservations

Phone ahead to make a reservation for eateries in the middle and upper price brackets. Nearly everyone speaks English. Many places let you book online.

Service

Service in Amsterdam may be impersonal, off-putting and slow. Don't take it personally; it's not directed at you.

Tipping

Diners do tip, but modestly. Round up to the next euro, or around 5%; a 10% tip is considered generous. If your bill comes to €9.50, you might leave €10.

Cash Rules

Many restaurants, even top-end, don't accept credit cards. Or if they do, there's a 5% surcharge. Check first.

Saving Money

Dagschotel is dish of the day; heartier appetites might go for a *dagmenu* (a set menu of three or more courses).

Best Websites

➡ **Amsterdam Foodie** (www.amsterdam foodie.nl) Restaurant reviews galore.

➡ **Dutchgrub** (www.dutchgrub.com) An expat's quest for great local food.

➡ **IENS** (www.iens.nl) Everyday eaters give their restaurant opinions; in Dutch.

Specialities

TRADITIONAL DUTCH

Traditional Dutch cuisine revolves around meat, potatoes and vegetables. Typical dishes include *stamppot* (mashed pot) – potatoes mashed with another vegetable

Vlaamse frites (Flemish fries; p46)

(usually kale or endive) and served with smoked sausage and strips of bacon. *Erwtensoep* is a thick pea soup with smoked sausage and bacon that's usually served in winter.

Pannenkoeken translates to pancakes – the Dutch variety is huge, served one to a plate and topped with sweet or savoury ingredients. The mini-version, covered in sugar or syrup, is *poffertjes*. You can often find these fresh at markets. Many snack bars and pubs serve *appeltaart* (apple pie). For breakfast it's common to eat *hagelslag* (chocolate sprinkles) on buttered bread.

CONTEMPORARY DUTCH

Fresh winds are blowing through the Dutch traditional kitchen, breathing new life into centuries-old recipes by giving them a contemporary twist. Creative Dutch chefs are taking concepts from the rest the world and melding them with locally sourced meats, seafood and vegetables. Amsterdam is ground zero for this type of 'contemporary Dutch' fare.

INDONESIAN & SURINAMESE

The most famous dish is *rijsttafel* (Indonesian banquet): a dozen or more tiny dishes such as braised beef, pork satay and ribs served with white rice. Other popular dishes are *nasi goreng* – fried rice with onion, pork, shrimp and spices, often topped with a fried egg or shredded omelette – and *bami goreng*, the same thing but with noodles in place of rice. Indonesian food is usually served mild for Western palates. If you want it hot (*pedis*, pronounced 'p-*dis*'), say so but be prepared for the ride of a lifetime.

Above: De Kaaskamer cheese shop (p116)

Right: *Rijsttafel* (Indonesian banquet)

JAMES BAIGRIE/GETTY IMAGES ©

Surinamese Caribbean–style cuisine features curries (chicken, lamb or beef) prominently. Roti are burrito-like flatbread wraps stuffed with curried meat or veg; they're delicious, filling and cheap.

Snacks

➡ **Vlaamse frites/patat** The iconic 'Flemish fries' are cut from whole potatoes and smothered in mayonnaise or myriad other gooey sauces.

➡ **Kroketten** Croquettes are dough balls with various fillings that are crumbed and deep-fried; the variety called *bitterballen* are a popular brown *café* snack served with mustard.

➡ **Haring** Herring is a Dutch institution, sold at stalls around the city. It's prepared with salt or pickled but never cooked, and served with diced onion and sometimes sweet-pickle chips.

Cheese

Locals love their *kaas* (cheese). Nearly two-thirds of all cheese sold is Gouda. The tastiest varieties have strong, complex flavours. Try some *oud* (old) Gouda, hard and rich in flavour and a popular bar snack with mustard. Edam is similar to Gouda but slightly drier and less creamy. Leidse or Leiden cheese is another export hit, laced with cumin or caraway seed and light in flavour.

Sweets

The most famous candy is *drop*, sweet or salty liquorice sold in a bewildering variety of flavours. It's definitely an acquired taste.

LOCAL EAT STREETS

These streets are stocked with popular local restaurants, where you can wander and choose whatever takes your fancy.

Amstelveenseweg Loads of international options along the western edge of Vondelpark.

Utrechtsestraat Chock-a-block with cafes where cool young Amsterdammers hang out; in the Southern Canal Ring.

Haarlemmerstraat & Haarlemmerdijk Adjoining streets north of the Jordaan that burst with trendy spots.

Stroopwafels hide their filling – usually thick caramel syrup – inside two cookie-esque waffles.

Quick Eats

Besides restaurants and *eetcafés* (pub-like eateries serving affordable meals), there are several quick options for feeding your face. *Broodjeszaken* (sandwich shops) are everywhere. Stroll up to the counter and pick the meat and/or cheese to go on a fluffy white or wheat roll for a few euros. Snack bars are also ubiquitous. FEBO is the most well-known, with its long rows of coin-operated yellow windows from which you pluck out a deep-fried treat. Branches are open into the wee hours, and stopping by for a greasy snack after a hard night of drinking is a Dutch tradition.

Eating by Neighbourhood

➡ **Medieval Centre & Red Light District** (p77) Name your price: from elegant Dutch to Zeedijk's Asian restaurants to alley-side sandwich shops.

➡ **Nieuwmarkt** (p98) The lively main square brims with locals digging in at outdoor terraces.

➡ **Western Canal Ring** (p110) Cute cafes and small restaurants surround the Negen Straatjes.

➡ **Southern Canal Ring** (p125) Cheap and cheerful around Leidseplein; diverse, quality options on Utrechtsestraat.

➡ **Jordaan & the West** (p146) Convivial little spots are the Jordaan's hallmark; scenester eats dot Westerpark.

➡ **Vondelpark & Around** (p162) International options along Amstelveenseweg; several squats serve organic vegan fare.

➡ **Old South** (p176) A scattering of chichi restaurants feed the genteel neighbourhood.

➡ **De Pijp** (p204) Grazing galore in the Albert Cuypmarket; exotic ethnic places west on Albert Cuypstraat and Ferdinand Bolstraat.

➡ **Plantage, Eastern Islands & Eastern Docklands** (p204) Options can be a trek to reach, but are worth it for the dramatic food/location combo.

➡ **Oosterpark & South Amsterdam** (p204) Indonesian, Moroccan, Turkish and Surinamese abounds.

Lonely Planet's Top Choices

Ron Gastrobar (p162) Ron Blaauw converted his swank, Michelin-starred eatery into this democratic spot serving Dutch-style tapas.

Pont 13 (p148) Vintage car ferry moored in the Western Docklands with a superb Mediterranean-inspired menu.

Café Restaurant Open (p151) Stunning glass restaurant atop a 1920 railway bridge, with an open kitchen cooking contemporary cuisine.

De Kas (p204) Dine in the greenhouse that grew your meal's ingredients.

Gartine (p79) Slow-food sandwiches and a dazzling high tea hide in the Medieval Centre.

Best by Budget

€

The Butcher (p183) Quite possibly the biggest, freshest burgers you'll ever taste, made right in front of you.

Little Collins (p183) Hip little hangout with extraordinarily good tapas and brunches.

'Skek (p81) Students serve thick-cut sandwiches and healthy main dishes for bargain prices.

€€

Brasserie De Joffers (p162) Beautiful art-deco brasserie with exquisite dishes and a table-lined terrace.

Wilde Zwijnen (p204) The Oost's rustic gem reaps praise for bold, eclectic seasonal fare.

Latei (p99) Cute-as-a-button cafe by day goes global Thursday through Saturday nights with Indonesian or Indian fare.

€€€

Ciel Bleu (p185) Mind-blowing, two-Michelin-starred haute cuisine with 23rd-floor views over Amsterdam.

Blauw aan de Wal (p81) 17th-century herb warehouse turned romantic restaurant in the Red Light District.

Best by Cuisine

Traditional Dutch

Bistro Bij Ons (p112) Honest-to-goodness classics include *stamppot*.

Letting (p110) Skip your hotel dining room and start the day with authentic Dutch breakfast dishes.

La Falote (p176) Stewed fish, meatballs with endives and other daily specials of home-style cooking.

Van Dobben (p126) Meaty goodness diner-style.

Contemporary Dutch

Greetje (p195) Resurrects and re-creates Dutch classics, with mouthwatering results.

Gebr Hartering (p195) In a seductive canal-side location, the menu changes daily but is unfailingly delicious.

Hemelse Modder (p99) North Sea fish followed by a heavenly mousse for dessert.

Indonesian

Blue Pepper (p165) Indonesian cuisine is elevated to an art form in this dramatic blue dining room.

Restaurant Blauw (p165) Feted Indonesian fare in contemporary surrounds.

Tempo Doeloe (p129) High-class *rijsttafel* without pretense, and one that knows how to fire up the spice.

Surinamese

Spang Makandra (p183) Fabulous array of astonishingly cheap dishes served in cosy surrounds.

Tokoman (p98) Crowds queue for the hot-spiced Surinamese sandwiches.

Best Bakeries & Sweets

Patisserie Holtkamp (p130) You're in good company as the gilded, royal coat of arms outside attests.

Bakken Met Passie (p183) Watch bakers at work while you dine amid the heavenly aromas.

Lanskroon (p78) One word: *stroopwafel*.

Best Vegetarian

SLA (p181) Super-chic spot with design-your-own organic salads.

Alchemist Garden (p165) Vegan heaven, serving delicious gluten-, lactose- and glucose-free dishes.

De Waaghals (p185) The menu emulates a different country each month, but it's always vegie.

Best Places to Eat Like a Local

Madelief (p165) Local foodies' secret near Vondelpark.

Worst Wijncafe (p150) Sausage-y tapas and a big Sunday brunch in the West.

Éénvistwéévis (p195) Fresh seafood from nearby waters; in the Plantage.

Preparing cocktails

🍷 Drinking & Nightlife

Amsterdam is one of the wildest nightlife cities in Europe and the world, and the testosterone-fuelled stag parties of young chaps roaming the Red Light District know exactly what they're doing here. Yet you can easily avoid the hardcore party scene if you choose to: Amsterdam also retains a café (pub) society where the pursuit of pleasure centres on cosiness and charm.

Amsterdam coffeeshop

Where to Drink
CAFÉS

When the Dutch say *'café'* they mean a pub, and there are more than 1000 of them in Amsterdam. In a city that values socialising and conversation more than the art of drinking itself, *cafés* aren't just about consuming alcohol: they're places to hang out, literally for hours of contemplation or camaraderie. Scores of *cafés* have outside seating on a *terras* (terrace), which are glorious in summer and sometimes covered and heated in winter. Most of these *cafés* serve food as well, ranging from snacks and sandwiches to excellent meals.

Brown cafés Amsterdam is famed for its historic *bruin cafés*. The name comes from the smoke stains from centuries of use (although recent aspirants slap on brown paint to catch up). You may find sand on the wooden floor to soak up spilt beer. Most importantly, the city's brown *cafés* provide an atmosphere conducive to deep, meaningful conversation – and inducing the nirvana of *gezelligheid* (conviviality, cosiness).

Grand cafés These are spacious, have comfortable furniture and are, well, grand. They all have food menus, some quite elaborate. Despite the name, there's no need to dress up for a visit to a grand *café*.

Theatre cafés Often similar to grand *cafés* and normally attached or adjacent to theatres, these serve meals before and drinks after performances. Generally they're good places to catch performers after the show, though they're lovely any time of day.

NEED TO KNOW
Coffeeshop vs Café

First things first: *café* culture should not be mistaken for coffeeshop (marijuana-smoking cafe) culture, and there's a *big* difference between a *café* (pub) or *koffiehuis* (espresso bar) and a coffeeshop. A coffeeshop may serve coffee (never alcohol) but it has a lot to do with cannabis.

Smoking (any substance) is banned by law in *cafés*.

Opening Hours

➡ *Cafés* serving breakfast tend to open around 9am or 10am, while others – notably many of the cosy brown *cafés* – are late risers, opening around noon.

➡ Bars usually open sometime between 5pm and 6pm.

➡ Coffeeshops generally open around noon.

➡ Closing times at all drinking and smoking establishments tends to be late – between midnight and 2am (as late as 3am at weekends).

➡ Most nightclubs close at 2am or 3am Sunday to Thursday and at 4am or 5am on Friday and Saturday nights. Most places are dead until after midnight on weeknights, or until 1am or 2am on weekends. Looking for an after-party? Head to an after-hours *nachtcafe* (night *café*).

Wi-fi

The majority of Amsterdam's bars and cafes, as well as some coffeeshops, have free wi-fi; you may need to ask for the code.

AMSTERDAM'S GAY SCENE

The Netherlands was the first country to legalise same-sex marriage (in 2001), so it's no surprise that Amsterdam's gay scene is one of the largest in the world. Five hubs party the hardest:

Warmoesstraat In the Red Light District (between the Dam and Centraal Station), it hosts the infamous, kink-filled leather and fetish bars.

Zeedijk Near Warmoesstraat, crowds spill onto laid-back bar terraces.

Above: Coffeeshop interior
Left: 't Smalle brown *café* (p151)

Drinking & Nightlife by Neighbourhood

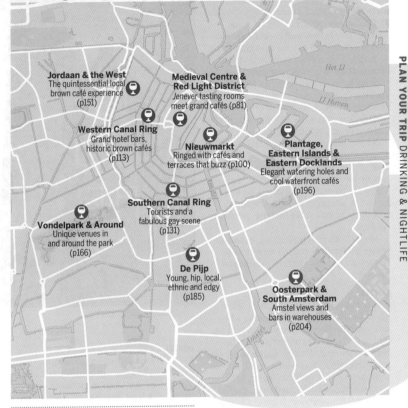

Jordaan & the West
The quintessential local brown café experience (p151)

Medieval Centre & Red Light District
Jenever tasting rooms meet grand cafés (p81)

Western Canal Ring
Grand hotel bars, historic brown cafés (p113)

Nieuwmarkt
Ringed with cafés and terraces that buzz (p100)

Plantage, Eastern Islands & Eastern Docklands
Elegant watering holes and cool waterfront cafés (p196)

Southern Canal Ring
Tourists and a fabulous gay scene (p131)

Vondelpark & Around
Unique venues in and around the park (p166)

De Pijp
Young, hip, local, ethnic and edgy (p185)

Oosterpark & South Amsterdam
Amstel views and bars in warehouses (p204)

Rembrandtplein In the Southern Canal Ring, this area has traditional pubs and brown *cafés*, some with a campy bent.

Leidseplein A smattering of trendy venues along Kerkstraat.

Reguliersdwarsstraat Draws the beautiful crowd.

Local gay and lesbian organisations (see p276) can help you tap into the city's scene.

Drinks
BEER

In stiff competition with a few of their European cohorts – the Belgians, Germans, Irish and Czechs – the Dutch take their beer very seriously (although they drink less per capita than any of them).

Lager beer is the staple, served cool and topped by a two-finger-thick head of froth to trap the flavour. Requests of 'no head please' will meet with a steely response. (Any Dutch bartender knows that a proper pour is a foamy one.) *Een bier, een pils* or *een vaasje* will get you a normal glass of beer; *een kleintje pils* is a small glass and *een fluitje* is a small, thin, Cologne-style glass. Many places also serve *een grote pils* (half-litre mugs) to please tourists, but it goes flat if you don't drink quickly.

Local brands include Heineken, Amstel, Grolsch, Oranjeboom, Dommelsch and Bavaria (which, despite its name, isn't German but Dutch). Stronger Belgian beers, such as Duvel and Westmalle Triple, are also very popular. *Witbier* (white beer) is a cloudy blonde beer drunk in summer with a slice of lemon. Dark, sweet *bokbier* comes out in the autumn.

Don't miss Amsterdam's wonderful microbreweries Brouwerij 't IJ (p197) and Brouwerij de Prael (p85).

WINE & SPIRITS

It's not just beer here: the Dutch also make the hard stuff. *Jenever* (ye-*nay*-ver; Dutch gin; also spelt *genever*) is made from juniper berries and is drunk chilled. It arrives in a tulip-shaped shot glass filled to the brim – tradition dictates that you bend over the bar, with your hands behind your back, and take a deep sip. Most people prefer *jonge* (young) *jenever*, which is smooth and relatively easy to drink; *oude* (old) *jenever* has a strong juniper flavour and can be an acquired taste.

A common combination, known as a *kopstoot* (head butt), is a glass of *jenever* with a beer chaser – few people can handle more than two or three of these. There are plenty of indigenous liqueurs, including *advocaat* (a kind of eggnog) and the herb-based Beerenburg, a Frisian schnapps.

More Dutch people drink wine than ever before, although almost all wine here is imported from elsewhere in Europe and beyond.

COFFEE

The hot drink of choice is coffee – after all, it was Amsterdam's merchants who introduced coffee to Europe. It should be strong and can be excellent if it's freshly made. If you simply order *koffie* you'll get a sizeable cup of java with a small, airline-style container of *koffiemelk*, similar to unsweetened condensed milk. *Koffie verkeerd* (wrong coffee) comes in a bigger cup or mug with plenty of real milk – it's similar to a caffe latte.

De Sluyswacht brown *café* (p100)

BORREL

Borrel in Dutch means, quite simply, 'drink' – as in a glass of spirits, traditionally *jenever*. But in social parlance, to be invited to *borrel* means to take part in an informal gathering for drinks, conversation and fun. It usually incorporates food too, especially *borrelhapjes* (bar snacks) like *borrelnootjes* (peanuts covered in a

COFFEESHOP & SMART SHOP DOS & DON'TS

➡ Do ask coffeeshop staff for advice on what and how to consume, and heed it, even if nothing happens after an hour.

➡ Don't ask for hard (illegal) drugs.

➡ Ask staff for the menu of products on offer. Most shops offer rolling papers, pipes or bongs to use; you can also buy ready-made joints.

➡ Don't drink alcohol – it's illegal.

➡ Don't smoke tobacco, whether mixed with marijuana or on its own; it is forbidden in accordance with the Netherlands' laws.

➡ 'Herbal ecstasy' – usually a mix of herbs, vitamins and caffeine – is sold in smart shops; ask staff what they recommend, as some varieties can have unpleasant side effects.

➡ Psilocybin mushrooms (aka magic mushrooms) are now illegal in the Netherlands, but many smart shops sell mushroom truffles, which have a similar effect.

crisp, spicy outer shell), and *kroketten* (croquettes) including *bitterballen* (small, round meat croquettes) – the name comes from the tradition of serving them with bitters, namely *jenever*.

Any occasion can be a reason for *borrel*: a birthday, a beautiful sunset that invites patio sitting, the end of a work day (*vrijdagmiddagborrel*, usually shortened to *vrijmibo* or just *vrimibo* is specifically Friday-afternoon work drinks with colleagues). When you see a group of locals spilling out of a brown *café* onto the street with a glass of beer in hand? That's *borrel*. Grab a beer (or buy someone one) and join in. The famously tolerant and open Dutch rarely mind an addition to the party.

Smoking
MARIJUANA & HASHISH

Despite what you may have heard, cannabis is not *technically* legal in the Netherlands – yet it is widely tolerated. Here's the deal: the possession and purchase of small amounts (5g) of 'soft drugs' (ie marijuana, hashish, space cakes and mushroom-based truffles) is allowed and users won't be prosecuted for smoking or carrying this amount. This means that coffeeshops are actually conducting an illegal business – but again, this is tolerated to a certain extent.

Most cannabis products sold in the Netherlands used to be imported, but today the country has high-grade home produce, so-called *nederwiet*. It's a particularly strong product – the most potent varieties contain 15% tetrahydrocannabinol (THC), the active substance that gets people high (since 2011, anything above 15% is classified as a hard drug and therefore illegal). In a nutshell, Dutch weed will literally blow your mind – perhaps to an extent that isn't altogether pleasant, which is why many native smokers have sworn off the local product. Newbies to smoking pot and hash should exercise caution; even many regular smokers can't stomach the homegrown stuff.

Space cakes and cookies (baked goods made with hash or marijuana) are sold in a rather low-key fashion, mainly because tourists often have problems with them. If someone is unused to the time they can take to kick in and the effects, they could be in for an intense and long-lasting experience.

PLAN YOUR TRIP DRINKING & NIGHTLIFE

Grey Area coffeeshop (p115)

THE DEATH OF AMSTERDAM COFFEESHOPS?

Since the decriminalisation of soft drugs in 1976, never has the 'right to smoke' been so threatened in Amsterdam. Coffeeshop restrictions, bans and outright closures have been the talk of the town since 2008, when the Dutch government announced plans to close all coffeeshops within 250m of schools, effectively condemning the majority of Amsterdam coffeeshops to their demise.

In 2011 the government proposed banning foreigners from cafes selling cannabis and requiring Dutch residents to sign up for a one-year pass in order to purchase 'soft drugs' at a coffeeshop. Although the top Dutch court declared that such legislation was unlawful, it indicated that restricting tourists and foreigners from entering coffeeshops would not necessarily be considered unconstitutional. The law was passed in 2012, however, Amsterdam's councillors declared their opposition to it – on the grounds of increased crime, street dealing and anti-social behaviour – and coffeeshops have turned a blind eye.

Despite the 2014 commencement of the Dutch law dictating that coffeeshops must not operate within 250m of primary schools and 350m of secondary schools in Amsterdam, authorities are also against enforcing this, arguing that minors are already forbidden, coffeeshops are monitored and that there are more effective ways to combat youth drug use, such as education.

For now, this means Amsterdam's coffeeshops remain open to anyone (foreigners or locals) aged 18 and above. But the 'coffeeshop issue' remains a wait-and-see situation.

Above: De Drie Fleschjes tasting house (p83)
Middle: Cannabis and menu at Grey Area coffeeshop (115)
Bottom: Coffee time near Sarphatipark (p181)

Lonely Planet's Top Choices

't Smalle (p151) Amsterdam's most intimate canal-side drinking in a former *jenever* distillery, with a gorgeous historic interior.

Café Belgique (p81) Belgium's best brews flow from the glinting brass taps.

Hannekes Boom (p196) A local secret with a waterside beer garden, summer barbecues and mellow live music.

Wynand Fockink (p85) This 1679 tasting house pours glorious *jenevers*.

In de Olofspoort (p85) The door of this brown *café*–tasting house was once the city gate.

SkyLounge (p196) A pinch-yourself 360-degree city panorama extends from this 11th-floor bar and vast terrace.

Best Brown Cafés

Hoppe (p81) An icon of drinking history beloved by journalists, bums and raconteurs.

De Sluyswacht (p100) Swig in the lock-keeper's quarters across from Rembrandt's house.

In 't Aepjen (p85) Candles burn all day long in the time-warped, 500-year-old house.

De Pieper (p152) Sand covers the floors and antique delft beer mugs hang from the bar here.

Het Papeneiland (p152) A 1642 gem once reached by a still-visible secret tunnel.

Eijlders (p131) Stained-glass artists' favourite with a lingering Resistance spirit.

Best Cafés

Luxembourg (p82) A quintessential sidewalk *café* on the Spui, prime for newspaper reading.

Bar Moustache (p131) This hip, loft-style local has a minimalist designer interior and a *bellissimo* Italian menu.

Welling (p177) A relaxed spot behind the Concertgebouw to unwind and hang with the *café's* cat.

Westergasterras (p154) In the former gasworks, with a fabulous terrace overlooking a reed-filled pond and weir.

Proust (p151) The centrepiece of this Noordermarkt trendsetter is a giant revolver-shaped chandelier.

Best Coffeeshops

Dampkring (p81) Hollywood made the hobbit-like decor and Cannabis Cup-winning product famous.

Abraxas (p82) A haven of mellow music, comfy sofas and milkshakes spread over three floors.

Greenhouse (p86) Psychedelic mosaics and stained glass plus a big menu for munchies.

Spirit (p153) State-of-the-art pinball machines.

Best Cocktail Bars

Canvas (p204) Edgy, artsy bar with great views atop the former Volkskrant newspaper building.

Twenty Third Bar (p185) Aerial 23rd-floor views, sublime champagne cocktails and two-Michelin-star bar snacks.

Door 74 (p132) Behind an unmarked door, this speakeasy-style bar mixes some of Amsterdam's wildest cocktails.

NJOY (p131) Creative cocktails are grouped according to patrons' personalities.

Lion Noir (p132) Ethereal designer bar with out-there cocktail creations.

Best Gay & Lesbian Hangouts

't Mandje (p85) Amsterdam's oldest gay bar is a trinket-covered beauty.

Café de Barderij (p85) Gay regulars and tourists mingle over canal views and meat specials.

Getto (p86) A younger crowd piles in for cheap food and Red Light District people watching.

Montmartre (p132) Legendary bar where Dutch ballads and old top-40 hits tear the roof off.

Vivelavie (p133) Flirty lesbian bar with a buzzing terrace and dancing.

The Other Side (p135) Groove to house and lounge music at this fab gay coffeeshop.

Best Coffee & Tea Houses

Koffiehuis De Hoek (p115) Charming old-fashioned coffee house experience.

Screaming Beans (p114) Has its own barista academy.

Pâtisserie Pompadour (p115) Top-notch teas and homemade chocolates and pastries.

Best Wine Bars

Worst Wijncafe (p150) Chequerboard-tiled wine bar with superb sausage tapas dishes.

Vyne (p114) Amsterdam's slickest wine bar with blond wood surrounds.

Pata Negra (p134) Wonderfully rustic Spanish-style bodega.

⭐ Entertainment

Amsterdam supports a flourishing arts scene, with loads of big concert halls, theatres, cinemas and other performance venues filled on a regular basis. Music geeks will be in their glory, as there's a fervent subculture for just about every genre, especially jazz, classical and avant-garde beats.

Music

JAZZ

Jazz is extremely popular, from far-out, improvisational stylings to more traditional notes. The grand Bimhuis is the big game in town, drawing visiting musicians from around the globe, though its vibe is more that of a funky little club. Smaller jazz *cafés* abound and you could easily see a live combo every night of the week.

CLASSICAL

Amsterdam's classical music scene, with top international orchestras, conductors and soloists crowding the agenda, is the envy of many European cities. Choose between the flawless Concertgebouw or dramatic Muziekgebouw aan 't IJ for the main shows.

ROCK & DANCE MUSIC

Amsterdam's dance-music scene thrives, with DJs catering to all tastes. Many clubs also host live rock bands. Huge touring names often play smallish venues such as the Melkweg and Paradiso; it's a real treat to catch one of your favourites here.

Comedy & Theatre

Given that the Dutch are fine linguists and have a keen sense of humour, it's natural that English-language comedy would thrive in Amsterdam, especially around the Leidseplein and Jordaan areas. Local theatre tends toward the edgy and experimental.

Cinema

The movies on holiday? Amsterdam's weather is fickle and even art lovers can overdose on museums. Luckily it is a cinephile's mecca, with oodles of art-house cinemas.

Entertainment by Neighbourhood

➡ **Medieval Centre & Red Light District** (p88) Several young rock/DJ clubs thrash throughout the 'hood, while avant-garde theatres line Nes.

➡ **Nieuwmarkt** (p101) A good place for a classical fix.

➡ **Western Canal Ring** (p115) Not many venues besides Felix Meritis, an oldie but a goodie.

➡ **Southern Canal Ring** (p135) Amsterdam's top spot for clubs, live music venues and jazz *cafés*, all around Leidseplein.

➡ **Jordaan & the West** (p154) Venues for comedy, blues, punk and cult films, plus the Westergasfabriek complex.

➡ **Vondelpark & Around** (p166) Free theatre in the park; an alternative scene at the squats-turned-culture-centres.

➡ **Old South** (p177) Home to the world-renowned, acoustically awesome Concertgebouw.

➡ **De Pijp** (p187) Vibrant, buzzy music *cafés* hold court here.

➡ **Plantage, Eastern Islands & Eastern Docklands** (p197) The Muziekgebouw aan 't IJ, Bimhuis and Conservatorium show off their style.

➡ **Oosterpark & South Amsterdam** (p205) Mega-venues and Amsterdam's beloved football team.

Lonely Planet's Top Choices

Melkweg (p136) Housed in a former dairy, it's a galaxy of diverse music, cinema and theatre.

Muziekgebouw aan 't IJ (p197) Acoustically and visually stunning performing arts venue on the IJ.

Westergasfabriek (p155) Options abound in this postindustrial former gasworks-turned-cultural-complex.

Felix Meritis (p115) It's more than 225 years old, but this arts centre is all about modern, experimental theatre and music.

Paradiso (p136) One-time church that preaches a gospel of rock and roll.

Best Jazz & Blues

North Sea Jazz Club (p154) Concerts by respected musicians, and jam sessions too.

Bimhuis (p197) The beating jazz heart of the Netherlands, inside the Muziekgebouw aan 't IJ.

Jazz Café Alto (p136) Excellent little club where you're practically onstage with the musicians.

Best Rock & Funk

CC Muziekcafé (p187) Live acts every night – from reggae to soul to rock.

De Nieuwe Anita (p154) Rock out by the stage behind the bookcase-concealed door.

Best Cinemas

EYE Film Institute (p87) New, old, foreign, domestic: the Netherlands' uber-mod film centre shows quality films of all kinds.

Movies (p154) Indie films screen alongside mainstream flicks at this art-deco gem.

Pathé Tuschinskitheater (p137) Amsterdam's most famous cinema, with a sumptuous art deco/Amsterdam School interior.

Best Classical & Opera

Concertgebouw (p177) World-renowned concert hall with superb acoustics.

Conservatorium van Amsterdam (p197) Catch recitals by students at Amsterdam's snazzy conservatory of music.

Orgelpark (p162) Listen to organ music in a lovely restored church on the edge of the Vondelpark.

Best Theatre & Comedy

Boom Chicago (p154) Laugh-out-loud improv-style comedy at the Jordaan's Rozentheater.

Stadsschouwburg (p136) Large-scale plays, operettas and festivals right on Leidseplein.

Best Free or Low Cost

Openluchttheater (p166) Open-air summertime performances in the Vondelpark.

Muziektheater (p101) Classical freebies fill the air Tuesdays at lunchtime.

Concertgebouw (p177) Wednesday's free lunchtime concerts are often rehearsals for the evening's big show.

Best for Kids

Amsterdams Marionetten Theater (p101) Fairy-tale stage

sets and stringed puppets bring operas to life.

Kriterion (p197) This cinema's kids' club screens loads of children's films with paired activities.

NEED TO KNOW

Ticket Shops

➡ Tickets to just about anything – comedy, dance and concerts – are available for a small surcharge at the Uitburo (www.amsterdam-suitburo.nl), a ticket shop located in the Stadsschouwburg (City Theatre) on the Leidseplein.

➡ In addition, the Uitburo's Last Minute Ticket Shop (www.lastminuteticketshop.nl) sells half-price seats on the day of performance. Available shows are announced daily at 10am. You can buy online with a credit card (usually only chip cards work), or in person.

➡ Last Minute shops are also in the **Centrale Bibliotheek Amsterdam** (p193) and **VVV Main Office** (p279) at Centraal Station, starting at 10am.

Resources

I Amsterdam (www.iamsterdam.com) Events listings.

Film Ladder (www.amsterdam.filmladder.nl) Movie listings.

A-Mag Magazine covering the local scene, published every two months and available at VVV offices, local newsagents and various hotels.

🛍 Shopping

During the Golden Age, Amsterdam was the world's warehouse, stuffed with riches from the far corners of the earth. The capital's cupboards are still stocked with all kinds of exotica (just look at that Red Light gear!), but the real pleasure here is finding some odd, tiny shop selling something you wouldn't find anywhere else.

Specialities

The city offers plenty of distinct wares, from cool-cat fashion to tulip bulbs. Whatever your price range, you'll find something to take home. Souvenir shops cluster around the Dam in the centre and the Bloemenmarkt in the Southern Canal Ring.

Dutch fashion Locals have mastered the art of casual style and it streams right out of the no-nonsense side of the national character. The result is hip, practical designs – such as floaty, layered separates and tailored denim (that don't get caught in bike spokes).

Dutch-designed homewares Dutch designers have shown a singular knack for bringing a creative, stylish touch to everyday objects. What started with a few innovators – such as Droog and Moooi – has morphed into a world-renowned industry. Items are colourful and sensible, with vintage and witty twists mixed in. They solve problems you didn't know you had. Once you own a hand towel with a rivet in one corner for hanging, you'll wonder how you ever lived without it!

Antiques and art Stores selling gorgeous antiques pop up all around the city. They're not cheap, but the quality is usually excellent. The Spiegel Quarter offers a long line of shops along Spiegelgracht and Nieuwe Spiegelstraat that attract moneyed browsers. Antiekcentrum Amsterdam is a knick-knack mini-mall in the Jordaan that's absorbing for those who like peculiar old stuff. On summer Sundays an outdoor antique market takes over Nieuwmarkt square.

Delftware The Dutch have been firing up the iconic blue-and-white pottery since the 1600s. Authentic delftware comes from only from Royal Delft and many visitors make the easy day-trip to the source. A few shops in Amsterdam sell the real deal, but it's much more common (and affordable) to buy replica pottery at souvenir shops.

Flower bulbs Exotic tulip bulbs and other flower seeds are popular gifts to take home. The Bloemenmarkt (aka Flower Market) in the Southern Canal Ring is ground zero for the colourful goods. Ask the vendors about custom regulations, since bringing bulbs into your home country can be prohibited. Those allowable in the USA are usually marked with a special label and you should receive a certificate to accompany the bulbs.

Cheese Dutch *kaas* is justifiably famous and makes a great economical souvenir. Gouda and Edam are the most common varieties. Visitors from the USA should be OK bringing back cheese as long it's hard cheese (like the aforementioned types) and it's properly wrapped (vacuum packed is best).

Alcohol *Jenever* (Dutch gin) is a distinctive souvenir. Bols is the main brand, and the House of Bols museum in the Old South has a shop that not only sells bottles but also cool bartending gear. Shops in the Red Light District sell more, er, colourful bottles of alcohol, such as absinthe in bottles painted a la Van Gogh and tequila in sperm-shaped bottles.

Bongs, pot-leaf-logoed T-shirts and sex toys This is Amsterdam after all, so it's no surprise that these items are legion in Red Light District shops.

Boutique Bonanza

Stumbling across offbeat little boutiques is one of the great joys of shopping in Amsterdam. A teeny store selling only antique eyeglass frames or juggling supplies or doll parts? They're here. The best areas for such finds are at the top of the Jordaan, along Haarlemmerstraat and Haarlemmerdijk, which are lined with hip boutiques and food shops. To the south the Negen Straatjes (Nine Streets) offers a satisfying browse among its pint-sized, one-of-a-kind shops. Staalstraat in Nieuwmarkt is another bountiful vein.

Iconic Places to Shop

De Bijenkorf is Amsterdam's famed department store, taking pride of place by the Royal Palace on the Dam. A lovely array of clothing, toys, household accessories and books spreads over five floors. It's quite welcoming and the cafe on the top floor is a must. Hema is the Netherlands' equivalent to UK-based Marks & Spencer or US-based Target. The thrifty chain carries a bit of everything: wine, homewares, clothing, and is great place for reasonably priced Dutch design goods.

Shopping Streets

The busiest shopping streets are Kalverstraat by the Dam and Leidsestraat, which leads into Leidseplein. Both are lined with clothing and department stores, including local retailers Hema and De Bijenkorf. The Old South's PC Hooftstraat queues up Chanel, Diesel, Gucci and other fancy fashion brands along its length.

Bargaining

For a nation of born traders the Dutch don't haggle much, if only because most retailers aren't set up for it. Flea markets, art galleries and antique shops are among the few places where you can try.

Markets

No visit to Amsterdam is complete if you haven't experienced one of its lively outdoor markets.

DAILY MARKETS

➡ **Albert Cuypmarkt** (p188) The largest, busiest market, offering food, clothing and everything else. Located in De Pijp; closed Sunday.

NEED TO KNOW

Opening Hours

➡ Department stores and large shops: 9am or 10am to 6pm Monday to Saturday, noon to 6pm Sunday.

➡ Smaller shops: 11am or noon to 6pm Tuesday to Saturday; from 1pm Sunday and Monday (if open at all).

➡ Many shops stay open late (to 9pm) Thursday.

Taxes

➡ The Dutch value-added tax (VAT) is 21%; it's reduced to 6% for groceries and books.

➡ Non-EU residents are entitled to a tax refund on purchases, as long as the store has the proper paperwork and you've spent €50 or more. Request a Tax Refund Cheque when paying.

➡ At the airport, present your goods, receipts and passport to customs and get your refund cheque stamped. Take it to the Global Refund office in Terminal 3 for cash or credit. The process can take a while, so give yourself ample time.

Cash Rules

A surprising number of stores do not accept credit cards.

➡ **Waterlooplein Flea Market** (p97) Bric-a-brac galore. Located in Nieuwmarkt; closed Sunday.

➡ **Dappermarkt** (p201) Multi-product bazaar similar to Albert Cuypmarkt, but smaller. Located near Oosterpark; closed Sunday.

➡ **Bloemenmarkt** (p128) The Flower Market. Located in the Southern Canal Ring; open daily.

➡ **Oudemanhuis Book Market** (p89) Old tomes, maps and sheet music. Located in the centre; closed Sunday.

WEEKLY MARKETS

➡ **Westermarkt** (p157) Mondays in the Jordaan for clothing.

➡ **Noordermarkt** (p157) Mondays in the Jordaan for flea market wares.

➡ **Postzegelmarkt** (Stamp & Coin Market; Nieuwezijds Voorburgwal 280; ◷10am-4pm Wed & Sat) Wednesdays and Saturdays in the centre; small group of vendors selling stamps and coins.

SHOPPING GLOSSARY

Virtually any sales clerk you meet in Amsterdam will speak English, but to make things quick, here's a short list of words you're likely to encounter:

kassa – cashier

kassakorting – discount taken at register

korting – discount, as in '25% korting'

laatste dagen – final days

opruiming, uitverkoop – clearance sale

soldes or sale – sale

tot or t/m – up to, as in 'tot 50% korting'

vanaf or va – literally 'and up', as in '€20 va' (€20 and up). Note that this can be a clever ploy in which, for example, a clothing rack marked '€10 va' includes just a few items at €10 – the rest can be priced much higher.

➤ **Lindengracht Market** (p157) Saturdays in the Jordaan for food and trinkets.

➤ **Boerenmarkt** (p103) Saturday farmers market in Nieuwmarkt and in the Jordaan.

➤ **Antiques Market** (p103) Sundays on Nieuwmarkt square.

➤ **Art Market** (p71) Sundays on the Spui in the centre and on Thorbeckeplein in the Southern Canal Ring.

Shopping by Neighbourhood

➤ **Medieval Centre & Red Light District** (p89) Red Light's vibrator shops, Spui's bookstores: there's something for everyone!

➤ **Nieuwmarkt** (p101) Waterlooplein Flea Market is the main draw, plus sweetly eccentric local shops on Staalstraat.

➤ **Western Canal Ring** (p115) The Negen Straatjes hold the mother lode of teensy, quirky speciality shops.

➤ **Southern Canal Ring** (p137) Hunt for art and antiques in the Spiegel quarter, and fashion, music and housewares in the surrounding lanes.

➤ **Jordaan & the West** (p155) Jordaan shops have an artsy, eclectic, homemade feel; Haarlemmerdijk has the newest, coolest boutiques.

➤ **Vondelpark & Around** (p166) Outdoors and travel shops fill the streets around the Vondelpark.

➤ **Old South** (p178) Ground zero for Van Gogh and Vermeer gear, plus shops on PC Hooftstraat.

➤ **De Pijp** (p187) Beyond the Albert Cuypmarkt are galleries and women's fashion boutiques.

➤ **Plantage, Eastern Islands & Eastern Docklands** (p198) Speciality shops for maritime books, smoked fish, corsets and caskets.

➤ **Oosterpark & South Amsterdam** (p205) Trawl the ethnically diverse Dappermarkt.

Lonely Planet's Top Choices

Moooi Gallery (p155) Dutch designer Marcel Wanders showcases his and others' extraordinary works.

Pied à Terre (p166) The world's largest travel bookshop will make anyone's feet itch.

Condomerie Het Gulden Vlies (p92) A fun setting with a wild array of condoms for sale.

De Kaaskamer (p116) This 'cheese room' is stacked to the rafters with goodness.

PGC Hajenius (p89) Gilded, art-deco tobacco emporium where the royal family has its humidor.

Best Markets

Albert Cuypmarkt (p188) Europe's largest daily (except Sunday) street market spills over with food, fashion and bargain finds.

Waterlooplein Flea Market (p97) Piles of curios, used footwear and cheap bicycle parts for treasure hunters.

Westermarkt (p157) Bargain-priced clothing and fabrics at 163 stalls.

Lindengracht Market (p157) Wonderfully authentic local affair, with bushels of fresh produce.

Best for Books

Books & Bubbles (p167) Sip champagne as you read or discuss literary works.

English Bookshop (p157) Cosy, canal-side shop hosting literary events and writers' workshops.

Mendo (p117) Sleek bookshop specialising in art, design, architecture, fashion and photography.

Oudemanhuis Book Market (p89) This old, atmospheric covered alleyway is lined with second-hand booksellers.

Best Fashion

SPRMRKT (p156) A major player in Amsterdam's fashion scene.

Young Designers United (p138) Tomorrow's big names jam the racks here.

By AMFI (p90) Students and alumni of the Amsterdam Fashion Institute sell their wares.

Tenue de Nîmes (p115) Ubercool denim wear and local designer fashions.

Buise (p166) Impeccably selected fashion on chic Cornelis Schuytstraat.

Best Souvenirs

Bloemenmarkt (p128) Bulbs, bulbs and more bulbs fill Amsterdam's 'floating' flower market.

Galleria d'Arte Rinascimento (p158) Royal Delftware ceramics (both antique and new).

Glas Kunst Winkel (p115) Gorgeous glass tulips, windmills and more.

Museum Shop at the Museumplein (p178) The one-stop shop for all your Rembrandt, Vermeer and Van Gogh items.

Best Dutch-Design Housewares

Droog (p101) The famed collective is known for sly, playful, repurposed and reinvented homewares.

Frozen Fountain (p115) Amsterdam's best-known showcase of Dutch-designed furniture and homewares.

Hutspot (p187) Funky store giving emerging designers an opportunity to sell their work.

Mobilia (p138) Dutch design is stunningly showcased at this three-storey 'lifestyle studio'.

Hema (p89) Design students put their spin on everyday objects at the frugal Dutch chain store.

Best Food & Drink

Unlimited Delicious (p116) Wildly flavoured chocolates and other irresistible treats.

Hart's Wijnhandel (p139) Historic shop selling tipples, including *jenever*.

Het Oud-Hollandsch Snoepwinkeltje (p156) All kinds of Dutch candies, including sweet and salty *drop* (Dutch liquorice).

Best Antiques & Vintage

Antiekcentrum Amsterdam (p156) Quirky indoor mall with stalls offering anything from 1940s dresses to 1970s Swedish porn.

Marbles Vintage (p102) Awesome selection of classic skirts, dresses and coats.

Gastronomie Nolstalgie (p90) Beautiful old china, goblets, candlesticks and other tableware from far-flung auctions.

Explore Amsterdam

AMSTERDAM'S
TOP SIGHTS

Neighbourhoods at a Glance

❶ Medieval Centre & Red Light District p66

Amsterdam's oldest quarter is remarkably preserved, looking much as it did in its Golden Age heyday. It's the busiest part of town for visitors. Some come to see the Royal Palace and Oude Kerk. Others barely get out of the train station before hitting the coffeeshops and Red Light District.

❷ Nieuwmarkt p93

Apart from its turreted Waag (Weigh House) and bar-lined square, Nieuwmarkt holds the keys to the Rembrandthuis – the master painter's studio – as well as to centuries-old synagogues, diamond factories and the daily Waterlooplein Flea Market in the old Jewish quarter.

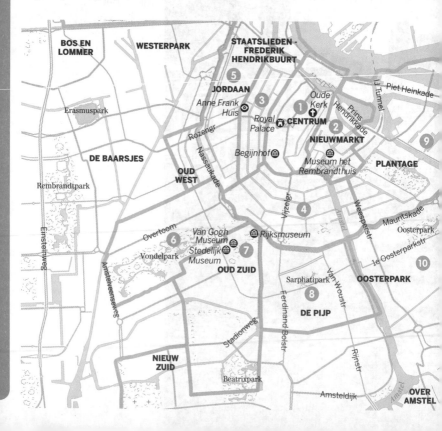

❸ Western Canal Ring p104

One of Amsterdam's most gorgeous areas. Grand old mansions and oddball little speciality shops line the glinting waterways. Roaming around them can cause days to vanish. But most people come here for a singular reason: to visit Anne Frank's house and see the famous diary.

❹ Southern Canal Ring p119

Two clubby nightlife districts anchor the Southern Canal Belt: Leidseplein and Rembrandtplein. Both are neon-lit, one-stop shops for partygoers. In between lie several intriguing museums – including the art blockbuster Hermitage Amsterdam – as well as the flower market, terrific restaurants, ritzy cafes and romantic canal views that'll get your camera flashing.

❺ Jordaan & the West p141

A former workers' quarter, the Jordaan teems with cosy pubs, cafes and galleries squashed into a grid of tiny lanes. It's short on conventional sights, but there's no better place to lose yourself for an afternoon stroll.

❻ Vondelpark & Around p159

Vondelpark is the city's bucolic playground where joggers, picnickers, dope smokers, accordion players and children all cheerfully coexist. It's a great place to experience a freewheeling slice of local life. Eclectic eat streets unfurl around the park's edges.

❼ Old South p168

Often called the Museum Quarter, the Old South holds the top-draw Van Gogh, Stedelijk and Rijksmuseum collections, as well as the Concertgebouw music hall. It's one of Amsterdam's richest neighbourhoods, and impressive manors line the leafy streets.

❽ De Pijp p179

Ethnic meets trendy in De Pijp, a gentrified area that mixes labourers, intellectuals, new immigrants, prostitutes and young urbanites. Marvel at the scene at colourful Albert Cuypmarkt and the eateries and free-spirited *cafés* (pubs) that surround it.

❾ Plantage, Eastern Islands & Eastern Docklands p189

Once a district of parks and gardens, the Plantage now hosts a sprawling zoo as well as a beery windmill. It segues into the Eastern Islands and Eastern Docklands, old warehouse hubs that have morphed into the cutting edge of Dutch architecture.

❿ Oosterpark & South Amsterdam p199

Oosterpark is a culturally diverse neighbourhood, with Moroccan and Turkish enclaves. South Amsterdam extends well beyond, offering art, greenery and goats in the forest.

Medieval Centre & Red Light District

MEDIEVAL CENTRE | RED LIGHT DISTRICT

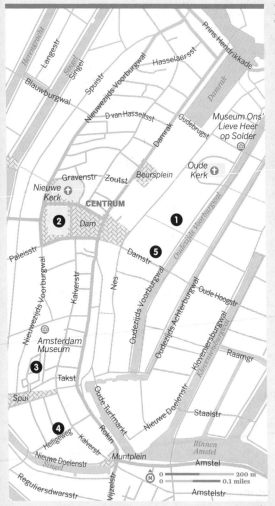

Neighbourhood Top Five

1 Wander through the **Red Light District** (p74), which will make your jaw go limp, even if near-naked women beckoning from backlit windows is the oldest Amsterdam cliché.

2 Ogle the chandeliered opulence and take a Dutch history lesson in the **Royal Palace** (p68).

3 Push open the door to the **Begijnhof** (p69) and behold the hidden gardens and churches.

4 Bite into a crisp golden spud slathered in mayonnaise, curry or peanut sauce at **Vleminckx** (p77).

5 Bowl up to a 17th-century tasting house such as **Wynand Fockink** (p85), to knock back a *jenever* (Dutch gin).

For more detail of this area, see Maps p300 and p304 ➡

Explore Medieval Centre & Red Light District

Amsterdam's heart beats in its medieval core, as well as in the centuries-old Red Light District. All visitors end up here at some point. Centraal Station is the main landmark. Indeed, it is the first thing most visitors see as they arrive by train from the airport or elsewhere in Europe. Damrak slices south from the station to the Dam – Amsterdam's central square and home to the Royal Palace.

A tourist-heavy crowd packs the neighbourhood day and night. While there are several intriguing sights, the big-ticket museums lie elsewhere. The main thing to do here is wander. The compact area is laced with atmospheric lanes, and 17th-century tasting rooms, brown *cafés*, hidden courtyards and wee speciality shops are the prizes for those who venture off the main drags.

Far from being a no-go area, the infamous Red Light District has some beautiful historic bars, as well as the stunning Oude Kerk, the city's oldest church. You'll probably find yourself on Warmoesstraat and Zeedijk while you're here, both commercial thoroughfares chock-a-block with shops and restaurants.

The charming thing about Amsterdam's core is its remarkable state of preservation. The overall layout has changed little since the 17th century, giving the district the air of a living museum – certain vistas look like they belong in a Golden Age landscape. You could easily spend your entire trip here, especially when factoring in the quick-ferry-ride-away northern region (p87), so remember: there are more neighbourhoods beyond.

Local Life

➡ **Café Hangouts** *Cafés* and bookstores ring the Spui (p71), a favoured haunt of academics and journalists.
➡ **Shopping Strip** With designer jeans, leather boots and fancy chain stores, Kalverstraat buzzes all day long.
➡ **Dam Bikes** A fair, a protest, a speech by the monarch – there's always something drawing people to Amsterdam's main square, evident by the sea of bicycles locked up in the middle.

Getting There & Away

➡ **Tram** Eleven of the city's 16 tram lines go through the neighbourhood en route to Centraal Station.
➡ **Boat** Free ferries run to NDSM-werf and elsewhere in Amsterdam-Noord, departing from the piers behind Centraal Station.

Lonely Planet's Top Tip

You're at the local tasting house, and you've ordered a *jenever*. It arrives filled to the brim. You can't pick it up without spilling it. What to do? Bend over the bar, with your hands behind your back, and take a deep sip. That's what tradition dictates.

✖ Best Places to Eat

➡ Gartine (p79)
➡ Blauw aan de Wal (p81)
➡ Vleminckx (p77)
➡ Thais Snackbar Bird (p80)
➡ De Laatste Kruimel (p77)

For reviews, see p77.➡

⚓ Best Places to Drink

➡ Wynand Fockink (p85)
➡ Hoppe (p81)
➡ In 't Aepjen (p85)
➡ Café Belgique (p81)
➡ In de Olofspoort (p85)

For reviews, see p81.➡

🔒 Best Places to Shop

➡ Condomerie Het Gulden Vlies (p92)
➡ American Book Center (p89)
➡ PGC Hajenius (p89)
➡ Hemp Works (p89)
➡ Kokopelli (p92)

For reviews, see p89.➡

TOP SIGHT
ROYAL PALACE (KONINKLIJK PALEIS)

Welcome to the King's house. If he's away, you're welcome to come in and wander around. Today's Royal Palace began life as a glorified town hall and was completed in 1665. The architect, Jacob van Campen, spared no expense to display Amsterdam's wealth in a way that rivalled the grandest European buildings of the day. The result is opulence on a big scale.

Pick up a free audio tour at the desk after you enter; it will explain everything you see in vivid detail. Most of the palace's rooms spread over the 1st floor, which is awash in chandeliers (51 shiners in total), damasks, gilded clocks and rich paintings by Ferdinand Bol and Jacob de Wit. The great *burgerzaal* (citizens' hall) that occupies the heart of the building was envisioned as a schematic of the world, with Amsterdam as its centre. Check out the maps inlaid in the floor; they show the eastern and western hemispheres, with a 1654 celestial map plopped in the middle.

In 1808 the building became the palace of King Louis, Napoleon Bonaparte's brother. In a classic slip-up in the new lingo, French-born Louis told his subjects here that he was the 'rabbit *(konijn)* of Holland', when he meant 'king' *(konink)*. Napoleon dismissed him two years later. Louis left behind about 1000 pieces of Empire-style furniture and decorative artworks. As a result, the palace now holds one of the world's largest collections from the period.

Officially King Willem-Alexander lives here and pays a symbolic rent, though he really resides in Den Haag. The palace is still used for state functions and often closes for such events, especially during April, May, November and December. The website posts the schedule.

DON'T MISS

➡ Chandeliers (all 51 of them)

➡ The *burgerzaal*

➡ Paintings by Ferdinand Bol and Jacob de Wit

➡ Empire-style decor

PRACTICALITIES

➡ Koninklijk Paleis

➡ Map p304

➡ ☏620 40 60

➡ www.paleisamster-dam.nl

➡ Dam

➡ adult/child €10/free

➡ ⊙11am-5pm Jul & Aug, noon-5pm Tue-Sun Sep-Jun

➡ ◰4/9/16/24/25 Dam

TOP SIGHT
BEGIJNHOF

It feels like something out of a story book. You walk up to the unassuming door, push it open and voilà – a hidden courtyard of tiny houses and gardens opens up before you. The 14th-century Begijnhof is not really a secret these days, but somehow it remains a surreal oasis of peace in the city's midst. The Beguines were a Catholic order of unmarried or widowed women who cared for the elderly and lived a religious life without taking monastic vows.

The last true Beguines died in the 1970s. Two churches hide in the *hof* (courtyard). The **Begijnhof Kapel** (Map p304; 1671) is a 'clandestine' chapel where the Beguines were forced to worship after the Calvinists took away their Gothic church. Go through the dog-leg entrance to find marble columns, paintings and stained-glass windows commemorating the Miracle of Amsterdam. (In short: in 1345 the final sacrament was administered to a dying man, but he was unable to keep down the communion wafer and – there's no way to put this delicately – vomited it up. Here's the miracle part: when the vomit was thrown on the fire, the wafer would not burn. Yes, it's all depicted in glass.)

The other church is known as the **Engelse Kerk** (Map p304; English Church), built around 1392. It was eventually rented out to the local community of English and Scottish Presbyterian refugees – including the Pilgrim Fathers – and it still serves as the city's Presbyterian church. Look for pulpit panels by Piet Mondrian, in a figurative phase. Note as this church is still in frequent use, it's sometimes closed to visitors.

Another sight to see is the **Houten Huis** (Map p304; Wooden House) at No 34. It dates from around 1465, making it the oldest preserved wooden house in the Netherlands.

DON'T MISS

➔ Taking a quiet seat in the garden
➔ Begijnhof Kapel
➔ Engelse Kerk
➔ Wooden House at No 34
➔ Miracle of Amsterdam windows

PRACTICALITIES

➔ Map p304
➔ ☑622 19 18
➔ www.begijnhofamsterdam.nl
➔ main entrance off Gedempte Begijnensloot
➔ ⊘8am-5pm
➔ ⊠1/2/5 Spui

TOP SIGHT
OUDE KERK

The Oude Kerk (Old Church) is Amsterdam's oldest building, dating back to around 1306. It has been undergoing extensive restoration work these past few years, so the interior gleams. The Gothic-style structure holds the city's oldest church bell (from 1450), a stunning Müller organ (1724) and 15th-century choir stalls with carvings that are far naughtier than you'd expect in a house of worship.

Many famous Amsterdammers lie buried under the worn tombstones set in the floor, such as Rembrandt's wife Saskia van Uylenburgh. Some 10,000 citizens in all lie beneath the church. Ask for a map when you enter. The church holds Sunday services at 11am, but generally it hosts exhibitions such as the World Press Photo Show, bringing big crowds between April and June. Carillon concerts, often on Tuesday and Thursday afternoons, also draw locals. Those who don't mind stair climbing can go up on a guided tour of the **tower** (Map p300; per person €7.50; ⏰1-5pm Thu-Sat Apr-Sep).

The church embodies a huge moral contradiction, as it's in full view of the Red Light District, with passers-by getting chatted up a stone's throw from the holy walls. Outside on Oudekerksplein is the **statue of Belle** (Map p300), erected in 2007 as a nod to sex-industry workers worldwide. The cobblestones nearby (by the church's main entrance) contain another bold statement: a **golden torso** of a naked woman held by a padlocked hand. The torso mysteriously appeared one day, was removed by police and then put back as most people seemed to like it. At the time of writing it had been removed again due to construction in the area, but supposedly it will return.

DON'T MISS

➡ World Press Photo exhibit (late April to late June)
➡ Floor tombstones, including Rembrandt's wife Saskia
➡ Choir stall carvings
➡ Golden Torso
➡ Surrounding Red Light ambience

PRACTICALITIES

➡ Old Church
➡ Map p300
➡ ☎625 82 84
➡ www.oudekerk.nl
➡ Oudekerksplein
➡ adult/child €5/free
➡ ⏰10am-6pm Mon-Sat, 1-5:30pm Sun
➡ 🚊4/9/16/24/25 Dam

◉ SIGHTS

◉ Medieval Centre

ROYAL PALACE   PALACE
See p68.

BEGIJNHOF   HISTORIC BUILDING
See p69.

CIVIC GUARD GALLERY   GALLERY
Map p304 (Kalverstraat 92; ⊙10am-5pm; 回1/2/5 Spui) FREE This cool gallery is part of the Amsterdam Museum – consider it the free 'teaser' – and fills an alleyway next to the museum's entrance. It displays grand posed group portraits, from medieval guards painted during the Dutch Golden Age (à la Rembrandt's *Night Watch*) to *Modern Civic Guards*, a rendering of Anne Frank, Alfred Heineken and a joint-smoking Personification of Amsterdam.

Evident here is the fact that guards were a captivating subgenre of Dutch painting. Divisions such as the *kloveniers* (named after the gun the guards used) protected the city and played a large part in deposing the Spanish government. The size of the paintings (typically enormous) was determined by the wall space in the guardhouses where the portraits were to be hung.

DAM   SQUARE
Map p304 (回4/9/16/24/25 Dam) The square is the very spot where Amsterdam was founded around 1270. Today pigeons, tourists, buskers and the occasional Ferris-wheel-dotted fair take over the grounds. It's still a national gathering spot, and if there's a major speech or demonstration it's held here.

Long before it hosted fun and games, the square was split into sections called Vissersdam, a fish market where the Bijenkorf department store now stands, and Vijgendam, probably named for the figs and other exotic fruits unloaded from ships. Various markets and events have been held here through the ages, including executions – you can still see holes on the front of the Royal Palace where the wooden gallows were affixed.

NATIONAAL MONUMENT   MONUMENT
Map p304 (Dam; 回4/9/16/24/25 Dam) The obelisk on the Dam's east side was built in 1956 to commemorate WWII's fallen. Fronted by two lions, its pedestal has a number of symbolic statues: four males (war), a woman with child (peace) and men with dogs (resistance). The 12 urns at the rear hold earth from war cemeteries of the 11 provinces and the Dutch East Indies. The war dead are still honoured here at a ceremony every 4 May.

SEXMUSEUM AMSTERDAM   MUSEUM
Map p300 (www.sexmuseumamsterdam.nl; Damrak 18; admission €4; ⊙9.30am-11.30pm; 回1/2/5/13/17 Martelaarsgracht) The Sexmuseum is good for a giggle. You'll find replicas of pornographic Pompeian plates, erotic 14th-century Viennese bronzes, some of the world's earliest nude photographs, an automated farting flasher in a trench coat and a music box that plays 'Edelweiss' and purports to show a couple in flagrante delicto. It's sillier and more fun than other erotic museums in the Red Light District.

Minimum age for entry is 16.

MADAME TUSSAUDS AMSTERDAM MUSEUM
Map p304 (www.madametussauds.nl; Dam 20; adult/child €22/17; ⊙10am-8.30pm Jul & Aug, to 5.30pm Sep-Jun; 國; 回4/9/16/24/25 Dam) Sure, Madame Tussauds wax museum is overpriced and cheesy, but its focus on local culture makes it fun: 'meet' the Dutch royals, politicians, painters and pop stars, along with global celebs (Bieber!). Kids love it. Buying tickets online will save you a few euros and get you into the fast-track queue. Going after 3pm also nets discounts.

SPUI   SQUARE
Map p304 (回1/2/5 Spui) Inviting *cafés* and brainy bookstores ring the Spui, a favoured haunt of academics, students and journalists. On Fridays a book market takes over the square; on Sundays it's an art market. And so you know: it's pronounced 'spow' (rhymes with 'now').

The statue in the middle is of a playful urchin called *Lieverdje* (Little Darling), a gift from a cigarette company. Lots of professors and students spill over from the University of Amsterdam next door.

BEURS VAN BERLAGE   ARCHITECTURE
Map p300 (✆530 41 41; www.beursvanberlage.nl; Damrak 243; 回1/2/5/13/17 Nieuwezijds Kolk) Master architect and ardent socialist HP Berlage (1856–1934) built the financial exchange in 1903. He filled the temple of capitalism with decorations that venerate labour. Look inside the *café* to see tile murals

of the well-muscled proletariat of the past, present and future. Within two decades trading had outgrown the building and moved elsewhere. The building now hosts orchestra concerts and art exhibitions.

ROKIN   STREET

Map p304 South of the Dam, this street is part of the route most visitors take from Centraal Station into town, the name being a corruption of *rak-in*, or inward reach. In the early 16th century the northern part was the site of the first Amsterdam stock exchange, which played a big part in spinning Golden Age riches.

The Rokin is now in the grip of the underground construction of a new metro line, which has brought forth a number of archaeological finds from the Amstel's old river bed. At the intersection of Rokin and Grimburgwal stands a **statue of Queen Wilhelmina** (Map p304) on horseback, a reminder of the monarch's trots through Amsterdam during official processions.

NOORD/ZUIDLIJN VIEWPOINT   VIEWPOINT

Map p304 (www.noordzuidlijn.amsterdam. nl; across from Rokin 96; ⊙1-6pm Tue-Sun; ⊞4/9/14/16/24/25 Rokin) Descend the stairs across from Rokin 96 and behold the North/South Metro line excavation in action. The massive engineering project is like a sci-fi movie: an abyss filled with welders' sparks and colossal digging machines. The whole place rumbles when a tram passes overhead. The displays and signage are in Dutch, but sometimes English-speaking guides are on hand. Look for the big red 'M' next to the bike path.

DAMRAK   WATERFRONT, STREET

Map p300 The Damrak is the original mouth of the Amstel river – *rak* being a reach, or straight stretch of water. The river flowed from a lock in the Dam into the IJ. In the 19th century the canal was filled in, except for the canal-boat docks on the east side. The gabled houses backing onto the water are among the town's most picturesque.

The west side of Damrak is like a giant stretch of flypaper, with cheap tourist hotels, fast-food restaurants and souvenir shops ready to catch visitors arriving at Centraal Station.

CENTRAAL STATION   ARCHITECTURE

Map p300 (Stationsplein; ⊞4/9/16/24/25 Centraal Station) Beyond being a transport hub, Centraal Station is a sight in itself. The turreted marvel dates from 1889. One of the architects, PJ Cuypers, also designed the Rijksmuseum, and you can see the similarities in the faux-Gothic towers, the fine red brick and the abundant reliefs (for sailing, trade and industry).

Built on an artificial island, the station was designed as a neo-Renaissance 'curtain', a controversial plan that effectively cut off Amsterdam from the IJ river. The garage in the right-hand wing was built to shelter the Dutch royal carriage, but it's rarely there (read: never).

ST NICOLAASKERK   CHURCH

Map p300 (www.nicolaas-parochie.nl; Prins Hendrikkade 73; ⊙noon-3pm Mon, 11am-4pm Tue-Fri, noon-3pm Sat; ⊞4/9/16/24/25 Centraal Station) In plain view from Centraal Station, the magnificent cupola and neo-Renaissance towers belong to the city's main Catholic church, the first built after Catholic worship became legal again in the 19th century. St Nicholas is the patron saint of seafarers, so the church became an important symbol for Amsterdam.

The interior is notable for its high altar, the theatrical crown of Emperor Maximilian I and depictions of the Stations of the Cross, on which tireless painter Jan Dunselman laboured for 40 years. Worship services take place daily at 12.30pm, except on Sunday (10.30am and 1pm).

SCHREIERSTOREN   HISTORIC BUILDING

Map p300 (www.schreierstoren.nl; Prins Hendrikkade 94-95; ⊞4/9/16/24/25 Centraal Station) Built around 1480 as part of the city's defenses, this tower is where Henry Hudson set sail for the New World in 1609; a plaque outside marks the spot. It's called the 'wailing tower' in lore – where women waved farewell to sailors' ships – but the name actually comes from the word 'sharp' (for how the corner jutted into the bay).

Step into the cozy VOC Café for a look inside the tower. The canal-side terrace is a dandy place for a drink.

RONDE LUTHERSE KERK   CHURCH

Map p300 (Round Lutheran Church; Singel 11; ⊙hours vary; ⊞1/2/5/13/17 Martelaarsgracht) The domed church, built from 1668 to 1671, has the curious distinction of being the only round Protestant church in the country. Falling attendances forced its closure in

TOP SIGHT
AMSTERDAM MUSEUM

The city's history museum keeps getting spiffier, thanks to ongoing renovations. Start with the multimedia DNA exhibit, which breaks down Amsterdam's 1000-year history into seven whiz-bang time periods. At the Revolt Against the King & Church display, you'll have a one-of-a-kind opportunity to wear a civic guard's ruffled collar and have a photo taken; it goes to the museum's Flickr page.

Afterward, plunge into the lower floors to see troves of religious artefacts, porcelains and paintings. Bonus points for finding Rembrandt's macabre *Anatomy Lesson of Dr Deijman*, showing the good physician cutting into a corpse's brain. There are also displays on the world wars, the spread of bicycle use and even a re-creation of the original Café 't Mandje, a touchstone in the gay-rights movement.

The museum building used to be Amsterdam's civic orphanage. While you're in the courtyard, note the cupboards in which the orphans stored their possessions (now filled with art). And don't forget to peak in the free Civic Guard Gallery in the arcade next door.

The museum is a good choice during soggy weather, since there rarely is a queue that requires you to wait outside, as at most other venues.

DON'T MISS

➡ *Anatomy Lesson of Dr Deijman*
➡ Café 't Mandje
➡ Civic Guard paintings
➡ Orphan cupboards

PRACTICALITIES

➡ Map p304
➡ ☑523 18 22
➡ www.amsterdammuseum.nl
➡ Kalverstraat 92
➡ adult/child €10/5
➡ ☉10am-5pm
➡ ▣1/2/5 Spui

1936. Ironically, the old church on the Spui that it was designed to replace is still in use.

NARROW HOUSE   BUILDING
Map p300 (Singel 7) It's often said that this house – which appears to be no wider than its door – is the narrowest abode in the city. But don't be deceived. The side facing the canal is actually the rear entrance of a house of normal proportions.

KALVERSTRAAT   STREET
Map p304 You're sure to end up on this crowded street at some point, so we might as well mention it. Named after the livestock markets held here in the 17th century, Kalverstraat is now a place where shoppers lather themselves into a fever pitch over the latest sales. (The Dutch Monopoly game has Kalverstraat as its most expensive street.)

PAPAGAAI   CHURCH
Map p304 (Kalverstraat 58; ☉10am-4pm; ▣1/2/5 Spui) An unexpected oasis in the sea of consumerism on Kalverstraat, the curious Petrus en Pauluskerk, aka Papagaai, is a Catholic church from the 17th century that was a clandestine house of worship.

Note the parrot over the door that gave the church its funny name. The slogan you'll see upon entering: '15 minutes for God'.

TORTURE MUSEUM   MUSEUM
Map p304 (www.torturemuseum.nl; Singel 449; adult/child €7.50/4; ☉10am-11pm; ▣1/2/5 Koningsplein) It's dilapidated and so dimly lit inside you can barely read the placards, but fans of kitsch and oddball lore will enjoy learning about devices like the Flute of Shame for bad musicians (the finger screws tighten), the Neck Violin for quarreling women (a shackle locked the two face-to-face), branding tongs, skull crackers, a guillotine and the Iron Maiden of Nuremberg (use your imagination).

The museum displays each torture tool and describes (in multiple languages) how it works. Graphic engravings show the instruments in action. The building lies across the canal from the flower market.

HEILIGEWEG   STREET
Map p304 (▣1/2/5 Koningsplein) The Heiligeweg (Holy Way) was once part of a route that pilgrims took to the spot where the Miracle of Amsterdam occurred. Halfway

along, and directly opposite Voetboog-straat, you'll see the **Rasphuis Gate** (Map p304), which led to a correctional institute in medieval times. The pedestal bears the sculpture of a woman with two criminals chained at her side, under the Latin word *castigatio* (punishment).

ALLARD PIERSON MUSEUM · MUSEUM

Map p304 (www.allardpiersonmuseum.nl; Oude Turfmarkt 127; adult/child €10/5; ⊙10am-5pm Tue-Fri, 1-5pm Sat & Sun; 🚊4/9/14/16/24/25 Spui) Run by the University of Amsterdam, this museum boasts one of the world's richest archaeological collections. You'll find an actual mummy, vases from ancient Greece and Mesopotamia, a very cool wagon from the royal tombs at Salamis (Cyprus) and galleries full of other items providing insight into daily life in ancient times.

Each section is explained in a detailed overview via English signage, although most individual items are labelled in Dutch only. It may not be in the same league as the British Museum or the Louvre, but the manageable scale of this museum makes it far more accessible.

UNIVERSITY LIBRARY · HISTORIC BUILDING

Map p304 (www.uba.uva.nl; Singel 421-425; ⊙8.30am-midnight Mon-Fri, 10am-5pm Sat & Sun; 🚊1/2/5 Koningsplein) Today's library is a concrete hulk, not nearly as beautiful building you'd expect from such a historic site, but its background is fascinating. Citizen militias used to meet here: the 'handbow' *(handboog)* militia in No 421, and the 'foot-bow' *(voetboog)* militia in No 425, which also served as headquarters for the Dutch West India Company.

Now you know where the names of the nearby streets Handboogstraat and Voetboogstraat come from. Their firing ranges at the back reached to Kalverstraat.

⊙ Red Light District

OUDE KERK · CHURCH
See p70.

PROSTITUTION
INFORMATION CENTRE · INFORMATION CENTRE

Map p300 (PIC; ✆420 73 28; www.pic-amster-dam.com; Enge Kerksteeg 3; ⊙1.30-8pm Sat or by appointment; 🚊4/9/16/24/25 Dam) Established by a former prostitute, the PIC provides frank information about the industry to sex workers, their customers and curious tourists. The centre's small shop sells enlightening reading material and souvenirs, but best of all is its excellent hour-long walking tour (p273) (5pm Saturday, €15 per person, no reservations needed), which takes you around the neighbourhood and into a prostitute's working room.

In summer the group adds an extra tour on Wednesdays at 6.30pm. You can also peek in the mini-museum set up like a historic brothel (free with tour, otherwise €1 per person). Proceeds go to the centre.

TROMPETTERSTEEG · STREET

Map p300 (🚊4/9/16/24/25 Dam) An intriguing place to view the Red Light action is Trompettersteeg, a teeny alley where the most desirable women are stationed. Claustrophobes beware: it's only 1m wide, but it's plenty busy. Look for the entrance in the block south of the Oude Kerk.

ZEEDIJK · STREET

Map p300 (🚊4/9/16/24/25 Centraal Station) This is one of Amsterdam's oldest streets. Initially a shipping district, it was a respectable place to be until the 17th century. Then the rich folk moved away to the Herengracht, and the Zeedijk turned to come-hither entertainment for sailors. It cleaned up again over the past decade, and is now the core of Amsterdam's Chinatown and sports lively cafes, bars and eateries.

You'll find a very mixed crowd of visitors bumping over the cobblestones.

GUAN YIN SHRINE · BUDDHIST TEMPLE

Map p300 (Fo Guang Shan He Hua Temple; www.ibps.nl; Zeedijk 106-118; ⊙noon-5pm Tue-Sat, 10am-5pm Sun year-round, plus noon-5pm Mon Jun-Aug; 🚊4/9/16/24/25 Dam) Europe's first Chinese Imperial–style Buddhist temple (2000) is dedicated to Guan Yin, the Buddhist goddess of mercy. Make a donation, light an incense stick and ponder the thousand eyes and hands of the Bodhisattva statue. Traditional Chinese-style recitations of the Sutras (sayings of the Buddha) are held every Sunday at 10.30am and are open to the public.

The ornate 'mountain gate' – an intriguing concept in the narrow confines of the Zeedijk – refers to the traditional setting of Buddhist monasteries. The middle section set back from the street was designed along principles of feng shui.

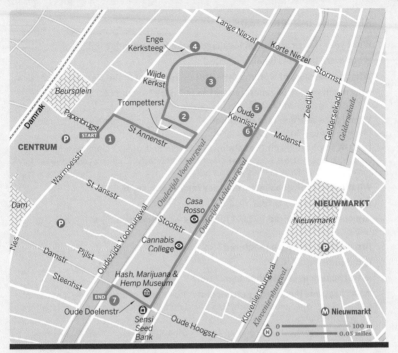

Neighbourhood Walk
Red Light Quickie

START CONDOMERIE HET GULDEN VLIES
END GREENHOUSE
LENGTH 1.25KM; 25 MINUTES

The typical 'quickie', according to Red Light District workers, is 15 minutes, and our walk shouldn't take you much longer.

What better way to set the mood than at **1 Condomerie Het Gulden Vlies** (p92)? Cherry red, hypoallergenic, cartoon character embodiments – the shop is a shrine to condom art, selling all sizes and colours.

It's easy to walk right by the teeny alley **2 Trompettersteeg** (p74). After turning onto Oudezijds Voorburgwal from St Annenstraat, it'll be the second little street you come to en route to the church. Claustrophobes beware: the medieval alley is only 1m wide, but the red-light windows keep it busy.

A contradiction if ever there was one: the 14th-century **3 Oude Kerk** (p70) is Amsterdam's oldest building, but the surrounding square has long been ground-zero for prostitution. Look near the entrance for the 'golden torso' pavement plaque, with a hand groping a breast.

The **4 Prostitution Information Centre** (p74) dispenses facts to sex workers and visitors. Next door is a room-rental shop, where workers book Red Light quarters. Further on, observe the separate zones for African, Asian and European women.

Bondage exhibits and dildo bikes educate visitors in the **5 Erotic Museum** (p76). For further browsing, multiple shops around here offer 'nonstop hard porno' and trinkets such as whips, masks and spiked collars.

It's rapid-fire vice as you continue down **6 Oudezijds Achterburgwal**: live sex shows at Casa Rosso, smoky vaporisers at the Cannabis College, botany lessons at the Hash, Marijuana & Hemp Museum and 'Big Bud' at the Sensi Seed Bank.

Wind down at surprisingly classy **7 Greenhouse** (p86), a Cannabis-Cup-worthy coffeeshop that serves up good food and funky music. Or choose among the many other coffee joints (pardon the pun!) in the district.

RED LIGHT DISTRICT FAQS

What year was prostitution legalised in the Netherlands? 1810.

When were brothels legalised? 2000.

What percentage of working prostitutes were born in the Netherlands? 5%.

How much money is generated by the industry? About €650 million annually, according to the Central Bureau of Statistics.

What is the average rent per window? €75 to €150 per eight-hour shift (paid by the prostitute), depending on location.

Is it OK to photograph the windows? No. Your first instinct might be to take a photo, but don't do it – out of simple respect, and to avoid having your camera tossed in a canal by the ladies' enforcers.

What is the typical base cost for sex (aka 'a quickie')? €50.

Do prostitutes pay taxes? Yes.

Are condoms required by law? No, but it's virtually impossible to find a prostitute who'll work without one.

Are medical check-ups required? No.

Is pimping legal? No.

Is trafficking in prostitutes legal? No.

What happens if a patron gets violent? Prostitutes' quarters are equipped with a button that, when pressed, activates a light outside. The police or other protectors show up in a hurry.

Why red light? Because it's flattering. Especially when used in combination with black light, it makes teeth sparkle. Even as early as the 1300s, women carrying red lanterns met sailors near the port.

CANNABIS COLLEGE   INFORMATION CENTRE
Map p304 (☎423 44 20; www.cannabiscollege. com; Oudezijds Achterburgwal 124; ◷11am-7pm; ▤4/9/16/24/25 Dam) This nonprofit centre educates visitors on tips and tricks to having a positive smoking experience, as well as providing the lowdown on local cannabis laws. Browse displays, try out a vaporiser (€3; bring your own smoking material), or view marijuana plants growing sky-high in the basement garden (€3 to see them; photos permitted).

Staff can provide maps and advice on where to find coffeeshops that sell organic weed and shops that are good for newbies. T-shirts, stickers, postcards and a few other trinkets with the logo are for sale, too.

HASH, MARIJUANA &
HEMP MUSEUM   MUSEUM
Map p304 (☎623 59 61; www.hashmuseum.com; Oudezijds Achterburgwal 148; admission €9; ◷10am-11pm; ▤4/9/16/24/25 Dam) Simple exhibits in this recently renovated museum cover dope botany and the relationship between cannabis and religion. Highlights

include an impressive pipe collection, an interactive vaporiser exhibit and a kiosk where you can create an e-postcard of yourself in a marijuana field. Admission also includes the **Hemp Gallery** (Map p304), filled with hemp art and historical items, in a separate building a few doors north.

The Sensi Seed company (conveniently attached to the museum) owns the whole thing, so it's no surprise that you get to peek at a roomful of growing plants as part of the deal. Visitors on a budget might prefer the Cannabis College, located on the same block, where you can see plants and vaporisers for less money.

EROTIC MUSEUM   MUSEUM
Map p300 (www.erotisch-museum.nl; Oudezijds Achterburgwal 54; admission €7; ◷11am-1am; ▤4/9/16/24/25 Dam) Ho hum. Your usual assortment of bondage exhibits, naughty photos and lewd cartoons. Although this museum has the advantage of location, it's less entertaining, not as well laid out and more expensive when compared with other sex museums in town.

WARMOESSTRAAT
STREET

Map p300 (🚇4/9/16/24/25 Centraal Station) Amsterdam's earliest canals grew out from the IJ river like the roots of a tree, and Warmoesstraat was one of the first streets to follow. Its historical pedigree pretty much pales next to its current line-up of leather bars, coffeeshops and fetish shops interspersed with galleries and cool cafes.

W139
ARTS CENTRE

Map p300 (www.w139.nl; Warmoesstraat 139; ⊘noon-6pm; 🚇4/9/16/24/25 Dam) Duck into this contemporary arts centre and ponder the multimedia exhibits, which often have an edgy political angle. Check the website for info on frequent artists talks.

OUDEMANHUISPOORT
BUILDING

Map p304 (Btwn Oudezijds Achterburgwal & Kloveniersburgwal; 🚇4/9/14/16/24/25 Spui) On the corner of Oudezijds Achterburgwal stands a distinctive gateway with spectacles over the pedestal, indicating its role as an almshouse for the elderly. It was built in 1601 from the proceeds of a public lottery. It's now the seat of the University of Amsterdam and closed to the public, although you can wander the courtyard. Note the bust of the learned Roman goddess Minerva over the courtyard entrance. A secondhand book market has operated in the passage since the mid-1700s.

NES
STREET

Map p304 (🚇4/9/14/16/25 Rokin) Beyond the glare of the Red Light District runs this dark, narrow lane, home to theatres for more than 150 years. In 1614 Amsterdam's first bank opened in a pawnshop here, at No 57.

✖ EATING

✖ Medieval Centre

★ VLEMINCKX
FRITES €

Map p304 (Voetboogstraat 31; small/large €2.10/2.70, sauces €0.70; ⊘noon-6pm Sun & Mon, 11am-6pm Tue-Sat; 🚇1/2/5 Koningsplein) This hole-in-the-wall takeaway has drawn the hordes for its monumental *frites* (French fries) since 1887. The standard is smothered in mayonnaise, though you can ask for ketchup, peanut sauce or a variety of spicy toppings.

DE LAATSTE KRUIMEL
CAFE €

Map p304 (The Last Crumb; www.delaatstekruimel. nl; Langebrugsteeg 4; mains €2-9; ⊘8am-8pm; 🚇4/9/14/16/24/25 Spui) Hmm, what to look at first: the uber-cute interior decorated with vintage objects from the Noordermarkt flea market and the recycled pallets being used as furniture and colanders as lampshades. Or the glass cases stacked with pies, quiches, breads, cakes and lemon poppy seed scones. Grandmothers, children, couples on dates and just about everyone else pack the place for the fantastic organic sandwiches and treats.

ROB WIGBOLDUS VISHANDEL
SANDWICH SHOP €

Map p300 (☎626 33 88; Zoutsteeg 6; sandwiches €2.50-4.50; ⊘9am-4pm Tue-Sat; 🚇1/2/5 Dam) A wee three-table oasis in the midst of surrounding tourist tat, this fish shop in a tiny alley serves excellent herring sandwiches

---

PUT OUT THE RED LIGHT?

Since 2007, city officials have been reducing the number of Red Light windows in an effort to clean up the district. They claim it's not about morals but about crime: pimps, traffickers and money launderers have entered the scene and set the neighbourhood on a downward spiral. Opponents point to a growing local conservatism and say the government is using crime as an excuse, because it doesn't like Amsterdam's current reputation for sin.

As the window tally decreases, fashion studios, art galleries and trendy cafes rise up to reclaim the deserted spaces, thanks to a program of low-cost rent and other business incentives. It's called Project 1012, after the area's postal code.

In 2013 the plan picked up steam after the city council won the right to introduce new zoning laws that make it possible to evict brothel owners who are 'uncooperative'. With these laws in effect, 62 more windows will have to shut down. In addition the city council raised the minimum age for prostitutes from 18 to 21 and introduced mandatory closing hours for Red Light windows between 4am and 9am. What's in store for the future remains to be seen.

on a choice of crusty white or brown rolls. Don't like fish? **Van den Berg's Broodjesbar** (similar prices and hours), right next door, prepares a variety of other sandwiches, from a humble cheese-filled roll to *gehakt* (thin meatball slices served warm with killer-hot mustard).

GEBR NIEMEIJER   CAFE €

Map p300 (www.gebroedersniemeijer.nl; Nieuwendijk 35; mains €4-8; ⊙8.30am-6.30pm Tue-Fri, to 5pm Sat, 9am-5pm Sun; 🐾; 🚊1/2/5/13/17 Martelaarsgracht) This French bakery is a real find amid the Nieuwendijk's head shops. Grab a newspaper and plop down at one of the sturdy wood tables to linger over flaky croissants for breakfast or fantastic sandwiches made with walnut bread and lamb sausage (or gruyére cheese, or fig jam...) for lunch.

LANSKROON   BAKERY & SWEETS €

Map p304 (✆623 74 43; www.lanskroon.nl; Singel 385; items from €2; ⊙8am-5.30pm Mon-Fri, 9am-5.30pm Sat, 10am-5.30pm Sun; 🚲; 🚊1/2/5 Spui) Other historic bakeries have prettier fixtures and daintier cakes, but only humble Lanskroon has such a remarkable *stroopwafel* – crispy, big as a dessert plate and

slathered with caramel, honey or a deceptively healthy-tasting fig paste. In winter locals come for spiced *speculaas* cookies and other holiday treats, and in summer there's thick nut- or fruit-swirled ice cream.

PANNENKOEKENHUIS
UPSTAIRS   TRADITIONAL DUTCH €

Map p304 (✆626 56 03; www.upstairspannenkoeken.nl; Grimburgwal 2; mains €7-11.50; ⊙noon-7pm Mon-Fri, to 6pm Sat, to 5pm Sun; 🚲; 🚊4/9/14/16/24/25 Spui) Climb some of the steepest stairs in town to reach this small-as-a-stamp restaurant. The lure? Pancakes that are flavoursome, inexpensive and filling. We like the one with bacon, cheese and ginger. It's a one-man show, so service operates at its own pace. Pass the time by admiring all the teapots hanging from the ceiling. Cash only. Opening hours can be erratic.

VILLA ZEEZICHT   CAFE €

Map p300 (✆626 74 33; Torensteeg 7; mains €5-12; ⊙9am-10pm; 🚊1/2/5/13/14/17 Raadhuisstraat) While it serves decent pastas and sandwiches, it's really all just clumsy foreplay for the homemade *appeltaart* (apple pie), a deserved Amsterdam legend. Fork

---

● TOP SIGHT
MUSEUM ONS' LIEVE HEER OP SOLDER

It's another one of those 'secret' Amsterdam places. What looks like an ordinary canal house in the Red Light District turns out to have an entire Catholic church stashed inside, with room for 150 worshippers. Ons' Lieve Heer op Solder (Our Dear Lord in the Attic) was founded in the mid-1600s, when local merchant Jan Hartman decided to build a covert church in his house so his son could study to be a priest. At the time, the country's Calvinist rulers had outlawed public worship of Catholicism.

So, as you wander through, you not only get to see the city's richest collection of Catholic art, but also period pieces from 17th-century canal-house life. There is a fantastic labyrinth of staircases, cubbyhole quarters, heavy oak furniture and a porcelain-tiled kitchen. Once upstairs – in the attic, so to speak – you'll see that the church itself is unexpectedly grand, with a marble-columned altar and a painting by Jacob de Wit, a steep gallery and a surprisingly good organ.

The museum continues its extensive restoration project, scheduled for completion sometime in 2014. It's open during construction, but many of the artefacts have been put away until work is finished.

DON'T MISS

➡ Free audio tour
➡ The altar
➡ Jacob de Wit painting
➡ Kitchen and other 17th-century restored rooms

PRACTICALITIES

➡ Map p300
➡ ✆624 66 04
➡ www.opsolder.nl
➡ Oudezijds Voorburgwal 40
➡ adult/child €8/4
➡ ⊙10am-5pm Mon-Sat, 1-5pm Sun
➡ 🚊4/9/16/24/25 Centraal Station

into a mountain of apples dusted in cinnamon, surrounded by warm pastry and fresh cream. In warm weather tables are set up on the bridge over the Singel.

BROODJE BERT
SANDWICH SHOP €

Map p304 (Singel 321; sandwiches €4-7; ⊗8am-5pm; ⚠; 🚃1/2/5 Spui) Join the locals sitting on wooden chairs in the sun (or the window seats inside) at this fabulous little sandwich shop in a winning canal-side location. In addition to huge sandwiches such as marinated grilled chicken or the eponymous house special 'Broodje Bert' (lamb meatballs on Turkish bread), there are burgers and omelettes made to order. Cash only.

MAOZ
MIDDLE EASTERN €

Map p300 (www.maozusa.com; Damrak 40; €4-7; ⊗11am-2am; 🚃1/2/5/13/17 Nieuwezijds Kolk) This outpost of the local felafel chain provides a dose of cheap, healthy vegetarian food amid the Damrak's waffle shops, *frites* stands and other tourist tat. Get your chickpea balls in a pita or salad box, then add your own toppings from the salad bar. It stays open until the wee hours.

★ GARTINE
CAFE €€

Map p304 (☎320 41 32; www.gartine.nl; Taksteeg 7; mains €6-12, high tea €12-21; ⊗10am-6pm Wed-Sun; ⚠; 🚃4/9/14/16/24/25 Spui) Gartine is magical, from its sly location in an alley off busy Kalverstraat to its mismatched antique tableware and its sublime breakfast pastries, sandwiches and salads (made from produce grown in its garden plot). The sweet-and-savoury high tea is a scrumptious bonus.

VAN KERKWIJK
INTERNATIONAL €€

Map p304 (www.caferestaurantvankerkwijk. nl; Nes 41; mains from €15; ⊗11am-late; ⚠🛗; 🚃4/9/16/24/25 Dam) Van Kerkwijk is so low-key you might not notice it, but locals sure know it's there. The small wooden tables are typically packed. They don't take reservations, and there's no menu, so you'll have to wait for the server to tell you what's available that day: perhaps an Indonesian curry, a North African tagine, or various French and Italian meaty classics.

It's quintessentially cosy, with candles burning even during the day – a true, personal-feeling spot in a somewhat generic part of the city.

> **TOP SPOTS FOR LOCAL SNACKS**
>
> The Centre is a great neighbourhood to sample some of Amsterdam's famed local specialities.
>
> **Vleminckx** (p77) *Frites* with mayo.
>
> **Rob Wigboldus Vishandel** (p77) Herring sandwich.
>
> **Lanskroon** (p78) Gooey, caramel-y *stroopwafel* (syrup waffle).
>
> **Pannenkoekenhuis Upstairs** (p78) Pancakes, sweet or savoury.

HAESJE CLAES
TRADITIONAL DUTCH €€

Map p304 (☎624 99 98; www.haesjeclaes.nl; Spuistraat 273-275; mains €16-25, set menus from €29.50; ⊗noon-10pm; 🛗; 🚃1/2/5 Spui) Haesje Claes' warm surrounds, a tad touristy but with lots of dark wood and antique knick-knacks, are just the place to sample comforting pea soup and *stamppot* (mashed pot: potatoes mashed with another vegetable). The fish starter has a great sampling of different Dutch fish.

TOMAZ
FRENCH, DUTCH €€

Map p304 (www.tomaz.nl; Begijnensteeg 6-8; mains €15-20; ⊗noon-9pm Sun-Wed, to 10pm Thu-Sat; ⚠; 🚃1/2/5 Spui) Charming little Tomaz hides near the Begijnhof, and is a fine spot for a light lunch or informal dinner, accompanied by a bottle of wine, of course. A vegetarian special is always available. Linger for a while over a game of chess.

D'VIJFF VLIEGHEN
CONTEMPORARY DUTCH €€€

Map p304 (☎530 40 60; www.vijffvlieghen.nl; Spuistraat 294-302; mains €26-33, set menus from €46; ⊗6-10pm; 🚃1/2/5 Spui) So what if every tourist and business visitor eats here? Sometimes the herd gets it right. 'The Five Flies' is a classic, spread out across five 17th-century canal houses. Old-wood dining rooms are full of character, featuring Delft-blue tiles and works by Rembrandt and Breitner. Some chairs have brass plates for the celebrities who have sat in them.

LUCIUS
SEAFOOD €€€

Map p304 (☎624 18 31; www.lucius.nl; Spuistraat 247; mains €20-30, set menu €39.50; ⊗5pm-midnight; 🚃1/2/5 Spui) Simple, delicious and consistently full, Lucius is known for both its fresh ingredients and for not mucking

TOP SIGHT
NIEUWE KERK

Don't let the 'New Church' name fool you – the structure dates from 1408 (though it *is* a good century fresher than its neighbour, the Oude Kerk). Located smack on the Dam, the basilica is the historic stage of Dutch coronations and royal weddings. The stained glass over the main entrance recalls Queen Wilhelmina, who ascended the throne in 1898, aged 18. Other than such ceremonies, the building no longer functions as a church, but rather a hall for multimedia exhibitions and organ concerts.

The interior is plain, but several key furnishings – the magnificent oak chancel, the bronze choir screen and the massive gilded organ (1645) – justify a look. Naval hero Admiral Michiel de Ruijter, as well as poets Joost van den Vondel and Pieter Cornelisz Hooft, are among the luminaries buried here.

It's possible to walk in and take a free peek, but you'll have to pay the admission to get up close. Pick up a 'welcome' brochure at the entrance, which maps out the highlights. Opening times and admission fees can vary, depending on what's going on.

DON'T MISS

➡ Queen Wilhelmina's inauguration window
➡ Main organ
➡ Monuments to De Ruijter, Vondel & Hooft
➡ Oak chancel

PRACTICALITIES

➡ New Church
➡ Map p300
➡ ✆638 69 09
➡ www.nieuwekerk.nl
➡ Dam
➡ admission €8-15
➡ ⊘10am-5pm
➡ ⌕1/2/4/5/9/16/24/25 Dam

---

them up with lots of sauce and spice. The interior, all fish tanks and tiles, is professional, just like the service.

SUPPERCLUB
CONTEMPORARY DUTCH €€€

Map p304 (✆638 05 13; www.supperclub.com; Jonge Roelensteeg 21; multi-course menus €50-70; ⊘from 7pm; ⌕1/2/5/14 Paleisstraat) If you're looking for a scene, you've found one. Enter the theatrical, white room, snuggle on the mattresses and snack on victuals as DJs spin house music. Shows are provocative and entertaining – if it's lamb night, live sheep may be led through to the kitchen. If it's hospital night, look out.

✕ Red Light District

DE BAKKERSWINKEL
CAFE €

Map p300 (✆489 80 00; www.debakkerswinkel.nl; Warmoesstraat 69; mains €5-10; ⊘8am-5.30pm Mon-Fri, 9am-6pm Sat & Sun; ⌕; ⌕4/9/16/24/25 Centraal Station) Family-friendly De Bakkerswinkel offers excellent baked goods (especially scones), sandwiches, soups, and breakfast fare such as quiche, French toast and omelettes. A smaller

De Bakkerswinkel (Map p300; Warmoesstraat 133) pops up nearby, serving sandwiches on wonderfully crusty bread and fresh-squeezed juices for takeaway.

KAM YIN
SURINAMESE €

Map p300 (✆625 31 15; www.kamyin.nl; Warmoesstraat 8; mains €7-13; ⊘noon-midnight; ⌕4/9/16/24/25 Centraal Station) It's nothing much to look at, but this plastic and fluorescent operation dispenses excellent versions of Surinamese standards such as roti and *tjauw min* (thick noodles with assorted meats). Its *broodje pom* (a chicken-casserole sandwich) ranks as one of the city's best.

THAIS SNACKBAR BIRD
THAI €€

Map p300 (✆420 62 89; www.thai-bird.nl; Zeedijk 77; mains €9-15; ⊘1-10pm; ⌕4/9/16/24/25 Centraal Station) Don't tell the Chinese neighbours, but this is some of the best Asian food on the Zeedijk – the cooks, wedged in a tiny kitchen, don't skimp on lemongrass, fish sauce or chilli. The resulting curries and basil-laden meat and seafood dishes will knock your socks off.

There's a bit more room to spread out in the (slightly pricier) restaurant across the street (No 72).

'SKEK
CAFE €€

Map p300 (☑427 05 51; www.skek.nl; Zeedijk 4-8; sandwiches €3-7, mains €12-14; ☺noon-10pm; 🛜; 🚊4/9/16/24/25 Centraal Station) Run by students for students (flashing your ID gets you one-third off), this friendly cafe-bar is an excellent place to get fat sandwiches on thick slices of multigrain bread, and healthy main dishes with chicken, fish or pasta. Bands occasionally perform at night (the bar stays open to 1am weekdays, and 3am on weekends).

DWAZE ZAKEN
CAFE €€

Map p300 (☑612 41 75; www.dwazezaken.nl; Prins Hendrikkade 50; sandwiches €7-8, mains €17-20; ☺9am-midnight Mon-Sat; 🚊4/9/16/24/25 Centraal Station) A refuge from red-light madness, this mosaic-trimmed corner cafe has big windows and a menu of spicy sandwiches, vegie-rich soups and creative fondue. A fine selection of beer (emphasis on Belgian elixirs) helps wash it down. Jazzy live music adds to the vibe on Mondays, when there are €6 dinners as well.

HOFJE VAN WIJS
CAFE €€

Map p300 (☑624 04 36; www.hofjevanwijs.nl; Zeedijk 43; mains €9-14; ☺noon-10pm Tue-Sun; 🚊4/9/16/24/25 Centraal Station) The 200-year-old coffee and tea vendor Wijs & Zonen (the monarch's purveyor) maintains this pretty courtyard cafe. It serves Dutch stews, fondue and a couple of fish dishes, plus local beers and liqueurs. But what you're really here for are the yummy cakes.

BLAUW AAN DE WAL
INTERNATIONAL €€€

Map p304 (☑330 22 57; www.blauwaandewal.com; Oudezijds Achterburgwal 99; mains from €27, set menu €55; ☺6-11.30pm Tue-Sat; 🚊4/9/16/24/25 Dam) Definitely a rose among thorns: a long, often graffiti-covered hallway in the middle of the Red Light District leads to this Garden of Eden. Originally a 17th-century herb warehouse, the whitewashed, exposed-brick, multilevel space still features old steel weights and measures, plus friendly, knowledgeable service and refined French- and Italian-inspired cooking. In summer grab a table in the romantic garden.

ANNA
CONTEMPORARY DUTCH €€€

Map p300 (☑428 11 11; www.restaurantanna.nl; Warmoesstraat 111; mains €22-26; ☺6pm-midnight Mon-Sat; 🚊4/9/16/24/25 Dam) It's quite a contrast: Anna's sleek line of white-clothed tables topped by plates of curry-sauced monkfish and truffle-and-veal risotto, while steps away the world's oldest profession is in full swing. The restaurant sits right by the Oude Kerk and the active Red Light windows surrounding it. A robust list of organic and global wines compliments the brilliantly executed fare.

🍷 DRINKING & NIGHTLIFE

🍸 Medieval Centre

★HOPPE
BROWN CAFE

Map p304 (www.cafehoppe.com; Spui 18-20; ☺8am-1am; 🚊1/2/5 Spui) Boasting the city's highest beer turnover rate, gritty Hoppe has been filling glasses for more than 300 years. Journalists, barflies, socialites and raconteurs toss back brews amid the ancient wood panelling. Most months the energetic crowd spews out from the dark interior and onto the Spui. Note that Hoppe has two parts: the brown *café* and a modern pub with a terrace, located next door (to the left).

★CAFÉ BELGIQUE
BEER CAFE

Map p300 (www.cafe-belgique.nl; Gravenstraat 2; ☺2pm-1am; 🚊1/2/5 Dam) Pull up a stool at the carved wooden bar and make your pick from the glinting brass taps. It's all about Belgian beers here, as you may have surmised. Eight flow from the spouts, and 30 or so are available in bottles. The ambience is quintessential *gezellig* (convivial, cosy) and draws lots of chilled-out locals. There's live music and DJs some nights.

DAMPKRING
COFFEESHOP

Map p304 (www.dampkring-coffeeshop-amsterdam.nl; Handboogstraat 29; ☺10am-1am; 🛜; 🚊1/2/5 Koningsplein) You saw it in *Ocean's Twelve;* now see it up close. Wood-carved, hobbit-like decor fills the moodily lit room. Consistently a winner of the Cannabis Cup, the coffeeshop is known for having the most comprehensive menu in town, including

82

MEDIEVAL CENTRE & RED LIGHT DISTRICT DRINKING & NIGHTLIFE

ⓘ ON YOUR BIKE

The Centre has the mother lode of options for bike rentals and tours. See p30 for details.

details about smell, taste and effect. Its name, by the way, means the ring of the earth's atmosphere where smaller items combust.

LUXEMBOURG GRAND CAFÉ
Map p304 (www.luxembourg.nl; Spui 24; ⊘8am-midnight Mon-Fri, from 9am Sat & Sun; ⊠1/2/5 Spui) Join gaggles of glam locals and tourists at this permanently busy café. Grab a paper (from the reading table or the Athenaeum newsagency across the square), procure a sunny seat on the terrace, order the 'Holland' snack platter (bread, cured meats, Dutch cheese and deep-fried croquettes) and watch the world go by. Inside are parquet floors, a marble bar and an art deco stained-glass skylight.

CAFÉ DE JAREN GRAND CAFÉ
Map p304 (www.cafedejaren.nl; Nieuwe Doelenstraat 20; ⊘9.30am-1am Sun-Thu, to 2am Fri & Sat; ⊠4/9/14/16/24/25 Muntplein) Watch the Amstel flow by from the balcony and waterside terraces of this soaring, bright and very grand café, one of our favourites. The great reading table has loads of foreign publications for whiling away hours over beers. If you're feeling peckish, hit the fabulous buffet salad bar (a rarity in Amsterdam).

DE ZWART BROWN CAFÉ
Map p304 (☎624 65 11; Spuistraat 334; ⊘9am-1am Mon-Sat, from 11am Sun; ⊠1/2/5 Spui) 'Not everyone has knowledge of beer, but those who have it drink it here' is the translation of the slogan on a panel above this atmospheric bar, which has an original tiled floor from 1921. Just across the alley from Hoppe, De Zwart gets a different (though amicable) crowd of left-wing journalists and writers, as well as local-government people.

IN DE WILDEMAN BEER CAFÉ
Map p300 (www.indewildeman.nl; Kolksteeg 3; ⊘noon-1am Mon-Thu, to 2am Fri & Sat; ⊠1/2/5/13/17 Nieuwezijds Kolk) This former distillery house has been transformed into an atmospheric yet quiet beer café with more than 250 bottled beers and 18 varieties on tap. Locals rave about the choice of

Trappist ales, the huge selection from Belgium and the Netherlands, and the potent French Belzebuth (13% alcohol).

GOLLEM BEER CAFÉ
Map p304 (www.cafegollem.nl; Raamsteeg 4; ⊘4pm-1am Mon-Thu, noon-3am Fri & Sat, noon-1am Sun; ⊠1/2/5 Spui) The pioneer of Amsterdam's beer cafés is a minuscule space covered all over in beer paraphernalia. The 200 beers on tap and in the bottle (mostly from Belgium) attract lots of connoisseurs. The bartenders are happy to advise.

PILSENER CLUB BROWN CAFÉ
Map p304 (☎623 17 77; Begijnensteeg 4; ⊘noon-1am Mon-Thu, to 2am Fri & Sat; ⊠1/2/5 Spui) Also known as Engelse Reet (ask the bartender for a translation), this small, narrow and ramshackle place doesn't allow you to do anything but drink and talk, which is what a 'real' brown café is all about. It opened in 1893 and has hardly changed since. Little name plates mark the seats of the bar's regulars through the years.

ABRAXAS COFFEESHOP
Map p304 (www.abraxas.tv; Jonge Roelensteeg 12; ⊘10am-1am; ☎; ⊠1/2/5/14 Paleisstraat) It's young stoner heaven: mellow music, comfy sofas, thick milkshakes and rooms with different energy levels spread across three floors. The considerate staff make it a great place for coffeeshop newbies (though the fairy-tale artwork can get a bit intense). Free wi-fi and computer terminals, too.

GRAND CAFE-RESTAURANT 1E KLAS GRAND CAFÉ
Map p300 (www.restaurant1eklas.nl; Stationsplein 15, platform 2b; ⊘8:30am-10pm; ⊠4/9/16/24/25 Centraal Station) This distinguished café in Centraal Station (upstairs by platform 2b) used to be the waiting room for first-class passengers, hence the name. It's a nice spot if you're waiting for a train, or even just to hang out in the afternoon for bitterballen (croquettes) and a Belgian beer while reading the newspapers. A white parrot named Elvis keeps you company by the bar.

There's also a same-named pub next door, though the café has more personality. Prices aren't bad considering the location.

DE SCHUTTER BROWN CAFÉ
Map p304 (www.deschutter.nl; Voetboogstraat 13-15; ⊘4pm-1am Mon-Thu, from noon Fri-Sun;

⊞1/2/5 Koningsplein) This large student *eet-café* (*café*/pub serving meals) has a brown-*café* look, a relaxed vibe and inexpensive, tasty *dagschotels* (dishes of the day) to accompany the swell selection of beer, wine and cocktails. It's open for lunch and dinner, and is a good place to fortify yourself on the cheap before a night on the town.

CAFÉ HET SCHUIM   BAR

Map p304 (⌖638 93 57; Spuistraat 189; ⊘noon-1am Sun-Thu, to 3am Fri & Sat; ⊞1/2/5 Dam/ Paleisstraat) *Schuim* means 'foam' (on beer) and this grungy, arty bar is extraordinarily popular with beer-swilling locals – it gets packed any time of day or night. While the people-watching can be distracting, it's wise to keep one eye on your belongings.

B VAN B CAFÉ   BAR, CAFÉ

Map p300 (⌖638 39 14; Beursplein 1; ⊘10am-6pm Mon-Sat, 11am-6pm Sun; ⊞1/2/5/13/17 Nieuwezijds Kolk) The cafe in this landmark building is a cool place to pop in for a beer or coffee so you can ogle the stunning 1903 murals by Jan Toorop representing the past, present and future. On nice days tables spill out into the adjoining plaza and fill with locals.

TARA   IRISH PUB

Map p304 (www.thetara.com; Rokin 85-89; ⊘10am-1am) This expat meeting place combines folkie Irish with Amsterdam chic. In its maze of rooms (the one-time home of German expressionist Max Beckmann) you'll find warm fireplaces, a cool bar, gorgeous wall carvings and seats salvaged from an old Irish church. Catch frequent musical happenings and sports on the telly. Meals include a full Irish breakfast, and burgers.

DE DRIE FLESCHJES   TASTING HOUSE

Map p300 (⌖624 84 43; www.dedriefleschjes. nl; Gravenstraat 18; ⊘2-8.30pm Mon-Sat, 3-7pm Sun; ⊞1/2/5 Dam) Behind the Nieuwe Kerk, the distiller Bootz' tasting room dates from 1650. It is dominated by 52 vats that are rented out to businesses that entertain clients here. It specialises in liqueurs (although you can also get *jenever*) – the macaroon liqueur is quite nice. Take a peek at the collection of *kalkoentjes,* small bottles with hand-painted portraits of former mayors.

DE BLAUWE PARADE   TASTING HOUSE

Map p300 (⌖624 48 60; Nieuwezijds Voorburgwal 176-180; ⊘noon-midnight; ⊞1/2/5/14

FROM OUD AMSTERDAM TO NIEUW AMSTERDAM

Among the wall plaques on the Schreierstoren, one explains that the English captain Henry Hudson set sail from here in 1609 in his ship, the *Halve Maen (Half Moon)*. The Dutch East India Company had enlisted him to find a northern passage to the East Indies, but instead he ended up exploring the North American river that now bears his name. On the return voyage his ship was seized in England and he was forbidden to sail again to a foreign nation.

The maverick Hudson disregarded the order. Commissioned by powerful private investors from Britain and Russia, he sailed to America in search of the elusive Northwest Passage. Though an accomplished navigator, the headstrong Hudson hardly endeared himself to his crew, who mutinied in the summer of 1611. The hapless Englishman and a handful of others were set adrift in a rowboat in what's now known as Hudson Bay, where they are presumed to have died.

In any event, Hudson's reports about the island at the mouth of the Hudson River made it back to base. The Dutch soon established a fort on an island called Manhattan that flowered into a settlement called Nieuw Amsterdam; in 1626 an agent of the recently established Dutch West India Company purchased the island from Native Americans for 60 guilders (often cited as the equivalent of US$24!). In 1664 the Dutch West India Company's local governor, the imperious, fanatically Calvinist Pieter Stuyvesant, surrendered the town to the British, who promptly renamed it New York. Stuyvesant retired to the Lower Manhattan market garden called Bouwerij, now known as the Bowery.

Fun fact: Manhattan's Wall St, one of the centres of world finance, was originally the site of a fortified wall erected by the Dutch to keep out the British.

Paleisstraat) The building, now the Hotel Die Poort van Cleve, was the site of the original Heineken brewery, so it seems an appropriate place for tastings (of *jenevers* though, not beers). While there, feast your eyes on the Delft-blue tile mural (1870s) of a parade of children bearing gifts to an emperor.

CAFÉ THE MINDS   BAR
Map p304 (www.theminds.nl; Spuistraat 245; ⊗9pm-3am Sun-Thu, to 4am Fri & Sat; 🚊1/2/5 Spui) Don't let the word *'café'* in the name fool you – this is a hardcore (but very friendly) punk bar where the beer's cheap, the music's loud and the party's rockin'. It's smack in the middle of a little strip of the Spui that's home to a few squats and plenty of graffiti.

CAFÉ VAN ZUYLEN   BROWN CAFÉ
Map p300 (www.cafevanzuylen.nl; Torensteeg 4; ⊗10am-1am Sun-Thu, to 3am Fri & Sat; 🚊1/2/5/13/14/17 Raadhuisstraat) Although the sun terrace is one of the prettiest spots for a drink on the Singel, the interior – with its cosy rooms featuring lots of wood and old leather banquettes – is just as appealing in the cooler months.

OPORTO   BROWN CAFÉ
Map p300 (☑638 07 02; Zoutsteeg 1; ⊗11am-1am; 🚊1/2/5 Dam) This tiny brown *café* is worth visiting just for the inlaid woodwork behind the bar (check out the Zodiac signs). Its wrought-iron-and-parchment lighting fixtures are said to have been the same for 60 years.

TWEEDE KAMER   COFFEESHOP
Map p304 (☑422 22 36; Heisteeg 6; ⊗10am-1am; 🚊1/2/5 Spui) The teeny, wood-panelled, original location of the Dampkring chain of coffeeshops feels more like a brown *café* than a coffeeshop. But weed there is, and the selection is vast (the chain is known for its detailed, informative menus). The Sativa is highly recommended for a special happy high. It's mostly locals creating the billows of smoke that spill out the door.

DUTCH FLOWERS   COFFEESHOP
Map p304 (☑624 76 24; Singel 387; ⊗10am-11pm Sun-Thu, to 1am Fri & Sat; 🚊1/2/5 Spui) Were it not for this shop's main wares, you'd be hard pressed to distinguish it from a brown *café*, with the game on TV and a lovely view

TASTING HOUSES
Several tasting houses hide among the Centre's streets, offering a prime opportunity to try *jenever* and other local liqueurs. Most have been pouring their wares for two to three centuries.

Wynand Fockink (p85)

In de Olofspoort (p85)

Proeflokaal de Ooievaar (p86)

De Drie Fleschjes (p83)

De Blauwe Parade (p83)

of the Singel. It means that you needn't slum it with the college kids in order to enjoy a toke.

CAFÉ DANTE   GRAND CAFÉ
Map p304 (☑638 88 39; www.amsterdamdante. com; Spuistraat 320; ⊗11am-1am Sun-Thu, 10am-3am Fri & Sat; 📶; 🚊1/2/5 Spui) This huge art deco space is quiet as auntie's back garden during the day, but after 5pm weeknights it transforms into a lively bar for the downtown business crowd. Plus, you get your choice of outside views: the busy Spui out front or the lovely Singel in the back.

PRIK   GAY BAR
Map p300 (www.prikamsterdam.nl; Spuistraat 109; ⊗from 4pm) 'Sexy snacks and lovely liquids' is the motto of this peppy retro bar with an 'I've just redone my loft' clientele of 20- to 30-year-olds. Live DJs spin pop, house and dance tunes.

HOMEGROWN FANTASY   COFFEESHOP
Map p300 (Nieuwezijds Voorburgwal 87a; ⊗10am-midnight; 📶) Organic Dutch-grown product, 3m-long glass bongs, vaporisers, rotating artwork on the walls and famous space cakes attract a good mixed crowd.

COFFEESHOP RUSLAND   COFFEESHOP
Map p304 (www.coffeeshop-rusland-amsterdam.com; Rusland 16; ⊗8am-12.30am; 🚊4/9/14/16/24/25 Spui) Rusland means 'Russia' in Dutch, so it's no surprise there's a different vibe to this coffeeshop. It's a young, mod group – including many expats from the mother country – puffing, sipping tea (more than 40 types are available) and playing the occasional game of chess. It's off the usual tourist path.

CUCKOO'S NEST — GAY BAR

Map p300 (www.cuckoosnest.gaynl.net; Nieuwezijds Kolk 6; ☺1pm-1am; ☐1/2/5/13/17 Nieuwezijds Kolk) A fetish-oriented clientele crowds into this busy bar, which has one of the largest 'playrooms' in Europe. You could spend a whole night exploring the labyrinth of cubicles and glory holes.

WEB — GAY BAR

Map p300 (www.thewebamsterdam.com; St Jacobsstraat 6; ☺from 1pm; ☐1/2/5/13/17 Nieuwezijds Kolk) Web is a well-established leather bar with darkrooms and a sling room for the more adventurous. Sundays are popular, adding DJs to the mix.

🍷 Red Light District

★WYNAND FOCKINK — TASTING HOUSE

Map p304 (www.wynand-fockink.nl; Pijlsteeg 31; ☺3-9pm; ☐4/9/16/24/25 Dam) This small tasting house (dating from 1679) serves scores of *jenever* and liqueurs in an arcade behind Grand Hotel Krasnapolsky. Although there are no seats or stools, it is an intimate place to knock back a taste or two with a friend. Guides give an English-language tour of the distillery every Saturday at 12.30pm (€9, reservations not required).

If you're stuck trying to decide on a flavour, try the house speciality *boswandeling* (secret of the forest), a vivacious combination of young *jenever*, herb bitters and orange liqueur – it tastes like cloves.

★IN 'T AEPJEN — BROWN CAFÉ

Map p300 (☎626 84 01; Zeedijk 1; ☺noon-1am; ☐4/9/16/24/25 Centraal Station) Candles burn even during the day at this bar based in a mid-16th-century house, which is one of two remaining wooden buildings in the city. The name allegedly comes from the bar's role in the 16th and 17th centuries as a crash pad for sailors from the Far East, who often toted *aapjes* (monkeys) with them.

Vintage jazz on the stereo enhances the time-warp feel. The place is stuffed with advertising signs and plenty of locals.

★IN DE OLOFSPOORT — TASTING HOUSE

Map p300 (☎624 39 18; www.olofspoort.com; Nieuwebrugsteeg 13; ☺4pm-2.30am Mon, Wed & Thu, 3pm-1.30am Fri & Sat, 3pm-10pm Sun; ☐4/9/16/24/25 Centraal Station) The door of this brown *café*-tasting room was once the city gate. A crew of regulars has *jenever*

bottles stocked just for them. Check out the jaw-dropping selection behind the back room bar. Occasional sing-alongs add to the atmosphere.

'T MANDJE — BROWN CAFÉ

Map p300 (www.cafetmandje.nl; Zeedijk 63; ☺5pm-1am Tue-Thu, from 4pm Fri, from 3pm Sat & Sun; ☐4/9/16/24/25 Centraal Station) Amsterdam's oldest gay bar opened in 1927, then shut in 1982, when the Zeedijk grew too seedy. But its trinket-covered interior was lovingly dusted every week until it reopened in 2008. The devoted bartenders can tell you stories about the bar's brassy lesbian founder. It's one of the most *gezellig* places in the centre, gay or straight.

BROUWERIJ DE PRAEL — BEER CAFÉ

Map p300 (☎408 44 69; www.deprael.nl; Oudezijds Armsteeg 26; ☺noon-midnight Tue-Sun; ☐4/9/16/24/25 Centraal Station) Sample organic beers named after classic Dutch singers at the multilevel tasting room of De Prael brewery, a do-gooder known for employing people with a history of mental illness. It's mostly a younger crowd that hoists suds and forks into well-priced stews and other Dutch standards at the comfy couches and big wood tables strewn about. Bands plug in some nights.

To see the brewery itself, head around the corner to Oudezijds Voorburgwal 30. Tours (€7.50) are offered every hour between 1pm and 5pm (from 2pm Sunday) and include a spicy, amber-coloured Johnny beer (named after the folk singer Johnny Jordaan). De Prael also makes liqueurs that you can taste at the brewery's shop.

CAFÉ DE BARDERIJ — BAR

Map p300 (www.barderij.com; Zeedijk 14; ☺4pm-1am; ☐4/9/16/24/25 Centraal Station) This friendly, candlelit bar draws a mixture of local gay regulars and tourists. It has killer views of the canal out back and Zeedijk in front. Come on Mondays and Wednesdays when the bar serves a two-course homemade Dutch meal (€13.50) in the basement. A gay crowd flocks here on Sundays for free meatballs.

CAFÉ-RESTAURANT KAPITEIN ZEPPO'S — BAR, CAFÉ

Map p304 (☎624 20 57; www.zeppos.nl; Gebed Zonder End 5; ☺noon-1am; ☐4/9/14/16/24/25 Spui) Tucked down an alleyway off Grimburgwal, the site has assumed many guises

LOW-KEY COFFEESHOPS

If loud music, trippy decor and big crowds aren't your thing, try one of these smaller, relaxed establishments:

Tweede Kamer (p84)

Dutch Flowers (p84)

Coffeeshop Rusland (p84)

throughout the centuries: a cloister during the 15th, a horse-carriage storehouse in the 17th and a cigar factory in the 19th. The *café* has a timeless bohemian feel, whether you're at the tiletop, candlelit tables or in the garden with its twinkling lights. It's a soulful little spot for a drink.

Between October and April there's live music on Sundays from 4pm (cover groups and big bands).

GREENHOUSE
COFFEESHOP

Map p304 (Oudezijds Voorburgwal 191; ⊙9am-1am; 🛜; 🚊4/9/16/24/25 Dam) It's one of the most popular coffeeshops in town. Smokers love the funky music, multicoloured mosaics, psychedelic stained-glass windows, and high-quality weed and hash. It also serves a breakfast, lunch and dinner to suit all levels of the munchies. It's mostly a young, back-packing crowd partaking of the wares.

GETTO
BAR

Map p300 (www.getto.nl; Warmoesstraat 51; ⊙4.30pm-1am Tue-Thu, to 2am Fri & Sat, to midnight Sun; 🚊4/9/16/24/25 Centraal Station) This groovy, long restaurant-bar is loved for its open, welcoming attitude, great people watching from the front and a rear lounge where you can chill. It's a haven for the younger gay and lesbian crowd and anyone who wants a little bohemian subculture in the Red Light District's midst. The food is good and cheap, too.

PROEFLOKAAL DE OOIEVAAR
TASTING HOUSE

Map p300 (www.proeflokaaldeooievaar.nl; St Olofspoort 1; ⊙noon-1am; 🛜; 🚊4/9/16/24/25 Centraal Station) Not much bigger than a vat of *jenever,* this magnificent little tasting house has been going since 1782. On offer are spirits of the De Ooievaar distillery, still located in the Jordaan. The house was built leaning over and has not subsided, as many people wrongly assume even before a shot of Old Dutch.

MOLLY MALONE'S
IRISH PUB

Map p300 (📞624 11 50; www.mollyinamsterdam.com; Oudezijds Kolk 9; ⊙3pm-1am Mon-Wed, from noon Thu & Fri, from 11am Sat & Sun) Regularly packed with Irish folk, this dark, woody pub holds spontaneous folk-music sessions. Bring your own guitar and let loose with the other Irish-folk fans. The mainly Irish pub grub is decent and there are specials (ie burger and a pint, curry and a pint, etc) on various weeknights.

BUBBLES & WINES
CHAMPAGNE BAR
WINE BAR

Map p304 (📞422 33 18; www.bubblesandwines.com; Nes 37; ⊙3.30pm-1am Mon-Sat, from 2pm Sun) Ignore the silly name; this stylish wine bar is a gem. There are more than 50 quality wines by the glass, tasting flights (several different wines to try) and the city's most scrumptious bar food: caviar blinis, cheese plates and our favourite, 'bee stings' (parmesan drizzled with white-truffle-infused honey).

QUEEN'S HEAD
GAY BAR

Map p300 (www.queenshead.nl; Zeedijk 20; ⊙4pm-1am Sun-Thu, to 3am Fri & Sat; 🚊4/9/16/24/25 Centraal Station) This beautifully decorated, canal-view, old-world-style *café* was once run by legendary drag queen Dusty. The place has toned down a bit: the crowd is more mixed, and straight people are welcome. Drag bingo nights and club DJ nights are some of the events that pop up throughout the week.

BABA
COFFEESHOP

Map p300 (www.babashops.nl; Warmoesstraat 64; ⊙9am-1am) The teak-and-Ganesha decor transport you to India – and that's before you indulge. It's not the cheapest weed in town, but it packs a punch. Pick up a bag of Silver Haze, plant yourself at the front window and watch the colourful types all run together along Warmoesstraat.

DE ENGEL VAN AMSTERDAM
GAY BAR

Map p300 (www.engelamsterdam.nl; Zeedijk 21; ⊙1pm-1am; 🚊4/9/16/24/25 Centraal Station) The 'Angel' draws a relaxed terrace crowd who toast the evening's promise with a flute of blended juice or champagne. On Sundays there's a meet and greet with a sing-along party, and the TGIF drink night sees action.

BRASSERIE HARKEMA
THEATRE CAFÉ

Map p304 (☑428 22 22; www.brasserieharkema. nl; Nes 67; ⊙11am-1am; ☎; ⊟4/9/16/24/25 Rokin) At the rear of the Frascati theatre, technicolour-walled Brasserie Harkema gets crammed with a young student crowd having a pre-theatre meal or post-theatre drinks.

DE BUURVROUW
BAR

Map p304 (www.debuurvrouw.nl; St Pieterspoort-steeg 29; ⊙10pm-3am Mon-Thu, to 4am Fri & Sat) This grungy late-night bar is where you inevitably end up when there's nowhere else to go. Take it easy because someone's watching: above the entrance is a painting of *De Buur-vrouw* (the woman next door). And yes, everyone *is* probably as drunk as you are.

DURTY NELLY'S
IRISH PUB

Map p300 (www.durtynellys.nl; Warmoesstraat 117; ⊙9am-1am Sun-Thu, to 3am Fri & Sat; ☎; ⊟4/9/16/24/25 Centraal Station) Huge, dark and always busy, Nelly's attracts foreign visitors from the cheap lodgings in the area (including the attached Durty Nelly's hostel) with a fun atmosphere, drinks, darts and pool. It serves a first-rate Irish breakfast.

WORTH A DETOUR

AMSTERDAM-NOORD

Free ferries depart behind Centraal Station and glide across the IJ to avant-garde destinations in northern Amsterdam.

EYE Film Institute & Around

The gleaming new **EYE Film Institute** (☑589 14 00; www.eyefilm.nl; IJpromenade 1; ⊙10am-6pm) is a five-minute ride from the train station, accessed via the 'Buikslot-erweg' ferry. Movies (mostly art house) from the 37,000-title archive screen in four theatres, sometimes with live music. Exhibits (admission €8 to €15) of costumes, digital art and other cinephile amusements run in conjunction with what's playing. A view-tastic bar-restaurant and free film displays in the basement (including pods where you can sit and watch classic Dutch- and English-language films in their entirety) add to the hep-cat feel. One quirk to keep in mind: EYE does not accept cash; you must use a credit or debit card.

Several cafes have sprouted a short distance north of the EYE around Van der Pekstraat. Midcentury-inspired **Cafe Modern** (☑494 06 84; www.modernamsterdam. nl; Meidoornweg 2; 5-course menu €40) is a popular one, serving excellent contemporary Dutch fare. A new, three-room boutique hotel sits above it.

This part of Amsterdam-Noord is also great for cycling. After you depart the ferry, pedal north along the Noordhollands Kanaal. Within a few kilometres you're in the countryside and the landscape morphs to windmills, cows and wee farming communities. You can buy cycling maps at the VVV office by Centraal Station. Many bike rental companies also sell maps, as well as offer guided tours that cover this very area (see p30 for more information on bicycling in Amsterdam).

The 'Buiksloterweg' ferry runs continuously, 24 hours a day.

NDSM-werf

NDSM-werf (www.ndsm.nl) is a derelict shipyard turned edgy arts community 15 minutes upriver. It wafts a post-apocalyptic vibe: an old submarine slumps in the harbour, abandoned trams rust by the water's edge and graffiti artists roam the streets tagging buildings, concrete walls and whatever else they find. Besides hanging out at ubercool **Pllek** (www.pllek.nl; TT Neveritaweg 59; mains €15-22; ⊙9.30am-10pm), a organic-focused cafe made out of old shipping containers and sporting an artificial sandy beach in front, or groovy **Café Noorderlicht** (www.noorderlichtcafe.nl; TT Never-itaweg 33; ⊙11am-late), set in a flag-draped greenhouse, the main thing to do is wander around and ogle the recycled-junk street art.

The whopping **IJ Hallen** (www.ij-hallen.nl; admission €4.50; ⊙9am-4.30pm) flea market provides a bonus for visitors who coincide with its one-weekend-per-month spread; check the website for the schedule.

The NDSM-werf ferry runs between 7am (9am on weekends) and midnight, departing Centraal Station at 15 minutes and 45 minutes past the hour.

ARGOS
GAY BAR

Map p300 (www.argosbar.nl; Warmoesstraat 95; ⊘10pm-3am Mon-Sat, from 6pm Sun; ▤4/9/16/24/25 Centraal Station) Amsterdam's oldest leather bar hosts randy men of all ages in its famous darkrooms. In addition to drinks, bartenders sell condoms and lube. There's lots of action on Sunday, including the occasional safe sex party, when the dress code is – that's right – naked.

WAREHOUSE AMSTERDAM
GAY BAR

Map p300 (www.warehouse-amsterdam.com; Warmoesstraat 96; ⊘11pm-4am Thu & Sun, to 5am Fri & Sat; ▤4/9/16/24/25 Centraal Station) It's mostly men dancing to the international array of hardcore DJs, but women are equally welcome.

★ ENTERTAINMENT

BITTERZOET
LIVE MUSIC, CLUB

Map p300 (www.bitterzoet.com; Spuistraat 2; ⊘from 8pm; ▤1/2/5/13/17 Nieuwezijds Kolk) Always full, always changing, this is one of the friendliest venues in town. One night it might be full of skater dudes; the next, relaxed 30-somethings. Music (sometimes live, sometimes a DJ) can be funk, roots, drum'n'bass, Latin, Afro-beat, old-school jazz or hip-hop groove.

WINSTON KINGDOM
LIVE MUSIC, CLUB

Map p300 (www.winston.nl; Warmoesstraat 127, Hotel Winston; ⊘9pm-4am Sun-Thu, to 5am Fri & Sat; ▤4/9/16/24/25 Dam) This is a club that even nonclubbers will love for its indie-alternative music beats, smiling DJs and solid, stiff drinks. No matter what's on – from 'dubstep mayhem' to Elvis Costello cover bands – the scene can get pretty wild in this goodtime little space.

CASA ROSSO
SEX SHOW

Map p304 (www.casarosso.nl; Oudezijds Achterburgwal 106-108; admission with/without drinks €50/40; ⊘7pm-2am; ▤4/9/16/24/25 Dam) It might be stretching it to describe a live sex show as 'classy', but this theatre is clean and comfortable and always packed with couples and hen's-night parties. Acts can be male, female, both or lesbian (although not gay...sorry boys!). Performers demonstrate everything from positions of the Kama Sutra to pole dances and incredible tricks with lit candles.

LOCAL KNOWLEDGE

MUSHROOMS, TRUFFLES & SMART SHOPS

Raoul Koning, manager at Kokopelli, gave us the lowdown on smart shops and their wares.

First, a bit of background. Smart shops – which deal in organic uppers and natural hallucinogens – have long been known for selling 'magic' mushrooms. But in 2008 the government banned them after a high-profile incident in which a tourist died. Nearly 200 varieties of fungus then went on the forbidden list – though conspicuously missing was the magic truffle...

What is the difference between magic mushrooms and truffles? Truffles come from a different part of the plant, but they contain the same active ingredients as mushrooms.

Why were truffles excluded from the ban? Technically and scientifically, truffles are not mushrooms.

How does a truffle trip compare to a mushroom trip? It's a little more like a body high than a visual experience, though this varies according to where you are when you trip, as well as how you are feeling mentally and physically.

What is the best advice you can give to those seeking a pleasant trip? Ask lots of questions. If you aren't satisfied with the answers, or the salesperson won't give you the answers, go to another shop. Once you've purchased the truffles, have the experience in an outdoor space, ideally a park. Avoid bars and other enclosed spaces. Don't drink alcohol during your trip and don't mix truffles with other drugs. Take the trip with friends, or better yet, do it accompanied by a friend who is not taking the truffles.

Interview by Caroline Sieg

FRASCATI
THEATRE

Map p304 (⌨626 68 66; www.theaterfrascati. nl; Nes 63; ⊙closed Aug; 🚋4/9/14/16/25 Rokin) This experimental theatre is a draw for young Dutch directors, choreographers and producers. Expect multicultural dance and music performances, as well as hip hop, rap and breakdancing. Check the website for upcoming events. Frascati also hosts a theatre, dance, art and music festival, **Breakin'Walls** (www.breakinwalls.nl), in both November (main festival) and April (mini-festival).

CASABLANCA
LIVE MUSIC

Map p300 (www.cafecasablanca.nl; Zeedijk 26; ⊙8pm-3am Mon-Sat; 🚋4/9/16/24/25 Centraal Station) Casablanca once had a hot reputation for jazz (combos still take the stage early in the week), but now it's better known as a karaoke madhouse on the weekends.

DE BRAKKE GROND
THEATRE

Map p304 (⌨626 68 66; www.brakkegrond.nl; Nes 45, Flemish Cultural Centre; 🚋4/9/14/16/25 Rokin) De Brakke Grond sponsors a fantastic array of music, experimental video, modern dance and exciting young theatre at its nifty performance hall. Visit the website to find out about upcoming events.

🛍 SHOPPING

🔒 Medieval Centre

★AMERICAN BOOK CENTER
BOOKS

Map p304 (ABC; www.abc.nl; Spui 12; ⊙11am-8pm Mon, from 10am Tue-Sat, 11am-6.30pm Sun; 🚋1/2/5 Spui) This excellent three-storey shop is the biggest source of English-language books in Amsterdam. Its greatest strengths are in the artsy ground-floor department, but on the upper floors there's fiction and oodles of special-interest titles, plus a good travel section. It also stocks foreign periodicals such as the *New York Times*.

PGC HAJENIUS
SPECIALITY SHOP

Map p304 (www.hajenius.com; Rokin 96; ⊙noon-6pm Mon, from 9.30am Tue-Sat, noon-5pm Sun; 🚋4/9/14/16/24/25 Spui) Even if you're not a cigar connoisseur, this tobacco emporium is worth a browse. Inside is all art-deco stained glass, gilt trim and soaring ceilings. Regular customers, including members of the Dutch royal family, have private humidors here. You can sample your Cuban stogie and other exotic purchases in the handsome smoking lounge.

HEMP WORKS
CLOTHING, ACCESSORIES

Map p300 (www.hempworks.nl; Nieuwendijk 13; ⊙11am-7pm Sun-Wed, to 9pm Thu-Sat; 🚋1/2/5/13/17 Martelaarsgracht) 🌿 Hempworks carries a big selection of eco-friendly clothing and bags, all made with organic hemp, cotton and bamboo. The locally made Dutch items sell under the label Hemp Hoodlamb. Some of the clothes have special touches such as hidden pockets for your stash.

OUDEMANHUIS BOOK MARKET
BOOKS

Map p304 (Oudemanhuispoort; ⊙11am-4pm Mon-Sat; 🚋4/9/14/16/24/25 Spui) Secondhand books weigh down the tables in the atmospheric covered alleyway between Oudezijds Achterburgwal and Kloveniersburgwal, where you'll rub tweed-patched elbows with University of Amsterdam professors thumbing through volumes of Marx, Aristotle and other classics. Old posters, maps and sheet music are for sale, too. Most tomes are in Dutch, though you'll find a few in English mixed in.

DE BIJENKORF
DEPARTMENT STORE

Map p304 (www.debijenkorf.nl; Dam 1; ⊙11am-8pm Sun & Mon, 10am-8pm Tue & Wed,10am-9pm Thu & Fri, 9.30am-8pm Sat; 🚋4/9/16/24/25 Dam) The city's most fashionable department store is in the highest-profile location, facing the Royal Palace. Design-conscious shoppers will enjoy the well-chosen clothing, toys, household accessories and books. It's a good place to stop in to use the bathrooms, which are free. The very snazzy cafe on the 5th floor has a terrace with steeple views.

HEMA
DEPARTMENT STORE

Map p300 (www.hema.nl; Nieuwendijk 174; ⊙9am-7pm Mon-Fri, 9am-6pm Sat, noon-6pm Sun; 🚋4/9/16/24/25 Dam) What used to be the nation's equivalent of Marks & Spencer, Woolworths or Target now attracts as many design aficionados as bargain hunters. Expect low prices, reliable quality and a wide range of products, including good-value wines and delicatessen goods.

LAUNDRY INDUSTRY — CLOTHING

Map p304 (www.laundryindustry.com; Spui 1; ⊘10am-6pm Mon-Sat, from noon Sun; 🚊4/9/14/16/24/25 Spui) Hip, urban types head here for well-cut, well-designed women's clothes by this Dutch design house. There are other branches at Utrechtsestraat 35 in the Southern Canal Ring and Van Baerlestraat 16 near Vondelpark, but the Spui location is the main shop.

GASTRONOMIE NOLSTALGIE — HOMEWARES

Map p304 (www.gastronomienostalgie.nl; 304 Nieuwezijds Voorburgwal; ⊘11am-7pm; 🚊1/2/5 Spui) The owner scours auctions in Paris and other cities for the gorgeous china plates, crystal goblets, silver candlesticks and other antique homewares spilling out of the jam-packed shop. Ring the brass bell to get in, then prepare to browse for a good long while.

MAGIC MUSHROOM GALLERY — SMART DRUGS

Map p304 (www.magicmushroom.com; Spuistraat 249; ⊘10am-10pm) This outlet of the local chain has an excellent choice of truffles, pipes and bongs. Feel free to wobble the garden swing while you nurse a smart drink, or check out the trippy mood lighting while you wait for the herbal ecstasy to kick in. Even non 'shroomers will appreciate the 3D shark playing cards, mushroom banks and other novelty toys for sale.

BY AMFI — FASHION

Map p304 (www.byamfi.nl; Spui 23; ⊘noon-6pm Tue-Sat; 🚊1/2/5 Spui) Students, teachers and alumni of the Amsterdam Fashion Institute show and sell their wares at this small shop. It's mostly clothing and decor that's wildly inventive in style, but sure to be one of a kind.

ATHENAEUM — BOOKS

Map p304 (www.athenaeum.nl; Spui 14-15; ⊘11am-6pm Mon, 9.30am-6pm Tue-Sat, noon-5.30pm Sun; 🚊1/2/5 Spui) Amsterdam's savviest bookshop is a bit of an intellectual and style hub. Its adjoining newsagency has a selection of cutting-edge international magazines, newspapers and guidebooks.

MARK RAVEN GRAFIEK — SOUVENIRS

Map p300 (www.markraven.nl; Nieuwezijds Voorburgwal 174; ⊘10.30am-6pm) Artist Raven's distinctive vision of Amsterdam is available as posters and on T-shirts – they make genuinely tasteful souvenirs. He also has a stand on Museumplein.

TIBETWINKEL — SPECIALITY SHOP

Map p304 (www.tibetwinkel.nl; Spuistraat 185a; ⊘1-6pm Mon-Fri, 11am-6pm Sat, 1-5pm Sun; 🚊1/2/5 Dam/Paleisstraat) Volunteers staff this tiny shop that sells fair-trade items from Tibet, including incense, prayer flags, yak-bone jewellery and spinning prayer wheels. Proceeds go to a non-profit group that supports Tibet's independence 'through peaceful actions'.

MARKS & SPENCER — FOOD, DRINK

Map p304 (www.marksandspencer.com; Kalverstraat 226; ⊘10am-8pm Mon, 9am-8pm Tue-Sat, 11am-8pm Sun) Britain's iconic retailer has a little supermarket on Kalverstraat, a prime place to get your genuine clotted cream, chocolate-covered Digestives, bangers, steak and kidney pie, and true cheddar cheese. There's also a little e-boutique with a smattering of clothing brands.

ANDRIES DE JONG BV — SPECIALITY SHOP

Map p304 (www.andriesdejong.nl; Muntplein 8; ⊘10am-6pm Mon-Sat) When seafarers need ship fittings, rope or brass lamps, they sail to Andries de Jong. Traditional clocks, bells, boats in bottles and other quaint maritime gifts fill the crowded shelves among the workers' items. It's perhaps best known as a supplier of strong, vividly coloured flags.

DE BIERKONING — DRINK

Map p304 (www.bierkoning.nl; Paleisstraat 125; ⊘11am Mon-Sat, 1-6pm Sun) Come here for beer – it stocks some 950 varieties (with an emphasis on Belgian, German, British and, of course, Dutch brews), the largest beer-glass selection we've ever seen, beer-logoed T-shirts and beer guidebooks to the region. It also carries a small selection of wines.

PRECINCT FIVE — FASHION

Map p304 (www.precinct-five.com; Singel 459; ⊘1-6pm Sun & Mon, noon-7pm Tue-Sat; 🚊1/2/5 Koningsplein) A popular DJ named Mr Wix runs this cool street-wear shop. Styles come from fashion designers such as Stussy and Enplus. The shop is set in an old police station across from the flower market.

CONCRETE — ART, CLOTHING

Map p304 (www.concrete.nl; Spuistraat 250; ⊘noon-7pm; 🚊1/2/5 Spui) This is part exhibition space, showing rotating exhibitions of adventurous photography, graphics and illustration, and part cool clothes store

STAYING ON TRACK: AMSTERDAM'S NEW METRO LINE

It's only 9.7km long, but the new Noord/Zuidlijn (north–south metro line) has stretched into a challenge of far greater size. The project begun in 2003 and originally targeted for completion by 2011, but the deadline has now been pushed back to 2017.

It's no wonder, given the massive task at hand. To build the metro's route between Amsterdam-Noord and the World Trade Centre in the south, engineers must tunnel under the IJ river and the centuries-old buildings of Amsterdam's city centre. The first part went OK, but when some of the historic monuments in the centre started to shift off their foundations, engineers halted construction.

Debates flared over what to do. Continue, even though the budget was running skyhigh? Quit, and lose the millions of euros already spent? How much longer would residents tolerate the inconvenience of their main streets being torn to bits?

The city ultimately decided to proceed. Engineers added additional support beams beneath the affected buildings. So far, so good. Take a peek at the project at the subterranean Noord/Zuidlijn Viewpoint (p72).

floating racks of zany T-shirts, jeans and trendy trainers.

MAISON DE BONNETERIE DEPARTMENT STORE
Map p304 (www.debonneterie.nl; Rokin 140; ⊙11am-6pm) Exclusive and classic clothes for the whole family are featured here. Men are particularly well catered for with labels such as Ralph Lauren and Armani, best purchased during the brilliant 50%-off sales, but there is still plenty for the ladies. Note the amazing chandeliers and beautiful glass cupola.

VROOM & DREESMANN DEPARTMENT STORE
Map p304 (V&D; www.vd.nl; Kalverstraat 201; ⊙noon-7pm Sun & Mon, from 10am Tue-Sat) Slightly more upmarket than Hema, this national chain is popular for its clothing and cosmetics. Its fabulous cafeteria, La Place, serves well-priced, freshly prepared salads, hot dishes and pastries.

FEMALE & PARTNERS EROTICA, CLOTHING
Map p300 (www.femaleandpartners.nl; Spuistraat 100; ⊙1-6.30pm Sun & Mon, from 11am Tue-Sat; 🚊4/9/16/24/25 Dam) Everything you need for your inner dominatrix...or the one who's waiting for you at home. Female & Partners is filled with clothing, undies, leather and toys for women and those who love them.

HANS APPENZELLER JEWELLERY
Map p304 (www.appenzeller.nl; Grimburgwal 1; ⊙11am-5.30pm Tue-Sat) Appenzeller is one of Amsterdam's leading designers in gold

and stone, known for the simplicity and strength of his designs. If his sparse work is not to your taste, along the same street is a row of jewellery shops of all kinds.

3-D HOLOGRAMMEN JEWELLERY, ART
Map p304 (www.3-dhologrammen.com; Grimburgwal 2; ⊙1-5.30pm Sun & Mon, noon-6pm Tue-Fri, noon-5.30 Sat) This fascinating (and trippy) collection of holographic pictures, jewellery and stickers will delight even the most jaded peepers. You can even get a hologram custom-made of yourself.

MAGNA PLAZA SHOPPING CENTRE
Map p304 (www.magnaplaza.nl; Nieuwezijds Voorburgwal 182; ⊙11am-7pm Mon, 10am-7pm Tue-Sat, noon-7pm Sun) This grand 19th-century landmark building, once the main post office, is now home to a marvellous upmarket shopping mall with more than 40 shops stocking fashion, gifts and jewellery – everything from Mango and Sissy Boy to a cashmere shop.

CHILLS & THRILLS SPECIALITY SHOP
Map p300 (www.chillsandthrills.com; Nieuwendijk 17; ⊙11am-8pm Sun-Thu, to 10pm Fri & Sat; 🚊1/2/5/13/17 Martelaarsgracht) Always packed with tourists straining to hear each other over thumping techno music, busy Chills & Thrills sells truffles, herbal trips, E-testing kits, psychoactive cacti, aminoacid and vitamin drinks, novelty bongs and life-sized alien sculptures.

KALVERTOREN
SHOPPING CENTRE
SHOPPING CENTRE

Map p304 (www.kalvertoren.nl; Kalverstraat 212-220; ⊙11am-6.30pm Mon, 10am-6.30pm Tue-Sat, from noon Sun) This popular, modern shopping centre contains a Vroom & Dreesmann, a small Hema, and big-brand fashion stores such as Replay, Quiksilver, Levi's, Timberland and DKNY.

INNERSPACE
SMART DRUGS

Map p300 (www.innerspace.nl; Spuistraat 108; ⊙11am-10pm) Known for good service and information, this big shop started as a supplier to large parties; it now sells truffles, herbal ecstasy, psychoactive plants and cacti. True to its origins, it's also a good place for party info and tickets.

🔒 Red Light District

★CONDOMERIE HET
GULDEN VLIES
SPECIALITY SHOP

Map p300 (www.condomerie.nl; Warmoesstraat 141; ⊙11am-6pm Mon-Sat, 1-5pm Sun; 🚇4/9/16/24/25 Dam) This is where the well-dressed johnson shops for variety. Perfectly positioned for the Red Light District, the boutique stocks hundreds of types of condoms (including the Coripa brand, which comes in 55 sizes), lubricants and saucy gifts. Some of the novelty condoms may remind you of your favourite cartoon character.

KOKOPELLI
SMART DRUGS

Map p300 (www.kokopelli.nl; Warmoesstraat 12; ⊙11am-10pm; 🚇4/9/16/24/25 Centraal Station) Were it not for its truffle trade you might swear this large, beautiful space was a fashionable clothing or homewares store. In addition to smart drugs, there's a coffee and juice bar and a chill-out lounge area overlooking Damrak.

COCA LEAF EXPERIENCE
FOOD, DRINK

Map p300 (www.agwabuzz.us/museum; Warmoesstraat 32; ⊙1.30-8.30pm; 🚇4/9/16/24/25 Centraal Station) Here's a one-of-a-kind shop for a browse. It's the retail outlet for a company that processes Bolivian coca leaves into liquor and energy drinks. Learn about the plant's traditional uses (and less savoury uses as an element of cocaine) in the 'museum' and sample the wares (per shot €2). The shop also sells sperm- and penis-shaped bottles of tequila.

NANA
EROTICA

Map p300 (www.happy-shops.com; Warmoesstraat 62; ⊙11am-midnight; 🚇4/9/16/24/25 Centraal Station) The 'most vibrating shop in town' is actually pretty classy. Choose from a massive assortment of devices that can battery-power your happiness.

HIMALAYA
GIFTS

Map p300 (www.himalaya.nl; Warmoesstraat 56; ⊙noon-6pm Sun & Mon, from 10am Tue-Sat; 🚇4/9/16/24/25 Centraal Station) What a surprise: a peaceful, New Age oasis in the Red Light District. Stock up on crystals, incense and oils, ambient CDs and books on the healing arts, then visit the lovely tearoom.

MR B
EROTICA

Map p300 (www.misterb.com; Warmoesstraat 89; ⊙10.30am-7pm Mon-Fri, to 9pm Thu, 11am-6pm Sat, 1-6pm Sun; 🚇4/9/16/24/25 Dam) *Kinky*! The tamer wares at this renowned Red Light District shop include leather and rubber suits, hoods and bondage equipment, all made to measure if you want. Horny toys add a playful (and somewhat scary) element.

ROB
EROTICA

Map p300 (www.rob.eu; Warmoesstraat 71; ⊙11am-7pm Mon-Sat, 1-6pm Sun; 🚇4/9/16/24/25 Centraal Station) RoB sells anything and everything for one's bondage and rough-sex fantasy: army gear, leather and rubber are just the start. Items from the 'Adonis pouch' to 'black stretchy ring' stock the shelves. Oh my!

WONDERWOOD
DESIGN, HOMEWARES

Map p304 (www.wonderwood.nl; Rusland 3; ⊙noon-6pm Wed-Sat & by appointment) As much a museum as a shop, here you can ogle the sensuous, delicate, moulded-plywood creations of George Nelson, Marcel Breuer and more – some of the vintage furniture pieces are for sale and some are available in reissue (ie old designs re-made). If the furniture's impractical, smaller art objects (made of wood, naturally) are also available.

MCCARTHY'S
FOOD, DRINK

Map p300 (Zeedijk 27a; ⊙noon-10pm, closed Tue) McCarthy's is a run-of-the-mill liquor shop, but it has good prices on absinthe in decorative bottles.

Nieuwmarkt

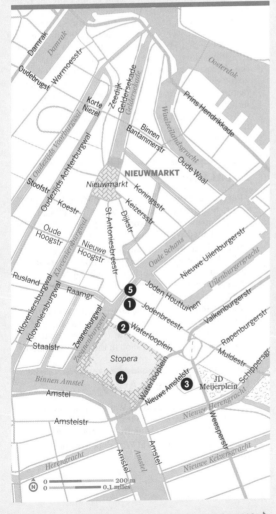

Neighbourhood Top Five

❶ View the inner sanctum of a master painter at **Museum het Rembrandthuis** (p95), where you can immerse yourself in the Dutch icon's studio and see his brushes, sketches and cabinet stuffed with seashells and Roman busts.

❷ Browse the **Waterlooplein Flea Market** (p97), where porcelain teapots, Buddha statues and other bric-a-brac tempt.

❸ Explore the **Joods Historisch Museum** (p96) for a look at life in Amsterdam's old Jewish quarter.

❹ Get a taste of classical music during Tuesday's free lunchtime concert at the **Muziektheater** (p101).

❺ Down a Dommelsch beer in the old lock-keeper's house at **De Sluyswacht** (p100).

For more detail of this area, see Map p308 ➡

Lonely Planet's Top Tip

Nieuwmarkt has heaps of intriguing architecture, from the imposing Scheep-vaarthuis (a classic example of the Amsterdam School style) to the mish-mash Stopera. Several unique buildings cluster near where Kloveniersburgwal and Oude Hoogstraat intersect, including Amsterdam's narrowest house and the mighty Oostindisch Huis, office of the 17-century, world-dominating Dutch East India Company. Keep an eye out as you wander the neighbourhood.

✕ Best Places to Eat

➡ Latei (p99)

➡ Hemelse Modder (p99)

➡ Tokoman (p98)

➡ Cafe Bern (p99)

➡ Moes (p99)

For reviews, see p98. ➡

🍺 Best Places to Drink

➡ De Sluyswacht (p100)

➡ Cafe de Doelen (p100)

➡ Cafe de Engelbewaarder (p100)

➡ Cafe Cuba (p100)

➡ De Bekeerde Suster (p100)

For reviews, see p100. ➡

🔒 Best Places to Shop

➡ Droog (p101)

➡ Het Fort van Sjakoo (p101)

➡ Henxs (p101)

➡ Juggle (p102)

➡ De Beestenwinkel (p102)

For reviews, see p101. ➡

Explore Nieuwmarkt

Nieuwmarkt (New Market) is a district as historic as anything you'll find in Amsterdam. Rembrandt painted canalscapes in Nieuwmarkt, and Jewish merchants generated a fair share of the city's wealth with diamonds and other ventures here.

The area's focal point is Nieuwmarkt square, just east of the Red Light District. This bright, relaxed place – ringed with *cafés* (pubs/bars), shops and restaurants – is arguably the grandest spot in town after the Dam. When the weather warms, the outdoor terraces boom with locals enjoying food and drink well into the evening.

The neighbourhood's top sight is Museum het Rembrandthuis, the master's impressive home/studio where he sketched and painted his finest works. It can get crowded, but never obnoxiously so. Nearby, the open-air Waterlooplein Flea Market provides fertile ground for treasure and bargain quests. Jodenbreestraat leads into the old Jewish quarter, which has a museum and synagogue worth checking out. The famed Gassan Diamond factory is also here, displaying its shiny baubles and offering free tours.

The neighbourhood is compact and its sights can easily be seen in a day, though the moody brown *cafés* and classical music venues may keep you longer.

Local Life

➡**Party at the Plaza** The *cafés* ringing Nieuwmarkt square buzz in the afternoon and evening. When the weather cooperates, everyone sits outside in the shadow of the turreted Waag (p96).

➡**Shops & Markets** Fill your bag with juggling balls, chilli-spiced chocolates or old film posters at the neighbourhood favourites along Staalstraat. Then plunge into the Saturday farmers market at Nieuwmarkt square.

➡**Best Broodjes** Follow the crowd for a spicy bite of Suriname at Tokoman (p98), famed for its *broodje pom* (chicken-and-tuber-mash sandwich). It's so popular it recently opened a second shop in the neighbourhood.

Getting There & Away

➡**Tram** Trams 9 and 14 go to Waterlooplein and the Jewish sights; there are no trams to Nieuwmarkt square, but it's a short walk from Waterlooplein.

➡**Metro** There are stops at Waterlooplein and Nieuwmarkt.

MUSEUM HET REMBRANDTHUIS

You almost expect to find the master himself at Museum het Rembrandthuis, set in the three-storey canal house where Rembrandt van Rijn lived and ran the Netherlands' largest painting studio between 1639 and 1658. He bought the abode at the height of his career. The atmospheric, tchotchke-packed interior gives a real feel for how Rembrandt painted his days away. Ask for a free audio guide, available downstairs past the entrance desk.

The house dates from 1606. Rembrandt bought it for a fortune in 1639, made possible by his wealthy wife, Saskia van Uylenburgh. On the ground floor is the living room/bedroom and the anteroom where Rembrandt entertained clients.

Climb the narrow staircase and you'll come to Rembrandt's light-filled studio, laid out as though he's just nipped down to the kitchen for a bite to eat. Artists give demonstrations here on how Rembrandt sourced and mixed paints. Across the hall is Rembrandt's 'cabinet', a mind-blowing room crammed with the curiosities he collected: seashells, glassware, Roman busts and stuffed alligators.

The top floor is devoted to Rembrandt's famous etchings. The museum has a near-complete collection of them (about 250), although they're not all on display at once. Expect to see between 20 and 100 inky works at any one time, depending on the exhibition. Demonstrators crank up an oak press to show etching techniques several times daily.

The house ultimately caused Rembrandt's financial downfall. He was unable to pay off the mortgage, and in 1656 the household effects, artworks and curiosities were sold to compensate his creditors. It's thanks to the debt collector's itemised list that the museum has been able to reproduce the interior so authentically. Rembrandt lived the rest of his years in cheaper digs in the Jordaan.

DON'T MISS...

➡ Free audio tour

➡ The paint-filled studio

➡ The cabinet stuffed with exotica

➡ Etchings collection and demonstrations

PRACTICALITIES

➡ Rembrandt House Museum

➡ Map p308

➡ ☎520 04 00

➡ www.rembrandt huis.nl

➡ Jodenbreestraat 4

➡ adult/child €12.50/4

➡ ⊙10am-6pm

➡ 🚊9/14 Water-looplein

SIGHTS

MUSEUM HET REMBRANDTHUIS   MUSEUM
See p95.

WAAG   HISTORIC BUILDING

Map p308 (www.indewaag.nl; Nieuwmarkt 4; ☺10am-1am; Ⓜ Nieuwmarkt) Multi-turreted Waag dates from 1488, when it was part of the city's fortifications. From the 17th century onwards it was Amsterdam's main weigh house, and later a spot for public executions. A bar-restaurant occupies it today. Out the front, Nieuwmarkt square hosts a variety of events, including a Saturday farmers market and a Sunday antiques market.

In its early days the Waag looked more like a castle, fronted by a moat-like canal and built into the old city walls. By the 17th century it was home to various guilds. The surgeons' guild, which occupied the upper floor, commissioned Rembrandt's famous *The Anatomy Lesson of Dr Tulp* (displayed in the Mauritshuis museum in Den Haag). The masons' guild was based in the tower facing the Zeedijk; note the superfine brickwork.

PORTUGUESE-ISRAELITE SYNAGOGUE   SYNAGOGUE

Map p308 (www.portugesesynagoge.nl; Mr Visserplein 3; adult/child €12/3; ☺10am-4pm Sun-Fri; 🚊 9/14 Mr Visserplein) This was the largest synagogue in Europe when it was completed in 1675, and it's still in use today. The interior features massive pillars and some two dozen brass candelabra. Outside (near the entrance) take the stairs underground to the 'treasure chambres' to see 16th-century manuscripts and gold-threaded tapestries. Admission tickets also provide entry to the Joods Historisch Museum.

The synagogue's architect, Elias Bouman, was inspired by the Temple of Solomon but the building's classical lines are typical of the Dutch capital. It was restored after WWII. The large library belonging to the Ets Haim seminary is one of the oldest and most important Jewish book collections in Europe.

GASSAN DIAMONDS   DIAMOND WORKSHOP

Map p308 (www.gassan.com; Nieuwe Uilenburgerstraat 173-175; ☺9am-5pm; 🚊 9/14 Waterlooplein) **FREE** This vast workshop demonstrates how an ungainly clump of rock is transformed into a girl's best friend. You'll get

---

TOP SIGHT
JOODS HISTORISCH MUSEUM

Impressive in scale and scope, the Jewish Historical Museum is housed in a beautifully restored complex of four Ashkenazic synagogues from the 17th and 18th centuries. The enormous Great Synagogue is home to two exhibitions: the 'History of the Jews in the Netherlands, 1600–1890' and 'Religion', about Judaism and Jewish traditions. Exhibits start with the pillars of Jewish identity and gradually give way to an engaging portrait of Jewish life in the city, with profiles of key figures and displays of religious items.

Even more enlightening is the New Synagogue and its 'History of Jews in the Netherlands, 1900–Present Day'. The WWII exhibits cover how 25,000 Dutch Jews went into hiding (18,000 survived) and what life was like after the war as they tried to repatriate.

The complex also has a children's museum set up as a Jewish home. Kids can bake challah bread in the kitchen and play tunes in the music room while learning about Jewish traditions.

The free, English-language audio tour that guides you through the collection is excellent, as is the bright cafe serving kosher dishes. Admission tickets are in conjunction with the Portuguese-Israelite Synagogue.

DON'T MISS

➡ WWII exhibits
➡ Children's Museum
➡ Free audio tour
➡ Kosher cafe
➡ Rotating art and photography exhibits

PRACTICALITIES

➡ Map p308
➡ ☎ 626 99 45
➡ www.jhm.nl
➡ Nieuwe Amstelstraat 1
➡ adult/child €12/3
➡ ☺ 11am-5pm
➡ 🚹
➡ 🚊 9/14 Mr Visserplein

a quick primer in assessing the gems for quality, and see diamond cutters and polishers in action. The one-hour tour is the best of its kind in town, which is why so many tour buses stop here. Don't worry: the line moves quickly.

The factory sits on Uilenburg, one of the rectangular islands reclaimed in the 1580s during a sudden influx of Sephardic Jews from Spain and Portugal. In the 1880s Gassan became the first diamond factory to use steam power.

WATERLOOPLEIN FLEA MARKET   MARKET
Map p308 (www.waterloopleinmarkt.nl; ⊙9am-5pm Mon-Sat; 🚊9/14 Waterlooplein) Covering the square once known as Vlooienburg (Flea Town), the Waterlooplein Flea Market draws sharp-eyed customers seeking everything from antique knick-knacks to imitation Diesel jeans, pot lollipops and cheap bicycle locks. The street market started in 1880 when Jewish traders living in the neighbourhood began selling their wares here.

Food vendors waft felafel sandwiches, *frites* and other quick bites around the market's periphery.

STOPERA   ARCHITECTURE & THEATRE
Map p308 (Waterlooplein 22; 🚊9/14 Waterlooplein) This odd, mod building houses both the *stadhuis* (town hall) and the opera hall (aka Muziektheater (p101)), hence the name 'Stopera'. It opened in 1986. For a neat peek behind the scenes, take a building tour (€6) on Saturdays at noon. The arcade between the town hall and the theatre has an intriguing display on NAP (ie Amsterdam's sea level) measurements (see also box on p102).

There are usually free lunchtime concerts (12.30pm to 1pm) on Tuesdays from September to June.

SCHEEPVAARTHUIS   ARCHITECTURE
Map p308 (Shipping House; Prins Hendrikkade 108; 🚊4/9/16/24/25 Centraal Station) The grand Scheepvaarthuis, built in 1916, was the first true example of Amsterdam School architecture. The exterior resembles a ship's bow and is encrusted in elaborate nautical detailing; look for figures of Neptune, his wife and four females that represent the compass points. Step inside (it's a luxury hotel now) to admire stained glass, gorgeous light fixtures and the art deco-ish central stairwell.

LOCAL KNOWLEDGE

DOCKWORKER STATUE

Beside the Portuguese-Israelite Synagogue, in triangular JD Meijerplein, Mari Andriessen's **Dockworker statue** (Map p308) (1952) commemorates the general strike that began among dockworkers on 25 February 1941 to protest against the treatment of Jews. The first deportation round-up had occurred here a few days earlier. The anniversary of the strike is still an occasion for wreath-laying, but has become a low-key affair since the demise of the Dutch Communist Party.

DE APPEL   ARTS CENTRE
Map p308 (📞625 56 51; www.deappel.nl; Prins Hendrikkade 142; adult/child €7/free; ⊙noon-8pm Tue-Sat, to 6pm Sun; 🚊4/9/16/24/25 Centraal Station) See what's on at this swanky contemporary arts centre. The curators have a knack for tapping young international talent and supplementing exhibitions with lectures, film screenings and performances. Moes (p99), the bar-restaurant in the centre's basement, rocks a local crowd of young hipsters.

ZUIDERKERK   CHURCH
Map p308 (www.zuiderkerkamsterdam.nl; Zuiderkerkhof 72; adult/child €7.50/3.75; ⊙1-5pm Mon-Sat Apr-Sep; Ⓜ Nieuwmarkt) Famed Dutch Renaissance architect Hendrick de Keyser built the 'Southern Church' in 1611. The interior is now used for private events, but you can still tour the tower. Guides lead visitors up lots of stairs every 30 minutes, past the bells to a swell lookout area for a sky-high city view.

This was the first custom-built Protestant church in Amsterdam – still Catholic in design but with no choir. The final church service was held here in 1929. During the 'Hunger Winter' of WWII it served as a morgue.

TRIPPENHUIS   ARCHITECTURE
Map p308 (Kloveniersburgwal 29; Ⓜ Nieuwmarkt) After making their fortune in arms-dealing, the Trip brothers commissioned a young Dutch architect, Justus Vingboons, to build the Trippenhuis in 1660. It's a greystone mansion with eight Corinthian

columns across two houses, one for each brother. In a nod to their ignoble profession, the chimneys are shaped like mortars. It's closed to the public, but worth a gander from the street.

OOSTINDISCH HUIS ARCHITECTURE

Map p308 (East Indies House; Oude Hoogstraat 24; MNieuwmarkt) This is the former office of the mighty Dutch East India Company (VOC), which was the globe's very first multinational corporation. You could easily walk past it, as there's no sign or plaque to identify it. The sweeping complex, built between 1551 and 1643, was attributed in part to Hendrick de Keyser, the busy city architect.

The mighty VOC sailed into rough waters and was dissolved in 1798.

MONTELBAANSTOREN HISTORIC BUILDING

Map p308 (Montelbaan Tower; Oude Schans 2; 🚊4/9/16/24/25 Centraal Station) The lower part of this striking tower was built to strengthen Amsterdam's eastern defences in 1512. Positioned on the old city wall, it gave sentries a good view of suspicious characters on the wharves along Oude Schans. The octagonal base and open wooden steeple were added in 1606 to dampen the bells on the clock after the neighbours complained.

SKINNY HOUSES

Amsterdam is chock-full of slender homes because property used to be taxed on frontage. So the narrower your facade, the less you paid.

Witness the **narrow house** (Map p308) at Oude Hoogstraat 22. It's 2.02m wide, 6m deep and several storeys tall, occupying a mere 12 sq metres per storey. This could well be the tiniest (self-contained) house in Europe.

Nearby, the **Kleine Trippenhuis** (Map p308; Kloveniersburgwal 26) is 2.44m wide. It stands opposite the mansion once owned by the wealthy Trip Brothers and, so the story goes, their coachman exclaimed: 'If only I could have a house as wide as my masters' door!' Webers fetish shop now occupies the skinny building.

Just a few years later the tower began to list under the weight, but residents attached cables and pulled it upright. The elegant tower has two sets of bellworks, four clock faces and a nautical vane like the one on top of the Oude Kerk (p70).

PINTOHUIS
(OPENBARE BIBLIOTHEEK) ARCHITECTURE

Map p308 (www.oba.nl; St Antoniesbreestraat 69; ⊙2-8pm Mon & Wed, 2-5pm Fri, 11am-4pm Sat; MNieuwmarkt) St Antoniesbreestraat was once a busy street, but it lost many of its old buildings during the metro's construction. One of the originals still standing is the Pintohuis, once owned by a wealthy Sephardic Jew, Isaac de Pinto, who had it remodelled with Italianate pilasters in the 1680s. It's now a *bibliotheek* (library) – pop inside to admire the beautiful ceiling frescoes.

✖ EATING

TOKOMAN SURINAMESE €

Map p308 (Waterlooplein 327; sandwiches €3-4, mains €7-9; ⊙11am-8pm Mon-Sat; 🚊9/14 Waterlooplein) Queue with the folks getting their Surinamese spice on at Tokoman. Chowhounds agree it makes the best *broodje pom* (a sandwich filled with a tasty mash of chicken and a starchy Surinamese tuber). You'll want the *zuur* (pickled-cabbage relish) and *peper* (chilli) on it, plus a cold can of coconut water to wash it down.

A second **branch** (Map p308; Zeedijk 136) recently opened in the neighbourhood.

TOKO JOYCE INDONESIAN €

Map p308 (www.tokojoyce.nl; Nieuwmarkt 38; mains €5-10; ⊙4-8pm Mon, 11am-8pm Tue-Sat, 1-8pm Sun; MNieuwmarkt) Pick and mix a platter of Indonesian-Surinamese food from the glass case. The 'lunch box' (you choose noodles or rice, plus two spicy, coconutty toppings) is good value. To finish, get a wedge of *spekkoek* (moist, layered gingerbread). Take your meal upstairs to the handful of tables, or head outside where canal-side benches beckon a few steps from the door.

TISFRIS CAFE €

Map p308 (www.tisfris.nl; St Antoniebreestraat 142; mains €4-9; ⊙9am-7pm; 🚊9/14 Waterlooplein) Tables splash out of mosaic-trimmed TisFris and over the canal, almost to Rembrandthuis' door. Pull up a chair and ask about the sandwich of the day.

★LATEI
CAFE €€

Map p308 (www.latei.net; Zeedijk 143; mains €6-16; ⊗8am-6pm Mon-Wed, to 10pm Thu & Fri, 9am-10pm Sat, 11am-6pm Sun; ☑; ⓂNieuwmarkt) Young locals throng groovy Latei, where you can buy the lamps (or any of the vintage decor) right off the wall. The cafe does unusual dinners Thursday through Saturday, often an Ethiopian, Indian or Indonesian dish by the local 'cooking collective'. Otherwise it serves sandwiches, apple pie and *koffie verkeerd* (milky coffee). A cat named Elvis roams the premises.

HEMELSE MODDER
CONTEMPORARY DUTCH €€

Map p308 (☑624 32 03; www.hemelsemodder.nl; Oude Waal 11; mains from €19.50, 3-course menu €32.50; ⊗6-11pm; ⓂNieuwmarkt) Celery-green walls and blond-wood tables are the backdrop for equally light and unpretentious food, which emphasises North Sea fish and farm-fresh produce. If there's no berry pudding for dessert, the namesake *hemelse modder* (heavenly mud) chocolate mousse is a good fallback. The back terrace makes for lovely alfresco dining. The restaurant is a bit out of the way, but worth it.

CAFÉ BERN
SWISS €€

Map p308 (☑622 00 34; www.cafebern.com; Nieuwmarkt 9; mains €12-18; ⊗6-11pm; ⓂNieuwmarkt) Indulge in a fondue frenzy at this delightfully well-worn cafe. People have been flocking here for more than 30 years for the gruyère fondue and the *entrecôte* (steak). Note: it's generally closed for a large part of the summer, when steamy weather lessens the hot-cheese demand. Reservations advised.

MOES
CONTEMPORARY DUTCH €€

Map p308 (☑623 54 77; www.totmoes.nl; Prins Hendrikkade 142; mains €12-20; ⊗noon-10pm Tue-Sat, to 7pm Sun; ☑; ☐4/9/16/24/25 Centraal Station) ✔ The mod, playful bar-restaurant in the basement of De Appel arts centre (p97) has a farm-to-fork credo. There's always a fish of the day and a daily vegetarian special made with local ingredients. Mains vary, but might be pasta with caramelised figs or roast lamb with summer vegetables. A fine selection of organic wines and ciders adds to the scrumptiousness.

GROENBURGWAL

If you ask Amsterdammers to pick the prettiest canal in the city, many will say the Groenburgwal. Step out onto the white drawbridge that crosses the waterway and look north toward the Zuiderkerk and you may well agree. Impressionist Claude Monet certainly took a shining to it, and painted it in 1874 as *The Zuiderkerk (South Church) at Amsterdam: Looking up the Groenburgwal.*

Every first Monday of the month is 'meatless Monday' when the whole menu goes vegetarian. Ask about hands-on lunches and dinners at farms around Amsterdam, which Moes sometimes arranges.

NYONYA
ASIAN €€

Map p308 (Kloveniersburgwal 38; mains €11-17; ⊗1-9pm, closed Tue; ⓂNieuwmarkt) Humble little Nyonya makes a mean bowl of *laksa* (spicy noodle soup), a complex *rendang* curry (spicy and coconutty) and several other Malaysian specialities. There's no alcohol, but you can sip milky tea or Sarsae (a Chinese root beer).

POCO LOCO
CAFE €€

Map p308 (Nieuwmarkt 24; mains €12-17; ⊗10am-10.30pm; ☑; ⓂNieuwmarkt) Beyond the fact it's open all day and has a great terrace overlooking the square, Poco Loco stacks up beyond-the-norm sandwiches for lunch, and concocts tapas with a Dutch twist for dinner. Vegetarians will usually find good options here. The retro, orange-and-brown '70s interior is cool if terrace seating is unavailable.

NAM KEE
CHINESE €€

Map p308 (☑638 28 48; Geldersekade 117; mains €9-19; ⊗4pm-midnight Mon-Fri, 2.30pm-midnight Sat, 2.30-11pm Sun; ☑; ⓂNieuwmarkt) The nicer branch of Amsterdam's Chinese icon (the other Nam Kee (p81) is in the Medieval Centre).

LASTAGE
FRENCH €€€

Map p308 (☑737 08 11; www.restaurantlastage.nl; Geldersekade 29; set menus from €39; ⊗from 6.30pm Wed-Sun; ☐4/9/16/24/25 Centraal Station) Small, cosy Lastage is a rose among thorns at the Red Light District's seedy

LOCAL KNOWLEDGE

TOWER TOURS

Amsterdam has three church towers to get high in: the Zuiderkerk (p97), the Westerkerk (p108) and the Oude Kerk (p70). The Westerkerk tour takes you highest and provides the best view of the canals. However, it's also the most crowded since it gets traffic from the Anne Frank Huis next door, and tours are limited to seven people at a time. The Zuiderkerk is quite similar looking (Hendrick de Keyser designed both), but the crowds are fewer and 15 people at a time can go up. The Oude Kerk tower is the same height as the Zuiderkerk, but its design is distinct from the other two.

edge. The changing menu might start with, say, stuffed guinea fowl atop red cabbage, followed by halibut with nutty Camargue wild rice and beetroot purée. It's all beautifully presented, and the elegant wine list matches to a tee.

🍷 DRINKING & NIGHTLIFE

★ DE SLUYSWACHT   BROWN CAFÉ
Map p308 (www.sluyswacht.nl; Jodenbreestraat 1; ⊙12.30pm-1am Mon-Sat, to 7pm Sun; 🚊9/14 Waterlooplein) Built in 1695 and listing like a ship in a high wind, this tiny black building was once a lock-keeper's house on the Oude Schans. Today the canalside terrace is one of the nicest spots in town to relax and down a Dutch beer (Dommelsch is the house speciality), and it has gorgeous views of the Montelbaanstoren.

CAFÉ DE DOELEN   BROWN CAFÉ
Map p308 (Kloveniersburgwal 125; ⊙10am-1am; 🚊4/9/14/16/24/25 Muntplein) Set on a busy canalside crossroad between the Amstel and the Red Light District, De Doelen dates back to 1895 and looks it: there's a carved wooden goat's head, stained-glass lamps and sand on the floor. In fine weather the tables spill across the street for picture-perfect canal views.

CAFE DE ENGELBEWAARDER   BROWN CAFÉ
Map p308 (www.cafe-de-engelbewaarder.nl; Kloveniersburgwal 59; ⊙11am-1am; 🚇Nieuwmarkt) Jazz-heads will want to settle in at this little *café* on Sunday afternoon (from 4.30pm) for an open session that has earned quite a following. The rest of the week, it's a tranquil place to sip a beer by the sunny windows.

CAFE CUBA   BROWN CAFÉ
Map p308 (www.cafecuba.nl; Nieuwmarkt 3; ⊙11am-1am; 🚇Nieuwmarkt) If a brown *café* was beamed to the tropical Atlantic, it would probably have Cafe Cuba's air of faded elegance. Slouch behind a table with names etched into it and quaff blender drinks like mai tais, Planter's Punch and the legendary mojito. It may remind you of Hemingway or the *Buena Vista Social Club*.

DE BEKEERDE SUSTER   BREWERY
Map p308 (www.debekeerdesuster.nl; Kloveniersburgwal 6-8; ⊙noon-1am; 🚇Nieuwmarkt) It's got the brew tanks, it's got the beautiful hardwood interior, it's even got the history – a 16th-century brewery-cloister run by nuns. Stop in for pub grub to go with the house suds, or hoist a glass to start an evening on Nieuwmarkt.

HILL STREET BLUES   COFFEESHOP
Map p308 (Nieuwmarkt 14; ⊙9am-1am; 🚇Nieuwmarkt) It feels more like a lounge bar than a coffeeshop, with jazzy music, an in-the-groove vibe and an international swath of visitors. Firm beanbag stools and comfy benches make great stations for watching the life forms on busy Nieuwmarkt while sipping a blended fruit-and-yogurt smoothie or one of the phenomenal shakes.

For a grungier vibe, check out its other location at Warmoesstraat 52, where graffiti covers every inch of the space and furniture.

LOKAAL 'T LOOSJE   BROWN CAFÉ
Map p308 (www.loosje.nl; Nieuwmarkt 32-34; ⊙9am-1am; 🚇Nieuwmarkt) With its beautiful etched-glass windows and tile tableaux on the walls, this is one of the oldest and prettiest *cafés* in the Nieuwmarkt area. It attracts a vibrant mix of students, locals and tourists.

AMSTELHOECK
GRAND CAFÉ

Map p308 (www.amstelhoeck.nl; Amstel 1; ⊙9am-1am; 🚋9/14 Waterlooplein) Located in the Stopera building, Amstelhoeck doesn't have the history of some of the other *cafés* in town, but that doesn't make it any less appealing. The great Amstel-side terrace is always busy in summer, with excellent views over the water and lots of sunlight.

GREEN PLACE
COFFEESHOP

Map p308 (www.thegreenplace.nl; Kloveniersburgwal 4; ⊙10am-1am; Ⓜ Nieuwmarkt) The staff at the Cannabis College recommend Green Place for its good selection, good quality product and fair prices. The gingersnap-like Twizzla wins praise.

 **ENTERTAINMENT**

MUZIEKTHEATER
CLASSICAL MUSIC

Map p308 (✆625 54 55; www.hetmuziektheater.nl; Waterlooplein 22; ⊙box office from noon, closed Aug; 🚋9/14 Waterlooplein) The Muziektheater is home to the Netherlands Opera and the National Ballet. Big-name performers and international dance troupes also take the stage here. Visitors aged under 30 can get tickets for €10 to €15 by showing up 90 minutes before show time. Free classical concerts (12.30pm to 1pm) are held most Tuesdays from September to June in its Boekmanzaal.

AMSTERDAMS MARIONETTEN THEATER
THEATRE

Map p308 (✆620 80 27; www.marionettentheater.nl; Nieuwe Jonkerstraat 8; adult/child €16/7.50; Ⓜ Nieuwmarkt) In a former blacksmith's shop, the marionette theatre has a limited repertoire (mainly Mozart operas such as *The Magic Flute*), but kids and adults alike are enthralled by the fairy-tale stage sets, period costumes and beautiful singing voices that bring the diminutive cast to life. From June to August the theatre performs only for groups; check the website for a schedule.

BETHANIËNKLOOSTER
CLASSICAL MUSIC

Map p308 (✆625 00 78; www.bethanienklooster.nl; Barndesteeg 6b; ⊙Sept-July; Ⓜ Nieuwmarkt) This former monastery near Nieuwmarkt has a glorious ballroom, and is a great place to take in exceptional chamber music. Jazz fills the air on Tuesdays.

🛍 SHOPPING

★ DROOG
DESIGN, HOMEWARES

Map p308 (www.droog.com; Staalstraat 7b; ⊙11am-6pm Tue-Sun; 🚋4/9/14/16/24/25 Muntplein) Droog means 'dry' in Dutch, and this slick local design house's products are strong on dry wit. You'll find all kinds of smart items you never knew you needed, like super-powerful suction cups. Droog has gone wild with expansion recently, adding gallery space, a whimsical blue-and-white cafe that's awesome for a respite, and a trippy courtyard garden that Alice in Wonderland would love.

HET FORT VAN SJAKOO
BOOKS

Map p308 (✆625 89 79; www.sjakoo.nl; Jodenbreestraat 24; ⊙11am-6pm Mon-Fri, to 5pm Sat; 🚋9/14 Waterlooplein) Get the low-down on the squat scene, plus locally produced zines and Trotsky translations, at this lefty bookshop, which has been in operation since 1977.

HENXS
CLOTHING

Map p308 (www.henxs.com; St Antoniesbreestraat 136; ⊙11am-6pm Mon-Sat, noon-6pm Sun; Ⓜ Nieuwmarkt) The two tiny floors of this indie clothes store are crammed with fave labels of skaters and graffiti artists,

---

LOCAL KNOWLEDGE

ALL ABOUT DIAMONDS

Two diamond factories in town offer free guided tours. Gassan Diamonds (p96) offers the slicker version. Coster Diamonds' (p176) perk is its convenient location at the Museumplein. You'll see lots of gems, and workers shining them, at both places.

For those in the market to buy, note that diamonds aren't necessarily cheaper in Amsterdam than elsewhere, but between the tours and extensive descriptions and factory offers, you'll know what you're buying.

And a bit of local diamond trivia: Amsterdam has been a diamond centre since Sephardic Jews introduced the cutting industry in the 1580s. The Cullinan, the largest diamond ever found (3106 carats), was split into more than 100 stones here in 1908, after which the master cutter spent three months recovering from stress.

such as Hardcore, Bombers Best, Evisu and G-Star. Graffiti supplies and edgy accessories are available in Henxs' space next door.

JUGGLE   SPECIALITY SHOP
Map p308 (www.juggle-store.com; Staalstraat 3; ⊙noon-5.30pm Tue-Sat; 🚊4/9/14/16/24/25 Muntplein) Wee Juggle puts more than mere balls in the air: it also sells circus supplies, from unicycles to fire hoops to magic tricks.

DE BEESTENWINKEL   TOYS
Map p308 (www.beestenwinkel.nl; Staalstraat 11; ⊙noon-6pm Sun & Mon, 10am-6pm Tue-Sat; 🚊; 🚊4/9/14/16/24/25 Muntplein) From teeny-tiny teddy bears to pink plastic pig snouts, this pleasantly crowded shop sells *de best* (the best) of *de beesten* (animals). Other bests: plush toys from great toy makers, lamps in animal shapes, and lots of plastic reptiles.

MARBLES VINTAGE   CLOTHING
Map p308 (Nieuwe Hoogstraat 12; ⊙11am-7pm; MNieuwmarkt) Pretty, feminine and reasonably priced, Marbles offers a wonderfully curated selection of vintage skirts, dresses, coats, shoes and jewellery. Items are sorted by colour and type. Clothes hounds can launch from here into several other hip new and used clothing stores on the same block.

FILMANTIQUARIAAT
CINE QUA NON   ART, BOOKS
Map p308 (www.cinequanonline.com; Staalstraat 14; ⊙1-6pm; 🚊4/9/14/16/24/25 Muntplein) An encyclopedic collection of film posters, arthouse DVDs and books on films fills this

dusty, crammed space. Amazingly, if you ask for something specific, the staff will know exactly where it is in the organised chaos.

PUCCINI BOMBONI   FOOD
Map p308 (www.puccinibomboni.com; Staalstraat 17; ⊙noon-6pm Sun & Mon, 9am-6pm Tue-Sat; 🚊4/9/14/16/24/25 Muntplein) It's pretty much impossible to walk by and resist the smell. Puccini fills its large, handmade chocolate bonbons with rich and distinctive flavours like anise, tamarind or calvados. There is another branch at Singel 184. Note: these shops have been known to close in warm weather – for the sake of the chocolates, of course.

HET HANZE HUIS AMSTERDAM   FOOD
Map p308 (www.hethanzehuis.nl; Staalstraat 20; ⊙noon-6.30pm Mon, 10.30am-6.30pm Tue-Sat, 11am-6pm Sun; 🚊4/9/14/16/24/25 Muntplein) This shop stocks wares from Amsterdam's old trading partners from the 12th through 16th centuries, including Copenhagen, Bruges, Hamburg, Riga and Tallinn (members of the once-powerful Hanseatic League). It also only uses suppliers who've been manufacturing from traditional recipes from 1800 onward. The result? You'll find unique coffee, tea, marzipan, wine and honey on the shelves.

JOE'S VLIEGERWINKEL   SPECIALITY SHOP
Map p308 (www.joesvliegerwinkel.nl; Nieuwe Hoogstraat 19; ⊙noon-6pm Tue-Fri, to 5pm Sat; 🚊; MNieuwmarkt) Whether you're after a kite that flies in nice patterns for the kids, or

---

NAP: AMSTERDAM'S SEA LEVEL MEASUREMENT

It is widely known that Amsterdam (and indeed more than half of the Netherlands) lies a couple of metres below sea level, but when's the last time you heard anyone ask 'which sea level'? In fact, sea levels vary around the globe and even around the Netherlands. The average level of the former Zuiderzee, in the lee of Holland, was slightly lower than that of the North Sea along Holland's exposed west coast.

A display in the arcade of the Stopera shows the ins and outs of Normaal Amsterdams Peil (NAP; Normal Amsterdam Level), established in the 17th century as the average high-water mark of the Zuiderzee. This still forms the zero reference for elevation anywhere in the country and is also used in Germany and several other European countries.

Water in the canals is kept at 40cm below NAP, and many parts of the city lie lower still. The Stopera display has water columns representing different sea levels, as well as the highest level of disastrous floods in 1953 (4.55m above NAP). Information sheets and a touch-screen explain the details. A paid-admission exhibit (€1) delves further into the subject.

you're looking for something more exotic, head to this specialised kite shop. You can also buy build-it-yourself kits.

JACOB HOOY & CO ALTERNATIVE MEDICINE
Map p308 (www.jacobhooy.nl; Kloveniersburgwal 12; ⊘1-6pm Mon, 10am-6pm Tue-Fri, 10am-5pm Sat; MNieuwmarkt) This charming chemist's shop – with its walls of massive wooden drawers – has been selling medicinal herbs, homeopathic remedies and natural cosmetics since 1743.

KNUFFELS TOYS, SHOES
Map p308 (www.knuffels.com; St Antoniesbreestraat 39-51; ⊘10am-6pm; ; MNieuwmarkt) Kids will be drawn to the bobbing mobiles hanging from the ceiling of this busy corner shop, as wells as the *knuffels* (soft cuddly toys), puppets, teddies and jigsaw puzzles. As a bonus, there's a clog shop downstairs with wooden shoes galore.

BOOK EXCHANGE BOOKS
Map p308 (www.bookexchange.nl; Kloveniersburgwal 58; ⊘10am-6pm Mon-Sat, 11.30am-4pm Sun; MNieuwmarkt) This rabbit warren specialises in secondhand English books, with temptingly priced literary titles as well as volumes on the social sciences and more. It's near the university.

WEBERS EROTICA
Map p308 (www.webersholland.nl; Kloveniersburgwal 26; ⊘1-7pm, from 11am Sat; MNieuwmarkt) Indulge in top-end versions of every kind of fetish-wear imaginable (and unimaginable).

'T KLOMPENHUISJE SHOES
Map p308 (www.klompenhuisje.com; Nieuwe Hoogstraat 9a; ⊘10am-6pm Mon-Sat; MNieuwmarkt) This children's clog shop has the traditional shoes in a rainbow of hues. It sells cute galoshes and other kids' footwear, too.

BOERENMARKT MARKET
Map p308 (Farmers Market; Nieuwmarkt; ⊘9am-4pm Sat; MNieuwmarkt) Stalls selling organic foods and produce draw crowds on Saturdays.

ANTIQUES MARKET MARKET
Map p308 (Nieuwmarkt; ⊘9am-5pm Sun May-Sep; MNieuwmarkt) Treasure hunters will find lots of old books and bric-a-brac to peruse.

🏃 SPORTS & ACTIVITIES

TUNFUN PLAYGROUND
Map p308 (www.tunfun.nl; Mr Visserplein 7; adult/child free/€8.50; ⊘10am-6pm, last entry 5pm; ; 9/14 Mr Visserplein) The cool indoor playground is located in a former traffic underpass. These days kids can build, climb, roll, draw, jump on trampolines and play on a soccer pitch. There's even a children's disco – this *is* Amsterdam – and a cafe serving *poffertjes* (small pancakes). Kids must be accompanied by an adult. It gets busy when the weather's bad.

The entrance is located opposite the Portuguese-Israelite Synagogue; look for the two green arches and stairs leading down.

Western Canal Ring

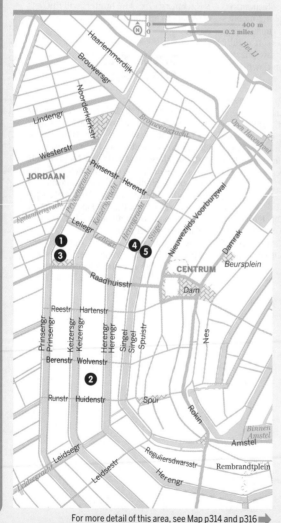

Neighbourhood Top Five

1 Contemplate the amazing life and tragic death of the most famous Dutch girl in history at the poignant **Anne Frank Huis** (p106) where she and her family hid from the Nazis.

2 Browse the speciality shops along the compact and captivating **Negen Straatjes** (p116).

3 Scale the bell tower of the mighty **Westerkerk** (p108) and see the Netherlands' largest nave.

4 Learn to distinguish an aged gouda from a young *boerenkaas* at **Reypenaer Cheese Tasting** (p118).

5 Explore the neighbourhood's standout canals on a **Western Canal Ring walking tour** (p111).

For more detail of this area, see Map p314 and p316 ➡

Explore Western Canal Ring

This whole area is a Unesco World Heritage Site and you could spend a full day admiring the architecture down one canal alone. And although the neighbourhood is loaded with high-profile sights, half the charm here is simply soaking up the atmosphere: from the street, from a boat, from a backyard garden or rooftop balcony, or from the terrace of a canal-side cafe.

Begin your first day at the neighbourhood's northern end around the hip Haarlemmerbuurt shopping area and work your way towards the south, weaving in and out of the lanes and canals to visit the Multatuli Museum, admire the architecture of the Huis Met de Hoofden and pay homage to the Homomonument and the Westerkerk until you wind up at Anne Frank Huis in the early evening, when the crowds are thinnest.

On your second day, start with some of Amsterdam's most enjoyable shopping along the Negen Straatjes (Nine Streets) in the neighbourhood's south. This tic-tac-toe board of *straatjes* (small streets) is full of quirky little boutiques stocking antiques, vintage fashions, homewares and one-off speciality shops dedicated to everything from toothbrushes to antique eye wear. The area is peppered with informal drinking and dining that spills out into the streets in warmer weather.

Tear yourself away to check out the Bijbels Museum, the canal-house museum Het Grachtenhuis and the Huis Marseille photography museum, before finishing up at the Prinsengracht's bars, cafes and restaurants.

Local Life

→ **Ad Life** Glance through the windows of the advertising agencies and design firms lining the Singel and Herengracht canals, whose arty designer interiors may cause serious job envy.

→ **Street Life** The Haarlemmerbuurt, incorporating Haarlemmerstraat, is a hotspot for restaurants, gourmet provisions and kitchen shops, interspersed with hip fashion boutiques.

→ **Snack Life** Join the locals queuing for fries slathered in mayonnaise or spicier sauces at Wil Graanstra Friteshuis (p112).

→ **Steam Life** The jewel-like art deco interior of Sauna Deco (p118) brightens any grey day.

Getting There & Away

→ **Trams** Trams 13, 14 and 17 have stops near the main attractions, and any tram or bus that stops near the Dam is just a short walk away.

Lonely Planet's Top Tip

In the spring and summer, take advantage of the later evening hours of the Anne Frank Huis. Go to an early dinner at one of the many excellent nearby cafes, and then spend the rest of the evening hours in Amsterdam's most moving sight – with few crowds and plenty of time to contemplate this remarkable Dutch girl's life and legacy.

✖ Best Places to Eat

→ De Belhamel (p112)
→ Bistro Bij Ons (p112)
→ Café Restaurant van Puffelen (p112)
→ Letting (p110)
→ Vinnies Deli (p110)

For reviews, see p110.➡

🍷 Best Places to Drink

→ 't Arendsnest (p113)
→ Café Tabac (p113)
→ Café Het Molenpad (p114)
→ Café de Vergulde Gaper (p113)
→ Werck (p114)

For reviews, see p113.➡

🔒 Best Places to Shop

→ Frozen Fountain (p115)
→ Tenue de Nîmes (p115)
→ Glas Kunst Winkel (p115)
→ Unlimited Delicious (p116)
→ Rock Paper Scissors (p116)

For reviews, see p115.➡

WESTERN CANAL RING

TOP SIGHT
ANNE FRANK HUIS

With its reconstruction of Anne's melancholy bedroom and her actual diary – sitting in its glass case, filled with sunnily optimistic writing tempered by quiet despair – visiting the Anne Frank Huis is a powerful experience.

It is one of the 20th century's most compelling stories: a young Jewish girl forced into hiding with her family and their friends to escape deportation by the Nazis. The house they used as a hideaway should be a highlight of any visit to Amsterdam; indeed, it gets nearly one million visitors a year. Stepping through the revolving bookcase of the 'Secret Annexe' and up the steep stairs into the living quarters – where the family lived for over two years before they were betrayed to the Gestapo – is to step back into a time that seems both distant and tragically real. Perhaps nowhere else in Europe does the brutal legacy of the Nazi rise to power – and the beauty and humanity that stubbornly persisted in spite of it – feel more palpable.

It seems impossible now, but it's true: it took the German army just five days to occupy all of the Netherlands, along with Belgium and much of France. And once Hitler's forces had swept across the country, many Jews – like Anne Frank and her family – eventually went into hiding. Anne's famous diary describes how restrictions were gradually imposed on Dutch Jews: from being forbidden to ride streetcars to being forced to turn in their bicycles and not being allowed to visit Christian friends. Ultimately, most of the Netherlands' Jewish population – more, in fact, than that of any other European country – perished in the Holocaust.

The Franks moved into the upper floors of the specially prepared rear of the building, along with another couple, the Van Pels (called the Van Daans

DON'T MISS

➡ Anne Frank's diary
➡ Anne's bedroom
➡ WWII news reels
➡ Peter van Pels' room
➡ The video of Anne's schoolmate Hannah Gisler

PRACTICALITIES

➡ Map p314
➡ 📞556 71 05
➡ www.annefrank.org
➡ Prinsengracht 267
➡ adult/child €9/4.50
➡ ⏰9am-10pm Jul & Aug; 9am-9pm Sun-Fri, to 10pm Sat Apr-Jun; Sep & Oct, 9am-7pm Sun-Fri, to 9pm Sat Nov-Mar
➡ 🚊13/14/17 Westermarkt

in Anne's diary), and their son Peter, and were joined later by a Fritz Pfeffer (called Mr Dussel in the diary). Here they survived until they were betrayed to the Gestapo in August 1944.

Ground Floor

After several renovations, the house itself is now contained within a modern, square shell that attempts to retain the original feel of the building (it was used during WWII as offices and a warehouse).

On this floor, be sure to watch the multilingual news reels of WWII footage narrated using segments of Anne's diary: it inextricably links the rise of Hitler with the Frank family's personal saga.

Offices

View the former offices of Victor Kugler, Otto Frank's business partner; his identity card and the film magazines he bought for Anne are on display. The other office area belonged to Miep Gies, Bep Voskuijl and Jo Kleiman, three women who worked in the office by day and provided food, clothing, school supplies and other goods – often purchased on the black market or with ration cards – for the eight members of the Secret Annexe. You can see some of their personal documents here.

Secret Annexe

While the lower levels are painstakingly curated in a way that boldly presents history with interactive modern technology, the former living quarters of the Frank family in the *achterhuis* (rear house) retain their stark, haunting austerity. It's as if visitors are stepping back into 1942. Notice how windows of the annexe were blacked out to prevent suspicion among people who might see it from surrounding houses (blackouts were common practice to disorient bombers at night).

Take a moment to observe the ingenious set-up of the Secret Annexe as you walk through. You then enter two floors of the dark and airless space where the Franks and their friends observed complete silence during the daytime, outgrew their clothes and read Dickens, before being mysteriously betrayed and sent to their deaths.

Anne's Bedroom

As you enter Anne's simple, small bedroom, which she shared with Fritz Pfeffer, you can still sense the remnants of a young girl's dreams: the physical evidence of her interests and longings is on the wall with her photos of Hollywood stars and postcards of the Dutch royal family.

WESTERN CANAL RING ANNE FRANK HUIS

◉ SIGHTS & ACTIVITIES

ANNE FRANK HUIS   MUSEUM
See p106.

WESTERKERK   CHURCH
Map p314 (Western Church; ☎624 77 66; www.
westerkerk.nl; Prinsengracht 281; ⊙10am-5pm
Mon-Sat; ☐13/14/17 Westermarkt) **FREE** The
main gathering place for Amsterdam's
Dutch Reformed community, this church
was built for rich Protestants to a 1620 design by Hendrick de Keyser. The nave is the
largest in the Netherlands and is covered by
a wooden barrel vault. The huge main organ dates from 1686, with panels decorated
with instruments and biblical scenes.

Rembrandt (1606–69), who died bankrupt at nearby Rozengracht, was buried in
a pauper's grave somewhere in the church.

A highlight is the **Westerkerk bell tower**
(Map p314; tours per person €7; ⊙by reservation
Mon-Sat Jun-Sep), topped by the blue imperial crown that Habsburg emperor Maximilian I bestowed to the city for its coat of
arms in 1489. Climbing the 85m tower can
be strenuous and claustrophobic (it's inside a tower, after all), but the guide takes
breaks on the landings while describing the
bells. Children under six aren't permitted.

Carillon recitals take place on Fridays
at 1pm (though check the schedule posted
by the entrance, as this can vary); best
listening is from the nearby Bloemgracht.
The bells also chime mechanically every 15
minutes.

HOMOMONUMENT   MONUMENT
Map p314 (cnr Keizersgracht & Raadhuisstraat;
☐13/14/17 Westermarkt) Behind the Westerkerk, this 1987 cluster of three 10m x 10m
x 10m granite triangles recalls persecution
by the Nazis, who forced gay men to wear
a pink triangle patch. One of the triangles
steps down into the Keizersgracht and is
said to represent a jetty from which gay
men were sent to the concentration camps.

Others interpret the step-up from the
canal as a symbol of rising hope. Note the
monuments are flush to the ground, and
can be easy to miss at first glance.

Just south of the Homomonument is the
Pink Point (Map p314; ☎428 10 70; www.pink-
point.org; Westermarkt; ⊙10am-6pm; ☐13/14/17
Westermarkt). Part information kiosk, part
souvenir shop, it's a good place to pick up
gay and lesbian publications, and news
about parties, events and social groups.

DE RODE HOED   CULTURAL BUILDING
Map p314 (The Red Hat; www.rodehoed.nl; Keizersgracht 102; ⊙8.30am-5.30pm, except during
special events; ☐13/14/17 Westermarkt) **FREE**
Occupying three glorious 17th-century
canal houses, this cultural centre offers
lectures by world-renowned authors and
debates on the topics of the day, sometimes
in English. Even if nothing is on it's worth a
visit to view the three-storey main auditorium, which was once the largest clandestine church in the Netherlands.

The centre was named for the hat shop
once located here (spot the tile on the facade that identified it).

HUIS MET DE HOOFDEN   HISTORIC BUILDING
Map p314 (House with the Heads; Keizersgracht
123; ☐13/14/17 Westermarkt) A whimsical
example of Dutch Renaissance style, this
canal house has a beautiful step gable
with six heads at door level representing
the classical muses. Folklore has it that the
heads depict burglars, decapitated in quick
succession by a fearless maid as they tried
to break in.

The facade drips with decorations – lion
masks, obelisks and vases – as well as the

HERENGRACHT

Dug out during the 17th century Golden Age, the Herengracht (Gentlemen's Canal)
takes its name from the wealthy landowners who built properties here. Notice how
some buildings lean forward and have hoists in the gables. Given the narrowness of
interior staircases, people used these hoists to haul large goods to upper floors.

Just north of the Herengracht, near the intersection of the Brouwersgracht, you'll
find the Herenmarkt, a small square that is home to the historic 17th-century West-
Indisch Huis (p109), the former headquarters of the Dutch West India Company.

The Herengracht is at its grandest along the Golden Bend (p121) in the Southern
Canal Ring.

famous heads (match 'em up): Apollo, Diana, Ceres, Bacchus, Minerva and Mars. The building now houses the Bureau Monumentenzorg, the city office of monument preservation.

VAN BRIENENHOFJE   COURTYARD
Map p314 (Prinsengracht 85-133; ⊘6am-6pm Mon-Fri, 6am-2pm Sat; ⌑1/2/5/13/17 Nieuwezijds Kolk) **FREE** This charming courtyard was named in the late 18th century for Jan van Brienen, who bought the Star Brewery located here, one of 13 breweries in town at the time. (The place is still called De Star Hofje by many.)

It was turned into an almshouse for older residents, who had a clear division of labour: the women cleaned house for the single men, who in turn toted water buckets from the outside pump (topped by a curious lantern). Hours can vary. If *hofjes* (almshouses or a series of buildings around a small courtyard) grab you, be sure to visit the Begijnhof (p69).

MULTATULI MUSEUM   MUSEUM
Map p314 (www.multatuli-museum.nl; Korsjespoortsteeg 20; ⊘10am-5pm Tue, noon-5pm Sat & Sun; ⌑1/2/5/13/17 Nieuwezijds Kolk) **FREE** Better known by the pen name Multatuli – Latin for 'I have suffered greatly' – novelist Eduard Douwes Dekker was best known for *Max Havelaar* (1860), a novel about corrupt colonialists in the Dutch East Indies. This small but fascinating museum-home chronicles his life and works, and shows furniture and artefacts from his period in Indonesia.

Dekker himself worked in colonial administration in Batavia (now Jakarta), and the book made him something of a social conscience for the Netherlands.

POEZENBOOT   ANIMAL REFUGE
Map p314 (Cat Boat; www.poezenboot.nl; Singel 38; admission by donation; ⊘1-3pm, closed Wed & Sun; ⌑1/2/5/13/17 Nieuwezijds Kolk) This boat on the Singel is a must for cat lovers. It was founded in 1966 by an eccentric woman who became legendary for looking after several hundred stray cats at a time. The boat has since been taken over by a foundation and holds a mere few dozen kitties in proper pens.

They're ready to be spayed or neutered, implanted with an identifying computer chip (as per Dutch law) and, hopefully, adopted out.

PRINSENGRACHT
The Herengracht and Keizersgracht might be grander, but locals love to hang out on the Prinsengracht, the liveliest of Amsterdam's inner canals. In summertime you could spend a whole weekend just enjoying its warm-weather charms – exploring the shops and kicking back on its cafe terraces – as boats glide by and houseboats sway in the breeze against the quays. During the chillier months, it's a winter wonderland where you might see skaters take to the iced-over canal.

WEST-INDISCH HUIS   HISTORIC BUILDING
Map p314 (West Indies House; Herenmarkt 97; ⌑18/21/22 Singel) Built in 1617 as a meat market and militia barracks, this historic building was rented by the Dutch West India Company (Geoctroyeerde Westindische Compagnie; GWC) as its headquarters in 1623. It was here that the GWC's governors signed off on the construction of a fort on the island of Manhattan in 1625, establishing New Amsterdam (now New York City).

The booty of Admiral Piet Heyn, the great naval hero, was stored here in 1628 after his men captured the Spanish silver fleet off the coast of Cuba.

Today this landmark on the Herenmarkt is used as a conference venue and houses offices including the John Adams Institute, which fosters cultural ties between the USA and the Netherlands. You can enter the courtyard to see the statue of Peter Stuyvesant (c 1612-1672), the colony of New Netherland's final Dutch Director-General until its British acquisition.

The Oost-Indisch Huis (p98), the headquarters of the Dutch East India Company (Vereenigde Oostindische Compagnie; VOC) is in Nieuwmarkt.

FELIX MERITIS BUILDING   CULTURAL BUILDING
Map p316 (www.felix.meritis.nl; Keizersgracht 324; ⌑1/2/5 Spui) This performing arts centre (p115) was built in 1787 by Jacob Otten Husly for Felix Meritis (Latin for 'happiness through achievement'), a society of wealthy residents who promoted the ideals of the Enlightenment through the study of science, arts and commerce. The colonnaded facade served as a model for that of the Concertgebouw.

Inside, its oval concert hall (where Brahms, Grieg and Saint Saëns performed) was copied as the Concertgebouw's Kleine Zaal (Small Hall) for chamber music.

HUIS MARSEILLE
MUSEUM

Map p316 (www.huismarseille.nl; Keizersgracht 401; adult/child €5/free; ⊙11am-6pm Tue-Sun; 🚊1/2/5 Keizersgracht) This well-curated photography museum stages large-scale, temporary exhibitions, drawing from its own collection as well as hosting travelling shows. Themes might include portraiture, nature or regional photography, spread out over several floors and in a 'summer house' behind the main house.

Huis Marseille is also located in a noteworthy building. The name refers to its original owner in 1665, a French merchant, and the original structure has remained largely intact. It retains some antique touches such as the 18th-century fountain in the library, and a painting of Apollo, Minerva and the muses in the garden room.

HET GRACHTENHUIS
MUSEUM

Map p316 (Canal House; www.hetgrachtenhuis. nl; Herengracht 386; adult/child €12/6; ⊙10am-5pm; 🚊1/2/5 Keizersgracht) If you're the kind of person who walks through the Canal Ring and marvels over what a true feat of engineering this area is, you won't want to miss the Canal House, which explains how the canals and the houses that line them became an integral part of Amsterdam city planning.

Prebook a spot on a small group tour as places are limited; unlike most Amsterdam museums you can't simply wander through. Tickets are cheaper when purchased online and cheaper still on weekdays.

BIJBELS MUSEUM
MUSEUM

Map p316 (Bible Museum; www.bijbelsmuseum. nl; Herengracht 366-368; adult/child €8/4; ⊙10am-5pm Tue-Sat, 11am-5pm Sun; 🚊1/2/5 Spui) This place first gained notoriety thanks to a dedicated minister, Leendert Schouten, who built a scale model of the Jewish Tabernacle described in Exodus. Now on the museum's 3rd floor, the model is said to have attracted thousands of visitors even before it was completed in 1851.

Another large exhibit examines the Temple Mount/Haram al-Sharif in Jerusalem from Christian, Jewish and Muslim perspectives. A collection of Dutch Bibles includes a delft Bible printed in 1477. On the ground floor you can sniff scents mentioned in the Good Book and stroll through a garden of biblical trees.

✖ EATING

The Western Canal Ring may not have the multicultural dining diversity of other parts of town, but bear in mind that the Jordaan is only a hop, skip and a jump away. The Negen Straatjes (p116) are filled with cute cafes and small restaurants to match their lovely boutiques.

LETTING
CAFE €

Map p314 (www.letting.nl; Prinsenstraat 3; dishes €4.50-15.50; ⊙8.30am-5.30pm; 🍴; 🚊13/14/17 Westermarkt) Start your day in traditional Dutch style with authentic breakfast dishes like *wentelteefjes* (sugar bread dipped in egg and cinnamon), *uitsmijter rosbief* (eggs served sunny side up, with cheese and roast beef) and scrambled eggs with smoked halibut. At lunch choose from soups and sandwiches. Or book ahead for royal high tea (€25), accompanied by tea and champagne.

VINNIES DELI
CAFE €

Map p314 (www.vinniesdeli.nl; Haarlemmerstraat 46; dishes €5-12; ⊙7.30am-6pm Mon-Fri, 9am-6pm Sat, 9.30am-6pm Sun; 🍴🚻; 🚊18/21/22 Singel) 🌿 Organic fare at this trendy spot spans sandwiches such as black-bean hummus and sweet peppers, pastrami, sauerkraut and gruyère, eggplant with buttermilk sauce and pomegranate, and smoked mackerel with grapefruit chutney. Cakes like beetroot-topped cheesecake are equally creative. Self-caterers can pick up products used in its dishes from the deli.

If you're imagining the designer furniture in your lounge room, you're in luck: all of the pieces are for sale.

SINGEL 404
CAFE €

Map p316 (Singel 404; dishes €3.50-8; ⊙10.30am-7pm; 🍴; 🚊1/2/5 Spui) It's easy to miss this tucked-away spot, despite its location near the bustling Spui (look for the cobalt-blue awning). Sure, the menu is as simple as can be – smoked salmon sandwiches, pumpkin soup – but the prices are rock bottom, portions are generous and the quality is superb.

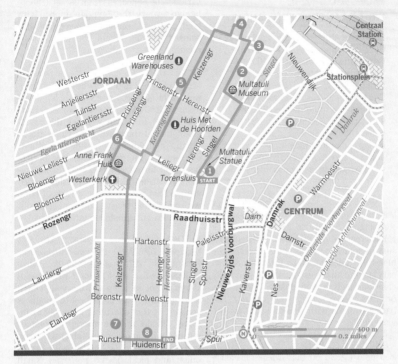

Neighbourhood Walk
Western Canal Ring

START SINGEL, TORENSLUIS
END NEGEN STRAATJES
LENGTH 3 KM; 1¼ HOURS

Get to know the Western Canal Ring's 17th-century beauties during this walk.

Originally a moat that defended Amsterdam's outer limits, the ❶ **Singel** is the first canal west of the centre. Torensluis, Amsterdam's oldest bridge (built in the mid-1600s), crosses it. Before you do too, stop to admire the Multatuli statue; the Dutch literary giant's museum is a few blocks north.

Amsterdam's wealthiest residents once lived along the ❷ **Herengracht** (Gentlemen's Canal; p108), named after the wealthy landowners here.

The Herengracht soon intersects with the pretty ❸ **Brouwersgracht** (Brewer's Canal), which took its name from the many suds makers located here in the

16th and 17th centuries. To the north is Herenmarkt, home to the 17th-century ❹ **West-Indisch Huis** (p109), where the Dutch West India Company's governors authorised establishing New Amsterdam (now New York City).

Turning south, cross the Brouwersgracht into the ❺ **Keizersgracht** (Emperor's Canal). You'll soon spot the imposing, red-shuttered Greenland Warehouses and, further on, the Huis Met de Hoofden, with carvings of Apollo, Ceres and Mars. At peaceful Leliegracht, turn west onto ❻ **Prinsengracht** (p109). You'll pass the Anne Frank Huis and the soaring towers of the Westerkerk. Back on Keizersgracht, you can't miss the quirky ❼ **Felix Meritis Building** (p109), a one-time Enlightenment society venue turned alternative theatre. Since you're probably hungry, thirsty or both by this point, head to one of the fetching little cafes lining the nearby ❽ **Negen Straatjes** (p116).

WIL GRAANSTRA FRITESHUIS

Legions of Amsterdammers swear by the crispy spuds at **Wil Graanstra Friteshuis** (Map p314; ☑624 40 71; Westermarkt 11; frites €2.50-4; ⊙noon-5pm Tue-Sat; 🚊13/14/17 Westermarkt). The family-run business has been frying on the square by the Westerkerk since 1956. Most locals top their cones with mayonnaise, though *oorlog* (a peanut sauce–mayo combo), curry sauce and *picalilly* (relish) rock the taste buds, too.

PANCAKES!   TRADITIONAL DUTCH €

Map p316 (☑528 97 97; www.pancakesamsterdam.com; Berenstraat 38; pancakes €5-13; ⊙10am-7pm; ☑ 📶; 🚊13/14/17 Westermarkt) Just as many locals as tourists grace the blue-tile tables at snug little Pancakes!, carving into all the usual options, plus daily creations such as ham, chicory and cheese, or goats cheese, spinach and pine nut. The batter is made with flour sourced from a local mill.

LUNCHCAFÉ NIELSEN   CAFE €

Map p316 (☑330 60 06; www.nielsen-ontbijtlunch.nl; Berenstraat 19; mains €5-11; ⊙8am-4pm Tue-Fri, to 6pm Sat, 9am-5pm Sun; ☑; 🚊13/14/17 Westermarkt) Looking for a locals' favourite in the Negen Straatjes? This bright, airy cafe is an institution, thanks to good value for money; fast, friendly service; Illy coffee and great food that spans hearty breakfasts, quiches, salads, sandwiches and fresh lemon and apple cakes that disappear as quickly as they're put out.

BAKKERIJ ANNEE   BAKERY, SWEETS €

Map p316 (☑623 53 22; Runstraat 25; dishes €2.50-7; ⊙7.30am-6pm Mon-Fri, 8am-5pm Sat; 🚊1/2/5 Spui) Once you've tasted the signature apple cake – moist, sweet and totally addictive – it's almost impossible to walk by this bakery without buying one. So why not pick up some bread and other goodies for your picnic while you're at it? At least it's all good for you.

PANCAKE BAKERY   CONTEMPORARY DUTCH €

Map p314 (www.pancake.nl; Prinsengracht 191; mains €6-14; ⊙noon-9.30pm; 📶; 🚊13/14/17 Westermarkt) This basement restaurant in a restored warehouse features a dizzying 79 varieties of pancakes, from sweet (chocolate) to savoury (the 'Egyptian', topped with lamb and garlic sauce; or 'Norwegian' with smoked salmon, cream cheese and sour cream).

★DE BELHAMEL   FRENCH €€

Map p314 (☑622 10 95; www.belhamel.nl; Brouwersgracht 60; lunch mains €15-24.50, dinner mains €22.50-24.50; ⊙noon-4pm & 6-11pm; 🚊22 Singel) In warm weather the canalside tables at the head of the Herengracht are an aphrodisiac, and the sumptuous art nouveau interior provides the perfect backdrop for superb French- and Italian-inspired dishes like truffle-parsley-stuffed guinea fowl with polenta, a rack of lamb with aubergine biscuit and pepper coulis, and honey- and mustard-marinated veal.

BISTRO BIJ ONS   TRADITIONAL DUTCH €€

Map p314 (☑627 90 16; www.bistrobijons.nl; Prinsengracht 287; mains €13.50-18; ⊙noon-10.30pm Tue-Sat; 📶; 🚊13/14/17 Westermarkt) If you're not in town visiting your Dutch *oma* (grandma), try the honest-to-goodness cooking at this charming retro bistro instead. Classics include *stamppot* (potatoes mashed with another vegetable) with sausage, *raasdonders* (split peas with bacon, onion and pickles), and *poffertjes* (small pancakes with butter and powdered sugar).

CAFÉ RESTAURANT
VAN PUFFELEN   GRAND CAFÉ €€

Map p316 (www.restaurantvanpuffelen.com; Prinsengracht 377; mains €8.50-19; ⊙3-10pm Mon-Thu, 1-10pm Fri, noon-10pm Sat & Sun; 🚊13/14/17 Westermarkt) Scallops with lemon cream and basil, beer tenderloins with Béarnaise sauce, game stew with cherry beer and bacon, and smoked, baked foie gras with artichokes and apple are among the innovative dishes at this large cafe-restaurant. Its nooks and crannies are enticing for a cosy drink.

VAN HARTE   INTERNATIONAL €€

Map p314 (☑625 85 00; www.vanharte.com; Hartenstraat 24; lunch mains €4-11.50, 3-course dinner menu €27.50; ⊙10am-9.30pm; 🚊13/14/17 Westermarkt) Behind floor-to-ceiling glass windows, a glistening mosaic-tiled bar and massive murals make Van Harte look like an ultrachic drinking spot but it's an even better place to dine, with an evening menu spanning brie and truffle dim sum with beetroot salad, roasted duck breast on Le

Puy lentils with duck liver sauce, or skin-baked cod with fennel and *beurre blanc*.

STOUT
INTERNATIONAL €€

Map p314 (🖉616 36 64; www.restaurantstout.nl; Haarlemmerstraat 73; mains €7-24, shared platters per person €29.50; ⊙noon-10pm; ☏; ☐22 Singel) In warm weather, sit on the benches outside this airy, contemporary cafe to watch the world go by. Indoors, you can share platters and individual dishes such as mushroom ravioli with sage butter. DJs spin during after-dinner dances on Saturday night.

CASA PERÚ
PERUVIAN €€

Map p316 (🖉620 37 49; www.casaperu.nl; Leidsegracht 68; mains €12-19; ⊙noon-11.30pm Apr-Sep, 5.30pm-11.30pm Oct-Mar; ☏; ☐1/2/5 Prinsengracht) There's nothing quite like enjoying a *chupe de camarones* (fisherman's soup) or *lomo saltado* (beef with onion, tomato and French fries) while looking out over the Leidsegracht and the Prinsengracht at this bright, busy spot – the Netherlands' only Peruvian restaurant.

DE STRUISVOGEL
FRENCH €€

Map p316 (🖉423 38 17; www.restaurantdestruisvogel.nl; Keizersgracht 312; 3-course menu €25; ⊙6pm-10pm; ☐13/14/17 Westermarkt) This former kitchen to some large canal houses is in the basement and offers good value. It doesn't serve the bird (*struisvogel* means 'ostrich'), but it does have a nightly rotating menu with French-inspired choices like veal tongue stewed in white wine followed by red mullet in prawn bisque and crème caramel for dessert. Book ahead.

LOCAL KNOWLEDGE

HAARLEMMERBUURT

Amsterdam's coolest neighbourhood-within-a-neighbourhood (or two – it straddles both the Western Canal Ring and the Jordaan), the Haarlemmerbuurt (www.haarlemmerbuurt-amsterdam.nl) is exploding with restaurants, food shops, designer workshops and funky boutiques. Its website (in Dutch but easy to navigate) has an interactive map of Haarlemmerstraat and its western extension, Haarlemmerdijk, and details of one-off events.

SPANJER EN VAN TWIST
CAFE €€

Map p314 (🖉639 01 09; www.spanjerenvantwist.nl; Leliegracht 60; mains €7-15; ⊙10am-10pm; ☐13/14/17 Westermarkt) Spanjer en van Twist's tables on Leliegracht are great for watching the boats cruise by. The eclectic lunch and dinner menu is good – say shrimp croquettes on pumpkin bread, Moroccan *tajine* (stew) with catfish, or traditional Dutch soup with smoked sausage – but a highlight is the divine apple tart.

🍷 DRINKING & NIGHTLIFE

Cafes in this refined district tend to have slick, polished interiors and elaborate menus. More down-to-earth brown *cafés* jam the nearby Jordaan.

'T ARENDSNEST
BEER CAFÉ

Map p314 (www.arendsnest.nl; Herengracht 90; ⊙2pm-midnight Sun-Thu, to 2am Fri & Sat; ☐1/2/5/13/17 Nieuwezijds Kolk) This gorgeous, restyled brown *café*, with its glowing copper *jenever* (Dutch gin) boilers behind the bar, only serves Dutch beer – but with more than 300 varieties (many from small breweries), including 23 on tap, you'll need to move here to try them all.

CAFÉ TABAC
BAR

Map p314 (www.cafetabac.eu; Brouwersgracht 101; ⊙4pm-1am Tue-Thu, to 3am Fri & Sat, 11am-1am Sun & Mon; ☏; ☐22 Buiten Brouwersstraat) Is Café Tabac a brown *café*, a designer bar or simply an effortlessly cool place to while away a few blissful hours at the intersection of two of Amsterdam's most stunning canals? The regulars don't seem concerned about definitions but simply enjoy the views and kicking back beneath the beamed ceilings.

CAFÉ DE VERGULDE GAPER
BROWN CAFÉ

Map p314 (Prinsenstraat 30; ⊙10am-1am Sun-Thu, to 3am Fri & Sat; ☏; ☐13/14/17 Westermarkt) Decorated with old chemists' bottles and vintage posters, this former pharmacy has amiable staff and a terrace with afternoon sun. It's popular with locals, especially for after-work drinks. The name translates to the 'Golden Gaper', for the open-mouthed bust of a Moor traditionally posted at Dutch apothecaries.

CAFÉ HET MOLENPAD
BAR, CAFÉ

Map p316 (Prinsengracht 653; ⊘noon-midnight Sun-Thu, to 1am Fri & Sat; ☎; ☒1/2/5 Prinsengracht) By day, this gem of a canal-side cafe is full of people poring over newspapers on the terrace. By night the atmosphere turns quietly romantic, with low lamps and candlelight illuminating little tables beneath pressed tin ceilings.

WERCK
DESIGNER BAR

Map p314 (☑627 40 79; www.werck.nl; Prinsengracht 277; ⊘noon-1am Sun-Thu, to 3am Fri & Sat; ☒13/14/17 Westermarkt) A big courtyard complete with a tropical tiki bar is the focal point of this buzzing bar, which is incongruently located between a historic church and the Anne Frank Huis. After Dark club nights kick off from 11pm on Friday and Saturday (no cover charge).

DE DOFFER
BROWN CAFÉ

Map p316 (www.doffer.com; Runstraat 12-14; ⊘noon-3am Sun-Thu, noon-4am Fri, 11am-4am Sat; ☒1/2/5 Spui) Writers, students and artists frequent this popular *café* (with adjoining bar) for affordable food and good conversation. The dining room, with its old Heineken posters, large wooden tables and, occasionally, fresh flowers, is particularly atmospheric at night.

DE ADMIRAAL
TASTING HOUSE

Map p316 (www.proeflokaaldeadmiraal.nl; Herengracht 319; ⊘5pm-midnight Mon-Sat; ☒1/2/5 Spui) The grandest and largest of Amsterdam's tasting houses, De Admiraal is also a restaurant and party venue. Although they pour only their own house brands (16 *jenevers* and 60 liqueurs), it's hard to quibble over the lovely setting and pleasant staff.

SCREAMING BEANS
CAFE

Map p314 (www.screamingbeans.nl; Hartenstraat 12; ⊘8am-5pm Mon-Fri, 9am-5pm Sat, 10am-5pm Sun; ☒13/14/17 Westermarkt) For a first-rate caffeine hit served by academy-trained baristas, drop by Screaming Beans' original Negen Straatjes location. And for a knockout gourmet meal, make a reservation at its Vondelpark branch (p164).

WOLVENSTRAAT 23
DESIGNER BAR

Map p316 (☑320 08 43; Wolvenstraat 23; ⊘8am-1am Sun-Thu, to 3am Fri & Sat; ☒1/2/5 Spui) This funky bar with no name – there's no sign anywhere – is especially popular with locals, who come for the good wines by the glass, great music and tasty Asian snacks. If this is your kind of place, check out their other bar, Finch (p152), in the Jordaan.

VYNE
WINE BAR

Map p316 (www.vyne.nl; Prinsengracht 411; ⊘6pm-midnight Mon-Thu, 5pm-1am Fri & Sat, 4-10pm Sun; ☒13/14/17 Westermarkt) With blond timber floors, walls and ceiling, the slickest wine bar in town looks like a stylish sauna (wine bottles notwithstanding). Knowledgeable staff guide you in the right direction, no matter your price point.

JAY'S JUICES
JUICE BAR

Map p314 (www.jaysjuices.nl; Haarlemmerstraat 14; ⊘9am-6pm Mon-Fri, 10am-6pm Sat & Sun; ☒22 Singel) Set yourself up for a day of sightseeing at Jay's. There's a huge range of fruit and vegetable juices, and combinations thereof, as well as wheatgrass shots and fresh coconut.

DAMPKRING
COFFEESHOP

Map p314 (www.dampkring.nl; Haarlemmerstraat 44; ⊘10am-1am; ☎; ☒22 Buiten Brouwersstraat) With lush ferns, comfy seats and open windows in warm weather, this multistoried stoner paradise is about as photogenic as these places get. Even nonsmokers might want to come for a coffee or a fresh fruit shake and dig the 1960s mod atmosphere.

CAFÉ DE PELS
BROWN CAFÉ

Map p316 (www.cafedepels.nl; Huidenstraat 25; ⊘10am-1am Sun-Thu, to 3am Fri & Sat; ☒1/2/5 Spui) This appealingly shabby traditional brown *café* is also a Sunday morning breakfast fave, with plenty of international newspapers to pore over as you sip your *koffie verkeerd* (milky coffee).

IL TRAMEZZINO
CAFE

Map p314 (www.iltramezzino.nl; Haarlemmerstraat 79; ⊘9am-6pm Wed-Mon; ☒22 Buiten Brouwersstraat) A perfect Haarlemmerstraat shopping break, this little slice of Milan in Amsterdam, with a white lacquer and red-cushioned interior, serves steaming espresso from a magnificent chrome contraption imported from Italy.

GREENHOUSE
COFFEESHOP

Map p314 (www.greenhouseseeds.nl; Haarlemmerstraat 64; 9am-1am; ☎; ☒22 Buiten Brouwersstraat) Yes, that stretch of the floor is glass and there really are koi swimming underfoot in this contemporary coffeeshop lounge.

Once you tire of the fish, peer into the microscope to see THC crystals or contemplate one of the pies spinning in the display case.

GREY AREA COFFEESHOP

Map p314 (www.greyarea.nl; Oude Leliestraat 2; ⊙noon-8pm; 📮1/2/5/13/14/17 Dam) Owned by a couple of laid-back American guys, this tiny shop introduced the extra-sticky, flavoursome 'Double Bubble Gum' weed to the city's smokers. It also keeps up the wonderful American tradition of free coffee refills (it's organic). It keeps shorter hours than most coffeeshops.

PÂTISSERIE POMPADOUR CAFE

Map p316 (📞623 95 54; www.patisseriepompadour.com; Huidenstraat 12; ⊙10am-6pm Mon-Fri, 9am-5pm Sat, noon-6pm Sun; 📮1/2/5 Spui) Join society ladies sipping top-notch tea and nibbling homemade Belgian-style chocolates and pastries at this chichi little tearoom in the Negen Straatjes.

KOFFIEHUIS DE HOEK CAFE

Map p316 (📞625 38 72; www.koffiehuisamsterdam.nl; Prinsengracht 341; ⊙7.30am-4pm Tue-Fri, 9am-3.30pm Sat; 📮13/14/17 Westermarkt) This *koffiehuis* (espresso bar; not to be confused with a coffeeshop) is one of the best places in the city to experience an old-fashioned Amsterdam coffee house experience. Come for *lekker* (tasty) cakes in a charming atmosphere.

SIBERIË COFFEESHOP

Map p314 (www.coffeeshopsiberie.nl; Brouwersgracht 11; ⊙11am-11pm Sun-Thu, to midnight Fri & Sat; 📷; 📮22 Singel) Popular among locals, Siberië's offerings go beyond marijuana – its owners regularly schedule cultural events such as art exhibits, poetry slams, concerts, DJ nights and even horoscope readings.

BRIX FOOD 'N' DRINX DESIGNER BAR

Map p316 (www.cafebrix.nl; Wolvenstraat 16; ⊙11am-11pm Sun-Thu, to 3am Fri & Sat; 📮1/2/5 Spui) The loungey setting makes this a great place to chill over a cocktail and enjoy nibbles from the starters-only menu, like raw oysters, beef sashimi and mini Peking duck. There's live jazz on Sunday (with established artists) and Monday nights (with an open stage) from about 9pm.

DULAC GRAND CAFÉ

Map p314 (📞624 42 65; www.restaurantdulac.nl; Haarlemmerstraat 118; ⊙7.30am-1am Sun-Thu, to

3am Fri & Sat; 📮22 Buiten Brouwersstraat) This former bank building is outrageously decked out in a kooky, kind of spooky, mixture of styles (art nouveau, Amsterdam School and Turkish, with a few Gothic accents). It has a pool table and an equally eclectic crowd.

☆ ENTERTAINMENT

FELIX MERITIS ARTS CENTRE

Map p316 (📞626 23 21; www.felix.meritis.nl; Keizersgracht 324, Felix Meritis Bldg; ⊙box office 9am-7pm; 📷; 📮1/2/5 Spui) Amsterdam's centre for arts, culture and science (p109) puts on innovative modern theatre, music and dance, as well as talks on politics, art, technology and literature. Its adjoining cafe is exceptional for coffee or cocktails by the huge windows or outside overlooking the canal.

🛍 SHOPPING

You could easily spend all of your shopping time in the Negen Straatjes (p116), but be sure to check out the Haarlemmerbuurt.

★ FROZEN FOUNTAIN DESIGN, HOMEWARES

Map p316 (www.frozenfountain.nl; Prinsengracht 645; ⊙1-6pm Mon, 10am-6pm Tue-Sat, 1-5pm Sun; 📮1/2/5 Prinsengracht) The city's best-known showcase of furniture and interior design. Prices are not cheap, but the daring designs are offbeat and very memorable (designer pen-knives, kitchen gadgets and that birthday gift for the impossible-to-wow friend).

TENUE DE NÎMES CLOTHING

Map p314 (www.tenuedenimes.com; Haarlemmerstraat 92-94; ⊙10am-6pm Mon-Wed, Fri & Sat, to 8pm Thu, noon-6pm Sun; 📮18/21/22 Buiten Brouwersstraat) Ubercool denimwear by legendary brands such as Levi's, Rogue Territory, Pure Blue Japan, Edwin, Naked & Famous and Rag & Bone are the speciality of this hip boutique. You'll also find hot new fashions such as t-shirts, stylishly cut jackets and dresses from local Amsterdam label Amatør.

GLAS KUNST WINKEL HOMEWARES

Map p314 (www.glaskunstwinkel.nl; Oude Leliestraat 8; ⊙11am-6pm Thu-Sat; 📮1/2/5/13/14/17 Dam) The Glass Art Shop has some beautiful and unique sculptures and tablewear, from tulips and windmills to owls, cats and more. You won't need to worry about added weight in your suitcase, or the fragility of the creations – items can be shipped worldwide.

UNLIMITED DELICIOUS
FOOD, DRINK

Map p314 (www.unlimiteddelicious.nl; Haarlemmerstraat 122; ⊘9am-6pm Mon-Sat; ◉22 Buiten Brouwersstraat) Is it ever! It's tempting to dive into the sculptural cakes and tarts, but – if you can – walk past them to the dozens of varieties of chocolates made in-house. Some of the more outlandish combinations (that somehow work) are rosemary sea salt, caramel cayenne and citron *witbier* (white beer). Also on offer are tastings, and bonbon and patisserie workshops.

ROCK PAPER SCISSORS
CLOTHING, ACCESSORIES

Map p314 (www.rockpaperscissorsamsterdam.com; Oude Leliestraat 10; ⊘1-6pm Mon, 11am-6pm Tue-Sat, noon-5pm Sun; ◉1/2/5/13/14/17 Dam) At this supercool little streetwear boutique you can find accessories like retro Casio digital watches (buttons and all), nifty bags and credit card holders and Lilla Bruket cosmetics, as well as cool denim and knitwear.

SCOTCH & SODA
CLOTHING

Map p316 (www.scotch-soda.com; Huidenstraat 3-5; ⊘noon-6pm Mon, 10am-6pm Tue, Wed, Fri & Sat, 10am-9pm Thu, noon-5pm Sun; ◉1/2/5 Spui) Styled by interior designer Marloes Hoedeman, Scotch & Soda's Negen Straatjes store is a prime place to check out offerings from this Amsterdam fashion label-gone-global. There are men, women and kids' ranges; the outerwear here is guaranteed to keep you looking impossibly cool even during the most tempestuous Dutch weather.

DENHAM THE JEANMAKER MEN'S STORE
CLOTHING

Map p316 (www.denhamthejeanmaker.com; Prinsengracht 495; ⊘noon-6pm Sun & Mon, 10am-6pm Tue, Wed, Fri & Sat, 10am-8pm Thu; ◉1/2/5 Spui) Next door to this Amsterdam label's Negen Straatjes studio, this flagship, 'zoned' boutique carries Denham the Jeanmaker's menswear lines. Jeans aside, you'll find jackets, knitwear and accessories. Cool vintage touches in-store include an antique haberdashery display case and a vintage scissor collection. Its **women's store** (Map p316; www.denhamthejeanmaker.com; Runstraat 17; ⊘noon-6pm Sun & Mon, 10am-6pm Tue-Sat; ◉1/2/5 Spui) is around the corner.

DE KAASKAMER
FOOD, DRINK

Map p316 (www.kaaskamer.nl; Runstraat 7; ⊘noon-6pm Mon, 9am-6pm Tue-Fri, 9am-5pm Sat, noon-5pm Sun; ◉1/2/5 Spui) The name means 'cheese room' and it is indeed stacked to the rafters with Dutch and organic varieties, as well as olives, tapenades, salads and other picnic ingredients. You can try before you buy, and if it's too much to take home a mondo wheel of gouda you can at least procure a cheese and/or meat baguette to take away.

GAMEKEEPER
GAMES

Map p314 (www.gamekeeper.nl; Hartenstraat 14; ⊘10am-6pm Mon & Sat, to 6.30pm Tue, Wed & Fri, to 9.30pm Thu, 11am-6pm Sun; ◉13/14/17 Westermarkt) The selection of board games is dizzying, as is the imagination that went into making them. Start with chequers, chess and mah jong, and move on to Cathedral (build a city in the style of the Great Wall of China or a souk in Marrakech) or Rush Hour (help a car get out of traffic). 'Cooperative' games encourage players to play with each other.

SHOPPING THE NEGEN STRAATJES

In a city packed with countless shopping opportunities, each seemingly more alluring than the next, the **Negen Straatjes** (Nine Streets; Map p316; www.de9straatjes.nl; ◉1/2/5 Spui) represent the very densest concentration of consumer pleasures. These nine little streets are indeed small, each just a block long. Their shops are tiny, too, and many are highly specialised. Eyeglasses? Cheese? Toothbrushes? Single-edition art books? Each has its own dedicated boutique.

The streets – from west to east, and north to south: Reestraat, Hartenstraat, Gasthuismolensteeg, Berenstraat, Wolvenstraat, Oude Spiegelstraat, Runstraat, Huidenstraat, Wijde Heisteeg – form a grid bounded by Prinsengracht to the west and Singel to the east.

To help navigate the welter of shops here, pick up a copy of *The Nine Streets* shopping guide, available at many tourist offices and in many of the shops themselves, as well as online. Many shops here are closed on Monday, and sometimes Tuesday too.

LOCK, STOCK & BARREL CLOTHING
Map p314 (http://lockstockbarrel.nl; Hartenstraat 26; ⊙noon-6pm Sun & Mon, 11am-6pm Tue, Wed, Fri & Sat, 11am-9pm Thu; ⏚13/14/17 Westermarkt) Up-to-the-minute men's and women's fashions, shoes and accessories ranging from hats and umbrellas to jewellery by a roll-call of designers like Filippa K, Vanessa Bruno, Christian Peau, Noguchi and Deux Souliers fill this gorgeous vintage-decorated, green Moroccan-tiled boutique.

BOEKIE WOEKIE BOOKS
Map p316 (http://boewoe.home.xs4all.nl; Berenstraat 16; ⊙noon-6pm; ⏚13/14/17 Westermarkt) This artist-run bookstore sells books created by artists. Some tell elegantly illustrated stories; others are riffs on graphic motifs.

BEBOB DESIGN HOMEWARES
Map p316 (☑624 57 63; http://bebob.eu; Keizersgracht 300; ⊙noon-6pm Thu-Sat & by appointment; ⏚13/14/17 Westermarkt) Apart from some smaller items like toasters and perfume bottles, most of the local and international designs here are larger pieces (sofas, chairs, tables, lamps), but it's worth a browse for an insight into the vintage influence on Dutch design.

MARLIES DEKKERS LINGERIE
Map p316 (www.marliesdekkers.com; Berenstraat 18; ⊙1-6pm Mon, 11am-6pm Tue & Wed, 11am-7pm Thu & Fri, 10am-6pm Sat, noon-5pm Sun; ⏚13/14/17 Westermarkt) The preeminent Dutch lingerie designer Marlies Dekkers is known for her subtle hints to bondage, detailed on exquisite undergarments. Summer sees an equally enticing range of swimwear. The shop itself is a sultry bastion of decadence, with handpainted wallpaper and a titillating lounge area with a fireplace.

AMSTERDAM WATCH COMPANY ACCESSORIES
Map p314 (www.awco.nl; Reestraat 3; ⊙11am-6pm Tue-Fri, 11am-5pm Sat; ⏚13/14/17 Westermarkt) A small, passionate and highly skilled team of watchmakers restores old watches (postwar to mid-1970s). The company is also the exclusive Amsterdam dealer of such brands as Germany's D Dornblüth and the Dutch Christiaan van der Klaauw, who makes fewer than 200 watches a year.

BRILMUSEUM ACCESSORIES
Map p314 (☑421 24 14; www.brilmuseum amsterdam.nl; Gasthuismolensteeg 7; ⊙11.30am-5.30pm Wed-Fri, to 5pm Sat; ⏚13/14/17 Westermarkt) This spectacles shop is an institution, both for its wares and for its presentation. You can take in the 700-year history of eyeglasses as well as a very 21st-century collection, some of which is pretty outlandish.

THE DARLING ACCESSORIES, CLOTHING
Map p316 (www.thedarling.nl; Runstraat 4; ⊙1-6pm Mon, 11am-6pm Tue-Sat, noon-6pm Sun; ☎; ⏚1/2/5 Spui) Funky, affordable, locally designed clothes. Whimsical accessories. And cupcakes! Shops like TD are why the Negen Straatjes continue to delight and surprise.

ARCHITECTURA & NATURA BOOKS
Map p314 (www.architectura.nl; Leliegracht 22; ⊙noon-6pm Mon, 10.30am-6.30pm Tue-Fri, 10.30am-6pm Sat; ⏚13/14/17 Westermarkt) This charming canal-side shop has art, architecture, design, landscape and coffee-table books. Its webshop, **Architectuurantiquariaat Opbouw** (Architectural Antiquarian Booksellers; ☑638 70 18; www.de8enopbouw.nl) has a selection of out-of-print and hard-to-find architectural antiquarian books.

ANTONIA BY YVETTE SHOES
Map p314 (www.antoniabyyvette.nl; Gasthuismolensteeg 18; ⊙10am-6pm Tue-Fri, 11am-6pm Sat; ⏚13/14/17 Westermarkt) Yvette Riemersma designs and develops shoes and works with Dutch designers. Shoes, boots, sandals and espadrilles run from supremely classy to just plain fun. There's a small section for guys.

EXOTA CLOTHING, ACCESSORIES
Map p314 (www.exota.com; Hartenstraat 10 & 13; ⊙10am-6pm Mon-Sat, noon-5pm Sun; ⏚13/14/17 Westermarkt) Exota sells its own hip King Louie label plus global brands such as Kookai and French Connection. Number 10 stocks sporty women's casual gear and kids' threads; men's and women's clothing is across the street at number 13.

MENDO BOOKS
Map p316 (www.mendo.nl; Berenstraat 11; ⊙10.30am-6pm Mon-Sat, noon-5pm Sun; ⏚13/14/17 Westermarkt) The Mendo graphic-design agency runs this smart, black-walled bookshop specialising in books in the creative realm: art, design, architecture, fashion and photography.

NUKUHIVA CLOTHING, ACCESSORIES
Map p314 (www.nukuhiva.nl; Haarlemmerstraat 36; ⊙noon-7pm Mon, 10.30am-7pm Tue-Fri, 10am-6pm Sat, noon-6pm Sun; ⏚22 Singel) 🌿

This eco-boutique stocks only ethical and fair-trade clothing and accessories, by brands such as Veja (vegan shoes) and Dutch designer Kuyishi (organic denim).

ZIPPER
CLOTHING, ACCESSORIES

Map p316 (www.zipperstore.nl; Huidenstraat 7; ☺noon-6pm Mon, 11am-6pm Tue, Wed, Fri & Sat, 11am-9pm Thu, 1-6pm Sun; ☒1/2/5 Spui) Amsterdam hipsters head here for seriously nostalgic, retro secondhand gear – wacky printed shirts, stovepipe jeans, '40s zoot suits, pork-pie hats and the like.

DE WITTE TANDEN WINKEL
DENTAL HYGIENE

Map p316 (☎623 34 43; www.dewittetanden-winkel.nl; Runstraat 5; ☺1-6pm Mon, 10am-6pm Tue-Fri, 10am-3pm Sat; ☒1/2/5 Spui) You've got to love shops that are obsessed, and 'The White-Teeth Shop' certainly is – with dental hygiene. There's a huge selection of toothbrushes, toothpastes from around the world, brushing accessories you never knew you needed, and friendly advice.

LAURA DOLS
VINTAGE CLOTHING

Map p316 (www.lauradols.nl; Wolvenstraat 6 & 7; ☺11am-6pm Tue, Wed, Fri & Sat, 11am-9pm Thu, 2-6pm Sun & Mon; ☒1/2/5 Spui) Compulsive style watchers head to this vintage-clothing store for fur coats, 1920s beaded dresses, lace blouses and '40s movie-star accessories like hand-stitched leather gloves.

BEADIES
JEWELLERY

Map p316 (www.beadies.com; Huidenstraat 6; ☺11am-6pm Mon, 10.30am-5pm Tue, Wed, Fri & Sat, 10.30am-9pm Thu; ☒1/2/5 Spui) Once the funky jewellery in the window draws you in, you'll find yourself here for hours, selecting gorgeous beads, gems, charms and trinkets to design your own necklaces and bracelets. If you don't want to start from scratch, opt for a variation on Beadies' designs.

HESTER VAN EEGHEN
SHOES, ACCESSORIES

Map p314 (www.hestervaneeghen.com; Harten-straat 1; ☺noon-6pm Wed-Sat, to 5pm Sun; ☒13/14/17 Westermarkt) Designed in Amsterdam and handcrafted in Italy from fine leather, internationally renowned Hester van Eeghen's unique shoes are for those who dare to dress their feet dramatically in bright colours, fur, suede, and geometric patterns and prints. Her handbags (available down the street at Hartenstraat 37) are just as attention-grabbing.

VAN RAVENSTEIN
CLOTHING

Map p316 (www.van-ravenstein.nl; Keizersgracht 359; ☺1-6pm Mon, 11am-6pm Tue-Fri, 10.30am-5.30pm Sat; ☒1/2/5 Spui) Chic men and women shop here for upmarket designers, including Dries van Noten, Ann Demeule-meester, Véronique Leroy and Amsterdam's own avant-garde design duo Viktor & Rolf.

EPISODE
VINTAGE CLOTHING

Map p316 (www.episode.eu; Berenstraat 1; ☺1-6pm Mon, 11am-6pm Tue & Wed, 11am-8pm Thu, 11am-7pm Fri, 10am-7pm Sat, noon-6pm Sun; ☒13/14/17 Westermarkt) Allow plenty of time to browse the seemingly endless racks of 1970s suede coats, folky peasant blouses, '80s jewellery and big, bright plastic sunglasses across Episode's two floors of fabulous vintage and secondhand gear.

SPORTS & ACTIVITIES

REYPENAER CHEESE TASTING
CHEESE TASTING

Map p314 (☎320 63 33; www.reypenaercheese.com; Singel 182; tastings from €15; ☺tastings by reservation; ☒1/2/5/13/14/17 Dam) Here's your chance to become a *kaas* (cheese) connoisseur. The 100-plus-year-old Dutch cheese maker Reypenaer offers tastings in a rustic classroom under its shop. The hour-long session includes six cheeses – two goat's milk, four cow's milk – from young to old, with wine and port pairings. Staff will guide you through them, helping you appreciate the cheeses' look, smell and taste.

SAUNA DECO
SAUNA

Map p314 (☎623 82 15; http://saunadeco.nl; Herengracht 115; adult/child €22/11, noon-3pm Mon & Wed-Fri €18/9, towel/robe rental €2/3; ☺noon-11pm Mon & Wed-Sat, 3-11pm Tue, 1-7pm Sun, closed mid-Jul–mid-Aug; ⚐; ☒1/2/5/13/17 Nieuwezijds Kolk) The exquisite 1920 art deco interior at this unisex sauna, including the stained glass, timber panelling and wrought-iron staircase balustrades, was salvaged from Paris' historic Le Bon Marché department store when it underwent a refit. Towels or bathrobes are optional (ie it's primarily nude); massage treatments are also available. Children are welcome up until 8pm. No credit cards.

Southern Canal Ring

Neighbourhood Top Five

1 Catch prestigious exhibitions at the **Hermitage Amsterdam** (p125), put together from the cache of treasures at the original St Petersburg museum.

2 Enjoy an *ahh*-inducing sunset or starry night by the **Reguliersgracht** (p124), aka 'the canal of seven bridges'.

3 Explore the **Museum Van Loon** (p126), Amsterdam's only complete canal house with its back coach house.

4 Shop for tulips, bulbs and colourful clogs at Amsterdam's famous 'floating' flower market, the **Bloemenmarkt** (p128).

5 Hit the cafes, bars, theatres and clubs on and around party central **Leidseplein** (p121).

For more detail of this area, see Map p310 ➡

Lonely Planet's Top Tip

Don't discount the areas around Leidseplein or Rembrandtplein as simply tourist traps for the tour-bus set or cheerfully drunk hooligans on pub crawls (although indeed they are both that). They can be serious (or not-so-serious) fun, with plenty of authentic bars and cafes just waiting to be discovered. To escape the hullabaloo and hang out with the locals, head to happening Utrechtsestraat.

✖ Best Places to Eat

➡ Buffet van Odette (p127)

➡ Tujuh Maret (p127)

➡ La Rive (p130)

➡ Stach (p125)

➡ Le Zinc...et les Autres (p130)

For reviews, see p125. ➡

♟ Best Places to Drink

➡ Bar Moustache (p131)

➡ Eijlders (p131)

➡ De Kroon (p131)

➡ Café Schiller (p131)

➡ NJOY (p131)

For reviews, see p131. ➡

☆ Best Entertainment

➡ Stadsschouwburg (p136)

➡ Air (p131)

➡ Van Dyck Bar (p132)

➡ Melkweg (p136)

➡ Sugar Factory (p136)

For reviews, see p135. ➡

Explore Southern Canal Ring

Diverse and buzzing with activity, the Southern Canal Ring spans the area from the radial Leidsegracht in the west to the Amstel in the east. With museums, restaurants, cafes and shops galore, not to mention miles of gorgeous canal photo-ops, it's best to give yourself some time here. The neighbourhood is anchored by two key nightlife hubs: Leidseplein and Rembrandtplein, so they're ideal end points for each day's exploration.

Begin your first day at the flower-filled Bloemenmarkt, then meander past the grand Golden Bend houses before checking out the antique and art shops of Nieuwe Spiegelstraat and the Museum Van Loon as you make your way to Leidseplein.

On the second day, beat the crowds by getting an early start at the Hermitage Amsterdam. Afterwards, stroll down the Amstel to marvel at the Amstelsluizen locks and the Gijsbert Dommer Huis ('House with the Blood Stains'). Around the corner is the Museum Willet-Holthuysen.

All that sightseeing is sure to make you hungry, so it's lucky Utrechtsestraat is in the hood – it's arguably the city's best restaurant strip thanks to its diverse, quality options. Take in the view of the seven bridges along Reguliersgracht and end the night on lively Rembrandtplein.

Local Life

➡ **Street Life** Many shops on Utrechtsestraat (p139) stay open even on Sunday, making this a popular local weekend shopping-eating-drinking trinity.

➡ **Snack Life** Do as the Dutch royals do and buy beautiful baked goods from Patisserie Holtkamp (p130), fronted by a royal coat of arms.

➡ **Café Life** Off Prinsengracht, tiny Weteringstraat feels like a secret passage; look out for local brown *café*, Café de Wetering (p131).

➡ **Cocktail Life** The door's unmarked and you'll need to send a text message to get in but the cocktails at speakeasy Door 74 (p132) are worth it.

➡ **Jazz Life** Locals pack lovable Jazz Café Alto (p136) every night of the week to chill out to smooth jazz by local and international musicians.

Getting There & Away

➡ **Tram** This area is well-served by trams. For the Leidesplein area, take tram 1, 2, 5, 7 or 10. To reach Rembrandtplein, take tram 4, which travels down Utrechtsestraat, or tram 9. Trams 16, 24 and 25 cut through the centre of the neighbourhood down busy Vijzelstraat.

◉ SIGHTS

LEIDSEPLEIN   SQUARE

Map p310 (🚊1/2/5/7/10 Leidseplein) Part historic architecture, part neon, part beer and plenty of tourists – welcome to Leidseplein. A one-stop shop for party-goers, this hyperactive square is a major tram intersection and a litmus test for nightlife. There are countless pubs and clubs, and a smorgasbord of restaurants. Pavement cafes at the northern end are perfect for watching street artists and eccentric passers-by.

On the square's eastern side, farmers would leave their horses and carts at the Leidsepoort (Leiden Gate) before entering town; it was demolished in 1870. The strip of greenery on the other side of the Singelgracht, with large chestnut trees is called Leidsebosje (Leiden Wood).

Entertainment venues radiate from its centre, and nearby Kerkstraat pulses with trendy gay establishments. For more intimate (but not necessarily more serene) bars and restaurants, explore the festive streets of Lange Leidwaarsestraat and Korte Leidwaarsestraat, as well as the streets behind the Stadsschouwburg (p136).

NEW YORK LIFE
INSURANCE BUILDING   HISTORIC BUILDING

Map p310 (Formerly Metz & Co Department Store; cnr Keizersgracht & Leidsestraat; 🚊1/2/5 Keizersgracht) This landmark building opened in 1890 to house the New York Life Insurance Company (hence the eagles), but soon passed to luxury furnishing purveyor Metz & Co. Functionalist designer/architect Gerrit Rietveld added the top-floor cupola in 1930. In 2012, American retailer Abercrombie & Fitch took over the building, while Metz & Co relocated to smaller premises at Leidsestraat 1–3.

FOAM   GALLERY

Map p310 (Fotografiemuseum Amsterdam; www.foam.org; Keizersgracht 609; adult/child €8.50/free; ⏲10am-6pm Sat-Wed, to 9pm Thu & Fri; 🚊16/24/25 Keizersgracht) Simple, functional but roomy galleries, some with skylights or grand windows for natural light, make this museum an excellent space for all genres of photography. Two storeys of exhibition space create a great setting for admiring changing exhibits from world-renowned photographers, including Sir Cecil Beaton, Annie Leibovitz and Henri Cartier-Bresson.

TASSENMUSEUM HENDRIKJE   MUSEUM

Map p310 (Museum of Bags & Purses; 📞524 64 52; www.tassenmuseum.nl; Herengracht 573; adult/child €9/5.50; ⏲10am-5pm; 🚊4/9/14 Rembrandtplein) At this handbag museum you'll find half a millennium's worth of arm candy. The largest collection in the Western world, it contains everything from a crumpled 16th-century pouch to dainty art deco and design classics by Chanel, Gucci and Versace, as well as Madonna's tasteful ivy-strewn 'Evita' bag from the film premiere.

Even if you don't see the '80s touch-tone phone bag, the 17th-century interiors alone are worth the entrance price.

GOLDEN BEND   ARCHITECTURE

Map p310 (Gouden Bocht; Herengracht, btwn Leidsestraat & Vijzelstraat; 🚊1/2/5 Koningsplein) One of the ultimate places to mutter 'if only my family had bought that property way back then', the Golden Bend is about the most prestigious stretch of real estate in Amsterdam, a monument to the Golden Age, when precious goods swelled in cellars of homes already stuffed with valuables.

The earliest mansions date from the 1660s, when the Canal Ring was expanded south. Thanks to some lobbying at city hall, the gables here were twice as wide as the standard Amsterdam model, and the rear gardens were deeper. The richest Amsterdammers lived, loved and ruled their affairs from here. Apart from the Kattenkabinet (p123) museum, the homes are only opened to the public on Open Monument Day (Open Monumentendag).

STADSARCHIEF   HISTORIC ARCHIVE

Map p310 (Municipal Archives; 📞251 15 11, tour reservations 251 15 10; www.stadsarchief.amsterdam.nl; Vijzelstraat 32; ⏲10am-5pm Tue-Fri, noon-5pm Sat & Sun; 🚊16/24/25 Keizersgracht) **FREE** The Amsterdam archives occupy a monumental bank building that dates from 1923. When you step inside, head to the left to the enormous tiled basement vault and displays of archive gems such as the 1942 police report on the theft of Anne Frank's bike. A small cinema at the back shows vintage films about the city.

Upstairs, a gallery space mounts temporary exhibits (for a small entry fee), and the fantastic Stadsboekwinkel (p139) sells city-oriented tomes. Building tours (€6) run at 2pm on Saturday and Sunday and must be reserved in advance.

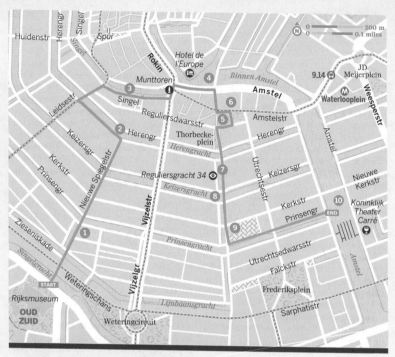

Neighbourhood Walk
Southern Canal Ring

START SPIEGEL QUARTER
END AMSTEL RIVER
LENGTH 4KM; 2 HOURS

Set off at the Singelgracht and head north into the nexus of art and antique shops, the **1 Spiegel Quarter**, along Nieuwe Spiegelstraat.

One of Amsterdam's swankiest patches of real estate, the aptly named **2 Golden Bend** (p121) on Herengracht is awash with classical French flourishes.

Stop by the bustling **3 Bloemenmarkt** (p128) and from the eastern end you'll see one of Amsterdam's most enduring emblems, the striking Munttoren (Mint Tower).

From the tower, head east along the Amstel river to take in the grand Hotel de l'Europe, where polished skiffs moor at the terrace restaurant. At the bridge, turn south into tiny Halvemaansteeg (Half-Moon Lane) and the beating heart of the entertainment district around **4 Rembrandtplein** (p123). As you cross the square, stop to admire the

statue of master painter Rembrandt, before making your way to **5 De Kroon** (p131), one of the most stylish grand *cafés* (bars).

Pass through shady Thorbeckeplein to the Herengracht, lean on the bridge and snap a postcard-perfect photo of **6 Reguliersgracht** (p124), 'the canal of the seven bridges'. The house at Reguliersgracht 34 has an unusual twin entrance and an eagle gable for the original owner, Arent van den Bergh (*arend* is a Dutch word for eagle).

Where the Keizersgracht and Reguliersgracht join up, there's a scene to outdo the mere seven bridges before: here you can count a whopping **7 15 bridges** as you peer east–west and north–south. A few steps further south you'll come to the **8 Amstelkerk** (p124), the curious wooden church with a belfry that still looks quite makeshift.

Head east down a quiet section of the Prinsengracht until you reach the shores of the **9 Amstel river**. From this vantage point you can admire the petite Magere Brug and, beyond the *sluizen* (locks), the neon-lit roof of the Koninklijk Theater Carré.

KATTENKABINET — MUSEUM

Map p310 (Cats Cabinet; ☑626 90 40; www.
kattenkabinet.nl; Herengracht 497; adult/child
€6/3; ☺10am-4pm Mon-Fri, noon-5pm Sat &
Sun; ☐1/2/5 Koningsplein) One Golden Bend
house that's open to the public is this offbeat museum, devoted to, of all things, the
feline presence in art. It was founded by a
wealthy financier, John Pierpont Morgan
III, in memory of his red tomcat. Among
the artists, Swiss-born Théopile-Alexandre
Steinlen (1859–1923) figures prominently.

There's also a small Rembrandt (a Madonna and child with a cat and snake) and
Picasso's *Le Chat*. You may get the chance
to admire the collection along with the cats
that live in the building.

GEELVINCK HINLOPEN HUIS — MUSEUM

Map p310 (☑639 07 47; www.museumgeelvinck.
nl; Keizersgracht 633; adult/child €8/4; ☺11am-
5pm Wed-Mon; ☐16/24/25 Keizersgracht) This
serene 17th-century house is well worth a
look. English-speaking guides are on hand
to show the rooms. Chamber music
concerts using the estate's vintage instruments take place on Sundays at 4.45pm.

REMBRANDTPLEIN — SQUARE

Map p310 (☐4/9/14 Rembrandtplein) Originally called Reguliersplein and then Boter-
markt, after the butter markets held here
until the mid-19th century, this square
now takes its name from the **statue** of the
painter erected in 1876. He's gazing pen-
sively towards the Jewish quarter, where he
lived until circumstances forced him to the
Jordaan.

Rembrandtplein soon evolved into a
nightlife hub as various cafes, restaurants
and clubs opened their doors. It's almost
genteel during the day, though often heaving with visitors. On the northern side of
the square, De Kroon (p131), opened 1898, is
one of the grandest *cafés* in town. Opposite,
Café Schiller (p131) (1892) is renowned for
its theatrical crowd and fabulous art deco
interior, including leadlight glass windows.
Come midnight, the Rembrandtplein club
crowd gets down to the serious business
of partying: it provides fascinating people
watching, even if you don't want to let loose.

GIJSBERT DOMMER HUIS — HISTORIC BUILDING

Map p310 (Amstel 216; ☐4 Keizersgracht) Look
closely at the facade of this sober residence
known locally as the 'House with the Blood

◉ TOP SIGHT
MUSEUM WILLET-HOLTHUYSEN

This sumptuous residence, now managed by the Amsterdam Museum (p73), is named after the widow who
bequeathed the property to the city in the late 19th
century. It's now a shining star in Amsterdam's vast
constellation of architectural treasures.

As you stroll through the elegant house, you'll be
surrounded by the inspiring art, design, and furniture
collection of former resident Abraham Willet, including
paintings by Jacob de Wit. Also look for the *place de mi-
lieu* (centrepiece) that was part of the family's 275-piece
Meissen table service, and the intimate French-style
garden with sundial – you can also peek at the garden
through the iron fence at the Amstelstraat end.

For a fascinating insight into the house through the
eyes of the servants, be sure to borrow the notebook
from the front desk, with details that make the house
(and indeed, an entire era) come alive, such as the tedi-
ous, back-breaking ways in which servants went about
their domestic tasks, such as roasting the meat and
cleaning the windows.

In addition to trams, you can travel by metro to
Waterlooplein.

DON'T MISS

➡ Jacob de Wit paint-
ings

➡ The French garden

➡ The notebook

➡ The Louis XVI–
style ground floor

PRACTICALITIES

➡ Map p310

➡ ☑523 18 22

➡ www.willetholt
huysen.nl

➡ Herengracht 605

➡ adult/child €8/4

➡ ☺10am-5pm Mon-
Fri, 11am-5pm Sat
& Sun

➡ ☐4/9/14 Rem-
brandtplein

Stains'. After losing his fortune, six-time mayor and diplomat Coenraad van Beuningen lost his mind and scribbled graffiti here, allegedly in his own blood, and his unfathomable message – including Hebrew letters and obscure cabal symbols – from the 17th century is still faintly visible.

Well-to-do businessman Gijsbert Dommer commissioned this house from 1671, but it's the mad mayor who is better known today.

BLAUWBRUG   BRIDGE
Map p310 (Blue Bridge; btwn Waterlooplein & Amstelstraat; ⓂWaterlooplein) Built in 1884, one of the city's most striking bridges replaced an old wooden version that had connected these shores of the Amstel since the 17th century. Inspired by the Alexander III bridge in Paris, it features tall, ornate street lamps topped by the imperial crown of Amsterdam, fish sculptures and foundations shaped like the prow of a medieval ship.

REGULIERSGRACHT   CANAL
Map p310 (🚊4/9/14 Rembrandtplein) Amsterdam's prettiest canal was dug in 1658 to link the Herengracht with the canals further south. It was named after an order of monks whose monastery was located nearby. From here you can peer through the arches of at least **seven bridges**. Many canal boats pass by.

A number of houses along the canal have intriguing gables, tablets and fancy decorations.

LOCAL KNOWLEDGE

PHOTOGRAPHING THE SEVEN BRIDGES

It's easy to focus on the raucous nightlife and forget that one of Amsterdam's most romantic canals flows in the neighbourhood. The Reguliersgracht, also known as 'the canal of seven bridges', is especially enchanting by night when its humpbacked arches glow with tiny white lights.

To get the money shot, stand with your back to the Thorbeckeplein and the Herengracht flowing directly in front of you to the left and right. Lean over the bridge and look straight ahead down the Reguliersgracht. Ahhh. Now kiss your sweetie.

AMSTELKERK   CHURCH
Map p310 (☎520 00 70; Amstelveld 10; ⊙9am-5pm Mon-Fri; 🚊4 Prinsengracht) The unique pinewood Amstelkerk was erected in 1668 as a *noodkerk* (makeshift church) under the direction of the city architect, Daniël Stalpaert. The idea was that the congregation would have somewhere to meet while a permanent church arose next to it but plans for this stone church were abandoned in the 1840s.

The Amstelkerk's square-shaped interior was updated with neo-Gothic alterations, including a pipe organ. It's now a popular concert venue, while the seats under the shady plane trees at the adjacent bar-restaurant NeL (p134) provide a wonderful refuge for a drink.

DE DUIF   CHURCH
Map p310 (The Dove; ☎520 00 90; http://deduif.home.xs4all.nl; Prinsengracht 756; 🚊4 Prinsengracht) In 1796, shortly after the French-installed government proclaimed freedom of religion, De Duif was the first Catholic church to be built with a public entrance for more than two centuries. These days De Duif is no longer Catholic but Ecumenical, and it's also a venue for concerts, opera and private events.

If you're able to peek inside, check out the clay friezes of the Stations of the Cross on the right-hand wall. The pulpit carvings are of St Willebrordus of Utrecht, and the organ is a sight in its own right, reaching up to the vaulted ceiling.

MAGERE BRUG   BRIDGE
Map p310 (Skinny Bridge; btwn Kerkstraat & Nieuwe Kerkstraat; 🚊4 Prinsengracht) The iconic 'Skinny Bridge' is the site of many a Dutch wedding photo. Dating from the 1670s, the nine-arched structure has been rebuilt several times in both concrete and timber. It's still operated by hand and remains photogenic even at night, when 1200 tiny lights make the bridge look like a Christmas decoration.

You can spot it in many films, including the 1971 James Bond thriller *Diamonds are Forever*. Stand in the middle and feel it sway under the passing traffic.

AMSTELSLUIZEN   ARCHITECTURE
Map p310 (Amstel Locks; Amstel river, near Koninklijk Theater Carré; 🚊4 Prinsengracht) These impressive sluices, or locks, date from 1674 and allowed the canals to be flushed with

TOP SIGHT
HERMITAGE AMSTERDAM

The long-standing ties between Russia and the Nether-lands – Tsar Peter the Great learned shipbuilding and Dutch cursing here in 1697 – led to the establishment of an Amsterdam branch of the State Hermitage Museum of St Petersburg. You'll experience prestigious exhibits on loan from the St Petersburg museum's amazing collection of more than three million art objects, such as treasures from the Russian palace or masterworks by Matisse and Picasso. Exhibits change about twice a year and they're as stately (and wildly popular) as you'd expect.

The Hermitage is magnificently housed in the Am-stelhof, a 17th-century former almshouse set around a sweeping courtyard. Facing the Amstel river, it offers breathtaking views from the west-side galleries.

Bear in mind that the museum has fast become one of the city's most popular attractions since its 2009 opening, and waiting times to enter can stretch up to 60 minutes during peak periods. To avoid the worst of the crowds, arrive before 11am daily or after 5pm on Wednesday (the museum's late night, perfect for art-loving night owls). In addition to trams, you can travel by metro to Waterlooplein.

DON'T MISS

➡ The permanent collection
➡ The lovely court-yard
➡ River views from the west-side galleries
➡ The dazzling tem-porary exhibits from St Petersburg

PRACTICALITIES

➡ Map p310
➡ ☑530 74 88
➡ www.hermitage.nl
➡ Amstel 51
➡ adult/child €15/free
➡ ⊗10am-5pm
➡ 🚇9/14 Water-looplein

SOUTHERN CANAL RING EATING

fresh water from lakes north of the city, rather than salt water from the IJ, an in-novation that made the city more liveable. The locks were still operated by hand until a couple of decades ago.

The locks are regularly shut so that fresh water flows in, while the sluices on the western side of the city are left open as the stagnant water is pumped out to sea.

KRIJTBERG CHURCH

Map p310 (☑623 19 23; www.krijtberg.nl; Singel 446; ⊗1-5pm Tue-Thu, Sat & Sun; 🚋1/2/5 Kon-ingsplein) The soaring turrets of this neo-Gothic church are an odd sight in this row of sedate Singel homes. Officially known as the St Franciscus Xaveriuskerk, it replaced a clandestine Jesuit chapel on the same site; these days it's still Jesuit. The lavish paint-ings and statuary make this one of the most beautiful church interiors in the city.

MAX EUWE CENTRUM CULTURAL BUILDING

Map p310 (☑625 70 17; www.maxeuwe.nl; Max Eu-weplein 30a-1; ⊗noon-4pm Tue-Fri, limited hours Jul & Aug; 🚋1/2/5/7/10 Leidseplein) FREE Max Euwe (1901–81) was the Netherlands' only world chess champion (in the 1930s) and at

this chess centre you'll find a permanent exhibition devoted to the history of the game. You can play against live or digital opponents. The pavement of the square out the front is often crowded with players and onlookers raptly watching games on the outsized chessboard.

🍴 EATING

All roads in Amsterdam seem to lead to Leidseplein, but there are better places to eat – try poking around the adjacent side streets or nearby canals. Much the same can be said for Rembrandtplein. Instead of dining here, walk a few steps to Utrechtsestraat, the finest restaurant row in town.

STACH CAFE €

Map p310 (www.stach-food.nl; Nieuwe Spiegel-straat 52; dishes €3-9; ⊗9am-10pm Mon-Sat, 10am-10pm Sun; ☑; 🚋7/10 Spiegelgracht) Stach's Southern Canal Ring branch is smaller than it's flagship De Pijp premises (p183). But even if you don't score a seat here, it's an equally good option for pastas

TOP SIGHT
MUSEUM VAN LOON

There's no better way to instantly whisk yourself back to 19th-century Amsterdam than by spending an hour or two at this wonderful house museum. The only complete replica of a canal house with its back coach house, where horse-drawn coaches arrived and were stored, the property has a luscious courtyard garden, opulent furniture and countless family portraits that seem to whisper secrets as you pass from room to gorgeous room.

Built in 1672, the property was first home to acclaimed painter Ferdinand Bol. By the late 1800s the Van Loons, a prominent patrician family, moved in and have lived here ever since (they still occupy the building's upper floors).

Take your time soaking up the quiet, calm atmosphere of each room, all of which are notable for the feeling of history, wealth and artistry they exude. Among some 150 portraits of the Van Loon family, you'll see important paintings such as *Wedding Portrait* by Jan Miense Molenaer. But the main exhibit is the house itself. Don't miss the intricate wedding-cake plasterwork on the ceilings, and the most fascinating room: the old-fashioned basement kitchen, where cook Leida presided for almost 40 years. Some of the family's favourite recipes are displayed.

DON'T MISS

➡ The coach house
➡ The gorgeous brass rococo banisters on the open staircase
➡ The 19th-century basement kitchen
➡ The dramatic red bedroom

PRACTICALITIES

➡ Map p310
➡ 624 52 55
➡ www.museumvanloon.nl
➡ Keizersgracht 672
➡ adult/child €8/4
➡ 11am-5pm Wed-Mon
➡ 16/24/25 Keizersgracht

(like spinach and ricotta ravioli) and amazing sandwiches (such as carpaccio, truffle mayonnaise and rocket, or buffalo mozzarella, basil mayonnaise and tomato) on organic bread to take to a canal-side bench.

SOUP EN ZO   SOUP BAR €
Map p310 (www.soupenzo.nl; Niewe Spiegelstraat 54; soup €3.50-7; 11am-8pm Mon-Fri, noon-7pm Sat & Sun; ; 7/10 Spiegelgracht) On a chilly day, you can't beat a steaming cup of soup from this little takeaway soup bar. Flavours change every hour but might include potato with roquefort, lentil and minced beef, prunes and pumpkin or spicy spinach and coconut. Cash only.

VAN DOBBEN   TRADITIONAL DUTCH €
Map p310 (624 42 00; www.eetsalonvandobben.nl; Korte Reguliersdwarsstraat 5-9; items €2.75-6.50; 10am-9pm Mon-Wed, 10am-2am Thu-Sat, 10.30am-8pm Sun; 4/9/14 Rembrandtplein) Open since the 1940s, Van Dobben has white-tile walls and white-coated staff who specialise in snappy banter. Traditional meaty Dutch fare is its forte: try the *pekelvlees* (something close to corned beef), or make it a *halfom* (if you're keen on that being mixed with liver).

The *kroketten* (meat croquettes) are up there with the best in town and compulsory after a late-night Rembrandtplein boozeup. There's a second branch in the De Pijp neighbourhood.

MAOZ   MIDDLE EASTERN €
Map p310 (420 74 35; www.maozusa.com; Muntplein 1; mains €4-8; 11am-1am Sun-Thu, to 3am Fri & Sat; ; 4/9/14/24/25 Muntplein) Felafel, saviour of vegetarians the world over, is perfected at this minichain, which has now expanded beyond the Netherlands. Around €5 gets you a felafel with unlimited access to a fresh, massive salad bar – a true test of your pita's strength. Other outlets are popping up like wildfire all over town.

LOEKIE   SANDWICH SHOP €
Map p310 (www.loekie.net; Utrechtsestraat 57; sandwiches €6.50-12.50; 9.30am-5.30pm Mon-Sat; 4 Keizersgracht) This delicatessen piles fresh, delicious ingredients into its takeaway sandwiches, such as smoked beef with egg and salt, or warm goat's cheese

with pine nuts and honey. Ask for the English menu if it's not on the counter already.

LITE/DARK   CAFE €

Map p310 (www.litedark.nl; Utrechtsestraat 22; items €4-12; ☻8am-7pm Mon-Fri, 10am-7pm Sat, 10am-6pm Sun; 🚊4 Keizersgracht) Somehow this hip, industrial-styled cafe manages to make a convincing case for the health benefits of chocolate (or at least the dark variety), serving chocolate shots and chocolate fondue alongside a huge range of 'lite' smoothies, energy shakes and wheatgrass shots. The short menu includes salads, bagels and sandwiches, as well as choc-dipped fruit.

WOK TO WALK   CHINESE €

Map p310 (www.woktowalk.com; Leidsestraat 96; mains €6-8; ☻11.30am-1am Sun-Thu, to 3am Fri & Sat; 🚊1/2/5 Prinsengracht) Many fast-food joints in these parts assume you're too drunk or stoned to care what you're eating. Wok to Walk, however, serves fresh fast food. Choose noodles or rice, meat or veg, and a sauce; add to a wok and stir.

This is the flagship outlet (it's now in 50 cities), and the culinary wasteland of Leidsestraat is where you'll need one most.

★ BUFFET VAN ODETTE   CAFE €€

Map p310 (✆423 60 34; www.buffet-amsterdam.nl; Prinsengracht 598; mains €7-21; ☻10am-9pm Wed-Mon; ✐; 🚊7/10 Spiegelgracht) Not a buffet but an airy, white-tiled sit-down cafe with a beautiful canal-side terrace, where Odette and Yvette show how good simple cooking can taste when you start with great ingredients and a dash of creativity. Soups, sandwiches, pastas and quiches are mostly organic with smart little extras like pine nuts or truffle cheese.

TUJUH MARET   INDONESIAN €€

Map p310 (✆427 98 65; www.tujuhmaret.nl; Utrechtsestraat 73; mains €7-22.50, rijsttafel veg/nonveg €23/28, makanan kecil €18; ☻noon-10pm; ✐; 🚊4 Prinsengracht) Tujuh Maret is just as good as its sibling Tempo Doeloe (p129) next door, but has a more casual atmosphere. Grab a wicker chair and tuck into Sulawesi-style dishes like dried, fried beef or chicken in red-pepper sauce. The *rijsttafel* (Indonesian banquet) is laid out according to spice intensity; *makanan kecil* is a mini-*rijsttafel*.

EVERYTHING ON A STICK   INTERNATIONAL €€

Map p310 (✆626 18 74; www.eoas.nl; Prinsengracht 478; adult/child €26/13; ☻6-11pm Tue, Wed & Sun, 6pm to midnight Thu-Sat; ♿; 🚊1/2/5 Prinsengracht) Everything at this cool, contemporary all-you-can-eat restaurant is served, you guessed it, on skewers. Designed for sharing (you get three sticks per round, for an unlimited number of rounds), options include seaweed-wrapped prawns, honey and lemon beef, bacon-wrapped scallops in rosemary oil and Dutch spiced chicken. Prices per adult drop to €24.50 on Tuesday and Wednesday. Different and delicious.

LOS PILONES   MEXICAN €€

Map p310 (✆320 46 51; www.lospilones.com; Kerkstraat 63; mains €17; ☻5pm-1am Mon-Thu & Sun, to 3am Fri & Sat; ☎; 🚊1/2/5 Keizersgracht) Set up by a trio of Mexican brothers, Los Pilones sets the standard among Amsterdam's handful of Mexican restaurants. If you're looking for grilled *bistek* (beefsteak), crispy chicken rolls and fruity mango or lime margaritas in a colourful, social environment, you're definitely in the right place.

A few shots from the 185-plus tequila list, and you'll be feeling brave enough to ask for the extra-hot salsa. There are branches in Nieuwmarkt and Jordaan. Food is served through to closing time.

BOUCHON DU CENTRE   FRENCH, LYONNAIS €€

Map p310 (✆330 11 28; www.bouchonducentreamsterdam.com; Falckstraat 3; mains €15-20; ☻noon-3pm & 5-8pm Wed-Sat; 🚊4/7/10/25 Frederiksplein) Classic red-and-white cloths cover the tables at this faithfully recreated Lyonnais *bouchon* (informal, rustic bistro). The daily changing menu of a few dishes only revolves around *bouchon* staples such as *andouillette* (offal sausage) and *quenelles de brochet* (pike dumplings). Don't miss a round of wonderfully gooey St Marcellin cheese and Rhône Valley wines such as Beaujolais.

PIET DE LEEUW   STEAKHOUSE €€

Map p310 (✆623 71 81; www.pietdeleeuw.nl; Noorderstraat 11; mains €12.50-21.50; ☻noon-11pm Mon-Fri, 5-11pm Sat & Sun; 🚊16/24/25 Keizersgracht) The building dates from 1900, but it's been a steakhouse and hang-out since the 1940s, and the dark and cosy atmosphere has barely changed since. If you don't get your own table, you may make friends

SOUTHERN CANAL RING EATING

TOP SIGHT
BLOEMENMARKT

One of the world's most famous flower markets, the Bloemenmarkt has a fascinating history. Since 1860 it's been located at the spot where nurserymen and women, having sailed up the Amstel from their smallholdings, would moor their barges to sell their wares directly to customers.

No longer floating (it's now perched on piles), the market here is a colourful sight and the place is packed with tourists (and pickpockets – stay alert). Prices are steep by Amsterdam standards but the quality is top notch. Before you buy a bag of burning heart or queen of night bulbs, do your research or ask the vendors about customs regulations at home. Look out for bulbs destined for the USA, which are marked with a special label.

You don't need to wait for a perfect sunny day to indulge in floral heaven – the Bloemenmarkt is lovely even in fog or cold weather, when the flowers only seem brighter against grey skies. Why not pick up a bunch to brighten up your hotel room? There's no better way to feel like a local than navigating Amsterdam's streets with flowers under the crook of your arm...

DON'T MISS
➡ Tulips in springtime
➡ Christmas trees in winter
➡ Seeds, bulbs and garden tools to take home
➡ Colourful wooden clogs and other unique souvenirs

PRACTICALITIES
➡ Flower Market
➡ Map p310
➡ Singel, btwn Muntplein & Koningsplein
➡ ⊙9am-5.30pm Mon-Sat, 11am-5.30pm Sun
➡ 🚊1/2/5 Koningsplein

at a common table. Good-value steaks come with toppings like onions, mushrooms or bacon, served with salad and piping-hot *frites* (French fries).

SLUIZER
INTERNATIONAL €€
Map p310 (📞622 63 76; www.sluizer.nl; Utrechtsestraat 43-45; mains €17-27.50; ⊙5-11pm; 🚊; 🚊4 Keizersgracht) This venerable institution, with its romantic, enclosed garden terrace, comprises two restaurants – a Parisian-style meat restaurant (No 43) and a fish restaurant (No 45) – though both menus are available in both restaurants (as is a vegetarian menu). Spare ribs are the speciality of the former and bouillabaisse the speciality of the latter.

It donates a small payment per diner to the UN's World Food Programme.

STACEY'S PENNYWELL
CAFE €€
Map p310 (www.staceys.nl; Herengracht 558; mains €9-19; ⊙9am-5.30pm Mon & Tue, 9am-10pm Wed-Sat, 9.30am-10pm Sun; 🚊4 Keizersgracht) Lovely crown mouldings and wrought ironwork chandeliers woo diners up to the second level, which is a perfect place to curl up on the comfy white leather chairs to dine on impressive fare like smoked mackerel in green curry or halibut with mash and carrot-and-ginger gravy. Cocktails are best on the lower level, with pillow-strewn couches overlooking the Herengracht canal.

TASTE OF CULTURE
CHINESE €€
Map p310 (📞427 11 36; www.tasteofculture.net; Korte Leidsedwarsstraat 139-141; dim sum €3.50-10, mains €9-32.50; ⊙from 5pm; 🚊1/2/5/7/10 Leidseplein) Freshly prepared regional dishes are enjoyed by a big Chinese clientele. Good options are the razor clams, Peking duck and pancakes, and various stir-fried greens. Added bonus: the kitchen is open till midnight, and later on weekends.

PASTINI
ITALIAN €€
Map p310 (📞622 17 01; www.pastini.nl; Leidsegracht 29; mains €13.50-22; ⊙6-10pm Mon-Sat; 🚊1/2/5 Keizersgracht) With a *gezellig* (convivial, cosy), rustic-Renaissance interior and a can't-beat-it location facing two canals, Pastini also wins praise for its pastas including its signature *tagliatelle gamberi* (Dutch prawns, sweet peppers, spicy chillies and anchovies and garlic) and exceptionally

reasonable prices. A speciality is the three-choice antipasto starter, but save room for *pastina di cioccolata* (dark chocolate tart) for dessert.

BOJO
INDONESIAN €€

Map p310 (☎622 74 34; www.bojo.nl; Lange Leidsedwarsstraat 51; mains €10.50-17; ☺4pm-1am Mon-Fri, noon-1.30am Sat & Sun; ◈1/2/5 Prinsengracht) After a night on the town, there's nothing like some Indonesian. Bojo is a late-night institution that's surprisingly peaceful, given the location. Clubbers come for sizzling satay, filling fried rice and steaming bowls of noodle soup, and generally leave smiling.

CAFÉ MORLANG
CAFE €€€

Map p310 (www.morlang.nl; Keizersgracht 451; lunch mains €8-17.50, dinner mains €16.50-21.50; ☺kitchen 11am-10pm; ☎; ◈1/2/5 Keizersgracht) Choose from a rotating menu with influences from Europe to Asia, such as pan-seared scallops in bacon with gin-and-tonic jelly and blueberry jus or chicken rendang. The canal-side terrace is fab in warm weather; indoors, check out the gigantic staff portraits painted on the back wall.

NA SIAM
THAI €€

Map p310 (www.nasiam.nl; Kerkstraat 332; mains €14-19; ☺5.30-11pm; ☎; ◈4 Prinsengracht) Get transported to Thailand amid the serenity of this wood-panelled dining room. Classics range from red and green curries to noodle dishes like pad thai; just don't underestimate the spicy dishes (rated on the menu).

LO STIVALE D'ORO
ITALIAN €€

Map p310 (☎638 73 07; www.lostivaledoro.nl; Amstelstraat 49; pizza €6-10.50, lunch mains €7.50, dinner mains €13.50-20; ☺11am-2.30pm & 5-10.30pm Wed-Mon; ◈4/9/14 Rembrandtplein) Enjoy awesome pizzas and pastas at this trattoria's chummy tables. The gregarious Italian owner Mario occasionally pulls out his guitar and strums for the crowd.

GOLDEN TEMPLE
VEGETARIAN €€

Map p310 (☎626 85 60; www.restaurantgoldentemple.com; Utrechtsestraat 126; mains €9-18.50; ☺5-9.30pm; ☎; ◈4 Prinsengracht) Golden Temple has a quietly upmarket setting and a diverse, very international menu of Indian thali, Italian pizzas and Middle Eastern and Mexican platters. The most sought-after seats are the floor cushions in the front window alcove.

JAPANS
SUSHI €€

Map p310 (☎624 46 72; www.japansrestaurantan.nl; Weteringschans 76; dishes €3-16; ☺11.30am-2pm Tue-Fri, 6-10pm Tue-Sat; ◈4/7/10/16/24/25 Weteringcircuit) The hardest decision at Japans isn't which sushi rolls to choose, it's where to sit: the intimate back patio opening up to a backyard garden reverie, or the serene, Zen-like front room? The streamlined menu of sushi and a handful of Japanese dishes is perfectly good, but the real draw is the atmosphere. No credit cards.

TEMPO DOELOE
INDONESIAN €€€

Map p310 (☎625 67 18; www.tempodoeloerestaurant.nl; Utrechtsestraat 75; mains €23.50-37.50, rijsttafel & set menus €29-49; ☺6pm-midnight Mon-Sat; ☎; ◈4 Prinsengracht)

SOUTHERN CANAL RING EATING

AMSTERDAM AMERICAN HOTEL

The reason the gorgeous **Amsterdam American Hotel** (Map p310; ☎556 30 00; www.edenamsterdamamericanhotel.com; Leidsekade 97; ◈1/2/5/7/10 Leidseplein) got its name is because the founder of the original hotel, CAA (Cornelis Alidus Anne) Steinigeweg, spent many years in the USA and helped establish a Dutch settlement on Grand Island, New York. Steinigeweg ensured that architect Ed Cuypers adorned the Viennese Renaissance-style building with abundant Americana – life-sized Native American chiefs and their squaws as well as a 4m heraldic eagle over the entrance.

Completed in the early 1880s, less than two decades later it had already become too small and was demolished to make way for the magnificent replacement you see today. Also in Viennese Renaissance style and topped by a bell tower, the new hotel (p230) opened at the turn of the 20th century; its art nouveau design is the work of architect Willem Kromhout. The hotel's Café Americain (p132), a heritage-listed showpiece with a beautifully restored art nouveau interior featuring stained glass, exquisite light fittings and murals, has long been affectionately dubbed 'Amsterdam's living room'.

Consistently ranked among Amsterdam's finest Indonesian restaurants, Tempo Doeloe's setting and service are elegant without being overdone. The same applies to the *rijsttafel*: a ridiculously overblown affair at many places, here it's a fine sampling of the range of flavours found in the country. Warning: dishes marked 'very hot' are indeed like napalm. The wine list is excellent.

LA RIVE
FRENCH €€€

Map p310 (☎520 32 64; www.restaurantlarive.com; InterContinental Amstel Amsterdam, Professor Tulpplein 1; 5-/6-course menu €95/110, wine pairings extra €75/85; ⊙6.30-10pm Tue-Sat, 5-9pm Sun; ⓂWeesperplein) A Michelin star and a formal dining room with graciously spaced white-clothed tables and Amstel views make La Rive the perfect venue for an out-to-impress dinner. The menu changes frequently, but might include lobster and veal filet mignon; optional extras include caviar and a selection from the trolley of Dutch farmhouse cheeses.

You'll need to dress the part: the dress code is strictly *tenue de ville* (business attire), so a suit and tie for guys.

LE ZINC...ET LES AUTRES
FRENCH €€€

Map p310 (☎622 90 44; www.lezinc.nl; Prinsengracht 999; mains €26.50-32.50, 3-/4-/5-course menu €37.50/46.50/55.50; ⊙5.30-11pm Tue-

---

LOCAL KNOWLEDGE

A PATISSERIE FIT FOR A KING

Esteemed **Patisserie Holtkamp** (Map p310; www.patisserieholtkamp.nl; Vijzelgracht 15; items €2.45-6.50; ⊙8.30am-6pm Mon-Fri, to 5pm Sat, closed late Jul–mid-Aug; ☐4/7/10/16/24/25 Weteringcircuit) has a storied history. There's been a bakery on this site since 1886, but the gorgeous art deco interior you see today was added in 1928 by leading Amsterdam School architect Piet Kramer. Outside, look up to spot the gilded royal coat of arms, topped by a crown and attached to the brick facade. It's not only the Dutch royals who appreciate this sweet and savoury delicacies – particularly its *kroketten* (meat croquettes) with fillings that include prawns, lobster and veal. They're also on the menu of some of the city's top restaurants.

Sat; ⓐ; ☐4 Prinsengracht) An unapologetically old-fashioned affair, this cosy canal-house restaurant is filled with candlelight, exposed timber beams, wine bottles, and romance to spare. The menu changes monthly but matches the atmosphere, with rustic dishes like venison and black pudding sausage or calf's liver and kidneys, and an option of matched reds and whites alongside each course.

Vegetarians aren't forgotten, with choices such as chestnut soup and cheese fondue.

VAN VLAANDEREN
FRENCH €€€

Map p310 (☎622 82 92; www.restaurant-vanvlaanderen.nl; Weteringschans 175; mains €25.50-29.50, 2-/3-/4-/5-course menu €29.50/36/42.50/59.50; ⊙noon-3pm Tue-Fri, 6-10pm Tue-Sat; ☐4/7/10/16/24/25 Weteringcircuit) One of the best French restaurants in town, Van Vlaanderen has lovely canal views from a raised deck. The fine nuances of dishes, such as crab ravioli with crab bisque, veal confit with sweetbread, and caramelised cheesecake with strawberry and pineapple yoghurt sorbet, make all the difference.

RISTORANTE D'ANTICA
ITALIAN €€€

Map p310 (☎623 38 62; www.dantica.nl; Reguliersdwarsstraat 80-82; mains €17-30; ⊙6-11pm Mon-Thu, 6pm to midnight Fri & Sat; ☐4/9/16/24/25 Muntplein) Although the Italian-owned d'Antica gets its share of celebrities, you'd be hard pressed to find a more welcoming restaurant in town (assuming you've made an all-important reservation). There's a familiar selection of pastas and meats, but cognoscenti order *spaghetti al parmigiano* – and everyone can watch as waiters turn steaming pasta inside a wheel of cheese.

SEGUGIO
ITALIAN €€€

Map p310 (☎330 15 03; www.segugio.nl; Utrechtsestraat 96; pastas €17-20, mains €24-30; ⊙6-11pm Mon-Sat; ☐4 Prinsengracht) This fashionably minimalist storefront with two levels of seating is the sort of place other chefs go for a good meal. It's renowned for inventive mains like crispy pork belly with lentils in dark beer sauce, a daily changing risotto, and high-quality ingredients; everything (bread, pasta, ice cream, chocolate) is made by hand. Book ahead – it's almost always busy.

DRINKING & NIGHTLIFE

Drinking in this area requires a serious strategy. With coffeeshops, theatre *cafés* (bars), brown *cafés* (pubs) and gay bars galore, it helps to consider the kind of atmosphere you want. Want to trade tales with other travellers? Head to the bars of Leidesplein. Want to dance? Rembrandtplein's the ticket. Utrechtestraat practically begs a *bruin café* (brown *café*) pub crawl. For some serious partying, head for the gay scene on Reguliersdwarsstraat.

★BAR MOUSTACHE   BAR, CAFÉ

Map p310 (www.barmoustache.nl; Utrechtsestraat 141; ⊙9am-1am Mon-Thu, 9am-3am Fri & Sat, 10am-1am Sun; 🚊4 Prinsengracht) With an exposed brick, minimalist interior designed by Stella Willing, this loft-style cafe/bar has a mix of communal and private tables that fill with hip locals, and a couple of coveted window-sill benches to watch the action along Utrechtsestraat. There's a stunning, pared-down Italian menu and a great drink selection including Italian wines by the glass.

★EIJLDERS   BROWN CAFÉ

Map p310 (www.eijlders.nl; Korte Leidsedwarsstraat 47; ⊙noon-1am Sun-Thu, to 2am Fri & Sat; 🚊1/2/5/7/10 Leidseplein) During WWII, this beautiful stained-glass brown *café* was a meeting place for artists who refused to toe the cultural line imposed by the Nazis, and the spirit lingers on. It's still an artists' *café*, hosting regular poetry readings (sometimes in English – call to be sure), jam sessions and exhibitions.

DE KROON   GRAND CAFÉ

Map p310 (www.dekroon.nl; Rembrandtplein 17-1; ⊙11am-1am Sun-Thu, to 4am Sat & Sat; 🚊4/9/14 Rembrandtplein) Restored to its original 1898 splendour, De Kroon has high ceilings, velvet chairs, and a beautiful art-deco-tiled staircase up the two floors above Rembrandtplein (there's also a lift/elevator). Sit at the atmospheric English-library-themed bar and be mesmerised by the curious display of 19th-century medical and scientific equipment.

AIR   CLUB

Map p310 (www.air.nl; Amstelstraat 24; ⊙11.30pm-4am Thu & Sun, 11pm-5am Fri & Sat; 🚊4/9/14 Rembrandtplein) One of Amsterdam's 'it' clubs, Air has an environmentally friendly design by Dutch designer Marcel Wanders including a unique tiered dance floor. Bonuses include free mini lockers and refillable drink cards that preclude fussing with change at the bar. Though the place gets packed, it has ultrahigh ceilings and plenty of room to get loose. The awesome sound system attracts cutting-edge DJs.

CAFÉ SCHILLER   BAR, THEATRE CAFÉ

Map p310 (www.cafeschiller.nl; Rembrandtplein 26; ⊙4pm-1am Mon-Thu, 4pm-2am Fri, 2pm-2am Sat, 2pm-1am Sun; 🚊4/9/14 Rembrandtplein) Most *cafés* would pay a fortune to recreate Schiller's fabulous art deco interior, but this is original. Walls are lined with portraits of Dutch actors and cabaret artists from the 1920s and '30s. Bar stools and booths are often occupied by pre- and post-theatre goers.

NJOY   COCKTAIL BAR

Map p310 (http://njoycocktails.com; Korte Leidsedwarsstraat 93; ⊙5pm-3am Sun-Thu, to 4am Fri & Sat; 🚻; 🚊1/2/5/7/10 Leidseplein) Creative cocktails at this little vixen of a bar are grouped by personality. If you're a 'trendsetter', you might go for a Blazing Mule (fresh ginger and chilli-infused vodka), if you're a 'dreamer', maybe Pandora's Potion (blackberries, mint and vanilla vodka), a 'sparkling star' might try Absolutely Flawless (strawberries, vanilla liqueur, and of course, champagne).

Other personalities span 'virgin' to 'connoisseur' and 'alchemist'. Its chilled-out vibe is a refreshing break from the madness of the street outside; under 23s aren't admitted. Ask about its cocktail-making courses.

CAFÉ DE WETERING   BROWN CAFÉ

Map p310 (Weteringstraat 37; ⊙4pm-1am Sun-Thu, to 3am Fri & Sat; 🚊7/10 Spiegelgracht) Bursting with locals of all ages, perennial favourite Café de Wetering is tucked into one of central Amsterdam's hidden streets, not far from the antiques corridor of Nieuwe Spiegelstraat. Perch on the upper level by the fireplace, or at the bar to chat with the wisecracking bartenders. On chilly days, it's an ideal refuge.

VAN DYCK BAR CLUB

Map p310 (www.vandyckbar.com; Korte Leidsed-warsstraat 28-32; ☉10pm-4am Thu & Sun, to 5am Fri & Sat; ☐1/2/5/7/10 Leidseplein) Opened in 2013, Van Dyck brings Ibiza-style clubbing to Amsterdam, with wicked lighting and sound systems and DJs who know how to pack the dance floor. Dress to impress.

ESCAPE CLUB

Map p310 (www.escape.nl; Rembrandtplein 11; ☉11pm-4am Thu, to 5am Sat, to 4.30am Sun; ☐4/9/14 Rembrandtplein) A fixture of Amsterdam nightlife for two decades, this cavernous club is the city's slickest. Its multispace layout includes the cream of local and international DJs rocking several dance floors, a video-screen-filled studio and an adjoining cafe. Dress up or you may not get in.

DOOR 74 COCKTAIL BAR

Map p310 (☑06 3404 5122; www.door-74.nl; Reguliersdwarsstraat 74; ☉8pm-3am Sun-Thu, to 4am Fri & Sat; ☐9/14 Rembrandtplein) You'll need to leave a voice message or, better yet, send a text for a reservation to gain entry to this cocktail bar behind an unmarked door. Some of Amsterdam's most amazing cocktails are served in a classy, dark-timbered speakeasy atmosphere beneath pressed tin ceilings. Themed cocktail lists change regularly. Very cool.

MONTMARTRE GAY BAR

Map p310 (www.cafemontmartre.nl; Halvemaan-steeg 17; ☉5pm-1am Sun-Thu, to 4am Fri & Sat; ☐4/9/14 Rembrandtplein) Regarded by many as the best gay bar in the Benelux, and a busy weekend will show why. Patrons sing along (or scream along) to recordings of Dutch ballads and old top-40 hits.

CAFÉ AMERICAIN GRAND CAFÉ

Map p310 (☑556 30 00; www.edenamsterdama-mericanhotel.com; Eden Amsterdam American Hotel, Leidsekade 97; ☉6.30am-10.30pm Mon-Fri, 7am-10.30pm Sat & Sun; ☐1/2/5/7/10 Leidseplein) Within the Amsterdam American Hotel (p129), this art nouveau monument, opened in 1902, was a grand café (bar) before the concept even existed. Its huge stained-glass windows overlook Leidseplein; there's a lovely, library-like reading table and a great terrace. High teas (Monday to Saturday) and jazz brunches (Sunday) are especially atmospheric – book ahead.

ODEON CLUB

Map p310 (www.odeonamsterdam.nl; Singel 460; ☉club 10pm-4am Sun-Thu, 11pm-5am Fri & Sat; ☐1/2/5 Koningsplein) Spread over three floors, this historic venue from the 1660s includes a classy restaurant, a swanky cocktail bar and a canal-side terrace to give your ears a rest. Its club is invariably pumping (despite – or maybe because of – the smallish dance floor); live music sometimes plays.

LION NOIR COCKTAIL BAR

Map p310 (www.lionnoir.nl; Reguliersdwarsstraat 28; ☉11.30am-1am Mon-Thu, to 3am Fri, 6pm-3am Sat, 6pm-1am Sun) With a Thijs Murré–designed interior of birdcages, taxidermied birds and plants, Lion Noir lures an A-list crowd with fine dining, a fabulous terrace, and inspired cocktails like Dutch Garden (lychees, sweet and sour soda, cucumber and *jenever* – a Dutch gin), Lionjito (rum, cointreau, mint, lime, vanilla and organic apple juice) and Flatliner (tequila, sambuca and tabasco).

CAFÉ DE SPUYT BEER CAFÉ

Map p310 (www.cafedespuyt.nl; Korte Leidsed-warsstraat 86; ☉4pm-3am Sun-Thu, to 4am Fri & Sat; ☐1/2/5/7/10 Leidseplein) Footsteps away from the bustling Leidseplein, the bar staff at this mellow, friendly *café* (bar/pub) will happily guide you through the massive chalkboard menu of more than 100 beers, from Belgian Trappist ales to American Sierra Nevada.

JIMMY WOO CLUB

Map p310 (☑626 31 50; www.jimmywoo.com; Korte Leidsedwarsstraat 18; ☉11pm-3am Thu, to 4am Fri-Sun; ☐1/2/5/7/10 Leidseplein) For a long time this club was the hottest thing

---

ⓘ THE GAY SCENE

For the best gay action in the hood, head to Reguliersdwarsstraat and cruise around to see what takes your fancy. Do keep in mind that venues on Reguliersdwarsstraat tend to come and go. Keep your eyes open for new bar and club openings.

Amsterdam's other major **hubs** of gay and lesbian life include Zeedijk and Warmoesstraat in the Red Light District.

in town, with zero serious competition. It's still a platform for the young and beautiful, with fab light-and-sound shows and various club nights that cater for divergent tastes. And really long queues: be patient, or call ahead to get on the list.

VIVELAVIE
LESBIAN BAR

Map p310 (www.vivelavie.net; Amstelstraat 7; ◷4pm-3am Sun-Thu, to 4am Fri & Sat; ☎; ◫4/9/14 Rembrandtplein) Flirty girls, good-natured staff, loud music, large windows and dancing make this one of Amsterdam's most popular lesbian *cafés*. In summer the outdoor terrace buzzes.

CAFÉ WALEM
CAFE

Map p310 (www.walem.nl; Keizersgracht 449; ◷9am-7pm Sun-Wed, to 9pm Thu-Sat; ◫1/2/5 Keizersgracht) The industrial-mod building by Gerrit Rietveld, two terraces, friendly service and a changing menu keep this place busy and perennially popular. DJs spin from 5pm on Friday and Saturday.

WEBER
DESIGNER BAR

Map p310 (Marnixstraat 397; ◷7pm-3am Sun-Thu, to 4am Fri-Sun; ◫1/2/5/7/10 Leidseplein) This buzzy bar is much loved for its indie and Brit rock, retro decor and unpretentious local vibe. Cheap drinks and friendly service are added incentives to head here on a Saturday night. As you sip your beer, ponder how the themes of American astronauts, elk heads and vaguely Asian decor all somehow make sense together.

CHICAGO SOCIAL CLUB
CLUB, BAR

Map p310 (☎530 73 03; www.chicagosocialclub.nl; Leidseplein 12; ◷bar 5pm-4am Mon-Thu, 5pm-5am Fri, noon-5am Sat, noon-4am Sun, club from 11pm Thu-Sat; ◫1/2/5/7/10 Leidseplein) Comedy club Boom Chicago (p154) has relocated to the Jordaan, but the intimate bar and club on Leidseplein is still going strong here, as it has been since 1923. Lots of techno and house, and a cool, unpretentious vibe.

CAFÉ LANGEREIS
CAFE

Map p310 (www.cafelangereis.com; Amstel 202; ◷11am-1am Sun-Thu, 11am to 3am Fri & Sat; ☎; ◫4/9/14 Rembrandtplein) Along the Amstel, Café Langereis feels like it's been here forever, in large part because the friendly young owner scoured the city for antique fixtures and furniture to recreate the lived-in vintage feel. Freshly ground coffee, fresh

flowers on the tables, an upright piano and a classic rock soundtrack keep things vibrant.

CAFÉ BRECHT
CAFE

Map p310 (www.cafebrecht.nl; Weteringschans 79; noon-1am Sun-Thu, to 3am Fri & Sat; ◫4/7/10/16/24/25 Weteringcircuit) Named after the seminal German dramatist and poet, Bertolt Brecht, this may be the only establishment in Amsterdam with German poetry inscribed on the walls. The young and gorgeously rumpled dig the funky, elegant lounge room vibe created by mismatched velvet chairs, vintage lamps, and plenty of books and board games.

MULLIGANS
IRISH PUB

Map p310 (www.mulligans.nl; Amstel 100; ◷4pm-1am Mon-Thu, 4pm-3am Fri, 2pm-3am Sat, 2pm-1am Sun; ☎; ◫4/9/14 Rembrandtplein) Amsterdam's most 'authentic' Irish pub, Mulligans has properly poured Guinness and Magners cider on tap and great *craic* (fun), with live Irish trad music most nights from 9.30pm or 10pm (no cover charge). Sunday sessions let you participate: BYOI (instrument) and T (talent). On Wednesdays, sing along to Irish tunes in the back room.

UP
CLUB, MUSIC

Map p310 (☎623 69 85; www.clubup.nl; Korte Leidsedwarsstraat 26; ◷11pm-4am Thu, to 5am Fri & Sat; ◫1/2/5/7/10 Leidseplein) You might catch DJs spinning anything from disco, funk, soul, hip hop and deep house to live bands or performance art at this small, quirky club. Occasionally entrance is through De Kring, at Kleine Gartmanplantsoen 7-9; check the website.

A BAR
COCKTAIL BAR

Map p310 (☎520 32 45; www.a-bar.nl; InterContinental Amstel Amsterdam, Professor Tulpplein 1; ◷noon-1am; Ⓜ Weesperplein) Freshly overhauled (and renamed) in 2013, the bar at the InterContinental Amstel Amsterdam takes full advantage of its riverside location, opening to a huge sofa-lined terrace. Cocktails such as a Lavender Gin Flip use homemade syrups; it also serves Scandinavian-style bar food. Chilled DJ sessions and live music regularly take place.

WHISKEY CAFÉ L&B
WHISKEY BAR

Map p310 (Korte Leidsedwarsstraat 92; ◷8pm-3am Sun-Thu, to 4am Fri & Sat; ◫1/2/5/7/10 Leidseplein) If whiskey's your poison, skip the beer *cafés* and head straight to this convivial (and usually packed) bar, which stocks 850 (yes, 850) different varieties.

NEL
CAFE, BAR

Map p310 (www.nelamstelveld.nl; Amstelveld 12; ☺10am-1am Sun-Thu, to 3am Fri & Sat; 🖫; 🚊4 Prinsengracht) Inside there's a mellow brasserie on one side and a stylish bar on the other, but on a sunny afternoon there's nothing better than sitting under the lush canopy of trees.

OOSTERLING
BROWN CAFÉ

Map p310 (Utrechtsestraat 140; ☺noon-1am Mon-Sat, 1-8pm Sun; 🚊4 Prinsengracht) Opened in the 1700s as a tea and coffee outlet for the Dutch East India Company, Oosterling has been run by the same family since 1877 and is one of the very few *cafés* that has a bottle-shop (liquor-store) permit.

PATA NEGRA
WINE BAR

Map p310 (www.pata-negra.nl; Utrechtsestraat 124; ☺noon-midnight Sun-Thu, to 1am Fri & Sat; 🚊4 Prinsengracht) The freshly squeezed margaritas are tops at this Spanish tapas bar. The alluringly tiled exterior is matched by a vibrant crowd inside, especially on weekends, downing sangria with garlic-fried shrimps and grilled sardines. It gets packed, and that's half the fun.

LELLEBEL
DRAG BAR

Map p310 (www.lellebel.nl; Utrechtsestraat 4; ☺8pm-3am Mon-Thu, to 4am Fri & Sat, to 3am Sun; 🖫; 🚊4/9/14 Rembrandtplein) This hole in the wall just off Rembrandtplein has karaoke, singing and comedy shows that bring out the best in any girl's wardrobe. It can get bitchy, but always in the funniest possible way.

CAFÉ KALE
BROWN CAFÉ

Map p310 (www.cafekale.nl; Weteringshans 267; ☺11am-1am Sun-Thu, to 3am Fri & Sat; 🖫; 🚊4/7/10/25 Frederiksplein) Stained-glass, funky light fittings and soft jazz make Café Kale a tad more contemporary than the average *bruin café* (brown *café*, pub). There's a well-stocked magazine rack and a great summer terrace.

DE KOFFIE SALON
CAFE

Map p310 (www.dekoffiesalon.nl; Utrechtsestraat 130; ☺7am-7pm; 🚊4 Prinsengracht) The airy, sophisticated vibe here is genuine, not a put-on affair, with communal tables that invite conversation, magazine sharing and gazing at that cute stranger who's lost in a novel. Friendly baristas whip up strong espresso that goes brilliantly with the *stroopwafels* (thin waffles filled with syrup) and other bakery goodies.

There are also branches in De Pijp and Vondelpark.

TWO FOR JOY
CAFE

Map p310 (www.twoforjoy.nl; Frederiksplein 29; ☺7.30am-7pm Mon-Fri, 8am-6pm Sat & Sun; 🚊4 Prinsengracht) Full of Francophiles drinking intense espresso on the umbrella-shaded sidewalk terrace, this skylit cafe on lush Frederiksplein takes coffee seriously. Pick your poison from among French press, lattes and several connoisseur styles of drip coffee (try the high-tech, Japanese-style 'Syphon' method). You can also get a jolt on Haarlemmerdijk in the West.

DE HUYSCHKAEMER
DESIGNER BAR

Map p310 (www.huyschkaemer.nl; Utrechtsestraat 137; ☺11.30am-1am Sun-Thu, 11.30am-3am Fri & Sat; 🖫; 🚊4 Prinsengracht) With conversation pieces of art – like a giant photo of a Dutch football team drinking beer in the buff – there's always plenty of buzzing chatter at De Huyschkaemer. Inside, the rock 'n' roll soundtrack veers from classic to indie.

Sipping a beer next to the big windows on Utrechtsestraat is tempting, but the real action spills out on the street, where a mixed crowd – gay and straight, expat and local, old and young – shakes off the work day.

TABOO BAR
GAY BAR

Map p310 (www.taboobar.nl; Reguliersdwarsstraat 45; ☺5pm-3am Sun-Thu, 6pm-4am Fri & Sat; 🖫; 🚊1/2/5 Koningsplein) Taboo's wicked two-for-one happy hours (6pm to 7pm and midnight to 1am, plus 6pm to 8pm Sunday) guarantee a good time.

BULLDOG
BAR, COFFEESHOP

Map p310 (www.thebulldog.com; Leidseplein 13-17; ☺coffeeshop 9am-1am daily, bar 10am-1am Mon-Thu, 10am-3am Fri & Sat, 10am-2am Sun; 🖫; 🚊1/2/5/7/10 Leidseplein) Amsterdam's most famous coffeeshop chain has evolved into its own empire, with multiple locations, a hotel, bike rental and even its own energy drink. The brawny, brassy Leidesplein flagship has two sides for its brand-name debauchery: one for smoking, one for drinking.

The crowds on either side are pretty much the same: a mix of stag parties, corporate travellers blowing off steam and backpackers. The gaudy decor only makes sense to the stoned.

KAMER 401 DESIGNER BAR

Map p310 (Marnixstraat 401; ⊘6pm-1am Wed & Thu, to 3am Fri & Sat; 🚊1/2/5/7/10 Leidseplein) DJs providing a funky soundtrack make Kamer 401 perfect for preclubbing drinks. If you can't breathe or move, see if you can snag a corner at **Lux** (Map p310; 📞422 14 12; Marnixstraat 403; ⊘7pm-3am Sun-Thu, to 4am Fri & Sat) next door – it's a similar scene, and equally popular.

SUZY WONG DESIGNER BAR

Map p310 (www.suzy-wong.nl; Korte Leidsedwarsstraat 45; ⊘6pm-1am Wed, Thu & Sun, to 3am Fri & Sat; 🚊1/2/5/7/10 Leidseplein) With red velveteen wallpaper and a bamboo garden, Suzy Wong's Victorian-drawing-room-on-speed look packs a visual punch. Order a fresh fruit mojito and nab a seat in the back along with local celebs.

THE OTHER SIDE GAY COFFEESHOP

Map p310 (www.theotherside.nl; Reguliersdwarsstraat 6; ⊘11am-1am; 🚊1/2/5 Koningsplein) House and lounge music make this brilliantly named coffeeshop a hopping and trendy place. It's in the neighbourhood's main gay street and welcomes a mixed gay, lesbian and straight crowd.

CAFÉ 'T LEEUWTJE GAY BAR

Map p310 (www.cafehetleeuwtje.nl; Reguliersdwarsstraat 105; ⊘5pm-1am Sun-Thu, to 3am Fri & Sat; 🚊4/9/16/24/25 Muntplein) 'The Little Lion' stands out from the rest of the venues on this street – snazzy it ain't, the music doesn't thump loudly and the interior feels a bit like a brown *café*. A fairly extensive beer selection makes it a prime place to chat or chill with a newspaper.

COFFEESHOP FREE COFFEESHOP

Map p310 (Reguliersdwarsstraat 70; ⊘10am-1am; 🚊4/9/16/24/25 Muntplein) Little Coffeeshop Free has been sporting its lazy tiki bar vibe in the Rembrandtplein area for more than 25 years. It's perfect for prepping to see that new arthouse film playing around the corner at Pathe Tuschinski (p137). The South Seas mural inspires a trip to paradise, regardless of the weather outside.

ON YOUR BIKE IN THE SOUTHERN CANAL RING

Contact the following for bike rentals and bike tours in the Southern Canal Ring:

MacBike (Map p310; 📞528 76 88; www. macbike.nl; Weteringschans 2; rental per 3/24hr €11/14.75; ⊘9am-5.45pm; 🚊1/2/5/7/10 Leidseplein) Rents bikes near Leidseplein.

Mike's Bike Tours (Map p310; 📞622 79 70; www.mikesbiketours.com; Kerkstraat 134; city tours per adult/child from €17/12, countryside tours per adult/child from €23/16; ⊘office 9am-6pm Mar-Oct, 10am-6pm Nov-Feb; 🚊16/24/25 Keizersgracht) Tours depart across the road from the office at Kerkstraat 123. You can also hire bikes (from €6 for four hours).

CHURCH GAY CLUB

Map p310 (www.clubchurch.nl; Kerkstraat 52; ⊘8pm-midnight Tue & Wed, 10pm-4am Thu, 10pm-5am Fri & Sat, 4-8pm Sun; 🚊1/2/5 Keizersgracht) This hardcore gay nightclub gives a whole new meaning to the phrase 'I'm going to church'. Unless you come dressed appropriately for the evening (S&M, leather...check the website for events) or with super-hot boys (or happen to be one yourself) you probably won't get in to this high-action cruise spot, but they'll be terribly nice about it.

☆ ENTERTAINMENT

Much of the Southern Canal Ring's after-dark action gravitates towards two of Amsterdam's busy pleasure centres, Leidseplein and Rembrandtplein. Both are surrounded by a plethora of live-music venues and nightclubs with cutting-edge DJs. On Leidseplein, the grand Stadsschouwburg theatre stages major plays and festivals; smaller theatres and cinemas are scattered throughout the neighbourhood.

KONINKLIJK THEATER CARRÉ HISTORIC BUILDING

Map p310 (📞524 94 52; www.theatercarre. nl; Amstel 115-125; ⊘box office 10am-8pm;

Ⓜ Weesperplein) This esteemed theatre was built in 1887 by the Carré family, who had started their career years earlier with a horse act at the annual fair. The first structure was of wood, but it was eventually rebuilt in concrete because of the fire hazard (early performances for 2000 spectators were lit by gas lamps).

The classical facade is richly decorated with faces of jesters, dancers and theatre folk. Today the Carré hosts high-calibre musicals, theatre and dance events; its Christmas circus is a seasonal highlight.

STADSSCHOUWBURG
THEATRE

Map p310 (Theatre; ☎624 23 11; www.stadsschouwburgamsterdam.nl; Leidseplein 26; ⊗box office noon-6pm Mon-Sat; ⓘ1/2/5/7/10 Leidseplein) In 1894, when this theatre with the grand balcony arcade was completed, public criticism was so fierce that funds for the exterior decorations never materialised. Architect Jan Springer couldn't handle this and promptly retired. The theatre is used for large-scale plays, operettas and festivals such as the Holland Festival and Julidans. Don't miss the chandeliered splendour of its **Stanislavski** theatre *café* (Map p310; www.stanislavski.nl; ⊗10am-1am Sun-Thu, 10am-1am Fri & Sat), and **International Theatre & Film Books** (Map p310; www.theatreandfilmbooks.com; ⊗noon-6pm Mon, 11am-6pm Tue-Sat) shop.

MELKWEG
LIVE MUSIC

Map p310 (www.melkweg.nl; Lijnbaansgracht 234a; ⊗6pm-1am; ⓘ1/2/5/7/10 Leidseplein) In a former dairy, the non-profit 'Milky Way' is a dazzling galaxy of diverse music. One night it's electronica, the next reggae or punk, and next heavy metal might lure a leather-jacketed biker crowd. Roots, rock and mellow singer-songwriters all get stage time too. Check out its website for cutting-edge cinema, theatre and multimedia offerings, too.

SUGAR FACTORY
LIVE MUSIC

Map p310 (www.sugarfactory.nl; Lijnbaansgracht 238; ⊗6pm-5am; ⓘ1/2/5/7/10 Leidseplein) The vibe at this self-described 'cutting-edge multidisciplinary night theatre' is always welcoming and creative. It's definitely not your average club – most nights start with music, cinema, or a dance or spoken-word performance, followed by late-night DJs and dancing. Sunday's Wicked Jazz Sounds party is a sweet one, bringing DJs, musicians, singers and actors together to improvise.

JAZZ CAFÉ ALTO
JAZZ

Map p310 (www.jazz-cafe-alto.nl; Korte Leidsedwarsstraat 115; ⊗from 9pm; ⓘ1/2/5/7/10 Leidseplein) Serious jazz and blues are played at this respected cafe near Leidseplein. Doors open at 9pm but music starts around 10pm – get here early if you want to snag a seat.

PARADISO
LIVE MUSIC

Map p310 (☎622 05 50; www.paradiso.nl; Weteringschans 6; ⊗from 6pm; ⓘ1/2/5/7/10 Leidseplein) Worship rock 'n' roll in a gorgeous old church where the Beatles once played. This historic, multistoreyed club opened in 1968 as 'Cosmic Relaxation Center Paradiso'. Midweek club nights with low cover charges lure the young and the restless, while the Small Hall upstairs provides an intimate venue to see up-and-coming international bands.

The real attraction, of course, is the chance to hear artists such as the White Stripes and Lady Gaga rock the Main Hall as you wonder if the stained-glass windows might shatter.

BOURBON STREET
JAZZ & BLUES CLUB
JAZZ, BLUES

Map p310 (www.bourbonstreet.nl; Leidsekruisstraat 6-8; ⊗10pm-4am Sun-Thu, to 5am Fri & Sat; ⓘ1/2/5 Prinsengracht) Catch blues, funk, soul and rock and roll in this intimate venue, with open jam sessions on Mondays when everyone's welcome to take part. Free entry before 11pm.

---

❶ LAST-MINUTE TICKETS

Not sure how to spend your evening? Head to the Last Minute Ticket Shop desk at the **Uitburo** (Map p310; ☎621 13 11; www.amsterdamsuitburo.nl; Leidseplein 26; ⊗10am-5pm; ⓘ1/2/5/7/10 Leidseplein), in the corner of the Stadsschouwburg on the Leidseplein. Comedy, dance, concerts, even club nights are often available at a significant discount (around 50% off). Productions and events are handily marked 'LNP' (language no problem) if understanding Dutch isn't vital.

The Uitburo has loads of free brochures and sells a huge range of regular tickets (with a surcharge).

DE HEEREN VAN AEMSTEL — LIVE MUSIC
Map p310 (www.deheerenvanaemstel.nl; Thorbeckeplein 5; ⊙noon-3am Mon-Thu, to 4am Fri & Sat; 🚊4/9/14 Rembrandtplein) Students in particular cram into this grand-*café*-style club to enjoy the roster of live big bands and pop and rock cover bands.

CINECENTER — CINEMA
Map p310 (www.cinecenter.nl; Lijnbaansgracht 236; ⊙3.30pm-midnight Mon-Sat, 10.30am-midnight Sun; 🚊1/2/5/7/10 Leidseplein) European and American indie and art-house films play in four small screening rooms. Don't miss the hip bar with white padded walls.

DE UITKIJK — CINEMA
Map p310 (www.uitkijk.nl; Prinsengracht 452; 🚊1/2/5 Prinsengracht) This fun art-house stalwart, located in a 1913 canal house is the city's second-oldest surviving cinema. For film buffs who know their Fuller from their Fellini.

PATHÉ TUSCHINSKITHEATER — CINEMA
Map p310 (www.pathe.nl/tuschinski; Reguliersbreestraat 26-34; ⊙4pm-12.30am; 🚊4/9/14 Rembrandtplein) Extensively refurbished, Amsterdam's most famous cinema is worth visiting for its sumptuous art deco/Amsterdam School interior alone. The *grote zaal* (main auditorium) is the most stunning and generally screens blockbusters; the smaller theatres play art-house and indie films.

DE LA MAR — THEATRE
Map p310 (www.delamar.nl; Leidsekade 90; ⊙closed Aug; 🚊1/2/5/7/10 Leidseplein) Big-name blockbuster musicals and crowd-pleasing plays shine in the most impressive venue to hit the theatre district in years. After the curtain comes down, head to the Grand Café De La Mar for a post-theatre glass of champagne.

COMEDY CAFÉ AMSTERDAM — COMEDY
Map p310 (www.comedycafe.nl; Max Euweplein 43-45; 🚊1/2/5/7/10 Leidseplein) The Comedy Café books Dutch and international stand-up comics.

DE KLEINE KOMEDIE — THEATRE
Map p310 (www.dekleinekomedie.nl; Amstel 56-58; ⊙vary; 🚊4/9/14 Rembrandtplein) This renowned little theatre, founded in 1786, puts on concerts, dance, comedy and cabaret, sometimes in English.

LOCAL KNOWLEDGE

LOUNGING LIZARDS
Slow down as you pass the Kleine Gartmanplantsoen park just near Leidseplein to spot forty lizards nestled in the grass and sunning themselves on the brickwork. Cast in bronze, the surreal life-size reptiles, created by Dutch artist Hans van Houwelingen in 1994, are collectively known as **Blauw Jan** (Map p310; Kleine Gartmanplantsoen; 🚊1/2/5/7/10 Leidseplein). The title comes from an old Amsterdam inn of the same name which, in the 17th and 18th centuries, had a menagerie of exotic animals that were brought to the port city from faraway lands.

DE BALIE — THEATRE
Map p310 (☎553 51 51; www.debalie.nl; Kleine Gartmanplantsoen 10; ⊙cafe/bar 10am-2am; 🛜; 🚊1/2/5/7/10 Leidseplein) The focus here is multicultural and political, with big international productions. De Balie also conducts short-film festivals and debates, and has new-media facilities. There's a breezy, bohemian vibe and a pre-theatre buzz in its cafe/bar, as actors, students and artists unfurl magazines or just knowing glances.

THEATER BELLEVUE — THEATRE
Map p310 (☎530 53 01; www.theaterbellevue.nl; Leidsekade 90; ⊙closed Aug; 🚊1/2/5/7/10 Leidseplein) Come here for experimental theatre, international cabaret and modern dance, mainly in Dutch. Its *café*, **De Smoeshaan** (Map p310; www.desmoeshaan.nl; Leidsekade 90; ⊙11am-1am Mon-Thu, 11am-3am Fri & Sat, restaurant 11.30am-4pm & 5.30-9pm Mon-Sat; 🚊1/2/5/7/10 Leidseplein), gets busy pre- and post-performance.

🛍 SHOPPING
From sleek Dutch fashion and design to colourful bouquets and rare Dutch *jenever*, the variety of goods on offer in the Southern Canal Ring is nothing short of staggering. The Nieuwe Spiegelstraat (aka the Spiegel Quarter) is renowned for its antique stores, bric-a-brac collectables, tribal and oriental art, and commercial art galleries.

SOUTHERN CANAL RING SHOPPING

YOUNG DESIGNERS UNITED CLOTHING
Map p310 (YDU; www.ydu.nl; Keizersgracht 447; ⊙1-6pm Mon, 10am-6pm Tue, Wed, Fri & Sat, 10am-8pm Thu; ⌂1/2/5 Keizersgracht) Angelika Groenendijk Wasylewski's boutique is a showcase for young designers (mainly Dutch). The racks are rotated regularly but you might spot durable basics by Agna K, minimalist knits by Andy ve Eirn, geometric dresses by Fenny Faber and soft, limited edition knits by Mimoods. Accessorise with YDU's select range of jewellery and bags.

MAISONNL HOMEWARES, CLOTHING
Map p310 (www.maisonnl.com; Utrechtsestraat 118; ⊙10.30am-6pm Tue-Sat, 1-5pm Sun; ⌂4 Prinsengracht) This gorgeous concept store looks like a cross between an art gallery and someone's stylish apartment. Artfully displayed products range from tea sets to baby shoes lamps to shawls and leather handbags; there's a clothing rack down the back.

MOBILIA HOMEWARES
Map p310 (www.mobiliawoonstudio.nl; Utrechtsestraat 62; ⊙9.30am-6pm Mon-Sat, 1-5pm Sun; ⌂4 Prinsengracht) Dutch and international design is stunningly showcased at this three-storey 'lifestyle studio'. Sofas, workstations, bookshelves, lighting, cushions, rugs and much more from both emerging and established designers offer a cornucopia of inspiration.

CENTRE NEUF CLOTHING
Map p310 (http://centreneuf.com; Utrechtsestraat 139; ⊙1-6pm Mon, 10am-6pm Tue-Sat, 1-5pm Sun; ⌂4 Prinsengracht) Exposed brick walls, parquet floors and a giant skylight make shopping in this spacious boutique a pleasure, as do to-die-for pieces from Marc by Marc Jacobs, Athé by Vanessa Bruno, Aaiko, Dante 6 and Avril Gau. Luscious handbags and shoes too.

WALLS GALLERY ART
Map p310 (☑616 95 97; http://walls.nl; Prinsengracht 737; ⊙noon-5pm Wed-Sun; ⌂1/2/5 Prinsengracht) A former garage now houses this edgy art gallery, which hosts six to eight exhibitions a year and also represents young, up-and-coming art students (meaning prices are reasonable).

RAAK CLOTHING
Map p310 (www.raakamsterdam.nl; Leidsestraat 79; ⊙noon-6pm Mon, 10am-6pm Tue-Sat;

⌂1/2/5 Prinsengracht) Alice + Olivia, Malene Birger and L'enfant Terrible are among the labels at this superbly stocked clothing shop, while shoes range from stilettos to Ugg boots. This is the place to find stylish evening dresses; the De Pijp branch (p187) has more casual wear.

REFLEX MODERN ART GALLERY ART
Map p310 (http://reflexamsterdam.com; Weteringschans 79a; ⊙11am-6pm Tue-Sun; ⌂7/10 Spiegelgracht) This prominent gallery, opposite the Rijksmuseum, is filled with contemporary art and photography, including works by members of the CoBrA and Nouveau Réaliste movements. Its **Reflex New Art Gallery** (Map p310; www.reflex-art.nl; Weteringschans 83; ⊙10am-6pm Tue-Sat; ⌂7/10 Spiegelgracht) exhibition space across the street specialises in new art, particularly photography.

MARAÑON HANGMATTEN OUTDOORS
Map p310 (www.maranon.com; Singel 488; ⊙11am-5.15pm Mon-Fri, 9.30am-5.30pm Sat, 11am-5pm Sun; ⌂1/2/5 Koningsplein) Anyone who loves hanging around should come here and explore Europe's largest selection of hammocks. The colourful creations, made of everything from cotton to pineapple fibres, are made by many producers, from indigenous weavers to large manufacturers. It ships worldwide.

CORA KEMPERMAN CLOTHING
Map p310 (☑625 12 84; www.corakemperman.nl; Leidsestraat 72; ⊙noon-6pm Sun & Mon, 10am-6pm Tue, Wed, Fri & Sat, 10am-9pm Thu; ⌂1/2/5 Prinsengracht) Kemperman was once a designer with large Dutch fashion houses, but since 1995 she's been working on her own empire – now encompassing nine stores, including three in Belgium. Her well-priced creations feature mainly solid colours, floaty, layered separates and dresses in linen, cotton and wool.

TINKERBELL CHILDREN
Map p310 (www.tinkerbelltoys.nl; Spiegelgracht 10; ⊙1-6pm Mon, 10am-6pm Tue-Sat, noon-5pm Sun; ⌂7/10 Spiegelgracht) The mechanical bear blowing bubbles outside this shop fascinates kids, as do the intriguing technical and scientific toys inside. You'll also find historical costumes, plush toys and an entire section for babies.

EDUARD KRAMER ANTIQUES

Map p310 (www.antique-tileshop.nl; Nieuwe Spiegelstraat 64; ⊘10am-6pm Tue-Sat, 1-6pm Sun & Mon; ⊞7/10 Spiegelgracht) Specialising in antique Dutch tiles, this tiny store is also crammed with lots of other interesting stuff – silver candlesticks, crystal decanters, jewellery and pocket watches.

JASKI ART

Map p310 (www.jaski.nl; Nieuwe Spiegelstraat 27-29; ⊘noon-6pm; ⊞16/24/25 Keizersgracht) This large commercial gallery sells paintings, prints, ceramics and sculptures by some of the most famous members of the CoBrA movement.

LIEVE HEMEL ART

Map p310 (www.lievehemel.nl; Nieuwe Spiegelstraat 3; ⊘noon-6pm Tue-Sat; ⊞16/24/25 Keizersgracht) You'll find magnificent contemporary Dutch realist paintings and sculptures at this smart gallery. It shows works by Dutch painters Ben Snijders and Theo Voorzaat, and astounding, lifelike representations of clothing – hewn from wood – by Italian Livio de Marchi.

VLIEGER STATIONERY

Map p310 (www.vliegerpapier.nl; Amstel 34; ⊘noon-6pm Mon, 9am-6pm Tue-Fri, 11am-5.30pm Sat; ⊞4/9/14 Rembrandtplein) Since 1869 this two-storey shop has been supplying upmarket paper to Amsterdam: Egyptian papyrus, lush handmade papers from Asia and Central America, papers inlaid with flower petals or bamboo and paper with a texture that looks like snake skin. It also sells indestructible, recycled Freitag messenger bags (to safely tote away all that paper on your bike?).

EH ARIËNS KAPPERS ART, ANTIQUES

Map p310 (⊘623 53 56; www.masterprints.nl; Prinsengracht 677; ⊘by appointment; ⊞16/24/25 Keizersgracht) This pretty gallery stocks original prints, etchings, engravings, lithographs, maps (primarily of the Netherlands) from the 15th to 20th centuries and Japanese woodblock prints.

CITYBOEK ART, BOOKS

Map p310 (⊘627 03 49; www.cityboek.nl; Kerkstraat 211; ⊘by appointment; ⊞16/24/25 Keizersgracht) Skip the commercial souvenir shops and head to this small publishing house for precisely drawn, multicoloured, architecturally faithful prints, books and postcards of Amsterdam's canal-scapes such as images of the entire Herengracht or Singel.

STADSBOEKWINKEL BOOKS

Map p310 (www.stadsboekwinkel.nl; Vijzelstraat 32; ⊘10am-3pm Tue-Fri, noon-5pm Sat & Sun; ⊞16/24/25 Keizersgracht) Run by the city printer, this is the best source for books about Amsterdam's history, urban development, ecology and politics. Most titles are in Dutch (if you don't speak it, you can always look at the pictures), but you'll also find some in English. It's in the Stadsarchief (p121) archives building.

GONE WITH THE WIND CHILDREN

Map p310 (www.gonewiththewind.nl; Vijzelstraat 22; ⊘noon-6pm Mon, 10am-6pm Tue-Sat, noon-5pm Sun; ⊞16/24/25 Keizersgracht) Most of the toys, train sets and games here are made from high-quality wood, as are the shop's speciality, fluttering baby mobiles from around the world. There are also adorable finger puppets, whimsical gifts and jewellery.

HART'S WIJNHANDEL FOOD, DRINK

Map p310 (www.hartswijn.nl; Vijzelgracht 27; ⊘noon-6pm Mon, 9.30am-6pm Tue-Fri, 10am-5pm Sat; ⊞4/7/10/16/24/25 Weteringcircuit) Listen to classical music as you peruse the large selection of *jenever* and French and Italian wines at this genteel shop. It's been around since 1880 and supplies many a local restaurant with top tipples.

UTRECHTSESTRAAT

Stocked with enticing shops, designer bars and one of the city's best concentration of quality eateries, popular local artery **Utrechtsestraat** (Map p310; ⊞4 Prinsengracht) seems a world away from the gaudy lights of Rembrandtplein, a stone's throw to the north.

The southern end of the street used to terminate at the Utrechtse Poort, a gate to the nearby city of Utrecht, hence the name. Lack of space becomes a charm as the trams, confined to a single line apart from passing points on the bridges, play a game of stop and go, and passers-by marvel at the choreography of it all.

LOOK OUT
CLOTHING

Map p310 (www.lookoutmode.com; Utrechtsestraat 91 & 93; ☺noon-6pm Mon, 10am-6pm Tue-Sat; ☒4 Prinsengracht) Searching through the racks at these wonderful neighbouring men's and women's stores is a real delight. Look out for super-stylish labels such as Philosophy, Etro, Kenzo, Bruuns Bazaar and Annemie Verbeke.

CONCERTO
MUSIC

Map p310 (Utrechtsestraat 52-60; ☺10am-6pm Mon-Wed, Fri & Sat, noon-6pm Sun; ☒4 Prinsengracht) Spread over several buildings, this rambling shop has Amsterdam's best selection of new and secondhand CDs and records in every imaginable genre, from pop to classical, dance to world music and much, much more. You could spend hours on end browsing here. It's often cheap and always interesting, and has good listening facilities.

CARL DENIG
OUTDOOR EQUIPMENT

Map p310 (www.denig.nl; Weteringschans 113-115; ☺noon-6pm Mon, 10am-6pm Tue, Wed & Fri, 10am-9pm Thu, 9.30am-5.30pm Sat; ☒7/10 Spiegelgracht) Opened in 1912 this is Amsterdam's oldest and best outdoor retailer, though you pay for the quality. There are five floors of packs, tents, hiking and camping accessories, snowboards and skis (not that you'll get much use out of the last two in the Netherlands, but still...).

KOM
HOMEWARES

Map p310 (www.komshop.nl; Utrechtsestraat 129; ☺1-6pm Mon, 11am-6pm Tue-Sat; ☒4 Prinsengracht) Alluring kitchen gear including delftware, pretty dishes, cake knives, and glasses, all wrapped up in pretty blue paper.

SHIRT SHOP
CLOTHING

Map p310 (www.shirtshopamsterdam.com; Reguliersdwarsstraat 64; ☺1-7pm; ☒4/9/16/24/25 Muntplein) On gay Amsterdam's main street, this funky, two-storey shop sells tight-fitting men's shirts to make you look fabulous and spurns global, mass-produced products.

HEINEKEN BRAND STORE
SOUVENIRS

Map p310 (www.heinekenthecity.nl; Amstelstraat 31; ☺11am-8pm Tue-Sat, noon-8pm Sun & Mon; ☒4/9/14 Rembrandtplein) Heineken's hip, multistorey concept store glows cool and green, just like a frosty bottle of the brew itself. Some of the logoed gear is over the top but the decorated beer bottles make groovy souvenirs. A 15-minute shuttle boat ride here is included in Heineken Experience (p186) admission.

EICHHOLTZ DELICATESSEN
FOOD, DRINK

Map p310 (http://eichholtzdeli.nl; Leidsestraat 48; ☺10am-6.30pm Mon, 9.30am-6.30pm Tue, Wed, Fri & Sat, 9.30am-9pm Thu, noon-6.30pm Sun; ☒1/2/5 Keizersgracht) Americans missing Hershey's, Brits wanting Hobnobs and Aussies craving Vegemite will find them all – and loads more – at this import-specialist grocery store, which has been in business for well over a century.

Jordaan & the West

JORDAAN | THE WEST

Neighbourhood Top Five

❶ Lose yourself in the labyrinth of narrow streets and charming canals while walking through the **Jordaan** (p143), before spending the evening in the neighbourhood's atmospheric brown *cafés* – nothing is more quintessentially Amsterdam.

❷ Learn about the fascinating history and production of the country's favourite bloom at the **Amsterdam Tulip Museum** (p145).

❸ Listen to rare jazz and classical tunes play on vintage pianolas at the **Pianola Museum** (p143).

❹ Discover what life is like on the city's waterways at the quaint **Houseboat Museum** (p143).

❺ Admire the Amsterdam School's revolutionary 1920s housing complex at the **Museum Het Schip** (p146).

For more detail of this area, see Map p303, p318 and p320 ➡

Lonely Planet's Top Tip

Be aware that trams 3 and 10 don't pass by Centraal Station, but take ring routes around the centre instead. If you're heading to areas such as Westerpark and Westergasfabriek from Centraal, a bus is by far your best bet.

✗ Best Places to Eat

➡ Balthazar's Keuken (p147)

➡ Café Restaurant Open (p151)

➡ Semhar (p148)

➡ Marius (p151)

➡ Pont 13 (p148)

For reviews, see p146.➡

☐ Best Places to Drink

➡ 't Smalle (p151)

➡ Finch (p152)

➡ Westergasterras (p154)

➡ De Pieper (p152)

➡ Café P 96 (p152)

For reviews, see p151.➡

☐ Best Places to Shop

➡ Moooi Gallery (p155)

➡ De Winkel Van Guus (p155)

➡ SPRMRKT (p156)

➡ Antiekcentrum Amsterdam (p156)

➡ Het Oud-Hollandsch Snoepwinkeltje (p156)

For reviews, see p155.➡

Explore Jordaan & the West

Though gentrified today, the Jordaan was a rough, densely populated *volksbuurt* (district for the common people) until the mid-20th century, and that history still shows. You'll discover that this neighbourhood is a curiously enchanting mix of its traditional gritty, hard-drinking, leftist character and its revitalised, trend-conscious sheen.

The area doesn't have many traditional sights, but that's not the point. It's the little things that are appealing here – the narrow lanes, the old facades, the funny little shops. The Jordaan is about taking your time wandering and not worrying if you get lost.

Start the day at the northern end of the Jordaan and criss-cross towards the neighbourhood's south, catching the area's museums, architecture and, if you time it right, markets, along the way. Take a coffee break at one of the many canal-side cafes along the Prinsengracht.

On day two, go west. Hop on a bike and wend through the Western Islands before a spin around verdant Westerpark. In the evening, revel in the possibilities that any evening in the Westergasfabriek presents, from an art-house film to jazz or rock and roll.

Local Life

➡**Market Life** Morning bliss in the Jordaan means cruising the weekly outdoor markets – Noordermarkt (p157), Lindengracht Market (p157) and Westermarkt (p157) – for mouthwatering food, bargain clothes and funky flea-market treasures.

➡**Cultural Life** Locals flock to the former gasworks turned cutting-edge cultural complex, Westergasfabriek (p155).

➡**Docklands Life** Two of Amsterdam's most extraordinary bars/restaurants – in a former offshore pirate radio and TV rig, and aboard a moored 1927-built ferry – are just north of the Western Islands in the **Western Docklands** (p148).

Getting There & Away

➡**Tram** Tram 3 and 10 along Marnixstraat skirt the neighbourhood's western edge; trams 13, 14 and 17 along Rozengracht go through its centre.

➡**Bus** Buses 18, 21, 22 and 48 provide the quickest access from Centraal to the neighbourhood's north, west and Western Islands.

➡**Car** Whatever you do, don't try to drive through the Jordaan's narrow streets. Seriously.

◉ SIGHTS

◉ Jordaan

BROUWERSGRACHT   CANAL

Map p318 (🏛3 Haarlemmerplein) Pretty as a Golden Age painting, the Brewers Canal took its name from the many breweries located here in the 16th and 17th centuries. Goods such as leather, coffee, whale oil and spices were stored and processed here in giant warehouses, such as those with the row of spout gables that still stand at Brouwersgracht 188–194.

A few years ago, the Brouwersgracht was voted the 'most beautiful street' in Amsterdam by newspaper *Het Parool*. It's a great a place to stroll and to see the waterborne action on King's Day.

NOORDERKERK   CHURCH

Map p318 (Northern Church; www.noorderkerk. org; Noordermarkt 48; ◷10.30am-12.30pm Mon, 11am-1pm Sat, 1.30-5.30pm Sun; 🏛3/10 Marnixplein) Near the Prinsengracht's northern end, this imposing Calvinist church was completed in 1623 for the 'common' people in the Jordaan. (The upper classes attended the Westerkerk further south.) It was built in the shape of a broad Greek cross (four arms of equal length) around a central pulpit, giving the entire congregation unimpeded access to the word of God.

This design, unusual at the time, would become common for Protestant churches throughout the country.

Noorderkerk hosts a well-regarded Saturday afternoon **concert series** (✆620 44 15; www.nooderkerkconcerten.nl; tickets from €15; ◷2pm Sat mid-Sep–mid-Jun).

PIANOLA MUSEUM   MUSEUM

Map p318 (✆627 96 24; www.pianola.nl; Westerstraat 106; adult/child €5/3; ◷2-5pm Sun; 🏛3/10 Marnixplein) This is a very special place, crammed with pianolas from the early 1900s. The museum has a stock of 50 pianolas, although only a dozen are on display at any given time, as well as nearly 20,000 music rolls and a player pipe organ. The curator gives demonstrations with great zest.

Every month except July and August, concerts are held on the player-pianos, featuring anything from Mozart to Fats Waller and rare classical or jazz tunes composed especially for the instrument. More eclectic musical offerings include a popular tango series.

EGELANTIERSGRACHT   CANAL

Map p318 (🏛13/14/17 Westermarkt) Many parts of the Jordaan are named after trees and flowers and this canal, lined by lovely houses built for artisans and skilled traders, takes its name from the eglantine rose, or sweetbrier.

BLOEMGRACHT   CANAL

Map p320 (Flower Canal; 🏛13/14/17 Westermarkt) In the 17th century the 'Herengracht of the Jordaan', as the gorgeous Bloemgracht was called, was home to paint and sugar factories, and a large number of fine gabled houses. A striking example is **De Drie Hendricken** (Map p320; Bloemgracht 87-91), built in a sober Renaissance style. The gable stones above the ground floor depict a townsperson, a farmer and a seafarer.

Many artists also lived on Bloemgracht, including Jurriaen Andriessen, whose work is displayed in the Rijksmuseum.

HOUSEBOAT MUSEUM   MUSEUM

Map p320 (✆427 07 50; www.houseboatmuseum.nl; Prinsengracht, opposite 296; adult/child €3.75/3; ◷11am-5pm Tue-Sun Mar-Oct, 11am-5pm Fri-Sun Nov-Feb, closed Jan; 🏛13/14/17 Westermarkt) This quirky museum, a 23m-long sailing barge from 1914, offers a good sense of how *gezellig* (convivial, cosy) life can be on the water. The actual displays are minimal, but you can watch a presentation on houseboats (some pretty and some ghastly) and inspect the sleeping, living, cooking and dining quarters with all mod cons.

JOHNNY JORDAANPLEIN   SQUARE

Map p320 (cnr Prinsengracht & Elandsgracht; 🏛13/14/17 Westermarkt) This shady little square is named for Johnny Jordaan (the pseudonym of Johannes Hendricus van Musscher), a popular musician in the mid-1900s who sang the romantic music known as *levenslied* (tears-in-your-beer-style ballads). The colourfully painted hut – a municipal transformer station – proudly displays one of his song lyrics 'Amsterdam, wat bent je mooi' (Amsterdam, how beautiful you are).

Behind the hut you'll find Johnny and members of the Jordaan musical hall of fame, cast in bronze. On King's Day, this is

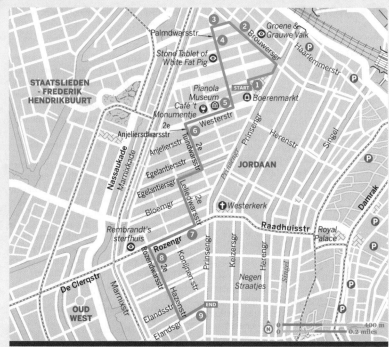

Neighbourhood Walk
Lost in the Jordaan

START NOORDERKERK
END JOHNNY JORDAANPLEIN
LENGTH 2.7KM; ONE HOUR

Begin at the ❶ **Noorderkerk** (p143). This impressive, cross-shaped church was revolutionary at the time, providing its working-class congregation with altar views from four transepts. Out front is the Noordermarkt, site of Amsterdam's most attractive *boerenmarkt* (farmers market), and a flea market.

Head north to ❷ **Brouwersgracht** (p143). As you move west along this 'Brewers Canal', you'll see the old warehouses Groene & Grauwe Valk. At the second drawbridge, turn left into Palmgracht and look out for the red door to the ❸ **Rapenhofje** (at 28–38). This little courtyard was home to one of Amsterdam's oldest almshouses (1648).

South along ❹ **Palmdwarsstraat** you'll pass tiny food shops. Note the stone tablet of the 'white fat pig' over the butcher/deli at 2e Goudsbloemdwarsstraat 26. Soon you'll reach ❺ **Westerstraat**, a main drag of the Jordaan, with the Pianola Museum, a weekly clothing market and alluring places for a bite or drink, such as Café 't Monumentje. At the 2e Anjeliersdwarsstraat, turn left to enter what locals call the '❻ **garden quarter**' of ivy-clad lanes and diminutive squares.

Zigzag down to Leliedwarsstraat and continue along until you hit ❼ **Rozengracht**, where speciality shops sell silk pillows and beaded saris. Rembrandt's *sterfhuis* (death house) is at 184, where the master painter died in 1669 (look upwards for a plaque marking the spot). The area on and around ❽ **2e Rozendwarsstraat** is a mad jumble of styles, and though the winch beams may appear decorative, they still see plenty of active duty. Secondhand stores, fancy boutiques and art shops pop up along the way.

Cross over the Lauriergracht, turning left into Elandsgracht to find ❾ **Johnny Jordaanplein** (p143), a square dedicated to the local hero and singer of schmaltzy tunes such as 'Bij ons in de Jordaan' (With Us in the Jordaan). As well as bronze busts of Johnny and his band, there's a colourful utility hut splashed with nostalgic lyrics.

where many Jordaanians head to rock out to live music.

ELECTRIC LADYLAND
MUSEUM

Map p318 (www.electric-lady-land.com; 2e Leliedwarsstraat 5; adult/child €5/free; ⊙2-5pm Tue-Sat; ☐13/14/17 Westermarkt) The world's first museum of fluorescent art features owner Nick Padalino's psychedelic sculpture work on one side and cases of naturally luminescent rocks and artificially glowing objects (money, government ID cards etc) on the other (his art gallery/shop is upstairs). Jimi Hendrix, the Beatles and other trippy artists play on the stereo while Nick lovingly describes each item in the collection.

STEDELIJK MUSEUM BUREAU AMSTERDAM
MUSEUM

Map p320 (☑422 04 71; www.smba.nl; Rozenstraat 59; ⊙11am-5pm Wed-Sun; ☐13/14/17 Westermarkt) FREE Don't blink or you might walk right past this unobtrusive outpost, a 'project space' of the leading Stedelijk Museum; it's in a one-time clothing workshop on a very quiet block. Exhibits here – from painting and sculpture to new media and installation pieces – present contemporary artists whose work reflects Amsterdam culture.

Shows change about every two weeks; check ahead to make sure the museum's not closed while exhibitions are being changed.

HAARLEMMERPOORT
GATE

Map p318 (Haarlem Gate, Haarlemmerplein; ☐3 Haarlemmerplein) Once a defensive gateway to the city, the Haarlemmerpoort marked the start of the busy route to Haarlem, which was a major trading route. The structure was finished just in time for King William II's staged entry for his 1840 investiture, hence its little-known official name of Willemspoort (see the plaque inside).

Traffic no longer runs through the gate since a bypass was built over the Westerkanaal. Today this grand archway is home to apartments with an alluring view of the canal and Westerpark beyond.

◉ The West

Amsterdam's west might be off the beaten tourist track but sights here are only a 20-minute walk from Centraal Station. Don't miss the former western gasworks, which have been transformed into the Westergasfabriek cultural complex (p155).

TOP SIGHT
AMSTERDAM TULIP MUSEUM

Don't be dissuaded – or distracted – by the gift shop overflowing with floral souvenirs at the front of this small museum. And yes, it is small, but the Amsterdam Tulip Museum offers a comprehensive overview of the history of the country's favourite bloom and is a fascinating way to spend half an hour or so, especially before taking a day trip to the **Keukenhof Flower Gardens** (p211) or the **Bloemenveiling Aalsmeer** (p220) flower auction, or strolling the Southern Canal Ring's 'floating' flower market, the **Bloemenmarkt** (p128).

Through exhibits, timelines and two short films (in English), you'll learn how Ottoman merchants came across the flowers in the Himalayan Steppes and began commercial production in Turkey (the word tulip derives from 'turban' due to the petals' resemblance to the head-wear). You'll also find out how fortunes were made and lost during Dutch '**Tulipmania**' (p241) in the 17th century, how bulbs were used as food in the war years and discover present-day methods of growing and harvesting the flower. The tulip paintings by 17th-century painter Judith Leijster (or Leyster), a student of Frans Hals, are a highlight; there's also a great collection of tulip vases designed to accommodate separate stems.

DON'T MISS
➡ The films
➡ Judith Leijster paintings
➡ The vase collection

PRACTICALITIES
➡ Map p318
➡ ☑421 00 95
➡ www.amsterdam tulipmuseum.com
➡ Prinsengracht 112
➡ adult/child €6/4
➡ ⊙10am-6pm
➡ ☐13/14/17 Westermarkt

WESTERPARK
PARK

Map p303 (Spaarndammerstraat & Zeehelden-buurt; ⊞3 Haarlemmerplein) The aesthetic around public green space of the Wester-park, which lends the surrounding neigh-bourhood its name, goes from urban plan to reedy wilderness, with marshes and shal-low waterfalls.

MUSEUM HET SCHIP
ARCHITECTURE, MUSEUM

Map p303 (✆418 28 85; www.hetschip.nl; Spaarn-dammerplantsoen 140; admission €7.50; ⊙11am-5pm Tue-Sun; ⊞22 Zaanstraat) Just north of Westerpark over the train tracks, this re-markable 1921-completed housing project is a flagship of the Amsterdam School of ar-chitecture. Designed by Michel de Klerk for railway employees and loosely resembling a ship, the triangular block's rocketlike tower links the wings of the complex. Admission is by guided tour (English available).

✕ EATING

✕ Jordaan

Restaurants here exude the conviviality that is a hallmark of the Jordaan. Many people gravitate to the eateries along Westerstraat, while the Haarlemmer-buurt offers increasingly trendy options. Or simply wander the narrow back streets, where the next hot spot may be opening up. Self-caterers shouldn't miss the neighbourhood's markets (p157).

WINKEL
CAFE €

Map p318 (www.winkel43.nl; Noordermarkt 43; mains €4.50-15.50; ⊙kitchen 7am-10pm Mon, 8am-10pm Tue-Fri, 7am-10pm Sat, 10am-10pm Sun; ⊛; ⊞3/10 Marnixplein) This sprawling, indoor-outdoor space is great for people watching, popular for coffees and small meals, and out-of-the-park for its tall, cakey apple pie. On market days (Monday and Sat-urday) there's almost always a queue out the door.

BOCA'S
CAFE €

Map p318 (✆820 37 27; www.bar-bocas.nl; West-erstraat 30; bar snacks €4-7, platters small/medium/large €14/22/30; ⊙10am-1am Sun-Thu, 10am-3am Fri & Sat; ⊞3/10 Marnixplein)

Fronted by a red-and-white-striped awning and white-timber facade, this hip little bar is a perfect place for a drink accompanied by bar snacks. Try the mini lasagnes, burg-ers, bruschetta and steak tartare, or bigger platters on wooden boards: cheese platters, vegie platters, seafood platters, meat plat-ters, sweet platters. If you can't decide, go for Boca's combination platter.

MONTE PELMO
ICE CREAM €

Map p318 (http://montepelmo.nl; 2e Anjeliersd-warsstraat 17; ice cream from €1.40; ⊙9am-4pm Mon-Fri, 1-10pm Sat & Sun; ⊞3/10 Marnixplein) Caramel cheesecake, blue Smurf sorbet, Red Bull and After Eight choc-mint are just some of the inventive flavours concocted by this ice-cream maker founded in 1957.

JORDINO
BAKERY, SWEETS €

Map p318 (✆420 32 25; www.jordino.nl; Haarlem-merdijk 25; ice cream from €1.50; ⊙1-7pm Sun & Mon, 10am-7pm Tue-Sat; ⊞18/21/22 Buiten Oranjestraat) It's the best of both worlds: Jordino makes rich chocolates and velvety ice cream and combines the two by scoop-ing the ice cream atop cones dipped in the house's chocolate or caramel. Of its 80 fla-vours, 24 (including fruit-based sorbets) are available at any one time.

À TABLE AMSTERDAM
FRENCH €

Map p320 (www.atableamsterdam.com; Kink-erstraat 10; dishes €4-7.50, Sunday brunch €17; ⊙8.30am-6pm Tue-Fri, 9.30am-6pm Sat, 11am-5pm Sun; ✍ ⊛; ⊞7/10/17 Elandsgracht) Flying the flag for French producers in Amsterdam (literally – look for the tricolour out front), this little cafe/deli minimises the need to hop down to France to pick up groceries such as LU biscuits, chestnut spread, Breton sardines and so on. But it really comes into its own for cheap, delicious lunchtime dish-es such as *tartines* (open-faced sandwiches) and quiches.

FESTINA LENTE
CAFE €

Map p320 (www.cafefestinalente.nl; Looiers-gracht 40b; sandwiches €5-7, small plates €4-8; ⊙kitchen noon-10.30pm Mon & Sun, 10.30am-10.30pm Tue-Sat; ✍; ⊞7/10/17 Elandsgracht) This canal-side neighbourhood hang out is typical Jordaan *gezelligheid* (convivial-ity/cosiness), packed with regulars playing board games, reading poetry and snacking on small-portion Mediterranean dishes and big sandwiches.

WESTERN ISLANDS

In the early 17th century, the wharves and warehouses of the **Western Islands** (Westelijke Eilanden; Map p303; ☒48 Barentszplein), north of the Jordaan, were abuzz with activity. The Golden Age was taking off, the Dutch still dominated the sea trade and money flowed into this old harbour like beer from a barrel. The wealthy Bicker brothers, both mayors of Amsterdam, even built their own Bickerseiland here to cater for their ships.

Few tourists visit here today, partly because the district is shielded from view by the railway line. Yet it's roughly a 10-minute walk (or five-minute bike ride) from Centraal and a wonderful area to explore, with cute drawbridges and handsome old warehouses nestled in quiet lanes. Many addresses have been converted to charming homes and artists' studios. The Prinseneiland (named in honour of the first three Princes of Orange) and Realeneiland (named after the 17th-century merchant Reynier Reael) are the two prettiest isles. The narrow bridge linking them, the **Drieharingenbrug** (Three Herrings Bridge; Map p303; Realengracht; ☒48 Barentszplein), is a quaint replacement for the pontoon that used to be pulled aside to let ships through.

On Realeneiland's eastern shore, be sure to visit the **Zandhoek** (Map p303; Realeneiland; ☒48 Barentszplein), a photogenic stretch of waterfront. It's now a modern yacht harbour, but back in the 17th century it was a 'sand market', where ships would purchase bags of the stuff for ballast. The street south of Zandhoek is the Galgenstraat (Gallows St), which on a clear day afforded a look at the executions in Amsterdam-Noord. In those days it was called entertainment.

The best place to eat and/or drink in the area is Café Restaurant Open (p151), atop an old railway bridge overlooking the IJ and the islands' striking contemporary architecture.

DUENDE
TAPAS €

Map p318 (☒420 66 92; www.cafe-duende.nl; Lindengracht 62; tapas €4-9; ⊙kitchen 5-11pm Mon-Fri, 4-11pm Sat & Sun; ☒; ☒3 Nieuwe Willemsstraat) Fiesty house specialities at this long-running tapas *café* include *picantes mejillones* (mussels in spicy tomato sauce) and *pimientos de piquillo con bacalao* (sweet peppers stuffed with cod). The casual buzz in the evenings is enlivened by sultry flamenco performances on many Saturday nights and lessons during the week.

PAZZI
PIZZA €

Map p320 (☒320 28 00; www.pazzislowfood.nl; Looiersdwarsstraat 4; pizzas €8-15; ⊙5-10pm; ☒7/10/17 Elandsgracht) Seating consists of a single, high banquette and there's one wood-burning oven. But each pizza – dripping with fresh buffalo mozzarella on a perfectly charred crust – is made with serious care. (Which gives you plenty of time to sip a beer and chat with your seatmates.)

RIAZ
SURINAMESE, INDIAN €

Map p320 (www.riaz.nl; Bilderdijkstraat 193; mains €5-14; ⊙1-9pm Mon-Fri, 2-9pm Sun; ☒ ☒; ☒7/17 Bilderdijkstraat) No-frills Riaz cooks up excellent rotis and an addictive, spicy peanut soup, as well as several Indian veggie dishes (the saag, aka spinach, is superb). Note that no alcohol is served and it closes on Saturdays.

BROODJE MOKUM
SANDWICH SHOP €

Map p320 (☒623 19 66; Rozengracht 26; sandwiches from €3; ⊙6.30am-6pm Mon-Fri, 8am-6pm Sat; ☒13/14/17 Westermarkt) This humble, vintage lunch room serves great sandwiches – just point and they'll tell you the price. More so than at most other *broodje* (bread roll) shops, there's room to sit down and spread out on one of the many window-facing seats.

★BALTHAZAR'S KEUKEN
MEDITERRANEAN €€

Map p320 (☒420 21 14; www.balthazarskeuken.nl; Elandsgracht 108; 3-course menu €32.50; ⊙5.30-10.30pm Wed-Sat; ☒7/10/17 Elandsgracht) In a former blacksmith's forge, with a modern-rustic look, this is consistently one of Amsterdam's top-rated restaurants. Don't expect a wide-ranging menu: the philosophy is basically to cook 'whatever we have on hand', which might mean wild sea bass with mushroom risotto or *confit* of rabbit, but it's invariably delectable. Reservations recommended.

SEMHAR
ETHIOPIAN €€

Map p320 (☑638 16 34; www.semhar.nl; Marnix-straat 259-261; mains €15.50-20; ⊙4-10pm Tue-Sun; ☑; ☐10 Bloemgracht) Owner Yohannes gives his customers a warm welcome (as do the heavenly aromas wafting from the kitchen) and is passionate about the quality of his *injera* (slightly sour, spongy pancakes) used to scoop up richly spiced stews and vegetable combos. The most romantic tables are the handful at the back overlooking the canal.

CINEMA PARADISO
ITALIAN €€

Map p318 (☑623 73 44; www.cinemaparadiso. info; Westerstraat 184-186; mains €11.50-18.50; ⊙6-11pm Wed-Sun; ☐3/10 Marnixplein) Action! Located in a former movie theatre, this spirited Italian restaurant pays homage to its cinematic roots with black-and-white movie stills, the visages of iconic directors on the walls and a glitterati clientele. Book a booth or table near the open kitchen and enjoy pastas, pizzas, antipasti and stargazing over cocktails.

RESTAURANT FRAÎCHE
FRENCH €€

Map p318 (☑627 99 32; http://restaurantfraiche. nl; Westerstraat 264; mains €22; ⊙6.30-11.30pm Tue-Sat; ☐3/10 Marnixplein) Cutting-edge French cuisine at this glass-fronted bistro changes seasonally but might include roast turbot and squid with pickled fennel and smoked carrot purée or roast duck breast with butterscotch and foie gras sauce. There are various tasting plates too, plus events such as brunch specials or a popular 'Dam hot wings night'.

XINH
VIETNAMESE €€

Map p320 (☑624 03 08; http://xinh.nl; Elands-gracht 2; mains €15.50-22.50, 3-course menus €28.50-37.50; ⊙5.30-11pm Sun-Thu, to midnight Fri & Sat; ☐7/10/17 Elandsgracht) The menu might be inspired by Vietnamese street food from around the country, such as *goi xoai* (mango salad) and *ca hap gung* (lime-and ginger-steamed fish), but the stream-lined, minimalist surrounds are much more upmarket. The three-course tasting menu includes a combination of three different mains, such as *bo luc lac* ('dancing beef', with garlic and spices).

YAM YAM
ITALIAN €€

(☑681 50 97; www.yamyam.nl; Frederik Hendrik-straat 88-90; mains €8-15.50; ⊙6-10pm Tue-Sat, 5.30pm-10pm Sun; ☐3 Hugo de Grootplein) Ask Amsterdammers to name the city's best pizza and chances are it's this hip, contem-

WORTH A DETOUR

WESTERN DOCKLANDS

Just north of the Western Islands, Amsterdam's Western Docklands are home to two utterly unique restaurants.

Towering 22m above the IJ, a vivid red, oil rig–like structure built in the 1960s as a pirate radio and TV broadcaster now houses **REM Eiland** (☑688 55 01; www.remei-land.com; Haparandadam 45; lunch mains €7.50-13.50, dinner mains €19, 3-/4-course menu €31/37; ⊙kitchen noon-4pm & 6-10pm; ☐48 Oostzaanstraat), with a 360-degree pano-rama over the industrial docklands and passing river traffic. Reached by steep metal staircases (or a lift/elevator), the dining rooms open onto wraparound platforms; the rooftop helipad has an outdoor bar. Bar snacks are served between casual lunches and evening mains such as baked wolffish with fregola, asparagus, roasted tomato and chimichurri, or gnocci with peas, artichoke and a *caciocavallo* beignet. Reserva-tions recommended, especially for window and platform tables.

Amazing views *of* REM Eiland extend across the pier from the sunny decks at either end of **Pont 13** (☑770 27 22; www.pont13.nl; Haparandadam 50 ; lunch mains €7.50-15, dinner mains €15; ⊙noon-10pm; ☎; ☐48 Oostzaanstraat). A vintage 1927 ex-car and passenger ferry, which once plied the IJ, now serves sublime Mediterranean fare such as seafood antipasti platters and mains such as rotolo stuffed with turnip, ricot-ta and sago, or smoked steak with girolles and garlic sauce from the open kitchen in its cavernous interior.

Both restaurants are a 10-minute walk from the Oostzaanstraat bus stop: from Spaarndammerdijk, turn north onto Archangelweg, then east on Haparandaweg and east again on to Haparandadam and follow it to the end. Alternatively, take a taxi from Centraal (around €10 to €15), or hop on a bike (15 minutes).

porary trattoria. The wood-fired oven turns out thin-crust pizzas such as salami and fennel seed, and the signature Yam Yam (organic smoked ham, mascarpone and truffle sauce). There are mouthwatering pastas and fish- and meat-based mains. Creative desserts include orange-caramel *panna cotta* with balsamic and strawberries. Reservations recommended.

MOEDERS
TRADITIONAL DUTCH €€

Map p320 (📞626 79 57; www.moeders.com; Rozengracht 251; mains €15-19.50, 3-course menus €26-30; ⊙5pm-midnight Mon-Fri, noon-midnight Sat & Sun; 🖬; 🚊10/13/14/17 Marnixstraat) Mum's the word at 'Mothers'. When this welcoming place opened in 1990 customers were asked to bring their own plates and photos of their mums as donations and the decor remains a delightful hotchpotch. So does the food, from pumpkin *stamppot* (potatoes mashed with another vegetable) to seafood and Moroccan dishes. Book ahead.

LA OLIVA
BASQUE €€

Map p318 (📞520 43 16; www.laoliva.nl; Egelantiersstraat 122-124; tapas €9-20, mains €22.50-25.50; ⊙noon-10pm; 🚊3/10 Marnixplein) Yes, there are perfectly lovely meat and fish mains here, but it's the *pintxos* (tapas from southwestern France/northwestern Spain's Basque region), skewered with wooden sticks and stacked on the gleaming bar, that everyone's raving about. Order some *cava* (Spanish sparkling wine) and deliberate over stuffed figs, mushroom Manchego tartlets and *Pata Negra* ham with pear. In summer the party spills out into the street.

JAPANESE PANCAKE WORLD
JAPANESE €€

Map p318 (📞320 44 47; www.japanesepancakeworld.com; 2e Egelantiersdwarsstraat 24a; mains €8-20; ⊙5-10pm Tue-Fri, noon-10pm Sat & Sun; 🚊3/10 Marnixplein) At the continent's only shop specialising in *okonomiyaki* (cook as you like), your pancakes come in a hot iron dish with your choice of fillings (meat, seafood, vegies, cheese) topped with flakes of dried fish. There are barely two dozen seats: book ahead to perch at the counter and watch the chef work his magic.

HOSTARIA
ITALIAN €€

Map p318 (📞626 00 28; 2e Egelantiersdwarsstraat 9; mains €13.50-21; ⊙6-10pm Tue-Sun; 🖉; 🚊3/10 Marnixplein) In a neighbourhood bursting with excellent Italian food, Hostaria holds its own, serving

fresh pastas, filling mains and sublime yet simple desserts, accompanied by decently priced wines. Tightly packed tables make it tricky to move about but add to the cosy, convivial atmosphere.

TOSCANINI
ITALIAN €€

Map p318 (📞623 28 13; http://restauranttoscanini.nl; Lindengracht 75; mains €15-19, 6-course menu €47.50; ⊙6-10.30pm Mon-Sat; 🖬; 🚊3 Nieuwe Willemsstraat) Classy Toscanini bakes its own bread, rolls its own pasta and pours Italian wines. The weekly changing dishes that grace the white tablecloths might include seared beef with tarragon or lamb shoulder stewed with white wine and rosemary. Desserts such as salted caramel *panna cotta* promise to weaken even the fiercest dietary resolves. Book ahead, even on weeknights.

MANZANO
SPANISH €€

Map p320 (📞624 57 52; www.manzano.nl; Rozengracht 106; tapas €2.50-10, mains €10.50-19.50; ⊙5-11pm Mon-Thu, noon-11pm Fri-Sun) The Dutch Golden Age remains palpable in this historic restaurant – never mind that the cuisine is Spanish. In a wood-beamed, enchanting 1648 building (once the private club for Bols employees who worked across the street), well-dressed folks sip on *vinos blancos* (white wine) while nibbling on paella and a wide selection of tapas and regional specialities.

Take your Catalan crème and Spanish coffee in the charming side courtyard after dinner.

BRASSERIE BLAZER
FRENCH €€

Map p320 (📞620 96 90; www.brasserieblazer.nl; Lijnbaansgracht 190; mains €14.50-23.50; ⊙kitchen 11am-6pm Mon & Tue, 10am-10pm Wed, Sat & Sun, 11am-10pm Thu, noon-10pm Fri; 🚊7/10/17 Elandsgracht) Inside the Antiekcentrum Amsterdam (p156) and opening out onto a narrow canal, Amsterdam's simplest French brasserie is also its most effortlessly sexy, with well-priced classic dishes – *confit de canard* (preserved duck), rib eye Béarnaise, et al.

BURGER'S PATIO
MEDITERRANEAN €€

Map p318 (📞623 68 54; www.burgerspatio.nl; 2e Tuindwarsstraat 12; mains €15.50-22.50; ⊙6-11pm; 🚊3/10 Marnixplein) Not a hamburger joint, but an easy-going Mediterranean restaurant with a modern interior and namesake patio. A seasonally changing menu features free-range meats and poultry, creative vegie dishes such as sweet potato pie with felafel and beetroot, and date and hazelnut crumble. Accompaniments such as crudités, aioli and tapenade make the prices seem more reasonable than they already are.

DE PRINS
CAFE €€

Map p318 (☑624 93 82; www.deprins.nl; Prinsengracht 124; mains €11.50-17.50; ⊙kitchen 10am-10pm; 🚊13/14/17 Westerkerk) On a picturesque stretch of the Prinsengracht , this brown *café* is a wonderful spot for a drink on the canal-side terrace or in the cosy bar. But these days it's best known for its excellent kitchen. Lunch specialities include prawn or meat *bitterballen* (croquettes), while the pick of the dinner menu is a divine four-cheese fondue.

DE REIGER
CONTEMPORARY DUTCH €€

Map p318 (☑624 74 26; www.dereigeramsterdam.nl; Nieuwe Leliestraat 34; mains €18.50-22.50; ⊙5-10:30pm, closed Mon; 🚊13/14/17 Westermarkt) Assiduously local and very atmospheric, this corner cafe has a quiet front bar and a noisy, more spacious dining section at the back serving a short but stunning menu (venison and stewed pear with honey cinnamon sauce, for instance). No reservations or credit cards.

KOEVOET
ITALIAN €€

Map p318 (☑624 08 46; Lindenstraat 17; mains €12-26; ⊙5.30-10.15pm Tue-Sun; 🖉; 🚊3 Nieuwe Willemsstraat) The congenial Italian owners of Koevoet took over a former cafe on a quiet side street, left the *gezellig* decor untouched and started cooking up their home-country staples such as handmade ravioli. Don't miss its signature, drinkable dessert, *sgroppino limone*: sorbet, vodka and prosecco whisked at your table and poured into a champagne flute.

BORDEWIJK
FRENCH, ITALIAN €€€

Map p318 (☑624 38 99; www.bordewijk.nl; Noordermarkt 7; mains €24-29, 3-/4-/5-course menus €39/49/59; ⊙6.30-10.30pm Tue-Sat; 🚊18/21/22 Buiten Oranjestraat) The interior at Bordewijk is so minimal that there's little to do but appreciate the spectacular French/Italian cooking. The chefs aren't afraid to take risks, resulting in dishes such as suckling pig with sausage in puff pastry, quail with foie gras or sea-salt-roasted ribs. Book ahead on weekends.

✕ The West

Those looking for nouveau, scenester eats will strike it rich in the West. For amazing fare in an even more amazing setting, head to the Western Docklands.

WORST WIJNCAFE
TAPAS, BAR €

Map p303 (☑625 61 67; http://deworst.nl; Barentszstraat 171; tapas €8-15, brunch mains €10; ⊙4pm-midnight Tue-Sat, 10am-5pm Sun; 🚊48 Barentszplein) Named for its sausage-skewed tapas dishes (veal tongue white sausage, chorizo, lobster sausage with spinach and asparagus), this chequerboard-tiled wine bar is the more casual sibling of esteemed restaurant Marius (p151) next door. Other dishes include pigs' trotters. There's a fantastic range of mostly French wines by the glass. Sunday brunch is a local event.

DE BAKKERSWINKEL
CAFE €

Map p303 (☑688 06 32; www.debakkerswinkel.nl; Polonceaukade 1, Westergasfabriek; dishes €5-10; ⊙9am-5pm Mon-Fri, 10am-6pm Sat & Sun; 🚊10 Van Limburg Stirumstraat) The wonderful 'Bakery' has seven branches throughout the city and country, but this one is uniquely situated by the drawbridge in the old regulator's house at the former gasworks, with mezzanine seating, comfy sofas and a great terrace. Quiches, fish terrines, soups and sourdough sandwiches are all good choices, and the carrot cake is unmissable.

LOCAL KNOWLEDGE

DROP THE LIQUORICE

The Dutch love their lollies, the most famous of which is *drop*, the word for all varieties of liquorice. It may be gummy-soft or tough as leather, shaped like coins or miniature cars, but the most important distinction is between *zoete* (sweet) and *zoute* (salty, also called *salmiak*). The latter is often an alarming surprise, even for avowed fans of the black stuff. But with such a range of textures and additional flavours – mint, honey, laurel – even liquorice sceptics might be converted. Het Oud-Hollandsch Snoepwinkeltje (p156) is a good place to do a taste test.

★**CAFÉ RESTAURANT OPEN** INTERNATIONAL €€
Map p303 (☑620 10 10; www.open.nl; Westerdoksplein 20-Brug; mains €18-19, 7-course tasting menu €45; ⊘kitchen noon-3.30pm & 6-10pm
Mon-Fri, 6-10pm Sat; ☑48 Westerdoksdijk) In-
geniously built on top of a disused 1920s
railway bridge (swung open), this glass box
has an outdoor terrace over the water and
a funky interior with pivoting windows,
lime-green seating, lounge music and an
open kitchen where chefs create stunning
dishes such as pea and feta ravioli or beef
with red lentil purée.

Bar snacks such as *bitterballen* or figs
stuffed with fresh cheese and *dukkah* (African spices) are served between meal times.
A lift/elevator provides wheelchair access.

RESTAURANT PS INTERNATIONAL €€
Map p303 (☑421 52 18; www.restaurantps.nl;
Planciusstraat 49; 1-/2-/3-/4-/5-course menu
€17.50/24.50/29.50/34.50/39.50; ⊘6pm-mid-
night Tue-Sat; ☑3 Zoutkeetsgracht) Run by an
unlikely yet vastly experienced pair – an
English chef and a Colombian maître d' –
this restaurant in the Western Islands has
an army of devoted fans. You can expect
reasonable prices, an excellent wine menu
and attentive service plus an artsy interior
with mosaics of Venetian glass. The set
menus change weekly and feature seasonal
ingredients.

RAÏNARAÏ ALGERIAN €€
Map p303 (☑486 71 09; www.rainarai.nl;
Polonceaukade 40, Westergasfabriek; mains
€14.50-19.50, 3-course menu €38.50; ⊘6-
11pm Tue-Sun, lunch by reservation; ☑21 Van
Hallstraat) This Algerian restaurant, in an
old industrial building in the Westergasfabriek, is decked out with Arabian-style
cushions and copper fixtures. The menu
changes constantly but might offer seared
salmon on chickpea-pumpkin-spiced couscous or grilled sardines with asparagus,
broad beans and tomatoes.

TOKO MC CARIBBEAN €€
Map p303 (☑475 04 25; www.tokomc.nl;
Polonceaukade 5, Westergasfabriek; mains €17-
20; ⊘5pm-1am Tue & Wed, noon-1am Thu,
noon-3am Fri & Sat, noon-1am Sun; ☑10 Van Limburg-
Stirumstraat) Toko MC is many things. It's a
'Caribbean soul food' restaurant, serving
dishes such as crab and mango salad. It's
a vibrant bar – with coconut-wood floors,
bright-hued walls and paper lanterns – that
pours cane-sugar cocktails. It's a late-night

club, where DJs spin world music. And it's
attached to the MC Theatre, which hosts
multicultural performances.

★**MARIUS** INTERNATIONAL €€€
Map p303 (☑422 78 80; http://deworst.nl; Barentszstraat 173; 4-course menu €47.50; ⊘6.30-
10pm Tue-Sat; ☑48 Barentszplein) Foodies
swoon over pocket-sized Marius, tucked in
amid artists studios in the Western Islands.
Chef Kees Elfring shops at local markets,
then creates his daily four-course, no-choice
menu from what he finds. The result might
be grilled prawns with fava bean purée or
beef rib with polenta and ratatouille. Marius also runs the fabulous wine/tapas bar
Worst Wijncafe (p150) next door.

🍷 DRINKING & NIGHTLIFE

🍷 Jordaan

**Anyone who seeks an authentic *café*
experience 'with the locals' will love the
Jordaan.**

★**'T SMALLE** BROWN CAFÉ
Map p318 (www.t-smalle.nl; Egelantiersgracht 12;
⊘10am-1am Sun-Thu, to 2am Fri & Sat; ☑13/14/17
Westermarkt) Dating back to 1786 as a *jenever* (Dutch gin) distillery and tasting house,
and restored during the 1970s with antique
porcelain beer pumps and lead-framed
windows, locals' favourite 't Smalle is one of
Amsterdam's charming *bruin cafés* (bars).
Dock your boat right by the pretty stone
terrace, which is wonderfully convivial by
day and impossibly romantic at night.

It's so gorgeous, so authentic and so
Dutch *gezellig* that there's a reproduction
of it in Japan.

PROUST BAR, CAFÉ
Map p318 (☑623 91 45; www.proust.nl; Noordermarkt 4; ⊘9am-1am Mon, 5pm-1am Tue-Thu,
noon-3am Fri, 9.30am-3am Sat, 11am-1am Sun;
☑3 Nieuwe Willemsstraat) Next door to Finch
(p152) – their terraces effectively merge into
one – this stylish bar is dominated by an
amazing chandelier in the shape of a giant
revolver that was created by Dutch designer
Hans van Bentum. There's a classy menu
and scrumptious hot chocolate.

FINCH
BAR, CAFÉ

Map p318 (☑626 24 61; Noordermarkt 5; ⊙9am-
1am Sun-Thu, 9am-3am Fri & Sat; ◻3 Nieuwe Willemsstraat) This funkalicious bar with its
retro decor (deliberately mismatched yet
somehow harmonious) is just the spot to
hang out and knock back a few beers after
a visit to the market. It attracts an arty-
designy clientele and is always packed on
the weekends.

DE PIEPER
BROWN CAFÉ

Map p320 (Prinsengracht 424; ⊙11am-1am Sun-
Thu, to 3am Fri & Sat; ◻7/10 Raamplein) Small,
unassuming and unmistakably old (1665), De
Pieper features stained-glass windows, fresh
sand on the floors, antique delft beer mugs
hanging from the bar and a working Belgian
beer pump (1875). Sip a Wieckse Witte as
you marvel at the claustrophobia of the low-
ceilinged bar (after all, people were shorter
back in the 17th century – even the famously
tall Dutch).

CAFÉ P 96
BROWN CAFÉ

Map p318 (www.p96.nl; Prinsengracht 96;
⊙10am-3am Sun-Thu, to 4am Fri & Sat; ☎;
◻13/14/17 Westermarkt) If you don't want the
night to end, P 96 is an amiable hangout.
When most other *cafés* in the Jordaan shut
down for the night, this is where everyone
ends up, rehashing their evening and striking up conversations with strangers. In
summertime head to the terrace across the
road aboard a houseboat.

DE TWEE ZWAANTJES
BROWN CAFÉ

Map p318 (☑625 27 29; www.detweezwaantjes.
nl; Prinsengracht 114; ⊙3pm-1am Sun-Thu, to 3am
Fri & Sat; ◻13/14/17 Westermarkt) The small,
authentic 'Two Swans' is at its hilarious
best on weekend nights, when you can join
locals and visitors belting out classics and
traditional Dutch tunes in a rollicking, un-
forgettable cabaret-meets-karaoke evening.
Everyone from the piano player to the patrons sing with ebullient relish, so don't be
afraid to join in.

The fact that singers are often fuelled
by liquid courage only adds to the spirited
fun.

CAFÉ DE KOE
BAR

Map p320 (www.cafedekoe.nl; Marnixstraat 381;
⊙4pm-1am Sun-Thu, to 3am Fri & Sat; ◻7/10
Raamplein) 'The Cow' is loved for its homey
gezellig atmosphere, with board games,
fun pop quizzes, darts tournaments, movie

DRINK LIKE A JORDAANIAN

There's a certain hard-drinking, hard-
living spirit left over from the Jordaan's working-class days when the
neigbourhood burst with 80,000 residents (compared to today's 20,000)
and *bruin cafés* (bars) functioned as
a refuge from the slings and arrows of
workaday life.

Local bastions that are still going
strong include the following:

➜ **De Reiger** (p150)
➜ **Café 't Monumentje** (p152)
➜ **Café de Jordaan** (p153)

---

nights and free gigs by local rock bands. A
down-to-earth neighbourhood crowd swills
beers upstairs by the funky cow mosaic,
while diners below gather around worn
wooden tables and order good, inexpensive
comfort food.

CAFÉ 'T MONUMENTJE
BROWN CAFÉ

Map p318 (☑624 35 41; Westerstraat 120;
⊙8.30am-1am Mon-Thu, 8.30am-3am Fri & Sat,
11am-1am Sun; ◻3/10 Marnixplein) This slightly
scruffy yet loveable *café* with sand on the
floor is always heaving with local barflies.
It's a good spot for a beer and a snack after
shopping at the Westermarkt (p157).

DE TUIN
BROWN CAFÉ

Map p318 (☑624 45 59; 2e Tuindwarsstraat 13;
⊙10am-1am Sun-Thu, to 3am Fri & Sat; ☎; ◻3/10
Marnixplein) Always a good place to start the
evening – join the youngish clientele enjoying the wide selection of Belgian beers
(many on tap), good food and funky soul
music. The small terrace has tables made
from *amsterdammertjes* (Amsterdam's
classic burgundy-brown traffic bollards
that separate the pavement from the street).

HET PAPENEILAND
BROWN CAFÉ

Map p318 (www.papeneiland.nl; Prinsengracht
2; ⊙10am-1am Sun-Thu, to 3am Fri & Sat; ◻3
Nieuwe Willemsstraat) You won't be the only
traveller at this *café* (even Bill Clinton
dropped by a couple of years ago), but that
doesn't make it any less worthwhile. It's a
1642 gem with Delft-blue tiles and a central stove. The name, 'Papists' Island', goes
back to the Reformation, when there was a

clandestine Catholic church on the canal's northern side.

Het Papeneiland was reached via a secret tunnel from the top of the stairs – ask the bar staff to show you the entrance.

CAFÉ DE LAURIERBOOM   CHESS PUB
Map p320 (www.laurierboom.nl; Laurierstraat 76; ⊗3pm-1am Sun-Thu, to 3am Fri & Sun; 🛜; 🚊13/14/17 Marnixstraat) The hub of the Jordaan chess circuit is one of its oldest *cafés*, still bearing a stone tablet labelled *tapperij en slijterij* (ask the bartender to explain what this is). Local masters test their wits over a drink; you can also play chess online here or play card or board games.

VESPER BAR   COCKTAIL BAR
Map p318 (☑420 45 92; www.vesperbar.nl; Vinkenstraat 57; ⊗8pm-1am Tue-Thu, 5pm-3am Fri & Sat; 🚊18/21/22 Buiten Oranjestraat) This luxe cocktail bar gains a certain ineffable mystique by its location on a low-key stretch of Jordaanian shops and businesses. Their martinis will coax out your inner James Bond – or Vesper Lynd (the Bond girl from *Casino Royale*).

If you're feeling adventurous, try the Wasabi Fizz: sake, ginger liqueur and homemade wasabi syrup with fresh lemon juice.

CAFÉ THIJSSEN   BAR, CAFÉ
Map p318 (☑623 89 94; www.cafethijssen.nl; Brouwersgracht 107; ⊗8am-1am Mon-Thu, 8am-3am Fri, 7.30am-3am Sat, 9am-1am Sun; 🚊3 Nieuwe Willemsstraat) The glowing umber (natural brown clay pigment), art deco–inspired interior with stained-glass windows and big tables is a crowd-puller. It's busy on weekends with groups of neo-Jordaanese young professionals meeting up for a late brunch and staying on until dinner.

LA TERTULIA   COFFEESHOP
Map p320 (☑623 85 03; Prinsengracht 312; ⊗11am-7pm Tue-Sat; 🚊7/10/17 Elandsgracht) A backpackers' favourite, this mother-and-daughter-run coffeeshop has a greenhouse feel. You can sit outside by the Van Gogh–inspired murals, play some board games or contemplate the Jurassic-sized crystals by the counter.

DE TRUT   LESBIAN CLUB
Map p320 (☑612 35 24; www.trutfonds.nl; Bilderdijkstraat 165e; ⊗11pm-4am Sun; 🚊7/17 Bilderdijkstraat) In the basement of a former squat, this Sunday-night club is a lesbian

institution (gay men also welcome). Its name means 'the tart' and it comes with an attitude; arrive well before 11pm (the space only fits 220 people).

GESPOT   DESIGNER BAR
Map p320 (www.restaurant-gespot.nl; Prinsengracht 422; ⊗11am-midnight; 🚊7/10 Raamplein) This contemporary spot has an impressive Italian restaurant upstairs and a bright light-filled bar downstairs serving classic cocktails and Italian *vino* by the glass. The waterside terrace has gorgeous views and the stylish interior retains an old canal-house ambience.

CAFÉ DE JORDAAN   BAR
Map p320 (☑627 58 63; Elandsgracht 45; ⊗10am-1am Thu-Sun, to 3am Fri & Sat; 🚊7/10/17 Elandsgracht) The epitome of an old-style Jordaan *café*. After midnight crooners link arms and sing along to classic Dutch tunes; the lyrics playing on the TV screens are a hoot. Earlier in the evening it's less vocal and a more relaxed spot for a *biertje* (glass of beer).

SPIRIT   COFFEESHOP
Map p318 (Westerstraat 121; ⊗noon-1am; 🚊3/10 Marnixplein) Setting this coffeeshop apart from the pack are its half-a-dozen state-of-the-art pinball machines, including Avatar, Metallica and AC/DC. You can also shoot pool here.

DI'VINO WIJNBAR   WINE BAR
Map p318 (www.wijnbardivino.nl; Boomstraat 41a; ⊗6pm-midnight Mon & Tue, 5pm-midnight Wed & Thu, 5pm-2am Fri, 4pm-2am Sat, 4pm-11pm Sun; 🚊3/10 Marnixplein) This wine bar serves only quality Italian wines by the glass and bottle, plus charcuterie and cheese plates. The polished wood bar, flickering candles and lofty corner windows draw you in – though the blankets strewn about the tables and chairs outside are equally inviting.

SAAREIN   GAY, LESBIAN
Map p320 (www.saarein.info; Elandsstraat 119; ⊗4pm-1am Tue-Thu, 4pm-2am Fri, noon-2am Sat, 2pm-1am Sun; 🚊7/10/17 Elandsgracht) Dating from the 1600s, this one-time feminist stronghold is still a meeting place for lesbians, although these days gay men are welcome too. There's a small menu with tapas, soups and specials.

JORDAAN & THE WEST DRINKING & NIGHTLIFE

STRUIK BAR, CAFÉ

Map p320 (☑625 48 63; Rozengracht 160; ☺11am-1am Mon-Thu, 11am-3am Fri & Sat, noon-midnight Sun; ☐10/13/14/17 Marnixstraat) If you prefer your beer with a background of hip hop, breakbeats and soul, come to this graffitied, split-level corner *café*, which does good food (including taco Tuesdays) then segues into drinking and chatting along to an old-school playlist or a DJ on weekends. Hours can vary; cash only.

THERMOS DAY SAUNA GAY SAUNA

Map p320 (☑623 91 58; www.thermos.nl; Raamstraat 33; under 26yr/26yr & over €10/20; ☺noon-8am; ☐7/10 Raamplein) Thermos is a sprawling, popular place for gay men looking to hook up, with porn movies, private (or not so private) darkrooms, a roof deck, a hair salon and a restaurant.

🍺 The West

Off the tourist radar, this up-and-coming area attracts an artsy crowd with its cultural amenities, particularly at the Westergasfabriek (p155) complex.

WESTERGASTERRAS BAR, CLUB

Map p303 (www.westergasterras.nl; Klönneplein 4, Westergasfabriek; ☺11am-1am Sun-Thu, 11am-3am Fri, 10am-3am Sun; ☐10 Van Limburg-Stirumstraat) Next to the 1903 Gasometer (which now hosts cultural events and club nights), this cool, postindustrial, indoor-outdoor *café* is screamingly popular every day of the week. There's a great range of tapas-style dishes; the massive decked outdoor terrace, overlooking reed-filled ponds and a weir, is hotly contested on sunny afternoons.

☆ ENTERTAINMENT

☆ Jordaan

MOVIES CINEMA

Map p318 (☑638 60 16; www.themovies.nl; Haarlemmerdijk 161; ☺restaurant 5.30-10pm; ☐3 Haarlemmerplein) This *gezellig* art-deco cinema (the oldest in Amsterdam, dating from 1912) screens indie films alongside mainstream flicks. From Sunday to Thursday you can treat yourself to a meal in the restaurant (a two- or three-course 'dinner and movie ticket' costs €30/37.50) or have a premovie tipple at its inviting *café*-bar.

CAFE SOUNDGARDEN LIVE MUSIC

Map p320 (www.cafesoundgarden.nl; Marnixstraat 164-166; ☺3pm-1am Mon-Thu, to 3am Fri & Sat; ☐10/13/14/17 Marnixstraat) In this grungy dive bar, the 'Old Masters' are the Ramones and Black Sabbath. Somehow a handful of pool tables, 1980s pinball machines, unkempt DJs and lovably surly bartenders add up to an ineffable magic. Bands occasionally make an appearance and the waterfront terrace scene is more like an impromptu party in someone's backyard.

All walks of life congregate here: the common denominator isn't fashion, age or politics, it's a diehard love of rock and roll.

BOOM CHICAGO COMEDY, CLUB

Map p320 (☑423 01 01; www.boomchicago.nl; Rozengracht 117, Rozentheater; ☺box office 4-8.30pm Wed-Fri, 3-11pm Sat; ☒; ☐13/14/17 Marnixstraat) Recently relocated from Leidseplein – which is still home to the Chicago Social Club (p133) – to the Rozentheater, Boom Chicago stages seriously funny improv-style comedy shows in English, including children's shows.

DE NIEUWE ANITA LIVE MUSIC

(☑06 4150 3512; www.denieuweanita.nl; Frederik Hendrikstraat 111; ☺8am-1am Mon, Tue & Thu, to 2am Fri & Sat; ☐3 Hugo de Grootplein) This living-room venue expanded for noise rockers has a great *café*. Behind the bookcase-concealed door, in the back, the main room has a stage and screens cult movies on Mondays.

MALOE MELO BLUES

Map p320 (☑420 45 92; www.maloemelo.com; Lijnbaansgracht 163; ☺9pm-3am Sun-Thu, to 4am Fri & Sat; ☐7/10/17 Elandsgracht) This is the freewheeling, fun-loving altar of Amsterdam's tiny blues scene. Music ranges from garage and Irish punk to Texas blues and rockabilly.

☆ The West

NORTH SEA JAZZ CLUB JAZZ

Map p303 (☑722 09 81; www.northseajazzclub.com; Pazzanistraat 1, Westergasfabriek; ☺concerts 10pm Thu, 9pm Fri & Sat, café noon-midnight daily; ☐10 Van Limburg Stirumstraat) Respected jazz musicians play at this welcoming venue. Three-course menus are available

WESTERGASFABRIEK

A stone's throw northwest of the Jordaan, the late-19th century Dutch Renaissance **Westergasfabriek** (Map p303; ☎586 07 10; www.westergasfabriek.nl; Haarlemmerweg 8-10; ☐3 Haarlemmerplein) complex and the area adjacent to the Westerpark (p146) were the city's western gasworks until gas production ceased in 1967. The site was heavily polluted and underwent a major clean-up before it re-emerged as a cultural and recreational park, with lush lawns, a long wading pool, cycle-ways and sports facilities.

The postindustrial buildings now house creative spaces including advertising agencies and TV production studios, as well as regular festivals and events.

A quality craft and gourmet food **market** (Map p303; www.sundaymarket.nl; Westergasfabriek; ◷noon-6pm 1st Sun of month, Jul-Sep) occasionally sets up here. Year-round, Westergasfabriek's slew of dining, drinking and entertainment options include the following:

De Bakkerswinkel (p150) Split-level cafe inside the gasworks' former regulator's house.

Raïnaraï (p151) Algerian cuisine amid exotic decor.

Toko MC (p151) Caribbean soul-food restaurant, bar, late-night club and theatre.

Westergasterras (p154) One of the hottest terraces in Amsterdam.

North Sea Jazz Club (p154) Swingin' live jazz.

Het Ketelhuis (p155) Art-house cinema.

Pacific Parc (p155) Indie gigs and DJ sets.

during concerts (€34); the cheapest tickets are standing only. On Wednesdays the *café* hosts regular jam sessions.

JET LOUNGE LIVE MUSIC
Map p303 (www.jetlounge.nl; Groen van Prinstererstraat 41; ☐10 Van Hallstraat) A cool, but not too cool, rock and roll hangout. Performances range from bands to songwriter showcases to open mic nights, as well as local DJs.

HET KETELHUIS CINEMA, CAFE
Map p303 (☎684 00 90; www.ketelhuis.nl; Pazzanistraat 4, Westergasfabriek; ◷cafe 2pm-1am Mon-Thu, 2pm-3am Fri, noon-3am Sat, 10.30am-6pm Sun; ☐10 Van Limburg-Stirumstraat) The three screening rooms at this art-house cinema have a chic postindustrial vibe and comfy seats. There's also a cosy *café*.

PACIFIC PARC LIVE MUSIC
Map p303 (☎488 77 78; www.pacificparc.nl; Polonceaukade 23, Westergasfabriek; ◷11am-1am Mon-Wed, to 3am Thu-Sat, to 11pm Sun; ☐10 Van Limburg Stirumstraat) In a tropical pirateship setting Pacific Parc is home to live music, DJ sets and plenty of rock and roll spirit to go along with the potent drinks and hearty food.

🛍 SHOPPING

Shops here have an artsy, eclectic, homemade feel. The area around Elandsgracht is the place for antiques and art, as well as speciality shops covering everything from hats to cats. Straddling the Jordaan and Western Canal Ring, the Haarlemmerbuurt, incorporating hip Haarlemmerdijk in the northern Jordaan, is teeming with trendy boutiques. The Jordaan also has some fabulous food and flea markets (p157).

⭐**MOOOI GALLERY** DESIGN, HOMEWARES
Map p318 (☎528 77 60; www.moooi.com; Westerstraat 187; ◷10am-6pm Tue-Sat; ☐3/10 Marnixplein) Founded by Marcel Wanders, this is Dutch design at its most over-the-top, from the life-sized black horse lamp to the 'blow away vase' (a whimsical twist on the classic delft vase) and the 'killing of the piggy bank' ceramic pig (with a gold hammer).

DE WINKEL VAN GUUS ACCESSORIES, HOMEWARES
Map p320 (www.dewinkelvanguus.nl; Rozengracht 104; ◷11am-6pm Tue-Fri, to 5pm Sat; ☐10/13/14/17) 🌿 Feel good about buying up at this light, bright concept store, which purely stocks eco-friendly products, such

as lighting, furniture made from salvaged materials, Swiss Freitag bags made from recycled truck tarpaulins, car seatbelts and bicycle inner tubes. You'll also find designer jewellery, kitchenware, plant pots, cute kids' toys and more.

HET OUD-HOLLANDSCH SNOEPWINKELTJE · FOOD, DRINK

Map p318 (📞420 73 90; www.snoepwinkeltje. com; Egelantiersdwarsstraat 2; ⊘11am-5pm Tue-Sat; 📵3/10 Marnixplein) This corner shop is lined with jar after apothecary jar of Dutch penny sweets with flavours from chocolate to coffee, all manner of fruit and the salty Dutch liquorice known as *drop*. It also stocks diabetic-friendly sweets.

ANTIEKCENTRUM AMSTERDAM · ANTIQUES

Map p320 (Amsterdam Antique Centre; www. antiekcentrumamsterdam.nl; Elandsgracht 109; ⊘11am-6pm Mon & Wed-Fri, to 5pm Sat & Sun; 📵7/10/17 Elandsgracht) Anyone with an affinity for odd antiques and bric-a-brac may enter this knick-knack mini-mall and never come out. Spanning 1750 sq m, there are 72 stalls, plus a handful of larger shops, displays and a private dealers' table market on Wednesday, Saturday and Sunday; you're just as likely to find 1940s silk dresses as you are 1970s Swedish porn.

Its cafe, Brasserie Blazer (p149), has bohemian street cred.

SPRMRKT · CLOTHING, DESIGN

Map p320 (📞330 56 01; www.sprmrkt.nl; Rozengracht 191-193; ⊘noon-6pm Mon, 10am-6pm Tue, Wed, Fri & Sat, 10am-8pm Thu,1-6pm Sun; 📵13/14/17 Marnixstraat) Whether you want a supertight pair of Acne jeans, a vintage Thor Larson Pod chair or the latest copy of *Butt* magazine, it's all here at this lofty industrial concept store, a major player in Amsterdam's fashion scene.

RAW MATERIALS · HOMEWARES

Map p320 (www.rawmaterials.nl; Rozengracht 229-233; ⊘noon-6pm Mon, 10am-6pm Tue, Wed, Fri & Sat, 10am-7pm Thu; 📵13/14/17 Marnixstraat) As its name suggests, Raw Materials stocks cool vintage furniture, steel cabinets and pieces made from reclaimed wood as well as a great array of fabrics, soft furnishings, ceramics and glassware that capture the spirit of Dutch design.

TENUE DE NÎMES · CLOTHING

Map p320 (www.tenuedenimes.com; Elandsgracht 60; ⊘noon-6pm Sun & Mon, 10am-6pm Tue, Wed, Fri & Sat, 10am-9pm Thu; 📵7/10 Elandsgracht) The Jordaan branch of the cool Western Canal Ring (p115) denim specialist.

ROCK ARCHIVE · ART

Map p318 (📞423 04 89; www.rockarchive.com; Prinsengracht 110; ⊘2pm-6pm Wed-Fri, noon-6pm Sat & by appointment; 📵13/14/17 Westermarkt) Limited-edition rock 'n' roll prints of Robert Plant, Debbie Harry, Sting and tons of others are all sold here for small change, in a format of your choice.

MECHANISCH SPEELGOED · TOYS

Map p318 (📞638 16 80; Westerstraat 67; ⊘10am-6pm Mon-Fri, 10am-5pm Sat; 📵3/10 Marnixplein) This adorable shop is crammed full of nostalgic toys, including snow domes, glow lamps, masks, finger puppets and wind-up toys. And who doesn't need a good rubber chicken every once in a while? Hours can vary.

KITSCH KITCHEN · HOMEWARES

Map p320 (📞622 82 61; www.kitschkitchen.nl; Rozengracht 8-12; ⊘10am-6pm Mon-Sat, noon-5pm Sun; 📵13/14/17 Westermarkt) You want it flowered, frilly, colourful, over-the-top or just made from plastic? The chances are you'll find it here – Kitsch Kitchen stocks homewares including Mexican tablecloths, pink plastic chandeliers from India, lamps, along with handbags, toys, dolls' dresses, and of course, bouquets of plastic flowers.

BOUTIQUE PETTICOAT · CLOTHING

Map p318 (Lindengracht 99; ⊘noon-3pm Mon, noon-5pm Wed & Thu, 11am-5pm Sat; 📵3 Nieuwe Willemsstraat) This is the pick of the Jordaan's vintage and secondhand shops, with a posh yet affordable collection of men's and women's fashions.

PERFUMES OF THE PAST · PERFUME

Map p318 (📞679 00 52; Binnen Oranjestraat 11; ⊘2-5pm Tue-Sat; 📵18/21/22 Buiten Oranjestraat) At this Aladdin's cave of hard-to-find fragrances from years gone by, owner Leo can help you identify long-lost scents. The retro bottles are a sight in themselves. If you're looking for a perfume that you or someone you know used to wear, chances are you'll find it here and be transported back in time.

LOCAL KNOWLEDGE

JORDAAN MARKETS

A market square since the early 1600s, the **Noordermarkt** (Northern Market; Map p318; www.jordaanmarkten.nl; Noordermarkt; ⊘flea market 9am-1pm Mon, farmers market 9am-4pm Sat; ⊠3/10 Marnixplein) plaza in front of the Noorderkerk hosts a couple of lively markets each week. Monday morning's **flea market** has some amazing bargains; Saturday mornings see local shoppers flock to the lush **boerenmarkt** (farmers market), overflowing with organic produce. There's a great selection of cafes surrounding the square, including Winkel (p146) on the southwest corner, home of some of the city's best apple pie.

On Saturdays, the **Lindengracht Market** (Map p318; www.jordaanmarkten.nl; Lindengracht; ⊘9am-4pm Sat; ⊠3 Nieuwe Willemsstraat) is a wonderfully authentic, even more local affair, with bountiful fresh produce, including fresh fish and magnificent cheese stalls, as well as gourmet goods, clothing and homewares. Arrive as early as possible for the best pickings and smallest crowds.

Bargain-priced clothing and fabrics are sold at 163 stalls at the **Westermarkt** (Map p318; www.jordaanmarkten.nl; Westerstraat; ⊘9am-1pm Mon; ⊠3/10 Marnixplein) (which isn't in fact on Westermarkt but on on Westerstraat, just near the Noordermarkt).

ENGLISH BOOKSHOP   BOOKS

Map p320 (www.englishbookshop.nl; Lauriergracht 71; ⊘11am-6pm Tue-Sat; 🛜🐾; ⊠7/10/17 Elandsgracht) Biblio-heaven. This cosy canal-side shop has a well-chosen selection of English-language biographies, novels and translations of the works of Dutch writers. Its in-store cafe serves British cream teas; the shop also organises literary and cultural walking tours, scrabble games, writers' workshops, literary quiz nights and a book club, plus story readings for one to three year olds.

A SPACE ODDITY   TOYS, BOOKS

Map p320 (www.spaceoddity.nl; Prinsengracht 204; ⊘1-5.30pm Mon, 11am-5.30pm Tue-Fri, 10.15am-5pm Sat; ⊠13/14/17 Westermarkt) This geekalicious shop will sate even the most hardcore *Star Wars* fanatic, DC comics collector or Stanley Kubrick obsessionist. Get lost in the memorabilia, action figures, comics, books and loads of other pop-culture ephemera.

CELLARRICH   ACCESSORIES

Map p318 (www.cellarrich.nl; Haarlemmerdijk 98; ⊘1-6pm Tue, 11am-5.30pm Wed, 11am-6pm Thu-Sat; ⊠3 Haarlemmerplein) Accessorise with colourful, creative, leather wallets, bags and gloves as well as jewellery and scarves. There are beautiful leather-bound notebooks too.

JOSINE BOKHOVEN   ART

Map p320 (⌀623 65 98; www.galerie-josinebokhoven.nl; Prinsengracht 154; ⊘1-6pm Tue-Sat & 1st Sun of every month; ⊠13/14/17 Westermarkt) The work of emerging young contemporary artists features alongside specialised exhibitions such as Welsh print making at this friendly canal-side gallery. Hours can vary.

BROWN CLOTHES   CLOTHING

Map p320 (⌀06 1444 6089; www.brownclothes.eu; Hazenstraat 28; ⊘noon-6pm Thu & Fri, 12.30-6pm Sat; ⊠7/10/17 Elandsgracht) Englishwoman Melanie Brown designs women's clothing with elegant lines and whimsical twists, such as feminine flowing tops with gathered sleeves and figure-hugging coats. Her studio is adjacent to the shop, so you may see her stitching as you contemplate the designs.

JEFFERSON HOTEL   CLOTHING

Map p320 (www.jeffersonhotel.nl; Elandsgracht 57; ⊘noon-6pm Mon, 10am-6pm Tue-Sat, 1-5pm Sun; ⊠7/10/17 Elandsgracht) Not a hotel, although it does resemble a classy lobby, this menswear shop wows with its discerning taste for edgy designers such as Vintage 66 and Girls Love DJs. Can't decide between quality shirts and rare denim? Mull it over while sipping a cappuccino at the in-store espresso bar.

CHOCOLÁTL   FOOD, DRINK

Map p320 (⌀755 50 47; www.chocolatl.nl; Hazenstraat 25a; ⊘11am-6pm Tue-Sat, 1-5pm Sun; ⊠7/10/17 Elandsgracht) Premium chocolate gifts for the serious chocoholic or connoisseur, including drinking chocolate. Ask about guided 'chocolab' tasting sessions.

LAB 13
CLOTHING, ACCESSORIES

Map p318 (Haarlemmerplein 13; ☺1-6pm Mon-Fri, noon-6pm Sat; ⬚3 Haarlemmerplein) Want a shop where soft T-shirts, handmade bags and jewellery, casual cotton blouses, bath products, floral dresses, spiffy retro pieces and Guatemalan worry dolls coexist? If so, Lab 13 is your spot.

NOU MOE STRIPWINKEL
COMICS, GIFTS

Map p318 (☎693 63 45; http://stripwinkelnou-moe.nl; Lindenstraat 1; ☺noon-6pm Mon-Sat; ⬚18/21/22 Buiten Oranjestraat) This tiny corner shop features everything from Asterix to Garfield, Tintin to *24* (yes, that *24*). More importantly it sells the merchandise: soft toys, notebooks, stickers, games, coffee mugs and bedroom slippers.

ARNOLD CORNELIS
FOOD, DRINK

Map p320 (www.cornelis.nl; Elandsgracht 78; ☺8.30am-6pm Mon-Fri, to 5pm Sat; ⬚7/10/17 Elandsgracht) Your dinner hosts will be impressed if you present them with something from this long-standing shop, such as fruitcake, cheesecake, chocolate-stuffed cookies or blue sphere biscuits made with Malaga wine. At lunchtime grab a flaky pastry filled with cheese, meat or vegetables.

'T ZONNETJE
FOOD, DRINK

Map p318 (www.t-zonnetje.nl; Haarlemmerdijk 45; ☺noon-6pm Sun & Mon, 9am-6pm Tue-Fri, 9am-5pm Sat; ⬚18/21/22 Buiten Oranjestraat) This charming place has been a teashop since 1642. You will find a selection teas from all over the world here, as well as coffees and accoutrements.

UKE BOUTIQUE
MUSIC

Map p320 (☎06 2981 4794; www.ukeboutique.nl; Lijnbaansgracht 191; ☺2-6pm Mon, Thu & Fri, noon-5pm Wed, noon-6pm Sat; ⬚7/10/17 Elandsgracht) In fact this shop just sells one musical instrument, the ukulele. All of its stock is quality checked and adjusted, ready for play; prices start from €35. Hours can vary. Ask about uke concerts and lessons.

> ### ON YOUR BIKE IN THE JORDAAN
>
> For bike rentals and bike tours in the Jordaan, contact Bike City (p30).

CATS & THINGS
GIFTS

Map p320 (☎428 30 28; www.catsandthings.nl; Hazenstraat 26; ☺11.30am-6pm Tue-Fri, 11.30am-5pm Sat; ⬚7/10/17 Elandsgracht) If you're a cat lover, or shopping for someone who is, this quirky shop – with its own resident cats – is a must. It stocks every feline-themed gift imaginable (statues, artworks, cat-adorned homewares) and presents for kitty too (baskets, food, collars and climbers).

DISCOSTARS
MUSIC

Map p318 (☎626 11 77; www.discostars-record-store.nl; Haarlemmerdijk 86; ☺1-6pm Sun & Mon, 10am-6pm Tue-Sat; ⬚18/21/22 Buiten Oranjestraat) The disco generation will enjoy this repository of the music of yesteryear. If the names Olivia Newton-John, Engelbert Humperdinck, Paul Young, Celia Cruz, Candy Dulfer, Buddy Holly, Yves Montand, Doris Day or Roy Rogers mean anything to you, you'll find lots more to like.

GALLERIA D'ARTE RINASCIMENTO
ART, ANTIQUES

Map p320 (☎622 75 09; www.delft-art-gallery.com; Prinsengracht 170; ☺9am-6pm; ⬚13/14/17 Westermarkt) This pretty shop sells Royal Delftware ceramics (both antique and new), all manner of vases, platters, brooches, Christmas ornaments and intriguing 19th-century wall tiles and plaques.

CALLAS 43
VINTAGE CLOTHING

Map p318 (☎427 37 90; Haarlemmerdijk 43; ☺noon-6pm Mon-Sat; ⬚18/21/22 Buiten Oranjestraat) Rummage through tightly packed vintage designer garments, creative secondhand finds, good-as-new samples and a large assortment of leather bags (some new, some not) for your next favourite outfit.

Vondelpark & Around

Neighbourhood Top Five

❶ Find your bliss in **Vondelpark** (p161) – laze over coffee, search out sculptures, enjoy a lunchtime picnic and catch an open-air theatre performance, followed by dinner and cocktails. No wonder the locals look so relaxed.

❷ Take a horse-riding lesson at the grand 1882 **Hollandsche Manege** (p162).

❸ Relive the area's hippie history at the entertainment spaces and vegan eateries of its **squats** (p164).

❹ Dream up round-the-world adventures at **Pied à Terre** (p166), Europe's largest travel bookshop.

❺ Admire the stately architecture surrounding Vondelpark on a **walking tour** (p163).

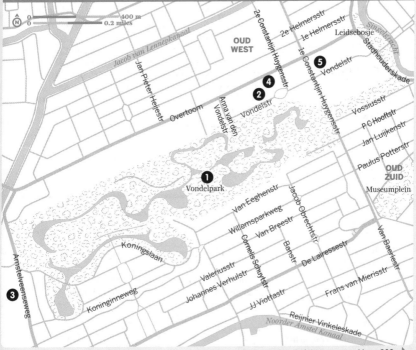

For more detail of this area, see Map p322 ➡

Lonely Planet's Top Tip

If you've worked up an appetite strolling or cycling through the park, you're spoilt for choice for places to dine along and just off Amstelveenseweg. Running along the western edge of the park, it's a fabulous eat street, with restaurants ranging from vegan to Chinese, Japanese, Indonesian, Indian, Thai, pan-Asian, Dutch, Italian, Brazilian, and American-style steaks, interspersed with stylish wine bars and cosy *cafés* (bars, pubs). Wander along and see what you find.

✕ Best Places to Eat

➡ Ron Gastrobar (p162)

➡ Brasserie De Joffers (p162)

➡ Madelief (p165)

➡ Blue Pepper (p165)

➡ Café Toussaint (p164)

For reviews, see p162.➡

🍷 Best Places to Drink

➡ Café Bédier (p166)

➡ Café Schinkelhaven (p166)

➡ Gollem's Proeflokaal (p166)

➡ 't Blauwe Theehuis (p166)

➡ Het Groot Melkhuis (p166)

For reviews, see p166.➡

🛍 Best Places to Shop

➡ Pied à Terre (p166)

➡ Buise (p166)

➡ Friday Next (p167)

➡ Books & Bubbles (p167)

For reviews, see p166.➡

Explore Vondelpark & Around

Though it's big enough to get lost in – at least metaphysically – Vondelpark itself is more epic for its near-pastoral beauty than it is for its actual size. Long and thin (about 1.5km long and 300m wide) the park itself can be easily explored in an afternoon. The easiest entry point is at the top (northeast) of the park. As you walk southwest, the path splits off to the left or right and makes a complete circle in either direction. Bring some bread to feed the ducks in the ponds.

Step out of the park through one of its several exits (you'll easily spot the iron gates) to soak up the gorgeous 19th-century houses of the many moneyed residents.

The streets around Overtoom burst with eateries and shops for all budgets, while shops along leafy Cornelis Schuytstraat are more stylish and exclusive. Come dinner time, you'll find the densest concentration of dining options on and around Amstelveenseweg at the park's western end.

Local Life

➡**Cycling Life** If you need a crash course in the art of Dutch biking away from the traffic-filled streets, Vondelpark is the perfect place to practise spinning your wheels like a local.

➡**Skating Life** Join local in-line skaters setting off from Vondelpark for a two-hour mass skate (p167) every Friday night.

➡**Shopping Life** Fashionable locals frequent the concentration of one-off boutiques such as Buise (p166) and chic retail outlets like French Connection a couple of blocks south of the park on Cornelis Schuytstraat, particularly around the intersection of Willemsparkweg.

➡**Bunker Life** Buried inside the 1e Constantjin Huygensstraat bridge (you could take the tram straight over it or walk right beneath it and never know it was here), the Vondelbunker (p164) hosts underground entertainment and activist activities.

Getting There & Away

➡**Tram** Trams 1, 2 and 5 stop near the main entrance of the park, on Hobbemastraat near Leidseplein. Tram 1 continues along Overtoom, while tram 2 travels along the southern side of the park along Willemsparkweg. Trams 3 and 12 cross the 1e Constantjin Huygensstraat bridge not far from the park's main entrance.

TOP SIGHT
VONDELPARK

The lush urban idyll of Vondelpark is one of Amsterdam's most magical places. On a sunny day, an open-air party atmosphere ensues when tourists, lovers, cyclists, in-line skaters, pram-pushing parents, cartwheeling children, football-kicking teenagers, spliff-sharing friends and champagne-swilling picnickers all come out to play. And while Vondelpark receives over 10 million visitors per year, it never feels too crowded to enjoy.

Originally known as Nieuwe Park (New Park), these sprawling, English-style gardens, with ponds, lawns, footbridges and winding footpaths, were laid out on marshland by architect Jan David Zocher and opened in 1865. Between 1875 and 1877, Zocher's son, Louis Paul Zocher, expanded the park to its current size of 47 hectares.

In 1867 a **statue** (Map p322) of poet and playwright Joost van den Vondel (1587–1679) was created by sculptor Louis Royer. Amsterdammers began referring to the park as Vondelspark (Vondel's Park), which led to it being renamed. The **rose garden** (Map p322), with some 70 different species, was added in 1936.

About a century after opening, the swampy location meant the park had actually sunk two to three metres. After it was listed as a national monument in the mid-1990s, major renovations incorporated an extensive drainage system and refurbished walking and cycling paths while retaining its historic appearance.

Near the eastern end, the 19th-century Italian Renaissance-style **Vondelparkpaviljoen** (Vondelpark Pavilion; Map p322) housed the EYE Filmmuseum before the museum relocated across the IJ; it's now set to become a media and cultural centre with a cafe in 2014. Plenty of art remains however, with 69 sculptures dotted throughout the park. Among them is Picasso's soaring abstract work **The Fish** (Map p322) (1965), which he donated for the park's centenary. Also here are cafes, playgrounds, and a wonderful Openluchttheater (p166).

Catch the park's highlights on a **walking tour** (p163). For bicycle rentals, MacBike (p135) is relatively close to the park's main entrance.

DON'T MISS

→ The rose garden
→ Picasso's *The Fish*
→ The Openluchttheater

PRACTICALITIES

→ Map p322
→ www.vondelpark.nl
→ 🚊2/5 Hobbemastraat

 SIGHTS & ACTIVITIES

VONDELPARK PARK
See p161.

HOLLANDSCHE MANEGE RIDING SCHOOL
Map p322 (📞618 09 42; www.dehollandsche-manege.nl; Vondelstraat 140; adult/child €6/4, private riding lessons per 30 min/1hr €36/60; ◷10am-5pm; 🚊1 1e Constantijn Huygensstraat) Just outside Vondelpark is the neoclassical Hollandsche Manege, an indoor riding school inspired by the famous Spanish Riding School in Vienna. Designed by AL van Gendt and built in 1882, it retains its charming horse-head facade. Take a riding lesson or watch the instructors put the horses through their paces during high tea (€24) at the elevated cafe.

ORGELPARK CONCERT HALL
Map p322 (📞515 81 11; www.orgelpark.nl; Gerard Brandtstraat 26; tickets €12.50-20; 🚊1 Jan Pieter Heijestraat) Not a park but a renowned stage for organ music, with four big organs in a lovely restored church on the edge of Vondelpark. More than 100 events take place each year, including concerts of classical, jazz and improvised music.

VONDELKERK HISTORIC BUILDING
Map p322 (www.vondelkerk.nl; Vondelstraat 120d; ◷9am-5pm; 🚊1 1e Constantijn Huygensstraat) Architect Pierre Cuypers' favourite church, which he designed and built between 1870 and 1880, suffered from a lack of funds during construction and a fire in 1904. Slated for demolition in 1978, it was saved by a group of architecture enthusiasts. It's a charming steepled church building featuring a fascinating series of shapes with an octagon at its base.

Workers at the offices inside are generally happy to let you in for a peek.

✖ EATING

International options abound around Amstelveenseweg. Head to Vondelpark's squats for organic vegan fare (p164). Picnickers should stock up at Marqt (p167).

MECH MAKE & TAKE SANDWICH SHOP €
(Willemsparkweg 152; dishes €4.50-7; ◷8am-5pm Mon-Fri, 9am-5pm Sat; 🚊2 Cornelis Schuytstraat) Jump-start the day with a French double espresso, croissant and freshly squeezed OJ or stop by for salads and baguettes with fillings such as smoked raw beef sausage with mustard mayo at this hip, red-brick cafe. The long bench out front is a prime spot to watch the action along Willemsparkweg and Cornelis Schuytstraat.

LUNCHROOM WILHELMINA CAFE €
Map p322 (📞618 97 78; www.lunchroomwilhelmina.nl; 1e Helmersstraat 83a; mains €5-9; ◷9am-5pm; 🚊1 1e Constantijn Huygensstraat) Lined with framed pictures of Dutch royalty beneath a chandelier, this corner cafe is ideal for a simple lunch (quiches, soups), brunch or *borrel* (drink).

TOASTY CAFE €
Map p322 (www.toasty.nl; Overtoom 437; toasties €3.50-6.50; ◷8am-5pm Mon-Fri, 9am-5pm Sat & Sun; 🛜; 🚊1 Rhijnvis Feithstraat) Delicious variations on the humble toasted sandwich here include pastrami and mustard, pear and honey, four-cheese, bacon, tomato, cheddar and chicken (it works), and a terrific tuna melt.

★RON GASTROBAR CONTEMPORARY DUTCH €€
Map p322 (📞496 19 43; www.rongastrobar.nl; Sophialaan 55; dishes €15; ◷noon-2.30pm & 5.30-10pm Mon-Fri, 3-10pm Sat, noon-9pm Sun; 🚊2 Amstelveenseweg) Until recently, Ron Blaauw ran his two-Michelin-star restaurant in these stunning designer premises. But he handed in the stars to transform the space into an egalitarian 'gastrobar', serving around 25 tapas-style dishes – Waldorf salad with crispy veal brains, Dutch asparagus and lobster-and-champagne sauce, wagyu burgers – at one flat price (with no restrictions on how few you can order).

The crafting and flavour combinations are still *haute cuisine* standard, and now they're affordable too.

BRASSERIE DE JOFFERS INTERNATIONAL €€
(📞673 03 60; www.brasseriedejoffers.nl; Willemsparkweg 163; mains €19-27; ◷8am-11pm Mon-Sat, 9am-8pm Sun; 🗙; 🚊2 Cornelis Schuytstraat) A timber and curved-glass shopfront, a table-lined terrace and a gorgeous interior with a chocolate-and-caramel-striped velour banquette entice you into this art deco brasserie. But what will keep you coming back through the day is the food, from flaky croissants to a quail egg–topped crayfish stack layered with wasabi-dressed lettuce, salmon and roe, or wild spinach and truffle ravioli.

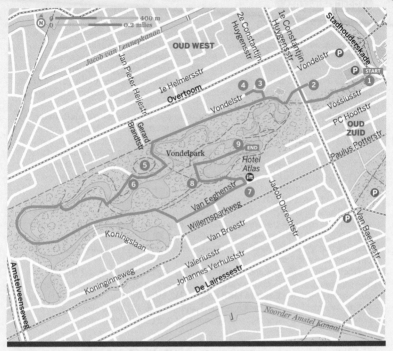

Neighbourhood Walk
Vondelpark

START VONDELPARK MAIN ENTRANCE
END 'T BLAUWE THEEHUIS
LENGTH 4.5KM; 2½ HOURS

While an unstructured stroll through the park is perfectly wonderful, this tour ensures you'll hit the key highlights in and around the park.

Enter the park through the **1 main entrance** and walk straight ahead; climb the stairs on the northern side of the bridge (look closely to spot the Vondelbunker) and exit the park along pretty **2 Roemer Visscherstraat**, where you'll come upon a row of houses built in 1894 in varying styles: English cottage, Dutch Renaissance, onion-domed Russian cathedral, Italian palazzo, Moorish-style Spanish, French Loire Valley chateau, and German Romantic.

Head back into the park, picking up the northwest walking loop path and passing the Vondelparkpaviljoen. Exit the park again on Vondelstraat to check out the lovely former-church-turned-offices **3 Vondelkerk** (p162). Staff generally don't mind if you take a peek at the inspiring interior. Continue west

along Vondelstraat to the magnificent riding school, the **4 Hollandsche Manege** (p162). Return to the park and head west. Take the right fork and go straight to the **5 Joost van den Vondel statue** (p161), which inspired the park's name. Continue southwest along the pond's edge until you reach the beautiful **6 rose garden** (p161).

Cross the footbridge and follow the path to the next footbridge; cross it too and turn west. Follow the path around the pond and head east. Take the second exit to detour down **7 Van Eeghenstraat** to see some of the city's most exquisite art nouveau architecture; the highlight is definitely the ornate Atlas Hotel (at number 64). Re-enter the park just west of Atlas Hotel and follow the western path. Where the path diverges, take the left-hand fork; Picasso's towering circa 6m-high sculpture **The Fish** (p161) is on your right. Return to the fork, walk north and take your right-hand path leading east over a footbridge past the Openluchttheater until you reach the space-agey looking cafe **'t Blauwe Theehuis** (p166).

LOCAL KNOWLEDGE

VONDELPARK SQUATS

Vondelpark and its surrounds have strong links to the cultural revolution, when Amsterdam became the *magisch centrum* (magic centre) of Europe. Hippies flocked to Amsterdam during the 1960s and '70s, a housing shortage saw speculators leaving buildings empty and squatting became widespread. The Dutch authorities turned the park into a temporary open-air dormitory. Although the sleeping bags are long gone today, an indie spirit persists.

Beneath the 1e Constantjin Huygensstraat bridge is the hidden **Vondelbunker** (Map p322; www.vondelbunker.nl; Vondelpark 8a; ⊙hrs vary; 📵1 1e Constantijn Huygensstraat). A fallout shelter dating from 1947, in 1968 it became Amsterdam's first youth centre and a hotbed of counterculture creativity and activism. If the unmarked black metal doors are open you might catch an underground gig, film or 'activist salon'.

Fringing Vondelpark are several **squats** that have gone legit and been turned into alternative cultural centres.

Graffiti-covered **OT301** (Map p322; www.ot301.nl; Overtoom 301; 📵1 Jan Pieter Heijestraat) hosts an eclectic roster of bands, international films, parties, dance workshops and DJs. There are two bars, plus the volunteer-run vegan kitchen **De Peper** (Map p322; ☑412 29 54; www.depeper.org; Overtoom 301; mains €7-10; ⊙7-8.30pm Tue, Thu, Fri & Sun; ☑; 📵1 Jan Pieter Heijestraat). Same-day reservations are required; call between 4pm and 6pm.

Occii (☑671 77 78; www.occii.org; Amstelveenseweg 134; ⊙vary; ☑; 📵2 Amstelveenseweg), in a 19th-century stable, also serves up alternative music and arts, plus vegan fare at the **Eetcafé MKZ** (☑679 07 12; http://binnenpr.home.xs4all.nl/mkz; 1e Schinkelstraat 16; mains from €5; ⊙from 7pm Tue-Fri; ☑; 📵2 Amstelveenseweg) – call between 2.30pm and 6pm to reserve your spot and confirm daily prices.

CAFÉ TOUSSAINT INTERNATIONAL €€

Map p322 (☑685 07 37; www.bosboom-toussaint. nl; Bosboom Toussaintstraat 26; mains €9-19; ⊙kitchen 10am-11pm; ☑; 📵7/10 Raamplein) On one of Amsterdam's prettiest streets, this casual neighbourhood gem feels like it's straight out of an Edith Piaf song. Come to sip cappuccino under the trees, or for creative twists on classics, from Thai beef salad to fish-filled ravioli in lobster sauce, in the candlelit evenings.

SCREAMING BEANS CAFE, RESTAURANT €€

Map p322 (☑616 07 70; www.screamingbeans.nl; 1e Constantijn Huygensstraat 35; 3-/4-/5-course menu €35/40/45, 7-/9-course menu incl wine €100/120; ⊙cafe 8.30am-midnight Tue-Fri, 9am-midnight Sat, 10am-11pm Sun, tasting menus by reservation; 📵1 1e Constantijn Huygensstraat) Screaming Beans' baristas take their coffee seriously (the company even runs its own training academy). But this off-shoot of the original Western Canal Ring branch (p114) is equally renowned for its chef-prepared dishes like salt-crusted Dutch buffalo mozzarella and beetroot with endives, and rabbit with olives, smoked garlic and sweet and sour raisins, accompanied by sommelier-picked wines.

THE SEAFOOD BAR SEAFOOD €€

Map p322 (www.theseafoodbar.nl; Van Baerlestraat 5; mains €13-19.50; ⊙noon-10pm; ☑; 📵2/5 Van Baerlestraat) White-tiled and exposed-brick walls give this seafood specialist a breezy, oceanside feel. Oysters, crabs and sardines are laid out behind glass, and the kitchen turns out freshly cooked fish and chips. No bookings required.

FONDUE & FONDUE FONDUE €€

Map p322 (☑612 91 04; www.restaurantfondue. nl; Overtoom 415; fondue €15.50-17.50; ⊙6pm-1am; 📵1 Rhijnvis Feithstraat) It's stylishly refitted with stripped herringbone floors and exposed brick, reasonably priced, and serves the most heavenly comfort food to ever come out of the Alps. Choose from fish (with tuna, salmon and prawns), meat (veal, steak, chicken and pork) or classic cheese fondue (with six different vegetables), all shared between two people. Desserts include a decadent chocolate fondue.

PASTIS FRENCH €€

Map p322 (☑616 61 66; www.pastisamsterdam. nl; 1e Constantijn Huygensstraat 15; mains €15.50-20; ⊙kitchen 9am-10pm Mon-Fri, 9am-10.30pm Sat, 10am-10pm Sun; 📵1 1e Constantijn Huygensstraat) With its red awning, pavement tables, rustic interior with old French advertising posters, and tomato- and garlic-laced dishes – as well as lavender crème brûlée for dessert – you could conceivably think you'd arrived in Provence (except for the Portuguese and Italian interlopers on the wine list).

PALOMA BLANCA
MOROCCAN €€

Map p322 (☑612 64 85; www.palomablanca.nl; Jan Pieter Heijestraat 145; mains €15-18; ☺6-10pm Tue-Sun; ☒1 Jan Pieter Heijestraat) The name is Spanish, but the lanterns, crockery and mosaic-topped tables are straight out of a Marrakesh souk. Start with a gorgeous *mezze* platter before moving on to savoury mains of couscous and *tajine* (Moroccan stew) dishes featuring an array of meats, vegetables and fish.

LALIBELA
ETHIOPIAN €€

Map p322 (☑683 83 32; www.lalibela.nl; 1e Helmersstraat 249; mains €11-15; ☺5-11pm; ☒☒; ☒1 Jan Pieter Heijestraat) Named after the ancient African city, this colourful restaurant, just north of Overtoom, was the Netherlands' first Ethiopian restaurant, and it's still as good as ever. You can drink Ethiopian beer from a half-gourd, and eat stews, egg and vegetable dishes using *injera* (slightly sour, spongy pancakes) instead of utensils, to a soundtrack of African music.

ALCHEMIST GARDEN
VEGAN €€

Map p322 (☑334 33 35; www.energieregie.nl; Overtoom 409; noon-8pm Tue-Sat; ☺mains €12-15; ☒; ☒1 Rhijnvis Feithstraat) ☑ Proving that gluten-, lactose- and glucose-free food can be delicious, this bright, contemporary space serves a vitamin-filled organic menu (raw vegetable pies, platters, sushi), plus smoothies, juices and guilt-free treats like mango-choc pie.

★BLUE PEPPER
INDONESIAN €€€

Map p322 (☑489 70 39; www.restaurantbluepepper.com; Nassaukade 366; mains €25, set menus €39-70; ☺6-10pm; ☒; ☒7/10 Raamplein) Chef Sonja Pereira elevates Indonesian cuisine to art in her dramatic blue dining room. The exquisite *rijsttafel* (Indonesian banquet) includes specialities from across the islands, such as spicy fish steamed in banana leaves, baby chicken soup with quail eggs, lamb satay with lime and soy sauce, and softshell crab with mango and pineapple.

MADELIEF
FRENCH €€€

Map p322 (☑612 20 00; Zocherstraat 10; mains €26-32; ☺7-10pm Tue-Sat; ☒1 Overtoomsesluis) Tucked away in a Vondelpark backstreet, this tiny charmer with stripped-back floors and walls is a local foodies' secret. Scallops with saffron risotto, veal with truffle madeira sauce and foie gras–stuffed quail are impeccably cooked and served with well-chosen wines. Reservations recommended.

RESTAURANT BLAUW
INDONESIAN €€€

Map p322 (☑675 50 00; www.restaurantblauw.nl; Amstelveenseweg 158; rijsttafel €26.50-32, mains €21-27; ☺6-10pm Mon-Fri, 5-10pm Sat & Sun; ☒2 Amstelveenseweg) The *New York Times* voted Blauw the 'best Indonesian restaurant in the Netherlands' and legions agree because the large, contemporary dining room is always packed (reserve well ahead). Menu standouts include *ikan pesmol* (fried fish with candlenut sauce) and *ayam singgand* (chicken in semi-spicy coconut sauce with tumeric leaf) and mouthwatering Indonesian desserts.

MOMO
ASIAN €€€

Map p322 (☑671 74 74; www.momo-amsterdam.nl; Hobbemastraat 1; mains €18-42; ☺noon-2.30pm & 6-10pm; ☒1/2/5/7/10 Leidseplein) Jungle curry with Alaskan king crab, scallops and prawns, rack of lamb with apricot miso and seared wagyu beef with truffle sauce are among the main-course choices at this stark, industrial-style restaurant, but there are also dim sum, sushi and bento box options.

HOW TO EAT A HERRING

'Hollandse Nieuwe' isn't a fashion trend – it's the fresh catch of super-tasty herring, raked in every June. The Dutch love it, and you'll see vendors selling the salty fish all over town. Although Dutch tradition calls for dangling the herring above your mouth, this isn't the way it's done in Amsterdam. Here the fish is served chopped in chunks and eaten with a toothpick, topped with *uitjes* (chopped onions) and *zuur* (sweet pickles). A *broodje haring* (herring roll) is even handier, as the fluffy white roll holds on the toppings and keeps your fingers fish-fat-free – think of it as an edible napkin.

DRINKING & NIGHTLIFE

CAFÉ BÉDIER
BROWN CAFÉ

Map p322 (Sophialaan 36; ⊙noon-1am Mon-Fri, 11am-3am Sat, 11am-1am Sun; 🚊2 Amstelveenseweg) At the end of the work day, the terrace out the front of Café Bédier is often so crowded it looks like a street party in full swing. Inside, the leather-upholstered wall panels, modular seats and hardwood floors put a 21st-century twist on classic brown *café* decor. Top-notch bar food too.

CAFÉ SCHINKELHAVEN
BROWN CAFÉ

(www.cafeschinkelhaven.nl; Amstelveenseweg 126; ⊙9am-1am Mon-Thu, 9am-3am Fri, 10am-3am Sat, 10am-1am Sun; 🚊; 🚊2 Amstelveenseweg) Exiting the park at the western end, Café Schinkelhaven's candle-topped terrace tables make an irresistible pit stop before heading along Amstelveenseweg in search of dinner. Super-friendly staff make you feel like a regular from the moment you arrive.

GOLLEM'S PROEFLOKAAL
BEER CAFÉ

Map p322 (www.cafegollem.nl; Overtoom 160-162; ⊙1pm-1am Mon-Thu, noon-3am Fri & Sat, noon-1am Sun; 🚊1 1e Constantijn Huygensstraat) Take a day trip to Belgium without leaving the Netherlands. Sip a Kriek (cherry beer) or a Trappist ale amid vintage beer signs and paintings of tippling monks, and soak it up with dishes like Trappist cheese fondue, croquettes and Flemish stew.

HET GROOT MELKHUIS
CAFÉ

Map p322 (☎612 96 74; www.grootmelkhuis.nl; Vondelpark 2; ⊙10am-6pm; 🚊🚊; 🚊1 Jan Pieter Heijestraat) At the forest's edge, this huge Swiss chalet-style timber house appears like something out of a fairytale. The vast drinking and dining forecourt and playground cater to families and all kidlike guests.

'T BLAUWE THEEHUIS
CAFÉ

Map p322 (www.blauwetheehuis.nl; Vondelpark 5; ⊙9am-11pm Sun-Thu, 9am-2am Fri & Sat; 🚊; 🚊2 Jacob Obreachtstraat) You might think a flying saucer landed in the park as you approach this wacky structure, but it's simply a fabulous cafe surrounded by greenery. In summer the terrace is packed with seemingly everyone in town enjoying coffee and cake or cocktails and dinner.

ENTERTAINMENT

For alternative entertainment including great live music, check out Vondelpark's squats (p164).

OPENLUCHTTHEATER
THEATRE

Map p322 (Open-Air Theatre; www.openluchttheater.nl; Vondelpark 5a; ⊙Jun-Aug; 🚊; 🚊1 1e Constantijn Huygensstraat) Each summer Vondelpark hosts free concerts in its intimate open-air theatre. It's a fantastic experience to share with others. Expect world music, dance, theatre and more. You can make a reservation (€2.50 per seat) on the website up to two hours in advance of showtime.

PLAN B
POOL HALL, BAR

Map p322 (www.planbovertoom.nl; Overtoom 209; ⊙3pm-1am Mon-Thu, 2pm-3am Fri & Sat, 2pm-1am Sun; 🚊1 Jan Pieter Heijestraat) If your Vondelpark football game's washed out, switch to Plan B and shoot some pool at this friendly hangout. It also hosts quiz nights on Wednesdays from 8pm.

SHOPPING

The winding paths of Vondelpark must inspire a certain wanderlust, as the nearby streets are full of outdoor and travel shops. Stylish Cornelis Schuytstraat is close to the Old South's ultra-luxe shopping avenue PC Hooftstraat (p178).

★PIED À TERRE
BOOKS

Map p322 (☎627 44 55; www.jvw.nl; Overtoom 135-137; ⊙1-6pm Mon, 10am-6pm Tue, Wed & Fri, 10am-9pm Thu, 10am-5pm Sat; 🚊1 1e Constantijn Huygensstraat) The galleried, sky-lit interior of Europe's largest travel-book shop feels like a Renaissance centre of learning. If it's travel or outdoor-related, it's likely got it: gorgeous globes, travel guides in multiple languages (including English) and over 600,000 maps. Order a cappuccino and dream up your next trip at the cafe tables.

BUISE
CLOTHING

Map p322 (www.buise.nl; Cornelis Schuytstraat 12; ⊙1-6pm Mon, 10am-6pm Tue-Fri, 10am-5pm Sat; 🚊2 Cornelis Schuytstraat) Impeccably selected pieces at this beautiful boutique include flatteringly cut jackets by Isabel Marant, shift dresses and stylish sweatshirts by Paul & Joe Sister and geometric prints by Laurence Dolige.

FRIDAY NEXT
HOMEWARES

Map p322 (🖉612 32 92; www.fridaynext.com; Overtoom 31; ⊙9am-6pm Tue-Fri, 10am-5pm Sat, noon-5pm Sun; 🕾; 🚊1 Constanijn Huygensstraat) Not only is this concept design store filled with designer furniture and homewares, it runs regular exhibitions and design workshops. A cafe is wedged amongst the stock.

BOOKS & BUBBLES
BOOKS

Map p322 (www.books-bubbles.com; Jan Pieter Heijestraat 168; ⊙noon-6pm Tue-Sat; 🕾; 🚊1 Jan Pieter Heijestraat) Quality literature (including in English) lines the shelves at this genteel bookshop. It runs a busy program of author readings and writing workshops (with plenty of room to spread out with a laptop or notebook and pen when they're not taking place), along with champagne tastings, conversational dinners and other events (many in English too).

ENNU
CLOTHING

(www.ennu.nl; Cornelis Schuytstraat 15; ⊙10am-6pm Mon-Fri, 10am-5pm Sat; 🚊2 Cornelis Schuytstraat) Both men and women can find edgy, up-to-the-minute high fashion at Ennu, stocking designers like Ann Demeulemeester, Rick Owens and Junya Watanabe in smoky grey surrounds.

MARQT
FOOD, DRINK

Map p322 (🖉422 62 11; www.marqt.com; Overtoom 21-25; ⊙9am-9pm Mon-Sat, 10am-8pm Sun; 🚊1 1e Constantijn Huygensstraat) 🌿 Pick up prepared gourmet food (often organic) like pastas or salads, cheese, fresh bread and a bottle of wine and you're set for a lazy afternoon in Vondelpark. Cards only; no cash. There are eight other branches around town.

WOMEN'S OUTDOOR WORLD
OUTDOORS

Map p322 (🖉412 28 79; www.bever.nl; Overtoom 51-53; ⊙9.30am-6pm Mon-Wed & Fri, to 9pm Thu, 9am-5pm Sat; 🚊1 1e Constantijn Huygensstraat) Owned by Bever, one of the country's leading sporting-equipment shops, WOW also sells non-gender-specific equipment such as tents.

🏃 SPORTS & ACTIVITIES

FRIDAY NIGHT SKATE
SKATING

(www.fridaynightskate.com; ⊙8.30pm Fri) `FREE` Every Friday night since 1997 (except in rain and snow), in-line skaters gather in Vondelpark to set off on a 20km, two-hour-long mass skate through Amsterdam. Anyone can join, providing you have reasonable skating proficiency (particularly knowing how to brake!). Arrive at the meeting point, adjacent to the Vondelparkpaviljoen, by 8pm (8.15pm in winter).

Check the website for details of skate (and safety gear) rental outlets.

Old South

Neighbourhood Top Five

1 Be awestruck by the tortured artist's vivid brushstrokes of yellow sunflowers and purple-blue irises at the **Van Gogh Museum** (p170).

2 Plunge into the Golden Age trove of Dutch master paintings, delft tiles and gilded dollhouses at the **Rijksmuseum** (p172).

3 Admire the abstractions of Mondrian, Matisse and their modern compadres at the **Stedelijk Museum** (p175).

4 Listen to music soar in pristine acoustics at the **Concertgebouw** (p177).

5 Wander past genteel homes and Amsterdam School **architecture** on streets throughout the Old South, such as Johannes Vermeerstraat.

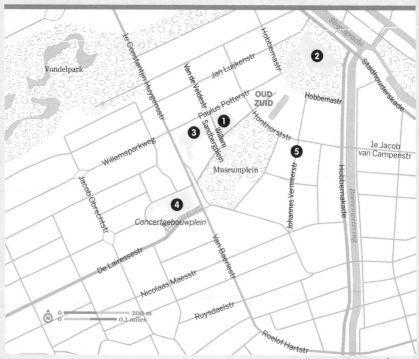

For more detail of this area, see Map p324

Explore Old South

The Old South is home to the city's big three art museums, all lined up in a walkable row. The gorgeously renovated Rijksmuseum, an 1885 Dutch Renaissance-style behemoth stuffed with Rembrandts, Vermeers and other Golden Age treasures, is the granddaddy. The Van Gogh Museum is the fan favourite, evidenced by the queues winding around the block. The Stedelijk is the triumvirate's third member, showing off its vast modern art collection via a wild new wing. No wonder they call it the Museum Quarter. You could easily spend a full day here seeing the sights.

The big patch of grass behind the museums is called Museumplein, handy for footsore tourists and well used by locals, especially in winter when an ice-skating rink is installed.

While most visitors clear out by late afternoon, there are plenty of reasons to linger. The Old South is one of Amsterdam's most gracious – and richest – neighbourhoods. Impressive manors rise on the leafy streets, and it's fun to wander around and see the cool architecture.

In the evening, the action shifts to the Concertgebouw, the grand music hall built in conjunction with the Rijksmuseum. Well-dressed locals flock to the neighbourhood and several genteel *cafés* spring to life.

Local Life

⇒**Plan for the Plein** Yes, the Museumplein (p176) is tourist-packed, but locals are out there, too, picnicking, smooching and tossing a frisbee.

⇒**Go Dutch** For eats, the eastern part of Van Baerlestraat leads to several traditional Dutch restaurants and cafes, such as Wildschut (p177).

⇒**Style Tips** Paulus Potterstraat, the street that runs by the museums, turns into Willemsparkweg as you move southeast. Continue along it and you'll pass cafes and local designers' shops where stylish locals sip coffee and get more, er, stylish.

⇒**Go Gliding** In winter, Museumplein's pond becomes a popular ice-skating rink, and the scene looks like the top of a wind-up jewellery box. In warmer weather, skateboarders head to the park's half-pipe.

Getting There & Away

⇒**Trams** Trams 2 and 5 are handy for getting to/from the city centre.

⇒**Bus** Bus 197 zips to the Museumplein from the airport, which is handy if you're staying in the neighbourhood.

Lonely Planet's Top Tip

The art museums all have cafes, and snack vendors pave the way between the institutions. But we prefer heading to the Albert Heijn at the Museumplein's foot on Van Baerlestraat. The supermarket has prepared salads and sandwiches, or you can buy cheese and a bottle of wine to take out for picnic on the lawn.

OLD SOUTH

Best Places to Eat

⇒ La Falote (p176)
⇒ Loetje (p176)
⇒ Renzo's (p176)
⇒ De Bakkerswinkel (p176)
⇒ Restaurant Elements (p177)

For reviews, see p176.➡

Best Places to Drink

⇒ Welling (p177)
⇒ Wildschut (p177)
⇒ Tunes Bar (p177)

For reviews, see p177.➡

Beyond the Art Museums

⇒ Concertgebouw (p177)
⇒ Museumplein (p176)
⇒ Coster Diamonds (p176)
⇒ House of Bols (p176)

For reviews, see p176.➡

TOP SIGHT
VAN GOGH MUSEUM

The world's largest Van Gogh collection packs the building – it's a superb line-up of masterworks. Opened in 1973 to house the collection of Vincent's younger brother, Theo, the museum comprises 200 paintings and 500 drawings by Vincent and his contemporaries, such as Paul Gauguin and Claude Monet. You'll see Van Gogh's evolution from depicting dark-hued peasants in the Netherlands to his giddy, colour-swirled landscapes in France, where he learned a few tricks from the Impressionists.

Museum Setup & Highlights

The museum is spread over four levels, from Floor 0 (aka the ground floor, where you enter) to Floor 3. It's a manageable size, and most visitors take a couple of hours or so to browse the galleries. The paintings tend to be moved around, depending on the current exhibit theme (say, Van Gogh's images of nature). Seminal works to look for include:

Potato Eaters & Skeleton with Burning Cigarette

Van Gogh's earliest works – shadowy, somber and crude – are from his time in the Dutch countryside and in Antwerp between 1883 and 1885. He was particularly obsessed with peasants and 'painting dark that is nevertheless light'. *The Potato Eaters* (1885) is his most famous painting from this period. *Still Life with Bible* (1885) shows his religious inclination. The burnt-out candle is said to represent the recent death of his father, who was a Protestant minister. *Skeleton with Burning Cigarette* (1886) – the print all the stoners are buying in the gift shop – was painted when Van Gogh was a student at Antwerp's Royal Academy of Fine Arts.

DON'T MISS

➡ *The Potato Eaters*
➡ *The Yellow House*
➡ *Wheatfield with Crows*
➡ *Sunflowers*
➡ *Skeleton with Burning Cigarette*

PRACTICALITIES

➡ Map p324
➡ ☎570 52 00
➡ www.vangogh museum.nl
➡ Paulus Potterstraat 7
➡ adult/child €15/ free, audioguide €5
➡ ⊙9am-6pm Sat-Thu, to 10pm Fri May-Aug, 9am-5pm Sat-Thu, to 10pm Fri Sep-Apr
➡ 🚊2/3/5/12 Van Baerlestraat

Self-Portraits

In 1886 Van Gogh moved to Paris, where his brother, Theo, was working as an art dealer. Vincent wanted to master the art of portraiture, but was too poor to pay for models. Several self-portraits resulted. You can see his palette begin to brighten as he comes under the influence of the Impressionists in the city.

Sunflowers & The Yellow House

In 1888 Van Gogh left for Arles in Provence to delve into its colourful landscapes. *Sunflowers* (1889) and other blossoms that shimmer with intense Mediterranean light are from this period. So is *The Yellow House* (1888), a rendering of the abode Van Gogh rented in Arles, intending to start an artists' colony with Gaugin. *The Bedroom* (1888) depicts Van Gogh's sleeping quarters at the house. In 1888 Van Gogh sliced off part of his ear.

Wheatfield with Crows

Van Gogh had himself committed to an asylum in St Remy in 1889. While there he painted several landscapes with cypress and olive trees, and went wild with *Irises*. In 1890 he went north to Auvers-sur-Oise. One of his last paintings, *Wheatfield with Crows* (1890), is an ominous work finished shortly before his suicide.

Extras

Intriguing displays enhance what's on the walls. For instance, you might see Van Gogh's actual sketchbook alongside an interactive kiosk that lets you page through a reproduction of the book. The museum has categorised all of Van Gogh's letters online at www.vangoghletters.org. Bring your smartphone so you can access them using the museum's free wi-fi.

Other Artists

Thanks to Theo van Gogh's prescient collecting and that of the museum's curators, you'll also see works by Vincent's contemporaries, including Gauguin, Monet and Henri de Toulouse-Lautrec. In addition, paintings by Van Gogh's precursors, such as Jean-François Millet and Gustave Courbet, pepper the galleries, as do works by artists Van Gogh influenced.

Exhibition Wing

Gerrit Rietveld, the influential Dutch architect, designed the museum's main building. Behind it, reaching toward the Museumplein, is a separate wing (opened in 1999) designed by Kisho Kurokawa and commonly referred to as 'the Mussel'. It hosts temporary exhibitions by big-name artists.

OLD SOUTH VAN GOGH MUSEUM

QUEUES & TICKETS

Entrance queues can be long, as only so many visitors are allowed inside at a time. Try waiting until after 3pm. I Amsterdam Card and Holland Pass holders have a separate 'fast' lane for entry, which moves pretty smoothly. E-ticket ticket holders and Museumkaart owners fare the best in their quick-moving lane. E-tickets are available online or at tourist information offices, with no surcharge. They must be printed.

While Van Gogh would come to be regarded as a giant among artists, he sold only one painting during his lifetime (Red Vineyard at Arles; it hangs at Moscow's Puskin Museum).

FRIDAY NIGHT

The museum stays open late on Friday, when it hosts special cultural events and opens a bar downstairs for patrons. There's usually live music or a DJ.

The museum's library has a wealth of reference material – 24,000 books to be exact – for serious study. It's open 10am to 12.30pm and 1.30 to 5pm Monday to Friday.

TOP SIGHT
RIJKSMUSEUM

The Rijksmuseum is the Netherlands' premier art trove, and no self-respecting visitor to Amsterdam can afford to miss it. The museum was conceived as a repository for several national collections, including art owned by the royal family. After a 10-year renovation, the building reopened in its entirety in 2013, with Rembrandts, Vermeers, porcelains and heaps of other treasures spilling out of its 1.5 kilometres' length of gallery space.

DON'T MISS

➡ Rembrandt's *Night Watch*
➡ Frans Hals' *The Merry Drinker*
➡ Vermeer's *Kitchen Maid*
➡ Delftware pottery
➡ Special collections

PRACTICALITIES

➡ National Museum
➡ Map p324
➡ ☎ 662 14 40
➡ www.rijksmuseum.nl
➡ Museumstraat 1
➡ adult/child €15/free
➡ ⊙ 9am-5pm
➡ 🚊 2/5 Hobbema-straat

Layout

The museum is spread over four levels, from Floor 0 (where the main atrium is) to Floor 3. The collection is huge. You can see the highlights in a couple of hours, but art buffs will want to stay much longer.

Pick up a floor plan from the information desk by the entrance. Galleries are well marked. When you enter a room it has the gallery's number and theme, which is easy to match to the floor plan.

Floor 2: 1600–1700

Most visitors make a beeline for the Golden Age masterpieces in the Gallery of Honour on Floor 2. It's a bit convoluted to reach. After you go through the ticket gate, head right past the audio tour desk and go up the stairs (the ones by the sign marked 'The Collection'). Walk back to the next set of stairs and ascend – you're following the '1600–1700' signs, though they're not easy to spot. Eventually you'll come to the Great Hall. Push open the glass doors to enter the Gallery of Honour, and here's what you'll see:

Frans Hals

The first room displays several paintings by Frans Hals, who painted with broad brushstrokes and a fluidity that was unique for the time. *The Merry Drinker* (1628–30) shows his style in action. No one knows who the gent with the beer glass is, but it's clear he's enjoying himself after a hard day of work.

Jan Vermeer

The next room draws big crowds to a couple of famed Vermeer works. Check out the dreamy *Kitchen Maid* (1658) for Vermeer's famed attention to detail. See the holes in the wall? The nail with shadow? In *Woman in Blue Reading a Letter* (1663) Vermeer uses a different style. He shows only parts of objects, such as the tables, chairs and map, leaving the viewer to figure out the rest.

Jan Steen

Another Jan hangs across the hall from Vermeer. Jan Steen became renowned for painting chaotic households, such as the one in *The Merry Family* (1668). Everyone is having such a good time in the picture, no one notices the little boy sneaking a taste of wine. Steen's images made quite an impression: in the 18th century the expression 'a Jan Steen household' entered the local lexicon to mean a crazy state of affairs.

Rembrandt

You'll pass through a room of landscape paintings, and then come to a gallery of Rembrandt's works. *The Jewish Bride* (1665), showing a couple's intimate caress, impressed Van Gogh. 'I would give 10 years of my life to be allowed to sit before this painting for 14 days with just a crust of bread to eat,' he said to a friend.

Night Watch & Civic Guards

Rembrandt's gigantic *Night Watch* (1642) hangs in the subsequent room. It shows the militia led by Frans Banning Cocq. The work is actually titled *Archers under the Command of Captain Frans Banning Cocq*. The *Night Watch* name was bestowed years later, thanks to a layer of grime that gave the impression it was evening. It's since been restored to its original colours and is surrounded by several other civic guard paintings. Fun fact: Captain Cocq, the main ruffed gentleman in Night Watch, once lived in the house at Singel 140–142.

Delftware & Dollhouses

Golden Age swag fills the rooms either side of the Gallery of Honour. Delftware was the Dutch attempt to reproduce Chinese porcelain in the late 1600s. Gallery 2.22 displays scads of the delicate blue-and-white pottery. Gallery 2.20 is devoted to mind-blowing dollhouses. Merchant's wife Petronella Oortman employed carpenters, glassblowers and silversmiths to make the 700 items inside her dollhouse, using the same materials as they would for full-scale versions.

Floor 3: 1900–2000

The upper-most floor holds a fairly limited collection. It includes avant-garde, childlike paintings by Karel Appel, Constant Nieuwenhuys and their CoBrA compadres (a post WWII movement) and cool furnishings by Dutch designers such as Gerrit Rietveld and Michel de Klerk.

Floor 1: 1700–1900

Highlights include the *Battle of Waterloo*, the Rijksmuseum's largest painting (in Gallery 1.12). Three Van Gogh paintings hang in Gallery 1.18. Gallery 1.16 recreates a gilded, 18th-century canal-house room.

Floor 0: 1100–1600

This is an awesome floor for lovers of curiosities and less-visited arts. The Special Collections present peculiar tidbits such as locks, keys, magic lanterns, old dresses, goblets and ship models. The Asia Pavilion, a separate structure that's often devoid of crowds, holds first-rate artworks from China, Indonesia, Japan, India, Thailand and Vietnam.

Facade & Gardens

Pierre Cuypers designed the 1885 building. The exterior mixes neo-Gothic and Dutch Renaissance styles. The museum's gardens (aka the 'outdoor gallery') host big-name sculpture exhibitions at least yearly. They're free to stroll, and offer roses, hedges, fountains and a cool greenhouse year round.

OLD SOUTH RIJKSMUSEUM

QUEUES & TICKETS

Entrance queues can be long. Friday, Saturday and Sunday are the busiest days. It's least crowded after 3pm. Buy and print your ticket online to save time. There's no surcharge. While you still must wait in the outdoor queue, once inside you can proceed straight into the museum (otherwise you must stand in another queue to pay). Museumkaart owners get the same privilege; I Amsterdam Card holders do not (the card provides a small discount, but not free admission).

Download the museum's free app (there's wi-fi onsite). It offers six tours through the collection, covering everything from Floor 2 Highlights to Golden Age masterpieces. Each jaunt takes 45 to 90 minutes.

AIRPORT ART

The Rijksmuseum has a free mini-branch at Schiphol Airport that hangs 10 to 15 stellar Golden Age paintings. It's located after passport control between the E and F Piers, and is open from 7am to 8pm daily.

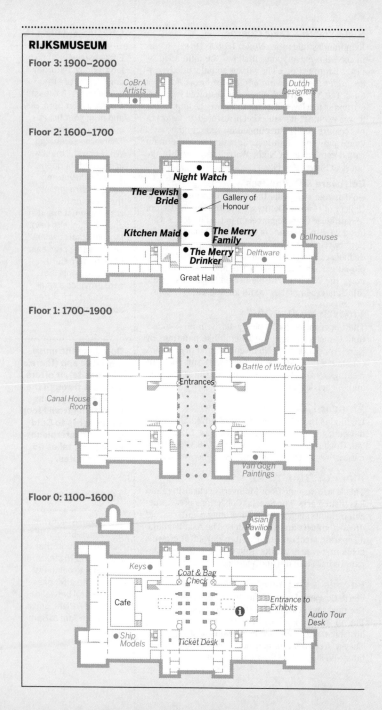

RIJKSMUSEUM

Floor 3: 1900–2000

CoBrA Artists

Dutch Designers

Floor 2: 1600–1700

Night Watch

The Jewish Bride

Gallery of Honour

Kitchen Maid

The Merry Family

The Merry Drinker

Dollhouses

Delftware

Great Hall

Floor 1: 1700–1900

Battle of Waterloo

Entrances

Canal House Room

Van Gogh Paintings

Floor 0: 1100–1600

Asian Pavilion

Keys

Coat & Bag Check

Cafe

Entrance to Exhibits

Audio Tour Desk

Ship Models

Ticket Desk

TOP SIGHT
STEDELIJK MUSEUM

Amsterdam's weighty modern art museum is among the world's best. The permanent collection includes works by Claude Monet, Pablo Picasso and all the blue chips of the 19th- and 20th-century art world. Displays of textiles, glassworks, posters and cool industrial design pieces add to the engaging scene. After a nine-year renovation, the museum reopened in late 2012 almost twice as large, thanks to a huge new wing where uber-contemporary installations show.

Main Building: Matisse to Wonder Woman

AM Weissman designed the 1895 main building. On the ground floor you'll see all sorts of masterpieces from the 90,000-work collection: Henri Matisse cut-outs, Picasso abstracts, Auguste Rodin sculptures and a vivid collection of paintings by Dutch homeboys Piet Mondrian, Willem de Kooning, Charlie Toorop and Karel Appel. The Design section – which takes up half of the floor – is particularly awesome, showing inventive jewellery, ceramics, homewares and furniture by masters such as Gerrit Rietveld and Ludwig Mies van der Rohe.

Head upstairs, and the works become more modern, ranging from 1950 to the present. Here you might view anything from a neon sign of fornicating couples to a *Wonder Woman* video installation or maybe a cluster of lava lights. Exhibits change regularly, so you never know what will be on hand, but count on it being offbeat and provocative.

The Bathtub: Mega Mod

The new wing, aka 'the Bathtub' (you'll know why when you see it), is accessed via a trippy, white-lit escalator that doubles as a piece of sound art. Big-name contemporary artists use the galleries here for temporary exhibitions.

That smooth, white tub material, by the way, is called Twaron, a synthetic fiber that's five times as strong as steel and typically used in yacht hulls.

Queues & Freebies

The Stedelijk doesn't have lengthy queues like its museum neighbours. Admission is free for Museumkaart, I Amsterdam Card and Holland Pass holders. Stop by the front desk when you enter to enquire about free guided tours (Sunday at 2.15pm in Dutch and 3.45pm in English) and gallery talks (typically Thursday, Friday and Sunday). Audio tours (€5) are also available to rent.

Kids will find games, drawing materials and other activities in the Family Lab. There's also a special audio tour (€2.50) for young ones.

The cafe on the main floor is a great post-museum refresher. Join the locals sipping from the swell list of wines, both still and sparkling varieties.

DON'T MISS

➡ Design collection
➡ Escalator to the Bathtub
➡ Piet Mondrian grid paintings
➡ Henri Matisse paper cut-outs
➡ Museum highlights tour (3.45 to 4.45pm Sun, in English)

PRACTICALITIES

➡ Map p324
➡ ☎573 29 11
➡ www.stedelijk.nl
➡ Museumplein 10
➡ adult/child €15/free
➡ ⏰10am-6pm Fri-Wed, 10am-10pm Thu
➡ 🚊2/3/5/12 Van Baerlestraat

OLD SOUTH STEDELIJK MUSEUM

◉ SIGHTS

VAN GOGH MUSEUM   MUSEUM
See p170.

RIJKSMUSEUM   MUSEUM
See p172.

STEDELIJK MUSEUM   MUSEUM
See p175.

MUSEUMPLEIN   SQUARE
Map p324 (Paulus Potterstraat) The grassy, people-filled square behind the museums entertains with its skateboard ramp, playground, ice-skating pond (in winter) and *I Amsterdam* sculpture (everyone's favourite photo op). Locals toss frisbees, couples hold hands, and everyone picnics here when the weather warms up. The space is also used for public concerts and special events.

Museumplein was laid out to host the World Exhibition in 1883, but gained its lasting title only when the Rijksmuseum opened two years later. One of many facelifts raised a triangle of turf at the southern end, dubbed the 'ass's ear' for its shape; it's now a popular spot for sun worshippers. There's a large supermarket, Albert Heijn, concealed below.

DIAMOND MUSEUM   MUSEUM
Map p324 (www.diamantmuseum.nl; Paulus Potterstraat 8; adult/child €7.50/5; ⊘9am-5pm; 🚊2/5 Hobbemastraat) Almost all of the exhibits at the small, low-tech Diamond Museum are clever recreations. Those on a budget can save money by going next door to **Coster Diamonds** (Map p324) (the company owns the museum and is attached to it) and taking a free workshop tour, where you can see gem cutters and polishers doing their thing.

Those who do venture into the museum will find exhibits on the history of the trade and the sparkling creations that have adorned the world's rich and powerful. You'll learn how Amsterdam was the globe's diamond-trade epicentre for many centuries, where local Jews dominated the cutting and polishing business, and how that trade moved to Antwerp after WWII once Amsterdam lost its Jewish population. Faux royal crowns and jewel-encrusted swords shine in the display cases.

HOUSE OF BOLS   MUSEUM
Map p324 (www.houseofbols.com; Paulus Potterstraat 14; admission €14.50; ⊘noon-5.30pm Sun-Thu, to 9pm Fri, to 7pm Sat; 🚊2/5 Hobbemas-

traat) An hour's self-guided tour through this *jenever* (Dutch gin) museum includes a confusing sniff test, a distilled history of the Bols company and a cocktail made by one of its formidable bartenders, who train at the academy upstairs. It's kind of cheesy (especially the 'flair booth' where you try out bottle-flipping skills), but fun. On Friday after 5pm admission is €9.50.

✖ EATING

Several snack vendors line the sidewalk between the Rijksmuseum and Van Gogh Museum, serving burgers, sandwiches, ice cream and drinks.

RENZO'S   ITALIAN €
Map p324 (⊠673 16 73; www.renzos.nl; Van Baerlestraat 67; items per 100g €1.50-3.25, sandwiches €5-6 ; ⊘11am-9pm; 🚊3/5/12/16/24 Museumplein) Most of this deli's pesto-y pastas, thickly cut sandwiches and omelettes are for takeaway, but don't be shy about eating at the tables on the mini terrace.

DE BAKKERSWINKEL   BAKERY €
Map p324 (www.debakkerswinkel.com; Roelof Hartstraat 68; mains €5-11; ⊘7.30am-6pm Tue-Fri, 7.30am-5pm Sat, 10am-4pm Sun; 📶; 🚊3/5/12/24 Roelof Hartplein) This is the original location of the local bakery mini-chain. Order one of the famed scones or a sandwich on wonderfully crusty bread, and take it to the big communal table in the bright lunchroom. Those with a sweet tooth can stroll two doors over to De Bakkerswinkel's cake shop.

LA FALOTE   TRADITIONAL DUTCH €€
Map p324 (⊠622 54 54; www.lafalote.nl; Roelof Hartstraat 26; mains €16-23; ⊘3-9pm Mon-Fri, 5-9pm Sat; 🚊3/5/12/24 Roelof Hartplein) Wee chequered-tableclothed La Falote is all about Dutch home-style cooking, such as calf liver, meatballs with endives, and stewed fish with beets and mustard sauce. The prices are a bargain in an otherwise ritzy neighbourhood. And wait till the owner brings out the accordion.

LOETJE   TRADITIONAL DUTCH €€
Map p324 (http://amsterdam.loetje.com; Johannes Vermeerstraat 52; mains €10-22; ⊘11am-10pm; 🚊16/24 Ruysdaelstraat) This cafe has a short chalkboard menu, but everyone orders thick steak, served medium-rare and swimming in delicious gravy. The staff are

PHOTO OP

You can't leave the Museumplein without stopping by the **I Amsterdam sculpture** for a photo. Feel free to climb in, around or on top of the 2m-high letters. It's located in the square's northwest corner, by the Rijksmuseum.

surprisingly good humoured, particularly considering the loud, meat-drunken mobs they typically serve.

RESTAURANT ELEMENTS   INTERNATIONAL €€

Map p324 (☑579 17 17; www.heerlijkamsterdam. nl; Roelof Hartstraat 6-8; 4-course set menu €26.50; ⊘seatings 5.30pm & 7pm Mon-Fri; ᠗3/5/12/24 Roelof Hartplein) Students – the same ones who run the nearby College Hotel – prepare and serve contemporary international dishes at this mod restaurant. The result is white-glove service at an excellent price. Reserve in advance.

RESTAURANT DE KNIJP   FRENCH €€

Map p324 (www.deknijp.nl; Van Baerlestraat 134; mains €18-26; ⊘5.30-12.30pm; ᠗3/5/12/16/24 Museumplein) Fork into French classics – snails in creamy garlic sauce, beef in buttery Béarnaise sauce, crème caramel – in this warm, inviting bistro. De Knijp serves its compact menu of fish and meat dishes later than most places in the neighbourhood. The snug wood tables tend to fill up when there's a show at the nearby Concertgebouw.

SAMA SEBO   INDONESIAN €€

Map p324 (☑662 81 46; www.samasebo.com; PC Hooftstraat 27; rijsttafel per person €29.50, mains from €16.50; ⊘noon-3pm & 5-10pm Mon-Sat; ᠗2/5 Hobbemastraat) Sama Sebo looks more like a brown *café* than a trip to the South Seas, and that's OK. The *rijsttafel* (Indonesian banquet) is 17 dishes (four to seven at lunchtime), but you can get individual plates if that's too much.

COBRA CAFE   CAFE €€

Map p324 (☑470 01 11; www.cobracafe.nl; Hobbemastraat 18; mains €7-13; ⊘10am-7pm; ᠗2/5 Hobbemastraat) This arty glass cube of a restaurant, which is full of original works by Corneille and Appel, sure is touristy. But when you're all museumed out and need a salad, a massive club sandwich or a slice of 'Karel Appel taart', you'll hardly notice.

🍷 DRINKING & NIGHTLIFE

WELLING   BROWN CAFÉ

Map p324 (www.cafewelling.nl; Jan Willem Brouwersstraat 32; ⊘4pm-1am Mon-Fri, from 3pm Sat & Sun; ᠗3/5/12/16/24 Museumplein) Tucked away behind the Concertgebouw, this is a relaxed spot to sip a frothy, cold *biertje* (glass of beer) and mingle with intellectuals and artists. Don't be surprised if the cafe's friendly cat hops onto your lap.

WILDSCHUT   CAFE

Map p324 (Roelof Hartplein 1; ⊘9am-1am Mon-Fri, from 10am Sat & Sun; ᠗3/5/12/24 Roelof Hartplein) This is a gathering place for the Old South. On a warm day, pretty much everyone heads to the terrace for views of the Amsterdam School. When the weather's not great, soak up the atmosphere in the art deco interior. Wildschut serves a fine menu of omelettes, sandwiches, burgers, frites and apple pie to accompany the drinks.

TUNES BAR   COCKTAIL BAR

Map p324 (www.conservatoriumhotel.com; Van Baerlestraat 27; ⊘4pm-1am Mon-Thu, to 2am Fri & Sat, 2pm-midnight Sun; ᠗2/3/5/12 Van Baerlestraat) Craving a tangerine-tinged gin and tonic with a side of shrimp *bitterballen* (small, round croquettes)? Or a glass of sparkling wine and plate of oysters? Then pull up a chair at the see-through bar at uber-mod Tunes, located in the posh Conservatorium Hotel. Gin drinks are the speciality, but the overall cocktail list is wide-ranging; prices start at €12.50 (beers around €5). Cigar aficionados can puff in the attached smoking lounge.

☆ ENTERTAINMENT

CONCERTGEBOUW   CLASSICAL MUSIC

Map p324 (☑671 83 45; www.concertgebouw. nl; Concertgebouwplein 2-6; ⊘box office 1-7pm Mon-Fri, 10am-7pm Sat & Sun; ᠗3/5/12/16/24 Museumplein) Bernard Haitink, former conductor of the venerable Royal Concertgebouw Orchestra, once remarked that the world-famous hall – built in 1888 with near-perfect acoustics – was the orchestra's best instrument. Free half-hour concerts take place every Wednesday at 12.30pm from mid-September until late June; arrive early. Try the Last Minute Ticket Shop (www.lastminuteticketshop.nl) for half-price seats to all other shows.

Those aged 30 or younger can queue at the box office for €12.50 tickets 45 minutes before shows. All tickets function as free transit passes before and after concerts (just show it to the driver), and as a voucher for a free drink in the concert hall lobby.

The literal name 'Concert Hall' scarcely does justice to the amazing facility. Architect AL van Gendt designed it in neo-Renaissance style. In spite of his limited musical knowledge, he managed to give the two-tiered Grote Zaal (Main Hall) acoustics that are the envy of sound designers worldwide. Add in baroque trim, panels inscribed with the names of classical composers, a massive pipe organ and a grand staircase via which conductors and soloists descend to the stage, and you have a venue where the best performers are honoured to appear. The facility offers 1.25-hour tours (per person €10) at 12.30pm Sunday, 5pm Monday and 1.30pm Wednesday that cover the hall's design in detail; buy tickets at the box office.

SHOPPING

The biggest concentration of shops is around PC Hooftstraat, which teems with brands that need no introduction: Chanel, Burberry, Hugo Boss, Cartier, Gucci, Armani, Hermes, Tommy Hilfiger and Lacoste, to name just a few.

BROEKMANS & VAN POPPEL   MUSIC

Map p324 (www.broekmans.com; Van Baerlestraat 92-94; ⊙9am-6pm Mon-Fri, to 5pm Sat; ⊞2/3/5/12 Van Baerlestraat) Near the Concertgebouw, this is the city's top choice for classical and popular sheet music, as well as music books. Head to the 1st floor for a comprehensive selection from the Middle Ages through to classical and contemporary.

DE WINKEL VAN NIJNTJE   TOYS

(www.dewinkelvannijntje.nl; Beethovenstraat 71; ⊙1-6pm Mon, 10am-6pm Tue-Fri, 10am-5pm Sat; ⊞; ⊞24 Stadionweg/Beethovenstraat) Dutch illustrator Dick Bruna's most famous character, Miffy (Nijntje in Dutch), is celebrated in toys and kids' merchandise. Items range from pencils and soap bubbles to plush toys, clothing and even Royal Delftware plates. It's a good 1km south of the Museumplein via Beethovenstraat en route to Beatrixpark.

MUSEUM SOUVENIRS

The Van Gogh Museum and Rijksmuseum jointly operate the **Museum Shop at the Museumplein** (Map p324; Hobbemastraat; ⊞2/5 Hobbemastraat), so you can pick up posters, cards and other art souvenirs from both institutions in one fell swoop (and avoid the museums' entrance queues). While the selection is not as vast as the in-house stores, the shop has enough iconic wares to satisfy most needs.

EDHA INTERIEUR   HOMEWARES

Map p324 (www.edha-interieur.nl; Willemsparkweg 5-9; ⊙10am-6pm Tue-Sat, noon-5pm Sun; ⊞2/3/5/12 Van Baerlestraat) You might not end up buying a sofa, kitchen unit or bathroom suite in these three adjoining 19th-century buildings but Edha is one of the best places in town to check out cutting-edge Dutch design. Smaller items more suitable to fit in your luggage (or at least ship) include textiles, groovy lights and kitchen gadgets.

VAN AVEZAATH BEUNE   FOOD & DRINK

Map p324 (www.vanavezaath-beune.nl; Johannes Verhulststraat 98; ⊙8am-6pm Mon-Fri, to 5pm Sat; ⊞2 Cornelis Schuytstraat) Counter staff in serious black aprons box up chocolate *amsterdammertjes* (the bollards along city sidewalks) – a great (if phallic-looking) gift, assuming you can keep from eating them.

FRETONS   SHOES

Map p324 (www.bretoniere.nl; Jacob Obrechtstraat 14; ⊙10.30am-6pm Tue-Fri, to 5pm Sat; ⊞2 Jacob Obrechtstraat) Fretons is shoemaker Fred de la Bretonniere's more relaxed brand. Think chunky sneakers that are comfy, sporty and urban-cool, and pretty much one of a kind.

SPORTS & ACTIVITIES

ZUIDERBAD   SWIMMING POOL

Map p324 (☎252 13 90; Hobbemastraat 26; adult/child €5/3; ⊞; ⊞2/5 Hobbemastraat) If you're looking for something to entertain the kids, consider this pool. The 1912 edifice behind the Rijksmuseum has been restored to its original glory, full of tiles, character and appreciative paddlers. Call for opening hours.

De Pijp

Neighbourhood Top Five

1 Feast your senses on the international free-for-all of fresh produce, cheese, fish, colourful clothing, accessories and quirky Dutch souvenirs at the **Albert Cuypmarkt** (p188), Europe's largest daily street market.

2 Picnic postmarket in the lush **Sarphatipark** (p181), an urban oasis of rolling lawns, statues and fountains.

3 **Bar hop** between exuberantly friendly neighbourhood watering holes (p182).

4 Tour the boisterously fun **Heineken Experience** (p186) before boarding its canal boat to its brand store.

5 Delve into De Pijp's adventurous **culinary offerings** (p181).

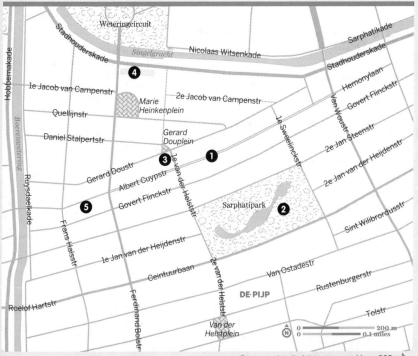

For more detail of this area, see Map p325 ➡

DE PIJP

Lonely Planet's Top Tip

Many people walk straight through the centre of the Albert Cuypmarkt's stalls and never realise that behind the stalls, on both sides, the street is lined with shops of all kinds. Some are run by the stallholders out front but most aren't, so it's well worth checking them out for bargains. Behind the stalls you'll also find hidden dining gems like **The Butcher** (p183) and **Bazar** (p184).

✗ Best Places to Eat

➡ Ciel Bleu (p185)
➡ SLA (p181)
➡ The Butcher (p183)
➡ Spang Makandra (p183)
➡ Brasserie Sent (p184)

For reviews, see p181.➡

🍷 Best Places to Drink

➡ Barça (p185)
➡ Café Binnen Buiten (p185)
➡ Café Berkhout (p185)
➡ Café Sarphaat (p185)
➡ Café de Greene Vlinder (p186)

For reviews, see p185.➡

🔒 Best Places to Shop

➡ Albert Cuypmarkt (p188)
➡ Hutspot (p187)
➡ Fietsfabriek (p187)
➡ Bleecker (p187)
➡ De Vredespijp (p187)

For reviews, see p187.➡

Explore De Pijp

No wonder De Pijp feels like a village smack in the centre of Amsterdam: the neighbourhood is actually a large island connected to the rest of the city by 16 bridges.

Originally known as the 'YY neighbourhood' (dating back to the classification of 1850, when neighbourhoods were designated from A to Z and AA to ZZ), this was Amsterdam's first 19th-century slum. Its present-day name, 'the Pipe', is thought to reflect its straight, narrow streets that resemble the stems of old clay pipes.

De Pijp is straightforward to explore. Start your day at the Albert Cuypmarkt with an open mind and keen eyes: deals and unique finds abound. Give yourself at least an hour to trawl through the sprawling street stalls before heading to peaceful Sarphatipark for a stroll, and chilling out in one of the nearby brown *cafés* (pubs).

The neighbourhood's streets are full of unique boutiques and speciality shops, so take some time exploring them (and be sure to stake out your dinner destination from the overwhelming options) before heading to the Heineken Experience. If you time it for the late afternoon, the tasting at the end provides a built-in happy hour. Of course in fun-loving De Pijp it almost always feels like happy hour. Chat with the friendly locals during a neighbourhood pub crawl and you'll see why this district earns its moniker of Amsterdam's Latin Quarter.

Local Life

➡**Red Light Life** On the western border of De Pijp, and within view of the Rijksmuseum, there's a little red-light district along Ruysdaelkade, opposite Hobbemakade. For a glimpse of the world's oldest profession, minus stag parties and drunken crowds, this is the place to sate your curiosity.

➡**Fishy Life** This is one Dutch delicacy you can smell from a block away: locals love to hit up De Pijp's raw herring stands on and around Albert Cuypmarkt. A tip: if you're feeling timid, order it in a bread roll, sans tail.

➡**Fashion Life** In addition to the bargain clothing sold at the Albert Cuypmarkt, local fashion mavens know that the streets surrounding the market are home to some of the best budget clothing stores in town.

Getting There & Away

➡**Tram** Trams 16 and 24 roll north–south from Centraal Station along Ferdinand Bolstraat right by De Pijp's main sights. Trams 4 and 25 travel from Rembrandtplein, while tram 3 cuts east–west across the neighbourhood.

◉ SIGHTS

Apart from the Albert Cuypmarkt and the Heineken Experience, sights in De Pijp are few. What's really enjoyable here is wandering through the neighbourhood and soaking up the bohemian atmosphere in the bars, cafes and shops. Note that the much beset Noord/Zuidlijn (north–south metro line; p91) will, eventually, travel through De Pijp. Expect to encounter construction on Ferdinand Bolstraat between Albert Cuypstraat and Ceintuurbaan for the foreseeable future.

SARPHATIPARK   PARK

Map p325 (Ceintuurbaan; ⧉16/24 Albert Cuyp-straat) While the Vondelpark is bigger in size and reputation, this tranquil English-style park delivers an equally potent shot of pastoral summertime relaxation, with far fewer crowds. Named after Samuel Sarphati (1813–66), a Jewish doctor, businessman and urban innovator, the grounds are a mix of ponds, gently rolling meadows and wooded fringes.

In the centre you'll see the **Sarphati memorial** (1886), a bombastic temple with a fountain, gargoyles and a bust of the great man himself.

DE DAGERAAD   ARCHITECTURE

Map p325 (Dawn Housing Project; Pieter Lodewijk Takstraat; ⧉4 Amstelkade) Following the key Housing Act of 1901, which forced the city to rethink neighbourhood planning and condemn slums, De Dageraad housing estate was developed between 1918 and 1923 for poorer families. One of the most original architects of the expressionist Amsterdam School, Piet Kramer, drew up plans for this idiosyncratic complex in collaboration with Michel de Klerk.

✕ EATING

Come hungry: anything and everything is fair game on De Pijp's cuisine scene. It's multicultural yet also quintessentially Dutch, with plenty of old brown cafés churning out hearty lunch specials, and bakeries selling lunchtime broodjes (bread rolls with fillings). Albert Cuypstraat, Ferdinand Bolstraat and Ceintuurbaan in particular are all lined with unique ethnic spots.

SLA   SALAD BAR €

Map p325 (www.ilovesla.com; Ceintuurbaan 149; salads €6-8.50; ⊙11am-9.30pm; ✎; ⧉3/25 2e Van der Helststraat) ✿ Amsterdam's fashionistas have been flocking to this super-stylish salad bar since its recent opening for its soups, juices and especially its extensive array of fresh, healthy salads that you design yourself. All of the meat, poultry and dairy products, 90% of the vegetables, and the wines are organic.

AMSTERDAM'S LATIN QUARTER

De Pijp uit gaan, which loosely translates to 'no one leaves De Pijp alive', was an old joke told for years around this historically working-class, close-knit neighbourhood. But these days its bohemian character means it's known as the 'Latin Quarter' of Amsterdam. De Pijp owes its spark and energy to a lively mix of people from all walks of life: labourers, intellectuals, new immigrants, prostitutes, corporate workers, gay and lesbian locals and visitors, movie stars, artists and more.

The area's roots are humble. Its early shoddy tenement blocks, some of which collapsed even as they were being built in the 1860s, provided cheap housing not just for newly arrived workers drawn by the city's industrial revolution, but also for students, artists, writers and other poverty-stricken individuals. In the 1960s and '70s many of the working-class inhabitants left for greener pastures and the government began refurbishing the tenement blocks for immigrants from Morocco, Turkey, Suriname and the Netherlands Antilles.

Professionals are now doing up apartments in grand style, lending the neighbourhood an increasingly gentrified air. Edgy advertising agencies and funky boutiques line the streets, and freelancers and their Mac Books crowd the cafes. Yet the neighbourhood retains an irrepressible appeal, with enough street smarts and grit to keep it authentic.

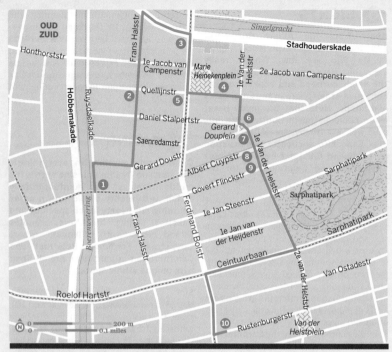

Neighbourhood Walk
De Pijp Pub Crawl

START CAFÉ BINNEN BUITEN
END CC MUZIEKCAFÉ
LENGTH 3.5KM; 2½ TO 3 HOURS

For a memorable pub crawl through the 'hood, begin by joining the after-work crowd on Ruysdaelkade, overlooking the Boerenwetering canal and bar-hop your way south towards Sarphatipark before ending the evening in a buzzing music *café*.

Start with a sundowner on the terrace of **1 Café Binnen Buiten** (p185), then head east on Gerard Doustraat and north on leafy Frans Halsstraat for a *biertje* (glass of beer) at the locals' local **2 Quinto** (p186). Continue north along Frans Halsstraat then east along Stadhouderskade to kick back on the window-side couches at sociable **3 Café Berkhout** (p185), across the road from the Heineken Experience. Head down Ferdinand Bolstraat and across Marie Heinekenplein to fortify yourself with tapas at **4 Barça** (p185), along with a glass of *cava* (Catalan sparkling wine). After soaking up the Iberian

vibe continue down Ferdinand Bolstraat to **5 Kingfisher** (p186). Sit at the bar and order some classic Dutch *bitterballen* (round meat croquettes) before sauntering to **6 Het Paardje** (p187), the see-and-be-seen nexus of De Pijp. As you leave, marvel at the festive impromptu street party that Gerard Douplein becomes in all kinds of weather.

If you're still going, the stretch south to Sarphatipark is awash with bars: stop in for some sangria at **7 Pilsvogel** (p186); sip an Amstel in the wooden interior or on the patio of **8 Café de Groene Vlinder** (p186) on Albert Cuypstraat and be amazed at how quiet this pedestrian street is when the market stalls have packed up for the night; or go for a glass of wine at retro-cool **9 Chocolate Bar** (p186) on 1e Jan van der Helststraat.

And if you're *still* going, continue south. At the end of Sarphatipark, turn west on Ceintuurbaan and south on Ferdinand Bolstraat; just east on Rustenburgerstraat catch live music at De Pijp's laidback little club **CC Muziekcafé** (p187).

THE BUTCHER
BURGERS €

Map p325 (📞470 78 75; www.the-butcher.com; Albert Cuypstraat 129; burgers €6.50-11; ⏱11am-late; 👶; 🚊16/24 Albert Cuypstraat) Burgers at this sizzling spot are cooked right in front of you (behind a glass screen, so you won't get splattered). Mouthwatering choices include 'Silence of the Lamb' (with spices and tahini), the 'Codfather' (beer-battered blue cod and homemade tartare sauce), an Angus beef truffle burger and a vegie version. Ask about its 'secret kitchen' supper club.

SPANG MAKANDRA
SURINAMESE, INDONESIAN €

Map p325 (📞670 50 81; www.spangmakandra.nl; Gerard Doustraat 39; mains €6-10; ⏱11am-10pm Mon-Sat, 1-10pm Sun; 🚊16/24 Albert Cuypstraat) There are just 26 seats at this cosy restaurant and it's a red-hot favourite with students and Surinamese and Indonesian migrants, so you'll need to book for dinner. The reward is a fabulous array of dishes like fish soups and satays with spicy sauces at astonishingly cheap prices. Friendly staff are happy to translate the Dutch-only menu.All the food is halal; no alcohol is served.

LITTLE COLLINS
TAPAS €

Map p325 (📞673 22 93; www.littlecollins.nl; 1e Sweelinckstraat 19; tapas €5.50-13, brunch €4.50-15; ⏱9am-10pm Wed-Sat, to 4pm Sun; 🚊16/24 Albert Cuypstraat) You could just drop in for a glass of wine or a cocktail at this hip little bar, but with a kitchen this good that would be missing the point. Small, shareable plates include pickled pumpkin and balsamic pear salad and marinated buffalo ricotta, house-made pâté, Korean-style beef with rice paper crisps, or date- and pancetta-stuffed roast quail with pomegranate jus.

It's hopping during brunch (9am to 4pm Wednesday to Sunday), when the food is equally inspired (coconut-crumbed French toast with lemon curd and baked apple, for instance).

TODAY'S
ITALIAN €

Map p325 (📞737 08 70; www.facebook.com/todaysamsterdam; Saenredamstraat 26hs; items €3-9; ⏱1-8pm Tue-Sat; 🖊; 🚊16/24 Albert Cuypstraat) Tiny and delightful, this deli/cafe functions as an impromptu Italian cultural centre. Charismatic chef Davide creates scrumptious Italian fare from focaccia to pumpkin lasagne, truffle and mushroom ravioli, and sinful tiramisu. Take away, eat in or book a private dinner in the lofted dining room.

TAART VAN M'N TANTE
BAKERY, SWEETS €

Map p325 (📞776 46 00; www.detaart.com; Ferdinand Bolstraat 10; items €4-7; ⏱10am-6pm; 👶; 🚊16/24 Stadhouderskade) One of Amsterdam's best-loved cake shops operates from this uber-kitsch parlour, turning out apple pies (Dutch, French or 'tipsy'), pecan pie and wish-you-could-bake-like-this cakes. Hot-pink walls accent cakes dressed like Barbie dolls – or are they Barbies dressed as cakes?

STACH
CAFE, DELI €

(📞754 26 72; www.stach-food.nl; Van Woustraat 154; dishes €3-9; ⏱9am-10pm Mon-Sat, 10am-10pm Sun; 🚊4 Lutmastraat) 🍃 An Aladdin's cave of fresh produce, jams, preserves, teas, coffees, juices and chocolates, this food emporium makes some of the best (and best-value) sandwiches around, loaded with gourmet ingredients. If it's not picnic weather, there's a mezzanine dining area inside; it also runs cooking courses. There's a second branch (p125) in the Southern Canal Ring.

BAKKEN MET PASSIE
BAKERY, SWEETS €

Map p325 (📞670 13 76; www.bakkenmetpassie.nl; Albert Cuypstraat 51-53; items €2-7; ⏱7.30am-6pm Tue-Sat; 🚊16/24 Albert Cuypstraat) 'Baking with passion' turns out treats like rich Valrhona chocolate and lighter lemon tarts and lighter-still macaroons. There's also a wide range of breads (including sourdoughs) and a sit-down area to eat amid the heavenly aromas while watching the bakers at work.

WILD MOA PIES
PIES €

Map p325 (www.pies.nu; Van Ostadestraat 147; mains €3-4; ⏱10am-6.30pm Tue-Sat; 📷🖊; 🚊3/25 2e Van der Helststraat) Just because this unassuming spot serves the only authentic New-Zealand-Australian-style meat pies in town (including NZ lamb) doesn't mean they aren't the best. Creative vegie and poultry varieties span Thai chicken, lentil and aubergine, spinach and feta, and pumpkin and paprika. The shelves are stocked with Aussie and Kiwi staples such as Tim Tam biscuits and Bundaberg ginger beer.

LUNCHROOM HANNIBAL
CAFE €

Map p325 (📞673 54 88; Ferdinand Bolstraat 92; mains €4-13; ⏱9am-5.30pm Mon-Wed, Fri & Sat, 9am-8pm Thu; 📷; 🚊16/24 Albert Cuypstraat) Diners unfurl newspapers over omelettes, pancakes and coffee at tables by big, bright windows. This quintessentially Dutch workers' cafe also serves knock-out homemade apple pie.

ALBINA
SURINAMESE, CHINESE €

Map p325 (☑370 02 23; Albert Cuypstraat 47-49; mains €5.50-13; ⊙noon-10pm Wed-Mon; 🚊16/24 Albert Cuypstraat) If you're looking for stylish surrounds, stop reading now. If, however, you're after quality Surinamese food (skip the rather bland Chinese selections), by all means take a seat for a colossal portion of *roti kip* (chicken curry, flaky roti, potatoes, cabbage and egg).

BRASSERIE SENT
INTERNATIONAL €€

Map p325 (☑676 24 95; www.restaurantsent.nl; Saenredamstraat 39; mains €16.50-18.50; ⊙6-10.30pm Tue-Sun; 🚊16/24 Albert Cuypstraat) The menu at this little restaurant is limited to around five mains, but that doesn't matter when they're this good. Many are cooked on the barbecue (including prawns and sirloin steak); dishes also include fillet of sea bass with lemon caper butter and bacon and walnut salad.

FRENCH CAFÉ
FRENCH €€

Map p325 (☑470 03 01; www.thefrenchcafe.nl; Gerard Doustraat 98; mains €23.50-28, 3-course menu from €32.50; ⊙6-11pm Mon-Sat; 🚊16/24 Albert Cuypstraat) Chef Grégory covers all the classics at this Parisian-chic bistro, from quiche lorraine to foie gras, snails and steak tartare. Cheeses are handmade Dutch farmhouse varieties but the wine list is overwhelmingly French.

FIRMA PEKELHAARING
ITALIAN €€

(www.pekelhaaring.nl; Van Woustraat 127-129; mains €10-18.50; ⊙10am-10pm; 🚇🛗; 🚊3/4/25 Van Woustraat) Sociable touches like the communal table, strewn with magazines and board games to play over dessert, belie the focused attention on fresh Italian flavours at arty, industrial Firma Pekelhaaring. Loads of fun and little pretence.

MAMOUCHE
MOROCCAN €€

Map p325 (☑670 07 36; www.restaurant-mamouche.nl; Quellijnstraat 104; mains €15.50-23.50; ⊙6-10pm; 🚊16/24 Stadhouderskade) One of De Pijp's most refined eateries, Mamouche gets serious acclaim for its French-accented North African cuisine. The sleek, minimalist design, with exposed flooring, mottled raw plaster walls and slat-

beam ceilings, complements the changing selection of *tajine* (Moroccan stew), candied duck with sweet potato mash and cinnamon, and couscous dishes such as spicy sea bass and saffron butter.

OP DE TUIN
MEDITERRANEAN €€

Map p325 (☑675 26 20; www.opdetuin.nl; Karel du Jardinstraat 47; €15.50–19.50; ⊙4-10pm Tue-Sun; 🚊3/25 2e Van der Helststraat) ✐ This is the kind of breezy, informal neighbourhood restaurant where you can while away an evening snacking on antipasti (let the chef decide on a mix of Mediterranean standards) or a beautiful three-course meal (€26.50–29.50) in the cosy, timber-floored dining room or flower-filled garden, and imagine living across the street.

BALTI HOUSE
INDIAN €€

Map p325 (☑470 89 17; www.baltihouse.nl; Albert Cuypstraat 41; mains €12.50-19.50; ⊙4-11pm; 🚇🛗; 🚊16/24 Albert Cuypstraat) Classics at this neighbourhood secret – from a smooth butter chicken masala to fiery tandooris and biryanis – never disappoint, and the three banquets offer a worthy culinary adventure for the seriously hungry.

ZEN
JAPANESE €€

Map p325 (☑627 06 07; Frans Halsstraat 38; mains €9-20; ⊙6-11pm Tue-Sat; 🚊16/24 Stadhouderskade) Zen offers cooking like *okāsan* (mum) used to make: *domburi* (bowls of rice with various ingredients on top), sushi and *tonkatsu* (deep-fried pork cutlet) are just the start. Decor is minimalist Dutch-meets-Japanese.

ORONTES
TURKISH €€

Map p325 (☑679 62 25; www.orontes.nl; Albert Cuypstraat 40; mains €14.50-18; ⊙5.30-11.30pm Mon-Sat; 🚇🛗; 🚊16/24 Albert Cuypstraat) The chef imports many of his ingredients (olives, pomegranates and chickpeas) from his southern Turkish homeland, and authentic flavours are the result. Charcoal-grilled meat and fish dishes wow in their savoury simplicity, like grilled sea bass stuffed with lemon. Vegetarians can proceed with enthusiasm: fantastic hummus and eggplant dishes ensure you won't miss out.

BAZAR AMSTERDAM
MIDDLE EASTERN €€

Map p325 (☑675 05 44; www.bazaramsterdam. nl; Albert Cuypstraat 182; mains €9-16; ⊙11am-midnight Sun-Thu, to 1am Fri & Sat; 🚇🛗; 🚊16/24 Albert Cuypstraat) Beneath a golden angel in the middle of the Albert Cuypmarkt, this one-time church has fab-u-lous tile murals and 1001 Arabian lights to complement the cuisine: from Moroccan to Turkish, Lebanese and Iranian. Fish and chicken dishes please meat eaters; eggplant and portobello mushroom dishes gratify vegetarians. Or just drop in for a beer and baklava.

DE WAAGHALS   VEGETARIAN €€
Map p325 (☎679 96 09; www.waaghals.nl; Frans Halsstraat 29; mains €11-19; ⏰5-9.30pm Tue-Sun; ☑; ☐16/24 Stadhouderskade) The popular white-walled 'Daredevil' is stylish enough for non-vegies to re-examine their dining priorities. The menu concentrates on one country each month – say, Thailand or Italy – plus a rotating array of inventive seasonal, organic dishes. Book ahead (it takes online reservations, too).

ZAGROS   KURDISH €€
Map p325 (☎670 04 61; www.zagrosrestaurant.nl; Albert Cuypstraat 50; mains €11-15; ⏰2.30-11.30pm Tue-Sat; ☑; ☐16/24 Albert Cuypstraat) Just as Kurdistan straddles multiple Middle Eastern regions, so does Kurdish cuisine, with grills and stews (mostly lamb and chicken), salads of cucumber, tomato or onion, and starters like hummus and *dumast* (thick, dry yoghurt). Book ahead on weekends.

★CIEL BLEU   FRENCH €€€
(☎678 74 50; www.cielbleu.nl; Ferdinand Bolstraat 333, Hotel Okura Amsterdam; mains €75-115, 4-/5-/6-course menu €110/135/160; ⏰6.30-10.30pm Mon-Sat, closed late Jul–mid-Aug; ☐12/25 Cornelius Trootsplein) Mindblowing, two-Michelin-star creations at this pinnacle of gastronomy change with the seasons, so spring might see scallops and oysters with vanilla sea salt and gin-and-tonic foam, or king crab with salted lemon, *beurre blanc* ice cream and caviar. Just as incomparable is the 23rd-floor setting with aerial views north across the city. If your budget doesn't stretch to dining here, head to the adjacent Twenty Third Bar (p185).

🍷 **DRINKING & NIGHTLIFE**

The neighbourhood that houses the old Heineken brewery is appropriately chock-full of places to drink it and much more. **In particular, the streets around Gerard Douplein heave with a spirited local crowd.**

BARÇA   DESIGNER BAR
Map p325 (www.barca.nl; Marie Heinekenplein 30-31; ⏰11am-1am Sun-Thu, to 3am Fri & Sat; ☐16/24 Stadhouderskade) One of the hottest bars in the 'hood, this 'Barcelona in Amsterdam'-themed club is the heart of Marie Heinekenplein. Hang in the plush red and dark-timber interior, or spread out on the terrace.

CAFÉ BINNEN BUITEN   BROWN CAFÉ
Map p325 (Ruysdaelkade 115; ⏰11am-1am Sun-Thu, to 3am Fri & Sat; ☐16/24 Ruysdaelkade) The minute there's a sliver of sunshine in the air, this *café* gets packed. Sure the food looks good (and the people even better) and the bar is candlelit and cosy. But what really brings in the crowds is simply the best canalside terrace in De Pijp – an idyllic spot to while away an entire afternoon.

TWENTY THIRD BAR   COCKTAIL BAR
(www.okura.nl; Ferdinand Bolstraat 333, Hotel Okura Amsterdam; ⏰6pm-1am Sun-Thu, to 2am Fri & Sat; ☐12/25 Cornelius Trootsplein) Twenty Third Bar has sweeping views to the west and south, a stunning bar-snack menu prepared in the kitchen of Ciel Bleu (p185) (dishes €7-15; caviar €36-60 per 10g), champagne cocktails and Heineken on tap.

CAFÉ BERKHOUT   BROWN CAFÉ
Map p325 (www.cafeberkhout.nl; Stadhouderskade 77; ⏰10am-1am Mon-Thu, to 3am Fri & Sat, 11am-1am Sun; ☐16/24 Stadhouderskade) Once a derelict spot, this beautifully refurbished brown *café* – with its dark-wood, mirrored and chandelier-rich splendour and shabby elegance – is a natural post-Heineken Experience wind-down spot. (No matter how much beer you've swilled at the Experience, you can't miss this *café*: it's right across the street.) Great food too, especially the burgers.

CAFÉ SARPHAAT   BROWN CAFÉ
Map p325 (☎675 15 65; Ceintuurbaan 157; ⏰9am-late; ☐3/4/25 Van Woustraat) Grab an outdoor table along Sarphatipark, order a frothy beer and see if you don't feel like a local. This is one of the neighbourhood's most genial spots, with a lovely old bar that makes sipping a *jenever* (Dutch gin) in broad daylight seem like a good idea. Free live jazz takes place most Sunday afternoons.

TOP SIGHT
HEINEKEN EXPERIENCE

Heineken, the Netherlands' world-famous brewery, wants you to know that this is not a museum – it's a multisensory experience. Heineken has been going strong since 1864 and the 'Experience' is an appropriately immodest (read: commercial) celebration of its place in Dutch brewing history.

On the site of the company's old De Pijp brewery, which closed in 1988, the 'Experience' is a rollicking self-guided tour. Allow at least 90 minutes to learn the storied history of the Heineken family, find out how the logo has evolved, and follow the brewing process from water and hops right through to bottling. Along the way you can watch Heineken commercials from around the world, sniff the mash in copper tanks, visit the horse stables and make your own music video. The crowning glory is Brew You – a 4-dimensional multimedia exhibit where you 'become' a beer as you get shaken up, heated up, sprayed with water and 'bottled'. True beer connoisseurs will shudder, but it's a lot of fun. Admission includes a 15-minute shuttle boat ride to the Heineken Brand Store (p140) near Rembrandtplein.

Prebooking tickets online saves you €2 and allows you to skip the queues.

DON'T MISS

➡ 'Becoming' a beer through Brew You
➡ Learning to pour a proper frothy pint, Dutch-style

PRACTICALITIES

➡ Map p325
➡ ☑5239435
➡ www.heinekenexperience.com
➡ Stadhouderskade 78
➡ adult/child €18/14
➡ ⊙11am-7.30pm Mon-Thu, 11am-8.30pm Fri-Sun
➡ 🚊16/24 Stadhouderskade

CAFÉ DE GROENE VLINDER   BROWN CAFÉ

Map p325 (Albert Cuypstraat 130; ⊙10am-1am Sun-Thu, to 3am Fri & Sat; 🚊16/24 Albert Cuypstraat) Right on Albert Cuypstraat, the Green Butterfly strikes just the right balance between hip and *gezellig* (cosy, convivial), meaning it's the perfect spot to go for a *koffie verkeerd* (coffee with lots of milk) in the warm wood interior before meeting up for a *biertje* (a beer) on the hopping patio.

QUINTO   CAFE

Map p325 (www.cafequinto.nl; Frans Halsstraat 42; ⊙noon-1am Sun-Thu, to 3am Fri & Sat; 🚊; 🚊tram 16/24 Albert Cuypstraat) On one of De Pijp's loveliest, leafiest side streets, this art deco–styled cafe takes full advantage of its corner location with a heated terrace filled with timber benches and tables. Fairy lights glow from the ceiling from its deceptively large interior. Its market-driven menus are fantastic value.

CHOCOLATE BAR   DESIGNER BAR

Map p325 (www.chocolate-bar.nl; 1e Van der Helststraat 62a; ⊙9am-1am Sun-Thu, to 3am Fri & Sat; 🚊16/24 Albert Cuypstraat) Chocolate isn't the draw here – it's the cool vibe, retro '60s/'70s interior and Euro soundtrack. The candlelit bar makes this place feel like a night out even at noon: curl up with a woolly blanket and a fashion mag on the patio on chilly days. At night, it's a scene; DJs hit the decks from Thursday to Sunday.

KINGFISHER   PUB

Map p325 (www.kingfishercafe.nl; Ferdinand Bolstraat 24; ⊙10am-1am Mon-Thu, to 3am Fri & Sat, noon-1am Sun; 🚊; 🚊16/24 Stadhouderskade) With friendly staff and loyal regulars, Kingfisher is a nucleus of De Pijp's signature feel-good vibe. The communal table welcomes laptops, newspapers and lunching by day. By happy hour the place is kicking.

PILSVOGEL   BROWN CAFÉ

Map p325 (www.pilsvogel.nl; Gerard Douplein 14; ⊙10am-1am Sun-Thu, to 3am Fri & Sat; 🚊16/24 Albert Cuypstraat) The kitchen dispenses small plates through to full meals to a young crowd but that's really secondary when you're sitting on De Pijp's most festive corner. A warm Mediterranean feel reigns at this casual tapas bar, with one of the neighbourhood's prime people-watching patios.

HET PAARDJE   BAR

Map p325 (⌨664 35 39; www.cafehetpaardje.nl;
Gerard Douplein 1; ⊙10am-midnight Mon-Wed, to
1am Thu, 10am-2am Fri & Sat, 11am-midnight Sun;
🚋16/24 Albert Cuypstraat) Inside the decor's
nothing flash (an updated, blander version of a brown *café*, pretty much), but Het
Paardje has one of best, most sprawling terraces in central De Pijp for people watching
(and people watching you).

KATSU   COFFEESHOP

Map p325 (www.katsu.nl; 1e Van der Helststraat
70; ⊙11am-11pm; 🚋16/24 Albert Cuypstraat)
Like the surrounding neighbourhood, this
relaxed coffeeshop brims with colourful
characters of all ages and dispositions. A
front table with newspapers lends a book-
ish vibe.

☆ ENTERTAINMENT

BADCUYP   JAZZ

Map p325 (⌨675 96 69; www.badcuyp.org; 1e
Sweelinckstraat 10; admission €5-10; ⊙Tue-Sun;
🚋4/25 Stadhouderskade) Every neighbourhood should be fortunate enough to have
a vibrant music *café* like this. Combining
a community feel with top-notch, international performers, Badcuyp brings a shot
of pure bohemian energy to the neighbourhood. From Sunday jazz sessions to salsa
nights, you can't walk out after an evening
here and not feel the love.

CC MUZIEKCAFÉ   LIVE MUSIC

Map p325 (⌨06 62436956; www.cccafe.nl;
Rustenburgerstraat 384; ⊙8pm-1am Sun-Thu, to
3am Fri & Sat; 📶; 🚋25 Cornelis Troostplein) A
low-key yet lively little nightclub, CC Muziekcafé is right at home in De Pijp. It dishes
up interesting live acts every night – from
reggae to soul to rock – along with zero
attitude.

RIALTO CINEMA   CINEMA

Map p325 (⌨676 87 00; www.rialtofilm.nl; Ceintuurbaan 338; 🚋3/25 2e Van der Helststraat) This
great old cinema near Sarphatipark focuses on premieres, and shows eclectic art-
house fare from around the world (foreign
films feature Dutch subtitles). The stylish
cafe buzzes with pre- and post-cinema
goers dissecting plot, theme and cinema-
tography.

🛍 SHOPPING

After you've hit the Albert Cuypmarkt,
head to the surrounding streets. They're
less crowded than the market, and
dotted with boutiques and galleries –
perfect for a quiet browse. You'll find
eclectic women's fashion and shoes on
Van Woustraat, off Ceintruurbaan.

★HUTSPOT   CONCEPT STORE

Map p325 (www.hutspotamsterdam.com; Van
Woustraat 4; ⊙noon-7pm Mon, 10am-7pm Tue-
Sat, noon-6pm Sun; 🚋4/25 Stadhouderskade)
Named after the Dutch dish of boiled and
mashed vegies, 'Hotchpotch' was founded
by four young guys with a mission to give
young entrepreneurs the chance to sell
their work. As a result, this concept store
is an inspired mishmash of Dutch-designed
furniture, furnishings, art, homewares and
clothing plus a cool in-store cafe.

FIETSFABRIEK   BICYCLES

Map p325 (www.fietsfabriek.nl; 1e Jacob van
Campenstraat 12; ⊙1-6pm Mon, 9am-6pm Tue-
Fri, 10am-6pm Sat; 🚋16/24 Stadhouderskade)
Wessel van den Bosch trained as an architect, and now he makes custom bicycles
from this wild and crazy workshop. Come
in and pick up a *bakfiets* (cargo bike), a
familiefiets (bike with covered 'pram') or a
standard *omafiets* (one-gear city bike). Just
browsing is a joy.

BLEECKER   CLOTHING

Map p325 (1e Jan Steenstraat 131; ⊙noon-5pm
Tue-Sat; 🚋16/24 Albert Cuypstraat) No rifling
through dusty racks here: this well-curated
store is a vintage lover's heaven, with a
thoughtful eye towards men's and women's
fashions, fab shoes and helpful staff.

DE VREDESPIJP   HOMEWARES

Map p325 (www.vredespijp-artdeco.com; 1e Van
der Helststraat 11a; ⊙noon-6pm Mon, 10am-6pm
Tue-Sat; 📶; 🚋16/24 Stadhouderskade) De Pijp's
ideal rainy day refuge is this art deco home
accessories and furniture shop, which has a
tiny cafe amongst the clutter serving excellent home-baked goods.

RAAK   CLOTHING

Map p325 (www.raakamsterdam.nl; 1e Van der Helststraat 46; ⊙noon-6pm Mon, 10am-6pm Tue-Sat;
🚋16/24 Albert Cuypstraat) Unique casual clothing, bags, jewellery and homewares by Dutch
and Scandinavian designers fill Raak's De

TOP SIGHT
ALBERT CUYPMARKT

Want to experience Amsterdam at its wonderfully chaotic, multicultural best? Head to Europe's most sprawling daily street market (bar Sunday).

Named after landscape painter Albert Cuyp (1620–91), Albert Cuypmart is Amsterdam's largest and busiest market, and is legendary for its huge variety. Scores of aromatic stalls sell Dutch cheese, fish, crustaceans, olives, oils, herbs and spices, and bushels of fresh fruit and vegies. Need some Saturday night bling or a new smartphone cover? How about a bike lock, hair-curling iron, or some flowers for your sweetheart or just to brighten your hotel room? There's also a staggering array of (mostly funky, sometimes junky) clothes and accessories. If you want it, it's likely the Albert Cuypmarkt's got it, and it's probably cheaper than anywhere else.

Don't miss the shops hidden behind the stalls too, selling everything from kitchen gadgets to backpacks and suitcases, bolts of fabric, more bike locks, soaps and shampoos, you name it.

Be sure to sample the cheese (just ask!), from a four-year-old gouda to a creamy *boerenkaas* (farmer's cheese) and indulge in a piping-hot *stroopwafel* (caramel syrup waffle).

DON'T MISS

➡ Cheese galore
➡ Only-in-the-Netherlands gifts (furry clog slippers, anyone?)
➡ *Stroopwafel* to nibble as you go

PRACTICALITIES

➡ Map p325
➡ www.albertcuypmarkt.nl
➡ Albert Cuypstraat, btwn Ferdinand Bolstraat & Van Woustraat
➡ ⏰10am-5pm Mon-Sat
➡ 🚊16/24 Albert Cuypstraat

Pijp store; its Southern Canal Ring branch (p138) has more formal, upmarket fashion.

TILLER GALERIE
ART
Map p325 (www.tillergalerie.com; 1e Jacob van Campenstraat 1; ⏰1-7pm Thu-Sun; 🚊16/24 Stadhouderskade) This intimate, friendly gallery has works by George Heidweiller (check out the surreal Amsterdam skyscapes), Peter Donkersloot's portraits of animals and iconic actors like Marlon Brando, and prints by the late Herman Brood.

HET IS LIEFDE
GIFTS
Map p325 (www.hetisliefde.nl; Gerard Doustraat 65; ⏰10am-6pm Mon & Fri, to 5pm Sat; 🚊16/24 Albert Cuypstraat) Feel the love in this wedding shop, where all forms of romance and general festivity are celebrated. Keepsakes and ephemera include whimsical cake toppers in boy-girl, boy-boy and girl-girl couplings.

STENELUX
GIFTS
Map p325 (📞662 14 90; 1e Jacob van Campenstraat 2; ⏰noon-5pm Thu-Sat; 🚊16/24 Stadhouderskade) Browse Stenelux' delightful collection of gems, minerals, stones and fossils. The fascinating collection from this world and beyond includes meteorites.

NOOR
CLOTHING
Map p325 (📞670 29 16; Albert Cuypstraat 145; ⏰9.30am-6pm Mon-Sat; 🚊16/24 Albert Cuypstraat) There are so many women's clothing stores on the Albert Cuypmarkt, you could spend a week browsing the bargains but the affordable, modern fashion at Noor may make you want to skip the competition altogether. Don't miss the jam-packed sale rack.

BLOND
GIFTS
Map p325 (www.blond-amsterdam.nl; Gerard Doustraat 69; ⏰10am-6pm Wed-Fri, 10am-5pm Sat; 🚊16/24 Albert Cuypstraat) The friendly blonde owners glaze plates and dishes in designs that are hilarious, adorable and colourful: ladies lunching, beach scenes, cakes and chocolates. Great gifts for anyone who likes modern kitsch with a sense of humour.

DE EMAILLEKEIZER
HOMEWARES
Map p325 (📞664 18 47; www.emaillekeizer.nl; 1e Sweelinckstraat 15; ⏰10.30am-6pm Mon-Sat; 🚊4/25 Stadhouderskade) This store brims with enamel treasures, including tableware with designs from China, Ghana and Poland. Dutch signs, such as the unmistakable 'coffeeshop', make interesting souvenirs.

Plantage, Eastern Islands & Eastern Docklands

PLANTAGE | EASTERN ISLANDS & EASTERN DOCKLANDS

Neighbourhood Top Five

1 Frolick with the animals at the gorgeous **Artis Royal Zoo** (p192), mainland Europe's oldest zoo and the world's third-largest.

2 Put yourself in the shoes of courageous WWII Dutch Resistance fighters at the inspiring **Verzetsmuseum** (p194).

3 Fathom the history of Dutch seafaring through the extensive maritime collection at the **Het Scheepvaartmuseum** (p191).

4 Experience live classical music or jazz at the acoustically and visually stunning **Muziekgebouw aan 't IJ** (p197).

5 Learn about science and technology in the striking, shiplike building that houses **NEMO** (p192).

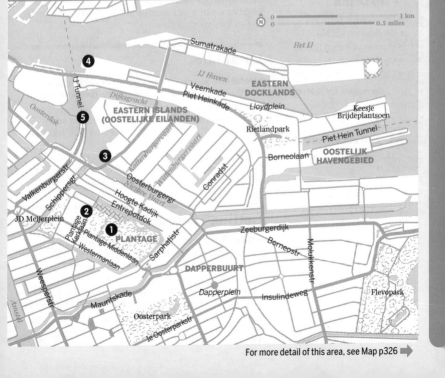

For more detail of this area, see Map p326 ➡

Lonely Planet's Top Tip

Too many travellers overlook the Eastern Islands and Docklands, thinking them too far out of the centre (when it's actually less than a 10-minute bike or tram ride). If you're remotely into boats, maritime history or modern architecture, don't even think about skipping this area.

✖ Best Places to Eat

➡ Greetje (p195)
➡ Gebr Hartering (p195)
➡ Zouthaven (p195)
➡ Éénvistwéévis (p195)
➡ Café Kadijk (p193)

For reviews, see p193.➡

🍷 Best Places to Drink

➡ Brouwerij 't IJ (p197)
➡ SkyLounge (p196)
➡ Hannekes Boom (p196)
➡ De Groene Olifant (p196)
➡ Café Scharrebier (p196)

For reviews, see p196.➡

☆ Best Entertainment

➡ Muziekgebouw aan 't IJ (p197)
➡ Conservatorium van Amsterdam (p197)
➡ Panama (p197)
➡ Kriterion (p197)

For reviews, see p197.➡

Explore Plantage, Eastern Islands & Eastern Docklands

The leafy district known as Plantage (Plantation) became a green recreation area during the 17th century. City planners reclaimed the land on the eastern side of the Amstel in a bid to capitalise on the city's flourishing overseas trade. This 'fourth city extension' did not take off, however, and in 1682, the area was converted into garden plots. By the 19th century construction boomed, and it became an entertainment district. Its darkest hour came during WWII when its large Jewish community was detained and deported from here.

Today the neighbourhood is a lovely place to stroll and admire the 19th-century architecture. Spend your first day here, allowing least a couple of hours at Artis Royal Zoo. Then walk through the Hortus Botanicus before visiting the Verzetsmuseum. End the day with a local brew beneath the De Gooyer Windmill at the Brouwerij 't IJ.

If you're looking to see the cutting edge of Dutch – and indeed European – architecture, the former shipyard and warehouse district of the Eastern Islands (Oostelijke Eilanden) and Eastern Docklands (Oostelijk Havengebied) is a must. Hop on a bike on your second day to explore traditional sights like the Het Scheepvaartmuseum, as well as mod designs such as the zinc-facade residential complex 'the Whale', the shiny Centrale Bibliotheek Amsterdam and the sparkling performance halls of the Muziekgebouw aan 't IJ. Finish up at NEMO, and head up to its roof for swooping views.

Local Life

➡**Hotel Life** You don't have to stay at the Lloyd Hotel (p234) to wine, dine and check out the fascinating hotel history exhibit.

➡**Architectural Life** Identify local landmarks and glimpse the city's future at the absorbing architectural centre, ARCAM (p193).

➡**Brewery Life** There's much more to Dutch beer than Heineken, as you can discover on a behind-the-scenes tour of the organic Brouwerij 't IJ (p197).

Getting There & Away

➡**Tram** Trams 9 and 14 are handy for reaching Plantage; tram 10 goes to the Eastern Islands and Eastern Docklands. Tram 26 travels along the IJ waterfront.

➡**Bus** Buses 22 and 48 are useful for areas of the Eastern Islands and Eastern Docklands that the tram doesn't reach.

⊙ SIGHTS

⊙ Plantage

HORTUS BOTANICUS   GARDEN

Map p326 (Botanical Garden; www.dehortus.nl; Plantage Middenlaan 2a; adult/child €8.50/4.50; ☺10am-5pm daily, to 7pm Sun Jul & Aug; 🚊9/14 Mr Visserplein) Established in 1638, this venerable garden became a repository for tropical seeds and plants brought in (read: smuggled out of other countries) by Dutch trading ships. From here, coffee, pineapple, cinnamon and palm-oil plants were distributed throughout the world. The 4000-plus species are kept in wonderful structures, including the colonial-era seed house and a three-climate glasshouse. The butterfly house is a hit with kids in particular.

Free one-hour guided tours take place at 2pm on Sunday year round – pick up a ticket from the entrance and give it to the guide.

On Sunday afternoons in July and August from 4pm, you can listen to Latin, jazz, tango, pop music or blues in idyllic tropical surrounds.

WERTHEIMPARK   PARK

Map p326 (Plantage Parklaan; ☺7am-9pm; 🚊9/14 Mr Visserplein) Opposite the Hortus Botanicus, this park is a brilliant, willow-shaded spot for lazing by the Nieuwe Herengracht. Its most significant feature is the Auschwitz Memorial, designed by Dutch writer Jan Wolkers: a panel of broken mirrors installed in the ground reflects the sky.

HOLLANDSCHE SCHOUWBURG   MEMORIAL

Map p326 (Holland Theatre; 🕿531 03 10; www.hollandscheschouwburg.nl; Plantage Middenlaan 24; suggested donation €2.50; ☺11am-5pm; 🚊9/14 Plantage Kerklaan) This historic theatre – first known as the Artis Theatre after its inception in 1892 – quickly became a hub of cultural life in Amsterdam, staging major dramas and operettas. During WWII the occupying Germans turned it into a Jewish theatre before, tragically, it became a detention centre for Jews held for deportation.

Up to 80,000 Jews passed through here on their way to the death camps. Glass panels have been engraved with the names of all Jewish families deported, and upstairs is a modest exhibit hall with photos and artefacts of Jewish life from before and during the war.

ENTREPOTDOK   ARCHITECTURE

Map p326 (🚊9/14 Plantage Kerklaan) The area northeast of the Plantage was the stomping ground of the Dutch East India Company (VOC), which grew rich on sea trade in the 17th century. The VOC owned this 500m row of warehouses – the largest storage depot in Europe at the time – located in a customs-free zone.

Some of the original facades have been preserved, and the facility has been converted into desirable offices, apartments and appealing dockside cafes, with tables perfect for lazing away an afternoon at the water's edge.

DE GOOYER WINDMILL   WINDMILL

Map p326 (Funenkade 5; 🚊10 Hoogte Kadijk) This 18th-century grain mill is the sole survivor of five windmills that once stood in this part of town. The mill was moved to its current position in 1814. It was fully renovated in 1925 and is now a private home. The public baths alongside the windmill were converted into Brouwerij 't IJ (p197) in 1985.

KADIJKSPLEIN   SQUARE

Map p326 (Kadijksplein; 🚊22/48 Kadijksplein) Flanked by *café* (pub) terraces, this tranquil square has twin views of 17th-century canals and cruise ships docking at the Docklands.

MUIDERPOORT   GATE

Map p326 (Alexanderplein; 🚊9 Alexanderplein) This grand, classical arch was built in 1770 as a gateway to the city. On the south side you'll see the Amsterdam emblem of three St Andreas' crosses, while on the other side there's a cog ship emblem, which appeared on Amsterdam's coat of arms in medieval times.

In 1811 Napoleon rode triumphantly through the gate with his royal entourage, and promptly demanded food for his ragged troops.

⊙ Eastern Islands & Eastern Docklands

HET SCHEEPVAARTMUSEUM   MUSEUM

Map p326 (Maritime Museum; 🕿523 22 22; www.scheepvaartmuseum.nl; Kattenburgerplein 1;

adult/child €15/7.50; ☺9am-5pm; ⊞; 🚊22/48 Kattenburgerplein) An immense 17th-century admiralty building houses one of the world's most extensive collections of maritime memorabilia. Early shipping routes, naval combat, fishing and whaling are all detailed, and there are some 500 models of boats and ships. A full-scale replica of the Dutch East India Company's 700-tonne *Amsterdam,* one of the largest ships of the fleet, is moored outside.

MUZIEKGEBOUW AAN 'T IJ — CONCERT HALL

Map p326 (☎tickets 788 20 00; www.muziekgebouw.nl; Piet Heinkade 1; admission to building free, performance prices vary; ☺ticket office noon-7pm Mon-Sat; 🚊26 Muziekgebouw) Even if you don't catch a performance here, the magnificent 'Music Building on the IJ' is a visual treat. The complex – with the main hall for varying shows and the smaller Bimhuis (p197) for jazz – was designed by the Danish firm 3xNielsen. Some 20 years in the making, it opened in 2005.

On the upper floor you'll find the computerised 'sound garden', a perfect diversion for children. You can visit the concert hall during box office opening hours, or during performances.

With huge windows overlooking the IJ, the venue's excellent Zouthaven (p195) restaurant specialises in seafood.

NEMO — MUSEUM

Map p326 (☎531 32 33; www.e-nemo.nl; Oosterdok 2; admission €13.50, roof terrace free; ☺10am-5pm, closed Mon Oct-May; ⊞; 🚊22/48 IJ-Tunnel) Perched atop the entrance to the IJ Tunnel is NEMO, the largest museum of science and technology in the Netherlands. The dramatic, green-copper building rises from the waterfront like a ship setting sail; Italian architect Renzo Piano (whose works include Paris' Centre Pompidou) conceived the design as the inverse of the IJ tunnel below.

Inside, Piano's design reflects a 'noble factory', with exposed wiring and pipes. It's really meant for kids, but most grown-ups will enjoy it, too. There are loads of interactive exhibits: drawing with a laser, 'antigravity' trick mirrors and a 'lab' where you can answer such questions as 'How black is black?' and 'How do you make cheese?'. Signage is in English and Dutch.

NEMO's stepped, decklike roof is the city's largest summer terrace, and worth a stair climb for the panoramic views.

PLANTAGE, EASTERN ISLANDS & EASTERN DOCKLANDS SIGHTS

⊙ TOP SIGHT
ARTIS ROYAL ZOO

A zoo, a bourgeois park or a manicured English garden? The Artis Royal Zoo is essentially all three, wrapped up in one elegant package.

The zoo is the world's third-largest, and the oldest zoo in mainland Europe. It's a beautifully curated experience, with plenty of room to observe and simply reflect on the wildness and the grandness of the animal kingdom.

In addition to the expected zoo attractions – big cats, apes and elephants – a highlight is the African savannah. Another must-see is the aquarium, a graceful purpose-built hall with a rainforest, a tropical coral reef and a cross-section of an Amsterdam canal. All-up there are 900 different animal species and 200 species of trees.

Locals as well as tourists visit to stroll the paths laid out through the former Plantage gardens. The grounds are packed with heritage-listed 19th-century buildings and monuments, making it feel more like a zoological museum than a zoo. It also has a lovely, airy cafe.

The Artis Royal Zoo Express (p193) is a nifty way to combine a canal-boat ride with a trip to the zoo.

DON'T MISS

➡ The aquarium
➡ The lion habitat
➡ The African savannah
➡ The planetarium

PRACTICALITIES

➡ Map p326
➡ ☎523 34 00
➡ www.artis.nl
➡ Plantage Kerklaan 38-40
➡ adult/child €19.50/16
➡ ☺9am-6pm Apr-Oct, to 5pm Nov-Mar
➡ ⊞
➡ 🚊9/14 Plantage Kerklaan

PERSMUSEUM MUSEUM

(Map p326 (☎692 88 10; www.persmuseum. nl; Zeeburgerkade 10; adult/child €4.50/3.25; ⏰10am-5pm Tue-Fri, noon-5pm Sun; 🚊22 Veelaan) The thoughtful and vigilant caretaker of Dutch journalism history, the press museum is much more interesting to non-Dutch speakers than it may sound. It's housed in sleek premises and has a large collection of historic newspapers (going all the way back to 1600), political and editorial cartoons and press photos, and a great stock of amusing old publicity posters.

CENTRALE BIBLIOTHEEK AMSTERDAM LIBRARY

Map p326 (Amsterdam Central Library; ☎523 09 00; www.oba.nl; Oosterdokskade 143; ⏰10am-10pm; 🚊4/9/16/24/25/26 Centraal) **FREE** Unveiled in 2007, this symmetrical, nine-storey 'tower of knowledge' (its self-appointed nickname) is the country's largest library and has claimed a commanding spot in Amsterdam's increasingly modern landscape. Inviting chairs and couches are scattered around every floor, as are loads of free internet terminals (there's also free wi-fi). Relax in the top-floor cafe overlooking the city and water.

ARCAM ARCHITECTURE

Map p326 (Stichting Architectuurcentrum Amsterdam; ☎620 48 78; www.arcam.nl; Prins Hendrikkade 600; ⏰1-5pm Tue-Sat; 🚊22/48 Kadijksplein) **FREE** This showpiece building of the Amsterdam Architecture Foundation is a one-stop shop for all your architectural needs. Expert staff are on hand to interpret

---

> **ℹ ARTIS ROYAL ZOO EXPRESS**
>
> Save money by combining a canal boat cruise and a visit to the zoo with the **Artis Royal Zoo Express** (Map p326; www.lovers.nl; adult/child return boat trip incl zoo entry €25/19; ⏰departures hourly 10am-1pm, return 3.20pm, 4.20pm & 5.20pm). Boats depart from the **Rederij Lovers** (www.lovers.nl; Prins Hendrikkade 25-27) dock on the western side of Centraal Station. From here it's a 20-minute ride to the zoo via the IJ, while the return trip to Centraal is a scenic 35-minute cruise via Herengracht and Prinsengracht.

---

the fascinating changing exhibits, and you can find books, guide maps and suggestions for tours on foot, by bike and by public transport.

WERFMUSEUM 'T KROMHOUT MUSEUM

Map p326 (☎627 67 77; www.machinekamer.nl; Hoogte Kadijk 147; adult/child €5/free; ⏰10am-3pm Tue; 🚊10 Hoogte Kadijk) Boats are still repaired at the 18th-century wharf on the outer side of the dyke. The eastern hall is a museum devoted to shipbuilding and to the indestructible marine engines that were designed and built here. Anyone with an interest in marine engineering will love the place; others will probably want to move on. Signage is primarily in Dutch only.

EATING

Plantage may be just footsteps from Nieuwmarkt, but what a difference those few steps make, taking you to an area that's blissfully quiet. In the Eastern Islands and Eastern Docklands, many of the best places to dine are by (or literally on) the water.

🍴 Plantage

BURGERMEESTER BURGERS €

Map p326 (www.burgermeester.eu; Plantage Kerklaan 37; burgers €7-9; ⏰noon-11pm; 🖊🔧; 🚊9/14 Plantage Kerklaan) This slick burger joint – a play on 'mayor' (burgemeester) – uses only organic beef (or lamb, felafel or fish), in huge portions that would pass as a main dish without a bun. Then come the toppings: feta, fresh mint, pesto, pancetta and more. Sides include roast potatoes and grilled corn on the cob (but no fries).

AGORA CAFETERIA €

Map p326 (www.uva.nl; Roetersstraat 11; mains €3-6; ⏰9.30am-3pm & 5-7pm Mon-Thu, 9.30am-3pm Fri; 🚊7/10 Weesperplein) When professors in suits are spotted eating in a student cafeteria, it's often out of desperation. But in Agora's case, the food is actually pretty good, with cheap and filling soups, sandwiches and daily changing hot dishes.

CAFÉ KADIJK INDONESIAN €€

Map p326 (☎06 1774 4441; www.cafekadijk.nl; Kadijksplein 5; mains €16-20; ⏰6-10pm Mon-Sat, 5-9pm Sun; 🚊22/48 Kadijksplein) This sunny, split-level *café* looks like it can serve no more than coffee from its tiny kitchen, but in fact it does quite good Indonesian food. Go for the *Eitjes van Tante Bea* (a spicy mix of egg, shrimp and beans), as well as a mini version of the normally gigantic *rijsttafel* (Indonesian banquet). No credit cards.

CAFÉ SMIT EN VOOGT
CAFE €€

Map p326 (www.cafesmitenvoogt.nl; Plantage Parklaan 10; lunch mains €4-7.50, dinner mains €14.50-17.50; ⏰kitchen 10am-9pm; ☎; 🚊9/14 Plantage Kerklaan) Equal parts refined and relaxed, this high-ceilinged, high-spirited cafe is an ideal spot to stop for lunch or a coffee when visiting the adjacent Wertheim-park. A lovely selection of simple salads and sandwiches is complemented by a handful of dinner choices like baked aubergine with goat's cheese, and duck breast with black-bean sauce.

KOFFIEHUIS VAN DEN VOLKSBOND
INTERNATIONAL €€

Map p326 (www.koffiehuisvandenvolksbond.nl; Kadijksplein 4; mains €16-20; ⏰6-10pm Mon-Sat, 5-9pm Sun; 🚊22/48 Kadijksplein) This laid-back place began life as a charitable coffeehouse for dockworkers and it still has a

fashionably grungy vibe – wood floors, tarnished chandeliers, a giant red-rose mural and an antique bath tub. Creative comfort food spans dishes like red onion tart with blue cheese, lamb with artichoke puree and a scrumptious Belgian chocolate terrine. No credit cards.

PAERZ
INTERNATIONAL €€

Map p326 (☎623 22 06; www.paerz.nl; Entre-potdok 64; lunch mains €6.50-11, dinner mains €18.50-22.50; ⏰noon-4pm & 6-10pm Wed-Sun; 🚊22/48 Kadijksplein) Along the Entrepotdok the former warehouse's double-height dining space with wooden beams and mezzanine seating sets the tone for stylish fare at lunch (gourmet burgers, salads and so on) and dinner (duck, premium steaks and skilfully cooked fish).

✖ Eastern Islands & Eastern Docklands

EINDE VAN DE WERELD
VEGETARIAN €

Map p326 (www.eindevandewereld.nl; Javakade 61; dishes €7-10; ⏰from 6pm Wed & Fri; ☎🍴; 🚊10 Azartplein) At 'the end of the world', look for the big yellow-and-green boat *Quo*

👁 TOP SIGHT
VERZETSMUSEUM

The Verzetsmuseum (Dutch Resistance Museum) shows, in no uncertain terms, how much courage it takes to actively resist an adversary so ruthless that you can't trust neighbours, friends or even family.

Ascend the spiral staircase to the mezzanine to watch an introductory film (available in multiple languages), then head anticlockwise around the main floor. Beginning with the build-up to WWII in the 1930s, the chronologically arranged exhibits give a powerful insight into the difficulties faced by those who fought the propaganda-steeped German occupation from within – as well as the minority who went along with the Nazis. Topics include the concepts of active and passive resistance, how the illegal resistance press operated, how 300,000 people were kept in hiding and how all this could be funded. Beneath the mezzanine an exhibit covers the Dutch role in the war in the Pacific, particularly in relation to Indonesian independence from the Netherlands. Labels are in Dutch and English.

Included in admission, the new Verzetsmuseum Junior relates the stories of four Dutch children, putting the resistance into context for kids.

Next door, the museum's cafe is a perfect sanctum for a post-museum discussion over coffee.

DON'T MISS
➡ The introductory film
➡ The Resistance press exhibits
➡ The Pacific exhibit

PRACTICALITIES
➡ Map p326
➡ ☎620 25 35
➡ www.verzets museum.org
➡ Plantage Kerklaan 61
➡ adult/child €8/4.50
➡ ⏰10am-5pm Tue-Fri, 11am-5pm Sat-Mon
➡ 🚊9/14 Plantage Kerklaan

Vadis. The volunteer-run onboard restaurant is cheap and very cheerful. Show up early: you can't book, and when the food's gone, it's gone. No credit cards.

GEBR HARTERING   CONTEMPORARY DUTCH €€

Map p326 (⚏421 06 99; www.gebr-hartering. nl; Peperstraat 10; 4-/7-course menu €40/65 Tue, Wed & Sun, 6-/9-course menu €50/75 Thu-Sat; ⊘6-10.30pm Tue-Sun; ⛴32/33 Prins Hendrikkade) At this jewel of a restaurant founded by two brothers, the menu changes daily so you never know what you'll be tasting, but dishes are unfailingly delicious and exquisitely presented. The wine list is succinct and the timber dining room and canal-side location impossibly romantic.

ZOUTHAVEN   SEAFOOD €€

Map p326 (⚏788 20 90; www.zouthaven.nl; Piet Heinkade 1, Muziekgebouw aan 't IJ; lunch mains €7.50-14.50, dinner mains €19-20; ⊘10.30am-11pm; ⛴26 Muziekgebouw) It's practically a commandment nowadays that any top performing space have a flash dining space, and the Muziekgebouw aan 't IJ's is hard to beat for location and views. Several storeys of glass and a sweeping terrace give you an IJ's-eye perspective, and the food, such as pan-fried gurnard and pistachio risotto, and green tea panna cotta, is superb.

The seafood is sustainable and/or organic.

ÉÉNVISTWÉÉVIS   SEAFOOD €€

Map p326 (⚏623 28 94; www.eenvistweevis.nl; Schippersgracht 6; mains €17.50-22.50; ⊘6-10pm Tue-Sat; ⛴22/48 Kadijksplein) This unassuming local favourite, with a shell-and-chandelier interior, has a short, handwritten menu utilising whatever's fresh from the sea, such as nettle soup with prawns, sole in butter, and great oysters.

MERCAT   SPANISH €€

Map p326 (⚏344 64 24; www.mercat.nl; Oostelijke Handelskade 4; tapas €3.50-7, mains €16.50-20.50; ⊘11am-10.30pm; ⛴26 Rietlandpark) This vast postindustrial space serves feisty Spanish fare such as chicken marinated in garlic oil, and chorizo, *morcilla* (blood sausage) and white-bean stew. On the last Wednesday of every month, there's unlimited paella, along with flamenco and sangria, while the final Saturday of the month has a dinner and dancing deal with neighbouring club Panama (p197).

FIFTEEN   INTERNATIONAL €€

Map p326 (⚏509 50 15; www.fifteen.nl; Jollemanhof 9; mains €15-24; ⊘noon-3pm & 5.30-10pm; ⛴26 Kattenburgerstraat) Celebrity chef Jamie Oliver has brought to Amsterdam a concept he began in London: take 15 young people from underprivileged backgrounds and train them for a year in the restaurant biz. Results: noble intention, patchy execution. The setting, however, is beyond question: Fifteen faces the IJ, and the busy, open-kitchen space is city-cool, with graffitied walls and exposed wood beams.

GARE DE L'EST   INTERNATIONAL €€

Map p326 (⚏463 06 20; www.garedelest.nl; Cruquiusweg 9; 4-course menu €32; ⊘6-10pm; ⛴22 Het Funen) You won't know what to expect from the four courses on the surprise menu until they arrive, but dietary requirements (including vegetarianism) can be accommodated. Portuguese tiles and glowing Middle Eastern lamps adorn the interior of the charming 1901 building, but in warm weather the best seats are in the courtyard.

DE WERELDBOL   INTERNATIONAL €€

Map p326 (⚏362 87 25; www.dewereldbol.nl; Piraeusplein 59; mains €17.50-20.50, 3-course menu €30; ⊘5-9pm Tue-Sun; ⛴10 Azartplein) A passionate and personable owner-chef, an ever-changing menu and an idyllic view of boats bobbing on the water make this small, dark-wood restaurant a fine place to end a day of sightseeing in the area.

SEA PALACE   CHINESE €€

(⚏626 47 77; www.seapalace.nl; Oosterdokskade 8; mains €14-28; ⊘noon-11pm; ⛴4/9/16/24/25/26 Centraal) It's a funny thing about floating Chinese restaurants: they look like tourist traps but so often serve superb food. The Sea Palace's three floors are busy with locals and visitors who aren't only here for the great views of the city from across the IJ. Try the dim sum or the excellent hot pot. Reservations recommended.

★GREETJE   CONTEMPORARY DUTCH €€€

Map p326 (⚏779 74 50; www.restaurantgreetje. nl; Peperstraat 23-25; mains €24-29; ⊘6-10pm; ⛴32/33 Prins Hendrikkade) Utilising market-fresh organic produce, Greetje resurrects and recreates traditional Dutch recipes like roasted Dutch rib eye with dried apricots and Frisian sausage, or pollock with fennel and Zeeland mussel foam. A good place to start is the two-person Big Beginning, with a sampling of hot and cold starters.

If you can't decide on dessert (which, with dishes like beetroot ice cream with white chocolate, or crème brûlée with sweet wood extract and liquorice ice cream, is no easy feat), go for the Grand Finale (for two people) to share all six.

🍷 DRINKING & NIGHTLIFE

In keeping with all the daring architecture out here, the Plantage, Eastern Islands and Eastern Docklands area has seen an invasion of back-lit designer bars and media-savvy cafés. Don't miss a tour or at least a beer at the Brouwerij 't IJ microbrewery adjacent to the De Gooyer Windmill.

★ HANNEKES BOOM
BAR

Map p326 (www.hannekesboom.nl; Dijksgracht 4; ⊘10am-1am Sun-Thu, to 3am Fri & Sat; ⊠26 Muziekgebouw) Just across the water from NEMO, yet a local secret, this laidback waterside *café* built from recycled materials has a beer garden that really feels like a garden, with timber benches, picnic tables and summer barbecues. Mellow live music such as jazz or singer-songwriters regularly takes place.

Its fascinating history dates back to 1662, when it was the site of a guard post monitoring maritime traffic into the city.

SKYLOUNGE
COCKTAIL BAR

Map p326 (http://doubletree3.hilton.com; Oosterdoksstraat 4, DoubleTree Amsterdam Centraal Station; ⊘11am-1am Sun-Thu, to 3am Fri & Sat; ⊠1/2/4/5/24/25 Centraal) A jaw-dropping 360-degree panorama of Amsterdam extends from the glass-walled SkyLounge on the 11th floor of the DoubleTree Amsterdam Centraal Station hotel, and just gets better when you head out to its vast SkyTerrace, with an outdoor bar and timber decking strewn with sofas.

Drinks don't come cheap (compared with its soft drinks, cocktails like 11th Heaven aren't actually bad value) but the view is unrivalled anywhere in town.

DE GROENE OLIFANT
BROWN CAFÉ

Map p326 (www.degroeneolifant.nl; Sarphatistraat 510; 11am-1am Sun-Thu, to 2am Fri & Sat; ⊠9 Alexanderplein) Steeped in Victorian-era opulence with intricate woodwork, the 'Green Elephant' transports you back in time. Sit at the circa-1880 bar with the locals and admire the art deco glass, or retreat to the lofted dining room for dinner like the the elegant residents of yesteryear's Plantage.

CAFÉ SCHARREBIER
BROWN CAFÉ

Map p326 (www.scharrebier.nl; Rapenburgerplein 1; ⊘11am-1am Sun-Thu, to 3am Fri & Sat; ⊠22 Kadijksplein) Overlooking the lock, the terrace at this snug little brown *café* is an inviting spot for a beer or *jenever*. (*Scharrebier*, incidentally, was beer mixed with water to make it more affordable.)

ODESSA
BAR

Map p326 (📞419 30 10; www.de-odessa.nl; Veemkade 259; ⊘4pm-1am Wed & Thu, to 3am Fri & Sat; ⊠26 Rietlandpark) With indoor and outdoor decks and a 1970s-themed 'plush-porno' decor, this groovy boat is just the sort of place where Hugh Hefner would hold a debauched pyjama party. Combining a sense of humour along with its unique brand of cool, it's a scene for people who normally hate scenes. DJs take over late at night.

KHL
BAR

Map p326 (www.khl.nl; Oostelijke Handelskade 44; ⊘4pm-1am Tue-Fri, noon-1am Sat & Sun; ⊠26 Rietlandpark) Set in a historic 1917 brick building with great tile work, KHL opens to a terrace that's idyllic for a glass of wine sourced from small vineyards. Regular live music ranges from Latin to pop and *klezmer* (traditional Jewish music).

KANIS & MEILAND
BAR

Map p326 (www.kanisenmeiland.nl; Levantkade 127; ⊘8.30am-1am Mon-Fri, 10am-1am Sat & Sun; 📶; ⊠10 Azartplein) A favourite among the 'islanders', this cavernous spot has an inviting wooden reading table, tall windows facing the 'mainland' and a quiet terrace directly on the water.

CAFÉ PAKHUIS WILHELMINA
CLUB

Map p326 (📞419 33 68; www.cafepakhuiswilhelmina.nl; Veemkade 576; ⊘8pm-1am Sun-Thu, to 3am Fri & Sat; ⊠26 Kattenburgerstraat) Well known for its hilariously fun hard-rock

BROUWERIJ 'T IJ

At the foot of the De Gooyer Windmill, Amsterdam's leading organic microbrewery, **Brouwerij 't IJ** (Map p326; www.brouwerijhetij.nl; Funenkade 7; tours €4.50; ⊗bar 2-8pm, English-language tours 3.30pm Fri-Sun; 📮10 Hoogte Kadijk) 🍺, produces fabulous brews, which you can taste on a 30-minute tour (admission includes a beer).

The tasting room has a cosy beer-hall feel, with dried hops and bottles lining the walls. If you're not taking a tour, definitely drop by for a pint (out on the terrace in warm weather). Most of the beer brewed here never leaves the premises, so it's fresh as well as eco-friendly.

In addition to seasonal brews, try Brouwerij 't IJ's latest success story, a dark blonde IPA (India Pale Ale); the sweet, 9% amber Columbus; or the Amsterdams Bruin (Amsterdam Brown Ale), also known as Collaboration #1 because it's the first brewing collaboration between Brouwerij 't IJ and Brouwerij de Prael (p85).

karaoke as well as its alternative dance nights, regular indie rock and other live music gigs, this is low-key clubbing at its best. Hours can vary.

CAFÉ ORLOFF BAR
Map p326 (www.orloff.nl; Kadijksplein 11; ⊗8am-1am Mon-Thu, 8am-3am Fri, 10am-3am Sat, 11am-1am Sun; 🚇; 📮22/48 Kadijksplein) On the picturesque Kadijksplein, Orloff's sprawling terrace is one of the most tranquil in town. Inside, there's a magazine-strewn communal table.

CAFÉ KOOSJE BROWN CAFÉ
Map p326 (www.koosjeamsterdam.nl; Plantage Middenlaan 37; ⊗9am-1am Sun-Thu, to 3am Fri & Sat; 📮9/14 Plantage Kerklaan) If the three catchwords for real estate are location, location and location, then Koosje – situated between the Artis Royal Zoo and the Hollandsche Schouwburg – has got a lock on the market. Perch at the window or on the terrace to soak up the street corner's vibrant atmosphere.

⭐ ENTERTAINMENT

MUZIEKGEBOUW AAN 'T IJ CONCERT VENUE
Map p326 (📞788 20 00; www.muziekgebouw.nl; Piet Heinkade 1; tickets €26-37; ⊗box office noon-6pm Mon-Sat; 📮26 Muziekgebouw) This dazzling performing-arts venue brings together several agendas under one roof. Behind the high-tech exterior, you'll find a dramatically lit main hall with flexible stage layout and great acoustics. Its jazz stage, Bimhuis (p197), is more intimate. Under-30s can get €10 tickets at the box

office 30 minutes before showtime, or online via http://earlybirds.muziekgebouw.nl.

Everyone else should try the **Last Minute Ticket Shop** (www.lastminuteticketshop.nl) for discounts.

CONSERVATORIUM VAN AMSTERDAM CLASSICAL MUSIC
Map p326 (📞527 75 50; www.ahk.nl/conservatorium; Oosterdokskade 151; 📮4/9/16/24/25 Centraal Station) Catch a delightful classical recital by students at the Netherlands' largest conservatory of music. It's in a snazzy contemporary building with state-of-the-art acoustics, endless glass walls and light-flooded interiors.

PANAMA CLUB
Map p326 (Oostelijke Handelskade 4; 📮26 Rietlandpark) Wildly diverse events at this always-happening venue span Latin, Ibiza vibes, Cuban big bands and more. Lots of retro music nights, R&B and hip-hop, and plenty of opportunities to get your groove on.

KRITERION CINEMA
Map p326 (📞623 17 08; www.kriterion.nl; Roetersstraat 170; ⊗10.30am-1am Sun-Thu, 10.30am-3am Fri, 12.30pm-3am Sat; 📮7/10 Weesperplein) Student-run since 1945, this cinema and *café* has a great array of premieres, themed parties, classics, kids' flicks and more. It also hosts several film festivals throughout the year.

BIMHUIS JAZZ
Map p326 (📞788 21 88; www.bimhuis.nl; Piet Heinkade 3; ⊗closed Aug; 📮26 Muziekgebouw) Bimhuis is the beating jazz heart of the Netherlands, and its stylish digs at the Muziekgebouw aan 't IJ (p192) draw international jazz greats.

SHOPPING

DATEMA AMSTERDAM
BOOKS, MAPS

Map p326 (427 77 27; www.datema-amsterdam. nl; Prins Hendrikkade 176/50; 10am-6pm Tue-Fri, to 5pm Sat; 22 Kadijksplein) Anyone with a passion for boats will enjoy browsing through the navigation charts and nautical books at this specialist maritime bookshop. If you're setting sail in the Netherlands, its personalised advice is indispensable.

FRANK'S SMOKEHOUSE
FOOD & DRINK

Map p326 (www.smokehouse.nl; Wittenburgergracht 303; 9am-4pm Mon, to 6pm Tue-Fri, to 5pm Sat; 22 Wittenburgergracht) Frank is a prime supplier to Amsterdam's restaurants, and his excellent Alaskan salmon, halibut and yellowfin tuna can be vacuum-packed for travelling (customs regulations permitting). He also sells stunning sandwiches (smoked halibut with pumpkin relish, king crab, wild boar and cranberry chutney).

LOODS 6
SHOPPING CENTRE

Map p326 (www.loods6.nl; KNSM-laan 143; 10 Azartplein) This isn't a shopping centre of the mall variety, but rather a string of shops in a 1900-built former Royal Dutch Steam Company (KNSM) customs warehouse and passenger terminal. Noteworthy shops include super-cool skateboarder clothing shop **Arrival/Departure** (www.arrivaldeparture. nl; 11am-6pm Tue-Sat, 1-6pm Sun), Dutch-designed pottery and homewares at **Pols Potten** (419 35 41; www.polspotten.nl; 10am-6pm Tue-Sat, noon-5pm Sun), art galleries and fashion including children's wear.

JC CREATIONS
CLOTHING

Map p326 (www.jc-creations.com; Baron GA Tindalstraat 150; 11am-6pm Tue-Sat, 1-6pm Sun; 10 C van Eesterenlaan) Take a deep breath when you enter this shop: classy corsets (for males and females) are the speciality. Plenty of ready-made options abound, but custom orders are welcome, too.

DE ODE
SPECIALITY SHOP

Map p326 (419 08 82; Levantkade 51; by appointment; 10 Azartplein) Send your loved ones off in style, with a creative casket from this one-of-a-kind shop. Open by appointment only, but a couple of interesting options are always on display in the window.

SPORTS & ACTIVITIES

GLOWGOLF
MINIGOLF

Map p326 (737 18 09; www.glowgolf.nl; Prins Hendrikkade 194, Noah's Arq; adult/child €7.75/6.75, 3D glasses €1.50; 10am-10pm Sun-Thu, to 11pm Fri & Sat; 22 Kadijksplein) From the street Noah's Arq looks like a normal pub but down in the basement it harbours this trippy-and-then-some minigolf course. The fifteen psychedelically coloured holes are played under black light, making them glow luridly in the dark (and making you feel like you're inside a giant pinball machine).

Definitely get the 3D glasses to max out the surreal experience.

Oosterpark & South Amsterdam

OOSTERPARK | SOUTH AMSTERDAM

Neighbourhood Top Five

❶ Spend the afternoon yodelling, sitting in a yurt and checking out Dutch colonial booty at the **Tropenmuseum** (p201).

❷ Take a trip through the big, bold, avant-garde paintings of Karel Appel and friends at the **CoBrA Museum** (p202).

❸ Sniff out the Turkish pide stall amid multipack sock vendors at the lively **Dappermarkt** (p201).

❹ Cycle through **Amster-damse Bos** (p202) and visit an organic farm-cafe for fresh goat's-milk ice cream.

❺ Seek out the political monuments and wild par-rots of sublime **Oosterpark** (p201).

For more detail of this area, see Map p317 ➡

Lonely Planet's Top Tip

With the Amstel river slicing through the area, Oosterpark and South Amsterdam have no shortage of riverside cafes that remind you of the age-old Dutch bond with water. On gorgeous summer evenings many patrons arrive by boat, settle at a terrace table and watch the freight barges, tugs and rowing teams ply the waters.

Best Places to Eat

➡ De Kas (p204)
➡ Wilde Zwijnen (p204)
➡ Roopram Roti (p204)
➡ Pata Negra (p204)

For reviews, see p204.➡

Best Places to Drink

➡ De Ysbreeker (p204)
➡ Distilleerderij 't Nieuwe Diep (p205)
➡ Canvas (p204)
➡ Trouw (p204)
➡ Spargo (p205)

For reviews, see p204.➡

Best Parks to Visit

➡ Amsterdamse Bos (p202)
➡ Amstelpark (p203)
➡ Oosterpark (p201)
➡ Park Frankendael (p201)

For reviews, see p201.➡

Explore Oosterpark & South Amsterdam

Oosterpark is one of Amsterdam's most culturally diverse neighbourhoods. Unlike De Pijp, it has seen only a tiny bit of gentrification and it's not (yet) on any trend-watchers' radar – which is precisely what makes it interesting.

The best sights are off the everyday tourist path. On the northern fringe you'll find the Tropenmuseum, which gives insights into Dutch colonial activities in the East Indies. The green expanse of Oosterpark itself makes a fine diversion afterwards, with its large pond and several monuments.

A walk east from the museum down 1e Van Swindenstraat leads to the street market on Dapperstraat and eventually into Javastraat, a Moroccan and Turkish enclave. Head to the neighbourhood's western edge, for urban-cool bars Trouw and Canvas.

Amsterdam extends well beyond here. The sights scatter as you head south, but you'll find wild art, lush greenery and goats in the forest, making it worth the trip. Reaching them is pretty straightforward by public transport; count on it taking between 30 and 60 minutes.

Local Life

➡**Moroccan & Turkish Delights** On Javastraat (which 1e Van Swindenstraat turns into) old Dutch fish shops and working-class bars sit adjacent to Moroccan and Turkish groceries.

➡**Garden Homes** Toward the northwest side of Park Frankendael lies a whole community of garden plots with teeny houses on them. The owners sit out on sunny days with wine and picnic fixings.

➡**Market Madness** If you're looking for an authentic place to shop, Dappermarkt is it. If organic fare is more your style, the monthly De Pure Markt in Park Frankendael is where everyone flocks.

Getting There & Away

➡**Tram** Tram 9 goes from the city centre to the Tropenmuseum. Trams 10 and 14 swing through the Oosterpark area on their east–west routes. Tram 5 heads south from the centre and ends near the CoBrA Museum.

➡**Bus** Buses 170 and 172 from Centraal Station go to Amsterdamse Bos and the CoBrA Museum, but note that if you're using a GVB transit pass, it's not valid on these particular routes (you'll need a regional day pass).

➡**Metro** The Wibautstraat stop is a stone's throw from the mod bars at the Oost's southwest edge. Amsterdam ArenA and Amsterdam RAI have their own Metro stops, all easy to reach from the centre.

◉ SIGHTS

◉ Oosterpark

OOSTERPARK   PARK

Map p317 ('s-Gravesandestraat; ⊙dawn-dusk; 🚹)
Oosterpark was laid out in 1891 to accommodate the diamond traders who found
their fortunes in the South African mines
and it still has an elegant, rambling feel,
complete with regal grey herons swooping
around the ponds and wild parrots chattering in the trees.

On the south side, look for two monuments: one commemorates the **abolition
of slavery** (Map p317) in the Netherlands in
1863; the other, **De Schreeuw** (The Scream;
Map p317), honours free speech and more
specifically, filmmaker Theo van Gogh,
who was murdered here in 2004. Another
(living) monument to Theo van Gogh is
the **Spreeksteen** (Map p317), a rock podium
marking a 'speakers' corner' established in
2005.

Families will enjoy the playground with
a wading pool on the the park's north side.

DAPPERMARKT   MARKET

Map p317 (www.dappermarkt.nl; Dapperstraat,
btwn Mauritskade & Wijttenbachstraat; ⊙10am-
4.30pm Mon-Sat; 🚊3/7 Dapperstraat) The larger Albert Cuypmarkt in De Pijp may be the
king of street bazaars, but the Dappermarkt
is a worthy prince. Reflecting the Oost's diverse immigrant population, it's a whirl of
people (Africans, Turks, Dutch), foods (apricots, olives, fish) and goods from sports
socks and shimmering fabrics to sunflowers, all sold from stalls lining the street.

FRANKENDAEL HOUSE   HOUSE, GARDENS

Map p317 (www.huizefrankendael.nl; Middenweg
72; tours per person €5; ⊙dawn-dusk, guided tours
2pm Sun; 🚊9 Hugo de Vrieslaan) As early as the
18th century, wealthy Amsterdammers
would spend their summers in plush country retreats south of Plantage on a tract of
drained land called Watergraafsmeer. The
last survivor of the era is Frankendael, an
elegant, restored Louis XIV–style mansion.
The **Merkelbach** (Map p317; ☎665 08 80; Middenweg 72; ⊙8.30am-11pm Tue-Sat, 8.30am-6pm
Sun & Mon) cafe sits in the adjoining coach
house and its patio overlooks Frankendael's
formal gardens (open to the public).

◉ TOP SIGHT
TROPENMUSEUM

Completed in 1926 to house the Royal Institute of the
Tropics, and still a leading research institute for tropical
hygiene and agriculture, the fascinating Tropenmuseum
(Tropics Museum) puts out a whopping collection of
colonial artefacts. Galleries are spread around a huge
central hall across three floors and present exhibits with
insight, imagination and lots of multimedia.

You can watch old Bollywood clips, stroll through a
recreated African market and sit inside a life-sized yurt
(traditional Central Asian felt hut). The galleries covering former Dutch territory are particularly rich, with gorgeous Indonesian jewellery and enormous Papuan war
canoes. 'World of Music' is a splendid exhibit, showing
how music and instruments travel throughout the world
and remix sounds; enter the Singing School to learn to
yodel or throat sing like a Tuvan.

The museum is especially great for kids. The gift
shop stocks lots of international goodies. The Ekeko
restaurant serves Indonesian, Indian and other global
specialities in a cafeteria-style set up if you need a bite
after all the activity.

DON'T MISS

➡ 'World of Music'
and Singing School
➡ Papuan war canoes
➡ Yurt
➡ Ekeko cafe
➡ Special exhibits

PRACTICALITIES

➡ Map p317
➡ ☎568 82 15
➡ www.tropen
museum.nl
➡ Linnaeusstraat 2
➡ adult/child €12/8
➡ ⊙10am-5pm Tue-
Sun
➡ 🚹
➡ 🚊9/10/14 Alexan-
derplein

Staff hold a free open house every Sunday from noon to 5pm when you can explore the building on your own, or go on a €5 guided tour. Be sure to view the house's forecourt with its gushing fountain and statues of Bacchus and Ceres. The property is swathed in a larger landscaped garden, Park Frankendael, with walking paths, flapping storks, decorative bridges and the remains of follies.

◉ South Amsterdam

AMSTERDAMSE BOS   PARK

(Amsterdam Forest; www.amsterdamsebos.nl; Bosbaanweg 5; ⊘park 24hr, visitors centre noon-5pm; 🚻; 🚌170, 172) Amsterdamse Bos is a vast tract of lakes, woods and meadows criss-crossed by paths. It's filled with activities and is especially great for children. You can rent bicycles, visit the goat farm, kayak the waterways, see a play at the open-air theatre, ascend to the treetops in the climbing park or hang out at the cafes and pancake restaurants.

In the densest thickets you can forget you're near a city at all (though, actually, you're right by Schiphol airport). The forest comprises roughly 2km by 5km of green

space. A lot of locals use the park but it rarely feels crowded.

Take bus 170 or 172 from Centraal Station; the trip takes about 40 minutes.

COBRA MUSEUM   MUSEUM

(www.cobra-museum.nl; Sandbergplein 1; adult/child €9.50/6; ⊘11am-5pm Tue-Sun; 🚌170, 172, 🚌5 Binnehof) Formed by artists from Copenhagen, Brussels and Amsterdam after WWII, the CoBrA movement produced semiabstract works known for their primitive, child-like qualities. This fascinating, canal-side museum holds a trove of boldly coloured, avant-garde paintings, ceramics and statues, including many by Karel Appel, the style's most famous practitioner. Asger Jorn, Anton Rooskens, Corneille and Constant are among the others. The CoBrA movement was active for just three years (1948–51).

The art is less of a unified whole than a philosophy, inspired by Marxism, of using materials at hand to create paintings, sculpture and even poetry. Changing exhibits by contemporary artists are on show as well.

The buses arrive right by the museum. The tram stop puts you about a kilometre from the museum; follow the 'CoBrA' signs through the mall to reach it.

AMSTERDAMSE BOS ITINERARY

You can easily spend a half-day in the thick trees and open fields here. Start at the **visitors centre** (open from noon to 5pm) by the main entrance. Rangers can tell you what sort of activities are happening throughout the park and you can buy a map (€2.50) to get your bearings. The **bicycle rental kiosk** (per 2hr/day €6/9.50; ⊘10am-6pm Tue-Sun) is also by the main entrance. If you plan to explore the park in depth, two wheels are vital. Likewise by the entrance is **Fun Forest** (www.funforest.nl; Bosbaanweg 3; adult/child €22/17; ⊘11am-7pm Jul & Aug, noon-6pm Wed & 11am-7pm Sat & Sun Sep-Jun; 🚻), a tree-top climbing park geared toward children that uses ropes, ladders and bridges.

From here head west for 2.5km and you'll come to the open-air theatre (p205). It stages classic plays (in Dutch) throughout the summer. Nearby at Grote Speelweide you can rent **canoes and kayaks** (per hour €6) and **pedal boats** (per hour €10).

About 0.75km south is the park's most delightful attraction. **De Ridammerhoeve** (www.geitenboerderij.nl; admission free; ⊘10am-5pm Wed-Mon) **FREE** is an organic, working goat farm where kids can feed bottles of milk to, well, kids (€8 for two bottles). The cafeteria sells goat's-milk smoothies and other dairy products.

There are couple of options for a meal after your park activities. A short distance from the theatre, on the northwest side of the Bosbaan (the long lake used for sculling) is **Boerderij Meerzicht** (www.boerderijmeerzicht.nl; Koenenkade 56; pancakes €6-11; ⊘10am-7pm Tue-Sun), an old farmhouse that has been converted into a kid-friendly pancake restaurant. The popular playground beside it lets little ones burn off excess energy. Back by the park entrance, **De Bosbaan Cafe** (www.debosbaan.nl; Bosbaan 4; mains €10-20 ; ⊘10am-9pm) is a lodge-like refuge for coffee or meals. Sit on the terrace to watch the rowers on the lake in front.

ELECTRISCHE MUSEUMTRAMLIJN
AMSTERDAM   MUSEUM

(Tram Museum Amsterdam; ☎673 75 38; www.
museumtramlijn.org; Amstelveenseweg 264; return adult/child €5/2.50; ⊙11am-5.30pm Sun
mid-Apr–Oct; ⓕ; ➔170 or 172, ➔16 Haarlemmermeer Station) Beyond the southwestern
extremities of Vondelpark, just north of the
Olympic Stadium, is the former Haarlemmermeer Station, which houses the tram
museum. Historic trams sourced from all
over Europe run between here and Amstelveen, making a great outing for kids
and adults alike. A return trip takes about
1¼ hours and skirts the large Amsterdamse
Bos recreational area.

The tram departs two to three times per
hour; see the website for details.

AMSTELPARK   PARK

(Europaboulevard; ⊙8am-dusk; ⓕ; ⓂRAI, ➔4
RAI) South of the Amsterdam RAI convention centre lies the vast Amstelpark. The
park is a paradise for kids, with a petting
zoo, minigolf and a playground. In summer
a miniature train chugs its way around the
park. Other attractions include rose and
rhododendron gardens; art exhibitions are
held in the Glazen Huis (Glass House), the
Orangerie and the Papillon Gallery.

Just outside the park's south edge, on the
west side of the Amstel river, you'll see a 1636
windmill called the **Riekermolen** (www.molens.nl). In a field southwest of the mill, you'll
find a statue of a sitting Rembrandt, who
made sketches here along the riverbank.

DE BIJLMER   NEIGHBOURHOOD

(ⓂBijlmer ArenA) Once a crime-ridden public
housing area, De Bijlmer today is known
for entertainment, shopping and innovative
architecture. Hop on the metro to the dramatic Nicholas Grimshaw–designed Bijlmer station, opened in 2007. To the west lies
Amsterdam ArenA (p205), the Heineken
Music Hall (p205) and Ziggo Dome (p205).
To the east is the Amsterdamse Poort shopping complex.

When you get off the train, walk toward
the Amsterdamse Poort shops. As you continue east you'll pass various mod, glassy
office buildings set next to chain stores
and exotic little ethnic shops. De Bijlmer
holds the city's largest Surinamese population, along with immigrants from west and
north Africa.

Eventually the commerce district gives
way to the few remaining 'honeycomb blocks'
of the original Bijlmer housing project, each
containing some 400 apartments. The 1960s
brochures touted 'a modern city where the
people of today can find the residential environment of tomorrow'. But the isolated,
austere project rapidly lost its lustre and,
in the 1970s, the city began to funnel poor
immigrants into the empty apartments. By
the 1980s crime was common and the infrastructure crumbling. Former residents
lament the trash-filled lawns and broken
elevators of those days, but many also wax
nostalgic about the tight-knit community
and the surrounding greenery.

In 1992 an El Al cargo plane crashed into
two of the blocks, killing 43 people, many of
them undocumented foreigners – a memorial stands in front of the missing buildings.
The tragedy kick-started a re-evaluation of
the neighbourhood, which has moved into
wholesale rebuilding, and shifted the balance in favour of privately owned property,
rather than publicly managed apartments.

The neighbourhood's park is the site of
the cultural bash **Kwaku** (http://kwakufestival.nl), drawing crowds on weekends from
mid-July through early August.

AMSTERDAM RAI   BUILDING

(www.rai.nl; Europaplein 22; ⓂRAI, ➔4 RAI) This
exhibition and conference centre (featured,
by the way, in Jacques Tati's 1971 film
Trafic) is the largest such complex in the
country. The building opened in 1961 and
just keeps expanding for the car, fashion,
horse-jumping and 50-odd other shows
held here every year. A huge, mod, sustainably designed new wing is scheduled to
open in 2015.

RAI stands for Rijwiel en Automobiel
Industrie, the bicycle and auto association.

OLYMPIC STADIUM   STADIUM

(www.olympischstadion.nl; Olympisch Stadion 21;
adult/child €6/5; ⊙11am-5pm Tue-Sun; ➔16/24
Stadionplein) The grand Olympic Stadium
was designed by Jan Wils, a protégé of
famous architect HP Berlage, and is functionalist in style. The arena was built for
the 1928 summer Olympic Games and has
a soaring tower from which the Olympic
flame burned for the first time during
competition. There's a little museum by
the entrance. The venue also hosts sporting
events and concerts.

Much of the housing in southwest
Amsterdam originates from the time of
the 1928 games. Many of the streets and

squares in the area bear Greek names such as Olympiaplein and Herculesstraat.

Trams 16 and 24 go from Centraal Station to the stadium; the trip takes about 30 minutes. The stadium is a few kilometres north of Amsterdamse Bos' main entrance.

 EATING

ROOPRAM ROTI SURINAMESE €
Map p317 (1e Van Swindenstraat 4; mains €4-10; ☺2-9pm Tue-Sun; 🚋9 1e Van Swindenstraat) There's often a line to the door at this bare-bones Surinamese place, but don't worry – it moves fast. Place your order – lamb roti 'extra' (with egg) and a *barra* (lentil doughnut) at least – at the bar and don't forget the fiery hot sauce. It's some of the flakiest roti you'll find anywhere.

It's super delicious for takeaway or to eat at one of the half-dozen tables.

WILDE ZWIJNEN CONTEMPORARY DUTCH €€
(☏463 30 43; www.wildezwijnen.com; Javaplein 23; mains €19-22, 3/4 courses €30.50/36.50; ☺6-10pm Mon-Thu, noon-4pm & 6-10pm Fri-Sun; 🚋; 🚋14 Javaplein) ✿ The name means 'wild boar' and if it's the right time of year, you may indeed find it on the menu. The rustic, wood-tabled restaurant serves locally sourced, seasonal fare with bold results. There's usually a vegetarian option and chocolate ganache with juniper berries for dessert.

It's about 1km east of Oosterpark; get here via 1e Van Swindenstraat, which turns into Javastraat, which runs into Javaplein.

PATA NEGRA SPANISH €€
Map p317 (☏692 25 06; www.pata-negra.nl; Reinwardtstraat 1; tapas €7-12, mains €12-18; ☺noon-11pm; 🚋3/7/9 Linnaeusstraat) This colourful tapas joint dishes up delicious morsels, such as super-garlicky prawns, grilled sardines and other savoury treats. On Sundays it adds a big ol' potful of paella to the mix, which is a belly-filling bonus indeed. Another branch of the restaurant can be found in the Southern Canal Ring (p134).

★DE KAS INTERNATIONAL €€€
Map p317 (☏462 45 62; www.restaurantdekas.nl; Kamerlingh Onneslaan 3, Park Frankendael; lunch/dinner menu €37.50/49.50; ☺noon-2pm & 6.30-10pm Mon-Fri, 6.30-10pm Sat; 🚋; 🚋9 Hogeweg) ✿ Admired by gourmets citywide, De Kas has an organic attitude to match its

chic glass greenhouse setting – try to visit during a thunderstorm! It grows most of its own herbs and produce right here and the result is incredibly pure flavours with innovative combinations. There's one set menu each day, based on whatever has been freshly harvested. Reserve in advance.

🍷 DRINKING & NIGHTLIFE

DE YSBREEKER BROWN CAFÉ
Map p317 (www.deysbreeker.nl; Weesperzijde 23; ☺8am-1am; 🚋; 🚋3 Wibautstraat) The terrace at this *café* on the Amstel is glorious for watching the river lined with houseboats as other vessels glide by. Inside, stylish drinkers hoist beverages in the plush booths and along the marble bar. It's great for organic and local beers (such as de Prael) and bar snacks such as lamb meatballs.

The building used to be an inn for the men who broke the ice on the Amstel so boats could pass (the art-glass windows in back depict the scene). Later it housed a major jazz and avant-garde music club – that institution became the Muziekgebouw aan 't IJ. The building also gained fame as a billiards centre – there's still a table to play on.

CANVAS BAR, CLUB
Map p317 (www.canvasopde7e.nl; Wibautstraat 150; ☺11am-1am Mon-Fri, from noon Sat & Sun; Ⓜ Wibautstraat) Take the elevator to the 7th floor for this restaurant-bar-club. It's edgy and improvisational, and is the social centre for all the artists with studios in the building (the former *Volkskrant* newspaper office). The sweet views are heightened by the creative cocktails (say, a lemongrass martini or Japanese gin fizz). Music is varied, from vintage voodoo to hippy psychedelic to funk. At the time of writing it was being renovated, so expect even more hipness. The Wibautstraat metro stop is a stone's throw away; follow signs saying 'Gijsbrecht van Aemstelstraat' as you exit the station.

TROUW BAR, CLUB
Map p317 (☏463 77 88; www.trouwamsterdam.nl; Wibautstraat 127; ☺24hr; Ⓜ Wibautstraat) Trouw is housed in a former newspaper printing warehouse, where the printing press floor has been transformed into an industrial-chic restaurant serving snack-sized plates of organic, Mediterranean-tinged dishes. You can also have a drink on the sculpture-

DISTILLEERDERIJ 'T NIEUWE DIEP

Set in an old pumping station in leafy Flevopark, **Distilleerderij 't Nieuwe Diep** (www.nwediep.nl; Flevopark 13; ⊘3-8pm Tue-Fri, noon-8pm Sat & Sun; 🚋7/14 Soembawastraat) makes around 100 small-batch *jenevers* (Dutch gin), herbal bitters, liqueurs and fruit distillates from organic ingredients according to age-old Dutch recipes. They're delicious, but the coolest part is the setting, which feels very rural and magical, like stumbling onto Hansel and Gretel's cottage in the woods. The outdoor terrace is on a little lake next to an orchard. Free guided tours of the distillery occur every Friday at 4pm. To get here, walk east from the tram stop; it's about a 10-minute jaunt into the park.

studded terrace. But Trouw is better known for its way-late club nights (with food served till 2am) and its salon series talks on culture, architecture and urban design.

The venue has one of Amsterdam's few 24-hour licenses, meaning it can stay open all night, though it doesn't always do so. Keep an eye out for the new 'night museum', a basement space set aside for late-night art exhibitions.

SPARGO   BEER CAFE

Map p317 (www.cafespargo.nl; Linnaeusstraat 37a; ⊘10am-1am; 🚋3/7/9 Linnaeusstraat) So you've done Oosterpark – sought out all the monuments and found the wild parrots chattering in the trees – and now you need a drink to replenish? Spargo's buzzy little terrace sends out its siren call from across the street. It pours several local Dutch brews, including Brouwerij 't IJ (the windmill-brewery a short distance away). FYI, the cafe's sign looks like 'Spar90'.

☆ ENTERTAINMENT

STUDIO K   ARTS CENTRE

(📞692 04 22; www.studio-k.nu; Timorplein 62; ⊘11am-1am; 🛜; 🚋14 Zeeburgerdijk) Sporting two cinemas, a club, a stage for bands and theatre, an eclectic restaurant (serving sandwiches for lunch, and vegetarian-friendly, international-flavoured dishes for dinner) and a huge terrace, the student-run Studio K is your one-stop shop for hip culture in the Oost. Stop in for a coffee and you might wind up staying all night for to dance. You can also rent bicycles at the shop next door.

AMSTERDAM ARENA   FOOTBALL

(www.amsterdamarena.nl; Arena Blvd 1; 🛜; Ⓜ️Bijlmer ArenA) Amsterdam ArenA is a high-tech complex with a retractable roof and seating for 52,000 spectators. Four-times European champion Ajax, the Netherlands' most famous football team, play here. Football games usually take place on Saturday evenings and Sunday afternoons from August to May. The arena is about 7km southeast of the centre; the metro will get you there with ease.

Fans can also take a one-hour guided tour of the stadium (adult/child €14.50/9.50). There are usually at least five tours daily; see the website for the schedule.

AMSTERDAMSE BOS THEATRE   THEATRE

(www.bostheater.nl; Bosbaanweg 5; ⊘Jun-Aug; 🚌170, 172) This large, open-air amphitheatre stages plays (Shakespeare, Brecht, Chekhov) in Dutch. We love it when the actors pause for planes passing overhead.

ZIGGO DOME   LIVE MUSIC

(www.ziggodome.nl; De Passage 100; 🛜; Ⓜ️Bijlmer ArenA) The 17,000-seat, indoor Ziggo Dome opened in 2012 and hosts big-name concerts. Beyoncé, Rihanna and Peter Gabriel are recent stage takers.

HEINEKEN MUSIC HALL   LIVE MUSIC

(www.heineken-music-hall.nl; Arena Blvd 590; Ⓜ️Bijlmer ArenA) This midsized venue is praised for its quality acoustics and lighting. Expect rock and pop acts from medium to big names.

🛍 SHOPPING

DE PURE MARKT   MARKET

Map p317 (www.puremarkt.nl; Park Frankendael; ⊘11am-6pm Sun Mar-Jun & Aug-Dec; 🚌9 Hogeweg) On the last Sunday of the month De Pure Markt sets up in Park Frankendael (near De Kas (p204) restaurant), with artisanal food and craft producers selling sausages, home-grown grapes and more. Check out to the market's west for the community of garden plots with wee houses on them.

Day Trips from Amsterdam

Haarlem p207
Alleys wind among grand 17th-century buildings, leafy *hofjes* (court-yards) and antique shops.

Keukenhof p211
See the world's largest, loveliest flower gardens in bloom during spring.

Leiden p211
Rembrandt's picturesque, canal-woven birthplace is home to the country's oldest university.

Delft p215
Gothic and Renaissance architecture rivals quaint Delftware pottery.

Alkmaar p218
Alkmaar's cheese market is one of the traditional cheese guilds' last bastions.

Scheveningen p218
Stroll the long, sandy beach and relax at a laidback seaside cafe.

Zaanse Schans p220
Watch windmills twirl and meet the millers at this open-air museum.

Bloemenveiling Aalsmeer p220
Walk above bustling flower warehouses and catch the auction action.

Haarlem

Explore

Strolling from glorious Haarlem Centraal to the old centre along Kruisweg and Kruisstraat, Haarlem's wealth and elegance becomes apparent as you pass exclusive stores, art galleries and antique shops. Stop at the Corrie Ten Boom House to pay homage to one of the Netherlands' most admired Resistance figures before heading to the lively Grote Markt for lunch. A few blocks south is the Frans Hals Museum. Haarlem was once more important in the art world than Amsterdam, and this incomparable museum possesses one of the country's finest assemblies of Dutch paintings. Garden lovers shouldn't miss the Provenierhuis *hofje,* a five-minute walk northwest of the museum.

Given Haarlem's easy access to Amsterdam, you can enjoy some sunset people-watching and check out live music amid the town's nightlife.

The Best...

→**Sight** Frans Hals Museum (p209)

→**Place to Eat** Jacobus Pieck (p210)

→**Place to Drink** Proeflokaal in den Uiver (p210)

Top Tip

Arrive early on a Monday or Saturday to hit the festive outdoor markets, then unwind with a leisurely lunch at a cafe on the Grote Markt.

Getting There & Away

→**Travel time** 15 to 20 minutes

→**Train** Services from Amsterdam's Centraal Station to Haarlem Centraal are frequent (€3.90, up to eight per hour); the Grote Markt is a 850m walk south of the station. When the trains stop running at night, the N30 night bus links Haarlem Centraal Station to Schiphol airport.

→**Car** From the ring road west of the city, take the N200, which becomes the A200.

Need to Know

→**Area Code** ☑023

→**Location** 20km west of Amsterdam

→**Tourist Office** (☑0900 616 16 00; www.haarlemmarketing.com; Verwulft 11; ☺9.30am-6pm Mon-Fri, 9.30am-5pm Sat, noon-4pm Sun Apr-Sep, 1-5.30pm Mon, 9.30am-5.30pm Tue-Fri, 10am-5pm Sat Oct-Mar)

◉ SIGHTS

HAARLEM CENTRAAL   TRAIN STATION

If you arrive in Haarlem by train, your first sight will be this glorious 1908-opened art nouveau station – the only one in the Netherlands and hands-down the country's most beautiful station.

GROTE MARKT   MARKET

Circled by elegant Renaissance and Gothic buildings and lined with lovely *cafés* (pubs, bars) and restaurants, this square is the city's beating heart. It's fronted by the 14th-century town hall, which features a balcony where judgements from the high court were pronounced. The Counts' Hall contains some amazing 15th-century panel paintings, and if it's open you can take a peek.

Don't miss the bustling market day each Saturday, when everyone in town floods the square to peruse the stalls selling everything from *stroopwafels* (thin, syrup-filled

---

TRAVEL TIPS ⓘ

All destinations in this chapter lie within an hour from Amsterdam by train (and, if need be, by connecting tram or bus). If you get an early start, it's possible to 'do' two locations in a day (Alkmaar and Zaanse Schans, for instance) without feeling rushed.

The fast, efficient Dutch railway network makes it a snap to get around. Rather than purchase a *dagkaart* (day pass; €49.20), buy a same-day return ticket from Amsterdam (around €8 to €24 for the towns in this chapter, depending on the distance), which allows you to hop on and off at multiple stops so long as you complete the journey in a single day.

Cycle paths are everywhere, but there's no need to bring a bike with you – rentals costing around €7.50 to €10 per day are widely available.

Haarlem

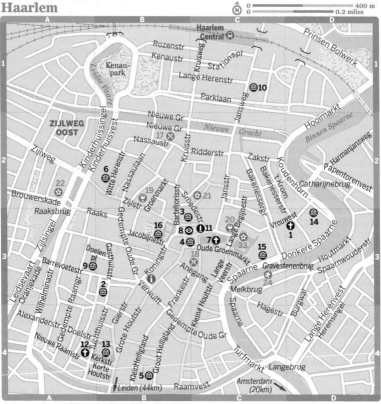

waffles) and tulips to locally made cheeses and that quintessential Dutch treat, raw herring. On Mondays you'll find a clothing market.

GROTE KERK VAN ST BAVO CHURCH
(www.bavo.nl; Oude Groenmarkt 23; adult/child €2.50/1.25; ☉10am-5pm Mon-Sat) Opposite the town hall looms the Grote Kerk van St Bavo, the Gothic cathedral with a towering 50m-high steeple. It contains some fine Renaissance artworks, but the star attraction is its stunning Müller organ – one of the most magnificent in the world, standing 30m high with about 5000 pipes. It was played by Handel and Mozart, the latter when he was just 10. There are free **organ recitals** (☉8.15pm Tue & 4pm Thu, Jul & Aug) in summer.

LAURENS COSTER STATUE STATUE
On the square north of the Grote Kerk is the Laurens Coster statue. Haarlemmers believe that Coster has a claim, along with

Gutenberg, to be called the inventor of moveable type.

DE HALLEN GALLERY
(www.dehallen.nl; Grote Markt 16; adult/child €6/free; ☉11am-5pm Tue-Sat, noon-5pm Sun) Haarlem's modern and contemporary art museum resides within two historic 'halls': the 17th-century Dutch Renaissance Vleeshal, a former meat market and the sole place that meat was allowed to be sold in Haarlem from the 17th to the 19th century, and the neoclassical Verweyhal. Eclectic exhibits rotate every three months and range from Dutch impressionists and CoBrA artists to innovative video, installation art and photography by cutting-edge international artists.

PROVENIERSHUIS HISTORIC BUILDING
(off Grote Houtstraat; ☉10am-5pm Mon-Sat) **FREE** Off Grote Houtstraat to the southwest of Grote Markt stands the Proveniershuis,

Haarlem

the former headquarters of St Joris Doelen (the Civic Guard of St George), which started life as a *hofje* (almshouse set around a garden). The wonderful old building is one of Haarlem's prettiest.

HOFJES HISTORIC BUILDINGS
(⊙generally 10am-5pm Mon-Sat) **FREE** In addition to Proveniershuis, other *hofjes* worth a look include the **Brouwers Hofje** (Tuchthuisstraat 8) which lodged the brewers' guild; the **Frans Loenen Hofje** (Witte Herenstraat 24), pared out of a merchant's estate; the **Hofje van Loo** (Barrevoetestraat 7), a former women's hospital; the **Hofje van Staats** (Jansweg 39), one of the town's largest and still occupied by older women; and the unusually grand **Teylers Hofje** (Koudenhorn 144) built by the founder of the Teylers Museum.

FRANS HALS MUSEUM GALLERY
(www.franshalsmuseum.nl; Groot Heiligland 62; adult/child €13/free; ⊙10am-5pm Tue-Fri, 11-6pm Sat & Sun) A short stroll south of Grote Markt, the Frans Hals Museum is a must for anyone interested in the Dutch Masters. Kept in a poorhouse where Hals spent his final years, the collection focuses on the 17th-century Haarlem School; its pride and joy are eight group portraits of the Civic Guard that reveal Hals' exceptional attention to mood and psychological tone. Look out for works by other greats such as Pieter Bruegel the Younger, and Jacob van Ruysdael.

Among the museum's other treasures are the works of Hals' teacher, Flemish artist

Carel van Mander: stunning illustrations of the human anatomy, all ceiling-high with biblical and mythological references.

TEYLERS MUSEUM MUSEUM
(www.teylersmuseum.eu; Spaarne 16; adult/child €10/2; ⊙10am-5pm Tue-Sat, 11am-5pm Sun) It's shocking, but depending on your tastes, the Teylers Museum may top Frans Hals Museum. It's the oldest museum in the country (1778) and contains an array of whiz-bang inventions, such as an 18th-century electrostatic machine that conjures up visions of mad scientists. The eclectic collection also has paintings from the Dutch and French schools and numerous temporary exhibitions.

The interiors are as good as the displays: the magnificent, sky-lighted Ovale Zaal (Oval Room) contains natural history specimens in elegant glass cases on two levels.

BAKENESSERKERK CHURCH
(cnr Vrouwestraat & Bakenesserstraat) Northeast of Teylers Museum stands the striking Bakenesserkerk, a late 15th-century church with a lamp-lit tower of sandstone. The stone was employed here when the Grote Kerk proved too weak to support a heavy steeple – hence the wooden tower. It's closed to the public.

CORRIE TEN BOOM HOUSE HISTORIC BUILDING
(www.corrietenboom.com; Barteljorisstraat 19; by donation; ⊙10am-3.30pm Tue-Sat Apr-Oct, 11am-3pm Tue-Sat Nov-Mar) Also known as 'the hiding place', the Corrie ten Boom House is named after the matriarch of a family who

lived in the house during WWII. Using a secret compartment in her bedroom, she hid hundreds of Jews and Dutch resistors until they could be spirited to safety. In 1944 the family was betrayed and sent to concentration camps where three died. Later, Corrie ten Boom toured the world preaching peace. There are daily tours in English.

NIEUWE KERK CHURCH
(Nieuwe Kerksplein; admission free; ⊙10am-5pm Mon-Sat Apr-Sep, 10am-4pm Mon-Sat Oct-Mar) Walk down charming Korte Houtstraat to find the 17th-century Nieuwe Kerk. The capricious Renaissance tower by Lieven de Key is supported by a rather boxy design by Jacob van Campen.

✖ EATING & DRINKING

DE HAERLEMSCHE VLAAMSE FRITES €
(Spekstraat 3; frites €2.10; ⊙11am-6.30pm Mon-Wed & Fri, 11am-9pm Thu, 11am-5pm Sat, noon-5pm Sun) Practically on the doorstep of the Grote Kerk, this *frites* (fries) joint, not much bigger than a telephone box, is a local institution. Line up for its crispy, golden fries made from fresh potatoes. Choose from one of a dozen sauces including three kinds of mayonnaise.

COMPLIMENTI PER VOI DELI €
(www.complimenti.nl; Nassaustraat 24; items from €3; ⊙noon-6pm Wed-Fri, 10am-5pm Sat) The scent of garlic wafts over the street from this picnicker's heaven of a deli. Varieties of fresh Italian bread, pesto, cheese and more are arrayed in display cases.

JACOBUS PIECK INTERNATIONAL €€
(www.jacobuspieck.nl; Warmoesstraat 18; lunch mains €5-10, dinner mains €12.50-18.50; ⊙11am-4pm & 5.30-10pm Tue-Sat) Touches such as

freshly squeezed OJ put this tidy bistro on a higher plane. The menu bursts with fresh dishes, from salads and sandwiches at lunch to more complex pasta and seafood choices at dinner. Staff are welcoming; snag a sunny table on the back patio.

PROEFLOKAAL IN DEN UIVER BROWN CAFÉ
(www.indenuiver.nl; Riviervismarkt 13; ⊙4pm-1am Mon-Wed, 4pm-2am Thu, 2pm-2am Fri & Sat, 4-9pm Sun) This nautical-themed place has shipping knick-knacks and a schooner sailing right over the bar. There's jazz on Thursday and Sunday evenings. It's one of many atmospheric places near the Grote Markt.

CAFÉ HET MELKWOUD BROWN CAFÉ
(Zijlstraat 63; ⊙4pm-2am Mon-Wed, 4pm-4am Thu-Sat) A fine place to nurse a beer (vast selection by the bottle) in ancient wooden surrounds behind ceiling-high windows. Cash only.

☆ ENTERTAINMENT

CAFÉ STIELS LIVE MUSIC
(www.stiels.nl; Smedestraat 21; ⊙8pm-2am Sun-Wed, to 3am Thu, to 4am Fri & Sat) Jazz and rhythm-and-blues bands play on the back stage almost every night of the week from 10pm onwards.

PATRONAAT LIVE MUSIC
(www.patronaat.nl; Zijlsingel 2; ⊙vary) At this cavernous music venue, bands with banging tunes usually start playing around 9pm.

PHILHARMONIE MUSIC
(☎023-512 12 12; www.theater-haarlem.nl; Lange Begijnestraat 11; ⊙vary) Haarlem's venerable concert hall, featuring music from every style imaginable.

🏃 SPORTS & ACTIVITIES

POST VERKADE CRUISES BOAT CRUISE
(☎023-535 77 23; www.postverkadegroep.nl; Spaarne 11a; adult/child €14.50/7.25; ⊙noon-5pm Tue-Sun Apr-Sep) Runs 50-minute canal boat tours through Haarlem's waterways. Commentary is available in English. Departure times vary.

HAARLEM'S SPANISH INVASION

When the Spanish invaded Haarlem in 1572, thousands of citizens were slaughtered during a seven-month siege. Against the odds, the community recovered quickly. The city then soared into the prosperity of the Golden Age, attracting painters and artists from around Europe.

KEUKENHOF FLOWER GARDENS

Covering more than 32 hectares, the glorious **Keukenhof flower gardens** (www.keuken-hof.nl; Lisse; adult/child €15/7.50, parking €6; ☺8am-7.30pm mid-Mar–mid-May, last entry 6pm) are the largest bulb-flower gardens in the world, attracting 800,000 visitors during eight weeks each year. Opening dates vary slightly from year to year, so check ahead and allow at least half a day here.

The historic park at Keukenhof's heart was originally castle kitchen gardens. Its present form dates from 1857 and was designed by Jan David Zocher (and his son Louis Paul), who also laid out Amsterdam's Vondelpark. The flower gardens were created in 1949 for European growers to show off their hybrids. Exhibitors supply more than 7 million bulbs each spring that are planted throughout the season by 30 horticulturists; they're harvested in autumn and the next spring the cycle begins again.

This isn't just any old trade show: nature's talents are combined with technical precision to create a wonder where tulips and daffodils blossom perfectly in place and exactly on time throughout the park's various themed gardens, along with some 150 sculptures. Other highlights include a century-old working windmill that you can enter. Special exhibits are held in the pavilions in the park and there are cafes and refreshment stands also.

Bike rental (€10 per day) is available at the main entrance for a spin through the flowering bulb fields (not through the park itself). You can also take an eco-friendly whisper boat ride (€7.50) on the surrounding canals.

Special buses run during the season from Amsterdam's Schiphol airport to Keukenhof (€6, 40 minutes, four per hour). Combination tickets including Keukenhof entry and return bus fares cost €22.50. Buses also run from Leiden Centraal Station (€3, 25 minutes, four per hour). Tickets can be purchased online, which helps avoid huge queues.

Leiden

Explore

Laced with canals and lined with gabled houses, enchanting Leiden resembles a mini version of Amsterdam.

As you walk south from the striking, hyper-modern Centraal Station, the city's traditional character unfolds. A five-minute stroll takes you to Leiden's historic waterways, the most notable being the Oude Rijn and the Nieuwe Rijn. They meet at Hoogstraat to form the Rijn canal.

Rembrandt, Jan Steen and Jan van Goyen all hailed from here and the city has a cache of artistic and historic treasures; take time to explore at least some of its 12 museums.

Leiden is also home to the Netherlands' oldest university, whose 20,000 students make up a big chunk of the population, so it's worth staying late to enjoy the dynamic ambience in its many *cafés* and bars.

The Best...

➡ **Sight** Rijksmuseum van Oudheden (p211)

➡ **Place to Eat** Annie's (p214)

➡ **Place to Drink** Café l'Esperance (p214)

Top Tip

Absorb Leiden's vibrant student life by exploring the university precinct, where such historic sights as one of Europe's oldest botanical gardens coexist with a contemporary cultural buzz.

Getting There & Away

➡ **Train** Services run from Amsterdam's Centraal Station six or seven times per hour (€8.40).

➡ **Car** Take the A4 from the southwest point of the A10 ring road.

Need to Know

➡ **Area Code** ☏071

➡ **Location** 45km southwest of Amsterdam

➡ **Tourist Office** (☏516 60 00; www.vvvleiden.nl; Stationsweg 41; ☺8am-6pm Mon-Fri, 10am-4pm Sat, 11am-3pm Sun)

◉ SIGHTS

RIJKSMUSEUM VAN OUDHEDEN MUSEUM
(National Museum of Antiquities; www.rmo.nl; Rapenburg 28; adult/child €9.50/3; ☺10am-5pm Tue-Sun) This museum has a world-class

collection of Greek, Roman and Egyptian artefacts, the pride of which is the extraordinary Temple of Taffeh, a gift from former Egyptian president Anwar Sadat to the Netherlands for helping to save ancient Egyptian monuments from floods.

PIETERSKERK
CHURCH

(Pieterskerkhof; ⊙10am-4pm Mon-Fri, 1.30-4pm Sat & Sun May-Sep, 1.30-4pm daily Oct-Apr) Follow the huge steeple to Pieterskerk, which is often under restoration (a good thing as it has been prone to collapse since it was built in the 14th century). The precinct here is as old Leiden as you'll get and includes

the gabled old **Latin School** (Lokhorststraat 16), which – before it became a commercial building – was graced by a pupil named Rembrandt from 1616 to 1620.

Across the square from the Latin School, look for the **Gravensteen**, which dates to the 13th century and was once a prison. The gallery facing the square was where judges watched executions.

DE BURCHT
PARK, MONUMENT

(⊙sunrise-sunset) **FREE** De Burcht, an 11th-century citadel on an artificial hill, lost its protective functions as the city grew around

Leiden

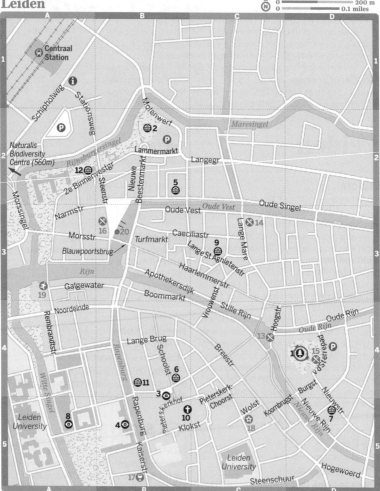

it. Now it's a park with lovely places to view the steeples and rooftops.

LEIDEN UNIVERSITY UNIVERSITY
(www.leiden.edu) The oldest university in the Netherlands was a gift to Leiden from Willem the Silent for withstanding two Spanish sieges in 1574. The campus comprises an interesting mix of modern and antique buildings that are scattered around town.

RIJKSMUSEUM VOLKENKUNDE MUSEUM
(National Museum of Ethnology; www.volkenkunde.nl; Steenstraat 1; adult/child €11/8, free Wed; ⊙10am-5pm Tue-Sun) Cultural achievements by civilisations worldwide are on show at the recently renovated Museum Volkenkunde. More than 200,000 artefacts span China, South America and Africa. There's a rich Indonesian collection; watch for performances by the museum's gamelan troupe.

HORTUS BOTANICUS GARDEN
(www.hortus.leidenuniv.nl; Rapenburg 73; adult/child €7/3; ⊙10am-6pm daily Apr-Oct, to 4pm Tue-Sun Nov-Mar) Established in 1590, the lush Hortus Botanicus is one of Europe's oldest botanical gardens, and home to the country's oldest descendants of the Dutch tulips. It's a wonderful place to relax, with explosions of tropical colour and a fascinating steamy greenhouse.

LAKENHAL MUSEUM
(www.lakenhal.nl; Oude Singel 28-32; adult/child €7.50/free; ⊙10am-5pm Tue-Fri, noon-5pm Sat & Sun) The 17th-century Lakenhal houses the Municipal Museum, with an assortment

of works by Dutch Masters (including the city's only Rembrandt, despite the fact that the Leiden native spent many years of his life here). The 1st floor has been restored to the way it would have looked when Leiden was at the peak of its prosperity. It also stages temporary exhibitions.

DE VALK MUSEUM
(The Falcon; ☎071-516 53 53; http://molendevalk.leiden.nl; 2e Binnenvestgracht 1; adult/child €4/2; ⊙10am-5pm Tue-Sat, 1-5pm Sun) Leiden's landmark windmill museum receives loving care (it recently underwent restoration), and many consider it the best example of its kind. The windmill's arms are free to turn 'whenever possible' and it can still grind grain.

NATURALIS
BIODIVERSITY CENTRE MUSEUM
(www.naturalis.nl; Darwinweg 2; adult/child €11/8; ⊙10am-5pm) A stuffed elephant greets you at this large, well-funded collection of all the usual dead critters. Its most notable acquisition, the million-year-old Java Man – discovered by Dutch anthropologist Eugène Dubois in 1891 – is held in the basement, though not displayed. The museum is 300m west of the town centre.

MUSEUM BOERHAAVE MUSEUM
(www.museumboerhaave.nl; Lange St Agnietenstraat 10; adult/child €9.50/4.50; ⊙10am-5pm Tue-Sun) Leiden University was an early centre for Dutch medical research. This museum displays the often-grisly results (five centuries of surgical tools, skeletons and pickled organs) plus you can have a gander at the anatomical theatre with skeletons in stiff relief.

DAY TRIPS FROM AMSTERDAM LEIDEN

Leiden

LEIDEN'S PILGRIM LINKS

In 1608 a group of Calvinist Protestants split from the Anglican church and left persecution in Nottinghamshire, England, for a journey that would span decades and thousands of miles. Travelling first to Amsterdam under the leadership of John Robinson, they encountered theological clashes with local Dutch Protestants.

In Leiden they found a more liberal atmosphere, thanks to the university and some like-minded Calvinist locals and refugees. However, in 1618 James I of England announced he would assume control over the Calvinists living in Leiden, and Leiden locals were becoming less tolerant of religious splinter groups.

The first group left Leiden in 1620 for Delfshaven in present-day Rotterdam. After several unsuccessful attempts to cross the Atlantic, they sailed to Southampton in England and eventually joined the *Mayflower* in Dartmouth before sailing into history as the Pilgrims. This legendary voyage was just one of many which took the Leiden group to the American colonies founded in what is today New England.

The **Leiden American Pilgrim Museum** (☎071-512 24 13; www.leidenamericanpilgrimmuseum.org/index.htm; Beschuitsteeg 9; admission €4; ☉1-5pm Wed-Sat) is a fascinating restoration of a one-room house occupied around 1610 by the soon-to-be Pilgrims. The house itself dates from 1375 (and retains original floor tiles), but the furnishings are from the Pilgrims' period. Curator Jeremy Bangs is an author with vast knowledge of the Pilgrims.

🍴 EATING & DRINKING

OUDT LEYDEN
PANCAKES €

(www.oudtleyden.nl; Steenstraat 49; pancakes €8-14, mains €15-22.50; ☉11.30am-9.30pm; 🖪 👪) Get ready to meet giant Dutch-style pancakes with creative fillings that make kids and adults wide-eyed and giddy. Whether you're feeling savoury (marinated salmon, sour cream and capers), sweet (warm cherries and vanilla ice cream) or adventurous (ginger and bacon, anyone?), this cafe hits the spot every time. Larger mains (steaks, fish, vegie lasagne) served too.

ANNIE'S
CAFE €€

(www.annies.nu; Hoogstraat 1a; lunch mains €6-13, dinner mains €11.50-21.50; ☉kitchen 11am-10pm, bar to 1am; 📶👪) At the confluence of canals and pedestrian zones, classy Annie's has a prime water-level location with dozens of tables on a floating pontoon. Even if you don't dine here (on steaks, pastas, satays or succulent spare ribs), at least stop for a drink.

BRASSERIE DE ENGELENBAK
CONTEMPORARY DUTCH €€

(www.brasseriedeengelenbak.nl; Lange Mare 38; lunch mains €6-11, dinner menus €26-32; ☉noon-10pm) 🖉 Right in the shadow of the 17th-century octagonal Marekerk, this elegant bistro serves a seasonally changing menu of fresh fare that takes its cues from across the continent. Local organic produce features in many of the dishes. Tables outside enjoy views of the hoi polloi. An adjoining cafe serves snacks until midnight.

HET KOETSHUIS
CAFE €€

(www.koetshuisdeburcht.nl; Burgsteeg 13; mains €14.50-20.50; ☉kitchen noon-9.30pm Sun-Fri, 10am-9.30pm Sat; 🖪) On a sunny day, it's hard to beat the terrace tables just outside the grand Burcht gate, where all of humankind gathers for an afternoon coffee or *borrel* (alcoholic drink of your choice). The wide-ranging menu spans sandwiches to steaks, with plenty of vegetarian options.

CAFÉ L'ESPERANCE
BROWN CAFÉ

(www.lesperance.nl; Kaiserstraat 1; ☉3pm-1am Sun-Wed, 11.30am-1am Thu, 11.30am-2am Fri & Sat) Decked out in nostalgic wood panelling, Café L'Esperance overlooks an evocative bend in the canal. Tables abound outside in summer; it has good meals too.

☆ ENTERTAINMENT

CAFÉ DE WW
LIVE MUSIC

(www.deww.nl; Wolsteeg 4; ☉2pm-2am Sun-Wed, to 3am Thu, to 4am Fri & Sat) On Friday and Saturday live rock in this glossy scarlet bar can expand to an impromptu stage in the alley with crowds trailing up to the main street. On other nights there's a DJ. Though the emphasis is on the music, there's a great beer selection.

⚡ SPORTS & ACTIVITIES

REDERIJ REMBRANDT   BOAT TOUR
(📞071-513 49 38; www.rederij-rembrandt.nl; Beestenmarkt; adult/child €10/6.50; ⏰11am-4pm Mar-Oct) There are leisurely one-hour canal boat tours of the channel around the old town centre with Rederij Rembrandt, including commentary (English language available).

BOTENVERHUUR 'T
GALGEWATER   BOAT RENTAL
(Boat Hire Galgewater; www.botenverhuurleiden.nl; Galgewater 44a; kayaks & canoes per hr from €6, boats per hr from €80; ⏰noon-7pm Mon-Thu, 11am-7pm Fri-Sun Apr–mid-May & mid-Aug–Oct, to 10pm mid-May–mid-Aug) Rent a canoe, kayak or motorised boat from Botenverhuur 't Galgewater and explore the canals.

Delft

Explore
Compact and charming, Delft is synonymous with its hand-painted blue-and-white porcelain. It's *very* popular with visitors strolling its narrow canals, gazing at the remarkable old buildings and meditating on the career of Golden Age painter Johannes Vermeer, who was born and lived here, so getting an early start helps beat the crowds.

After touring Royal Delft's porcelain factory, Koninklijke Porceleyne Fles, pick up a copy of the *Historic Walk through Delft* brochure (€3.50) from the tourist office and explore the city's riches at your own pace. Be sure to allow time for shopping and wining and dining around the Markt. Although just an hour from Amsterdam, gracious hotels cater to daytrippers who don't want to go home quite yet.

The Best...
➡ **Sight** Koninklijke Porceleyne Fles (p215)
➡ **Place to Eat** Stads-Koffyhuis (p217)
➡ **Place to Drink** Belgisch Bier Café Belvédère (p217)

Top Tip
It's not all pottery, really: take time to wander the streets of one of the Netherlands' prettiest cities, a veritable treasure trove of Gothic and Renaissance architecture.

Getting There & Away
➡ **Travel time** One hour
➡ **Train** Services from Amsterdam's Centraal Station to Delft are frequent (€12, up to six per hour).
➡ **Car** Take the A13/E19, which passes through Den Haag en route to Rotterdam.

Need to Know
➡ **Area Code** 📞015
➡ **Location** 55km southwest of Amsterdam
➡ **Tourist Office** (VVV; 📞015-215 40 51; www.delft.nl; Kerkstraat 3; ⏰11am-4pm Mon, 10am-4pm Tue-Sat, 10am-3pm Sun)

◉ SIGHTS

KONINKLIJKE
PORCELEYNE FLES   PORCELAIN FACTORY
(Royal Delft; www.royaldelft.com; Rotterdamseweg 196; adult/child €12/free; ⏰9am-5pm, closed Sun Nov–mid-Mar) Pottery fans, and even those new to the iconic blue-and-white earthenware, will enjoy this factory-meets-gallery-meets-shopping experience. This Royal Delft factory is the only original factory, and has been operating since the 1650s. Regular tickets include an audio tour which leads you through a painting demonstration, the company museum and the factory production process. The truly delftware-obsessed will want to take a workshop (€46) in which you get to paint your own piece of Delft blue.

For many, of course, the real thrills begin and end in the gift shop.

The factory is a 15-minute walk southwest of the train station.

VERMEER CENTRUM DELFT   MUSEUM
(www.vermeerdelft.nl; Voldersgracht 21; adult/child €8/4; ⏰10am-5pm) Along with viewing life-sized images (though no actual paintings) of Delft native Vermeer's oeuvre, you can tour a replica of his studio, which gives insight into the way the artist approached the use of light and colour in his craft.

Delft

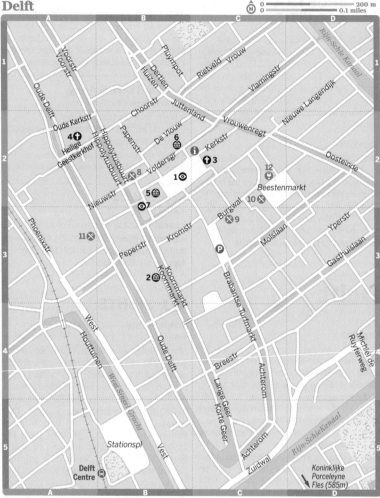

Exhibits offer a biographical insight into Vermeer's environment and upbringing and showcase the ways in which his work continues to inspire other artists.

MARKT
SQUARE

The pedestrian city plaza is worth a stroll for its pleasant collection of galleries, antique stores, clothing boutiques and quirky speciality shops. Most stores are open to 9pm on Friday. On Thursday you'll find the general market, while on Saturday, from April to September, the antiques, bric-a-

brac and book market attracts those seeking treasures and deals alike.

Before you leave the crowded Markt, check out the **town hall** (Markt), with its unusual combination of a Renaissance construction surrounding a 13th-century tower. Behind it, the 1644 weigh house (the Waag) is now a bar and restaurant.

OUDE KERK
CHURCH

(Old Church; www.oudekerk-delft.nl; Heilige Geestkerkhof 25; adult/child incl Nieuwe Kerk €3.50/2; ⊙9am-6pm Apr-Oct, 11am-4pm Nov-

Delft

Mar, closed Sun) The Gothic Oude Kerk, founded in 1246, is a surreal sight: its 75m-high tower leans nearly 2m from the vertical due to subsidence caused by its canal location, hence its nickname 'Scheve Jan' ('Leaning Jan'). One of the tombs inside the church is Vermeer's.

NIEUWE KERK   CHURCH
(New Church; www.nieuwekerk-delft.nl; Markt; adult/child incl Oude Kerk €3.50/1.50, Nieuwe Kerk tower extra €3.50/2; ☺9am-6pm Apr-Oct, 11am-4pm Nov-Mar, closed Sun) Construction on Delft's Nieuwe Kerk began in 1381; it was finally completed in 1655. Amazing views extend from the 108.75m-high tower: climbing its 376 narrow, spiralling steps will reward you with incredible views of the city and beyond (as far as Rotterdam and Den Haag on a clear day). It's the resting place of William of Orange, in a mausoleum designed by Hendrick de Keyser.

MUSEUM PAUL TETAR VAN ELVEN   MUSEUM
(www.museumpaultetarvanelven.nl; Koornmarkt 67; adult/child €5/2.50; ☺1-5pm Tue-Sun) A former studio and home of the 19th-century Dutch artist Paul Tetar van Elven, the museum features several Rembrandts and a Vermeer, along with reproductions of notable paintings by the artist himself. The evocative 17th-century interior retains its original furnishings and lived-in feel.

✖ EATING & DRINKING

DE VISBANKEN   SEAFOOD €
(Camaretten 2; snacks from €3; ☺10am-6pm) Fish has been sold on this spot since 1342. The present vendors line the display cases in the old open-air pavilion with all manner of things fishy. Enjoy marinated and smoked treats or go for something fried.

STADS-KOFFYHUIS   CAFE €
(www.stads-koffyhuis.nl; Oude Delft 133; mains €10-13) The best seats at Stads-Koffyhuis are on the terrace, aboard a barge moored out the front of the cafe. Tuck into burgers and the house-speciality pancakes while admiring the view of the Oude Kerk, just ahead at the end of the canal.

NATUURLIJK 015   VEGETARIAN €
(www.natuurlijk015.nl; Burgwal 11; mains €6.50-8.50, 3-course menu €27.50; ☺10am-6pm Mon-Wed, 10am-10pm Thu-Sat, 11am-5pm Sun; 🐾) 🍃 This organic cafe delights visitors and locals alike, who congregate on the terrace for creative sandwiches, smoothies and salads. On Thursday, Friday and Saturday evenings it serves a three-course dinner (choices include lentil salad, pearl-barley risotto and pineapple with soy ice cream). Most dishes are vegan; it also has weekly high tea and 'high wine' events.

SPIJSHUIS DE DIS   CONTEMPORARY DUTCH €€
(www.spijshuisdedis.com; Beestenmarkt 36; mains €17-23; ☺5-9.30pm Tue-Sat; 🐾) Fresh fish and amazing soups served in bread bowls take centre stage at this romantic eatery, but meat eaters and vegetarians are well catered for too. Creative starters include smoked, marinated mackerel on sliced apple with horseradish. Don't skip the Dutch pudding served in a wooden shoe.

BELGISCH BIER CAFÉ BELVÉDÈRE   BEER CAFÉ
(www.bbcbelvedere.nl; Beestenmarkt 8; ☺11am-1am Mon-Thu, 11am-2am Fri, 10am-2am Sat, noon-1am Sun) You can choose from six beers on tap and many more by the bottle at this Belgian beer temple in an old historic house.

Alkmaar

Explore

If ever there was a cheese town, Alkmaar is it. Most visitors come to this picturesque town for the traditional cheese market dating back to the 17th century. It only takes place on Friday mornings from April to the beginning of September, so you'll need to time your trip right to catch it.

After spending the morning at the cheese market, you'll be understandably hungry. So head to lunch, or make your own gouda or *boerenkaas* (farmer's cheese) sandwiches from the shops on Magdalenenstraat. Spend the afternoon at the Stedelijk Museum and the National Beer Museum. And after that, why not a have beer on one of the laidback cafe terraces?

The Best...

→ **Sight** Cheese Market (p218)
→ **Place to Eat** Heeren van Sonoy (p219)
→ **Place to Drink** Cafe Restaurant De Buren (p219)

Top Tip

While most people come for the cheese, don't miss the wonderful Stedelijk Museum, which houses an impressive collection of Dutch Masters.

Getting There & Away

→ **Train** Services run at least three times per hour from Amsterdam's Centraal Station (€7, 45 minutes). Note that faster Intercity trains terminate at Uitgeest, where you'll need to change to the slower Sprinter train to Alkmaar, so it's easier (and about the same travel time overall) to take a Sprinter train straight through from Amsterdam. Alkmaar's canal-bound centre is 1km southeast of the train station.
→ **Car** Take the A9 in the west of Amsterdam, which goes directly to Alkmaar.

Need to Know

→ **Area Code** ☑072
→ **Location** 35km northwest of Amsterdam
→ **Tourist Office** (VVV; ☑511 42 84; www.vvvalkmaar.nl; Waagplein 2; ⊗10am-4pm Mon-Thu & Sat, 9am-4pm Fri Apr-Sep; 10am-5pm Mon-Sat Oct; 1-5pm Mon, 10am-5pm Tue-Sat Nov-Mar)

◉ SIGHTS

CHEESE MARKET   MARKET
(Waagplein; ⊗10am-noon Fri Apr-early Sep) On Friday mornings in season, waxed wheels of *kaas* (cheese) are ceremoniously stacked on the main square. Soon, porters appear in colourful hats (denoting the cheese guild), and dealers in white smocks insert a hollow rod to extract a cheese sample, and

---

SCHEVENINGEN

Arguably the Netherlands' most popular beach, **Scheveningen** (www.scheveningen.com) is a great family destination 65km southwest of Amsterdam and just a 15-minute tram ride from Den Haag. Even if it's too chilly to swim, it's a lovely spot to stroll along the beach, shop at the Palace Promenade or dine in a seaside cafe. With its swirling sand dunes and forest, the beach is also popular with walkers who come to hike the 'Dutch Dune' from Scheveningen to Noordwijk.

The beach itself is about 3km long. The Noorderstrand (North Beach) is built up with modern hotel and condo developments, and is home to a pier and a shopping promenade with restaurants and bars that get insanely packed on summer days. Retreat to the Zuiderstrand (South Beach) to find solitude, but mind the current, which is known to be strong.

Trains run from Amsterdam's Centraal Station to Den Haag (€10.60, 45 minutes, at least four per hour). To reach the Noorderstrand, take tram 1 or 9 from the city centre of Den Haag, or take bus 22 from Den Haag's Centraal Station. To get to Zuiderstrand take tram 11 from Hollands Spoor, Den Haag's smaller train station. Tickets from Den Haag to Scheveningen cost €3.

sniff and crumble to check fat and moisture content. Once deals are struck, the porters whisk the cheeses on wooden sledges to the old cheese scale, accompanied by a zillion camera clicks.

It's primarily for show – nowadays the dairy co-ops have a lock on the cheese trade. Still, as living relics go it's a colourful show.

STEDELIJK MUSEUM   MUSEUM
(www.stedelijkmuseumalkmaar.nl; Canadaplein 1; adult/child €8/free; ⊙10am-5pm Tue-Sun) The Stedelijk Museum's collection of oil paintings by Dutch Masters, including impressive life-sized portraits of Alkmaar nobles, is worth the entry fee alone. Other works show the city in post–Golden Age decline; sombre scenes of almswomen caring for the poor recall how the church's role grew as trade declined. Modern works on display include Charley Toorop's odd oil painting of the Alkmaar cheese market; her cheese-bearers with grotesque features remain controversial.

WAAGGEBOUW   HISTORIC BUILDING
(weigh-house; Waagplein 2; ⊙carillon 6.30pm & 7.30pm Thu, 11am & noon Fri, noon & 1pm Sat mid-Apr–mid-Sep) Built as a chapel in the 14th century, the Waaggebouw was pressed into service as a weigh house two centuries later. This handsome building houses the tourist office and the Hollands Kaasmuseum. The mechanical tower **carillon** with jousting knights still springs to life.

HOLLANDS KAASMUSEUM   MUSEUM
(Dutch Cheese Museum; www.kaasmuseum.nl; Waagplein 2; adult/child €3/1.50; ⊙10am-4pm Mon-Thu & Sat, 9am-4pm Fri Apr-Oct, 10am-4pm Sat Nov-Mar) Upstairs from the tourist office in the Waaggebouw, this cheesy museum has a reverential display of cheese-making utensils, photos and a curious stock of paintings by 16th-century female artists.

NATIONAAL BIERMUSEUM   MUSEUM
(www.biermuseum.nl; Houttil 1; adult/child €4/2; ⊙11am-5pm Mon-Sat) Housed in the attractive old De Boom brewery, the Nationaal Biermuseum has a decent collection of beer-making equipment and wax dummies showing how the suds were made. The video of Dutch beer commercials since the 1950s will have you in stitches. Choose from 30 beers (eight on draught) in the

friendly bar after your tour (included in adult admission).

GROTE KERK   CHURCH
(www.alkmaarorgelstad.nl; Kerkplein; admission free; ⊙10am-5pm Tue-Sun Jul & Aug, Wed & Fri-Sun only Sep-Jun) FREE The Grote Kerk is renowned for its organs, the most famous of which is the little 'Swallow Organ' (1511) in the north ambulatory. The 17th-century organ built by Jaco van Campen dominates the nave. Organ recitals – which will thrill any fan of 1930s horror movies – take place on Wednesday evenings and at noon on days when the church is open. Be sure to get the English-language guide. The pastel stained-glass windows bathe the interior in colour.

EATING & DRINKING

Running northwest from the Waagplein cheese marketplace, Magdalenenstraat is lined with cheese shops and bakeries.

HEEREN VAN SONOY   INTERNATIONAL €€
(☏072-511 28 85; www.heerenvansonoy.nl; Hof van Sonoy 1; lunch mains €5-15, dinner mains €18.50-25.50; ⊙10am-9pm Tue-Sun) Heeren van Sonoy occupies a former 15th-century nunnery with a rustic dining room overlooking the *hofje* and umbrella-shaded courtyard tables. Cooking is global: satays, roasts and more. Lunchtime sandwiches are a treat.

CAFE RESTAURANT
DE BUREN   CONTEMPORARY DUTCH €€
(www.restaurant-deburen.nl; Mient 37; mains €14.50-24.50; ⊙9.30am-10pm) Outside tables at this vintage cafe span the canal and wrap around to the old fish market. The menu is a fresh take on Dutch fare. There's a sprightly mustard soup and curries.

SPORTS & ACTIVITIES

WOLTHEUS CRUISES   BOAT CRUISE
(www.woltheuscruises.nl; adult/child €5.90/4.40; ⊙11am-4pm Apr-Oct) Tours depart from Mient near the Waaggebouw and last 45 minutes. Offers multilingual commentary.

Zaanse Schans

Explore

People come for an hour and stay for several at this working and fully inhabited village, which functions as a kind of open-air windmill gallery on the Zaan river. It's *the* place to see windmills operating, although only a few of the formerly more than 1000 windmills in the area have been restored. While the village has a strong touristy element, the mills are completely authentic and are operated with enthusiasm and love.

Spend your time exploring the six working mills. One sells fat jars of its freshly ground mustard, while the others turn out oils, flour and sawed planks. Most are open for inspection, and it's a delight to clamber about the creaking works while the mills shake in the North Sea breeze.

Top Tip

Hire a bike and pedal from Amsterdam to Zaanse Schans. It only takes about 90 minutes, and the picturesque trip is a highlight of many travellers' holiday.

Getting There & Away

➡ **Train** Take the Sprinter (or Intercity) train from Amsterdam's Centraal Station towards Alkmaar (or Uitgeest) and get off at Koog-Zaandijk (€2.90, 17 minutes, four times hourly), then walk 1.5km via the Julianabrug spanning the Zaan river to Zaanse Schans.

➡ **Car** Travel to the northwestern side of Amsterdam on the A10 ring road, and take the A8 turn-off. Exit at Zaandijk.

Need to Know

➡ **Area Code** ✆075
➡ **Location** 10km northwest of Amsterdam
➡ **Tourist Office** (Zaanse Schans Information Desk; ✆075-681 00 00; www.zaanseschans.nl; Schansend 7, reception area, Zaans Museum; ◷10am-5pm)

◉ SIGHTS

WINDMILLS   WINDMILLS

You can explore Zaanse Schans' working windmills at will, seeing first-hand the

---

BLOEMENVEILING AALSMEER

The world's biggest flower auction, **Bloemenveiling Aalsmeer** (www.floraholland.com; Legmeerdijk 313; adult/child €6/3.50; ◷7-11am Mon-Wed & Fri, to 9am Thu), is a heady combination of hard-nosed business and sweet-smelling pleasure. Run by vast flower conglomerate FloraHolland, it's fascinating even for those who don't have tulip fever.

The auction takes place in Europe's largest commercial complex (1 million sq metres), and one look at the car park and truck fleets will tell you why so much space is necessary. Some 90 million flowers and two million plants change hands here every single day, racking up some €7 million in business. Monday is the busiest time; Thursday is quietest. Be prepared to get an early start: the later you arrive, the less there is to see.

Admission includes an aromatic self-guided tour on a 3km-long, wheelchair-accessible elevated walkway above the frenetic warehouse floor, overlooking the choreography of flower-laden forklifts and trolleys. Along the route, signboards with push-button audio recordings interpret the action.

The route also passes windows where you can peek into the auction rooms and see arrangers prepping the blooms for display as the carts go to auction. Selling is conducted – surprise! – by Dutch auction, with a huge clock showing the starting price. From the starting bell, the hand keeps dropping until someone takes up the offer and a deal is struck. More and more transactions are taking place online, so catch the action while it's still here.

Bloemenveiling Aalsmeer is just 22km from Amsterdam. Take bus 172 from Amsterdam Centraal Station (€3.50, 45 minutes, four per hour) to the FloraHolland Hoofdingang (FloraHolland main entrance) stop. Services start running at 4.59am so arriving in time shouldn't be a problem.

vast moving parts that make these devices a combination of intricate machinery and sailing ship. As a bonus, the riverbank setting is lovely. While most attractions are free, some charge an entrance fee.

The mill selling paint pigments will delight artists, as you see the actual materials used in producing Renaissance masterpieces turned into powders. Ask to see the storeroom of ground pigments for sale.

The other buildings have been brought here from all over the country to re-create a 17th-century community. There's an early Albert Heijn supermarket, a cheese maker and a clog factory that turns out wooden shoes as if grinding keys (and which has a surprisingly interesting museum). The engaging pewtersmith will explain the story behind dozens of tiny figures while the soft metal sets in the moulds.

The impressive **Zaans Museum** (☑075-616 28 62; www.zaansmuseum.nl; Schansend 7; adult/child €9/5; ☺10am-5pm) shows how the harnessing of wind and water was done.

Once you've finished poking about the village, take a **boat** (adult/child €5/3; ☺9am-6pm May-Sep) across the Zaan river, saving you part of the walk back to the train station. It runs on demand.

Sleeping

In its typically charming way, Amsterdam has loads of hotels in wild and wonderful spaces: inspired architects have breathed new life into old buildings, from converted schools and industrial lofts to entire rows of canal houses joined at the hip. Many lodgings overlook gorgeous waterways or courtyards. But charm doesn't come cheap...

Seasons & Prices

Rates and crowds peak in summer and on weekends at any time of the year. Book well in advance if you're travelling then. Prices are lowest from October to April (excluding Christmas/New Year and Easter).

Hotels

Any hotel with more than 20 rooms is considered large, and most rooms themselves are on the snug side. You'll see a 'star' plaque on the front of every hotel, indicating its rating according to the Benelux Hotel Classification. The stars (from one to five) are determined by the existence of certain facilities, rather than their quality. This means that a two-star hotel may be in better condition than a hotel of higher rank, though admittedly with fewer facilities.

B&Bs

Amsterdam has a scattering of B&Bs but most don't have exterior signage and access is by reservation only, giving an intimate feel. A couple of particularly cool ones are on houseboats.

Youth Hostels

Jeugdherbergen (youth hostels) are popular in Amsterdam. The Netherlands hostel association goes by the name **Stayokay** (www.stayokay.com) and is affiliated with **Hostelling International** (www.hihostels.com).

Party & Stoner Hotels

A number of hotels in the budget category welcome party guests as well as pot smokers. By and large they're pretty basic affairs. If in doubt whether smoking marijuana is permitted, ask when you make your reservation. Many hotels have strict no-drugs policies.

Amenities

Wi-fi is nearly universal across the spectrum, but air-conditioning and lifts are not.

TOP END

Expect lifts (elevators), minibars and room service. At the top end of top end, facilities such as air-conditioning and fitness centres are standard. Breakfast is rarely included.

MIDRANGE

Most hotels in this category are big on comfort, low on formality and small enough to offer personal attention. Rooms usually have a toilet and shower, a TV and a phone. Not many midrange hotels with more than two storeys have lifts, and their narrow stairwells can take some getting used to, especially with luggage. Rates typically include breakfast.

BUDGET

Lodgings in the lowest price bracket, other than hostels, are thin on the ground. Some are nothing short of rundown flophouses. The better options tend to be spick and span, with furnishings that are, at best, cheap and cheerful. Rates often include breakfast.

Lonely Planet's Top Choices

Collector (p232) Offbeat B&B in the Old South with backyard chickens.

Hotel Pulitzer (p227) As Amsterdam as it gets, spread over 25 historic canal houses.

Andaz Amsterdam (p227) A wonderland envisioned by iconic Dutch designer Marcel Wanders.

Hotel Brouwer (p225) Eight rooms get artsy in a 17th-century canal house.

Hotel Fita (p232) Sweet little family-owned hotel a stone's throw from the Museumplein.

Best by Budget

€

Cocomama (p228) Red-curtained boutique hostel in a former brothel.

Stayokay Amsterdam Stadsdoelen (p226) Bustling backpacker digs near Nieuwmarkt square.

Christian Youth Hostel 'The Shelter Jordaan' (p230) Oasis of sobriety, with pancake breakfasts and a piano.

€€

Hotel Résidence Le Coin (p225) Shiny, university-owned apartments in the centre.

Hotel V (p229) Retro-chic hotel facing lush Frederiksplein.

Conscious Hotel Vondelpark (p231) Eco innovations extend to pressed cardboard benchtops.

€€€

Hotel Okura Amsterdam (p233) Rare-for-Amsterdam views and three Michelin stars in the building.

Toren (p227) Blends 17th-century opulence with a sensual decadence.

College Hotel (p233) Celebrity-favourite boutique run by hotel-school students.

Best Canal Views

Canal House (p227) Gorgeous water views out front and a sofa-strewn garden out back.

Seven Bridges (p229) One of the city's most exquisite little hotels on one of its loveliest canals.

Best Only-in-Amsterdam

Hemp Hotel (p228) Chilled-out, individually themed rooms are decked out with hemp soap and fabrics.

B&B Le Maroxidien (p234) Wonderful houseboat B&B aboard a 1920s freighter.

Xaviera Hollander's Happy House (p233) B&B owned by the famed author and former madam.

Best Design Savvy

Hotel Notting Hill (p230) A lobby wall of vintage suitcases is among designer Wim Hoopman's touches.

Lloyd Hotel (p234) Rooms are so one-of-a-kind they'll even impress travellers who think they've seen it all.

Best for Romantics

Houseboat Ms Luctor (p231) Hide away on your own houseboat, with a breakfast basket delivered to your door.

Seven One Seven (p230) Nine spacious, breathtakingly beautiful rooms that you won't want to leave.

Where to Stay

Neighbourhood	For	Against
Medieval Centre & Red Light District	In the thick of the action; close to sights, nightlife, theatres and transport	Can be noisy, touristy and seedy; not great value for money
Nieuwmarkt	Still near the action, but with a slightly more laid-back vibe than the Centre	Some parts are close enough to the Red Light District to get rowdy spillover
Western Canal Ring	Tree-lined canals. Oddball boutiques and the Jordaan's cafes are nearby. Within walking distance of Amsterdam's most popular sights	Given all the positives, rooms book out early and can be pricey
Southern Canal Ring	Swanky hotels, not far from the dining hub of Utrechtsestraat and Nieuwe Spiegelstraat's antique shops	Can be loud, crowded, pricey, and touristy – especially around the high-traffic areas of Leidseplein and Rembrandtplein
Jordaan & the West	Cosy cafes, quirky shops and charming village character surround you	Sleeping options are few, due in part to the paucity of big-name sights close by
Vondelpark & Around	An aura of wealth and history surrounds Vondelpark, and the serene, designer hotels mirror it	High prices reflect the ideal location, which is also near Museumplein and Leidseplein
Old South	Quiet, leafy streets; walking distance to Museumplein; small, gracious properties; lots of midrange options	Not much nightlife
De Pijp	Ongoing explosion of dining/drinking cool in the area; located near Museumplein and Southern Canal Ring	Easy walking distance to Museumplein, Vondelpark and Leidseplein, but a hike from the Centre; options are fairly limited
Plantage, Eastern Islands & Eastern Docklands	Abundant greenery, cutting-edge architecture and the rippling expanse of the IJ dotted with riverboats	Not an easy walk to Amsterdam's major sights; you'll need to tram or bike
Oosterpark & South Amsterdam	Lower prices due to remote location (which is really just a short tram/metro ride away); quiet area amid locals	Fewer options for food and drink

🛏 Medieval Centre & Red Light District

ST CHRISTOPHER'S
AT THE WINSTON
PARTY HOTEL, HOSTEL €

Map p300 (📞623 13 80; www.winston.nl; Warmoesstraat 123; dm €35-45, r €80-120; 📶; 🚊4/9/16/24/25 Dam) This place is party central for touring bands, with rock 'n' roll rooms and a busy club, bar, beer garden and smoking deck downstairs; it hops 24/7. Dorm rooms (all en suite) sleep up to eight. Most private rooms are 'art' rooms: local artists were given free rein, with results from super-edgy (entirely stainless steel) and playful to questionably raunchy.

There's no internet in the rooms, but the ground-floor wi-fi (lobby and bar) is free. Rates include breakfast.

AIVENGO YOUTH HOSTEL
HOSTEL €

Map p300 (📞421 36 70; www.aivengoyouthhostel.com; Spuistraat 6; dm €20-30, r €80-100; @📶; 🚊1/2/5/13/17 Nieuwezijds Kolk) Aivengo spreads out across two buildings – one with a Middle Eastern interior, the other with exposed wood beams. Rooms come in a variety of shapes: there's a 10-bed female dorm, a 20-bed mixed dorm and a couple of private en suite doubles among the stock. As far as in-the-thick-of-the-scene hostels go, Aivengo has a quiet, respectful vibe.

There's no real common room though, and the 'lounge' area meant to fill the gap sits right next to the bathroom.

FLYING PIG
DOWNTOWN HOSTEL
STONER HOSTEL €

Map p300 (📞420 68 22; www.flyingpig.nl; Nieuwendijk 100; dm €30-42; @📶; 🚊1/2/5/13/17 Nieuwezijds Kolk) Hang out with hundreds of young, dope-smoking backpackers at this very relaxed, massive, 250-bed hostel. It's pretty grungy, but no one seems to mind, especially when there's so much fun to be had in the throbbing lobby bar, which has a pool table and DJs some nights. There's also an indoor smoking area, full-service kitchens and a cushion-lined basement nicknamed the 'happy room'.

Rates include a continental breakfast.

★HOTEL BROUWER
HOTEL €€

Map p300 (📞624 63 58; www.hotelbrouwer.nl; Singel 83; r €60-100; @📶; 🚊1/2/5/13/17 Nieuwezijds Kolk) A bargain-priced favourite, Brouwer has just eight rooms in a house dating back to 1652. Each chamber is named for a Dutch painter and furnished with simplicity, but all have canal views. There's a mix of Delft-blue tiles and early-20th-century decor, plus a tiny lift. Staff dispense friendly advice.

Reserve well in advance. No credit cards accepted.

HOTEL RÉSIDENCE LE COIN
APARTMENT €€

Map p304 (📞524 68 00; www.lecoin.nl; Nieuwe Doelenstraat 5; s €125, d €145-160, f €240; 📶; 🚊4/9/14/16/24/25 Muntplein) This shiny inn, owned by the University of Amsterdam, offers 42 small, high-class apartments spread over seven historical buildings, all equipped with designer furniture, wood floors and kitchenettes – and all reachable by lift. It's in the thick of things, opposite the popular grand Café de Jaren and just a five-minute stroll to pretty Nieuwmarkt.

Breakfast costs €11.50 per person and wi-fi costs €5 per 24 hours.

HOTEL LUXER
HOTEL €€

Map p300 (📞330 32 05; www.hotelluxer.nl; Warmoesstraat 11; r €90-150; ❄📶; 🚊4/9/16/24/25 Centraal Station) A pleasant surprise if ever there was one, this smart little number is probably the best option for your money in the thick of the Red Light District. Rooms are small but well equipped (air-con!) and at night the breakfast area becomes a chic little bar. Breakfast is €8.

HOTEL THE EXCHANGE
BOUTIQUE HOTEL €€

Map p300 (📞561 36 99; www.exchangeamsterdam.com; Damrak 50; r €100-400; @📶; 🚊1/2/5/13/17 Nieuwezijds Kolk) The Exchange has 61 rooms that have been done up in crazy, eye-popping style by students from the Amsterdam Fashion Institute. Anything goes, from eye paintings on the walls to a Marie Antoinette dress tented over the bed. If you like plain decor, this isn't your place. Rooms span one star (very small and no view) to five stars; all have a private bathroom.

Rooms fronting the Damrak can be noisy, but the young and groovy guests don't seem to mind.

BELLEVUE HOTEL
HOTEL €€

Map p300 (📞530 95 30; www.bellevuehotel.nl; Martelaarsgracht 10; r €100-170; ❄📶; 🚊1/2/5/13/17 Martelaarsgracht) Of the small hotels around Centraal Station, this three-star place is the only one we'd stay at. The

77 rooms are small, white and tidy, and feature mod loos and themes of sand, water and grass.

If you're sensitive to noise, get a room in the back. Breakfast costs €12.50.

HOTEL HOKSBERGEN — BOUTIQUE HOTEL €€

Map p304 (②626 60 43; www.hotelhoksbergen. nl; Singel 301; d €70-135; ☎; ☐1/2/5 Spui) You sure can't beat Hoksbergen's fantastic canal-side location, and there's a free breakfast buffet, but be warned: even sardines would have trouble squishing into the microscopically small rooms (with clean but plain furnishings).

HOTEL DE L'EUROPE — LUXURY HOTEL €€€

Map p304 (②531 17 77; www.leurope.nl; Nieuwe Doelenstraat 2-8; r from €340; ✳@☎☒; ☐4/9/14/16/24/25 Muntplein) Owned by the Heineken family, who recently gave it an €85 million renovation, L'Europe mixes classical elements (glass chandeliers, doorkeepers in top hats) with whimsical Dutch design. The 111 rooms are grand, with iPads, canal views, heated floors and white marble bathtubs; wi-fi is free. The on-site cigar lounge and Freddy's Bar, with brass-topped tables and leather chairs, attract a professional crowd.

ART'OTEL AMSTERDAM — BOUTIQUE HOTEL €€€

Map p300 (②719 72 00; www.artotels.com; Prins Hendrikkade 33; r €259-339; ✳☎☒; ☐4/9/16/24/25 Centraal Station) This stylish hotel, part of a European chain, opened in 2013. Located opposite Centraal Station, the 107 rooms have mod decor and original artworks on the wall. To add to the creative theme, there's an open-to-the public gallery in the basement. The lobby is a swank refuge with a fireplace and library.

NH GRAND HOTEL KRASNAPOLSKY — HOTEL €€€

Map p304 (②554 91 11; www.nh-hotels.com; Dam 9; d from €220; ✳@☎; ☐4/9/16/24/25 Dam) Pride of place belongs to this 468-room edifice across from the Royal Palace. One of the city's first grand hotels (1866), it has elegant if compact rooms and spectacular public spaces. The 19th-century 'winter garden' dining room, with its soaring steel-and-glass roof, is a national monument, and there are fitness and business centres.

⊨ Nieuwmarkt

★ STAYOKAY AMSTERDAM STADSDOELEN — HOSTEL €

Map p308 (②624 68 32; www.stayokay.com; Kloveniersburgwal 97; dm €22-36, r €60; @☎; ☐4/9/14/16/24/25 Muntplein) Efficient Stadsdoelen is always bustling with backpackers and we can understand why. Staff are friendly and the 11 ultraclean single-sex and mixed rooms (each with up to 20 beds and free lockers) offer a modicum of privacy. There's a big TV room, a pool table, laundry, free lobby wi-fi, bicycle storage (€2 per day) and free continental breakfast.

Laptop rental costs €3 per hour.

CHRISTIAN YOUTH HOSTEL 'THE SHELTER CITY' — HOSTEL €

Map p308 (②625 32 30; www.shelter.nl; Barndesteeg 21; dm €25-39; @☎; ⊠Nieuwmarkt) The price is right at this rambling hostel just outside the Red Light District, but only if you can handle a bit of religious zeal and a tough no-drugs-or-alcohol policy. The pros of staying here include large, airy, single-sex dorms, filling free breakfasts, a quiet cafe, and a garden courtyard with a ping-pong table. There's a partner hostel in the Jordaan.

MISC EAT DRINK SLEEP — BOUTIQUE HOTEL €€€

Map p308 (②330 62 41; www.misceatdrinksleep. com; Kloveniersburgwal 20; r €155-245; @☎; ⊠Nieuwmarkt) Steps from Nieuwmarkt square, the Misc's six themed rooms range from 'baroque' (quite romantic) to 'the room of wonders' (a modern Moroccan escapade); two rooms contain quirky 'bumblebee' ceiling fans. Canal View rooms cost more, but the Garden View rooms are equally charming (and bigger).

Bonus: all nonalcoholic in-room snacks and beverages (minibar) and coffee (your own Nespresso machine) are free. Breakfast is also included in the rate.

⊨ Western Canal Ring

CHIC & BASIC AMSTERDAM — DESIGN HOTEL €€

Map p314 (②522 23 45; www.chicandbasic.com; Herengracht 13-19; s/d from €130/145; @☎; ☐18/21/22 Singel) Spread across three canal houses, the all-white, modern rooms here merge minimalism with cosiness and flair.

Try for a room facing the quaint footbridge across the Herengracht canal. Rates include breakfast.

FREDERIC RENTABIKE
APARTMENT, HOUSEBOAT €€

Map p314 (☎624 55 09; www.frederic.nl; Brouwersgracht 78; d/apt/houseboat from €87/133/138; ☎; ☐18/21/22 Brouwersstraat) Frederic offers nicely outfitted houseboats on the Prinsengracht, Brouwersgracht and Bloemgracht that are bona fide floating holiday homes with all mod cons. On land, the company also offers various rooms and apartments in central locations. (And yes, bikes too.)

MAES B&B
B&B €€

Map p314 (☎427 51 65; www.bedandbreakfastamsterdam.com; Herenstraat 26hs; s €95-115, d €115-135, apt €135-260; @☎; ☐13/14/17 Westermarkt) If you were designing a traditional home in the Western Canal Ring, it would probably turn out a lot like this property: oriental carpets, wood floors and exposed brick. It's actually fairly spacious for such an old building, but the kitchen (open all day for guests to use) is definitely *gezellig* (convivial, cosy).

HOTEL CLEMENS AMSTERDAM
HOTEL €€

Map p314 (☎624 60 89; www.clemenshotel.nl; Raadhuisstraat 39; s/d/tr €90/110/135; @☎; ☐13/14/17 Westermarkt) Freshly renovated in 2013, Clemens has private bathrooms with rain showers in all 14 rooms – but alas, still no lift/elevator. If you don't score a room with a private balcony (some others have window seats or fireplaces), there's a lovely terrace for breakfast (included in the rate).

SEBASTIAN'S
BOUTIQUE HOTEL €€

Map p314 (☎433 23 42; www.hotelsebastians.nl; Keizersgracht 15; s/d from €100/120; ✳@☎; ☐13/14/17 Westermarkt) The younger, more affordable sister of Toren (p227), a few blocks along the same picturesque canal. Sebastian's rocks its sibling's brand of dramatic cool, with striking purple and gold colour schemes, big vases and a backlit bar.

SUNHEAD OF 1617
B&B €€

Map p314 (☎626 18 09; www.sunhead.com; Herengracht 152; d €105-145, apt €115-160; @☎; ☐13/14/17 Westermarkt) The fabulous and funny Carlos is your host at these two flower-themed suites along some of Amsterdam's prettiest stretches of canal. There's a delightful balance of modern design and traditional Dutch charm, and an excellent breakfast.

★HOTEL PULITZER
LUXURY HOTEL €€€

Map p314 (☎523 52 35; www.pulitzeramsterdam.com; Prinsengracht 315-331; d from €359; ✳@☎; ☐13/14/17 Westermarkt) Starring in the heist film *Ocean's Twelve* (worth watching for the backdrop of Amsterdam alone), the Pulitzer's individually decorated, mod-con-equipped rooms spread over 25 historic canal houses. Extras range from the cigar bar and art gallery to a sleek gym and private canal cruises, along with lush garden courtyards and a superb restaurant and bar. Wi-fi is €19 for 24 hours.

CANAL HOUSE
BOUTIQUE HOTEL €€€

Map p314 (☎622 51 82; www.canalhouse.nl; Keizersgracht 148; d from €240; ✳☎; ☐113/14/17 Westermarkt) A large, leafy sofa-strewn garden is an unexpected find behind these adjoining 17th-century canal houses. Inside, the 23 rooms – in categories ranging from Good and Better to Exceptional and Best – have purple, grey and brown tones, soaring ceilings and king-size beds. There's a clubby cocktail bar; rates include breakfast.

★ANDAZ AMSTERDAM
DESIGN HOTEL €€€

Map p316 (☎523 12 34; www.amsterdam.prinsengracht.andaz.hyatt.com; Prinsengracht 587; d €375-480; @☎; ☐1/2/5 Prinsengracht) Visionary Dutch designer Marcel Wanders has transformed Amsterdam's former public library into a fantasy of giant gold and silver cutlery, fish murals, delftware-inspired carpets, library-book pages writ large on the walls and other flights of imagination. The 122 guest rooms have Geneva sound systems with iPod docks, king-size beds, and complimentary snacks and non-alcoholic drinks.

Views extend over the Prinsengracht canal or the Marcel Wanders–designed garden. It's part of the Hyatt's Andaz luxury boutique hotels collection.

TOREN
BOUTIQUE HOTEL €€€

Map p314 (☎622 60 33; www.toren.nl; Keizersgracht 164; s/d/garden patio with Jacuzzi from €140/275/385; historic boat rental per hour €140-345; ✳@☎; ☐13/14/17 Westermarkt) A title-holder for room size and personal service, the Toren's communal areas mix 17th-century opulence – gilded mirrors, fireplaces and magnificent chandeliers – with sensual decadence that whispers Parisian boudoir. Guest rooms are elegantly furnished with modern facilities (including Nespresso coffee machines).

It also rents historic boats (from €140 to €345 per hour) for private canal cruises.

DYLAN
LUXURY HOTEL €€€

Map p316 (⌂530 20 10; www.dylanamsterdam.com; Keizersgracht 384; d/ste from €295/500; ❄@☎; ⊕1/2/5 Spui) The Dylan consistently upholds its reputation as a temple of style. Slink through the 17th-century canal house's courtyard garden entrance to ensconce yourself in the restaurant or the black-and-white lobby. The 41 sumptuous rooms each have a unique theme, whether you're after flamboyant colours, Zen minimalism or the Dylan Thomas suite's fully stocked cocktail cabinet.

⌂ Southern Canal Ring

★COCOMAMA
HOSTEL €

Map p310 (⌂627 24 54; www.cocomama.nl; Westeinde 18; dm/r from €37/108; @☎; ⊕4/25 Stadhouderskade) Amsterdam's first self-proclaimed 'boutique hostel' plays up its salacious past (the building was once home to a high-end brothel) in some themed bunk rooms, while others are more demure with delftware or windmill themes. Private rooms (check out the monarchy-themed 'Royal' room) have iPod docking stations and flat-screen TVs.

Amenities are way above typical hostel standard, with en suite bathrooms, in-room wi-fi, a relaxing back garden, well-equipped kitchen, book exchange and a super-comfy lounge for movie nights.

CITY HOTEL
HOTEL €

Map p310 (⌂627 23 23; www.city-hotel.nl; Utrechtsestraat 2; 1-2 people €69, 3-6 people €99-189, 5-8 people without bathroom €149-239; @☎; ⊕4/9/14 Rembrandtplein) Above the Old Bell pub, practically on Rembrandtplein, is this unexpectedly fabulous budget hotel, run by a friendly family. Rooms sleeping two to six have private bathrooms; larger rooms sleeping five to eight people share bathroom facilities. All come with crisp linen; the attic annexe has a wonderful view of town.

HEMP HOTEL
STONER HOTEL €

Map p310 (⌂625 44 25; www.hemp-hotel.com; Frederiksplein 15; s/d without bathroom €55/70, d with bathroom €75; @☎; ⊕4 Prinsengracht) In the capital of the northern 'hempisphere' this chilled-out hotel serves hemp-flour rolls with breakfast (included in the rate) and the tattooed bartenders pour hemp teas and beer as they groove to reggae in the cafe. The colourful, individually themed rooms (Tibetan, Afghani) are decked out with hemp soap and fabrics, adding to the 'just back from Goa' vibe.

HOTEL ASTERISK
BOUTIQUE HOTEL €

Map p310 (⌂626 23 96; www.asteriskhotel.nl; Den Texstraat 16; s/d from €68/72; @☎; ⊕16/24/25 Wetering Circuit) Some rooms are miniscule but you'll sleep soundly on the comfy mattresses at this central, family-owned 42-room hotel. Little touches of elegance include crown mouldings, crystal chandeliers and a pretty breakfast room.

AIRPORT ACCOMMODATION

If you need a bed by the airport, try these reasonably priced hotels:

Citizen M (⌂811 70 80; www.citizenmamsterdamairport.com; Plezierweg 2; r €79-139; ❄@☎) A five-minute walk from the terminals, the Starship Enterprise–like rooms are snug but maximise space to the utmost, with plush, wall-to-wall beds, and shower and toilet pods. Each room includes a lighting control – command central for the lighting (purple, red or white), blinds, flat-screen TV (free on-demand movies), music, temperature and rain shower. Sushi, sake and self-service snacks are for sale in the club-like canteen. There's a second Citizen M (⌂811 70 90; www.citizenmamsterdamcity.com; Prinses Irenestraat 30; r €79-159), not far from the Amsterdam RAI convention centre, with an identical look and feel.

Yotel (⌂in UK 020-7100 1100; www.yotel.com; Schiphol Airport Plaza; r from €42 per 4hr; @☎) Yotel's Japanese-style capsule hotel at Schiphol is a blessing for travellers who need to catch some shut-eye. Prices for the standard 7-sq-metre glam cabins are time-based (four-hour minimum) for short layovers. The standards and twins have bunks and fold-up desks, while the premiums contain regular beds; all are stylish, with crisp white bedspreads and light wood. Located in Lounge 2, near Pier D.

HOTEL PRINSENHOF HOTEL €

Map p310 (☑623 17 72; www.hotelprinsenhof.
com; Prinsengracht 810; s/d without bathroom
€55/75, s/d €75/95; ☎; ☒4 Prinsengracht) This
good-value, 18th-century house features
lovely canal views and a breakfast room
with some Delft-blue tiles. Staff are affable
and the rooms are spacious.

HANS BRINKER
BUDGET HOTEL PARTY HOSTEL €

Map p310 (☑622 06 87; www.hans-brinker.com;
Kerkstraat 136; dm €25-35, d from €40; @☎;
☒1/2/5 Keizersgracht) The lobby is mayhem
and spartan rooms have the ambience of
a public hospital, but its beds are almost
always filled to capacity with boisterous
backpackers and groups who pack into the
bright and happy bar, the pulsating disco
and the inexpensive restaurant. Rooms
have private bathrooms and lockers; wi-fi is
available in public areas.

SEVEN BRIDGES BOUTIQUE HOTEL €€

Map p310 (☑623 13 29; www.sevenbridgesho-
tel.nl; Reguliersgracht 31; d €115-215; @☎; ☒4
Keizersgracht) Sophisticated and intimate,
the Seven Bridges is one of the city's most
exquisite little hotels on one of its loveliest canals. It has eight tastefully decorated
rooms (all incorporating lush oriental rugs
and elegant antiques). The urge to sightsee
may fade once breakfast (€12.50), served on
fine china, is delivered to your room.

HOTEL ORLANDO BOUTIQUE HOTEL €€

Map p310 (☑638 69 15; www.hotelorlando.nl; Prinsengracht 1099; s €105-140, d €125-160; ❋@☎;
☒4 Prinsengracht) There are just seven
rooms at this jewel of a 17th-century canal
house, all with a blend of antiques, designer
furniture and contemporary art, as well as
solid oak floors and silk curtains, but each
is uniquely different. Higher priced rooms
have more space and canal views. Breakfast
(included in the rate) comes with freshly
squeezed orange juice.

Note that stairs between the hotel's three
floors are steep and there's no lift/elevator.

HOTEL V BOUTIQUE HOTEL €€

Map p310 (☑662 32 33; www.hotelv.nl; Weteringschans 136; d €69-249, apt €199-399; @☎;
☒4/7/10/25 Frederiksplein) Facing lush Frederiksplein and footsteps away from Utrechtsestraat, the retro-chic Hotel V offers
fantastic value given its style and location.
Its 48 artsy rooms are done up in charcoal

colours and feature stone-wall bathrooms;
the four-person loft apartment has a private
entrance and a kitchenette.

BACKSTAGE HOTEL HOTEL €€

Map p310 (☑624 40 44; www.backstagehotel.
com; Leidsegracht 114; s without bathroom €65,
d without/with bathroom €125/155; @☎; ☒7/10
Raamplein) Seriously fun, this music-themed
hotel is a favourite among musicians jam-
ming at nearby Melkweg and Paradiso,
as evidenced by the lobby bar's band-
signature-covered piano and pool table. Gig
posters (many signed) line the corridors,
and rooms are done up in neo-retro black
and white, with iPod docking stations, and
drum kit overhead lights.

Late at night, bands (and their fans) hold
court in the lively bar.

HOTEL FREELAND HOTEL €€

Map p310 (☑622 75 11; www.hotelfreeland.com;
Marnixstraat 386; s without bathroom from €60,
s/d from €70/110; @☎; ☒1/2/5/7/10 Leidseplein) In a prime canal-side location, Free-
land has tidy themed rooms (tulips, roses
and sunflowers, and a few with Moroccan
details). Add in a tasty breakfast and it pretty much kills the Leidseplein competition.
It's gay-friendly and all-welcoming.

HOTEL AMSTELZICHT HOTEL €€

Map p310 (☑623 66 93; www.hotelamstelzicht.
nl; Amstel 104; d €149-209, apt €279-299; @☎;
☒4/9/14 Rembrandtplein) The view out front
is straight from a 17th-century painting, so
make sure you get one of the rooms facing
the Amstel river and the gabled houses beyond. From the blue tiles in the lobby to the
elegant rooms it's smooth and refined.

HOTEL ADOLESCE HOTEL €€

Map p310 (☑626 39 59; www.adolesce.nl; Nieuwe
Keizersgracht 26; s/d without bathroom €80/110,
s/d €85/130; @☎; ☒Waterlooplein) Simple
rooms are brightened by artistic prints
at this little family-owned hotel in an old
canal house. You can help yourself all day
to coffee, tea and snacks, including fruit.
Some but not all rooms have wi-fi – ask
when you book.

HOTEL KAP HOTEL €€

Map p310 (☑624 59 08; www.kaphotel.nl; Den
Texstraat 5b; d €125-140; @☎; ☒16/24/25
Weteringcircuit) Affordable rates, a buffet
breakfast served in an attractive dining
room or courtyard garden, and courteous,

gay-friendly owners make up for the plain rooms and lack of lift/elevator at this simple hotel. Wi-fi costs €5 per stay, and bikes are available for hire. A handful of cheaper single and twin rooms with shared bathrooms are available.

AMISTAD HOTEL
BOUTIQUE HOTEL €€

Map p310 (☑624 80 74; www.amistad.nl; Kerkstraat 42; s without bathroom from €97, s/d from €130/158; @🛜; 🚋1/2/5 Keizersgracht) Rooms at this bijou gay hotel are adorned with Philippe Starck chairs, CD players and computers. The breakfast room (with ruby-red walls and communal tables) becomes a hopping cafe later in the day.

GOLDEN BEAR
BOUTIQUE HOTEL €€

Map p310 (☑624 47 85; www.goldenbear.nl; Kerkstraat 37; s/d without bathroom from €67/92, s/d from €107/122; 🛜; 🚋1/2/5 Keizersgracht) Amsterdam's oldest gay and lesbian hotel has been operating since 1948. It straddles two 18th-century buildings, and the rooms are individually decorated in bright colours (some very bright).

★SEVEN ONE SEVEN
LUXURY HOTEL €€€

Map p310 (☑427 07 17; www.717hotel.nl; Prinsengracht 717; d €500-680; ✱@🛜; 🚋1/2/5 Prinsengracht) The nine hyperplush, deliciously appointed rooms at this breathtaking hotel come with that all-too-rare luxury: space. Step into the prodigious Picasso suite – with its soaring ceiling, elongated sofa, and contemporary and antique decorations – and you may never, ever want to leave. Rates include breakfast, afternoon tea, house wine and personalised service.

BANKS MANSION
HOTEL €€€

Map p310 (☑420 00 55; www.carlton.nl/banksmansion; Herengracht 519-525; d/ste from €229/429; ✱@🛜; 🚋16/24/25 Keizersgracht) You get far more than a fancy bed here: refreshments are complimentary at the self-service bar in the Frank Lloyd Wright–designed lobby. When you retire to your contemporary room, you'll enjoy a plasma-screen TV, DVD player (with free films), a huge rain shower and gin, whisky and cognac on the house.

HOTEL NOTTING HILL
DESIGN HOTEL €€€

Map p310 (☑523 10 35; www.hotelnottinghill.nl; Westeinde 26; d €188-345; ✱🛜; 🚋4/25 Stadhouderskade) Styled by Dutch designer Wim Hoopman of Hoopman Interior Projects (aptly abbreviated to HIP), this stunning former office block features a wall of vintage suitcases in the lobby, quirky sculptures and outsized contemporary art, with richly patterned wallpaper in the 67 guest rooms. Higher-priced rooms have canal views. It's in a bulls-eye location between Utrechtsestraat and De Pijp.

EDEN AMSTERDAM AMERICAN HOTEL
HOTEL €€€

Map p310 (☑556 30 00; www.edenamsterdamamericanhotel.com; Leidsekade 97; d from €220; ✱@🛜; 🚋1/2/5/7/10 Leidseplein) You can't get closer to the action than this ornate, tower-topped landmark (p129) on Leidseplein, a short walk to the Museum Quarter. Furnishings are sleek and contemporary; guests have use of a gym with a sauna.

🛏 Jordaan & the West

CHRISTIAN YOUTH HOSTEL 'THE SHELTER JORDAAN'
HOSTEL €

Map p320 (☑624 47 17; www.shelter.nl; Bloemstraat 179; dm €25-38.50; @🛜; 🚋13/14/17 Marnixstraat) Putting up with the 'no-everything' (drinkin', partyin', stumblin') policy at this small hostel isn't hard because it's such a gem. Single-sex dorms are quiet and clean, breakfasts – especially the fluffy pancakes – are great, and there's a piano. The cafe serves cheap meals the rest of the day.

INTERNATIONAL BUDGET HOSTEL
STONER HOSTEL €

Map p320 (☑624 27 84; www.internationalbudgethostel.com; Leidsegracht 76; dm €25-45, tw €70-100; @🛜; 🚋7/10 Raamplein) Reasons to stay: canal-side location in a former warehouse; really close to nightlife; four-person limit in rooms; cool mix of backpackers from around the world; clean rooms with lockers; printer access and bike rental; staff who are more pleasant than they need to be. There's a two-night minimum stay on weekends.

ALL INN THE FAMILY B&B
B&B €€

Map p318 (☑776 36 36; www.allinnthefamily.nl; 2e Egelantiersdwarsstraat 10; d €130; 🛜; 🚋3/10 Marnixsplein) In a charming old Amsterdam canal house, this welcoming B&B embodies the qualities of the inimitable Jordaan itself. Spirited hosts speak five languages, a bountiful organic Dutch breakfast is served in the garden in fine weather, and it's set in a quiet location in the heart of the neighbourhood. Lunch and dinner are available on request. Minimum stay three nights.

AMSTERDAM WIECHMANN HOTEL   HOTEL €€
Map p320 (✆626 33 21; www.hotelwiechmann. nl; Prinsengracht 328; s/d from €85/155; @🛜; ☐7/10/17 Elandsgracht) Lovingly cared-for rooms at this family-run hotel in three canal houses are furnished like an antique shop, with country quilts and chintz, while the lobby *tchotchkes* (knick-knacks) have been here for some 70 years. Rates include breakfast.

HOTEL VAN ONNA   HOTEL €€
Map p320 (✆626 58 01; www.hotelvanonna.nl; Bloemgracht 102-108; s €45-65, d €65-120; @🛜; ☐10 Bloemgracht) Some of these simple, reasonably priced rooms occupy a lovely c 1644 canal house in a gorgeous section of the Jordaan. The bells of the Westerkerk are within earshot, which is either charming or not (in which case get a room in the back).

Try to book one of the two attic rooms with old wooden roof beams and views over the Bloemgracht (Flower Canal).

HOUSEBOAT MS LUCTOR   HOUSEBOAT €€€
Map p303 (✆06 2268 9506; www.boatbedandbreakfast.nl; Westerdok 103; d from €170; 🛜; ☐48 Barentszplein) 🌿 A brimming organic breakfast basket is delivered to you each morning at this self-contained mahogany-panelled 1913 boat, moored in a quiet waterway 10 minutes' walk from Centraal (five from the Jordaan). Eco initiatives include solar power, two bikes to borrow and a canoe for canal explorations. Minimum stay two nights.

🛏 Vondelpark & Around

STAYOKAY AMSTERDAM
VONDELPARK   HOSTEL €
Map p322 (✆589 89 96; www.stayokay.com; Zandpad 5; dm €26-44, tw €71-100; @🛜; ☐1 1e Constantijn Huygensstraat) A frisbee's throw away from the Vondelpark, this 536-bed hostel attracts over 75,000 guests a year – no wonder the lobby feels like a mini-UN. The renovated rooms sport lockers, private bathrooms and well-spaced bunks. Chill out in the congenial bar/cafe, or shoot some pool.

HOTEL DE FILOSOOF   BOUTIQUE HOTEL €€
Map p322 (✆683 30 13; www.sandton.eu/nl/amsterdam; Anna van den Vondelstraat 6; s/d/tr from €95/100/179; @🛜; ☐1 Jan Pieter Heijestraat) It's easy to clear your mind in rooms named

after philosophers. Each room has its own theme representing its namesake, from Thoreau (with a mural of Walden Pond) to Nietzsche (lots of red, representing his book *Morgenröte*, meaning 'The Dawn'). There's an elegant bar and the tranquil English garden is a pastoral pleasure come summer.

CONSCIOUS HOTEL
VONDELPARK   BOUTIQUE HOTEL €€
Map p322 (✆820 33 33; www.conscioushotels. com; Overtoom 519; d €90-165; 🛜; ☐1 Rhijnvis Feithstraat) 🌿 At the Vondelpark branch of Europe's first officially eco-certified hotel, enviro-friendly features are both practical and stylish, from a growing wall in the stunning lobby and live plants in the rooms to recycled materials made into artful furnishings (including pressed cardboard bathroom benchtops) and the organic breakfast buffet (€13.50).

HOTEL ZANDBERGEN   HOTEL €€
Map p322 (✆676 93 21; www.hotel-zandbergen. com; Willemsparkweg 205; s €75-85, d €95-115, tr €125-145, studio apt €145-165; @🛜; ☐2 Emmastraat) The Zandbergen stands out like sterling silver in a tray of plastic cutlery. The staff at this peacefully situated hotel go overboard to help; rooms at the rear have balconies overlooking a quiet, flower-filled courtyard. Excellent value for money.

HOTEL PIET HEIN   BOUTIQUE HOTEL €€
Map p322 (✆662 72 05; www.hotelpiethein. com; Vossiusstraat 52-53; s/d €100/150; @🛜; ☐2/5 Van Baerlestraat) Overlooking the Vondelpark's fine old arbour, this immaculate hotel offers a startling variety of contemporary rooms (including snug, single 'business' rooms). There's a sublime garden and a relaxing bar. Wi-fi costs €12 per 24 hours.

FLYNT B&B   B&B €€
Map p322 (✆618 46 14; www.flyntbedandbreakfast.nl; 1e Helmersstraat 34; d €85-120; @🛜; ☐1 1e Constantijn Huygensstraat) The spacious slate bathrooms make you feel like you're in a mod boutique hotel, but the friendly owner, the cosy breakfast nook (with breakfast goodies available round the clock) and their pet-friendly policy are pure Vondelpark neighbourhood B&B.

OWL HOTEL   HOTEL €€
Map p322 (✆618 94 84; www.owl-hotel.nl; Roemer Visscherstraat 1; s/d from €84/112; @🛜; ☐1 1e Constantijn Huygensstraat) Some guests

love this place so much that they send in owl figurines from all over the world to add to the hotel's collection. Staff are warm and welcoming, and rooms are bright and quiet. The buffet breakfast (included in the rate) is served in a serene, light-filled room overlooking a delightful garden.

HOTEL VONDEL
BOUTIQUE HOTEL €€€

Map p322 (☎612 01 20; www.vondelhotels.com; Vondelstraat 28-30; d €89-285; @☎; ☐1 1e Constantijn Huygensstraat) Named after the famed Dutch poet Joost van den Vondel (as is the nearby park), the rooms in this chic hotel have a calm, comfortable decor (lots of plush grey). Alternatively, lounge next to goldfish and koi ponds in the Zen-like back gardens, opening out from the bar. Wi-fi is €10 per 24 hours.

Bike rental is available; the dramatic, art-lined restaurant is excellent.

FUSION SUITES
LUXURY HOTEL €€€

Map p322 (☎618 46 42; www.fusionsuites.com; Roemer Visscherstraat 40; ste €245-275; ✳@☎; ☐1 1e Constantijn Huygensstraat) Four-poster beds with luxury mattresses, flat-screen computers and TVs, free-standing baths and tasteful decor in Eastern earth tones with fresh flowers are just a few reasons you may choose never to leave these three spacious suites.

PARK HOTEL
HOTEL €€€

Map p322 (☎671 12 22; www.parkhotel.nl; Stadhouderskade 25; s/d/ste €69/169/269; ☎; ☐1/2/5/7/10 Leidseplein) Adjustable mood lighting, incense, and stunning George Heidweiller cityscapes on the walls are some of this individual hotel's design features. Downstairs, curl up with a cappuccino in the 'Living Room' with its changing gallery of modern art. It has a well-equipped fitness room and is within spitting distance of Vondelpark, so there's little excuse to not work out.

An Asian-inspired breakfast costs €23.50; wi-fi is free in the lobby and €10 per 24 hours in the rooms.

🛏 Old South

VAN GOGH HOSTEL & HOTEL
HOSTEL, HOTEL €

Map p324 (☎262 92 00; www.hotelvangogh.nl; Van de Veldestraat 5; dm €25-45, r €90-170; ✳@☎; ☐2/3/5/12 Van Baerlestraat) No false advertising here: it sits about 14 steps from the Van

Gogh Museum, and every room has a Van Gogh mural. The set-up puts the 200-bed hostel on one side, the hotel on the other, and the common area for breakfast (€5) divides them. The hostel dorms have six to eight beds, en suite bathroom and flat-screen TV.

The hotel rooms have balconies on the higher floors (ask for one when booking).

★COLLECTOR
B&B €€

Map p324 (☎673 67 79; www.the-collector.nl; De Lairessestraat 46hs; d from €95; @☎; ☐5/16/24 Museumplein) This spotless B&B near the Concertgebouw is furnished with museum-style displays of clocks, wooden clogs and ice skates – things the owner, Karel, collects. Each of the three rooms has balcony access and a TV. Karel stocks the kitchen for guests to prepare breakfast at their leisure (the eggs come from his hens in the garden).

The kitchen is open all day if you want to cook your own dinner. There are also a couple of bikes Karel lends out to guests.

★HOTEL FITA
HOTEL €€

Map p324 (☎679 09 76; www.hotelfita.com; Jan Luijkenstraat 37; r €115-175; @☎; ☐2/3/5/12 Van Baerlestraat) Family-owned Fita, on a quiet street off the Museumplein and PC Hooftstraat, has 15 handsome rooms with nicely appointed bathrooms; a bountiful free breakfast of eggs, pancakes, cheeses and breads; and an elevator. The dynamic young owner has been making lots of upgrades (new furniture, new artwork, fresh paint), and service could not be more attentive. It's one of the area's best-value digs, and tends to book up fast with older Americans.

HOTEL AALDERS
HOTEL €€

Map p324 (☎662 01 16; www.hotelaalders.nl; Jan Luijkenstraat 13-15; r €107-205; @☎; ☐2/3/5/12 Van Baerlestraat) There are fancier hotels in town, but family-owned Aalders is homey and well situated near the museums. The 28 rooms are spread among two tall, adjoining buildings and come in varying sizes and styles (some with wood panelling and decorative-glass windows). In the morning, munch free homemade pastries in the chandelier-adorned breakfast room. Aalders also rents out bikes.

CONSCIOUS HOTEL MUSEUM SQUARE
BOUTIQUE HOTEL €€

Map p324 (☎671 95 96; www.conscioushotels. com; De Lairessestraat 7; r €120-190; @☎; ☐5/16/24 Museumplein) 🌿 This is your place to go green. It starts with the living plant wall in the lobby and the organic breakfast (€10 extra). Then come modern rooms – beds made with 100% natural materials, desks constructed from recycled yoghurt containers, and energy-saving plasma TVs. There is a second location (p231) near Vondelpark.

HOTEL BEMA
HOTEL €€

Map p324 (☑679 13 96; www.bemahotel.com; Concertgebouwplein 19b; without/with bathroom from €65/80; @📶; 🚊5/16/24 Museumplein) Climb the stairs to this six-room hotel in a converted movie theatre: the old velvet seats decorate the halls, and the place is filled with African art. Expect tidy doubles and a nice continental breakfast (included in rates) delivered to your room. Staff can also arrange private apartments for up to four people. It's across from the Concertgebouw.

XAVIERA HOLLANDER'S HAPPY HOUSE
B&B €€

Off Map p324 (☑673 39 34; www.xavierahollander .com; Stadionweg 17; r/ste from €110/130; @📶; 🚊5/24 Gerrit van der Veenstraat) The former madam and author of *The Happy Hooker* welcomes guests to her home in the ritzy Beethovenstraat neighbourhood. The two rooms (which share a bathroom) are decked out with erotic photos, red heart pillows and books, such as her most recent *Guide to Mind-Blowing Sex*. There's also a garden hut with its own facilities (bathroom, refrigerator, terrace).

Xaviera's still something of a media star, and if you're lucky enough to meet her during your stay you'll quickly understand her charisma. The B&B is a good 1km south of the Museumplein. Two-night minimum stay required.

POET HOTEL
HOTEL €€

Map p324 (☑662 05 26; www.poethotelamsterdam.com; Jan Luijkenstraat 44; d €90-170; @📶; 🚊2/5 Hobbemastraat) The big bed pretty much takes up the entire space in the Poet's rooms, and the white-and-black colour scheme is a bit stark, but on the plus side is decent prices for a leafy location a couple blocks from the museums. It's mostly a younger crowd that stays here. The welcoming bar is filled with photos of old Amsterdam.

COLLEGE HOTEL
BOUTIQUE HOTEL €€€

Map p324 (☑571 15 11; www.thecollegehotel. com; Roelof Hartstraat 1; r from €225; ✳@📶; 🚊3/5/12/24 Roelof Hartplein) Originally a 19th-century school, College Hotel has fashioned its 40 chambers – with high ceilings, tasteful furnishings and the occasional stained-glass window – from former classrooms. Hospitality-school students now staff the hotel to earn their stripes, while celebs from Brooke Shields to Fatboy Slim enjoy the swanky end product. The hotel is well situated between the Museum Quarter and De Pijp's sights and cafes (about 1km from both).

🛏 De Pijp

BICYCLE HOTEL AMSTERDAM
HOTEL €€

Map p325 (☑679 34 52; www.bicyclehotel.com; Van Ostadestraat 123; d €115, s/d without bathroom €65/80; @📶; 🚊3/25 Ferdinand Bolstraat) 🌿 Run by Marjolein and Clemens, this casual, friendly, green-minded hotel has rooms that are comfy and familiar. It also rents bikes, and serves a killer organic breakfast (included in the rate).

BETWEEN ART & KITSCH B&B
B&B €€

Map p325 (☑679 04 85; www.between-art-and-kitsch.com; Ruysdaelkade 75-2; s/d from €85/105; @📶; 🚊16/25 Ruysdaelkade) Mondrian once lived here – that's part of the art – while the kitsch includes the crystal chandelier in the baroque room and a smiling brass Buddha. The art deco room has gorgeous tile work and views of the Rijksmuseum. Husband and wife hosts Ebo and Irene couldn't be friendlier. Note that it's on the third floor, with no lift/elevator.

CAKE UNDER MY PILLOW
B&B €€

Map p325 (☑751 09 36; www.cakeundermypillow. nl; 1e Jacob van Campenstraat 66; d with/without bathroom from €170/140; @📶; 🚊16/24 Stadhouderskade) Run by the owners of bakery Taart van m'n Tante (p183), this B&B above the cafe (no lift/elevator) has comfy rooms decorated with plates. A two-night minimum stay is required.

HOTEL OKURA AMSTERDAM
LUXURY HOTEL €€€

(☑678 71 11; www.okura.nl; Ferdinand Bolstraat 333; d €216-380, ste from €400; ✳@📶♨) Rare-for-Amsterdam amenities that elevate this business-oriented hotel way above the competition are panoramic city views (particularly from higher-priced north-facing rooms), a total of three Michelin stars on the premises (two at top-floor Ciel Bleu (p185), and one at lobby-level Japanese res-

SLEEPING DE PIJP

taurant Yamazato), and an amazing health club with an 18m-long jet-stream swimming pool. Wi-fi costs €12 per 24 hours.

Plantage, Eastern Islands & Eastern Docklands

HOTEL HORTUS   HOTEL €

Map p326 (☑625 99 96; www.hotelhortus.com; Plantage Parklaan 8; s €40-45, d €70-80; @☜; 🚋9/14 Plantage Kerklaan) Facing the botanical garden, this well-worn, comfortable 20-room hotel is terrific value for this area and contains a large common area with a pool table and several TVs. There are only two doubles, with or without shower (luck of the draw); all have a safe and a sink. Larger, dorm-style rooms sleep up to six people (€35 per person per night).

★B&B LE MAROXIDIEN   HOUSEBOAT, B&B €€

Map p326 (☑400 40 06; www.lemaroxidien.com; Prins Hendrikkade 534; s/d without bathroom €80/120; ☜; 🚋22/32/34/35/48 Prins Hendrikkade) ✐ Moored within easy reach of Centraal Station, Kathrin Rduch's wonderful houseboat (a 1920s former freighter) has a guest wing with three exotic cabins – the sky-blue Morocco, spacious Mexico and small India – which share two bathrooms and a cosy lounge. Kathrin provides an organic feast each morning for breakfast; sociable evening meals (€47.50) often take place. There's a minimum two-night stay; children over six are welcome. No credit cards.

LLOYD HOTEL   BOUTIQUE HOTEL €€

Map p326 (☑561 36 36; www.lloydhotel.com; Oostelijke Handelskade 34; r €120-525; @☜; 🚋26 Rietlandpark) Not only a 'one- to five-star' hotel but a cultural centre and local gathering place, the Lloyd was originally a hotel for migrants back in 1921, and many of the original fixtures still exist alongside contemporary Dutch design. Budget (bathroom down the hall) to top-end (racquetball-court-sized) rooms are so one-of-a-kind (bathtub in the centre, fold-away bathrooms, a giant bed for eight...) they'll even impress travellers who think they've seen it all.

HOTEL ALLURE   HOTEL €€

Map p326 (☑627 27 14; www.hotelallure.com; Sarphatistraat 117; s €139, d €149-179, tr €195; @☜; 🚋7/10 Weesperplein) Scarlet drapes, carpets,

and a vivid red dining room add a dramatic flair to this gleaming contemporary hotel. It's within walking distance of the Hermitage Amsterdam and the Artis Royal Zoo.

HOTEL REMBRANDT   HOTEL €€

Map p326 (☑627 27 14; www.hotelrembrandt.nl; Plantage Middenlaan 17; s/d from €75/115; @☜; 🚋9/14 Plantage Kerklaan) With its spotless modern rooms, the Rembrandt shines. Most rooms contain pop-art prints of Rembrandt himself, but room 8 is graced with a nearly life-sized mural of *Night Watch*. Breakfast (€10) is served in a wood-panelled room with chandeliers and 17th-century paintings on linen-covered walls. Take care not to let cute resident cat Bink out of the building.

Oosterpark & South Amsterdam

STAYOKAY AMSTERDAM ZEEBURG   HOSTEL €

Off Map p317 (☑551 31 90; www.stayokay.com; Timorplein 21; dm €21-37, r €30-100; @☜; 🚋14 Zeeburgerdijk) The sibling of Stayokay Vondelpark and Stayokay Stadsdoelen, Zeeburg might be the best of the bunch. It has 508 beds spread over three floors; most of the spick-and-span rooms are four- or six-bed dorms, all with en suite bathroom and bright orange decor. Hot breakfast is included, wi-fi (lobby only) is free.

Next door is Studio K, a cool arts centre/cinema/cafe, and a bike rental shop (€11 per day). Dappermarkt and Javaplein – with great restaurants – are a short stroll away. Take tram 14 from the Dam, a 15-minute journey.

HOTEL ARENA   HOTEL €€

Map p317 (☑850 24 00; www.hotelarena.nl; 's Gravesandestraat 51; d from €105; @☜; 🚋3/14 Beukenweg) With more facelifts than a Hollywood star, this building bordering Oosterpark has morphed from chapel to orphanage to backpackers hostel to, now, a modern, four-star, 116-room hotel with a trendy restaurant, cafe and nightclub. A recent makeover means minimalist rooms have a designer-industrial feel, and most of the chic, black-tiled bathrooms were designed by Philippe Starck. Some rooms are multi-level, so the bathroom is on a separate level from the bed.

Understand Amsterdam

Amsterdam Today

Amsterdam's famed tolerance is on display wherever you wander, despite right-leaning national policies that almost snuffed out the coffeeshops. Despite the economy taking a hit, dramatic architecture and grand urban projects continue to rise up and transform the cityscape, merging Golden Age charm with hypermodernity. Meanwhile, a new king has the keys to the palace, but it's his stylish, practical wife who steals the spotlight.

Best on Film

Zwartboek (Black Book; directed by Paul Verhoeven; 2006) This action-packed story explores some of the less heroic aspects of the Dutch Resistance in WWII. It launched the international career of today's hottest Dutch actor, Carice van Houten.

Het Diner (The Dinner; directed by Menno Meyjes; 2013) Two brothers and their wives go out to a fancy dinner together. As the meal progresses, it's revealed that their sons are linked by a terrible crime.

Best in Print

The Diary of Anne Frank (Anne Frank; 1952) A moving account of a young girl's thoughts and yearnings while in hiding from the Nazis in Amsterdam. The book has been translated into 60 languages.

Rock Bottom (Michael Shilling; 2009) A washed-up Los Angeles band ends up in Amsterdam for their last show on tour. The rockers wander the city on various paths of destruction, excitement, stupidity and possibly redemption.

A New King

Amsterdammers aren't obsessed with their royal family as some other cultures are, but when Queen Beatrix stepped down after 33 years, it was the headline of 2013. Her son, Willem-Alexander (b 1967), became king – the first male to accede to the Dutch throne since 1890. The invesiture took place at the Nieuwe Kerk on April 30, followed by a city-rocking party. (Incidentally, the nation's biggest holiday – known as Queen's Day – has become King's Day and now takes place on Willem-Alexander's birthday on 27 April.)

If locals had to admit to one royal fascination, it would be Queen Máxima. The stylish, blonde Argentinean, married to the king since 2002, has been known to ride her bike to royal functions and reuse her elegant dresses.

Tolerant Culture

Laid-back. Progressive. Fun-loving. Bilingual (sometimes trilingual). Industrious. Aware. International. Amsterdam's locals embody these qualities in spades for their famously tolerant attitudes toward diversity and differences. Perhaps this is why Amsterdam is celebrated for being a consummately easy and relaxed place to travel.

It's an open society in the literal sense. Walk down any street and notice the abundance of open windows – even in the ritziest neighbourhoods – where families and couples cook, eat, watch TV and play with their children in full view.

And while the economy has sputtered a bit over the past few years, the Dutch still rank among world's most satisfied people, according to the 2013 World Happiness Report by Columbia University. Only citizens of Denmark, Norway and Switzerland are happier with their lot in life.

Sex & Drugs

In 2010 the nation had a brief foray into conservative politics (with a right-of-centre minority VVD-CDA government supported by Geert Wilders' right-wing PVV party) that tightened immigration policies, slashed arts and culture funding, and even passed what was thought to be a near-death sentence for the country's coffeeshops. After a period when it seemed tourists would be banned from smoking pot in Amsterdam, the national 'weed pass' law fell by the wayside in late 2012. That's when the government that passed the act – whereby coffeeshops could sell pot only to registered locals – lost power. The new government (formed by the right-of-centre VVD and left-of-centre PvdA parties) let individual municipalities decide for themselves whether to enforce it. In Amsterdam, where one in three tourists visits a coffeeshop, the city decreed it would conduct business as usual.

But Amsterdam's other 'vice' industry – prostitution – faces continued restrictions. In 2013 the city won the right to introduce new zoning laws that will, in effect, shut down more than 60 Red Light District windows. These will be converted to galleries, cafes and other 'more wholesome' businesses. The city says organised crime has entered the scene and must be stopped; opponents say the city simply doesn't like its reputation for sin. The industry won't disappear anytime soon, but it will likely end up being confined to a couple of distinct areas.

Innovation Continues

Amsterdam has had the knack for innovation from the get-go. Just look at the canal ring, which celebrated its 400th birthday in 2013. City planners built it to drain and reclaim waterlogged land to accommodate the exploding population during the Golden Age. Flash-forward to today and it's a similar story. Amsterdam is running out of room for its growing number of denizens, and urban planners are using visionary architecture to solve the problem.

The shores along the IJ have seen the most action, with swooping modern developments transforming industrial areas such as the Eastern Docklands and Western Docklands (on either side of Centraal Station), as well as Amsterdam-Noord across the water. These are the new 'it' neighbourhoods for eye-popping, sustainably designed housing, offices and public buildings like the EYE Film Institute.

The innovation extends underground, too, as engineers build the new Noord/Zuidlijn – aka North–South Metro Line – from Amsterdam-Noord to the World Trade Centre in south Amsterdam, tunneling under the IJ and historic centre en route. The project, which is the source of all the torn-up streets you see around town, should be finished by 2017. Amsterdam also remains a world leader in eco-design and by 2015 all new construction here will be carbon neutral.

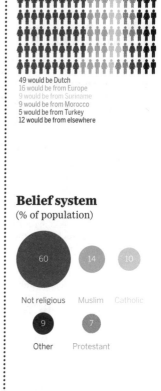

if Amsterdam were 100 people

49 would be Dutch
16 would be from Europe
9 would be from Suriname
9 would be from Morocco
5 would be from Turkey
12 would be from elsewhere

Belief system
(% of population)

60 Not religious
14 Muslim
10 Catholic
9 Other
7 Protestant

population per sq km

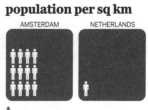

AMSTERDAM   NETHERLANDS

♦ ≈ 400 people

History

Amsterdam may have spawned one of the world's great trading empires, but this area was once an inhospitable patchwork of lakes, swamps and peat, at or below sea level; its contours shifted with the autumn storms and floods. The oldest archaeological finds in what is now Amsterdam date from Roman times, when the IJ river lay along the northern border of the Roman Empire. Maritime trading, egalitarian attitudes and engineering ingenuity all paved the way for the modern city today.

Historical Reads

The Embarrassment of Riches (Simon Schama)

Amsterdam: The Brief Life of a City (Geert Mak)

Tulip Fever (Deborah Moggach)

Max Havelaar (Eduard Douwes Dekker)

From the Beginning

The mighty Romans – who had conquered the lands now known as the Netherlands in the 1st century – left behind no colosseums or magnificent tombs. In uncharacteristic style, they left practically no evidence, much less any grand gestures, of settlement. While the swampy, sea-level topography made the construction of grand edifices challenging, the Romans had been known to bypass such challenges before in other regions. In the end, they simply had other more important lands south of the Low Countries to inhabit and rule.

Around 1200, a fishing community known as Aemstelredamme ('the dam built across the Amstel') emerged at what is now the Dam, and the name Amsterdam was coined.

Early Trade

Farming was tricky on the marshland and, with the sea on the doorstep, early residents turned to fishing. But it was commercial trade that would flourish. While powerful city-states focused on overland trade with Flanders and northern Italy, Amsterdam shrewdly levelled its sights on the maritime routes. The big prizes? The North and Baltic Seas, which were in the backyard of the powerful Hanseatic League, a group of German trading cities.

Ignoring the league's intimidating reputation, Amsterdam's clever *vrijbuiters* (buccaneers) sailed right into the Baltic, their holds full of cloth and salt to exchange for grain and timber. It was nothing short of

TIMELINE	1150–1300	1275	1380
	Dams are built to retain the IJ river between the Zuiderzee and Haarlem. A tiny community of herring fishermen settles on the banks of the Amstel river.	Amsterdam is founded after toll-free status is granted to residents along the Amstel. The city gains direct access to the ocean via the Zuiderzee, now the IJsselmeer.	Canals of the present-day Medieval Centre are dug. Amsterdam flourishes, winning control over the sea trade in Scandinavia and later gaining free access to the Baltic.

a coup. By the late 1400s the vast majority of ships sailing to and from the Baltic Sea were based in Amsterdam.

By this time sailors, merchants, artisans and opportunists from the Low Countries (roughly present-day Netherlands, Belgium and Luxembourg) made their living here.

At the time, Amsterdam was unfettered by the key structures of other European societies. With no tradition of Church-sanctioned feudal relationships, no distinction between nobility and serfs, and hardly any taxation, a society of individualism and capitalism took root. The modern idea of Amsterdam – free, open, progressive and flush with opportunity – was born.

Independent Republic

The Protestant Reformation wasn't just a matter of religion; it was also a classic power struggle between the 'new money' (an emerging class of merchants and artisans) and the 'old money' (the land-owning, aristocratic order sanctioned by the established Catholic Church).

The Protestantism that took hold in the Low Countries was its most radically moralistic stream, known as Calvinism. It stressed the might of God and treated humans as sinful creatures whose duty in life was sobriety and hard work. The ascetic Calvinists stood for local decision-making and had a disdain for the top-down hierarchy of the Catholic Church.

Calvinism was key to the struggle for independence by King Philip II of Spain. The hugely unpopular Philip, a fanatically devout Catholic, had acquired the Low Countries in something of a horse trade with Austria. His efforts to introduce the Spanish Inquisition, centralise government and levy taxes enraged his subjects and awoke a sense of national pride.

In 1579 the seven northern provinces, with mighty Amsterdam on their side, declared themselves to be an independent republic, led by William of Orange: the seed that grew into today's royal family. William was famously dubbed 'the Silent' because he wisely refused to enter into religious debate. To this day, he remains the uncontested founder – and father – of the Netherlands.

The Dutch 'bought' (a concept foreign to North American tribes at the time) the island of Manhattan from the Lenape in 1626 for the equivalent of US$24 worth of beads.

Golden Age (1580–1700)

In 1588, Den Haag was established as the seat of the Dutch republic, but Amsterdam grew rapidly to become the largest and most influential city in the Netherlands.

By 1600 Dutch ships controlled the sea trade between England, France, Spain and the Baltic, and had a virtual monopoly on North

1452	1519	1543	1578
Following the second 15th-century fire to devastate the city, laws decree that brick and tile are the only building materials that can be used in the city.	Spain's Charles V is crowned Holy Roman Emperor. Treaties and dynastic marriages make Amsterdam part of the Spanish empire, with Catholicism the main faith.	Charles V unites the Low Countries (roughly the area covering what is now the Netherlands, Belgium and Luxembourg) and establishes Brussels as the region's capital.	Amsterdam is captured in a bloodless coup. A Dutch Republic made up of seven provinces is declared a year later, led by William the Silent.

Sea fishing and Arctic whaling. Jewish refugees taught Dutch mariners about trade routes, giving rise to the legendary Dutch East India and Dutch West India Companies. For a while, the Dutch ran rings around the fleets of great powers, which were too slow or cumbersome to react. In the absence of an overriding religion, ethnic background or political entity, money reigned supreme.

Two decades on, Dutch traders had gone global, exploring the far corners of the earth, and by the mid-17th century the Dutch had more seagoing merchant vessels than England and France combined. Half of all ships sailing between Europe and Asia belonged to the Dutch, and exotic products – coffee, tea, spices, tobacco, cotton, silk and porcelain – became commodities. Amsterdam became home to Europe's largest shipbuilding industry, and the city was veritably buzzing with prosperity and innovation.

In 1651, England passed the first of several Navigation Acts that posed a serious threat to Dutch trade, leading to several thorny, inconclusive wars on the seas. Competitors sussed out Dutch trade secrets, regrouped and reconquered the sea routes. In 1664 the Dutch lost the colony of New Netherland, including the provincial capital New Amsterdam (now New York City) to the British, in exchange for Suriname in South America (which the Dutch governed until 1954). Louis XIV of France seized the opportunity to invade the Low Countries two decades later, and the period of prosperity known as the Golden Age ended. While the city hardly went into decay or ruin, the embattled economy would take more than a century to regain its full strength.

Tulipomania: The Story of the World's Most Coveted Flower by Mike Dash is an engaging look at the bizarre bulb fever that swept the nation in the 17th century.

Amsterdam is the official (constitutional) capital of the Netherlands, but Den Haag is the seat of government and the site of the royal family's residence, Huis ten Bosch. All embassies are located in Den Haag, although some countries also have consulates general in Amsterdam.

Wealthy Decline (1700–1814)

If you can't beat them, pacify them: while the Dutch Republic didn't have the resources to fight France and England head-on, it had Amsterdam's money to buy them off and ensure freedom of the seas.

As the costs mounted, Amsterdam went from being a place where everything (profitable) was possible, to a lethargic community where wealth creation was a matter of interest rates. Gone were the daring sea voyages, the achievements in art, science and technology, and the innovations of government and finance. Ports such as London and Hamburg became powerful rivals.

The decline in trade brought poverty, and exceptionally cold winters hampered transport and led to serious food shortages. The winters of 1740 and 1763 were so severe that some residents froze to death.

Amsterdam's support of the American War of Independence (1776) resulted in a British blockade of the Dutch coast, followed by British

1600s

The Golden Age places Amsterdam firmly on the cultural map. While Rembrandt paints in his atelier, the grand inner ring of canals is constructed. The city's population surges to 200,000.

1602

Amsterdam becomes the site of the world's first stock exchange when the offices of the Dutch East India Company trade their own shares.

LONELY PLANET/GETTY IMAGES ©

Cycling in the Golden Bend (p121)

THE CURIOUS HISTORY OF TULIPMANIA

When it comes to investment frenzy, the Dutch tulip craze of 1636–37 ranks alongside the greatest economic booms and busts in history.

Tulips originated as wildflowers in Central Asia and were first cultivated by the Turks, who filled their courts with these beautiful spring blooms. In the mid-1500s the Habsburg ambassador to Istanbul brought some bulbs back to Vienna, where the imperial botanist Carolus Clusius learned how to propagate them. In 1590 Clusius became director of the Hortus Botanicus in Leiden – Europe's oldest botanical garden – and had great success growing and cross-breeding tulips in Holland's cool, damp climate and fertile delta soil.

The more exotic specimens of tulip featured frilly petals and 'flamed' streaks of colour, which attracted the attention of wealthy merchants, who put them in their living rooms and hallways to impress visitors. Trickle-down wealth and savings stoked the taste for exotica in general, and tulip growers arose to service the demand.

A speculative frenzy ensued, and people paid top florin for the finest bulbs, many of which changed hands time and again before they sprouted. Vast profits were made and speculators fell over themselves to outbid each other. Bidding often took place in taverns and was fuelled by alcohol, which no doubt added to the enthusiasm.

Of course, this bonanza couldn't last, and when several bulb traders in Haarlem failed to fetch their expected prices in February 1637, the bottom fell out of the market. Within weeks many of the country's wealthiest merchants went bankrupt and many more people of humbler origins lost everything.

However, love of the unusual tulip endured, and cooler-headed growers perfected their craft. To this day, the Dutch continue to be the world leaders in tulip cultivation and supply most of the bulbs planted in Europe and North America. They also excel in other bulbs such as daffodils, hyacinths and crocuses.

So what happened to the flamed, frilly tulips? They're still produced but have gone out of fashion, and are now known as Rembrandt tulips because of their depiction in so many 17th-century paintings.

conquests of Dutch trading posts around the world, forcing the closure of the Dutch West and East India Companies.

Enter the French: in 1794 French revolutionary troops invaded the Low Countries. In a convenient act of nepotism, the Dutch Republic became a monarchy in 1806, when Napoleon installed his brother Louis Napoleon as king.

After Napoleon's defeat in 1813, Amsterdam's trade with the world recovered only slowly; domination of the seas now belonged to the British.

1618	1664	1688	1795
The world's first weekly broadsheet newspaper, the *Courante uyt Italien, Duytslandt, &c.*, is printed in Amsterdam. Catholicism is outlawed, with clandestine worship permitted.	The Dutch infamously lose the colony of New Netherland (now the northeastern US), including New Amsterdam (now New York City), to the British.	William III of Orange repels the French with the help of Austria, Spain and Brandenburg. William then invades England, where he and his wife are proclaimed king and queen.	French troops occupy the Netherlands and install the Batavian Republic. The fragmented United Provinces become a centralised state, with Amsterdam as its capital.

New Infrastructure (1814–1918)

Hans Brinker, who supposedly stuck his finger in a dyke and saved the Netherlands from a flood, is an American invention and unknown in the Netherlands. He starred in a 19th-century children's book.

In the first half of the 19th century, Amsterdam was a gloomy, uninspiring place. Its harbour had been neglected and the sandbanks in the IJ proved too great a barrier for modern ships. Rotterdam was set to become the country's premier port.

Things began to look up as the country's first railway, between Amsterdam and Haarlem, opened in 1839. Trade with the East Indies was the backbone of Amsterdam's economy, and a canal, later extended to the Rhine, helped the city to benefit from the Industrial Revolution under way in Europe.

Amsterdam again attracted immigrants, and its population doubled in the second half of the 19th century. Speculators hastily erected new housing beyond the Canal Ring – dreary, shoddily built tenement blocks.

The Netherlands remained neutral in WWI, but Amsterdam's trade with the East Indies suffered from naval blockades. Food shortages brought riots, and an attempt to bring the socialist revolution to the Netherlands was put down by loyalist troops.

Boom & Depression (1918–40)

After WWI, Amsterdam remained the country's industrial centre. The Dutch Shipbuilding Company operated the world's second-largest wharf and helped carry a large steel and diesel-motor industry. The harbour handled tropical produce that was processed locally, such as tobacco and cocoa (Amsterdam is still the world's biggest centre for cocoa distribution).

The 1920s were boom years. In 1920 KLM (Koninklijke Luchtvaart Maatschappij; Royal Aviation Company) began the world's first regular passenger air service between Amsterdam and London from an airstrip south of the city, and bought many of its planes from Anthony Fokker's factory north of the IJ. There were two huge breweries, a sizeable clothing industry and even a local car factory. The city hosted the Olympic Games in 1928.

The world Depression in the 1930s hit Amsterdam hard. Make-work projects did little to defuse the mounting tensions between socialists, communists and a small but vocal party of Dutch fascists. The city took in 25,000 Jewish refugees fleeing Germany; many were turned back at the border because of the country's neutrality policy.

ROYALTY

The official website of the Dutch royal family (www.koninklijk huis.nl) features minibiographies and virtual tours of the palaces.

1813–14	1830	1865–76	1889
The French are overthrown and William VI of Orange is crowned as Dutch King William I.	With French help, the southern provinces secede to form the Kingdom of Belgium. The country is not formally recognised by the Dutch government until 1839.	In a period of rapid economic and social change, the North Sea Canal is dug, the Dutch railway system is expanded and socialist principles of government are established.	Centraal Station makes its grand debut, and – in an instant – Amsterdam is connected by rail to the rest of Europe.

JEWISH AMSTERDAM

It's hard to overstate the role Jews have played in the evolution of civic and commercial life in Amsterdam. The first documented Jewish presence goes back to the 12th century, but it was expulsion from Spain and Portugal in the 1580s that brought a large number of Sephardic (Jews of Spanish, Middle Eastern or North African heritage) refugees.

As in much of Europe, Jews in Amsterdam were barred from many professions. Monopolistic guilds kept most trades firmly closed. But some Sephardim were diamond cutters, for which there was no guild. Other Sephardic Jews introduced printing and tobacco processing, or worked in unrestricted trades such as retail, finance, medicine and the garment industry. The majority, however, eked out a meagre living as labourers and small-time traders. They lived in the Nieuwmarkt area, which developed into the Jewish quarter.

Yet Amsterdam's Jews had some human rights unheard of elsewhere in Europe. They were not confined to a ghetto and, with some restrictions, could buy property. Although the Protestant establishment sought to impose restrictions, civic authorities were reluctant to restrict such productive members of society.

The 17th century saw more Jewish refugees arrive, this time Ashkenazim (Jews from Europe outside of Iberia), fleeing pogroms in Central and Eastern Europe. Amsterdam became the largest Jewish centre in Europe – some 10,000 strong by Napoleonic times. The guilds and all remaining restrictions on Jews were abolished during the French occupation, and Amsterdam's Jewish community thrived in the 19th century.

All that came to an end, however, with WWII. The Nazis brought about the near-complete annihilation of Amsterdam's Jewish community. Before the war about 140,000 Jews lived in the Netherlands, of whom about 90,000 lived in Amsterdam (comprising 13% of the city's population). Only about 5500 of Amsterdam's Jews survived the war, barely one in 16.

Today there are roughly 41,000 to 45,000 Jews in the Netherlands, nearly half of whom live in Amsterdam.

WWII (1940–45)

The Netherlands tried to remain neutral in WWII, but Germany invaded in May 1940. For the first time in almost 400 years, Amsterdammers experienced war firsthand. Few wanted to believe that things would turn really nasty (the Germans, after all, had trumpeted that the Dutch were of the 'Aryan brotherhood').

In February 1941, dockworkers led a protest strike over the treatment of Jews, commemorated as the 'February Strike'. By then, however, it was already too late. Only one in every 16 of Amsterdam's 90,000 Jews

1914–20	1939	1940	1944–45
The Netherlands remains neutral in WWI. Food shortages cripple the country, leading to strikes, unrest and growing support for the Dutch Communist Party.	The Dutch government establishes Westerbork as an internment camp to house Jewish refugees.	Germany invades the Netherlands. Rotterdam is destroyed by the Luftwaffe, but Amsterdam suffers only minor damage before capitulating.	The Allies liberate the southern Netherlands, but the north and west of the country are cut off from supplies. Thousands of Dutch perish in the bitter 'Hunger Winter'.

SIGHTS FOR HISTORY BUFFS

Amsterdam Museum (p73) Lift the veil on the city's storied past.

Stadsarchief (p121) Plumb the city's rich archives.

Anne Frank Huis (p106) See the annexe where the Frank family hid, and pages from Anne's poignant diary.

Verzetsmuseum (p194) Learn about Dutch Resistance efforts during WWII.

West-Indisch Huis (p109) Ponder the 17th-century building where the Dutch West India Company's governors authorised the establishment of New Amsterdam (now New York City).

survived the war (one in seven in the Netherlands), the lowest proportion of anywhere in Western Europe.

The Dutch Resistance, set up by an unlikely alliance of Calvinists and communists, only became large-scale when the increasingly desperate Germans began to round up able-bodied men to work in Germany.

Towards the end of the war, the situation in Amsterdam was dire. Coal shipments ceased; many men aged between 17 and 50 had gone into hiding or to work in Germany; public utilities were halted; and the Germans began to plunder anything that could assist their war effort. Thousands of lives were lost to severe cold and famine. Canadian troops finally liberated the city in May 1945 in the final days of the war in Europe.

Postwar Growth (1945–62)

The city's growth resumed after the war, with US aid through the Marshall Plan.

Massive apartment blocks arose in areas annexed west of the city to meet the continued demand for housing, made more acute by the demographic shift away from extended families. The massive Bijlmermeer housing project (now called De Bijlmer) southeast of the city, begun in the mid-1960s and finished in the 1970s, was built in a similar vein.

John Lennon and Yoko Ono took to bed at the Amsterdam Hilton for a week in 1969 and invited the world's press to join them. Rather than salacious entertainment, however, they offered bromides about world peace.

Cultural Revolution (1962–82)

For nearly a century leading up to the 1960s, Dutch society had become characterised by *verzuiling* (pillarisation), a social order in which each religion and political persuasion achieved the right to do its own thing, with its own institutions. Each persuasion represented a pillar that supported the status quo in a general 'agreement to disagree'. In the 1960s

1976	1980	2001	2002
The Netherlands' drugs laws distinguish soft from hard drugs; possession of small amounts of marijuana is decriminalised.	Queen Beatrix's investiture in Amsterdam is disrupted by smoke bombs and riots instigated by squatters reacting against the lack of affordable housing.	The Netherlands becomes the first country in the world to legalise same-sex marriage. In the next few years Belgium, Spain, Canada and South Africa follow suit.	Pim Fortuyn, a hard-line politician on immigration and integration, is assassinated. The ruling Dutch parties shift to the right after suffering major losses in the national election.

the old divisions were increasingly irrelevant and the pillars came tumbling down, but not the philosophy they spawned.

Amsterdam became Europe's 'Magic Centre': hippies smoked dope on the Dam, camped in Vondelpark and tripped at clubs such as the Melkweg, an abandoned dairy barn. In 1972 the first coffeeshop opened and in 1976 marijuana was decriminalised to free up police resources for combating hard drugs. With soaring housing prices, squatters began to occupy buildings left empty by speculators. In the process, they helped save several notable historical structures from demolition.

Since 2010, squatting has been illegal, and some former squats have become legitimate cultural centres.

New Consensus (1982–2000)

Twenty years after the cultural revolution began, a new consensus emphasised a decentralised government. Neighbourhood councils were established with the goal of creating a more liveable city, through integration of work, schools and shops within walking or cycling distance; decreased traffic; renovation rather than demolition; friendly neighbourhood police; a practical, nonmoralistic approach towards drugs; and legal recognition of homosexual couples.

By the early 1990s, the families and small manufacturers that had dominated inner-city neighbourhoods in the early 1960s had been replaced by professionals and a service industry of pubs, coffeeshops, restaurants and hotels. The city's success in attracting large foreign businesses resulted in an influx of high-income expats.

Testing Times (2000–Present)

The first decade-and-a-half of the new century have been full of ups and downs for Amsterdam. After smouldering for years, a noisy debate erupted over the Netherlands' policy towards newcomers, which quickly led to a tightening of immigration laws. The limits of tolerance, a core value of Dutch identity, were called into question. Pim Fortuyn, a right-wing politician, declared the country 'full' before he was assassinated in 2002.

Social tensions flared in the wake of the Fortuyn murder, and the number of people leaving the country reached a 50-year high, although most departed for economic and family reasons. The mood was edgy, like a cauldron about to boil over.

It finally did in the autumn of 2004, when filmmaker Theo van Gogh – known for his anti-Muslim views – was murdered on an Amsterdam street. The leading political parties in the Netherlands responded with a big shift to the right. In 2006 the government passed

Dubbed the 'most famous bleached blond since Marilyn Monroe', parliamentary leader Geert Wilders has been a divisive, controversial politician in the Netherlands, comparing the Koran to *Mein Kampf*, calling for immigrants to be deported and demanding churches preach in Dutch.

2004	2006	2008	2009
Activist filmmaker Theo van Gogh, a fierce critic of Islam, is murdered, touching off intense debate over the limits of Dutch multicultural society.	The government passes a law requiring immigrants (except from countries with pre-existing treaties) to have competency in Dutch language and culture in order to get a residency permit.	The city announces Project 1012. The goal is to clean up the Red Light District and to close prostitution windows and coffeeshops believed to be controlled by organised crime.	Amsterdam courts prosecute Dutch parliamentary leader Geert Wilders for 'incitement to hatred and discrimination'. (He is acquitted of all charges in 2011.)

King Willem-Alexander and his wife Queen Máxima have three daughters: Princess Catharina-Amalia (the Princess of Orange), Princess Alexia and Princess Ariane.

a controversial immigration law requiring newcomers – except those from countries with reciprocal arrangements or pre-existing treaties – to have competency in Dutch language and culture before they could get a residency permit. This meant the policy mostly affected immigrants from non-Western countries. Indeed, immigration from these countries has slowed considerably over the past few years – though immigration overall has ticked upwards, thanks to newcomers from Eastern Europe.

In 2008, the Dutch government made waves – both locally and abroad – by announcing its plans to reduce the number of coffeeshops and legal brothels. The legal age of prostitutes was raised from 18 to 21 in 2013, and other measures are under way to reduce associated crime and clean up the Red Light District (see p77). And for now, at least, it's 'business as usual' for Amsterdam's famous coffeeshops.

A budget crisis over austerity measures as a result of the global financial crisis led to the fall of the Dutch government in 2012. Subsequent elections saw Prime Minister Mark Rutte retain the position of de facto head of government and form a new coalition government with his liberal VVD party and the centre-left Labour party.

The Dutch monarchy recently experienced changes too: in 2013 Queen Beatrix abdicated (in the Royal Palace) in favour of her eldest son Willem-Alexander, who became king on 30 April that year. His investiture took place in the Nieuwe Kerk.

2010	2010	2013
Members of the Dutch government officially apologise to the Jewish community for failing to protect the Jewish population from genocide.	For the third time, the Netherlands football team make it to the World Cup Final – only to lose to Spain by a single goal in extra time.	After a 33-year reign, Queen Beatrix abdicates in favour of her eldest son, Willem-Alexander, who becomes the Netherlands' first king in 123 years.

Dutch football supporter

Dutch Painting

They don't call them the Dutch Masters for nothing. The line-up includes Rembrandt, Frans Hals and Jan Vermeer – these iconic artists are some of world's most revered and celebrated painters. And then, of course, there's Vincent van Gogh, who toiled in ignominy while supported by his loving brother Theo, and 20th-century artists including De Stijl proponent Piet Mondrian, and graphic genius MC Escher. Understanding these quintessential Dutch painters requires a journey back into history.

16th Century

Flemish School

Prior to the late 16th century, when Belgium was still part of the Low Countries, art focused on the Flemish cities of Ghent, Bruges and Antwerp. Paintings of the Flemish School featured biblical and allegorical subject matter popular with the Church, the court and (to a lesser extent) nobility, who, after all, paid the bills and called the shots.

Among the most famous names of the era are Jan van Eyck (c 1385–1441), founder of the Flemish School, who was one of the earliest artists to use oils in detailed panel painting; Rogier van der Weyden (1400–64), whose religious portraits showed the personalities of his subjects; and Hieronymus (also known as Jeroen) Bosch (1450–1516), with his macabre allegorical paintings full of religious topics. Pieter Bruegel the Elder (1525–69) used Flemish landscapes and peasant life in his allegorical scenes.

Dutch School

In the northern Low Countries, artists began to develop a style of their own. Although the artists of the day never achieved the level of recognition of their Flemish counterparts, the Dutch School, as it came to be called, was known for favouring realism over allegory. Haarlem, just west of Amsterdam, was the centre of this movement, with artists such as Jan Mostaert (1475–1555), Lucas van Leyden (1494–1533) and Jan van Scorel (1494–1562). Painters in the city of Utrecht were famous for using chiaroscuro (deep contrast of light and shade), a technique associated with the Italian master Caravaggio.

17th Century (Golden Age)

When the Spanish were expelled from the Low Countries, the character of the art market changed. There was no longer the Church to buy artworks and no court to speak of, so art became a business, and artists were forced to survive in a free market – how very Dutch. In place of Church and court emerged a new, bourgeois society of merchants, artisans and shopkeepers who didn't mind spending money to brighten up their houses and workplaces. The key: they had to be pictures the buyers could relate to.

Painters became entrepreneurs in their own right, churning out banal works, copies and masterpieces in factory-like studios. Paintings were mass-produced and sold at markets alongside furniture and chickens. Soon the wealthiest households were covered in paintings from top to bottom. Foreign visitors commented that even bakeries and butcher shops seemed to have a painting or two on the wall. Most painters specialised in one of the main genres of the day.

Rembrandt van Rijn

The 17th century's greatest artist, Rembrandt van Rijn (1606–69), grew up a miller's son in Leiden, but had become an accomplished painter by his early 20s.

In 1631 he came to Amsterdam to run the painting studio of the wealthy art dealer Hendrick van Uylenburgh. Portraits were the studio's cash cow, and Rembrandt and his staff (or 'pupils') churned out scores of them, including group portraits such as *The Anatomy Lesson of Dr Tulp*. In 1634 he married Van Uylenburgh's niece Saskia, who often modelled for him.

Rembrandt fell out with his boss, but his wife's capital helped him buy the sumptuous house next door to Van Uylenburgh's studio (the current Museum het Rembrandthuis). There Rembrandt set up his own studio, with staff who worked in a warehouse in the Jordaan. These were happy years: his paintings were a success and his studio became the largest in Holland, though his gruff manner and open agnosticism didn't win him dinner-party invitations from the elite.

Rembrandt became one of the city's biggest art collectors. He was a master manipulator not only of images; the painter was also known to have his own pictures bid up at auctions. He often sketched and painted for himself, urging his staff to do likewise. Residents of the surrounding Jewish quarter provided perfect material for his dramatic biblical scenes.

Night Watch

In 1642, a year after the birth of their son Titus, Saskia died and business went downhill. Although Rembrandt's majestic group portrait *Night Watch* (1642) was hailed by art critics (it's now the Rijksmuseum's prize exhibit), some of the influential people he depicted were not pleased. Each subject had paid 100 guilders, and some were unhappy at being shoved to the background. In response, Rembrandt told them where they could shove their complaints. Suddenly he received far fewer orders.

Rembrandt began an affair with his son's governess but kicked her out a few years later when he fell for the new maid, Hendrickje Stoffels, who bore him a daughter, Cornelia. The public didn't take kindly to the man's lifestyle and his spiralling debts, and in 1656 he went bankrupt. His house and rich art collection were sold and he moved to the Rozengracht in the Jordaan.

Etchings

No longer the darling of the wealthy, Rembrandt continued to paint, draw and etch – his etchings on display in the Museum het Rembrandthuis are some of the finest ever produced. He also received the occasional commission, including the monumental *Conspiracy of Claudius Civilis* (1661) for the city hall, although authorities disliked it and had it removed. In 1662 he completed the *Staalmeesters* (The Syndics) for the drapers' guild and ensured that everybody remained clearly visible, though it ended up being his last group portrait.

Later Works

The works of his later period show that Rembrandt had lost none of his touch. No longer constrained by the wishes of clients, he enjoyed

Great Rembrandt Paintings
....
Night Watch (Rijksmuseum)
....
Peter Denies Christ (Rijksmuseum)
....
Self Portrait (Rijksmuseum)

Great Frans Hals Paintings
....
The Merry Drinker (Rijksmuseum)
....
Wedding Portrait (Rijksmuseum)

new-found freedom. His works became more unconventional yet showed an ever-stronger empathy with their subject matter, as in *The Jewish Bride* (1667). The many portraits of Titus and Hendrickje, and his ever-gloomier self-portraits, are among the most stirring in the history of art.

A plague epidemic between 1663 and 1666 killed one in seven Amsterdammers, including Hendrickje. Titus died in 1668, aged 27 and just married; Rembrandt died a year later, a broken man.

Frans Hals

Another great painter of this period, Frans Hals (c 1581-1666), was born in Antwerp but lived in Haarlem. He devoted most of his career to portraits, dabbling in occasional genre scenes with dramatic chiaroscuro. His ability to capture his subjects' expressions was equal to Rembrandt's, though he didn't explore their characters as much. Both masters used the same expressive, unpolished brush strokes and their styles went from bright exuberance in their early careers to dark and solemn later on. The 19th-century Impressionists also admired Hals' work. In fact, his *The Merry Drinker* (1628–30) in the Rijksmuseum's collection, with its bold brush strokes, could almost have been painted by an Impressionist.

Group Portraits

Hals also specialised in beautiful group portraits in which the participants were depicted in almost natural poses, unlike the rigid line-ups produced by lesser contemporaries – though he wasn't as cavalier as Rembrandt in subordinating faces to the composition. A good example is the pair of paintings known collectively as *The Regents & the Regentesses of the Old Men's Alms House* (1664) in the Frans Hals Museum in Haarlem. The museum is a space that Hals knew intimately; he lived in the almshouse.

Vermeer

The grand trio of 17th-century masters is completed by Johannes (also known as Jan) Vermeer (1632–75) of Delft. He produced only 35 meticulously crafted paintings in his career and died poor with 10 children; his baker accepted two paintings from his wife as payment for a debt of more than 600 guilders. Yet Vermeer mastered genre painting like no other artist. His paintings include historical and biblical scenes from his earlier career, his famous *View of Delft* (1661) in the Mauritshuis in Den Haag, and some tender portraits of unknown women, such as the stunningly beautiful *Girl with a Pearl Earring* (1666), also hanging in the Mauritshuis.

To comprehend Vermeer's use of perspective, study *The Love Letter* (1670) in the Rijksmuseum.

The Little Street (1658) in the Rijksmuseum's collection is Vermeer's only street scene.

Great Vermeer Paintings

....

Kitchen Maid (Rijksmuseum)

....

Woman in Blue Reading a Letter (Rijksmuseum)

Other Golden Age Painters

Around the middle of the century, the focus on mood and subtle play of light began to make way for the splendour of the baroque. Jacob van Ruysdael (c 1628–82) went for dramatic skies while Albert Cuyp (1620–91) painted Italianate landscapes. Van Ruysdael's pupil Meindert Hobbema (1638–1709) preferred less heroic, more playful, scenes full of pretty bucolic detail. (Note that Cuyp, Hobbema and Van Ruysdael all have main streets named after them in the Old South and De Pijp districts, and many smaller streets here are named after other Dutch artists.)

GREG GIBB PHOTOGRAPHY/GETTY IMAGES ©

1. Jordaan (p141)
Get lost among the narrow lanes, old facades and little shops of this curiously enchanting neighbourhood.

2. Herengracht (p108)
Amsterdam's wealthiest residents built their mansions along the aptly named 'Gentlemen's Canal'.

3. Cheese (p46)
The Dutch love their *kaas* (cheese), especially Gouda, which is served with mustard as a popular bar snack.

4. Cycling (p30)
Amsterdam's flat terrain makes it ideal for cycling – more locals get around by bike than by car.

REZA ESTAKHRIAN/GETTY IMAGES ©

The genre paintings of Jan Steen (1626–79) show the almost frivolous aspect of baroque. A good example is the animated revelry of *The Merry Family* (1668) in the Rijksmuseum; it shows adults having a good time around the dinner table, oblivious to the children in the foreground pouring themselves a drink.

18th Century

The Golden Age of Dutch painting ended almost as suddenly as it began when the French invaded the Low Countries in 1672. The economy collapsed and the market for paintings went south with it. Painters who stayed in business concentrated on 'safe' works that repeated earlier successes. In the 18th century they copied French styles, pandering to the fashion for anything French.

The results were competent but not groundbreaking. Cornelis Troost (1697–1750) was one of the best genre painters, and is sometimes compared to the British artist William Hogarth (1697–1764) for his satirical as well as sensitive portraits of ordinary people; Troost, too, introduced scenes of domestic revelry into his pastels.

Gerard de Lairesse (1640–1711) and Jacob de Wit (1695–1754) specialised in decorating the walls and ceilings of buildings – de Wit's trompe l'oeil decorations (painted illusions that look real) in the Bijbels Museum are worth seeing.

VAN GOGH

Van Gogh produced an astonishing output of art during his 10-year artistic career, of which 864 paintings and almost 1200 drawings and prints have survived.

19th Century

The late 18th century and most of the 19th century produced little of note, save for the landscapes and seascapes of Johan Barthold Jongkind (1819–91) and the gritty, almost photographic Amsterdam scenes of George Hendrik Breitner (1857–1923). They appear to have inspired French Impressionists, many of whom visited Amsterdam.

Jongkind and Breitner reinvented 17th-century realism and influenced the Hague School of the last decades of the 19th century. Painters such as Hendrik Mesdag (1831–1915), Jozef Israels (1824–1911) and the three Maris brothers (Jacob, Matthijs and Willem) created landscapes, seascapes and genre works, including Mesdag's impressive *Panorama Mesdag* (1881; located in Den Haag), a gigantic, 360-degree cylindrical painting of the seaside town of Scheveningen viewed from a dune.

Vincent van Gogh

Without a doubt, the greatest 19th-century Dutch painter was Vincent van Gogh (1853–90), whose convulsive patterns and furious colours were in a world of their own and still defy comfortable categorisation. (A post-Impressionist? A forerunner of expressionism?)

While the Dutch Masters were known for their dark, brooding paintings, it was Van Gogh who created an identity of suffering as an art form, with a morbid style all his own. Even today, he epitomises the epic struggle of the artist: the wrenching poverty; the lack of public acclaim; the reliance upon a patron – in this case his faithful brother, Theo; the mental instability; the untimely death by suicide. And of course, one of the most iconic images of an artist's self-destruction, the severed ear.

For a moving window into the inner life of Vincent van Gogh, and the extraordinary friendship and artistic connection he shared with his brother, Theo, read *Vincent van Gogh: the Letters*. It contains all 902 letters to and from Van Gogh to his brother and other confidantes.

The Artist's Legend

Vincent Van Gogh may have been poor – he sold only one painting in his lifetime – but he wasn't old. It's easy to forget from his self-portraits, in which he appears much older (partly the effects of his poverty), that he was only 37 when he died. But his short life continues to influence art to this day.

Born in Zundert in 1853, the Dutch painter lived in Paris with his younger brother Theo, an art dealer, who financially supported him from his modest income. In Paris he became acquainted with seminal artists including Edgar Degas, Camille Pissarro, Henri de Toulouse-Lautrec and Paul Gauguin.

Van Gough moved south to Arles, Provence, in 1888. Revelling in its intense light and bright colours, he painted sunflowers, irises and other vivid subjects with a burning fervour. He sent paintings to Theo in Paris to sell, and dreamed of founding an artists' colony in Provence, but only Gauguin followed up his invitation. Their differing artistic approaches – Gauguin believed in painting from imagination; Van Gogh painting what he saw – and their artistic temperaments, fuelled by absinthe, came to a head with the argument that led to Van Gogh lopping his ear (which he gave to a prostitute acquaintance) and his subsequent committal in Arles.

In May 1889, Van Gogh voluntarily entered an asylum in St-Rémy de Provence, where he painted prolifically during his one-year, one-week and one-day confinement, including masterpieces like *Irises* and *Starry Night*. While there, Theo sent him a positive French newspaper critique of his work. The following month, Anna Boch, sister of his friend Eugène Boch, bought *The Red Vines* (or *The Red Vineyard*; 1888) for 400 francs (less than €100 today). It now hangs in Moscow's Pushkin Museum.

Legacy of a Tortured Genius

On 16 May 1890 Van Gogh moved to Auvers-sur-Oise, just outside Paris, to be closer to Theo, but on 27 July that year he shot himself, possibly to avoid further financial burden on his brother, whose wife had just had a baby son, named Vincent, and who was also supporting their ailing mother. Van Gogh died two days later with Theo at his side. Theo subsequently had a breakdown, was also committed, and succumbed to physical illness. He died, aged 33, just six months after Van Gogh.

It would be less than a decade before Van Gogh's talent would start to achieve wide recognition and by the early 1950s, he had become a household name. In 1990 he broke the record for a single painting (*A Portrait of Doctor Gachet*) at Christie's, which fetched US$82.5 million. Accounting for inflation, it's still the highest price paid at a public auction for art to this day.

DUTCH PAINTING 19TH CENTURY

Van Gogh Museum's Famous Five

Sunflowers

Wheatfield with Crows

Self Portrait with Felt Hat

Almond Blossom

The Bedroom

Jan Steen was also a tavern keeper, and his depictions of domestic chaos led to the Dutch expression 'a Jan Steen household'.

MONDRIAN

A major proponent of De Stijl was Piet Mondrian (originally Mondriaan, 1872–1944), who initially painted in the Hague School tradition. After flirting with Cubism, he began working with bold rectangular patterns, using only the three primary colours (yellow, blue and red) set against the three neutrals (white, grey and black). He named this style neoplasticism and viewed it as an undistorted expression of reality in pure form and pure colour. His *Composition in Red, Black, Blue, Yellow & Grey* (1920), in the Stedelijk Museum's collection, is an elaborate example.

Mondrian's later works were more stark (or 'pure') and became dynamic again when he moved to New York in 1940. The world's largest collection of his paintings resides in the Gemeentemuseum (Municipal Museum) in his native Den Haag.

20th Century

De Stijl

De Stijl (The Style), also known as neoplasticism, was a Dutch design movement that aimed to harmonise all the arts by bringing artistic expressions back to their essence. Its advocate was the magazine of the same name, first published in 1917 by Theo van Doesburg (1883–1931). Van Doesburg produced works similar to Piet Mondrian's, though he dispensed with the thick, black lines and later tilted his rectangles at 45 degrees, departures serious enough for Mondrian to call off the friendship.

Throughout the 1920s and 1930s, De Stijl also attracted sculptors, poets, architects and designers. One of these was Gerrit Rietveld (1888–1964), designer of the Van Gogh Museum and several other buildings, but best known internationally for his furniture, such as the *Red Blue Chair* (1918) and his range of uncomfortable zigzag seats that, viewed side-on, formed a 'z' with a backrest.

MC Escher

One of the most remarkable graphic artists of the 20th century was Maurits Cornelis Escher (1898–1972). His drawings, lithos and woodcuts of blatantly impossible images continue to fascinate mathematicians: a waterfall feeds itself; people go up and down a staircase that ends where it starts; a pair of hands draw each other. You can see his work at Escher in het Paleis in Den Haag.

CoBrA

After WWII, artists rebelled against artistic conventions and vented their rage in abstract expressionism. In Amsterdam, Karel Appel (1921–2006) and Constant (Constant Nieuwenhuys, 1920–2005) drew on styles pioneered by Paul Klee and Joan Miró, and exploited bright colours and 'uncorrupted' children's art to produce lively works that leapt off the canvas. In Paris in 1945 they met up with the Danish Asger Jorn (1914–73) and the Belgian Corneille (Cornelis van Beverloo, 1922–2010), and together with several other artists and writers formed a group known as CoBrA (Copenhagen, Brussels, Amsterdam). It's been called the last great avant-garde movement.

Their first major exhibition, in the Stedelijk Museum in 1949, aroused a storm of protest (with comments such as 'my child paints like that too'). Still, the CoBrA artists exerted a strong influence in their respective countries, even after they disbanded in 1951. The Cobra Museum in Amstelveen displays a good range of their works, including colourful ceramics.

Vermeer's work is known for serene light pouring through tall windows. The calm, spiritual effect is enhanced by dark blues, deep reds, warm yellows and supremely balanced composition. Good examples include the Rijksmuseum's *Kitchen Maid* (aka *The Milkmaid*, 1658) and *Woman in Blue Reading a Letter* (1664).

Even Van Gogh's last words ring with the kind of excruciating, melancholic beauty that his best paintings express. With Theo at his side, two days after he shot himself in the chest, he's said to have uttered in French *'la tristesse durera toujours'* (the sadness will last forever).

Architecture in Amsterdam

It is difficult not to be struck by Amsterdam's well-preserved beauty: the lovely canal-scapes depicted in centuries-old paintings remain remarkably unchanged. Historian Geert Mak once described Amsterdam as 'a Cinderella under glass', spared as it was from wartime destruction and ham-fisted developers. In fact, the enchanting old centre boasts no fewer than 7000 historical monuments, more humpback bridges than Venice and more trees per capita than Paris.

A City Built on Freedom

Unlike many capitals, Amsterdam has few grand edifices to trumpet. There is hardly the space for a Louvre or a Westminster Abbey, which would be out of keeping with Calvinist modesty anyway. But you'll be pressed to find another city with such a wealth of residential architecture, and with an appeal that owes more to understated elegance than to power and pomp.

Amsterdam's beauty was built on freedoms – of trade, religion and aesthetics. Many of its gabled mansions and warehouses were erected by merchants in the Golden Age, with little meddling by city officials. Thus its leading citizens determined the look of the city, in what amounted to an early urban experiment.

Dutch architecture today is one of the country's most successful exports, with names such as Rem Koolhaas and Lars Spuybroek popping up on blueprints from Seattle to Beijing. Back home, rivalry can be intensely local as talents in Amsterdam and Rotterdam jostle for a spot in the architectural pantheon.

Middle Ages

Around the year 1200, Amsterdam was a muddy little trading post on the Amstel river. The soft marshland couldn't support brick, so the earliest houses were made of timber, often with clay and thatched roofs (similar to ones still standing in Amsterdam-Noord today), but even these modest abodes would list into the soggy ground.

Two fires burned down much of the city centre in 1421 and 1452, and wood was sensibly outlawed as a main building material. There was plenty of clay to make brick, but this was too heavy, as was stone.

Engineers solved the problem by driving piles into the peat. Timber gave way to heavier brick, and thatched roofs were replaced by sturdier tile. Eventually brick and sandstone became *de rigueur* for most structures.

Dutch Renaissance

As the Italian Renaissance filtered north, Dutch architects developed a rich ornamental style that merged the classical and the traditional, with their own brand of subtle humour. They inserted mock columns, known as

Notable Historic Buildings

....
Oude Kerk (Old Church; Red Light District)
....
Nieuwe Kerk (New Church; Medieval Centre)
....
Royal Palace (Koninklijk Paleis; Medieval Centre)
....
Amsterdam American Hotel (Southern Canal Ring)
....
Rijksmuseum (Old South)

TIMBER HOUSES

Particularly as a result of Amsterdam's devastating 15th-century fires, only two early houses with timber facades have survived to this day. Near Spui, the house at Begijnhof 34 is the oldest preserved wooden house in the country, dating from 1465. The other, at Zeedijk 1, dates from the mid-16th century.

pilasters, into facades and replaced old spout gables with step gables. Sculptures, columns and little obelisks suddenly appeared all over the Canal Ring. Red brick and horizontal bands of white were all the rage too.

Key commercial buildings include the 1620-built Greenland Warehouses. Whale oil was a sought-after ingredient for soap, lamp oil and paint, and wells in these warehouses held 100,000L of the precious stuff. Nowadays they're chic apartments, but the facade is well maintained.

Without a doubt, the best-known talent of this period was Hendrick de Keyser (1565–1621), the city sculptor. He worked with Hendrick Staets, a canal-ring planner, and Cornelis Danckerts, the city bricklayer, to produce some of Amsterdam's finest masterpieces, including magnificent canal architecture (p264). He also put his stamp on three 'directional churches': the Zuiderkerk (p97) (Southern Church) and Westerkerk (p108) (Western Church), both Gothic in style, and the Noorderkerk (p143) (Northern Church), built for impoverished Jordaaners and laid out like a Greek cross inside – a veritable revolution at the time.

For a glimpse into the city's medieval seafaring past, visit its oldest monument, the 1480-built Schreierstoren, located next to Centraal Station. It's thought to be the embarkation point for Henry Hudson's legendary journey to what became New Amsterdam – now New York City.

Dutch Classicism

During the Golden Age of art in the 17th century, architects such as Jacob van Campen, and Philips Vingboons and his brother Justus decided to stick to Greek and Roman classical design, dropping many of De Keyser's playful decorations.

Influenced by Italian architects, the Dutch made facades look like temples and pilasters like columns. All revolved around clever deception. Neck gables with decorative scrolls came into fashion, often crowned by a temple-like roof. Garlands appeared under windows, and red brick, which was prone to crumbling, was hardened with dark paint.

The Vingboons designed the Bijbels Museum (p110) and the fine example at Keizersgracht 319. Don't miss Justus Vingboons' Trippenhuis (p97): it's about as austere as it gets. It was built between 1660 and 1664 for the wealthy Trip brothers, who made their fortune in metals, artillery and ammunition. The most striking hallmarks are up at roof level – chimneys shaped like mortars.

In the mid- to late-17th century, facades became plainer as attention shifted to sumptuous interiors. Adriaan Dortsman, a mathematician by training, was a leader of this austere style. Dortsman's greatest hits include the Ronde Lutherse Kerk (Round Lutheran Church; 1671) and the 1672 residence that now houses the Museum Van Loon.

18th-Century 'Louis Styles'

As the Netherlands' trading might faded, the wealthy fell back on fortunes amassed in the mercantile era. Many invested or turned to banking, and conducted business from their opulent homes. Traders no longer stored goods in the attic because they could afford warehouses elsewhere.

The Gallic culture craze proved a godsend for architect and designer Daniel Marot, a Huguenot refugee who introduced matching French interiors and exteriors to Amsterdam. Living areas with white stuccoed ceilings were bathed in light that streamed in through sash windows. As the elegant bell gable became a must, many architects opted for the next big thing: a horizontal cornice.

The dignified facades and statuary of the Louis XIV style hung on until about 1750. In rapid succession it was followed by Louis XV style – rococo rocks, swirls and waves – and Louis XVI designs, with pilasters and pillars making a comeback.

Standing in front of the late-Louis-style Felix Meritis Building (p109), step back to take in the enormous Corinthian half-columns, with a pomp that architect Jacob Otten Husly was skilled in imparting.

The **Maagdenhuis** (Spui 21), designed by city architect Abraham van der Hart, is a more sober brand of this classicism. Built in 1787 as a Catholic orphanage for girls, the building is now the administrative seat of the University of Amsterdam.

19th-Century Neostyles

After the Napoleonic era, the Dutch economy stagnated, merchants closed their pocketbooks and fine architecture ground to a halt. Seen as safe and sellable, neoclassicism held sway until the more prosperous 1860s, when planners again felt free to rediscover the past.

The late 19th century was all about the neo-Gothic, harking back to the grand Gothic cathedrals, and the neo-Renaissance. It was around this time that Catholics regained their freedom to worship openly, and built churches like mad in neo-Gothic style.

A leading architect of the period was Pierre Cuypers, known for a skilful design of several neo-Gothic churches, something he had in common with CH Peters. Their contemporary, AC Bleijs, created some of the greatest commercial buildings of the era.

Pierre Cuypers designed two of Amsterdam's iconic buildings: Centraal Station (p72) and the Rijksmuseum (p172), both of which display Gothic forms and Dutch Renaissance brickwork. A similar melange in CH Peters' General Post Office, now Magna Plaza (p91). The ebullient neo-Renaissance facade of the **Melkfabriek**, a former milk factory, was built in 1876 to a design by Eduard Cuypers (Pierre's nephew).

Bleijs designed the high-profile St Nicolaaskerk (p72) as well as the intimate 1881 former **PC Hooft Store** (Map p310; Keizersgracht 508). The latter, a Dutch Renaissance throwback with a Germanic tower, was built to commemorate the 300th birthday of the poet and playwright Pieter Cornelisz Hooft.

The facade of AL van Gendt's Concertgebouw (p177) is neoclassical, but its red brick and white sandstone are all Dutch Renaissance.

Around the turn of the century, the neo-Goths suddenly fell out of favour as art nouveau spread its curvy plant-like shapes across Europe. Art nouveau's influence can be seen in the former headquarters of Greenpeace International, still referred to as the **Greenpeace Building** (Keizersgracht 174-176). The towering edifice was built in 1905 for an insurance company, and its tiled facade shows a guardian angel that

One of the city's signature buildings and a Rembrandt favourite, the Montelbaanstoren was built as a defensive tower in 1516. Its octagonal steeple was designed by master architect Hendrick de Keyser in 1606 to house a clock that's still in use today.

ACCESSING AMSTERDAM'S ARCHITECTURE

Clad in curved aluminium and glass, ARCAM (p193, Architectuurcentrum Amsterdam) is a fantastic resource for anyone interested in Amsterdam's architecture – past, present and future.

ARCAM also publishes four free *Archishuttle* booklets (in English), covering trips on designated tram and bus routes, with descriptions of architectural highlights you'll see along the way.

Guided architectural walking and bus tours are generally only available for groups, but bike tour company Orangebike (p30) offers a couple of architecturally themed cycling tours focussing on the Eastern Harbour and Amsterdam School.

ROYAL
PALACE

seems to be peddling a life policy. Other art nouveau structures are the Amsterdam American Hotel (p129) and the riotous Pathé Tuschinskitheater (p137).

Berlage & the Amsterdam School

The father of modern Dutch architecture was Hendrik Petrus Berlage (1856–1934). He criticised the lavish neostyles and their reliance on the past, instead favouring simplicity and a rational use of materials.

In Berlage's view, residential blocks were a holistic concept rather than a collection of individual homes. Not always popular with city elders, Berlage influenced what became known as the Amsterdamse School (Amsterdam School) and its leading exponents Michel de Klerk, Piet Kramer and Johan van der Mey.

The titans of the Amsterdam School designed buildings of 'Plan South', an ambitious project mapped out by Berlage. It was a productive period: the Beurs van Berlage (p71) displayed the master's ideals to the full, with exposed inner struts and striking but simple brick accents.

Johan van der Mey's remarkable Scheepvaarthuis (p97) was the first building in the Amsterdam School style. It draws on the street layout to reproduce a ship's bow.

De Klerk's Het Schip (p146) and Kramer's De Dageraad (p181) are like fairytale fortresses rendered in a Dutch version of art deco. Their eccentric details are charming, but the 'form over function' ethic meant these places weren't always great to live in.

The most impressive example of Dutch Classicism is Jacob van Campen's town hall (now the Royal Palace). It was the largest town hall in Europe, and was given a precious shell of Bentham sandstone and a marble interior inspired by the Roman palaces.

Functionalism

As the Amsterdam School flourished, a new generation began to rebel against the movement's impractical and expensive methods. In 1927 they formed a group called 'de 8', influenced by the German Bauhaus school, America's Frank Lloyd Wright and France's Le Corbusier.

Architects such as Ben Merkelbach and Gerrit Rietveld believed that form should follow function and advocated steel, glass and concrete. The Committee of Aesthetics Control didn't agree, however, which is why you'll see little functionalism in the Canal Ring.

After WWII, entire suburbs such as the sprawling Bijlmermeer in Amsterdam-Zuidoost were designed along functionalist lines. By the late 1960s, however, resistance had grown against such impersonal, large-scale projects.

Rietveld left Amsterdam the Van Gogh Museum (p170), where the minimalist, open space allows the artist's works to shine.

Aldo van Eyck's work remains controversial, with critics arguing it looks out of place against the 17th- and 18th-century surrounds. His designs include the **Moederhuis** (Map p326; Plantage Middenlaan 33), built for 'fallen women'.

The Amsterdam School ushered in a new philosophy of city planning, given a boost by the 1928 Olympic Games held in Amsterdam. Humble housing blocks became brick sculptures with curved corners, odd windows and rocket-shaped towers, to the marvel (or disgust) of traditionalists.

The Present

Since the 1970s, designers have lent a human scale to the suburbs by integrating low- and medium-rise apartments with shops, schools and offices.

On the shores of the IJ just east of Centraal Station stands the Oosterdokseiland, a row of landmark buildings that includes the Centrale Bibliotheek Amsterdam (p193) and features a high-density mix of shops, restaurants, offices, apartments and a music conservatorium (p197), as well as the **DoubleTree Amsterdam Centraal Station hotel** (Oosterdoksstraat 4; ⊞1/2/4/5/24/25 Centraal).

CONCRETE

Named Dutch Architect of the Year in 2012, Concrete is one of the most innovative practices impacting architecture today. Concrete was founded in 2004 by Dutch-born architect Rob Wagemans (b 1973), who trained in Utrecht and Amsterdam. The 40-person interdisciplinary team also embraces interior, urban and brand development. Its HQ is the House of Concrete, an 1880 listed building in Amsterdam's Red Light District overhauled by the Concreters to incorporate space-saving measures like a staircase library and spider-like overhead lighting.

Among Concrete's Amsterdam projects are the platformed rig housing the REM Eiland (p148) restaurant and bar, the Mendo (p117) graphic design agency's black-walled bookshop, and the retro-futuristic VIP lounge at Schiphol airport. You'll also see Concrete's work in the lounge-like central hall of the Van Gogh Museum (p170), where the blue seating and carpet allow the hall to act as a 'blue screen': when a Van Gogh painting is projected onto the central hall's wall, the furnishings become 'invisible' and the hall's visitors appear to be in the middle of the painting.

Beyond Amsterdam, Concrete's projects span the Netherlands and the globe, from London's Spice Market and Leicester Square W hotel to Stuttgart's Mercedes-Benz Museum, Seoul's Hyundai finance outlets and New Jersey's Harborside Plaza skyscrapers on the Hudson River opposite the Manhattan skyline.

ARCHITECTURE IN AMSTERDAM THE PRESENT

Looking southeast from Centraal Station, you can't miss the green copper snout of NEMO (p192), a science museum designed by Renzo Piano that resembles the prow of a ship. The cubelike glass shell of the Muziekgebouw aan 't IJ (p192) stands not far to the north, on the IJ waterfront. In the Plantage district, a must-see is the huge Entrepot-dok (p191). Sprawling half a kilometre along a former loading dock, the crusty shipping warehouses have been recast as desirable apartments, studios and commercial spaces.

Heading east, the Eastern Islands and Eastern Docklands were full of derelict industrial buildings until the 1980s and early '90s, when they got a new lease of life. Borneo, Java and KNSM islands are home to innovative residential projects as well as stylishly repurposed buildings. The docklands' historic Lloyd Hotel (p234) started off as a hotel, but went through various incarnations as a Nazi prison and a juvenile facility, before it was re-imagined by a bunch of visionary Dutch artists, designers and architects. Striking new Docklands' buildings include the residential and commercial complex dubbed the Whale.

Further east is the burgeoning IJburg neighbourhood, on a string of artificial islands some 10km from the city centre. About 50,000 residents are predicted to inhabit the islands by 2025. The curvaceous Enneüs Heerma Brug, dubbed Dolly Parton Bridge by locals, links it to the mainland.

Northwest of Centraal Station and also on the IJ, you'll find the Westerdokseiland, a harbour that has been repurposed. One of the most striking sites in the Western Docklands is the REM Eiland (p148), a 22m-high former pirate-broadcasting rig transformed into a restaurant and bar.

Across the IJ river in Amsterdam-Noord, housing blocks and office towers are springing up on a former industrial estate at the Overhoeks development, where the architectural centrepiece is the EYE Film Institute (p87).

Exciting projects continue to sweep through the city – watch this space.

Notable Contemporary Buildings

NEMO (Eastern Islands & Eastern Docklands)

EYE Film Institute (Amsterdam-Noord)

Muziekgebouw aan 't IJ (Eastern Islands & Eastern Docklands)

The Whale (Eastern Islands & Eastern Docklands)

Centrale Bibliotheek Amsterdam (Eastern Islands & Eastern Docklands)

IWAN BAAN/IMAGE COURTESY OF RIJKSMUSEUM ©

3

LONELY PLANET/GETTY IMAGES ©

1. Street Art
Art in Amsterdam is not just about Golden Age masters – keep your eyes peeled for contemporary street art.

2. Rijksmuseum (p172)
The recently refurbished Rijksmuseum is home to the Netherlands' premier art collection.

3. Café de Pels (p114)
This traditional brown *café* (pub) doubles as a Sunday morning breakfast spot.

4. Cannabis College (p76)
This nonprofit information centre educates visitors about recreational cannabis use.

JEAN-PIERRE LESCOURRET / GETTY IMAGES ©

1. Keizersgracht (p35)
The 'Emperor's Canal' was named as a nod to Holy Roman Emperor Maximilian I.

2. La Tertulia (p153)
This coffeeshop on lively Prinsengracht is decorated with Van Gogh–inspired murals.

3. Dutch fashion (p268)
In recent decades, unique Dutch fashion design has attracted international attention.

4. Bloemenmarkt (p128)
Full of colourful blooms, the flower market is always lovely, even in fog or cold weather.

JEAN-PIERRE LESCOURRET / GETTY IMAGES ©

Canal Architecture

The labyrinthine canals that create Amsterdam's enchanting landscape reflect the soul, spirit and physical history of the city, telling a thousand stories in the ripples of their waters.

Canal Rings

Far from being simply decorative or picturesque, or even as waterways for transport, the canals were crucial to drain and reclaim the water-logged land. It is likely that none of the elegant canal houses would have been constructed – and they would certainly not be still standing – had the canals not solved Amsterdam's essential problem: keeping the land and the sea separate.

Above: Herengracht (p108)

The key to understanding the canals' significance in the evolution of the city is that much of the region is polder: land that once lay at the bottom of lakes or the sea. The land was reclaimed by building dykes across sea inlets and rivers, and pumping the water out with windmills (and later with steam and diesel pumps).

The turn of the 17th century brought one of Europe's greatest engineering and architectural marvels to Amsterdam: the canal ring, an intricate network of waterways that were built beginning with the Western Canal Ring in the late 1600s. The entire 17th-century canal ring became the eighth Dutch treasure to land on the coveted Unesco World Heritage list (in 2010).

Of all of the engineers and architects who contributed to the canal-ring project, Hendrick de Keyser was perhaps the most definitive influence on this singular triumph of Amsterdam's Golden Age. De Keyser's work is celebrated for originating the Amsterdam Renaissance style of architecture.

Many of De Keyser's buildings line 17th-century canals (eg Herengracht, Keizergracht and Prinsengracht), including grand houses like the 1609 Huis aan de Drie Grachten, which is notable for its steep gables, leaded-glass windows and handsome shutters.

Must-See Canal Buildings

Bartolotti House (Western Canal Ring)

Entrepotdok (Plantage)

Huis aan de Drie Grachten (Medieval Centre)

Melkfabriek (Southern Canal Ring)

Huis met de Hoofden (Western Canal Ring)

Canal Houses

Gables

Among Amsterdam's great treasures are its magnificent gables – the roof-level facades that adorn the elegant houses along the canals. The gable hid the roof from public view, and helped to identify the house, until the French occupiers introduced house numbers in 1795. Gables then became more of a fashion accessory.

There are four main types of gable: the simple **spout gable**, with diagonal outline and semicircular windows or shutters, that was used mainly for warehouses from the 1580s to the early 1700s; the **step gable**, a late-Gothic design favoured by Dutch Renaissance architects; the **neck gable**, also known as the bottle gable, a durable design introduced in the 1640s; and the **bell gable**, which appeared in the 1660s and became popular in the 18th century.

Hoists & Houses That Tip

Many canal houses deliberately tip forward. Given the narrowness of staircases, owners needed an easy way to move large goods and furniture to the upper floors. The solution: a hoist built into the gable, to lift objects up and in through the windows. The tilt allowed loading without bumping into the house front. Some houses even have huge hoist-wheels in the attic with a rope and hook that run through the hoist beam.

The forward lean also makes the houses seem larger, which makes it easier to admire the facade and gable – a fortunate coincidence.

Wall Tablets

Other house features include historic wall tablets. Before street numbers were introduced near the turn of the 19th century, many Amsterdam homes were identified by their wall tablets. These painted or carved stone plaques were practical decorations that earmarked the origin, religion or profession of the inhabitants.

Beautiful examples of these stones are still found on many buildings along the main canals. Occupations are a frequent theme: tobacconists, milliners, merchants, skippers, undertakers and even grass-mowers are depicted.

The tablets also provide hints about the city's past. On the Singel, a stone depicting the scene of Eve tempting Adam with an apple harkens back to a fruit market of yesteryear.

By Numbers

Number of canals: 165

Kilometres of canals: 100

Number of bridges: 1281

Number of islands: 90

Number of houseboats: 2500

Narrowest canal house (front): 2.02m

Narrowest canal house (rear): 1m

Widest canal house (front): 22m

Canal boat cruise passengers per year: 3.1 million

Contemporary Dutch Design

Contemporary Dutch design has a reputation for minimalist, creative approaches to everyday furniture and homewares products, mixed with vintage twists and tongue-in-cheek humour to keep it fresh. In the past two decades or so, what started out as a few innovators has accelerated to become a movement that is putting the Netherlands at the forefront of the industry. Dutch fashion is also reaching far beyond the country's borders, with designs that are vibrant and imaginative, yet practical too.

Dutch Design Online Resources

....

www.design.com: Interior, furniture, product and fashion news

....

www.fashionnl. com: Blogs, events, shops and designers

....

www.dutch fashionherenow. com: Promotes Dutch fashion from academy to industry

The Beginning of a Movement

The Dutch design movement today can be traced back to a handful of designers working in different materials and mediums around the same time, who started gaining respect at home and abroad.

Providing a key platform was Droog (p101), established in 1993. This design collective works with a community of designers to help them produce their works and sell them to the world, with the partners to make it happen and the connections to facilitate collaborations with big brands.

Signature Droog designs employ surreal wit, such as a chandelier made of 80-plus light bulbs clustered like fish eggs, or an off-centre umbrella, surely inspired by the country's blustery weather.

Dutch Design Pioneers

Among the contemporary pioneers was Marcel Wanders, who first drew international acclaim for his iconic Knotted Chair, produced by Droog in 1996. Made from a knotted aramid and carbon fibre thread and resin, Wanders' air-drying technique meant it was ultimately shaped by gravity. It's now in the permanent collection of the Museum of Modern Art in New York. In 2001 Wanders founded Moooi (p155) (the name is a play on the Dutch word for 'beautiful', with an additional 'o' symbolising extra beauty and uniqueness). Now a world-leading design label, Moooi also showcases other pioneering designers such as Maarten Baas (best known for his Smoke series of charred timber furniture) and Studio Job (Job Smeets and Nynke Tynagel's neo-Gothic decorative arts).

Other pioneering designers include Droog designer Jurgen Bey who has strong architectural links, working with interior and public space design; Hella Jongerius, whose designs include porcelain plates and tiles using new printing techniques; Piet Hein Eek's works with reclaimed wood; Scholten & Baijings (Stefan Scholten and Carole Baijings), producing colourful textiles and kitchenware; Hans van Bentum (check out his extraordinary giant revolver chandelier in the Jordaan *café* Proust (p151)); and Ineke Hans, whose celebrated recyclable plastic Ahrend 380 chair incorporates a table.

Furniture, product and interior designer Richard Hutten has been involved with Droog since its foundation. Famed for his 'no sign of design' humorous, functional furniture, his works have been exhibited worldwide and are held in the permanent collections of museums including Amsterdam's Stedelijk Museum.

Gaining Momentum

The momentum that the first wave of contemporary Dutch designers generated inspired young designers who thought 'if they can do it, I can too', according to Dutch interior designer Marloes Hoedeman. Trained as a stylist at Amsterdam's Artemis Styling Academie, Hoedeman began her career freelancing as a stylist for magazines including *Elle Decoration*, going on to design residential interiors and commercial spaces such as Scotch & Soda's retail stores.

Hoedeman says the buzz generated by Dutch design's growing reputation led to the advent of events like **Inside Design** (www.elle.nl/inside design), which in turn inspired more designers to create and produce works. Her take on Dutch design is that it's 'colourful, young, mixed with vintage and reclaimed materials. It's influenced by tradition and old techniques, but it's uniquely Dutch. It's open to designers from other countries, but it's not trying to do the same thing as anyone else'.

Following on from the Dutch design pioneers, second-generation designers – who tend to focus as much on aesthetics as concept and function – include Wieki Somers, awarded for designs like her Merry-go-round Coat Rack and rowboat-shaped Bathboat tub.

The Future

Up-and-coming Dutch designers to watch for include Lex Pott, working with raw materials including wood, stone and metal at his studio in an old shipyard on the NDSM-Terrein, and Pepe Heykoop, whose recycled objects include his 'Skin Collection' of leftover leather covering modified second-hand pieces.

The waves of designers have also triggered an explosion of new design stores stocking innovative pieces by established and emerging designers, which continue to feed the industry. Not simply places to view the artistic designs, gain inspiration, or even pick up products for your own home or workplace (although they are all that), these accessible galleries incorporate cafes where you can browse design magazines amid the wares (often, even the chair you're sitting on is for sale).

Designer Living

'Interior design is much slower than the fashion world due to production time and basic items you keep for years, like a sofa – it's an investment', Marloes Hoedeman says, making it 'harder to come up with new trends – in furniture you're almost always too soon'. Yet fashion brands are now encompassing furnishings. 'It's becoming more like a lifestyle'.

Droog itself has now extended beyond design – its new Hôtel Droog houses shops including the Droog store, along with a gallery and cafe, and a guest room (really an apartment, complete with a kitchen and separate bedroom) on the top floor.

Another inspired hotel intersecting the design and fashion spheres is the independent Hotel The Exchange (p225) in Amsterdam's former stock exchange. Created by Otto Nan and Suzanne Oxenaar, who also worked on Amsterdam's Lloyd Hotel (p234), Hotel The Exchange's 61 rooms are dressed 'like models' by young designers from the Amsterdam Fashion Institute. Ranging from snug one-star boltholes to spacious five-star rooms, decor ranges from details like buttons or embroidery hoops on the walls to wild whole-room concepts such as a gigantic knitted jumper, crinoline skirt or Rembrandt-esque collar.

Marcel Wanders has recently put his talents to work on the Hyatt's fantastical Andaz Amsterdam (p227), in the city's former public library.

Best Dutch Design Stores

Droog (Nieuwmarkt)

Moooi (Jordaan)

Frozen Fountain (Western Canal Ring)

Hutspot (De Pijp)

Mobilia (Southern Canal Ring)

Raw Materials (Jordaan)

Edha (Old South)

Friday Next (Vondelpark)

Pols Potten (Eastern Islands & Eastern Docklands)

BeBoB (Western Canal Ring)

Dutch Design Events

Inside Design: Held over three days in late September and open to the public, showcasing emerging Dutch-designed furniture and products

Amsterdam Fashion Week: Twice-yearly runway shows of new season collections

Woonbeurs Amsterdam: Interior-design fair with over 300 stalls, held over six days in early October

---

CONTEMPORARY DUTCH DESIGN GAINING MOMENTUM

Fashion

Around the same time as the Dutch furniture, product and interior designers were taking flight, so too was a generation of cutting-edge fashion designers.

Veterans of today's contemporary Dutch fashion scene include Cora Kemperman (p138), the label founded by Cora Kemperman and Gloria Kok (who previously worked together at Mac & Maggie), focuses on well-priced creations – mainly solid colours, floaty, layered separates and dresses in linen, cotton and wool.

Marlies Dekkers' (p117) lingerie label Undressed was hailed as a new approach in lingerie design; her spin-off lines include Undressed Men, Undressed Secrets (her vintage lingerie collection), Sundressed (beachwear and sunglasses), and Nightdressed (evening wear).

Shoe and accessory designer Hester van Eeghen (p118) creates eye-catching leather shoes and handbags in bright colours, fur, suede, and geometric patterns and prints.

Headed up by Anja Klappe, Agna K teams up with different young designers to build its classic, well-cut women's wear collections.

Amsterdam fashion house Viktor & Rolf, founded by Viktor Horsting and Rolf Snoeren, is enjoying huge international success. From prize-winning haute couture to ready-to-wear collections, their range now spans men's and women's apparel, shoes, accessories including eyewear, and fragrances. Collaborations such as with retail giant H&M have broadened their appeal and accessibility.

Dutch retail brands making a global impact include Amsterdam success story Scotch & Soda (p116), selling its own-label affordable designs. Collections cover Scotch & Soda for men, Maison Scotch for women, Scotch Shrunk for boys, Scotch R'belle for girls and Amsterdams Blauw denim, as well as its perfume, Barfly. A new vintage furniture collection was launched in 2013. Amsterdam brand Denham the Jeanmaker (p116) is also making a name for itself in denim wear, both here in the city and as far afield as Japan.

Emerging designers are making their mark too. Names to watch include Daisy Kroon, producing brightly coloured, minimally cut women's wear, and Jivika Biervliet, who seeks out and subverts boundaries in her conceptual, wearable menswear lines.

Best Boutiques for Dutch Fashion

SPRMRKT (Jordaan)

Young Designers United (Southern Canal Ring)

By AMFI (Medieval Centre)

Tenue de Nîmes (Western Canal Ring)

Van Ravenstein (Western Canal Ring)

Centre Neuf (Southern Canal Ring)

ELINE STARINK, DESIGNER, AMATØR

Dutch-born fashion designer Eline Starink, who founded her label **Amatør** (www.amatorcollection.com) in Amsterdam in 2011, studied business psychology in the city and worked in marketing and branding for Heineken. It was then that she spotted a gap in the market for young, ambitious business women to have clothes that were 'sophisticated, powerful and individual but not boring'.

Starink spent many years living in Norway before returning to the Netherlands, and incorporates Scandinavian influences in her designs, combining the 'quality and minimalistic simplicity' of Scandinavian design with 'Dutch humour and more detail'. Her view of Dutch fashion is that 'it dares to be different and out of the box. It's humorous, nonchalant and cool, and not afraid to experiment with colour and material mixes'. Yet, she says, it's practical, especially due to the Dutch cycling lifestyle – 'you don't see high heels often. The Dutch are sophisticated but sporty, and their clothes need to adapt from work to *borrel* (drinks) to weekend parties'.

Starting a label in the Netherlands is easier than in many countries, in Starink's experience, due to its 'social instinct – people are really friendly and social here, and they want to help. Dutch people are entrepreneurial and up-tempo and energetic; there's an attitude of "let's get this done". It's the Dutch way'.

Survival Guide

Transport

ARRIVING IN AMSTERDAM

Most visitors arrive by air at Schiphol International Airport or by train at Centraal Station.

Schiphol is Europe's fourth-busiest airport and has copious air links worldwide, including many on low-cost European airlines. It's the hub of Dutch passenger carrier KLM.

National and international trains arrive at Centraal Station. There are good links with several European cities. The high-speed **Thalys** (www.thalys.com) runs from Paris (3½ hours) via Brussels nearly every hour between 6am and 7pm. **Eurostar** (www.eurostar.com) runs from London (around five hours); it stops in Brussels, where you transfer onward via Thalys. German ICE trains run six times a day between Amsterdam and Cologne (2½ hours); many continue on to Frankfurt (four hours). For more information on international trains (including ICE), see **NS Hispeed** (www.nshispeed.nl).

Flights, cars and tours can be booked online at lonelyplanet.com.

Schiphol International Airport

Schiphol International Airport (AMS; www.schiphol.nl) is 18km southwest of the city centre. It has ATMs, currency exchanges, tourist information, car hire, train ticket sales counters, luggage storage, food and free wi-fi (for one hour). It's easy to reach the city from Schiphol.

Train Trains run to Amsterdam's Centraal Station (€3.90 one way, 20 minutes) 24 hours a day. From 6am to 12.30am they go every 10 to 15 minutes; hourly in the wee hours. The rail platform is nearby, down the escalator.

Shuttle bus There is a shuttle bus every 30 minutes from 6am to 9pm (www.schipholhotelshuttle.nl; one-way/return €16.50/26.50). It runs from the airport to several hotels. Look for the **Connexxion** desk by Arrivals 4.

Bus Bus 197 (€4 one way, 25 minutes) is the quickest way to places by the Museumplein, Leidseplein or Vondelpark. It departs outside the arrivals hall door.

Taxi Taxis take 20 to 30 minutes to the centre (longer in rush hour), costing around €47. The taxi stand is just outside the arrivals hall door.

Centraal Station

Centraal Station is in the city centre, with easy transport connections onward. The station has ATMs, currency exchanges, tourist information, restaurants, shops, luggage storage (€8 per day), and national and international train-ticket sales.

CLIMATE CHANGE & TRAVEL

Every form of transport that relies on carbon-based fuel generates CO_2, the main cause of human-induced climate change. Modern travel is dependent on aeroplanes, which might use less fuel per kilometre per person than most cars but travel much greater distances. The altitude at which aircraft emit gases (including CO_2) and particles also contributes to their climate change impact. Many websites offer 'carbon calculators' that allow people to estimate the carbon emissions generated by their journey and, for those who wish to do so, to offset the impact of the greenhouse gases emitted with contributions to portfolios of climate-friendly initiatives throughout the world. Lonely Planet offsets the carbon footprint of all staff and author travel.

TRAIN TRIBULATIONS

Buying a train ticket is the hardest part of riding Dutch trains. Among the challenges:
➡ Only some ticket machines accept cash, and those are coins-only, so you need a pocketful of change.
➡ Ticket machines that accept plastic will not work with most non-European credit and ATM cards.
➡ Ticket windows do not accept foreign credit or ATM cards, although they will accept paper euros. Lines are often quite long and there is a surcharge for the often-unavoidable need to use a ticket window.

Train

➡ **NS** (Nederlandse Spoorwegen; www.ns.nl), aka Dutch Railways, runs the nation's rail service. Trains are frequent from Centraal Station and serve domestic destinations such as Haarlem, Leiden and Delft several times per hour, making for easy day trips.

➡ The main service centre to buy tickets for both national and international trains is on the station's west side. The left-luggage lockers are on the east side.

DOMESTIC TICKETS

➡ Tickets can be bought at the NS service desk windows (for a €0.50 surcharge) or at ticketing machines.

➡ The ticket windows are easiest to use, though there is often a queue. Non-European credit cards (ie those that lack chip technology) are not accepted.

➡ To use the ticketing machines, find one that accepts coins (paper bills aren't usable, and many machines only take chip cards). Start by choosing 'single' (ie one-way) or 'day return'. Enter the first few letters of your destination, which should bring it up. Select it, then choose 1st or 2nd class (there's little difference in comfort, but if the train is crowded there are usually more seats in 1st class). Choose 'full fare' and the period of validity (ie 'today' or 'without date' for a future trip). For

tickets without a date, be sure to validate the ticket in a yellow punch gadget near the platform before you board.

➡ At Centraal Station, there are change machines at the entrance to the main Ticket Service Centre.

➡ Day-return tickets (aka *dagretour*) are 10% to 15% cheaper than two one-way tickets.

➡ There are basically two types of domestic train: Intercity (faster, with fewer stops) and Sprinter (slower, stops at each station).

INTERNATIONAL TICKETS

➡ **NS Hispeed** (www.nshispeed.nl) has separate windows to buy international tickets. Queues can be long. Upon entering, an agent will give you a numbered ticket. When your number is called, you can proceed to the window.

➡ Unless you have a credit card with chip technology, you'll need to use cash to buy your ticket on site. There's also a €3.50 to €7.50 booking charge for on-site purchases.

➡ An alternative is to buy tickets online (where credit cards are accepted), and print your tickets at home or via NS Hispeed's kiosks at the station. Online purchases do not incur booking fees.

➡ Be sure to reserve in advance during peak periods.

Tram

Eleven of Amsterdam's 16 tram lines stop at Centraal Station, and then fan out to the rest of the city. For trams 4, 9, 16, 24, 25 and 26, head far to the left (east) when you come out the station's main entrance; look for the 'A' sign. For trams 1, 2, 5, 13 and 17, head to the right and look for the 'B' sign.

Taxi

Taxis queue near the front entrance. Fares are meter-based. It should be €10 to €15 for destinations in the centre, canal ring or Jordaan.

Bus Station

Eurolines (www.eurolines.com) connects with all major European capitals. Buses arrive at Amstelstation, south of the centre, which has an easy metro link to Centraal Station (about a 15-minute trip). The **Eurolines Ticket Office** (Rokin 38a) is near the Dam. Bus travel is typically the cheapest way to get to Amsterdam.

Car

If you're arriving by car, it's best to leave your vehicle in a park-and-ride lot near the edge of town. A nominal parking fee (around €8 per 24 hours) also gets you free public-transport tickets. For more info see www.bereikbaar.amsterdam.nl.

GETTING AROUND AMSTERDAM

Central Amsterdam is relatively compact and best seen on foot or by bicycle.

The GVB operates the public-transport system, a mix of tram, bus, metro and ferry. Visitors will find trams the most useful option.

The excellent **Journey Planner** (www.9292.nl) calculates routes, costs and travel times, and will get you from door to door, wherever you're going in the city.

Tram

➡ Most public transport within the city is by tram. The vehicles are fast, frequent and ubiquitous, operating between 6am and 12.30am.

➡ On trams with conductors, enter at the rear; you can buy a disposable **OV-chipkaart** (www.ov-chipkaart.nl; 1hr €2.80) or day pass (€7.50) when you board. On trams without conductors (line 5, and some on line 24), buy a ticket from the driver.

➡ When you enter and exit, wave your card at the pink machine to 'check in' and 'check out'.

➡ Most tram lines start at Centraal Station and then fan out into the neighbourhoods. Common routes:

Jordaan & Western Canals Tram 1, 2, 5, 13

Southern Canal Ring Tram 1, 2, 5 for Leidseplein; 4, 9 for Rembrandtplein

Old South & Vondelpark Tram 1, 2, 5

De Pijp Tram 16, 24

Nieuwmarkt & Plantage Tram 9

➡ You can pick up tickets, passes and maps at the **GVB Information Office** (www.gvb.nl; Stationsplein 10; ⊙7am-9pm Mon-Fri, 8am-9pm Sat & Sun). It's across the tram tracks from Centraal Station, and attached to the main VVV tourist information office.

Metro & Bus

➡ Amsterdam's buses and metro (subway) primarily serve outer districts. Fares are the same as for trams.

➡ *Nachtbussen* (night buses) run after other transport stops (from 1am to 6am, every hour). A ticket costs €4.50.

➡ Note that Connexxion buses (which depart from Centraal Station and are useful to reach sights in South Amsterdam) and the No 197 airport bus are not part of the GVB system. They cost more (around €4).

Bicycle

The vast majority of Amsterdammers get around town on their *fietsen* (bikes). Cycling is such a big deal here, we've devoted an entire chapter to the pursuit. See p30 for details on rentals, tours and road rules.

Boat

Canal Bus

The **Canal Bus** (www.canal.nl; day pass adult/child €22/11) offers a unique hop-on, hop-off service among its 17 docks around the city and near the big museums.

Ferry

Free ferries to Amsterdam-Noord depart from piers behind Centraal Station. The ride to Buiksloterweg is the most direct (five minutes) and runs 24 hours; this is how you reach the EYE Film Institute. Another boat runs to NDSM-werf (15 minutes) between 7am and midnight (from 9am weekends). Another goes to IJplein (6.30am to midnight). Bicycles are permitted.

Taxi

➡ Taxis are expensive and not very speedy given Amsterdam's maze of streets.

➡ You don't hail taxis on the road. Instead, find them at stands at Centraal Station, Leidseplein and other busy spots around town. You needn't take the first car in the queue.

➡ Another method is to book a taxi by phone. **Taxicentrale Amsterdam** (TCA; ☎777 77 77; www.tcataxi.nl) is the most reliable company.

➡ Fares are meter-based. The meter starts at €2.83, then it's €2.08 per km thereafter. A ride from Leidseplein to the Dam runs about €12; from Centraal Station to Jordaan is €10 to €15.

➡ Bicycle taxis are a nice alternative. They often have lower rates, and can be flagged down in the street, especially near Leidseplein, Rembrandtplein and Dam. Contact **Amsterdam Bike Taxi** (☎06 4541 2725; www.amsterdambiketaxi.info) if you don't see its three-wheelers circulating around.

Car & Motorcycle

We absolutely advise against having a car in Amsterdam, but if you must, read on.

Parking

➡ Pay-and-display applies in the central zone from 9am to midnight Monday to Saturday, and noon to midnight on Sunday.

➡ Costs are around €5/30 per hour/day in most of the city centre, and around €4/25 elsewhere within the Canal Ring.

Prices ease as you move away from the centre.

➡ Parking garages include locations at Damrak, near Leidseplein and under Museumplein and the Stopera, but they're often full and cost more than street parking.

➡ It's best to leave your vehicle in a park-and-ride lot near the edge of town. See www.bereikbaar.amsterdam.nl for details.

Road Rules

➡ Drive on the right-hand side of the road.

➡ Seat belts are required for everyone in a vehicle.

➡ Children under 12 must ride in the back if there's room.

➡ Be alert for bicycles, and if you are trying to turn right, be aware that bikes going straight ahead have priority.

➡ Trams always have right of way.

➡ On roundabouts (traffic circles), approaching vehicles have right of way, unless there are traffic signs indicating otherwise.

➡ The blood-alcohol limit when driving is 0.05%.

Automobile Association

The **ANWB** (www.anwb.nl) is the Netherlands' auto association. Members of auto associations in their home countries (the AAA, CAA etc) can get assistance, free maps, discounts and more.

Rental

Requirements for renting a car in the Netherlands:

➡ Show a valid driving license from your home country.

➡ Be at least 23 years of age (some companies levy a small surcharge – €10 or so – for drivers under 25).

➡ Have a major credit card. Note most cars do *not* have an automatic transmission. If you need this, request it and be prepared for a hefty surcharge.

All the big multinational rental companies are here; many have offices on Overtoom, near Vondelpark. Rates start at around €45 per day, but they change frequently, so call around. Rentals at Schiphol airport incur a surcharge. Companies include:

Avis Autoverhuur (www.avis.nl)

easyCar (www.easycar.nl)

Europcar (www.europcar.com)

Hertz (www.hertz.nl)

National (www.nationalcar.com)

Sixt (www.sixt.com)

TOURS

For cycling tours, see p30. For boat tours, see p38. Our favourite walking tours include the following:

Randy Roy's Redlight Tours (06 4185 3288; www.randyroysredlighttours.com; tours €15; 8pm Sun-Thu, 8pm & 10pm Fri & Sat, closed Dec-Feb; 4/9/16/24/25 Centraal Station) Fun guides provide in-the-know anecdotes about the city's sex life and celebrity secrets on Randy Roy's lively 1½-hour tour. The jaunt ends at a local bar with a free drink. Meet in front of the Victoria Hotel (Damrak 1-5), opposite Centraal Station, rain or shine. Reserving in advance is a good idea.

Prostitution Information Centre Red Light District Tour (Map p300; www.pic-amsterdam.com; Enge Kerksteeg 3; tours €15; 5pm Sat year-round, plus 6.30pm Wed Jun-Aug; 4/9/16/24/25 Dam) The nonprofit **Prostitution Information Centre** (PIC; Map p300; 420 73 28; www.pic-amsterdam.com; Enge Kerksteeg 3; 1.30-8pm Sat or by appointment; 4/9/16/24/25 Dam) offers fascinating one-hour tours of the Red Light District, where guides explain the details of

---

TRAVEL PASSES

➡ Travel passes are extremely handy and provide substantial savings over per-ride ticket purchases.

➡ The GVB offers unlimited-ride passes for one to seven days (€7.50/12/16/21/26/29.50/32), valid on trams, some buses and metro.

➡ Passes are available at the GVB office, VVV offices (one- to four-day passes only) and from tram conductors (one-day passes only).

➡ The **I Amsterdam Card** (www.iamsterdam.com; per 24/48/72hr €42/52/62) and **Holland Pass** (www.hollandpass.com; 2/5/7 attractions €33/48/68) both include a GVB travel pass in their fee.

➡ A wider-ranging option is the Amsterdam & Region Day Ticket (€13.50), which goes beyond the tram/metro system, adding on night buses, airport buses, Connexxion buses and regional EBS buses that go to towns such as Haarlem and Zaanse Schans. The pass is available at the GVB office and at VVV offices.

how the business works and take you into a Red Light room. Profits go to the centre; reservations are not necessary.

Sandeman's New Amsterdam Tours (www. newamsterdamtours.com; donations encouraged; ⊙11.15am & 1.15pm; 🚊4/9/16/24/25 Dam) Energetic young guides working on a tip-only basis lead a three-hour jaunt past the top sights of the Medieval Centre and Red Light District (with a dip into the Jordaan). Meet at the Nationaal Monument on the Dam, regardless of the weather. The tour is first come, first served; to guarantee a spot you can make a reservation (€3).

Drugs Tour (www.drugstour. nl; tours by donation; ⊙6pm Fri; 🚊4/9/16/24/25) The illuminating, 1½-hour itinerary looks at Amsterdam's drug culture, both its myths and reality. It includes smart shops, a 'user room' (the tour doesn't go inside) and a look at fake drugs being sold on the street. Tours depart by the Oude Kerk. Reserve in advance. Private tours also can be arranged (€40 per four people) in multiple languages.

Urban Home & Garden Tours (📞06 2168 1918; www. uhgt.nl; tours incl drink €34; ⊙10.30am Fri, 11.30am Sat, 12.30pm Sun mid-Apr–mid-Oct) These well-regarded tours visit 18th-century, 19th-century and contemporary Amsterdam dwellings. Tours take 2½ to three hours. Reserve ahead – the meeting point for tours (near Rembrandtplein) will be revealed after you do. Call for last-minute bookings.

Mee in Mokum (www. gildeamsterdam.nl; Kalverstraat 92; tours €7.50; ⊙11am & 2pm Tue-Sun; 🚊1/2/5 Spui) Mee in Mokum's low-priced walkabouts are led by senior-citizen volunteers who often have personal recollections to add. The tours can be a bit hit or miss, depending on the guide, but are well worth it. They depart from the cafe in the Amsterdam Museum.

Directory A–Z

Customs Regulations

For visitors from EU countries, limits only apply for excessive amounts. Log on to www.douane.nl for details.

Residents of non-EU countries are limited to the following:

Alcohol 1L of spirits, wine or beer.

Coffee 500g of coffee, or 200g of coffee extracts or coffee essences.

Perfume 50mL of perfume and 250mL of eau de toilette.

Tea 100g of tea, or 40g of tea extracts or tea essences.

Tobacco 200 cigarettes, or 250g of tobacco (shag or pipe tobacco), or 100 cigarillos, or 50 cigars.

Discount Cards

Visitors of various professions, including artists, journalists, museum conservators and teachers, may get discounts at some venues if they show accreditation.

Students regularly get a few euros off museum admission; bring ID.

Seniors over 65, and their partners of 60 or older, benefit from reductions on public transport, museum admissions, concerts and more. You may look younger, so bring your passport.

I Amsterdam Card (www.iamsterdam.com; per 24/48/72hr €42/52/62) Provides admission to more than 30 museums, a canal cruise, and discounts at shops, attractions and restaurants. Also includes a GVB transit pass. Available at VVV offices (tourist offices) and some hotels.

Museumkaart (Museum Card; www.museumkaart.nl; adult/child €50/25, plus €5 for first-time registrants) Free and discounted entry to some 400 museums all over the country for one year. Purchase at participating museum ticket counters or at Uitburo ticket shops.

Holland Pass (www.hollandpass.com; 2/5/7 attractions €33/48/68) Similar to the I Amsterdam Card, but without the rush for usage; you can visit sights over a prolonged period. Prices are based on the number of attractions, which you pick from 'tiers' (the most popular/expensive sights are top-tier). Also includes a transit pass. Available from GWK Travelex offices and various hotels.

Cultureel Jongeren Paspoort (Cultural Youth Passport; www.cjp.nl; card €15) Big discounts to museums and cultural events nationwide for people under the age of 30.

PRACTICALITIES

➡ Dutch-language newspapers include *De Telegraaf*, the Netherlands' biggest seller; and *Het Parool*, Amsterdam's paper, with the scoop on what's happening around town.

➡ Keep abreast of news back home via the *International Herald Tribune* or the *Guardian*, or weeklies such as the *Economist* or *Time*, all widely available on newsstands.

➡ *Uitkrant* and *NL20* are free Dutch-language listings magazines you can pick up around town.

➡ The metric system is used for weights and measures.

➡ Amsterdam banned smoking in all bars and restaurants in 2008, but you'll find some establishments ignore the order and will let people light up freely.

Electricity

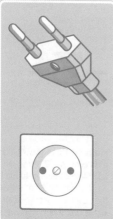

230v/50hz

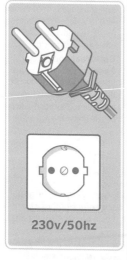

230v/50hz

Embassies & Consulates

Amsterdam is the country's capital but, confusingly, Den Haag is the seat of government. So the embassies (including those for Australia, Canada, New Zealand and Ireland) are in Den Haag, but Amsterdam has several consulates:

France (☎530 69 69; www.consulfrance-amsterdam.org; Vijzelgracht 2; ⬚16/24/25 Keizersgracht)

Germany (☎574 77 00; www.den-haag.diplo.de; Honthorststraat 36-8; ⬚2/5 Hobbemastraat)

UK (☎676 43 43; www.britain.nl; Koningslaan 44; ⬚2 Valeriusplein)

US (☎575 53 09; http://amsterdam.usconsulate.gov; Museumplein 19; ⬚3/5/12/16/24 Museumplein)

Emergency

Police, fire, ambulance: ☎112

Gay & Lesbian Travellers

The Netherlands was the first country to legalise same-sex marriage (in 2001), so it's no surprise that Amsterdam's gay scene is among the world's largest.

Five hubs party hardest. **Warmoesstraat** in the Red Light District hosts the infamous kink-filled leather and fetish bars. Nearby on the upper end of the **Zeedijk**, bright crowds spill onto laid-back bar terraces. In the Southern Canal Ring, the area around **Rembrandt-plein** (aka the 'Amstel area') has traditional pubs and brown *cafés*, some with a campy bent. **Leidseplein** has a smattering of trendy venues along Kerkstraat. And **Reguliersdwarsstraat**, located one street down from the flower market, draws the beautiful crowd (though financial and legal problems have taken a toll on many venues here in recent years).

➡ **Gay Amsterdam** (www.gayamsterdam.com) Lists hotels, shops, restaurants and clubs, and provides maps.

➡ **Pink Point** (Map p314; ☎428 10 70; www.pinkpoint.org; Westermarkt; ◷10am–6pm; ⬚13/14/17 Westermarkt) Located behind the Westerkerk, Pink Point is part information kiosk, part souvenir shop. Get details on GLBT hang-outs and social groups, and pick up a copy of the candid *Bent Guide*.

➡ **Reguliers** (www.reguliers.net) Info on the Reguliers-dwarsstraat scene, including current club openings and closings.

➡ **Gay News Amsterdam** (www.gay-news.com) Free monthly listings magazine available around town.

Internet Access

➡ Free wi-fi is common in lodgings across the price spectrum; many places also have a computer on-site for you to use.

➡ Most bars and *cafés* and some coffeeshops have free wi-fi. You may need to ask for the code.

➡ Outlets of the public library (Openbare Bibliotheek) offer free wi-fi; there's usually a small fee (€1 per half hour) to use the computer terminals to go online.

➡ Internet cafes have become less common, though a few scatter around Centraal Station. Expect to pay around €3 per hour.

➡ For free wi-fi hot spots around the city, check www.wifi-amsterdam.nl.

➡ We've identified listings that have wi-fi with a 🛜. We've denoted lodgings that offer internet terminals for guest use with a @.

Legal Matters

Amsterdam *politie* (police) are pretty relaxed and helpful unless you do something clearly wrong, such as littering or smoking a joint right under their noses.

Police can hold offenders for up to six hours for questioning (plus another six hours if they can't establish your identity, or 24 hours if they consider the matter serious). You won't have the right to a phone call, but they'll notify your consulate. You're presumed innocent until proven guilty.

ID Papers

Anyone over 14 years of age is required by law to carry ID. Foreigners should carry a passport or a photocopy of the relevant data pages; a driver's licence isn't sufficient.

Drugs

➡ Technically, marijuana is illegal. However, possession of soft drugs (eg cannabis) up to 5g is tolerated. Larger amounts are subject to prosecution.

➡ Don't light up in an establishment other than a coffeeshop without checking that it's OK to do so.

➡ Hard drugs are treated as a serious crime.

➡ Never buy drugs of any kind on the street.

Prostitution

Prostitution is legal in the Netherlands. The industry is protected by law, and prostitutes pay tax. Much of this open policy stems from a desire to undermine the role of pimps and the underworld in the sex industry.

In Amsterdam's Red Light District you have little to fear as the streets are well-policed, but the back alleys are more dubious.

Medical Services

The Netherlands has reciprocal health arrangements with other EU countries and Australia. If you're an EU citizen, a European Health Insurance Card (EHIC), available from health centres (or, in the UK, post offices), covers you for most medical care. You still might have to pay on the spot, but you should be able to claim it back at home.

Citizens of other countries are advised to take out travel insurance; medical or dental treatment is less expensive than in North America but still costs enough.

For minor health concerns, see a local *drogist* (chemist) or *apotheek* (pharmacy, to fill prescriptions).

For more serious problems, go to the casualty ward of a *ziekenhuis* (hospital).

Referrals

Contact the **Centrale Doktersdienst** (Central Doctors Service; ☎900 15 15; www.cdd.nl; ☺24hr) for doctor, dentist or pharmacy referrals.

Emergency Rooms

Hospitals with 24-hour emergency facilities:

Onze Lieve Vrouwe Gasthuis (☎599 91 11; www.olvg.nl; Oosterpark 9; ☺24hr; ▣3/14 Beukenweg) At Oosterpark, near the Tropenmuseum. It's the closest public hospital to the centre of town.

VU Medisch Centrum (☎444 44 44; www.vumc.com; De Boelelaan 1117; ☺24hr; ▣16/24 VU Medisch Centrum) Hospital of the Vrije Universiteit (Free University).

Pharmacies

Forget about buying flu tablets and antacids at supermarkets; for anything stronger than toothpaste you'll have to go to a pharmacy.

Dam Apotheek (☎624 43 31; www.dam-apotheek.nl; Damstraat 2; ☺8.30am-5.30pm Mon-Fri, 10am-5pm Sat, noon-5pm Sun; ▣4/9/16/24/25 Dam) is conveniently located just off the Dam.

Money

The Netherlands uses the euro (€). Denominations of the currency are €5, €10, €20, €50, €100, €200 and €500 notes, and €0.01, €0.02, €0.05, €0.10, €0.20, €0.50, €1 and €2 coins (amounts under €1 are called cents).

To check the latest exchange rates, visit www.xe.com.

ATMs

Automatic teller machines can be found outside most banks, at the airport and at Centraal Station. Most accept credit cards such as Visa and MasterCard/Eurocard, as well as cash cards that access the Cirrus and Plus networks. Check with your home bank for service charges before leaving.

ATMs are not hard to find, but they often have queues or run out of cash on weekends.

Cash

A surprising number of businesses do not accept credit cards, so it's wise to have cash on hand.

Changing Money

Generally your best bet for exchanging money is to use **GWK Travelex** (☎0900 05 66; www.gwk.nl), with several branches around town:

GWK Travelex (Centraal Station) (Stationsplein; ☺8am-10pm Mon-Sat, 9am-10pm Sun; ▣4/9/16/24/25 Centraal Station)

GWK Travelex (Leidseplein) (Leidseplein 31a; ☺9.30am-5.30pm Mon-Sat, 10.30-5.30pm Sun; ▣1/2/5/7/10 Leidseplein)

GWK Travelex (Schiphol airport) (☺6am-10pm)

Credit Cards

All the major international credit cards are recognised,

and most hotels and large stores accept them. But a fair number of shops, restaurants and other businesses (including Dutch Railways and supermarket chain Albert Heijn) do not accept credit cards, or accept only European cards with security chips.

Some establishments levy a 5% surcharge (or more) on credit cards to offset the commissions charged by card providers. Always check first.

For a backup plan against the security chip issue, consider getting a preloaded debit card that has the security chip embedded. Many banks provide such cards.

PIN Cards

While in Amsterdam you'll notice people using 'PIN' cards everywhere, from shops to public telephones and cigarette vending machines. These direct-debit cards look like credit or bank cards with little gold-printed circuit chips on them, but they won't be of much use to visitors without a Dutch bank account.

Tipping

Tipping is not essential, as restaurants, hotels, bars etc include a service charge on their bills. A little extra is always welcomed though, and common in certain instances.

➡ Hotel porters: €1–2

➡ Restaurants: round up, or 5–10%

➡ Taxis: 5–10%

Travellers Cheques

Travellers cheques are rare – you'll be hard-pressed to find a bank that will change them for you.

Opening Hours

The list below provides general opening hours for businesses. Reviews throughout the book show specific hours. Note that hours can vary by season. Our listings depict operating times for peak season (from around May to September). Opening hours often decrease during off-peak months.

Banks 9am-4pm Mon-Fri, some Sat morning.

Cafés, bars & coffeeshops Open noon (exact hours vary); most close 1am Sun-Thu, 3am Fri & Sat.

Clubs Open around 10pm (exact hours vary); close 4am or 5am Fri & Sat (a few hours earlier on weekdays).

General office hours 8.30am-5pm Mon-Fri.

Museums 10am-5pm daily, some close Mon.

Restaurants Lunch 11am-2.30pm, dinner 6-10pm.

Shops Large stores: 9am or 10am to 6pm Mon-Sat, noon-6pm Sun. Smaller shops: 11am or noon to 6pm Tue-Sat, from 1pm Sun & Mon (if open at all). Many shops stay open late (to 9pm) Thu.

Supermarkets 8am-8pm, though some in the central city will stay open until 9pm or 10pm.

Post

The national post office in the Netherlands is privatised and has gone through various name changes. The current operator is **PostNL** (www.postnl.nl). It has closed most city post offices and to mail a letter or package you'll need to go to a postal service shop which may be a supermarket or tobacco shop or something else. Use the website to find a location near you, although the website is only in Dutch. Note that if you're trying to mail a parcel abroad, the staff at the third-party shop may have no idea how to help you.

Public Holidays

Many restaurants and other businesses close for two to six weeks in summer, usually in July or early August.

Banks, schools, offices and most shops close on these days:

Nieuwjaarsdag New Year's Day, 1 January.

Goede Vrijdag Good Friday, 18 April 2014, 3 April 2015.

Eerste & Tweede Paasdag Easter Sunday and Easter Monday, 20/21 April 2014, 5/6 April 2015.

Koningsdag King's Day, 27 April (but celebrated 26 April in 2014).

Bevrijdingsdag Liberation Day, 5 May. It's celebrated officially every five years; the next is in 2015.

Hemelvaartsdag Ascension Day, 29 May 2014, 14 May 2015.

Eerste & Tweede Pinksterdag Whit Sunday (Pentecost) and Whit Monday, 8/9 June 2014, 24/25 May 2015.

Eerste & Tweede Kerstdag Christmas Day and Boxing Day, 25/26 December.

Telephone

The Dutch phone network, **KPN** (www.kpn.com), is efficient, and prices are reasonable by European standards. It's free to make a **collect call** (collect gesprek; domestic 0800 01 01, international 0800 04 10).

Costs

Calls are time-based, anytime and anywhere. Here is a rough guide to costs (note phones in cafés and hotels often charge more):

National call to landline or mobile phone €0.09 per minute plus €0.10 connection fee

International call from €0.20 per minute plus €0.10 connection fee

Incoming calls to Dutch mobile phones are generally free to the recipient.

Internet Calls

Services such as **Skype** (www.skype.com) and **Google Voice** (www.google.com/voice) can make calling home quite cheap. Check the websites for details.

Mobile Phones

The Netherlands uses GSM phones compatible with the rest of Europe and Australia but not with some North American GSM phones. Smartphones such as iPhones will work – but beware of enormous roaming costs, especially for data (buy an international plan from your carrier before you leave home).

Prepaid mobile phones are available at mobile-phone shops. Prices start from around €35 when on special. You can also buy SIM cards (from €5) for your own GSM mobile phone that will give you a Dutch telephone number. Look for Phone House, Orange, T-Mobile and Vodafone shops along Kalverstraat and Rokin.

New prepaid phones generally come with a small amount of call time already stored. To top it up, purchase more minutes at one of the branded stores, newsagencies or supermarkets, and follow the instructions.

Phone Codes & Dialling

To ring abroad, dial 00 followed by the country code for your target country, the area code (you usually drop the leading 0 if there is one) and the subscriber number.

Netherlands country code 31

Amsterdam city code 020

Free calls 0800

Mobile numbers 06

Paid information calls

0900, cost varies between €0.10 and €1.30 per minute.

Drop the leading 0 on city codes if you're calling from outside the Netherlands (eg 20 for Amsterdam instead of 020). Do not dial the city code if you are in the area covered by it.

Phonecards

➡ For public telephones, cards (for €5, €10 and €20) are available at train station counters, VVV and GWK offices, and tobacco shops for €5, €10 and €20.

➡ KPN's card is the most common but there are plenty of competitors (Orange, T-Mobile and Vodaphone among them) that usually have better rates.

Time

Amsterdam is in the Central European time zone (same as Berlin and Paris), GMT/UTC plus one hour. Noon in Amsterdam is 11am in London, 6am in New York, 3am in San Francisco and 9pm in Sydney. For daylight savings time, clocks are put forward one hour at 2am on the last Sunday in March and back again at 3am on the last Sunday in October.

When telling the time, be aware that the Dutch use 'half' to indicate 'half before' the hour. If you say 'half eight' (8.30 in many forms of English), a Dutch person will take this to mean 7.30.

Toilets

Public toilets are not a widespread facility on Dutch streets, apart from the redolent, free-standing public urinals for men in places such as the Red Light District. Many people duck into a *café* or department store. The standard fee for toilet attendants is €0.50.

Tourist Information

The **VVV** (Vereniging voor Vreemdelingenverkeer; www.vvv.nl) is the Netherlands Tourism Board. In Amsterdam, the VVV runs offices in conjunction with the **Amsterdam Tourism & Convention Board** (www.iamsterdam.com).

VVV Main Office (Stationsplein 10; ⊙9am-6pm Mon-Sat, 10am-5pm Sun; 🚊4/9/16/24/25 Centraal Station) Located outside Centraal Station, this office can help with just about anything: it sells the I Amsterdam discount card; theatre and museum tickets; a good city map (€2.50); cycling maps; public transit passes (the GVB transport office is attached); and train tickets to Schiphol Airport. It also books hotel rooms (commission charged).

Queues can be long; be sure to take a number when you walk in.

VVV Leidseplein Office (Map p310; Leidseplein 26; ⊙10am-7pm Mon-Fri, 10am-6pm Sat, noon-6pm Sun; 🚊1/2/5/7/10 Leidseplein) Run in conjunction with the Uitburo ticket shop.

Holland Tourist Information (⊙7am-10pm) A VVV-run office at Schiphol International Airport.

Travellers with Disabilities

➡ Travellers with reduced mobility will find Amsterdam moderately equipped to meet their needs.

➡ Most offices and museums have lifts and/or ramps and toilets for the disabled.

➡ Many budget and midrange hotels have limited accessibility, as they are in old buildings with steep stairs and no lifts.

➡ The city's many cobblestone streets are rough for wheelchairs.

➡ Restaurants tend to be on ground floors, though 'ground' sometimes includes a few steps.

➡ Most buses are wheelchair accessible, as are metro stations. Trams are becoming more accessible as new equipment is added. Lines 1, 5, 13, 17 and 26 have lots of elevated stops for wheelchair users. The GVB website denotes which stops are wheelchair accessible.

➡ For access details at entertainment venues and museums, contact the **Uitburo** (www.amsterdamsuitburo.nl) or the **VVV** (Vereniging voor Vreemdelingenverkeer; www.vvv.nl).

➡ More questions? Check the accessibility guide at **Accessible Amsterdam** (www.toegankelijkamsterdam.nl).

Visas

Tourists from nearly 60 countries – including Australia, Canada, Israel, Japan, New Zealand, Singapore, South Korea, the USA and most of Europe – need only a valid passport to visit the Netherlands for up to three months. EU nationals can enter for three months with just their national identity card or a passport that expired less than five years ago.

Nationals of most other countries need a so-called Schengen visa, valid within the EU member states (except the UK and Ireland), plus Norway and Iceland, for 90 days within a six-month period. Schengen visas are issued by Dutch embassies or consulates overseas and can take a while to process (up to two months). You'll need a passport that's valid until at least three months after your visit, and will have to prove you have sufficient funds for your stay and return journey.

The **Netherlands Foreign Affairs Ministry** (www.government.nl) lists consulates and embassies around the world. Visas and extensions are handled by the **Immigratie en Naturalisatiedienst** (Immigration & Naturalisation Service; ☎per min €0.10 0900 123 45 61; www.ind.nl). Study visas must be applied for via your college or university in the Netherlands.

Women Travellers

In terms of safety, Amsterdam is probably as secure as it gets in Europe's major cities. There's little street harassment, even in the Red Light District, although it's best to walk with a friend to minimise unwelcome attention.

Language

The official language of Amsterdam and the rest of the Netherlands is Dutch, which has around 20 million speakers worldwide. As a member of the Germanic language family, Dutch has many similarities with English.

The pronunciation of Dutch is fairly straightforward. The language does distinguish between long and short vowels, which can affect the meaning of words, for example, *man* (man) and *maan* (moon). Also note that aw is pronounced as in 'law', eu as the 'u' in 'nurse', ew as the 'ee' in 'see' (with rounded lips), oh as the 'o' in 'note', öy as the 'er y' (without the 'r') in 'her year', and uh as in 'ago'.

The consonants are pretty simple to pronounce too. Note that kh is a throaty sound, similar to the 'ch' in the Scottish *loch*, r is trilled and zh is pronounced as the 's' in 'pleasure'. This said, if you read our coloured pronunciation guides as if they were English, you'll be understood just fine. The stressed syllables are indicated with italics.

Where relevant, both polite and informal options in Dutch are included, indicated with 'pol' and 'inf' respectively.

BASICS

Hello.	*Dag./Hallo.*	dakh/ha·*loh*
Goodbye.	*Dag.*	dakh
Yes./No.	*Ja./Nee.*	yaa/ney
Please.	*Alstublieft.* (pol)	al·stew·*bleeft*
	Alsjeblieft. (inf)	a·shuh·*bleeft*
Thank you.	*Dank u/je.* (pol/inf)	dangk ew/yuh

WANT MORE?

For in-depth language information and handy phrases, check out Lonely Planet's *Dutch Phrasebook*. You'll find it at **shop.lonelyplanet.com**, or you can buy Lonely Planet's iPhone phrasebooks at the Apple App Store.

You're welcome.	*Graag gedaan.*	khraakh khuh·*daan*
Excuse me.	*Excuseer mij.*	eks·kew·*zeyr* mey

How are you?
Hoe gaat het met u/jou? (pol/inf) — hoo khaat huht met ew/yaw

Fine. And you?
Goed. — khoot
En met u/jou? (pol/inf) — en met ew/yaw

What's your name?
Hoe heet u/je? (pol/inf) — hoo heyt ew/yuh

My name is ...
Ik heet ... — ik heyt ...

Do you speak English?
Spreekt u Engels? — spreykt ew *eng*·uhls

I don't understand.
Ik begrijp het niet. — ik buh·*khreyp* huht neet

ACCOMMODATION

Do you have a ... room?	*Heeft u een ...?*	heyft ew uhn ...
single	*éénpersoons-kamer*	eyn·puhr·sohns·kaa·muhr
double	*tweepersoons-kamer met een dubbel bed*	twey·puhr·sohns·kaa·muhr met uhn du·buhl bet
twin	*tweepersoons-kamer met lits jumeaux*	twey·puhr·sohns·kaa·muhr met lee zhew·*moh*

How much is it per ...?	*Hoeveel kost het per ...?*	hoo·*veyl* kost huht puhr ...
night	*nacht*	nakht
person	*persoon*	puhr·*sohn*

Is breakfast included?
Is het ontbijt inbegrepen? — is huht ont·*beyt* in·buh·khrey·puhn

Signs

Ingang	Entrance
Uitgang	Exit
Open	Open
Gesloten	Closed
Inlichtingen	Information
Verboden	Prohibited
Toiletten	Toilets
Heren	Men
Dames	Women

bathroom	*badkamer*	*bat*·kaa·muhr
bed and breakfast	*gasten-kamer*	*khas*·tuhn·kaa·muhr
campsite	*camping*	*kem*·ping
guesthouse	*pension*	pen·*syon*
hotel	*hotel*	hoh·*tel*
window	*raam*	raam
youth hostel	*jeugd-herberg*	*yeukht*·her·berkh

DIRECTIONS

Where's the ...?
Waar is ...? — waar is ...

How far is it?
Hoe ver is het? — hoo ver is huht

What's the address?
Wat is het adres? — wat is huht a·*dres*

Can you please write it down?
Kunt u dat alstublieft opschrijven? — kunt ew dat al·stew·*bleeft* op·skhrey·vuhn

Can you show me (on the map)?
Kunt u het mij tonen (op de kaart)? — kunt ew huht mey *toh*·nuhn (op duh kaart)

at the corner	*op de hoek*	op duh hook
at the traffic lights	*bij de verkeerslichten*	bey duh vuhr·*keyrs*·likh·tuhn
behind	*achter*	*akh*·tuhr
in front of	*voor*	vohr
left	*links*	lingks
near (to)	*dicht bij*	dikht bey
opposite	*tegenover*	tey·khuhn·*oh*·vuhr
right	*rechts*	rekhs
straight ahead	*rechtdoor*	rekh·*dohr*

EATING & DRINKING

What would you recommend?
Wat kan u aanbevelen? — wat kan ew aan·buh·vey·luhn

What's in that dish?
Wat zit er in dat gerecht? — wat zit uhr in dat khuh·*rekht*

I'd like the menu, please.
Ik wil graag een menu. — ik wil khraakh uhn me·*new*

Delicious!
Heerlijk/Lekker! — *heyr*·luhk/*le*·kuhr

Cheers!
Proost! — prohst

Please bring the bill.
Mag ik de rekening alstublieft? — makh ik duh *rey*·kuh·ning al·stew·*bleeft*

I'd like to reserve a table for ...	*Ik wil graag een tafel voor ... reserveren.*	ik wil khraakh uhn *taa*·fuhl vohr ... rey·ser·*vey*·ruhn
(two) people	*(twee) personen*	(twey) puhr·*soh*·nuhn
(eight) o'clock	*(acht) uur*	(akht) ewr

I don't eat ...	*Ik eet geen ...*	ik eyt kheyn ...
eggs	*eieren*	*ey*·yuh·ruhn
fish	*vis*	vis
(red) meat	*(rood) vlees*	(roht) vleys
nuts	*noten*	*noh*·tuhn

Key Words

bar	*bar*	bar
bottle	*fles*	fles
breakfast	*ontbijt*	ont·*beyt*
cafe	*café*	ka·*fey*
cold	*koud*	kawt
dinner	*avondmaal*	*aa*·vont·maal
drink list	*drankkaart*	*drang*·kaart
fork	*vork*	vork
glass	*glas*	khlas
grocery store	*kruidenier*	kröy·duh·*neer*
hot	*heet*	heyt
knife	*mes*	mes
lunch	*middagmaal*	*mi*·dakh·maal
market	*markt*	markt
menu	*menu*	me·*new*
plate	*bord*	bort
pub	*kroeg*	krookh
restaurant	*restaurant*	res·toh·*rant*

spicy	pikant	pee·kant
spoon	lepel	ley·puhl
vegetarian (food)	vegetarisch	vey·khey·taa·ris
with	met	met
without	zonder	zon·duhr

Meat & Fish

beef	rundvlees	runt·vleys
chicken	kip	kip
duck	eend	eynt
fish	vis	vis
herring	haring	haa·ring
lamb	lamsvlees	lams·vleys
lobster	kreeft	kreyft
meat	vlees	vleys
mussels	mosselen	mo·suh·luhn
oysters	oester	oos·tuhr
pork	varkensvlees	var·kuhns·vleys
prawn	steurgarnaal	steur·khar·naal
salmon	zalm	zalm
scallops	kammosselen	ka·mo·suh·luhn
shrimps	garnalen	khar·naa·luhn
squid	inktvis	ingkt·vis
trout	forel	fo·rel
tuna	tonijn	toh·neyn
turkey	kalkoen	kal·koon
veal	kalfsvlees	kalfs·vleys

Fruit & Vegetables

apple	appel	a·puhl
banana	banaan	ba·naan
beans	bonen	boh·nuhm
berries	bessen	be·suhn
cabbage	kool	kohl
capsicum	paprika	pa·pree·ka
carrot	wortel	wor·tuhl
cauliflower	bloemkool	bloom·kohl
cucumber	komkommer	kom·ko·muhr
fruit	fruit	fröyt
grapes	druiven	dröy·vuhn
lemon	citroen	see·troon
lentils	linzen	lin·zuhn
mushrooms	paddestoelen	pa·duh·stoo·luhn
nuts	noten	noh·tuhn
onions	uien	öy·yuhn

KEY PATTERNS

To get by in Dutch, mix and match these simple patterns with words of your choice:

When's (the next bus)?
Hoe laat gaat (de volgende bus)? — hoo laat khaat (duh vol·khun·duh bus)

Where's (the station)?
Waar is (het station)? — waar is (huht sta·syon)

I'm looking for (a hotel).
Ik ben op zoek naar (een hotel). — ik ben op zook naar (uhn hoh·tel)

Do you have (a map)?
Heeft u (een kaart)? — heyft ew (uhn kaart)

Is there (a toilet)?
Is er (een toilet)? — is uhr (uhn twa·let)

I'd like (the menu).
Ik wil graag. (een menu) — ik wil khraakh (uhn me·new)

I'd like to (hire a car).
Ik wil graag (een auto huren). — ik wil khraakh (uhn aw·toh hew·ruhn)

Can I (enter)?
Kan ik (binnengaan)? — kan ik (bi·nuhn·khaan)

Could you please (help me)?
Kunt u alstublieft (helpen)? — kunt ew al·stew·bleeft (hel·puhn)

Do I have to (get a visa)?
Moet ik (een visum hebben)? — moot ik (uhn vee·zum he·buhn)

orange	sinaasappel	see·naas·a·puhl
peach	perzik	per·zik
peas	erwtjes	erw·chus
pineapple	ananas	a·na·nas
plums	pruimen	pröy·muhn
potatoes	aardappels	aart·a·puhls
spinach	spinazie	spee·naa·zee
tomatoes	tomaten	toh·maa·tuhn
vegetables	groenten	khroon·tuhn

Other

bread	brood	broht
butter	boter	boh·tuhr
cheese	kaas	kaas
eggs	eieren	ey·yuh·ruhn
honey	honing	hoh·ning
ice	ijs	eys
jam	jam	zhem

noodles	noedels	noo·duhls
oil	olie	oh·lee
pastry	gebak	khuh·bak
pepper	peper	pey·puhr
rice	rijst	reyst
salt	zout	zawt
soup	soep	soop
soy sauce	sojasaus	soh·ya·saws
sugar	suiker	söy·kuhr
vinegar	azijn	a·zeyn

Drinks

beer	bier	beer
coffee	koffie	ko·fee
juice	sap	sap
milk	melk	melk
red wine	rode wijn	roh·duh weyn
soft drink	frisdrank	fris·drangk
tea	thee	tey
water	water	waa·tuhr
white wine	witte wijn	wi·tuh weyn

EMERGENCIES

Help!
Help! — help

Leave me alone!
Laat me met rust! — laat muh met rust

I'm lost.
Ik ben verdwaald. — ik ben vuhr·dwaalt

Call a doctor!
Bel een dokter! — bel uhn dok·tuhr

Call the police!
Bel de politie! — bel duh poh·leet·see

I'm sick.
Ik ben ziek. — ik ben zeek

Where are the toilets?
Waar zijn de toiletten? — waar zeyn duh twa·le·tuhn

I'm allergic to (antibiotics).
Ik ben allergisch voor (antibiotica). — ik ben a·ler·khees vohr (an·tee·bee·yoh·tee·ka)

Question Words		
How?	Hoe?	hoo
What?	Wat?	wat
When?	Wanneer?	wa·neyr
Where?	Waar?	waar
Who?	Wie?	wee
Why?	Waarom?	waa·rom

SHOPPING & SERVICES

I'd like to buy ...
Ik wil graag ... kopen. — ik wil khraakh ... koh·puhn

I'm just looking.
Ik kijk alleen maar. — ik keyk a·leyn maar

Can I look at it?
Kan ik het even zien? — kan ik huht ey·vuhn zeen

Do you have any others?
Heeft u nog andere? — heyft ew nokh an·duh·ruh

How much is it?
Hoeveel kost het? — hoo·veyl kost huht

That's too expensive.
Dat is te duur. — dat is tuh dewr

Can you lower the price?
Kunt u wat van de prijs afdoen? — kunt ew wat van duh preys af·doon

There's a mistake in the bill.
Er zit een fout in de rekening. — uhr zit uhn fawt in duh rey·kuh·ning

ATM	pin-automaat	pin·aw·toh·maat
foreign exchange	wisselkantoor	wi·suhl·kan·tohr
post office	postkantoor	post·kan·tohr
shopping centre	winkelcentrum	wing·kuhl·sen·trum
tourist office	VVV	vey·vey·vey

TIME & DATES

What time is it?
Hoe laat is het? — hoo laat is huht

It's (10) o'clock.
Het is (tien) uur. — huht is (teen) ewr

Half past (10).
Half (elf). — half (elf)
(lit: half eleven)

am (morning)	's ochtends	sokh·tuhns
pm (afternoon)	's middags	smi·dakhs
pm (evening)	's avonds	saa·vonts

yesterday	gisteren	khis·tuh·ruhn
today	vandaag	van·daakh
tomorrow	morgen	mor·khuhn

Monday	maandag	maan·dakh
Tuesday	dinsdag	dins·dakh
Wednesday	woensdag	woons·dakh
Thursday	donderdag	don·duhr·dakh
Friday	vrijdag	vrey·dakh
Saturday	zaterdag	zaa·tuhr·dakh
Sunday	zondag	zon·dakh

January	januari	ya·new·waa·ree
February	februari	fey·brew·waa·ree
March	maart	maart
April	april	a·pril
May	mei	mey
June	juni	yew·nee
July	juli	yew·lee
August	augustus	aw·khus·tus
September	september	sep·tem·buhr
October	oktober	ok·toh·buhr
November	november	noh·vem·buhr
December	december	dey·sem·buhr

TRANSPORT

Public Transport

Is this the ... to (the left bank)?	Is dit de ... naar (de linker-oever)?	is dit duh ... naar (duh ling·kuhr·oo·vuhr)
ferry	veerboot	veyr·boht
metro	metro	mey·troh
tram	tram	trem

| platform | perron | pe·ron |
| timetable | dienst-regeling | deenst·rey·khuh·ling |

When's the ... (bus)?	Hoe laat gaat de ... (bus)?	hoo laat khaat duh ... (bus)
first	eerste	eyr·stuh
last	laatste	laat·stuh
next	volgende	vol·khun·duh

A ticket to ..., please.
Een kaartje naar ... graag. — uhn kaar·chuh naar ... khraakh

What time does it leave?
Hoe laat vertrekt het? — hoo laat vuhr·trekt huht

Does it stop at ...?
Stopt het in ...? — stopt huht in ...

What's the next stop?
Welk is de volgende halte? — welk is duh vol·khuhn·duh hal·tuh

I'd like to get off at ...
Ik wil graag in ... uitstappen. — ik wil khraak in ... öyt·sta·puhn

Is this taxi available?
Is deze taxi vrij? — is dey·zuh tak·see vrey

Please take me to ...
Breng me alstublieft naar ... — breng muh al·stew·bleeft naar ...

Numbers

1	één	eyn
2	twee	twey
3	drie	dree
4	vier	veer
5	vijf	veyf
6	zes	zes
7	zeven	zey·vuhn
8	acht	akht
9	negen	ney·khuhn
10	tien	teen
20	twintig	twin·tikh
30	dertig	der·tikh
40	veertig	feyr·tikh
50	vijftig	feyf·tikh
60	zestig	ses·tikh
70	zeventig	sey·vuhn·tikh
80	tachtig	takh·tikh
90	negentig	ney·khuhn·tikh
100	honderd	hon·duhrt
1000	duizend	döy·zuhnt

Cycling

I'd like ...	Ik wil graag ...	ik wil khraakh ...
my bicycle repaired	mijn fiets laten herstellen	meyn feets laa·tuhn her·ste·luhn
to hire a bicycle	een fiets huren	uhn feets hew·ruhn

I'd like to hire a ...	Ik wil graag een ... huren.	ik wil khraakh uhn ... hew·ruhn
basket	mandje	man·chuh
child seat	kinderzitje	kin·duhr·zi·chuh
helmet	helm	helm

Do you have bicycle parking?
Heeft u parking voor fietsen? — heyft ew par·king vohr feet·suhn

Can we get there by bike?
Kunnen we er met de fiets heen? — ku·nuhn wuh uhr met duh feets heyn

I have a puncture.
Ik heb een lekke band. — ik hep uhn le·kuh bant

bicycle path	fietspad	feets·pat
bicycle pump	fietspomp	feets·pomp
bike repairman	fietsen-maker	feet·suhn·maa·kuhr
bicycle stand	fietsenrek	feet·suhn·rek

GLOSSARY

bibliotheek – library

bier – beer

biertje– glass of beer

bitterballen – small, round meat croquettes

broodje – bread roll (with filling)

bruin café – brown *café*; traditional Dutch pub

café – pub, bar; also known as *kroeg*

coffeeshop (also spelt *koffieshop* in Dutch) – cafe authorised to sell cannabis

CS – Centraal Station

dagmenu – set menu

dagschotel – daily special in restaurants

drop – salted or sweet liquorice

dwarsstraat – street connecting two (former) canals

eetcafé – *café* serving meals

fiets – bicycle

frites – French fries; also known as *patat*

gezellig – convivial, cosy

gezelligheid – conviviality/ cosiness

gracht – canal

Grachtengordel – Canal Ring

GVB – Gemeentevervoerbedrijf; Amsterdam municipal transport authority

GWK – Grenswisselkantoor; official currency exchanges

hof – courtyard

hofje – almshouse or series of buildings around a small courtyard or garden, such as the Begijnhof

jenever – Dutch gin; also spelled *genever*

kaas – cheese

kade – quay

kerk – church

koffiehuis – coffee house (distinct from a *coffeeshop*)

koninklijk – royal

kroketten – croquettes

markt – town square, market

NS – Nederlandse Spoorwegen; Dutch railway company

OV-chipkaart – fare card for Dutch public transit

pannenkoeken – pancakes

paleis – palace

plein – square

proeflokaal – tasting house

Randstad – literally 'rim city'; the urban agglomeration including Amsterdam, Utrecht, Rotterdam and Den Haag

stadhuis – town hall

stamppot – potatoes mashed with another vegetable (eg sauerkraut or kale), served with bacon bits and a smoked sausage

stedelijk – civic, municipal

steeg – alley, lane

straat – street

strand – beach

stroopwafel – thin, syrup-filled waffle

toren – tower

VVV – tourist office

waag – old weigh house

De Wallen – Red Light District

zaal – hall

Behind the Scenes

SEND US YOUR FEEDBACK

We love to hear from travellers – your comments keep us on our toes and help make our books better. Our well-travelled team reads every word on what you loved or loathed about this book. Although we cannot reply individually to postal submissions, we always guarantee that your feedback goes straight to the appropriate authors, in time for the next edition. Each person who sends us information is thanked in the next edition – and the most useful submissions are rewarded with a selection of digital PDF chapters.

Visit **lonelyplanet.com/contact** to submit your updates and suggestions or to ask for help. Our award-winning website also features inspirational travel stories, news and discussions.

Note: We may edit, reproduce and incorporate your comments in Lonely Planet products such as guidebooks, websites and digital products, so let us know if you don't want your comments reproduced or your name acknowledged. For a copy of our privacy policy visit lonelyplanet.com/privacy.

OUR READERS

Many thanks to the travellers who used the last edition and wrote to us with helpful hints, useful advice and interesting anecdotes:

Andre Ancion, Dave Jarvis, Jet Oesterreicher, Jonathan Brach, Joyel Dhieux, Kathryn Ashwell, Martijn Brussaard, Ugis Godmanis

AUTHOR THANKS
Karla Zimmerman

Many thanks to Kimberley Melger and the Amsterdam Press Office, and Roel de Haas and staff at Hotel Fita. Deep gratitude to ace co-author Catherine Le Nevez, James Smart, Jo Cooke, Barbara Delissen and all at Lonely Planet. Thanks most of all to Eric Markowitz, the world's best partner-for-life, who fed me and kept the house from falling apart while I wrote this book.

Catherine Le Nevez

Hartelijk bedankt first and foremost to Julian, and to everyone in and around Amsterdam who provided insights and information. *Dank u wel* in particular to Pamela Sturhoofd, Jeffrey Liong-A-Kong, Annemarie Gerards-Adriaansens, Willemien van der Veen (and Kareltje-de-kat), and fashion designer Eline Starink and interior designer Marloes Hoedeman for the interviews. Huge thanks too to Karla Zimmerman, James Smart, Jo Cooke, Annelies Mertens, Jennifer Johnston and all at Lonely Planet. As ever, *merci encore* to my parents, brother, belle-sœur and neveu.

ACKNOWLEDGMENTS

Cover photograph: Leidsegracht canal, Amsterdam; Herva Hughes/Getty.

THIS BOOK

This 9th edition of Lonely Planet's *Amsterdam* guidebook was researched and written by Karla Zimmerman and Catherine Le Nevez. The 8th edition was written by Karla Zimmerman and Sarah Chandler, and the 7th by Karla Zimmerman, Caroline Sieg and Ryan Ver Berkmoes, with additional content by Jeremy Gray and Simon Sellars.

This guidebook was commissioned in Lonely Planet's London office, and produced by the following:

Commissioning Editors James Smart, Korina Miller

Coordinating Editors Barbara Delissen, Luna Soo, Amanda Williamson

Senior Cartographers Jennifer Johnston, Anthony Phelan

Book Designers Katherine Marsh, Mazzy Prinsep

Managing Editors Brigitte Ellemor, Annelies Mertens, Angela Tinson

Assisting Editors Penny Cordner, Samantha Forge, Jodie Martire, Kate Mathews

Cover Research Naomi Parker

Thanks to Elin Berglund, Lauren Egan, Ryan Evans, Larissa Frost, Briohny Hooper, Genesys India, Jouve India, Andi Jones, Elizabeth Jones, Catherine Naghten, Trent Paton, Gerard Walker

See also separate subindexes for:

🍴 EATING P292

🍺 DRINKING & NIGHTLIFE P294

☆ ENTERTAINMENT P295

🛍 SHOPPING P295

🛏 SLEEPING P296

Index

Amsterdam Maps

Map Legend

Sights
- Beach
- Buddhist
- Castle
- Christian
- Hindu
- Islamic
- Jewish
- Monument
- Museum/Gallery
- Ruin
- Winery/Vineyard
- Zoo
- Other Sight

Eating
- Eating

Drinking & Nightlife
- Drinking & Nightlife
- Cafe

Entertainment
- Entertainment

Shopping
- Shopping

Sleeping
- Sleeping
- Camping

Sports & Activities
- Diving/Snorkelling
- Canoeing/Kayaking
- Skiing
- Surfing
- Swimming/Pool
- Walking
- Windsurfing
- Other Sports & Activities

Information
- Post Office
- Tourist Information

Transport
- Airport
- Border Crossing
- Bus
- Cable Car/Funicular
- Cycling
- Ferry
- Monorail
- Parking
- S-Bahn
- Taxi
- Train/Railway
- Tram
- Tube Station
- U-Bahn
- Underground Train Station
- Other Transport

Routes
- Tollway
- Freeway
- Primary
- Secondary
- Tertiary
- Lane
- Unsealed Road
- Plaza/Mall
- Steps
- Tunnel
- Pedestrian Overpass
- Walking Tour
- Walking Tour Detour
- Path

Boundaries
- International
- State/Province
- Disputed
- Regional/Suburb
- Marine Park
- Cliff
- Wall

Geographic
- Hut/Shelter
- Lighthouse
- Lookout
- Mountain/Volcano
- Oasis
- Park
- Pass
- Picnic Area
- Waterfall

Hydrography
- River/Creek
- Intermittent River
- Swamp/Mangrove
- Reef
- Canal
- Water
- Dry/Salt/Intermittent Lake
- Glacier

Areas
- Beach/Desert
- Cemetery (Christian)
- Cemetery (Other)
- Park/Forest
- Sportsground
- Sight (Building)
- Top Sight (Building)

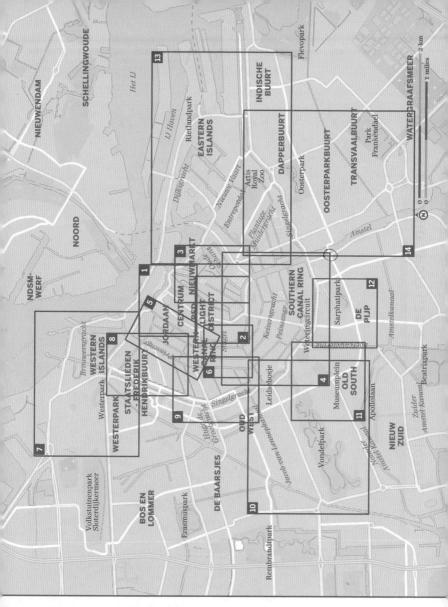

MAP INDEX

Key on p302

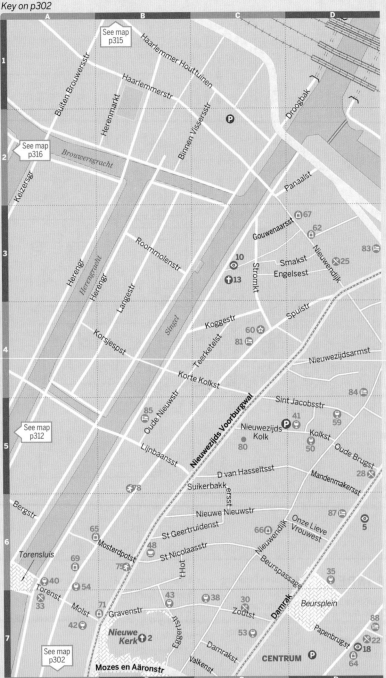

See map p315

See map p316

See map p312

See map p302

Buiten Brouwersstr

Haarlemmer Houttuinen

Haarlemmerstr

Herenmarkt

Binnen Visserssstr

Droogbak

Keizersgr

Brouwersgracht

Panaalst

Gouwenaarsst

67
62
83
25
Nieuwendijk
Smakst
Engelsest

Herengr

Herengr

Roommolenstr

Langestr

Singel

10
13

Stromkt

Koggestr

60
81

Spuistr

Teerketelst

Korsjespst

Korte Kolkst

Nieuwezijdsarmst

85
Oude Nieuwstr

Sint Jacobsst

84

41
59

Nieuwezijds Voorburgwal

Nieuwezijds Kolk

80

Kolkst
50

Oude Brugst

Lijnbaanst

28

D van Hasseltsst

Mandenmakersst

78

Suikerbakk

Nieuwe Nieuwstr

87
5

Bergstr

65
Mosterdpotst

48

St Geertruidenst

St Nicolaasstr

66
Nieuwendijk

Onze Lieve Vrouwest

Beurspassage

35

Torensluis

69
75

'tHof

40
Torenst
33

54

71
Gravenst

42

Molst

43

38

30
Zoutst

Damrak

Beursplein

88

Nieuwe Kerk

2

Eggertstr

Damrakst

53

Papenbrugst

22
18
64

Valkenst

CENTRUM

Mozes en Aäronstr

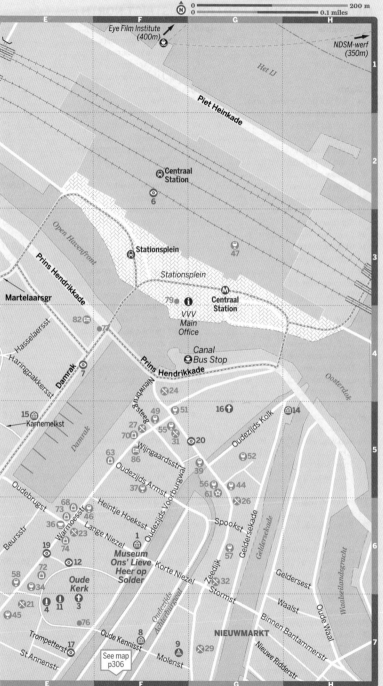

0   200 m
0   0.1 miles

Eye Film Institute
(400m)

NDSM-werf
(350m)

Het IJ

Piet Heinkade

Centraal
Station

6

Open Havenfront

Stationsplein

Prins Hendrikkade

47

Stationsplein

Martelaarsgr

79

Centraal
Station

VVV
Main
Office

Hasselaersst

82

77

Haringpakkersst

Canal
Bus Stop

Prins Hendrikkade

Damrak

7

Oosterdok

24

15

Karnemelkst

49   51

16

14

Nieuwendijksteeg

Damrak

27
70

55

31

20

Oudezijds Kolk

63
86

Wijngaardsstraat

52

Oudezijds Armst

39

Oudezijds Voorburgwal

37

56   44

61

26

Oudebrugst

Heintje Hoekst

68
73

46

Spookst

Geldersekade

Beursst

36

Warmoesst

23

Lange Niezel

19

74

1

Geldersekade

57

72

12

Museum
Ons' Lieve
Heer op
Solder

Korte Niezel

Zeedijk

Gelderseст

58
34

Oude
Kerk

Stormst

32

Geldersest

21
45

4

11

3

Oudezijds Achterburgwal

Waalst

Binnen Bantammerstr

Oude Waal

Waalseilandsgracht

76

8

NIEUWMARKT

Oude Kennisst

Oude Bantammerstr

Trompetterst

17

9

29

Nieuwe Ridderstr

St Annenstr

Molenst

See map
p306

MEDIEVAL CENTRE & RED LIGHT DISTRICT NORTH *Map on p300*

The West

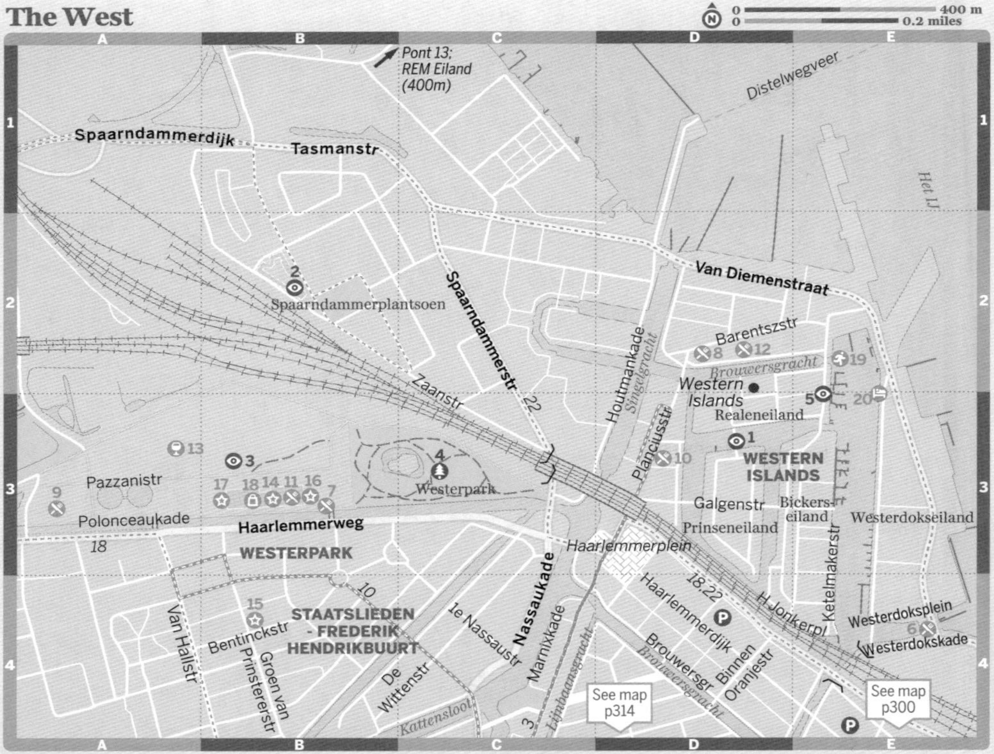

Spaarndammerdijk
Tasmanstr
Pont 13; REM Eiland (400m)
Distelwegveer
Het IJ
Van Diemenstraat
Spaarndammerplantsoen
Spaarndammerstr
Zaanstr
Barentszstr
Brouwersgracht
Houtmankade
Singelgracht
Western Islands
Realeneiland
Planciusstr
WESTERN ISLANDS
Galgenstr
Bickerseiland
Prinseneiland
Westerdokseiland
Ketelmakerstr
Westerdoksplein
Westerdokskade
Pazzanistr
Polonceaukade
Westerpark
Haarlemmerweg
WESTERPARK
Haarlemmerplein
Haarlemmerdijk
H Jonkerpl
Binnen Oranjestr
Brouwersgr
Nassaukade
Marnixkade
Lijnbaansgracht
1e Nassaustr
De Wittenstr
Kattensloot
STAATSLIEDEN - FREDERIK HENDRIKBUURT
Bentinckstr
Groen van Prinstererstr
Van Hallstr
See map p314
See map p300
0 400 m
0 0.2 miles

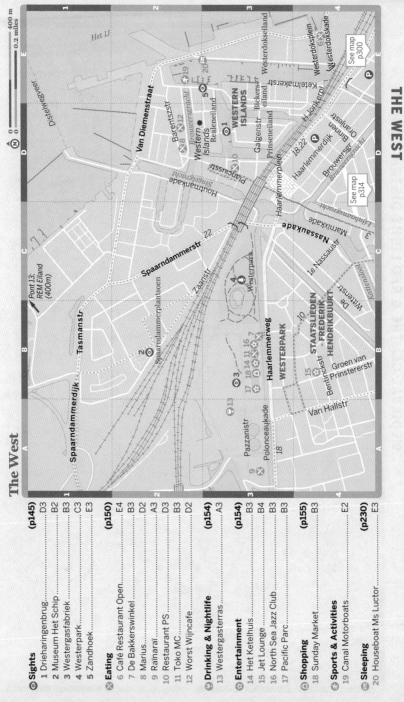

Sights (p145)

1 Drieharingenbrug ... D3
2 Museum Het Schip ... B2
3 Westergasfabriek ... B3
4 Westerpark ... C3
5 Zandhoek ... E3

Eating (p150)

6 Café Restaurant Open ... E4
7 De Bakkerswinkel ... B3
8 Marius ... D2
9 Raïnaraï ... A3
10 Restaurant PS ... D3
11 Toko MC ... B3
12 Worst Wijncafe ... D2

Drinking & Nightlife (p154)

13 Westergasterras ... A3

Entertainment (p154)

14 Het Ketelhuis ... B3
15 Jet Lounge ... B4
16 North Sea Jazz Club ... B3
17 Pacific Parc ... B3

Shopping (p155)

18 Sunday Market ... B3

Sports & Activities

19 Canal Motorboats ... E2

Sleeping (p230)

20 Houseboat Ms Luctor ... E3

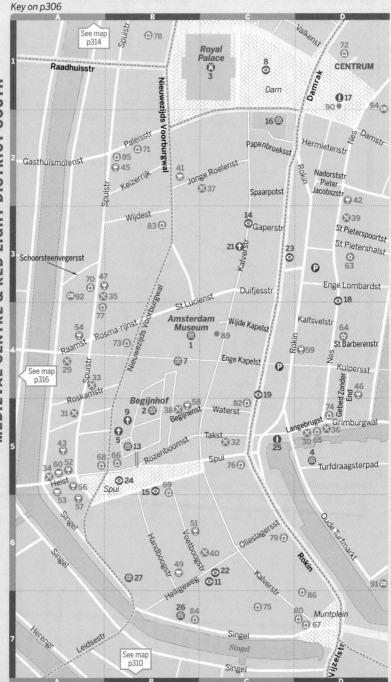

MEDIEVAL CENTRE & RED LIGHT DISTRICT SOUTH

See map p314

Raadhuisstr

Royal Palace
3

Dam

8

CENTRUM

72

17
90

94

16

Papenbroeksst

Hermietenstr

Nadorststr
Pieter Jacobszstr

42

Spaarpotst

39

St Pieterspoortst
St Pietershalst

63

Gasthuismolenst

Paleisstr

71

85
45

Keizerrijk

Jonge Roelenst

41

37

14
Gaperstr

21

23

P

Enge Lombardst

18

Wijdest

83

Schoorsteenvegersst

70
47

92

35

77

St Lucienst

Duifjesst

Kalfsvelstr

64
St Barberenstr

54

Rosma-rijnst

73

Amsterdam Museum
1

Wijde Kapelst

89

Rokin

59

Raamst

29

Spuist

33

7

Enge Kapelst

P

Nes

Kuipersst

See map p316

Roskamstr

Begijnhof

9

2

38

58
Begijnenst

Waterst

82

19

46

74

Grimburgwal

Gebed Zonder End

31

5

13

Rozenboomst

Takst

32

36

30 65

43

68 66

Spui

76

25

4
Turfdraagsterpad

Langebrugst

34 60 52
Heist

56

53 57

24

Spui

15

69

51

Voetboogstr

79

Oude Turfmarkt

Oude Turfmarkt

Rokin

40

Olieslagersst

Handboogstr

49

Heiligeweg

27

22

11

Kalverstr

86

91

26

84

75

80
67

Muntplein

Herengr

Leidsestr

Singel

Singel

Singel

Singel

Singel

Vijzelstr

See map p310

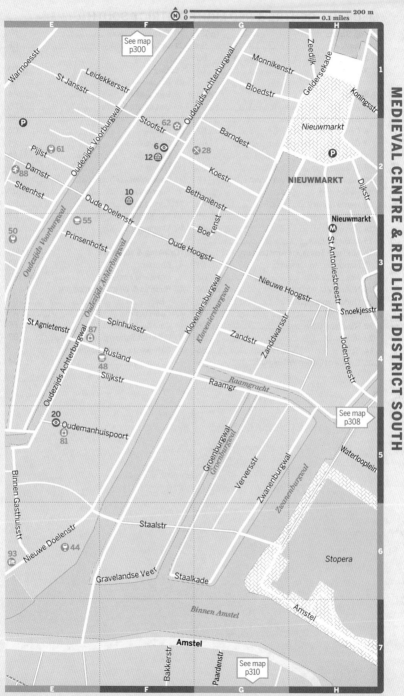

MEDIEVAL CENTRE & RED LIGHT DISTRICT SOUTH *Map on p304*

⊕ Entertainment (p88)

⊞ Shopping (p89)

⊕ Sports & Activities

⊟ Sleeping (p225)

MEDIEVAL CENTRE & RED LIGHT DISTRICT SOUTH

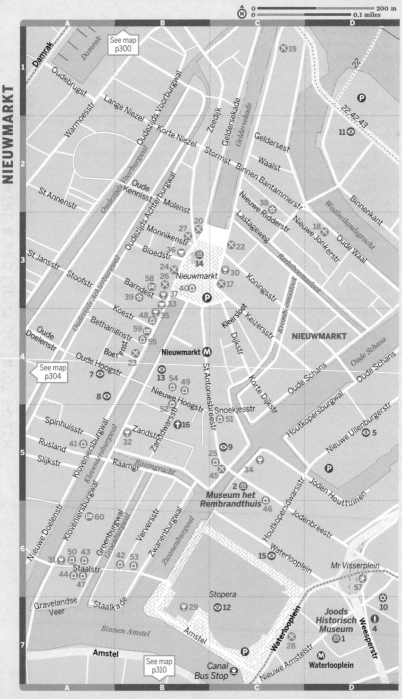

See map
p300

See map
p304

See map
p310

See map
p326

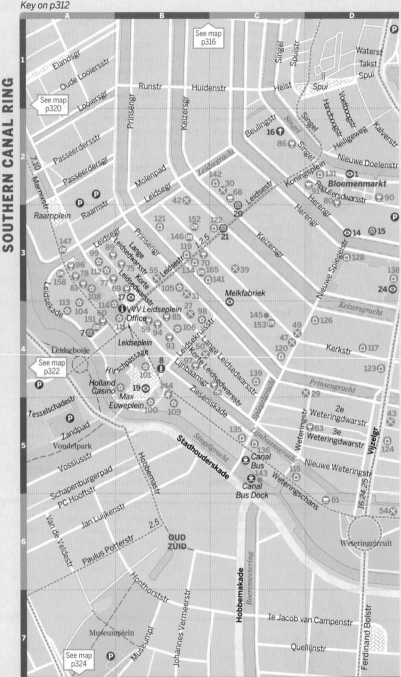

SOUTHERN CANAL RING

See map p316
See map p320
See map p322
See map p324

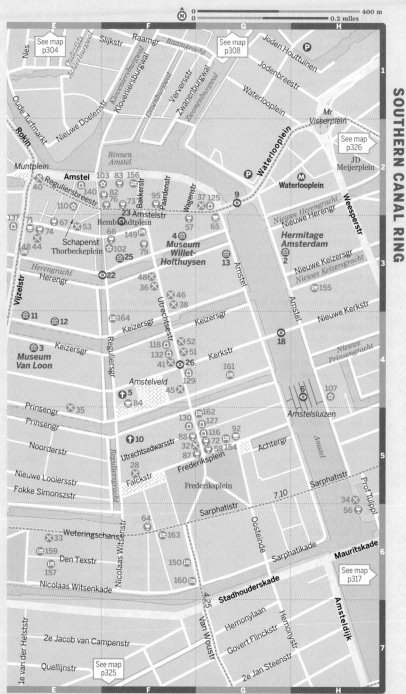

SOUTHERN CANAL RING

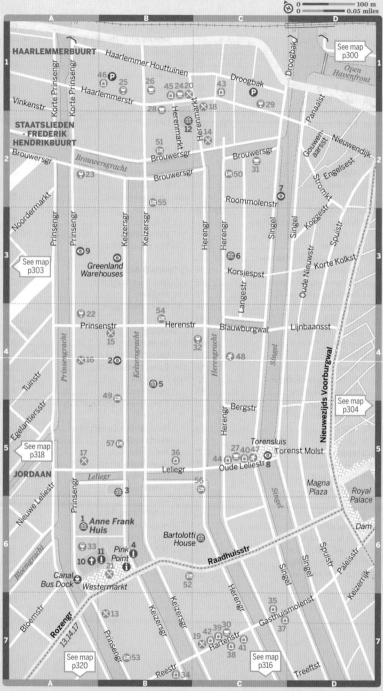

HAARLEMMERBUURT

Haarlemmer Houttuinen

Vinkenstr

Korte Prinsengr

Korte Prinsengr

Haarlemmerstr

Droogbak

STAATSLIEDEN
- FREDERIK
HENDRIKBUURT

Brouwersgr

Brouwersgracht

Brouwersgr

Brouwersgr

Brouwersgr

Herenmarkt

Roommolenstr

Noordermarkt

Prinsengr

Prinsengr

Keizersgr

Keizersgr

Herengr

Herengr

Singel

Singel

Singel

Korsjespst

Korte Kolkst

Oude Nieuwstr

Nieuwendijk

Panaalst

Gouwen-
aarsst

Engelsest

Stromkt

Koggestr

Spuistr

Greenland
Warehouses

Prinsenstr

Herenstr

Blauwburgwal

Lijnbaansst

Prinsengracht

Keizersgracht

Herengracht

Singel

Nieuwezijds Voorburgwal

Tuinstr

Egelantiersstr

Bergstr

Torensluis

Torenst Molst

Oude Leliestr

Leliegr

Leliestr

JORDAAN

Nieuwe Leliestr

Prinsengr

Anne Frank
Huis

Pink
Point

Bartolotti
House

Raadhuisstr

Magna
Plaza

Royal
Palace

Dam

Bloemgr

Canal
Bus Dock

Westermarkt

Bloemstr

Rozengr

Keizersgr

Keizersgr

Herengr

Herengr

Gasthuismolenst

Spuistr

Singel

Singel

Paleisstr

Keizerrijk

Treeftst

Hartenstr

Reestr

Prinsengr

See map
p300

Open
Havenfront

See map
p303

See map
p304

See map
p318

See map
p320

See map
p316

WESTERN CANAL RING NORTH

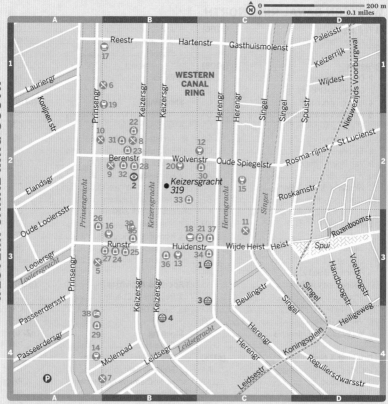

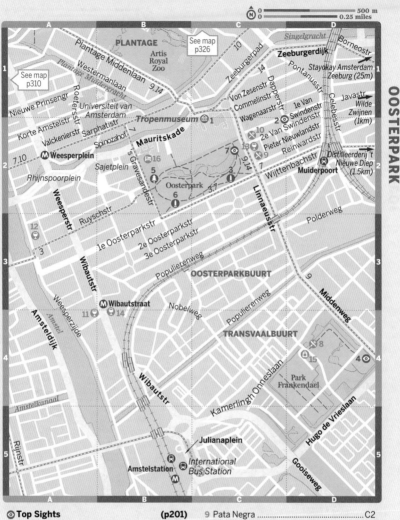

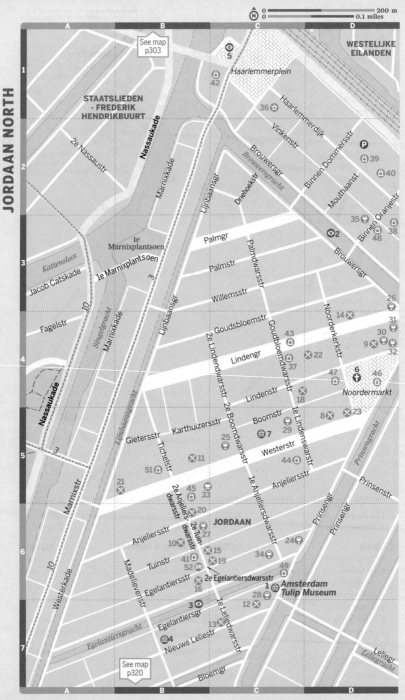

See map
p303

WESTELIJKE
EILANDEN

Haarlemmerplein

STAATSLIEDEN
- FREDERIK
HENDRIKBUURT

2e Nassaustr

Nassaukade

Marnixkade

Haarlemmerdijk

Vinkenstr

Binnen Donmersstr

Mouthaanstr

Brouwersgr

Brouwersgracht

Binnen Oranjestr

Brouwersgr

Lijnbaansgr

Driehoekstr

1e
Marnixplantsoen

Palmgr

Palmstr

Palmdwarsstr

Kattensloot

Jacob Catskade

Fagelstr

1e Marnixplantsoen

Singelgracht

Marnixkade

Lijnbaansgr

Willemsstr

Goudsbloemstr

Lindengr

Goudsbloemdwarsstr

Noorderkerkstr

Nassaukade

Lindengr

2e Lindendwarsstr

Lindenstr

Lindenstr

2e Boomdwarsstr

Gietersstr

Karthuizersstr

Boomstr

1e Lindensdwarsstr

Noordermarkt

Tichelstr

Westerstr

Marnixstr

Anjeliersstr

1e Anjeliersdwarsstr

Prinsengracht

Prinsengr

Prinsenstr

Prinsengr

Prinsengr

2e Anjeliers dwarsstr

JORDAAN

Anjeliersstr

2e Tuin dwarsstr

Tuinstr

Madelievenstr

Egelantiersstr

2e Egelantiersdwarsstr

Amsterdam
Tulip Museum

Egelantiersgr

3

Egelantiersgr

1e Leliedwarsstr

Nieuwe Leliestr

4

Bloemgr

Leliegr

Leliegracht

Westerkade

See map
p320

JORDAAN NORTH

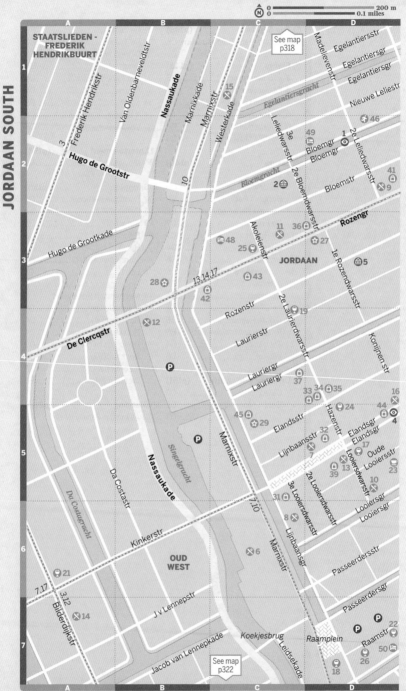

JORDAAN SOUTH

STAATSLIEDEN - FREDERIK HENDRIKBUURT

JORDAAN

OUD WEST

See map p318

See map p322

◎ **Sights** (p143)
1 Bloemgracht.........................D2
2 De Drie Hendricken C2
3 Houseboat Museum.............E5
4 Johnny Jordaanplein...........D5
5 Stedelijk Museum Bureau
    Amsterdam......................D3

✕ **Eating** (p146)
6 À Table Amsterdam C6
7 Balthazar's Keuken..............D5
8 Brasserie Blazer.................C6
9 Broodje Mokum D2
10 Festina Lente......................D5
11 Manzano C3
12 Moeders B4
13 Pazzi D5
14 Riaz A7
15 Semhar..............................C1
16 Xinh D4

◎ **Drinking & Nightlife** (p151)
17 Café de Jordaan..................D5
18 Café de Koe D7
19 Café de Laurierboom C4
20 De Pieper...........................E7
21 De Trut A6
22 Gespot................................D7
23 La Tertulia..........................D5
24 Saarein D5
25 Struik C3
26 Thermos Day Sauna............D7

✪ **Entertainment** (p154)
27 Boom Chicago.....................D3

28 Cafe Soundgarden B3
29 Maloe Melo C5

◎ **Shopping** (p155)
30 A Space Oddity E3
31 Antiekcentrum
    Amsterdam C5
32 Arnold Cornelis D5
33 Brown Clothes D4
34 Cats & Things D4
35 Chocolátl............................D4
36 De Winkel Van Guus D3
37 English Bookshop................C4
38 Galleria d'Arte
    Rinascimento E2
39 Jefferson Hotel D5
40 Josine Bokhoven E2
41 Kitsch Kitchen D2
42 Raw Materials.....................B3
43 SPRMRKT...........................C3
44 Tenue de Nîmes..................D5
45 Uke Boutique......................C5

◎ **Sports & Activities**
46 Bike City.............................D2

◎ **Sleeping** (p230)
47 Amsterdam Wiechmann
    Hotel................................E5
48 Christian Youth Hostel
    'The Shelter
    Jordaan'...........................C3
49 Hotel van Onna D2
50 International Budget
    Hostel...............................D7

VONDELPARK & AROUND

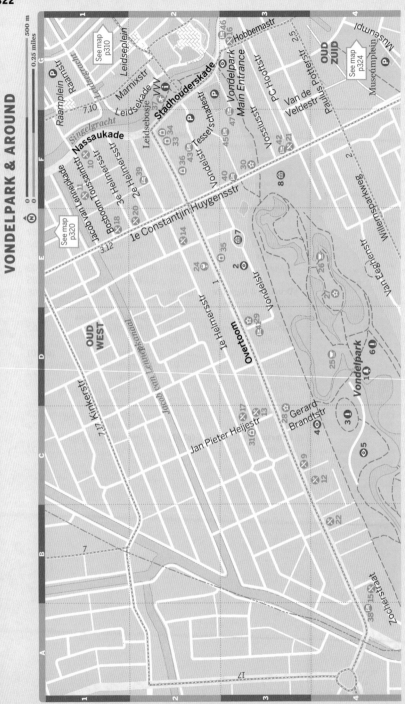

See map p310

See map p320

See map p324

0 500 m
0 0.25 miles

Raamplein
Raamstr
Leidseplein
Leidsekade
Leidsebosje
Marnixstr
Nassaukade
Singelgracht
Jacob van Lennepkade
Bosboom Toussaintstr
Jacob van Lennepkanaal
Kinkerstr
Jan Pieter Heijestr
1e Helmersstr
Overtoom
1e Constantijn Huygensstr
2e Helmersstr
3e Helmersstr
Vondelstr
Tesselschadestr
Vondelpark Main Entrance
Stadhouderskade
Hobbemastr
PC Hooftstr
Vossiusstr
Van de Veldestr
Paulus Potterstr
Van Eeghenstr
Willemsparkweg
Museumplein
Gerard Brandtstr
Zocherstraat
Vondelpark
OUD WEST
OUD ZUID

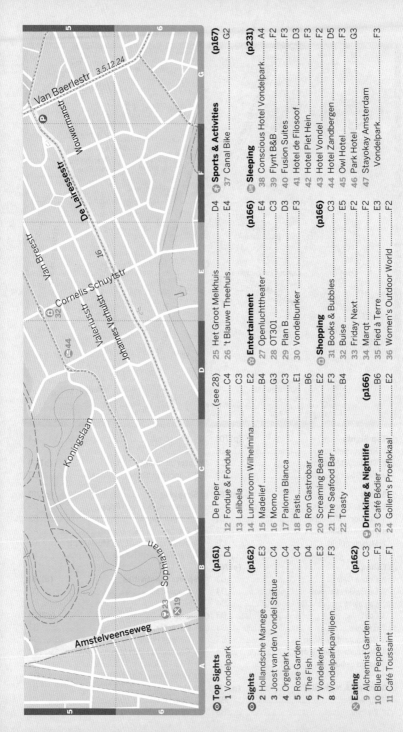

OLD SOUTH

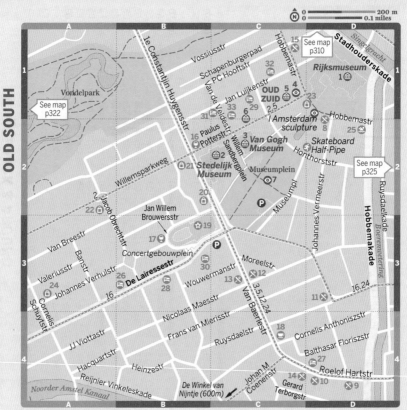

DE PIJP

PLANTAGE, EASTERN ISLANDS & EASTERN DOCKLANDS

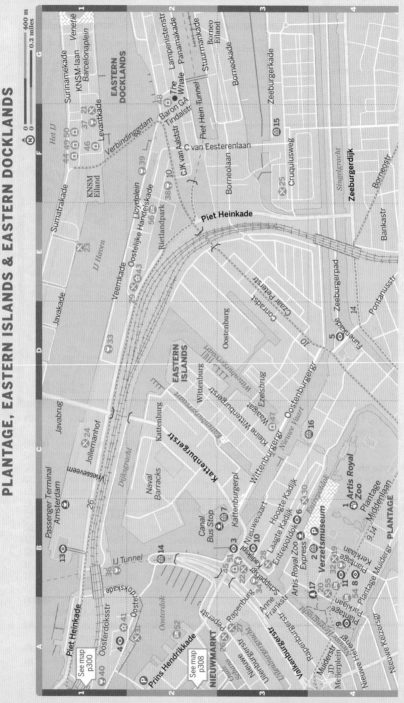

PLANTAGE, EASTERN ISLANDS & EASTERN DOCKLANDS

Molukkenstr
Sumatrastr
Javastr
1e Atjehstr
Insulindeweg
INDISCHE BUURT
Celebesstr
Dapperplein
DAPPERBUURT
Dapperplein
Dapperstr
Commelinstr
Reinwardstr
Linnaeusstr
9,14
Oosterpark
See map p317
Mauritskade
Alexander-plein
Sarphatistr
Alexander
7
Roetersstr
Nieuwe Prinsengr
Universiteit van Amsterdam
42
Nieuwe Achtergr
53
Nieuwe Valckenier Str
Spinozastr
18
12
Weesperstr
Nieuwe Kerkstr
See map p310
Weesperplein
Amstel

JUN 2015

Our Story

A beat-up old car, a few dollars in the pocket and a sense of adventure. In 1972 that's all Tony and Maureen Wheeler needed for the trip of a lifetime – across Europe and Asia overland to Australia. It took several months, and at the end – broke but inspired – they sat at their kitchen table writing and stapling together their first travel guide, *Across Asia on the Cheap*. Within a week they'd sold 1500 copies. Lonely Planet was born.

Today, Lonely Planet has offices in Melbourne, London and Oakland, with more than 600 staff and writers. We share Tony's belief that 'a great guidebook should do three things: inform, educate and amuse'.

Our Writers

Karla Zimmerman

Coordinating Author, Medieval Centre & Red Light District, Nieuwmarkt, Old South, Oosterpark & South Amsterdam During her Amsterdam travels, Karla admired art, bicycled crash-free, ate an embarrassing quantity of *frites* and bent over to take her *jenever* like a local. She has been visiting Amsterdam since 1989, decades that have seen her trade space cakes for *stroopwafels*, to a much more pleasant effect. She never tires of the city's bobbing houseboats, cling-clinging bike bells and canal houses tilting at impossible angles. Karla writes travel features for books, magazines and online outlets. She has authored or co-authored several Lonely Planet guidebooks covering the USA, Canada, Caribbean and Europe. For this guide, Karla also wrote Welcome to Amsterdam, Amsterdam's Top 10, What's New, Need to Know, First Time, Top Itineraries, If You Like, Museums & Galleries, Eating, Entertainment, Shopping, Amsterdam Today and the Survival Guide. Learn more by following her on Twitter (twitter./karlazimmerman).

Read more about Karla at:
lonelyplanet.com/members/karlazimmerman

Catherine Le Nevez

Western Canal Ring, Southern Canal Ring, Jordaan & the West, Vondelpark & Around, De Pijp, Plantage, Eastern Islands & Eastern Docklands, Day Trips Catherine's wanderlust kicked in when she first roadtripped across Europe, including Amsterdam, aged four, and she's been returning to this spirited, innovative and *gezellig* city ever since, completing her Doctorate of Creative Arts in Writing, Masters in Professional Writing, and post-grad qualifications in editing and publishing along the way. Catherine has worked as a freelance writer for many years and during the past decade or so she's written dozens of Lonely Planet guidebooks and articles covering destinations all over Europe and beyond. For this guide Catherine also wrote Month by Month, With Kids, Like a Local, For Free, By Bike, Canals, Drinking & Nightlife, History, Dutch Painting, Contemporary Dutch Design, Canal Architecture and Architecture in Amsterdam.

Read more about Catherine at:
lonelyplanet.com/members/catherinelenevez

Published by Lonely Planet Publications Pty Ltd
ABN 36 005 607 983
9th edition – March 2014
ISBN 978 1 74220 874 9
© Lonely Planet 2014   Photographs © as indicated 2014
10 9 8 7 6 5 4 3 2
Printed in China